European Casebook on

Finance

Edited by

Paul Stonham
and
Keith Redhead

Prentice Hall

London   New York   Toronto   Sydney   Tokyo   Singapore
Madrid   Mexico City   Munich

First published 1995 by
Prentice Hall International (UK) Limited
Campus 400, Maylands Avenue
Hemel Hempstead
Hertfordshire, HP2 7EZ
A division of
Simon & Schuster International Group

Typeset in Palatino and Times
by Hands Fotoset, Leicester

Printed and bound in Great Britain
at Redwood Books, Trowbridge, Wiltshire.

Library of Congress Cataloging-in-Publication Data

Library of Congress Cataloging-in-Publication data
are available from the publisher

British Library Cataloguing in Publication Data

A catalogue record for this book is available from
the British Library

ISBN 0-13-291030 6

1   2   3   4   5   99   98   97   96   95

European Casebook on

Finance

WITHDRAWN

The European Casebook Series on Management

Series Editor: Paul Stonham, EAP European School of Management, Oxford

Contents

Series Editorial

The idea of a series of European Casebooks on Management arose from discussions during the annual case writing competition organized by the European Foundation for Management Development (EFMD) in Brussels. The case writing competition itself was set up to encourage the production of more case studies in management with a specifically European content, to meet the growing demand in European business schools and training programmes of corporations. Begun in 1989, the competition has now established itself as a major focus of interest for case study writers.

However, knowing that many European cases were being produced outside the context of the competition, it was decided to extend the search for cases more widely. The project was taken up by Prentice Hall International in 1991, who undertook to publish the series, and appointed a Series Editor to manage the academic aspects of the collection of volumes.

From the inception of the project, the EAP European School of Management, a *grande école* of the Paris Chamber of Commerce and Industry, agreed to finance the costs of the Series Editor, and Prentice Hall funded secretarial assistance. As well as its financial support, EAP is well positioned to supply an appropriate academic infrastructure to the editorial management of the Series. From its headquarters in Paris, it maintains establishments in Berlin, Madrid and Oxford, and its masters' level students train in three countries. EAP is one of the leaders in European multicultural management education and, of course, a major user of case studies with a European focus in its courses.

Early market research showed a strong and largely unsatisfied demand for case studies in European management at a time when interest in the completion of the Single European Market was at its height. Calls for case study writers and for volume editors met a good response, and the major fields of management were quickly covered as well as several important specialized areas not originally considered.

There is an increasing number of titles available in this Series of European Casebooks on Management on a wide range of topics including Business Alliances, Business Ethics, Competing Through Services, Cooperative Strategies, Entrepreneurship and New Ventures, Environmental Issues, Finance, Human Resource Management, Managing Industrial and Business-to-Business Marketing, Industrial and Trade Policy, Information Technology, International Business, Leadership, Management in Eastern Europe, Production and Operations Management, Research and Technology Management and Strategy. A full list of current titles is available from the publisher's UK address shown on page iv.

The case studies are intended to draw on the main developments and changes in their respective fields of management in recent years, focusing on managerial issues in corporations trading in or with the European Union. Although the principal concentration is on the non-governmental sector, the experience of governments and governmental agencies is included in some of the volumes to the extent that they affect the corporate sector. In the light of the title of the Series, cases dealing with European cross-border involvements have been given priority in inclusion, but material that relates to national experience or is conceptual or global in nature has been considered relevant if it satisfies the criteria for good cases.

A driving motive for developing the Series of European Casebooks on Management has been the wish to encourage the production of cases with a specifically European dimension. Not only have the regulatory background, institutional framework and behavioural traits of cases developed in the American business schools like Harvard always been barriers to their use in European management education, but the developing European Union has emphasized aspects of corporate development and strategy completely ignored in most American cases. With the build-up of cross-border business activity in Europe have come difficulties in cultural adjustment. The growing legislation of the European Commission in its '1992 programme' has imposed constraints and given freedoms not known in an American context, in such fields as technology, patents, competition, take-overs and mergers, freedom of establishment and workers' rights. There was clearly a need for case studies which took account of the rapid changes occurring in the European Union and which analysed corporations' responses to them. It is recognized in the kind of terminology which is now much more current in management thinking: 'European management', 'Euromanagers' and 'Pan-Europeanization' no longer raise eyebrows even if not everyone believes these are totally valid terms.

In selecting cases for their volumes, the Editors and the Series Editor asked the leading question again and again – what is a good case? It was not sufficient to take the accepted Harvard view. Cases are critically important to teaching at the Harvard Business School and have been since they were first produced in 1910. For example, in 1986 Benson Shapiro said that 'one must understand the fundamentals of course design, because each case must fit into the rubric of the course'. Shapiro also said the case writer should 'Ensure the case includes a balanced conflict'. In 1955, Robert Davies, also of Harvard, wrote that 'There are two kinds of cases . . . the *issue case* in which the writer poses a particular problem and the reader prepares a recommendation designed to overcome the problem, and an *appraisal case* in which the writer describes a management decision already made and the reader evaluates this decision'. Generally, cases now being written in Europe are less rigid and constrained. They reflect the multifunctional and multicultural aspects of modern European business. They are pedagogical, but less tied to functional disciplines than the Harvard cases described by Shapiro, and this again is probably because the boundaries of the functional disciplines themselves, like marketing and finance, are becoming less distinct. However, according to Paul Lawrence, in 1953, many of the 'good' points of Harvard case study teaching are nonetheless incorporated into European case writing: the emphasis on complex, real-life situations, the degree of interest aroused, the use of 'springboard cases', and the need for good reporting.

The essentials of 'good' case writing in European management have been discussed extensively by the judges of the annual case writing competition organized by EFMD. They can be summarized as follows from the main points of a presentation by Robert Collins of IMD Lausanne at the annual conference workshop and prize-giving in Jouy-en-Josas, Paris, in September 1993.

Although writing case studies in management involves an element of opportunistic, investigative journalism, the pedagogical needs of students should be paramount. The case writer should be objective; there is no place for personal opinion or advocacy – the case writer or teacher is neither judge nor jury.

As far as the audience for cases is concerned, the case must be interesting. The setting or topic should be attractive and the case raise compelling issues. A decision-forcing case is more likely to turn students on than a descriptive or expository one – but the snag is that students do not generally like open-ended and vague cases. The case should be transferable – across faculty members, programmes and institutions.

In terms of product quality, the case should exceed audience expectations of both performance and conformance. The length of a case is important – it should give optimal time for reading and analysis, and the quality and quantity of data should be right. Assimilation is made easier when the case focuses on characters or issues, is structured, has internally consistent data, avoids jargon and is written in high-quality prose. It should be remembered that inexperienced students have a low tolerance of ambiguity and of data/ information.

Writing a good case involves creating a favourable climate among all the stakeholders in a company. They will not assist if there is not confidence, discretion and cooperation. In a company there are archetypal executives who must all be managed, for example, the 'champion' may steer the case writer through the company (but only when he or she is on hand); the 'guerilla' will appear to help, but snipe from out of sight; the 'security guard' will consider everything classified and not for discussion. The reality for a case writer on site in a company is that not everyone will love you.

The teacher can maximize the benefits of a good case. Opportunities for customization and experimentation should always be sought – among different sets of participants, programmes and in-team teaching. A good teacher can exploit the richness of a case and the acuity of the participants.

Clearly, the case method is not the only pedagogical method of teaching management. Charles Croué of the École Supérieure de Commerce de Tours believes it is the most revolutionary, because unlike teacher-centred or self-tutoring methods, it is an active and interactive method.

The method encourages students to organize their work, to exchange different points of view in complex discussions, to find compromise by negotiating, and to improve their skills at oral presentation. They learn to compare different solutions and to synthesize information and decisions. They can observe the relationships between different disciplines of management – like marketing and strategy, and understand the difference between theory and practice. In the case-study method they do all this in a situation of reality, solving a real management problem. All of these skills prepare students well for manager status.

The case method has three main distinguishing characteristics which set it aside from other teaching methods. It is *cooperative* – students work in groups, they exchange information, and it improves their communicative abilities. It is *dynamic* – students are stimulated from passivity to effort. And it is *democratic* – teachers and students have equal roles; there are no preset solutions, and ideas are freely exchanged.

Finally, the case method is well suited to the changing nature of management and business at the present time. The current environment is moving very quickly: case studies can 'catch' new events and issues as they happen (likewise, they may quickly date). They lend themselves well to performance measurement, as the managerial qualities of the students improve. The current wish for 'action-learning' is satisfied, and cases can be delivered using multiple media like videos and computers.

The present volume, by Paul Stonham and Keith Redhead, covers a field, finance, in which there has hitherto been a paucity of case study material, even from American case study writers. The shortage is even more acute when it comes to case studies with a European dimension. The editors, both on the finance faculty of the European School of Management, were acutely aware of the need for European case studies in finance relevant to the needs of their students, and the current volume is in part a response to that.

The *European Casebook on Finance* is structured to reflect three main areas of activity and concern in European financial affairs: alliances, acquisitions and privatizations; corporate finance and restructuring; and risk management. These three areas have themselves been brought to prominence by the development of the European Union (EU), but global financial considerations have also had a major part to play. The cases deal with both corporate finance (finance from the focused perspective of the company) and international finance (cases dealing with issues and problems that have a global impact on markets, governments, public and private institutions as well as companies), but often the distinction between corporate and international becomes blurred.

In Part 1, alliances, acquisitions and privatizations, all the cases are company-focused even though wider issues like regulation, government policy on competition, and directives of the European Commission may be involved. Manufacturing and services industries of the EU are still in a state of high activity as far as mergers and acquisitions are concerned, and all the governments of the EU have embarked on large-scale, long-term privatization programmes. The intensity and fervour of take-overs in recent times is shown in the hard-won victory of Seagram over Grand Metropolitan for the hand of Martell, the French cognac producer, and the creation of the world's second-largest non-Japanese banking group when HSBC Holdings acquired Midland Bank in the face of a hostile counter-bid by Lloyds Bank. Two early examples of national privatizations in Spain and The Netherlands (Repsol SA and PTT Netherlands) are good examples of the wave of privatizations now sweeping Europe, nearly all successful.

In Part 2, corporate finance and restructuring, the emphasis is again on cases in which companies deal with problems of competition, structure and growth, many of them linked to effects emanating primarily from EU legislation. The two Eurotunnel cases (debt and equity) illustrate well the financing problems of Europe's largest-ever infrastructure investment project. There is a special focus on the offer of shares and capital-raising in a European context, from the Wellcome Share Offering Case in which Wellcome plc had to cope with a huge sale of its equity base through the London Stock Market to GPA, Saatchi and Saatchi, IBC, Amazonia Plantations and EuroDisney who all used various techniques and went through various experiences to raise money. Only when the section turns to a case on foreign direct investment do rather more macroeconomic considerations arise. Cases in this section reflect well the kinds of restructuring decision which involve a financial dimension that companies are currently considering in the European context.

In the final section, risk management, the cases are mainly concerned with currency risk management as a result of fluctuating and volatile currencies, a concern which is now heightened by the virtual break-up of the discipline of the Exchange Rate Mechanism. The emphasis is on financial products designed effectively to hedge currency risk from a corporate viewpoint.

The Editors believe that this selection of cases satisfies good pedagogical practice in relation to current academic thinking, and that they display the features of good cases described earlier in this editorial. Above all, they hope the fact that most of the cases are recently written about currently 'hot' topics in European finance and involve companies of importance will provide readers with an up-to-date spectrum of corporate activity in finance in the European context.

Paul Stonham, Series Editor,
EAP European School of Management, Oxford

About the Authors

Dr Oriol Amat is associate professor at the University Pompeu Fabra in Barcelona and is a member of the Case Committee of the European Foundation for Management Development. He has held visiting appointments at universities in Europe and America and is the author of a number of finance and accounting books published in Spanish, Catalan, English and French.

Grahame Boocock is a lecturer in banking at Loughborough University Business School and an associate member of Loughborough University Banking Centre. Prior to joining the university in 1987 he was a senior lecturer at Sheffield Polytechnic and prior to this he was employed at Lloyds Bank plc. He has close links with the Chartered Institute of Bankers and has been an assistant examiner for a number of years. In 1993 he was seconded to the Universiti Utara Malaysia as the British Aerospace Associate Professor.

Clive Collis, formerly head of the department of economics at Coventry University, is currently director of its Centre for Local Economic Development. He has lectured in North America, Germany and Russia as well as in the UK. His main current research area is the role of foreign direct investment in regional and local economies. He has authored, co-authored and contributed to numerous books and journals including chapters in *Regional Economic Prospects* (Cambridge Econometrics) and articles in *Local Economy*, *British Review of Economic Issues* and *European Business Review*.

Dr Kees Cools, a chartered accountant, received his master's degrees in business administration and philosophy in The Netherlands. He started his professional career as a corporate planner at the Dutch chemicals giant Akzo and then worked at the finance departments of the University of Maastricht and Tilburg University. Most of his articles deal with corporate finance issues, in particular capital structure. Kees Cools is working as a management consultant at Horringa & de Koning, a member of the Boston Consulting Group.

Matthew Davis joined Aston University in 1993 as a teaching fellow in the Corporate Management Division of Aston Business School. He is a chartered accountant, having trained with Price Waterhouse in Birmingham. He has a first-class degree in accounting and finance from Brighton Polytechnic.

Professor Elroy Dimson is chair of the finance department and formerly director of the Institute of Finance and Accounting at the London Business School, where he is also Prudential Research Fellow in Investment. He has held positions at Chicago, Berkeley, Hawaii, Geneva, Brussels and the Bank of England. Professor Dimson co-edits the School's *Risk Management Service* and edits the Elsevier book series, *Advances in Finance, Investment and Banking*. He serves on the editorial boards of *Journal of Banking and Finance* and *Journal of Investing*. He is a director of the German Investment Trust, Mobil Trustee Company, Hoare Govett Indices Ltd and LBS Financial Software Ltd. His interests include index design, risk measurement, capital adequacy, performance evaluation and asset allocation. His degrees are from the universities of Newcastle, Birmingham and London.

Dr Gerhard Fink is professor of managerial economics and applied microeconomics at the Institute for European Affairs at the Vienna University of Economics. In the past he taught at universities in Linz, Munich, Vienna, and at the Johns Hopkins University Bologna Center. During 1973–1990 he was affiliated to the Vienna Institute for Comparative Studies (director during 1984–1990). He also has a certificate of the Austrian Chamber of Commerce as business consultant. Professor Fink has published nearly 90 books and articles. He has presented his research on several lecture tours in the northern hemisphere in 24 countries, at universities and leading research institutes in more than 80 major cities worldwide, and has organized and co-organized more than 50 international conferences. He is a member of the board of two Austrian associations on east and Central European Affairs, member of four national and seven international learned societies, among these the European Economic Association and the Japanese Foundation for Advanced Information and Research.

Barry Howcroft is senior lecturer in banking and director of Loughborough University Banking Centre. Prior to joining the university in 1978 he was employed by National Westminster Bank plc and has experience in both domestic and international banking. Since joining the university he has written a large number of articles and is the author of and contributor to eleven books on banking. In 1992 he received the Literati Club award for excellence for the most outstanding paper.

He has lectured extensively throughout the UK and the Middle East and is a management consultant for the Royal Bank of Scotland and Sundridge Management Centre where he has considerable experience of the training needs of delegates from Eastern Europe.

Dr Rezaul Kabir is associate professor of finance at the Department of Business Administration, Tilburg University, The Netherlands. From 1986 to 1990 he held a research-cum-teaching position at the University of Limburg, Maastricht from where he received his doctorate in finance. He received his MBA from the University of Dhaka, Bangladesh (1981), and his MBA (1984) and MA in economics (1985) from the Catholic University of Leuven, Belgium. His research interests lie in the areas of corporate finance, corporate control and regulation.

Dr Evi Kaplanis is assistant professor of finance at the London Business School, Citibank Research Fellow and joint director of the Master of Science in finance. Her research and publications are on international portfolio investment, the welfare effects of exchange controls, foreign exchange risk, hedging and the regulation of EC capital markets. She was previously convenor of the PhD programme in finance and a former director of the London Business School's short course on options. She has been a consultant on international portfolio investment, options and developing capital markets.

Donald R. Lessard is professor of international management at the MIT Sloan School of Management. His research and teaching interests include international aspects of corporate finance; the interaction between corporate strategy and corporate finance; and financing the less developed countries, especially Latin America.

One of the originators of the concept of operating exposure to foreign exchange rate movements, his publications on foreign exchange risk management include articles in the *Harvard Business Review*, *Journal of Applied Corporate Finance*, and *Journal of International Financial Management and Accounting*.

He has been consultant to banks, firms and government agencies including Argentaria (Spain), General Re Financial Products, Merck, Pepsi Co, Repsol (Spain), Chemical Bank, Santander Investments (Spain), Marakon Associates, The World Bank, USAID, UNIDO, UNCTAD, and the governments of Canada, Ecuador, Peru, Kuwait and Slovenia.

He has been at MIT since 1973 and has been a visiting professor at the London Business School, Stanford University, IESE (Barcelona), STOA (Naples), and the Stockholm School of Economics.

Paul Marsh, professor of management and finance and joint director of the Masters' Programme, was previously with Esso Petroleum and Scion. He was formerly faculty dean and deputy principal and director of the London Business School's Sloan Programme, and was a member of the CBI Task Force on City/Industry relations. Director of the Corporate Finance Evening Programme. Author of *Short-Termism on Trial*, co-author of *Cases in Corporate Finance*. Director of M&G Investment Management and Hoare Govett Indices. Research, publications and consulting in corporate finance, finance and strategy, smaller companies, the stock market and short-termism.

Ralf W. H. Martens is a management consultant in Europe. He received his MBA degree from the Stern School of Business, New York University in 1992.

Dr Eduardo Martínez-Abascal is associate professor of finance at IESE (International Graduate School of Management, Barcelona) and deputy dean for the MBA programme. His research work covers capital markets and portfolio management. He is author of *Weak Form Efficiency in the Spanish and European Stock Markets* and *Portfolio Management with Options and Futures*. He has studied the Spanish IPO' experience, covering the past eight years, and published several articles and research papers. Before joining IESE, Professor Martínez-Abascal was managing director of an investment company running a group of mutual funds and closed-end investment companies. Professor Martínez-Abascal has been visiting scholar at the Sloan School of Management, MIT.

Dr Antonio Mello has an MA and MBA, both from Columbia University, and a PhD from the University of London. After spending four years teaching in the Sloan School of Management, MIT, he has joined the research and statistics department of the Banco de Portugal. He has written articles in the *Journal of Banking and Finance* and has acted as consultant both for government agencies and for several financial institutions.

Professor Roger W. Mills is professor of accounting and finance at Henley Management College, where he is director of studies of the faculty. He has a first degree in psychology, sociology and economics, a master's degree in management studies and a PhD in finance. He trained as an accountant in industry and is a fellow of the Chartered Institute of Management Accountants, a fellow of the Chartered Institute of Secretaries and Administrators and a fellow of the Association of Corporate Treasurers. He is a co-author of a number of books on accounting and finance and is the author of numerous articles on such subjects as strategic, financial and value analysis, project appraisal and business evaluation.

David Myddelton is a chartered accountant, and a graduate of the Harvard Business School. He has been professor of finance and accounting at the Cranfield School of Management since 1972 where he has held a number of senior posts, including acting director of the School of Management and dean of the Faculty of Management. He has written textbooks on financial accounting, management accounting, financial management and economics, and other books on tax reform and on inflation accounting. He is on the council of the University of Buckingham, and is a member of the advisory council of the Institute of Economic Affairs.

Bill Neale is lecturer in accounting and finance at the University of Bradford Management Centre. He began his academic career at the University of Sheffield as a temporary lecturer in finance, and then spent many years at Sheffield City Polytechnic teaching managerial economics and corporate finance. His research interests are in investment appraisal systems, especially post-auditing procedures, and international trade, in particular, counter-trade. He has nearly one hundred publications to his name in a variety of academic and professional outlets and has recently written *Corporate Finance and Investment* (jointly with R.H. Pike) for Prentice Hall. He has close links with the accountancy bodies, being an examiner for ACCA and a contributor to CIMA's Mastercourses programme, and has lectured in numerous overseas countries including Holland, Ireland, Turkey, Hungary and Lithuania.

Dr Anthony Neuberger is an assistant professor at the London Business School (LBS) where he holds the S.G. Warburg Research Fellowship. He teaches corporate finance, capital markets and investment management. His research interests include options, derivative instruments and the structure of financial markets. Before joining the faculty of LBS in 1985, he worked for 10 years in the UK civil service, first in the cabinet's Central Policy Review Staff and latterly in the Department of Energy.

Reinhard Petschnigg has a master's degree in European management from the Community of European Management Schools (CEMS) and a PhD from the University of Business Administration and Economics, Vienna. In 1993 he was research assistant at the Institute for European Affairs, Brussels, investigating bank strategies and European monetary union. Since October 1993 he has been with the Austrian National Bank, Division for Integration Affairs and International Financial Institutions.

Serge Platonow completed his MBA degree at INSEAD in Fontainebleau, France, in 1992, and is employed by the government of Canada in Ottawa.

Xavier Puig is associate professor at the University Pompeu Fabra in Barcelona. He has held visiting appointments at universities in Europe and America. He is the author of two finance books published in Spanish and French and is financial consultant to several governments and multinational companies operating in Spain.

Dr Ahmad Rahnema is professor of finance at IESE (International Graduate School of Management) where he teaches international finance in the MBA programme and executive education programmes. He received his MBA from Western Michigan University and his PhD from IESE in 1979 and 1991, respectively. He has worked for a variety of consulting and financial institutions internationally, specializing in international business. His research has dealt mainly with international finance and risk management. Professor Rahnema has also acted as consultant to various industrial and financial institutions.

Keith Redhead is principal lecturer in financial economics at Coventry University. He also teaches at the City University Business School, the European School of Management in Oxford, the University of Birmingham and Loughborough University. His publications include about forty articles and three books: *Financial Risk Management* (with S. Hughes), *Introduction to Financial Futures and Options*, and *Introduction to the International Money Markets*. He was the first chief examiner for the Securities Institute examination in financial futures and options. He has carried out in-house training for Salomon Brothers, Merrill Lynch and DKB International as well as operating as an ongoing consultant for Hyperion Training Ltd.

H. Lee Remmers is professor of finance and director of the 'Alpha' programme at INSEAD, France. Co-author of *The Strategy of Multinational Enterprises: Organization and Finance, The International Firm*, and *The Multinational Company in Europe*, he has also written journal articles on investment decisions, financial markets, capital structure of firms and foreign exchange management, as well as case studies, computer models of financial problems, and the international finance simulation, FORAD. He has organized many executive development programmes for multinationals worldwide.

Dr Ken Robbie has been research fellow of the Centre for Management Buy-out Research (CMBOR) at the University of Nottingham since it was founded by Barclays Development Capital Limited and Touche Ross in 1986. Prior to joining CMBOR he held positions at the Bank of England, the Moscow Narodny Bank and Tanganyika Holdings where he was actively involved in corporate restructuring through management buy-out of Elbar Industrial. As well as contributing to the Centre's research and statistical publications, he is co-author (with M. Wright and J. Normand) to *Touche Ross Management Buy-outs* and (with M. Wright, B. Chiplin and S. Thompson) of *Buy-ins and Buy-outs: New Strategies in Corporate Management* and contributed to buy-out handbooks published by *The Economist* and *Euromoney*. He has published in a variety of journals including *Journal of Business Venturing, Omega, Journal of Applied Corporate Finance, Strategic Management Journal* and *Entrepreneurship: Theory and Practice*.

Thomas Ryan acts as a consultant to financial firms and other firms in the service sector on strategic and financial management. He is a graduate of the London Business School MBA programme, and has also qualified as a chartered accountant in Ireland. He has held accounting and financial management positions in the film, computer and advertising industries.

Karel Scheepers studied business administration at Tilburg University, The Netherlands. After graduation in 1991 he started working at Koninklijke PTT Nederland as a junior corporate finance officer, where he took part in the flotation process of the KPN. In 1993 he completed a postgraduate study of financial economics at the Tilburg Institute of Academic Studies (TIAS).

Ian Shepherdson graduated with first-class honours in banking and finance at Loughborough University and subsequently obtained a PhD in economics at the same university. He is now senior UK economist with Midland Global Markets.

Roy C. Smith has been on the faculty of the Stern School of Business at New York University since September 1987 as a professor of finance and international business. Prior to assuming this appointment he was a general partner of Goldman, Sachs & Co., specializing in international investment banking and corporate finance. Upon his retirement from the firm to join the faculty, he was the senior international partner. During his career at Goldman Sachs he set up and supervised the firm's business in Japan and the Far East, headed business development activities in Europe and the Middle East and served as president of Goldman Sachs International Corporation while resident in the firm's London office from 1980 to 1984.

His principal areas of research include international banking and finance, global capital market activity, mergers and acquisitions, leveraged transactions, foreign investments, the problems of third world debt, and privatization of Eastern European businesses. In addition to various articles in professional journals and special features, he is the author of *The Global Bankers*, *The Money Wars*, and *Comeback: The Restoration of American Banking Power in the New World Economy*. He is also co-author with Ingo Walter of *Investment Banking in Europe: Restructuring in the 1990s*, and *Global Financial Services*.

Dr Mike Staunton completed his PhD in finance from the London Business School on the pricing of airline assets and their valuation by securities markets. His research interests include project evaluation and the costs of financial regulation. He also has written case studies on treasury management and corporate foreign exchange hedging. He has lectured extensively on finance, especially equity portfolio management and spreadsheet modelling. He has a background in commercial and merchant banking and holds an MBA from the London Business School.

Dr Paul Stonham is associate professor of finance and editor of *European Management Journal* at EAP European School of Management, Oxford. He is the author of two books and over 30 papers in academic journals. His career includes assistant director at the Bank of England, Committee on Invisible Exports, Training Officer at UNCTAD, Geneva, and director, Commonwealth Bureau of Agricultural Economics, Oxford. He has undertaken many consulting projects for the Statistical Office of the European Communities and the World Bank in Europe, Africa and Australia. His current research is into European stock markets and banking. He is also a member of EFMD's jury for the annual case writing competition in European management.

Hugh Thomas is assistant professor of finance at McMaster University in Hamilton, Ontario. He completed his doctorate in finance and international business at New York University in 1991.

Theo Vermaelen is professor of finance at the University of Limburg and at INSEAD, France, where he teaches in undergraduate, MBA, PhD and executive programmes. He has taught at the University of British Columbia, the Catholic University of Leuven, the London Business School, UCLA and the University of Chicago. He has published several articles on corporate finance and investment in leading academic journals, including the *Journal of Finance, Journal of Financial Economics*, and *Journal of Banking and Finance*. He is editor of the *Journal of Empirical Finance*, associate editor of the *Journal of Corporate Finance* and of the *Journal of Financial Management*. He is also a consultant to various corporations and government agencies and programme director of the Amsterdam Institute of Finance.

Ingo Walter is Charles Simon Professor of Applied Financial Economics at the Stern School of Business, New York University, and also serves as director of the New York University Salomon Center, an independent academic research institute founded in 1972 to focus on financial institutions, instruments and markets. He also holds a joint appointment as Swiss Bank Corporation Professor of International Management, INSEAD, Fontaine-bleau, France. Dr Walter's principal areas of academic and consulting activity include international trade policy, international banking, environmental economics, and economics of multinational corporate operations. He has published papers in various professional journals in these fields and is the author or editor of 21 books, the most recent of which is *Universal Banking in the United States*, co-authored with Professor Anthony Saunders. At present his interests focus on competitive structure, conduct, and performance in the international banking and financial services industry, as well as international trade and investment issues.

Christian C.P. Wolff is professor of finance and chairman of the finance department at the University of Limburg and a research fellow of the Centre for Economic Policy Research, London. Prior to his current post he held positions at the London Business School and University of Chicago. He has published in leading academic journals such as the *Journal of Finance, Journal of Business, Journal of Business and Statistics* and the *Journal of International Money and Finance,* and is editor of the *Journal of Empirical Finance.* He has taught in a number of MBA and executive programmes, is consultant to various financial institutions and is program director of the Amsterdam Instituut of Finance.

Mike Wright is professor of financial studies and director of the Centre for Management Buy-out Research at the University of Nottingham. He has published extensively on management buy-outs, mergers and divestment, corporate strategy and organizational control in both academic and professional journals. He has published in the *Journal of Business Venturing, Journal of Applied Corporate Finance, Strategic Management Journal, Entrepreneurship: Theory and Practice, Journal of Management Studies, British Journal of Management, Accounting and Business Research* and *Journal of Business Finance and Accounting.* His major books include *Management Buy-outs* (edited with J. Coyne), *Divestment and Strategic Change* (with J. Coyne), *The Logic of Mergers* (with B. Chiplin), and *The Economist Guide to Management Buy-outs* (editor, 5th edition). He has acted as consultant on venture capital and buy-outs/buy-ins to a number of venture capital organizations and the National Audit Office among others.

Amir Zafar joined Aston University in 1993 as a teaching fellow in the Corporate Management Division of Aston Business School. He is a chartered accountant, having trained with Price Waterhouse in Birmingham. He has a first-class degree in economics from the University of London.

PART 1

Alliances, Acquisitions, Privatizations

Introduction

Some of the cases in this section illustrate the many and often large-scale mergers and acquisitions which are currently taking place in the European Union (EU), such as the acquisition of Martell by Seagrams, and the takeover of Midland Bank by HSBC Holdings – both in the face of hostile counter-offers. These two bids were successful. Another case, BAT Industries, illustrates an abortive takeover (by Hoylake, a consortium specially formed by three wealthy entrepreneurs for the purpose). The three cases provide a lesson in logic; the HSBC Holdings and Seagrams' bids did fulfil a market logic, and the stock markets generally approved of the synergy, competition and market share aspects of these bids. In the case of BAT Industries, the intended 'unbundling' of BAT's assets did not take place as a result of takeover, but surprisingly, the firm later unbundled itself to some extent, focusing on two (unrelated) core activities. The Girozentrale case shows a complex situation of competition between banks in Austria where alliances and participations are changing the balance of competitive advantage in the Austrian banking business.

Another group of cases is concerned with the other large-scale ownership transformation of hitherto state-owned companies in Europe – taking state enterprises to the stock markets or, in the case of Eastern Europe, placing the enterprises with private buyers. The scale of the current privatization exercise in all the major countries of the EU is daunting; capitalization of the stock markets will be tremendously increased, and the financial implications of the privatization programmes will last a long time. The sale of Repsol, a state-owned company that heads the most important industrial group in Spain and which focuses on energy, is a good example. The impact of such a large flotation on the fledgling Spanish stock exchange was critical.

Another huge privatization (initial public offer) is that of Koninklijke

PTT Nederland in 1994, the biggest flotation in the history of the Amsterdam Stock Exchange, and a state enterprise operating in a rapidly evolving and growing industry. A different picture is painted in the case of Jenapharm, a pharmaceutical manufacturer owned by the erstwhile East German government. Although considered a successful agency of privatization, the Treuhandanstalt was motivated by the need to sell off the company as rapidly as possible to any potential buyer in an environment where buyers were scarce. The lessons of the three privatization projects are very relevant to the wave of many privatizations currently planned or in progress in Europe, particularly in terms of financial techniques adopted and market impact.

Our three remaining cases include one which focuses on the market position of a large, pan-European bank, Crédit Lyonnais, in its attempt to break into profitable European business and to increase its competitive advantage both geographically and in customer segments. For Crédit Lyonnais, it concerned the personal strategy of a high-profile chief executive officer attempting to create a 'European champion' bank by increasing its size, being very pan-European, controlling tightly its corporate banking customers and having a 'special relationship' with the French government. In the second case, Lucas Industries was faced with the problem of how to distribute profits at a time when a final dividend was due, and involves consideration of future profit policy. Finally, the international news and media company, Reuters, provides a case study of a company with cash in excess of its operating and strategic requirements, which decided, in 1993, to return a large part of this excess to shareholders in the form of a share repurchase. At the time, this involved a decision to reject other ways of rewarding shareholders (the increased dividend return) and consequently led the company to examine carefully the technical effects of the buy-back, the implications for the stock market, and the longer-return strategic inferences for the company including attitude towards market positioning and its competitors.

HSBC Holdings/Midland Bank Takeover (A)

Strategy, Tactics and Logic

In 1992, the Hong Kong and Shanghai Banking Corporation successfully took over Midland Bank plc following a non-hostile bid. The takeover also represented the culmination of a long-term strategy on the part of HSBC Holdings. The result was the creation of the second largest non-Japanese bank in the world and the largest in the UK, measured by 1992 market capitalisation. However, the bid was strongly contested by Lloyds Bank in a counter-bid in the spring of 1992.

Part A of this case study analyses the competing bidders' strategies in attempting to acquire Midland Bank, the logic of each bidder's offer, and the tactics employed in wooing Midland's directors and shareholders. The role of regulation had a major effect on the outcome.

The Announcement

The headquarters of HSBC Holdings (the parent company of the Hong Kong and Shanghai Banking Corporation, or 'Hongkong Bank') is a futuristic building in Queen's Road Central, Hong Kong. That of Midland Bank is a Lutyens-designed, rather impractical edifice in Poultry, London. On 17 March 1992, the chairman of HSBC Holdings, William Purves, and Group Chief Executive of Midland Bank, Brian Pearse, jointly made an historic announcement – that HSBC Holdings would make an offer for the whole of Midland's share capital. Although the proposed deal was announced as a merger, it would in fact be a takeover. The takeover would create a huge transcontinental banking group; ranked by 1991 tier one capital the enlarged HSBC would have been the eighth largest bank in the world. Measured by

This case was written by Paul Stonham as a basis for class discussion rather than to illustrate either effective or ineffective handling of an administrative situation. The case has been compiled from published sources. © Paul Stonham, EAP European School of Management, Oxford, 1993.

1992 market capitalisation it would rank as the second largest non-Japanese bank in the world and the largest in the UK.

The news came as a surprise to some and not to others. Earlier, on 10 March, William Purves, in announcing an end of financial year 1991 rise of 83% in profits, went on to say that he wished to scotch two rumours then currently making the rounds of financial markets. One was that the bank would make a rights issue in 1992 and the other that it would be making a European acquisition. In the event, both rumours proved correct. On the question of an acquisition, Purves went further to say that the bank's preference remained for an 'alliance' along the lines of the one it currently enjoyed with the American Bank, Wells Fargo.

First reaction by analysts and the press in the UK and Hong Kong was not favourable. In the *Financial Times* of 8 May, John Plender wrote that:

> All recent History suggests that acquisitive financial institutions with grandiose global aspirations have a marked tendency to come unstuck.

Plender pointed to the US commercial banks' incursion into the UK securities market in the mid-1980s, Barclays and National Westminster's 'recent adventures' in North America, Fuji Bank's 'disastrous' acquisition of Chicago-based Walter E. Heller and, most hurtfully, Midland Bank's 'catastrophic' acquisition of Crocker in California, and HSBC's 'unhappy experience' with Marine Midland in the USA. 'Lex', in the *Financial Times* of 15 April said, 'There is something not quite right about the marriage contract between the Midland and Hongkong Bank'. The *Investors Chronicle* was nastier: on 20 March it said that HSBC's coded message was, 'We're so desperate to get out of Hong Kong before the Chinese overwhelm us that even Midland seems attractive', and Midland's coded message was, 'If we shrink much more we'll have little choice but to become a glorified building society – what else can we do but shack up with these guys?'

Although rather simplistically put, these views were not out of touch with the general feeling at the time. The perceived wisdom of the banking industry then, and even after the HSBC bid was consolidated, was that cross-border bank mergers do not work. A major reason they did not work lay in cultural problems – these have prevented cross-border bank mergers taking place on the Continent of Europe. One of the biggest deals in European banking that never came off was that between AB/AMRO and Generale Bank where cross-shareholdings were made. The idea was to combine the two banks and form a truly 'European' one. It failed because they did not speak the same language, have the same culture, or even have the same attitude towards banking. Cross-border banking mergers were seen in banking circles as merely an extension of the internationalisation strategy which had failed in the 1970s and 1980s.

On the other hand, in-market mergers did work because they took excess capacity out of the banking system. Not only was this reduction in capacity badly needed, but also such mergers or acquisitions could *aggressively* cut costs. Analysts generally reckon that a target bank's costs can be reduced by an in-market merger within two to three years of completion and that in fact in the USA the figure is closer to 40%.

The 'in-market' argument was in fact used persuasively following the next surprise announcement on 28 April by Lloyds Bank – that it was considering making a counter-offer for Midland's share capital. The markets had known that Sir Jeremy Morse, Chairman of Lloyds Bank, had approved a bid at a directors' meeting on 24 April. So by the end of April 1992 the stage had been set for a courtship of Midland Bank by two suitors with the suspicion of a stormy affair.

Antecedents to the Bid

The bid of 17 March 1992 was in fact the culmination of a long-term strategy on the part of HSBC Holdings to achieve a substantial operating presence in Europe. As early as 1981 the Hong Kong and Shanghai Banking Corporation (Hongkong Bank) had made a counter-offer for the Royal Bank of Scotland, which was already subject to a bid from Standard Chartered Bank. Both bids failed when they were disapproved by the Monopolies and Mergers Commission, not least because of the strength of Scottish nationalism.

Having been unsuccessful in this move, the Hong Kong and Shanghai Banking Corporation's next step was to acquire 14.9% of new equity in Midland Bank in December 1987. From 1987 onwards, the two banks co-operated to rationalise their overlapping banking operations in 13 countries, establish systems of cross-referral of business, co-operate in information technology, form joint ventures and develop joint business plans for complementary products.

Discussions between Hongkong Bank and Midland were held again in 1990 on the possibility of a full merger, but the time was not held to be auspicious. Nineteen ninety was a poor trading year for both banks, and a major inflection point for the global banking industry generally. Hongkong Bank had large and very badly managed exposure in Australia and the USA (through Marine Midland) and Midland was just coming into recession and dealing with a severe treasury structural problem. Nineteen ninety was a year when profits collapsed for both banks. It made it difficult for either bank to value itself in terms of a merger and therefore to give true value to shareholders. On top of all that, both banks had intense management problems within their own organisations of actually coping with recession and the effects it would have on their organisations. Following that, Midland Bank ran out of distributable reserves and became the first British bank since the 1930s to cut its dividend. The erstwhile chairman, Sir Kit McMahon, departed.

The Players' Strategies

At the end of 1991, the three banks were in different positions from the point of view of financial strength and competitiveness. Hongkong Bank, after a poor 1990, turned in good 1991 results, and the 1992 results were remarkable: 1991 saw an 83% rise in net income after minorities. Hang Seng Bank – Hongkong Bank's subsidiary – returned even better results, with both banks disclosing inner reserves for the first time, which all had underestimated. HSBC was a strong international bank in a growth and recovery situation. One-third of its operating revenues came from Hong Kong where the Hongkong Bank and Hang Seng Bank had a powerful technological lead and market penetration. This dependence on the domestic Hong Kong market was a plus, since it was clearly high-growth. In 1991, HSBC's equity/assets ratio was 5.62%, return on assets 0.83%, and return on equity 12.7%. Its market capitalisation at the end of 1991 was £5 billion.

Midland Bank, the target, presented a much less rosy picture, although it confounded its critics by actually earning a small pre-tax profit of £36 million and maintaining a dividend of 1.7p following a heavy cut in dividend in the last half of 1990. The size of Midland's problem could be judged by the scale of its charges to cover the risk of bad debts – £903 million – even though that was lower than expected by analysts. On the other hand, the second half of 1991 saw a decline in the bad debt charge. Despite Midland being the smallest and weakest of the UK clearing banks (it was among the world's largest banks in the 1950s) it was believed to have passed the worst in 1991 and be on the road to recovery: 1991 EPS was 6.3p, and dividend 3.4p; in 1992 it was estimated that ROE was 7.9%, but tier one capital had improved to 5.5% and BIS total ratio to 10.3%. Its market capitalisation in 1991 was £3.1 billion.

Finally, Lloyds Bank, the other contender, was easily the strongest of the UK clearers, and generally agreed to be the best managed of the clearing banks at the forefront of developing a successful banking strategy compatible with generating a high level of profitability. Nineteen ninety-one results showed post-tax profit of £449 million in 1991 with an EPS of 28.6p and a dividend of 16.7p. In 1991, Lloyds Bank had an ROE of 18% and a tier one ratio of 6.2%. Its market capitalisation was £5.3 billion. Although Lloyds Bank faced the same UK market conditions as Midland, it did so from a far healthier competitive position.

Exhibit 1.1 compares major indicators for HSBC Holdings with the four largest UK clearing banks in 1991.

The Strategy – HSBC

HSBC's strategy for the acquisition of Midland Bank was set out clearly in its offer document dated 8 May 1992. The document emphasised that HSBC was a UK-based international banking group and that the merger (sic) would establish Midland as a major part of that new group.

From HSBC's point of view it had already built up cross-border trade and investment flows based on its trading origins in the Far East. It was, of course, the dominant banking force in Hong Kong and its growth had been driven mainly by the dynamic Hong Kong economy and its links with China. Many of HSBC's customers were international in their activities and outlook and HSBC was called upon increasingly to provide services in markets other than the Far East. Through natural expansion and acquisition HSBC had operations throughout the Asia-Pacific region, North America and the Middle East.

For HSBC, though, an important area in which they had little market penetration was Europe. Although HSBC already had a 15% stake in Midland, although many of its assets and much of its revenue was located in the UK and although it had some capital markets business in Continental Europe, it did not have any significant corporate or retail banking operations in the European Union which was clearly a key banking market. Midland Bank had a presence in Europe through Trinkhaus and Burkhardt in Germany, Euromobiliare in Italy and Midland SA in France. The takeover would also give HSBC a presence in Switzerland through Guyerzeller. Apart from this, Midland had a network in Continental Europe offering wholesale and investment services to corporate and private clients. HSBC wished to take advantage of this, especially as it believed SEM trade with Asia would continue to increase. The *quid pro quo*, of course, would be Midland's participation in the fast-growing economies of Asia.

The size argument was quite powerful for the enlarged group, with the combined market capitalisation of the two banks increasing by nearly 50% over HSBC's total. Hong Kong was already one of the world's top ten

Exhibit 1.1   *HSBC Holdings compared with the four major UK clearing banks*

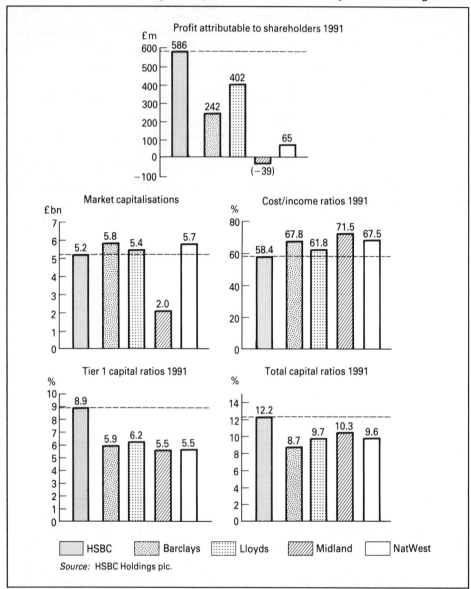

Source: HSBC Holdings plc.

banks in foreign exchange, deposits and capital market instruments. A combination with Midland would place it in the top three in these categories. HSBC would benefit from the fact that business in the major financial centres London, New York and Tokyo would be transacted in the Midland name because of its OECD status, and Midland would co-ordinate the group's activities. The increased size of the group reflected in its stronger capital position and international presence meant that it would also be able to take advantage of the higher pricing available in the international lending markets.

HSBC, at the time of the offer, also realised that UK banking in early 1992 had long-term recovery prospects – not only from loan-loss provisions, but also from improving operating profits. All of the UK banks had demonstrated a strong control of costs in 1991 and had reasonable rates of growth in income, particularly in fees. Midland also returned a modest pre-tax profit in its interim 1992 results, a good sign that things were improving. Midland itself represented one of the best recovery prospects because of its low level of profits, and although it appeared to make a negative contribution originally to the combination, prospects were good.

Clearly, HSBC's strength lay in Hong Kong. The Hongkong Bank accounted for approximately one-third of the group's assets and half of its operating revenues. It was the largest bank in Hong Kong and its very profitable subsidiary, Hang Seng, was the second largest bank, so it had a grip on the banking business of a dynamic economy. Hang Seng's business was almost entirely local; it was a very liquid bank with negligible debt problems, and had big reserves on which it was earning interest. Banking in Hong Kong was currently a dream, the banks had the best of all worlds – high lending volume, low deposit rates, high lending rates and, because of fast economic growth and inflationary asset values, low bad debts. HSBC's strong local retail banking business was really its core business and was the strength it brought to the new combination.

Midland could also count on the powerful *entrée* Hongkong Bank had into China. More than 60 million people live in China's Guandong Province, just across the border from Hong Kong. Fuelled by trade and investment from Hong Kong, the province has averaged 12% growth per year in real terms for a decade, in effect doubling in size every six years. China itself has experienced average annual growth of 8.7% in real terms for 12 years. HSBC has 13 offices in China whose foreign trade has averaged 12.2% growth per year for the past 12 years. In 1991, 45% of China's export business passed through Hong Kong.

Whilst there is rising competition from Chinese People's Republic banks in the local domestic market of Hong Kong, Hongkong Bank and Hang Seng Bank have strong leads in market share and organisation of the local banking cartel (there is no central bank) and by the high savings rate typical of Hong Kong Chinese. The Chinese community is very conscious of security and if there are any banking runs it is always Hongkong Bank and Hang Seng that are the principal beneficiaries.

HSBC was in fact challenging the prevailing wisdom of the international banking industry by attempting a global takeover. As mentioned earlier, only in-market mergers have really received approval. The main rationale of HSBC's takeover was to increase revenue-generation through the enhancement of its global capabilities and to consolidate the group's position in the foreign exchange, trade finance and treasury markets. HSBC's offer document spells out synergy benefits it expects from the takeover, which would result in growth through increased business. The key areas of growth were expected to be treasury, trade-related services and corporate banking, but big improvements were also expected in other areas like correspondent banking and private banking. The growth would arise from a combination of higher market share and cross-selling of fee-earning products and services.

As well as expected business growth, HSBC expected the enlarged group would cut out duplicated services and streamline cost structures. Since not much of HSBC and Midland's retail business overlapped, there was limited scope for rationalising branches, but the rationalisation would instead be mostly achieved in information technology and from operational back office and premise savings in London, Tokyo, New York and other locations as the enlarged group consolidated businesses and standardised head office functions. HSBC made a provision of £190 million for restructuring costs – costs of redundancies and closing offices – but the benefits of the resulting lower running costs would feed through immediately to income.

HSBC had strong treasury, international and corporate operations and, following the takeover, would merge these functions of Midland and HSBC, so that there would not be the costs of running two businesses. There would be just one global/forex operation. HSBC's strong capital base would allow the enlarged group to benefit from higher pricing of international loans likely to be sustained for several years.

Hongkong Bank had particular strengths in technology; its electronic banking service 'Hexagon' had proved very successful. Its cost of processing is very low in comparison with other banks, especially Midland, and therefore should have given rise to big savings in the enlarged group. In 1991, information technology would have accounted for about 15% of the enlarged group's total costs. In fact, production processing costs would have been brought down by combining data centres and communications networks. The introduction of common application processing systems across the enlarged HSBC group would have brought down costs in systems development and maintenance.

Hongkong Bank had especial strength in small and medium-sized businesses, the traditional customer base of the bank in Hong Kong. This, of course, was an asset to the enlarged group. Many of HSBC's small to medium-sized corporate customers were owned by high net worth individuals. HSBC saw these customers attracted to Midland's well-established European-based private banking services.

HSBC was an international bank operating through a system of regional franchises. This had been an engine of growth for the group and should have continued to support the enlarged group.

The Downside to HSBC

International banking is a risky business, as many organisations have found out to their cost. HSBC faced uncertainty from its particular focus of business – Asia. In 1997 the colony of Hong Kong will revert to the People's Republic of China and the run-up is presenting political and economic tensions. Although Hong Kong is a high-growth economy, it is currently experiencing high inflation, rising manufacturing costs and rising property prices.

In theory, the Chinese authorities could have been very obstructive to HSBC's enlargement, for example by refusing banking licences for a new branch. But Hongkong Bank was vital for China's trade and financing, and it was not likely to wish to damage that business relationship. Wisely, Hongkong Bank had not lent on a large scale to China or bought into property there on a large scale. Confining itself to financing customers who have established manufacturing bases in China and financing Chinese trade has been, largely, a non-interventionists, pragmatic and profitable way of benefiting from China's high growth rate.

HSBC operates in countries like Malaysia where nationalism is a powerful factor affecting local business. In Malaysia, for example, incorporation will be required in 1994, with possible local shareholding participation.

A final weakness of HSBC related to its exposure as an international bank. In the past it had had to make provisions for shipping, property and LDC debt. It had large exposure to Olympia and York, the developers of Canary Wharf, London, recently declared bankrupt. It amounted to about US$750 million.

Midland Bank's Strategy

In early 1992, Midland Bank was the weakling of UK banking. It entered the year as the smallest of the UK clearers, barely scraping a profit and, although bad debt provision had fallen, operating income fell even faster (at 4%) than the rate at which the bank managed to cut its costs (2%). Later, in 1992, costs were reduced by 4% (excluding Thomas Cook).

In fact, the 1992 results pointed to a recovery situation. It had increased its ratio of provisions to lending to 4.19% (the highest of all the UK clearers), it also had the strongest ratio of domestic provision to lendings (5.09%), which, if personal mortgages were included, was twice the ratios achieved by its competitors. Similarly, its credit quality improved in 1992, with provisionable exposure falling continually to £2.77 billion in June 1992. Its strategy had been to reduce developing country debt and improve the quality of its portfolio. This had been achieved by debt sales, debt swaps and Brady-style restructuring arrangements. By June 1992 Midland's provisions had risen to 57% of exposure. Net exposure to developing countries as a proportion of shareholder funds had fallen from 93% in 1988 to 50% in June 1992 (18% less than that of Lloyds at the last date).

The bank had increased its liquid assets as a proportion of total assets from 16.8% in 1989 to 19.2% in June 1992, and had its entity rating upgraded by Bank Watch in July 1992, although, in common with all corporate groups in the USA, Western Europe and the Far East, saw its senior debt rating fall.

This picture shows Midland as weak in financial terms, but it was considered a recovery stock. Its general strategy still remained to increase its share of the stagnating UK banking market, but of course, it was up against institutions with the same aim – also trying to offer improved service without sacrificing margin. Although the UK banks had recently been successful at prising business away from the building societies, the next stage was fiercer inter-bank competition.

Midland's problem in 1992, in an overbanked UK market, was to sustain a steady flow of UK profits in order to pay dividends without incurring a large bill for unrelieved ACT. But the prospects for this were not certain. The UK recession had been long and deeply entrenched although it may have then turned the corner. The recession's effect could be clearly seen in the drop in such basic services as money transmission. Since Midland's customers had been making fewer banking transactions, fees and commissions paid had fallen, and the bank had cut the value of loans, although in 1991 there was a big improvement in UK banking loan and overdraft spreads (the difference between the interest on assets and funds).

One of Midland's major costs was maintaining a network of high street branches – it had 1,800, and 57,640 employees, of which 51,000 were in the UK (at the end of 1991). Clearly, Midland had in mind considerable cost savings to be achieved by branch closures and staff rationalisation, and this in fact was a major part of Lloyds' takeover strategy. During the year, Midland changed the regional structure of its UK branch banking to devolve management power to new regional units – this would assist any rationalisation strategy.

Midland's strategy in 1992, therefore, consisted of consolidating its 1991 gains, cutting costs, recovering profits, and strengthening its capital ratios. But, although it had studied its future as an independent bank, it clearly had an overstretched retail banking network, and was under-capitalised to compete strongly. Some parts of Midland's business, like treasury, continued to be strong.

In the background to Midland's strategy lay the knowledge that HSBC had a 14.9% stake in the bank's equity, and that it had tried earlier to bring about an integration of the two banks. It was vulnerable to a bid. During 1991 Midland had had conversations with about 15 banks who said they were interested in buying parts of the bank; about one-third of these said they might be interested in a full-scale merger. At the same time, the Kuwait Investment Office, the investment arm of the Kuwait government, had a 10% equity stake in Midland which it had acquired in the 1980s, as one of its strategic holdings. Midland Bank could do little until it knew what HSBC intended to do with its shareholding. The possibility of merger or takeover, and the knowledge that HSBC would probably be a strong contender lay behind Midland's strategic thinking in 1992.

The Strategy – Lloyds

At the beginning of 1992 Lloyds Bank was the strongest of the UK clearing banks. This was not always so. When Brian Pitman was appointed chief executive in 1983, he asked his senior colleagues if the bank was successful. They said it was. In fact Pitman quoted research which said that, 'We had happy customers and happy staff'. Unfortunately, the stock market said otherwise, and Lloyds' shares were priced at only 50% of the value of assets at that time.

But by June 1992 much had been achieved by Brian Pitman. He refocused on a mission to manage the bank primarily for shareholders, and this he believed would automatically be in the interests of customers and employees. He began ruthlessly to pull out of businesses making a low return, and embarked on a policy of cutting costs. In 1991 alone, £150m was saved by reducing staff by 8,500. By June 1992, Lloyds had tier one capital of 6.7% and a total capital ratio of 10.2%, both the highest of all the UK clearing banks. At end 1991 its pretax profits were £645m, its EPS 28.6p, P/E 14.7 and net dividend 16.7p. Over the past 10 years it had returned 27% per annum compound for its shareholders.

Like Midland, it had a large staff, 57,877, including its insurance subsidiary, Lloyds Abbey Life, most of whom were UK-based. It also had a large number of branches, 2,000. Its strategy was to increase profits by focusing on productivity, by cutting costs. This had been a strategy which succeeded in the past, and still promised potential in the future – particularly by closing branches. When HSBC made its first move to bid for Midland, Lloyds knew it had a strong case which fitted in with its own internal strategy of increasing profitability by rationalisation.

Lloyds clearly had an interest in a merger with Midland. It had previously made evaluations of the TSB Group, Royal Bank of Scotland and Standard Chartered Bank. To keep up its superior profits record, it needed an acquisition. A combination with Midland, however, would have created the most profitable banking group in the UK sector and provided a real challenge to the position of currently dominant Barclays and National Westminster Banks. Mergers succeed for reasons of cost-saving or revenue-enhancement or both. In the case of Lloyds, a Midland takeover strategy would probably have maximised benefits via cost savings, although there would have been revenue-enhancing prospects, particularly by Lloyds Abbey Life assurance business accessing the Midland customer base – in effect doubling the customer base for Black Horse Life.

But Lloyds believed it could have been onto a winner based on the savings it could have achieved by rationalisation and restructuring should it have combined with Midland. The cost savings were estimated at the time at £700 million or 14% of total 1991 operating costs, attainable mainly by reducing staff numbers by some 20,000 over a four-year period – equivalent to a 5% reduction each year on the combined group, with most of it accounted for by natural wastage. Of course, there would have been restructuring costs, estimated at £550 million, but these could have been charged to reserves of a combined group. Branch closures would probably have totalled 1,000, bringing the combined group branch network down to 2,845 – similar to Barclays and Natwest. There would also have been some geographical complementarity – Midland stronger in the north of UK and Lloyds stronger in the south. Lloyds would probably have sold parts of Midland's business that did not meet target returns. It would certainly have merged head office functions and eliminated duplication in technology.

By early 1992, Lloyds, a strong bank in a recessionary industry, and a bank which was concentrated on the UK market, eyed Midland Bank as a way of instantly curing the over-capacity of distribution in UK banking, and positioning the Lloyds/Midland combine as the dominant player on the UK banking scene, with its competitive strength firmly based on superior productivity. The UK banking scene was characterised by enormous scope for rationalising the operating base. The future held little hope for strong economic growth, and the banks' best hope for better profits lay through productivity gains, i.e. cost reductions.

Tactics and Logic

The HSBC Bid

On 17 March 1992 HSBC Holdings and Midland announced proposals to combine through a recommended offer of HSBC shares in exchange for Midland shares. It was widely believed at the time that Midland had previously been in serious negotiations with Lloyds, and that in fact HSBC's public announcement was prompted by the fear that Lloyds 'would get there first'. Nonetheless, up to 17 March, none of the rumours which abounded had any real underpinning. From this date, things became much more open. Probably the announcement was made at this time under Rule 2 of the UK City Code on Takeovers and Mergers, because both parties feared their plans would leak. The announcement said that the offer would be made at a 'significant premium' to the 253p price at which Midland's shares closed on Monday, 16 March. On Tuesday, 17, Midland's share price rose 79p to 329p.

At this stage, no formal offer from HSBC was on the table, and after 17 March both HSBC and Midland were constrained from making any further public statements about the deal by the Takeover Panel and the Stock Exchange. Bankers are precluded from making statements which might put a value on their businesses. If they do, the regulators can insist that these implied valuations can be used as merger terms. Nor could formal terms be agreed until HSBC and Midland had examined each other's books for valuation by the process known as 'due diligence'.

In fact, HSBC and Midland reached agreement on 14 April, and Sir Peter Walters, chairman of Midland, wrote to Midland shareholders advising them that HSBC's offer was 'fair and reasonable' and that he, and the other appropriate directors of Midland, intended 'unanimously to recommend Midland shareholders to accept the offer'. The basic offer was an exchange of one new HSBC share and 100p nominal of new HSBC bonds for each Midland ordinary share. This offer valued Midland at £3.1 billion and each Midland share at 378p, based on the closing price of HSBC shares on Monday, 13 April plus the estimated value of the new HSBC bonds. The basis of the offer valuation and the valuation of the combined group is examined in Part B of this case study.

Shortly after this, the offer was revised to 1.18 HSBC shares plus £50 nominal HSBC bonds for every one Midland share. It represented a more attractive offer for Midland shareholders because HSBC's share price in Hong Kong was rising.

Later, on 8 May, Schroder Wagg issued a formal offer document which set out the terms above and detailed substantial synergy benefits from combining the two banks. In the offer document they were stated to be £800 million pre-tax in the first four years of the takeover, reaching at least an annualised £300 million by 1996. This figure was arrived at by a combination of cost savings and income generation. The figure was somewhat inflated because the reorganisation itself would have cost £190 million, but this would have been charged to reserves when the offer was implemented.

At this time, Lloyd's Bank was bitterly disappointed that Midland had come out with a public announcement of an offer by HSBC when it emerged that Lloyds had been a secret suitor. It was believed Midland preferred the HSBC bid for two reasons. One was that Lloyds would almost certainly have sought to increase profitability by drastically closing branches and shedding staff. The second was that Midland did not believe the competition authorities in Brussels and the UK would have sanctioned such a large in-market combination.

At the time of making its bid, HSBC was reassured that China was not questioning the fundamental soundness of its bid for Midland Bank. HSBC had been at pains to keep the Chinese authorities informed of its intentions. There still remained, however, some suspicion that HSBC could later use Midland as a means of switching assets out of Kong Kong. The Hong Kong stock market did not, on the whole, react favourably at first to the announcement of the deal.

On 28 April, Lloyds announced plans for a hostile offer for Midland Bank. The proposed (not formal) offer was for an exchange of one new Lloyds Bank share plus 30p cash for each Midland Bank share. At that time the bid was worth 464p per Midland Bank share. Lloyds placed two preconditions on the offer becoming formal. The first was that Lloyds and HSBC should be treated equally by the regulatory authorities (specifically, if the Lloyds' offer was referred to the UK Monopolies and Mergers Commission, HSBC's offer should also be referred). Second, Lloyds should receive the same financial and other information necessary for 'due diligence' from Midland that it had supplied previously to HSBC.

The Trade and Industry secretary, Michael Heseltine, immediately met Department of Trade and Industry officials to discuss Lloyds' bid plan. The question was whether or not to refer. The Office of Fair Trading also have an advisory role here.

There are also statutory requirements to banking acquisitions or mergers in the UK. Under the Banking Act 1987, a person intending to acquire 15% or more of the voting power of a UK incorporated bank, and therefore become a 'shareholder controller' of that bank, must receive Bank of England approval.

The other area of regulatory banking control is the European Commission. Based on a ruling in 1989 (EEC Merger Regulation 4064/89), the European Commission can scrutinise a proposed takeover if the combined assets of the two banks concerned do not exceed two-thirds of their total assets in the same EC member state. If two-thirds are exceeded, the offer is referred back to the national authorities. In the case of Midland Bank, clearly two-thirds of its loans were to UK customers; HSBC was more problematic to analyse. It was also not automatically clear whether the Commission should examine the Lloyds/Midland proposed deal. Lloyds, of course, would have preferred that the Commission referred both proposals back to the UK – it wanted a 'level playing field'.

During May, the contest became intensely political. William Purves for HSBC wrote a letter to all heads of relevant UK ministries, and MPs received a letter from Sir Jeremy Morse at Lloyds. On 8 May, Brian Pearse, chief executive of Midland, wrote to all shareholders quoting his chairman, as follows:

> What is clear at the moment, in this very complex situation, is that Lloyds' hostile approach does not amount to an offer for Midland and that Lloyds recognises that it may never be able to make an offer because of competition issues. Merging with HSBC is the right strategy for Midland's future.

On 8 May, Sir Leon Brittan, EC Competition Commissioner, announced that the HSBC/Midland takeover offer, according to his calculations, fell under the jurisdiction of the European Commission but the Lloyds' bid did not.

On 19 May, HSBC announced that the Bank of England had written to say it had no objection to the HSBC/Midland takeover. At about this time, Lloyds challenged Midland's refusal to supply commercial information needed for a formal bid that Midland had already provided to HSBC. On 15 May, Lloyds won its appeal to the Panel on Takeovers and Mergers which recommended Midland should release the information to Lloyds.

On 21 May, Sir Leon Brittan stated there was no need for an extended investigation into the HSBC/Midland offer, as the two banks competed in different sectors. Lloyds' proposal did not fall within the EEC Merger Regulation since more than two-thirds of the EC assets were held in the UK. Following this news, Lloyds' only hope would have been that the European Commission would refer the HSBC's offer back to the UK regulatory authorities and get the rival bids back onto a 'level playing field'. But this hope was doomed. There were strong legal reasons why the HSBC offer could not be referred back to the Monopolies and Mergers Commission (MMC). Once the European Commission had decided that the matter fell under its jurisdiction, it could only be referred back to the national authorities if the merger 'threatened to create or strengthen a dominant position as a result of which effective competition would be significantly impeded.' (Article 9 of the Merger Regulations). Since there was very little overlap between the activities of HSBC and Midland in the UK market, there was no realistic possibility of Article 9 being invoked. One more possibility remained – Article 21 allowed referral if a British bank was taken over by an 'overseas' bank. But during 1992 HSBC had become incorporated in the UK with the Bank of England becoming the lead supervisor for the enlarged HSBC group. The European Commission's decision also removed the need for HSBC to comply with competition regulations in other EC states.

On 22nd May, the final blow was delivered to Lloyds Bank's hopes. Michael Heseltine announced that he had decided to refer Lloyds' proposed bid to the MMC. At the same time, he said there was no reason to review HSBC's proposed takeover of Midland. Earlier, the Office of Fair Trading had made these recommendations to Mr Heseltine, although he was not obliged to follow them. The MMC was asked to produce its ruling by 25 August. Only if the bid was cleared would Lloyds be able to make a formal offer.

Lloyds was now left at a considerable disadvantage. Several months would have to elapse before it got an MMC decision. All this time there was a firm offer on the table from HSBC. Midland's shareholders were obliged to accept or reject HSBC's offer before the MMC had ruled, since HSBC's offer expired in June. Also, there was no guarantee that, if turned down, HSBC would come back.

The news for Lloyds got worse. Earlier, HSBC had applied to the US Federal Reserve Board for a temporary exemption permitting it to acquire Midland's non-banking activities in the USA. This would normally require approval under the US Bank Holding Company Act. Lloyds challenged this application on a number of grounds. On 3 June, the US regulators granted approval to HSBC. It was approved on the grounds that HSBC would not be given a significant competitive advantage over a US bank holding company. Midland Bank was cock-a-hoop. In a letter of 3 June headed 'Midland Calls on Lloyds to Withdraw', the chairman, Sir Peter Walters, said:

> Lloyds should recognise reality and withdraw. There is only one offer available and that is the recommended final offer from HSBC. It is no more likely today than it was in March that Lloyds can make an offer for Midland likely to be acceptable to the Competition authorities.

It was not mentioned in the letter, but was well understood, that Lloyds had another fundamental problem in acquiring Midland. HSBC made it clear it would not sell its 15% stake in Midland. Lloyds would then never be able to buy more than 90% of Midland's shares which it would need to integrate the two businesses completely.

Lloyds Bank put out a news release on 22 May noting that its proposed offer for Midland had been referred to the MMC, and indicating that it would be advocating a strong case for clearance before the MMC, and underlining to the world at large the superiority of its proposed offer to that of HSBC.

On 2 June, HSBC made its next move, and sweetened its offer again. It announced that a new and final recommended offer would be made to Midland shareholders. For each 100 shares in Midland, shareholders were offered 120 new shares in HSBC and either £65 nominal of new HSBC bonds of £65 in cash. This offer valued each Midland share at 471p and the whole of the share capital of Midland including the shares owned by HSBC and assuming full exercise of all share options, at approximately £3.9 billion. This represented an 86% increase in value of the Midland share price since 17 March when takeover talks were announced. The announcement was joint between the boards of HSBC and Midland that agreement had been reached.

On 9 June, Lloyds threw in the towel and withdrew its offer. In a letter to Lloyds' shareholders its explanation was that:

> Given the delay and uncertainty introduced by the MMC enquiry, we considered that a substantial premium over HSBC's offer would have been needed to persuade shareholders of Midland Bank to reject that offer and wait for our own. To establish this premium, we would have had to increase our proposed offer to a level which would have given most of the benefits to Midland Bank shareholders and which accordingly we believed would not be in the interests of Lloyds Bank shareholders.

William Purves was lunching on the eleventh floor of HSBC's Bishopsgate offices in London when he was told the news. Before catching his plane back to Hong Kong he said:

> We can't afford to relax yet. But I'm glad Lloyds has gone away. I'm also glad the smokescreen has cleared. Lloyds has been a diversion and getting the institutional shareholders to concentrate on our offer was a little difficult.

He also said:

> I don't anticipate anyone appearing on the horizon in the next 18 days. But until the offer is closed and declared unconditional one cannot be certain.

He went on to say that he did not expect any of Midland's large shareholders to hold out and not accept the bid. 'If we do not have 50% acceptance on 25 June, then the offer is dead.' The waiting period was clearly going to be a tense one for HSBC.

HSBC Holdings/Midland Bank Takeover (B)

Financial Offer, Valuation and
Stock Market Reaction

The successful takeover bid for Midland Bank PLC by Hong Kong and Shanghai Bank in 1992 resulted in the creation of the second largest non-Japanese bank in the world and the largest in the UK. The bid was strongly contested by Lloyds Bank plc.

Part B of this case study focuses on HSBC Holdings' acquisition offer for Midland Bank. It involves the valuation of HSBC's and Lloyds Bank's offers and theoretical questions of the valuation of target companies' shares under a paper exchange. Valuation is made of the successfully achieved HSBC/Midland enlarged group and estimates made of shareholder value before and after the takeover as well as for Lloyds Bank pre- and post-theoretical takeover. Dilution of earnings and transfer of shareholder value as a result of the takeover are interesting aspects and an evaluation is made. Finally, the reaction of the stock market to the takeover terms is interesting and provides the basis of comparison with similar large-scale acquisitions and their effect on stock market behaviour

The Story So Far

The takeover of Midland Bank by HSBC Holdings (Hong Kong and Shanghai Banking Corporation), which had been launched on 17 March 1992, became complete (went unconditional) on 25 June 1992 when more than 50% of Midland Bank accepted HSBC's offer of a share exchange of 120 new HSBC shares plus £65 nominal new HSBC bonds for 100 Midland

This case was written by Paul Stonham as a basis for class discussion rather than to illustrate either effective or ineffective handling of an administrative situation. The case has been compiled from published sources. © Paul Stonham, EAP European School of Management, Oxford, 1993.

shares or 120 new HSBC shares and £65 cash alternative for 100 Midland shares. In a hotly-fought contest, Lloyds Bank withdrew its hostile proposed offer of 1 new Lloyds Bank share and 30p cash for each Midland share. Lloyds Bank withdrew its offer on 9 June leaving the field clear for HSBC. HSBC's offer had remained open until 25 June.

When the excitement had died down a little, analysts went to work on evaluating the prospects for the enlarged HSBC Holdings Bank and looking at some of the consequences for the banking industry. Several technical aspects of HSBC's offer created intense interest at the time, like the valuation of the offer, dilution, and the behaviour of share price: aspects like these clearly had an effect on shareholders' perceptions of the takeover. Part B of this case study looks at the financial aspects of the takeover contest.

The Financial Offer

HSBC's offer document of 11 June 1992, 'Recommended Final Offer for Midland', revised its 17 March offer of 1 new HSBC share plus 100p nominal of new HSBC bonds for each Midland share to a new offer of 120 new HSBC shares of 75p each and £65 in either new HSBC bonds due 2002 or cash for every 100 Midland shares. The HSBC shares were issued fully paid and ranked identical with the existing HSBC shares. They were denominated in sterling but equivalent to the HKS-denominated shares but not fungible (could not be traded in both London and Hong Kong). HSBC set up primary listings in both London and Hong Kong. The addition of bonds to the offer was quite innovative, since these were classed as listed, subordinated bonds, in bearer and registered form. Midland shareholders could in fact accept equivalent cash value instead of bonds and the cash was provided for in the form of an underwriting by a small group of banks led by Crédit Suisse First Boston Ltd. These banks agreed to subscribe at par for those bonds which accepting Midland shareholders who elected to receive cash instead of bonds did not wish to take up. The bonds were similar in nature to Eurobonds and were constituted as such for UK tax purposes, as long as they were in bearer form. The registered bonds were interchangeable into bearer bonds and vice versa. They satisfied the Bank of England's requirements for subordinated loan capital and ranked as tier two capital of the enlarged group. After the issue went unconditional, approximately £148 million net proceeds arising from the use of the subscribed bonds was used to pay Midland shareholders who elected to receive a cash payment.

At the completion of the transaction there were 2,440 million shares in issue, 1,638.1 million were old HSBC shares with a par value of HK$10 and the balance were new shares with a nominal value of 75p. All of the shares were included in the Hang Seng index, the FTSE 100 and the All Share Index with effect from 13 July 1992. Approximately 703 million new shares and 703 million nominal new bonds were issued by HSBC.

The valuation of HSBC's offer proved a moving target as the current share prices of HSBC and Midland varied according to the whole variety of factors affecting the takeover and share prices. In the offer document from HSBC dated 11 June 1992 an optimistic illustrative valuation was attempted as follows:

(a) *Capital Value*

	£
Market value of 120 new HSBC shares[1]	383.72
Estimated value of £65 nominal new HSBC bonds or cash under the cash election	65.00
Value of the final offer	448.72
Market value of 100 Midland shares[2]	253.00
Increase	195.72
This represented an increase of	77.4%

Notes
1. Middle market quotation of £319.77p on 8 June 1992 at the current HK$/£ rate of exchange.
2. Middle market quotation of 253p ex-div. on 16 March 1992, the day prior to the announcement of the offer by HSBC for Midland. If 8 June was taken, the middle market quotations for a Midland share were 420p per share, and the increase in capital value would have been 6.8%.

(b) *Income*

	Final offer £	Cash election £
Gross income from 120 new HSBC shares[1]	15.64	15.64
Gross income from £65 nominal new HSBC bonds[2]	7.74	–
Gross income from £65 cash[3]	–	5.98
Total gross income	23.38	21.62
Gross income from 100 Midland shares[4]	4.53	4.53
Increase	18.85	17.09

This represented an increase of   415.9%   377.0%

Notes
1. Based on interim dividend of HK$0.54(3.81p) per existing HSBC share and final dividend of HK$1.31(9.23) per existing HSBC share paid at year ended 31 December 1991.
2. Based on estimated coupon of 11.91% as at 8 June 1992.
3. Assumed cash reinvested to yield 9.20% p.a. (government medium-term 5-year securities average gross redemption yield as at 5 June 1992).
4. Based on interim dividend of 1.7p per share and second interim dividend of 1.7p per share paid at 31 December 1991.

Note 2 of the capital value table shows how capital value could be affected by changes in the price of shares. What this sort of information did not do was show accurately how merger value estimated from enhanced revenue or cost savings was divided between target shareholders and bidder company shareholders. And, of course, set out in this way it did not indicate the extent of any dilution of value of bidder shares.

Projected and Total Returns

Observers of the takeover contest for Midland were concerned not only for the share price bid and valuations of Midland as a result of the offer. Investors, in particular, were also interested to know what cost and revenue enhancement did for compounded future returns. In June 1992 Morgan Stanley Research, London, made long-term financial and earnings forecasts for HSBC, Midland and Lloyds, and the for two combinations which were still possible at the time – HSBC/Midland and Lloyds/Midland.

Exhibit 2.1 shows a pro-forma analysis to 1996 of estimated earnings for the combined HSBC/Midland group. The forecasts were based on the final recommended offer by HSBC of 1.2 HSBC shares plus 65p nominal HSBC bond or 65p cash alternative/1 Midland share. The table incorporates forecasts for Midland Bank which were based on steady but unexciting growth in income by the standards of Hong Kong, combined with a gradual reduction from the current high bad debt charge as a result of the recession in the UK coming to an end. There was provision of £200 millions for restructuring etc. The synergy benefits were stated by HSBC at £800 million, and this had been spread over the first four years of the takeover, reaching an annualised £200 million net by 1996. Dividend growth was restrained in the first two years, to absorb provision, but was expected to be more aggressive and reaching three times cover in 1996. The table also contains some writing down of equity as a consequence of the merger.

Exhibit 2.1   *HSBC/Midland Bank pro-forma earnings analysis – latest offer (£m)*

	1991	1992E	1993E	1994E	1995E	1996E
Attributable income						
Hongkong Bank (£)	585	760	953	1,159	1,365	1,538
Midland Bank	(49)	190	369	551	617	717
Total	536	950	1,322	1,710	1,982	2,255
Adjustments (net)						
HSBC dividend from Midland	(5)	(11)	(17)	(23)	(29)	(34)
Tax adjustment	–	26	39	26	–	–
Estimated cost savings	0	40	105	130	160	200
Loan stock cost[2]	(44)	(44)	(44)	(44)	(44)	(44)
Pro-forma attributable	486	960	1,405	1,799	2,069	2,377
Dividends	n/a	(363)	(429)	(510)	(644)	(7,815)
Retained earnings	n/a	597	975	1,288	1,424	1,596
Balance sheet						
Assets						
Hongkong Bank	85,786	96,819	102,728	112,616	123,600	135,811
Midland	59,408	61,780	65,487	70,071	74,976	79,474
Adjustments	(531)	(531)	(531)	(531)	(531)	(531)
Pro-forma	144,663	158,068	167,684	182,156	198,045	214,754
Equity	5,545	6,142	7,118	8,406	9,831	11,427
Key ratios and per share figures						
EPS (p)	19.6	38.4	55.6	70.5	80.3	91.3
Dilution[3]	n/a	(17.2)	(4.4)	(0.3)	(3.6)	(2.7)
Dividend (p)	n/a	14.5	17.0	20.0	25.0	30.0
ROE (%)	n/a	16.4	21.2	23.2	22.7	22.4
Equity/assets (%)	3.83	3.89	4.24	4.61	4.96	5.32

1. Based on 1.2 HSBC shares and 65p bond or cash/Midland share.
2. Cost of 12.15% per annum.
3. Dilution from HSBC stand alone EPS.
4. Hongkong Bank earnings based on HK$/£ exchange rate of 14.56 in 1991 and 13.80 for 1992–96.

E = Morgan Stanley Research estimate.
Source: Company data and Morgan Stanley Research Estimates.

Exhibit 2.1 shows that there was not a great deal of dilution in HSBC earnings as a result of the merger, although there was some. ROE, EPS, and the ratio of equity to assets all showed good growth in the combined scenario. The improvement in the combined equity/assets ratio indicated that HSBC's current strong capital ratios would be maintained or even improved upon.

Exhibit 2.2 'Summary 1996 projections and total business returns –
HSBC new offer and projected Lloyds offers' undertook an interesting
exercise. It compared total returns for Lloyds, Midland and HSBC as
independent organisations and the proposed Lloyds/Midland takeover under
two options: (a) that Lloyds increased its original proposed offer from 1
Lloyds share plus 30p cash/1 Midland share to 1.1 Lloyds shares plus 50p
cash/1 Midland share, and (b) the offer is increased to 1.2 Lloyds shares plus
50p cash/1 Midland share. These two assumed options were put in to reflect
the reality that *had not* Lloyds withdrawn its offer, it would *have had* to raise
its bid to compete effectively against HSBC. The table also included two
options for the HSBC/Midland projections: (a) an HSBC offer of 1.2 HSBC
shares plus 65p nominal HSBC nominal bonds/1 Midland share, and (b) an
offer of 1.2 HSBC shares plus 65p cash/1 Midland share with the cash
reinvested in HSBC shares.

Exhibit 2.2 shows that Midland alone as an independent bank could
have achieved a compounded return of 12.1% in 1996, which was not bad,
and reflected its recovery stock position. Lloyds and HSBC's compounded
returns reflected the basic strength of these two banks and their growth
situation. HSBC shareholders stood to fare very much the same in terms of
compounded return whether HSBC had stood alone or combined with
Midland. In a way this was success. Midland contributed little short-term
strength to the combination. Most of the gains from the HSBC/Midland deal
came about from synergy benefits and growth. These were not likely to show
their best results until around 1996. Midland shareholders, however, did well
out of the combination. From a 'stand-alone' compounded return of 12.1%
in 1996, they achieved 20.5% under the bond offer option and 21.6% under
the cash alternative option. Clearly, there was a strong transfer of value to
Midland shareholders in this deal.

As far as Lloyds shareholders are concerned, they would have seen a
better compounded return than the case where Lloyds stood alone, but
Midland shareholders would have done a lot better under both possible share
exchange options – increasing from 12.1% to 25.1% and 26.5% respectively
under options (a) and (b) – an even stronger transfer of value.

The same degree of result applied to EPS for the organisations
concerned. HSBC actually saw a small decrease in 1996. Midland in the
HSBC/Midland combination did much better. Lloyds increased modestly
from stand-alone to merged situation and Midland jumped up a lot in the
Midland/Lloyds combination.

Another message from Exhibit 2.2 is that HSBC appeared to have
reached the limit of its financial offer as far as dilution was concerned, shown
by EPS. Already there was some. If HSBC had been forced to increase its

Exhibit 2.2 Summary 1996 projections and total business returns – HSBC new offer and projected Lloyds offers (£m)

	Lloyds	Midland	HSBC	Lloyds/[3] Midland	Lloyds/[4] Midland	HSBC/ Midland[1]	HSBC/ Midland[2]
NAV (p)	418	514	539	407	390	438	438
ROE (%)	25.5	18.2	18.7	29.0	29.0	22.4	22.4
Required ROR (%)[5]	14.1	14.7	15.3	14.4	14.4	15.0	15.0
P/BV	1.81	1.24	1.22	2.01	2.03	1.49	1.49
Theoretical price (p)	756	636	659	821	790	654	654
Dividend (p)	32.6	29.2	31.5	35.0	34.0	30.0	30.0
Yield to a UK shareholder (%)	5.75	6.12	6.38	5.69	5.74	6.12	6.12
EPS (p)	97.8	87.6	94.8	107.5	103.6	91.3	91.3
P/E	7.7	7.3	6.9	7.6	7.6	7.2	7.2
Current price (p)	432	452	351	432	432	351	351

Increase in shareholder value	Lloyds	Midland	HSBC	Lloyds[3] share-holder	Midland[3] share-holder	Lloyds[4] share-holder	Midland[4] share-holder	Lloyds[1] share-holder	Midland[1] share-holder	Lloyds[2] share-holder	Midland[2] share-holder
Capital appreciation (p)	324	184	308	389	451	358	497	303	333	303	333
Dividend reinvested (p)[6]	201	130	153	215	236	213	256	155	186	155	186
Cash/bond coupon reinvestment (p)[7]	–	–	–	–	134	–	135	–	36	–	146
Bond (p)	–	–	–	–	–	–	–	–	65	–	–
Compounded return (%)	18.8	12.1	19.9	20.8	25.1	20.0	26.5	19.8	20.5	19.8	21.6

1. Based on HSBC offer of 1.2 shares and 65p bond/Midland share.
2. Based on HSBC offer of 1.2 shares and 65p cash/Midland share.
3. Assumes Lloyds increases its indicated offer to 1.1 shares and 50p cash/Midland share.
4. Assumes Lloyds increases its indicated offer to 1.2 shares and 50p cash/Midland share.
5. The required rate of return is based on an average target return for UK banks of 13.5% (long-term bond yield 9.5% plus risk premium of 4% adjusted for the beta of the stock). For HSBC we use the beta of Standard Chartered as the best proxy for a UK bank. In a merger situation we use the weighting average of the betas of the two companies.
6. Dividends reinvested is made on the basis of our projections of dividends for the banks individually and in a merger situation for the five years 1992–96. The full payment for 1996 is included even though it will not be received until 1997. Dividends for 1992 to 1995 have been reinvested in shares of the company at the ROE for the following year.
7. The cash element of the bids is assumed to be invested in shares and therefore appreciates in line with the share price. The net dividend on the HSBC loan stock is assumed to be reinvested in HSBC shares each year.

Source: Morgan Stanley Research.

bid yet again against an increased Lloyds bid such as that hypothesised in Exhibit 2.2, there would have been greater dilution of HSBC stock in a basically paper exchange and HSBC shareholders would have seen more value transferred to Midland shareholders. Lloyds, on the other hand, could have increased its bid quite significantly from the original proposed offer and still have added value for its own shareholders.

Another estimate of earnings and dilution was made by S.G. Warburg and Company in London, as shown in Exhibit 2.3. The estimates did not include synergy benefits and therefore showed uncompensated dilution. For HSBC shareholders the dilution was still modest. Its extent and duration would, of course, have depended on the timing of Midland's recovery and therefore the strength of the UK economy. In its offer document, HSBC estimated that the takeover would have brought profit benefits of at least £300 million by 1996 and savings of £800 million split equally between revenue additions and cost savings. It proposed that information technology rationalisation would have saved £70 million and combined treasury operations would have brought in £50 million.

In Exhibit 2.3 Warburgs calculated the amount of synergies needed to make the acquisition non-dilutive for holders of old HSBC shares. For example, in 1993, an additional £158 million of pre-tax income would have been required – equivalent to arrange 55% of the synergies identified as achievable by 1996. This should not have been too difficult to achieve.

In practice, there was little danger of much dilution of HSBC earnings in 1992, despite the theoretical calculations, for the amount of money that Hongkong Bank was going to earn in 1992. When the results came out they were substantially ahead of market expectations. There was then a transfer

Exhibit 2.3   *Earnings and dilution estimates – HSBC and HSBC/Midland Bank*

	1992E	1993E	1994E
Forecast EPS (pence per share)			
HSBC	37.5	58.2	75.1
Enlarged HSBC	33.3	52.8	68.6
Forecast EPS (HK$ per share)			
HSBC	5.52	8.57	11.05
Enlarged HSBC	4.90	7.77	10.10
Dilution (%)	11.2	9.3	8.6
Required synergies (£m)	145	158	185
(HK$m)	2,146	2,338	2,700
E = Morgan Stanley Research estimates.			

of value to Midland shareholders who got this unexpected windfall. Second, HSBC's shares did not fall back because the Hong Kong market had always known that HSBC intended to make a large acquisition, so that this knowledge had been discounted in the share price. At the end of the day, the Hong Kong market believed HSBC had got a realistic value for the shares it had issued. The shares held their value because the Hong Kong market believed Midland's shares had been bought at the bottom of the banking cycle, that Midland would recover, that dilution would be bearable and that HSBC was not going to make another large acquisition in Europe. In fact, HSBC's shares performed strongly in Hong Kong during the offer period and helped prevent dilution.

Exhibit 2.4 summarises the compounded returns for Lloyds, Midland and HSBC including also the two original HSBC offers: 1 HSBC share and 100p bond/Midland share and 1.18 HSBC shares and 50p bond/Midland share. Exhibit 2.5 summarises similarly for estimated earnings per share.

Exhibit 2.6 shows the effect on the FT-A Bank Index as a result of the final recommended offer by HSBC of 1.2 HSBC shares plus 65p bond or 65p cash/Midland share. The final offer included more shares than the original one; this increased both the FT-A Bank Index in the FT-A All Share Index to 6.5% and HSBC shares in the FT-A Bank Index to 24% (the largest constituent) respectively. As the table shows, an investment fund wishing to keep its current weighting in the FT-A Bank Index would have needed to increase its shareholding in value by 17%. This was one reason why there was a good aftermarket in the enlarged HSBC Holdings group shares.

Exhibit 2.4 *Summary of compound returns expressed as percentages for Lloyds, Midland and HSBC*

	Stand alone		Original offers		Increased offers	
Lloyds shareholders	18.8		21.8		20.8[3]	20.0[4]
HSBC shareholders	19.9	20.9[1]		19.9[2]	19.8[5]	19.8[6]
Midland shareholders	12.1		–		–	
Merger with Lloyds	–		22.5		25.1[3]	26.5[4]
Merger with HSBC	–	18.7[1]		19.7[2]	20.5[5]	21.6[6]

1. Based on 1 HSBC share and 100p bond/Midland share.
2. Based on 1.18 HSBC share and 50p bond/Midland share.
3. Assumes 1.1 Lloyds shares and 50p or/Midland share.
4. Assumes 1.2 Lloyds shares and 50p cash/Midland share.
5. Based on 1.2 HSBC shares and 65p bond/Midland share.
6. Based on 1.2 HSBC shares and 65p cash/Midland share.
Source: Morgan Stanley Research.

Exhibit 2.5 *Summary of 1996 estimated earnings per share (pence)*

	Stand alone		Original offer		Increased offer	
Lloyds shareholders	97.8		112.4		107.5[3]	103.6[4]
HSBC shareholders	94.8	96.5[1]		92.6[2]	91.3[5]	91.6[6]
Midland shareholders	87.6		–		–	
Merger with Lloyds	–		112.4		118.3	124.3
Merger with HSBC		96.5[1]		109.3[2]	109.6[5]	109.6[6]

1. Based on 1 HSBC share and 100p bond/Midland share.
2. Based on 1.18 HSBC share and 50p bond/Midland share.
3. Assumes 1.1 Lloyds shares and 50p cash/Midland share.
4. Assumes 1.2 Lloyds shares and 50p cash/Midland share.
5. Based on 1.2 HSBC shares and 65p bond/Midland share.
6. Based on 1.2 HSBC shares and 65p cash/Midland share.
Source: Morgan Stanley Research.

Exhibit 2.6 *Hongkong Bank in the FT-A Bank Index*

Current FT-A Bank Index	£30,750 m
Current bank sector weighting	5.6%
Increase in size of FT-A Bank Index (including new HSBC)	£5,180 m
New value of FT-A Bank Index	£35,930 m
New increased weighting	6.5%
HSBC merged value	£8,500 m
Group as a % of index	24%

Therefore a fund wishing to maintain its current weighting needs to increase its shareholding in value by 17%.

The Stock Market and Aftermarket

At the time Lloyds Bank was making its proposed offer for Midland, UK institutions favoured Lloyds over HSBC. Lloyds was known, HSBC was much less known in the UK. It was clear Lloyds, with 1.5 times the market capitalisation of Midland, could have absorbed it without any serious dilution in the short run and achieved substantial earnings enhancement – particularly if it had got its way on cost-cutting. Investors thought this would have pushed up the value of Lloyds' shares a lot and had a knock-on effect on other bank shares which they owned.

However, because the two offers were basically paper bids, there could not have been much difference in their valuation. Once Lloyds Bank ran into regulatory problems, and especially when its offer was referred to the Monopolies and Mergers Commission (MMC), a brake was applied to Lloyds' share price, and HSBC's shares were buoyant. By the time HSBC had increased its bid and its offer had become unconditional, market attitudes had changed in the UK and Hong Kong. UK institutional fund managers bought because they were underweight in the new giant combination (Exhibit 2.6), and there was substantial arbitrage in Midland shares – especially after the Kuwait Investment Office had placed 10% of Midland's shares in the market during the early stages of HSBC's bid.

In the aftermarket for HSBC's shares in the UK and Hong Kong there was heavy stock turnover, partly based on the arbitrage position built up. Midland Bank's shares rose dramatically until August 1992 when they were absorbed into HSBC's (Exhibit 2.7). The price of HSBC's shares, post the takeover, soared between August and November 1992 and only fell at that point due to turmoil in Hong Kong, but later recovered well in January 1993 (Exhibit 2.8). Lloyds Bank shares showed a strong performance during 1992 which continued in 1993 (Exhibit 2.9). The share performance of HSBC (enlarged group) and Lloyds Bank can be compared in Exhibit 2.10.

Exhibit 2.7   *Midland Bank indexed share prices*

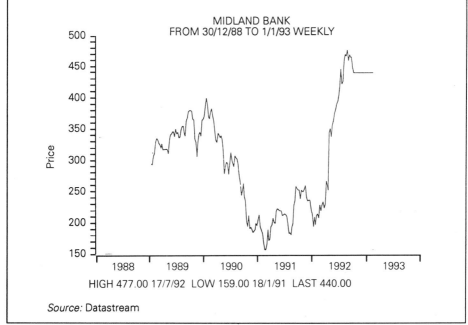

Source: Datastream

Exhibit 2.8 *HSBC Holdings indexed share prices*

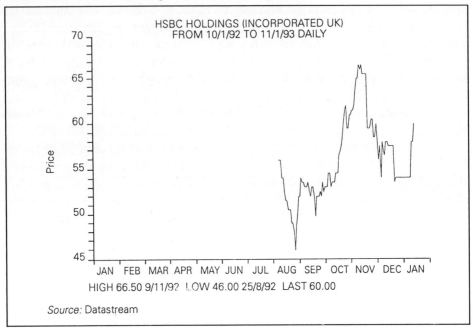

Exhibit 2.9 *Lloyds Bank indexed share prices*

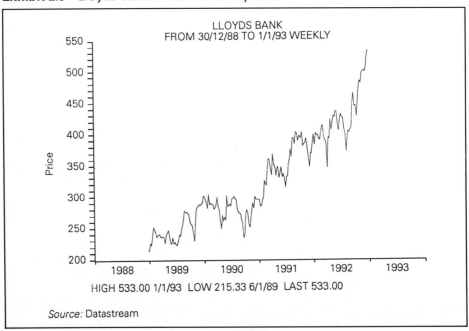

Exhibit 2.10   *HSBC, Midland and Lloyds indexed share prices*

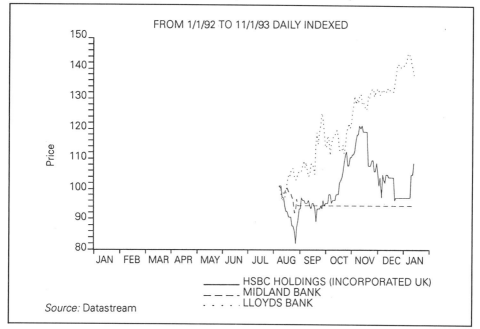

On 11 November 1992, HSBC showed its strength on the stock market again by offering 80 million new shares. The bank said the main reason for raising this new money was to repay loans made by its subsidiary Hongkong Bank to other parts of the HSBC group. These were loans that had helped to finance the group's acquisition of Midland Bank in June. HSBC knew that there was strong demand for its shares and was not disappointed. They sold for £435.3 million (HK$5.12 billion). The issue increased HSBC's ratio of tier one capital from 6.4% to 6.9%, well above the internationally agreed minimum of 4%.

At this point, HSBC's shares had doubled in price since the beginning of 1992, and the company's value in the UK stock market reached 2.5% from 2% at the beginning of the year. Since most UK investment institutions had missed the opportunity to correct their investment weighting in this stock in the FT-A Bank Index, they immediately took up the placing with them. These institutions had also missed the 50% rise in HSBC's share price since the Midland acquisition took place and believed there was still growth in the stock.

All in all, HSBC directors could look back on 1992 and the acquisition of Midland Bank with pleasure.

The Acquisition of Martell

*This is a case study of the acquisition of the prominent French Cognac
producer, Martell, by the Canadian multinational Seagram in a
competitive cross-border bidding situation involving the British-based
diversified multinational Grand Met. Following an earlier acquisition of
part of Martell's stock by Grand Met, Seagram reached an agreement
with Martell to purchase a controlling share with an intention later to buy
out all remaining minority shareholders. Grand Met then announced a
competitive bid. Despite allegations of impropriety by Seagram, Grand
Met argued that its bid did not appear to violate regulations of the French
authorities.*

New Year's Eve 1987 brought with it, in addition to festive good cheer,
confrontation among three parties – two of the foremost wine and spirits
companies in the world and the government of France – over the fate of the
prominent French cognac producer Martell. Grand Metropolitan plc (Grand
Met) and The Seagram Company Limited were on the verge of a bidding
war that neither had anticipated, and one which Martell had striven to avoid.

Cognac

Since the rise of maritime trade during the seventeenth century, when
shipping of 'burnt' (distilled) wines proved to be more profitable than
shipping bulky wine, the brandy of the Charente district of western France
on the Bay of Biscay has been renowned. Though the sour, acidic white wines
grown in the district's chalky soils are disagreeable to the palate, when twice
distilled and aged in casks made out of Limousin oak cut from the nearby
Limoges forests, Charente white wine is transformed into golden spirits of

*This case was prepared by research assistant Hugh Thomas under the direction of Professors
Ingo Walter and Roy C. Smith, Stern School of Business, New York University, as a basis for
classroom discussion. Acknowledgement is gratefully made to the Salomon Center Case Series,
Stern School of Business, New York University, and INSEAD, Fontainebleau, France. Case
reprinted with kind permission of Professor Walter.* © *Ingo Walter, Roy C. Smith, 1989.*

unparalleled flavor and body. Those spirits, blended and bottled locally, are known by the name of the district's principal town, Cognac.

By the time Napoleon demonstrated preference for the brandy of Charente by hauling casks of it around Europe on his military campaigns, purveyors of brandy throughout the western world had taken to calling their liquor cognac. However, the ire of the Charente distillers, expressed through the commercial policies of subsequent French governments, succeeded in limiting the use of the term. By the time of the Fifth Republic (the government of France in the late twentieth century), 'cognac' was an *appellation controllée*. The French government insisted that the word be applied only to Charente brandy, and the world respected its wish.

In 1987, as in the seventeenth century, the mainstay of commerce in cognac continued to be international trade, with only 8.6% of production sold domestically in France. The United States accounted for 23.9% of sales followed by Great Britain with 12.0%, Japan with 9.9%, France with 8.6%, Germany with 7.9%, East Asia (excluding Japan) with 12.8% and the rest of the world 24.9%. But shares were not stable. US sales were volatile, being sensitive to changes in the exchange rate, but not exhibiting a noticeable trend – unlike sales of other spirits, whose consumption was in decline.

In Japan and the Far East, in contrast, sales were rising rapidly with increasing affluence. There, cognac was being increasingly regarded as a ceremonial drink of choice, consumed by the tumbler-full at weddings and other celebrations, and frequently favored as a present. Hong Kong residents were already the world's largest consumers of cognac per capita. The ability to supply cognac was considered critical for any significant distributor of wines and spirits to the Far East.

Although in the 1980s the number of private producers of Cognac still numbered in the hundreds (if one counted every farmer who operated a still) most of the 11.5 million cases of cognac shipped annually was accounted for by the large houses of Hennessy (21%), Martell (19%), Courvoisier (14%) and Remy Martin (15%).

In the mid-1980s the cognac market had been unusually competitive. The stock-to-sales ratios, which had risen to 6.02 in 1986 before falling to 5.62 in 1987, still remained above their normal level of 5.0. The need for exporting firms to market and distribute worldwide had led to consolidation. Hennessy, a cognac house which dated from an eighteenth century Irishman who established the firm, combined with the houses of Moët et Chandon in 1970s and Louis Vuitton in 1987. Courvoisier was bought out by Hiram Walker of the US, which was acquired in turn by Allied Lyons of the UK. Remy Martin, however, remained private with 51% in the hands of

Heriard family. Although publicly listed on the Paris stock exchange, Martell remained a family concern.

Martell

From 1715 to 1987, the house of Martell was largely owned and completely controlled by its members of the founding Martell family, originally merchants from the Channel Islands. However, to meet the requirements for increased capital, the firm went public on the Paris stock exchange in 1975. Thereafter, family ownership eroded to 41% of the shares and 57% of the voting rights. The family group comprised some 50 individuals between the ages of 18 and 95, only six of whom were actively involved in the cognac trade.

In 1987, Martell's chairman was M. René Firino Martell, a member of the eighth generation of Martells to manage the firm. His record was mixed. Analysts gave him high marks for running the cognac business, his strong control over costs, and keeping worldwide staff down to a trim 1,387 employees. Martell's inventory of aging Cognac – reportedly the industry's largest with the bulk equivalent of about 100 million bottles aging in oak casks – showed that the firm was planning to increase the proportion of older cognacs in its sales. That inventory and M. Martell's successful introduction of a new top-of-the-line cognac, XO Cordon Suprême, showed his keen insight into market trends.

Under his leadership, however, Martell had tried and failed to diversify away from spirits. The sale in 1987 of the perfumes and cosmetics subsidiary Jacomo marked the end of an attempt started in 1981–82 to penetrate the Middle Eastern market for French perfumes. Prior to and immediately after the sale, Martell's sales by product were as follows:

| | Fiscal year ended 30 June | |
	1986	1987
Cognac	77.3%	81.5%
Other spirits	11.0%	13.4%
Perfumes and cosmetics	9.7%	0.0%
Other products	2.0%	5.1%
Total	100.0%	100.0%

'Other spirits' consisted primarily of Armagnac and brandies produced by subsidiaries in Mexico, Venezuela and South Africa. 'Other products' primarily comprised boutique leather goods.

In 1987, Martell exported 97% of its cognac to 135 countries, with 44.4% going to other countries of the EC (primarily the UK), 30.4% to the Far East, 19% to the USA and 6.1% to the rest of the world. That summer, under the premise that the outlays for global distribution and marketing were beyond its capabilities, Martell entered into a marketing and distribution agreement with Grand Met, giving that firm exclusive distribution rights to Martell cognac throughout the Far East and the EC outside of the UK. To consummate the alliance, Grand Met, with Martell's blessing, acquired 10% of Martell stock.

Nineteen eighty-seven also saw a significant change in the Martell organization. All of the cognac activities were consolidated into a newly established subsidiary, while the listed parent company became a pure holding company. Since the operating subsidiary had not remitted its dividend in fiscal year 1987 (ending June 30) the financial statements of 1986 and 1987 were not comparable (see Exhibits 3.1 and 3.2). Calculated on the same basis as in 1986, 1987 income was only ½% below 1986 income, with losses due to the depreciation of the US dollar, the Hong Kong dollar and British pound with respect to the French franc being offset by increased sales volumes.

Exhibit 3.1 *Martell financial statement summaries*

	US$m[1]	FFr m	
	1987	1987	1986
Statement of income (year ended June 30)			
Total operating revenues	4.62	28.2	1333.0
Cost of goods sold	0.10	0.6	463.0
Other direct costs	0.87	5.3	391.7
Value added	3.65	22.3	478.3
Absorbed taxes and tariffs	0.00	0.0	21.7
Personnel expenses	0.00	0.0	181.8
Amortization and depreciation	0.28	1.7	30.5
Other production changes	0.13	0.8	1.3
Operating income	3.24	19.8	243.0
Financial income	2.51	15.3	32.2
Financial charges	3.82	23.3	73.6
Current period income	1.93	11.8	201.6
Net loss on disposal of assets	1.03	6.3	16.5
Profits distributed to employees	0.00	0.0	9.7
Profit taxes	0.00	0.0	71.0
	0.90	5.5	104.4

Exhibit 3.1 *continued*

	US$m[1]	FFr m	
	1987	1987	1986
Balance sheet (year ended June 30)			
Goodwill	0.41	2.5	2.5
Land	0.00	0.0	6.6
Buildings (net)	4.67	28.5	113.4
Other fixed assets	0.00	0.0	149.6
Shareholdings	199.07	1215.4	226.2
Other financial fixed assets	0.00	0.0	8.0
Total fixed assets	204.14	1246.4	506.3
Raw materials and provisions	0.00	0.0	856.0
Goods in process	0.00	0.0	475.2
Merchandise	0.00	0.0	0.5
Pledged deposits	0.00	0.0	22.3
Accounts receivable	0.00	0.0	163.2
Other receivables	31.89	194.7	104.7
Negotiable securities and cash	4.57	27.9	176.7
Total current assets	36.46	222.6	1798.6
Prepaid expenses	2.80	17.1	32.5
Total assets	243.40	1486.1	2337.4
Share capital and issue premium	8.21	355.4	327.4
Revaluation discrepancy	2.06	12.6	37.8
Reserves/regulatory provision	118.67	724.6	704.1
Carry forward	8.24	50.3	47.1
Income in current year	0.92	5.6	104.4
Total shareholders' equity	188.11	1148.5	1220.8
Provisions	1.64	10.0	26.2
Convertible bonds	40.09	244.8	278.9
Bank debt	2.19	13.4	528.4
Other debt	9.02	55.1	140.6
Suppliers' accounts and payables	0.15	0.9	63.9
Wages payable	2.19	13.4	78.6
Total liabilities	53.66	327.6	1090.4
Total liabilities and equity	243.40	1486.1	2337.4

[1] Translated at the June 30, 1987 rate of FFr6.1055 per US$.
Source: Martell Annual Report 1987.

Exhibit 3.2 *Martell stock market and dividend data*

Year	Number of shares	Dividends per share			Price range			Dividend yield per share
		Final	Interim	Total	High	Low	Close	
1984	1,053,782	34.00	17.00	51.00	2,075	1,568	1,705	2.99%
1985	1,155,649	37.00	18.50	55.50	1,942	1,310	1,560	3.56%
1986	1,307,408	38.00	19.00	57.00	1,939	1,260	1,592	5.58%
1987	1,381,953	39.00	19.50	58.50	2,269	1,470	1,690	3.46%

Source: Martell Annual Report 1987.

Seagram

Seagram had its origins in the family distilling firm of Joseph E. Seagram & Sons of Waterloo, Ontario, Canada, founded in 1857. Its rise to maturity as a multinational corporation started in 1928, when it was acquired by Samuel Bronfman. A Russian immigrant who had successfully developed a Canadian liquor mail order business in the early 1900s, Bronfman found his business being undercut in the early 1920s as the provincial governments of Canada took over the sale of alcoholic beverages. Bronfman responded by building a distillery in 1924 at LaSalle, Quebec. His company, Distillers Corporation Limited, was further expanded through the purchase in 1928 of Joseph E. Seagram & Sons, and Distillers Corporation–Seagrams Limited was born. The company enjoyed a brief association with Distillers Company Limited of the UK, but Distillers sold its shares when Samuel Bronfman turned his energies to the American market.

With five years left before the repeal of Prohibition, sales of Canadian whisky of all grades were booming. Bronfman capitalized on the demand while simultaneously emphasizing product quality and brand reputation. Moreover, confident that repeal of Prohibition was inevitable, Bronfman built up what became, by 1933, the largest stock of aged rye and bourbon whiskies in the world. Even after repeal he waited six months until he could be assured of marketing a quality product before moving into the virgin market. Six weeks after his entry, he commanded 60% of the US market. From the 1930s through the 1980s Seagram led the US whisky market.

By the time Samuel Bronfman died in 1971, Seagram had grown through export sales and acquisitions of well-known beverage producers in Europe, the USA and Latin America into one of the foremost spirits companies in the world. The USA, however, continued to be its main market. Seagram brands included Seven Crown, Seagrams VO, Seagrams

Gin, Kessler, Paul Masson, Calvert and Chivas Regal. Together, Seagram's brands held one-fifth of the total market share in spirits.

The Bronfman family continued to own a controlling 40% of the shares of Seagram. Samuel Bronfman's sons Edgar (chairman of the board and chief executive officer) and Charles (co-chairman of the board and chairman of the executive committee) were the dominant figures in the company. Institutions held a further 21% of the Seagram stock and the remainder of the shares was widely held by the general public.

Notwithstanding the diverse interests of the family, Seagram itself continued to be predominantly an alcoholic beverage company, with the notable exception of large investments in the oil, gas and chemicals industries. Since the 1960s, Seagram had acquired a reputation for diversifying in and out of those industries. As of 1988, the main legacy of that activity was a 22.9% stake in EI du Pont de Nemours & Co., the largest producer of chemicals in the USA and itself the owner of Conoco, Inc., the ninth largest American oil company. As Exhibit 3.3 shows, the du Pont investment accounted for about half the assets and over half of the income of Seagram in 1987.

Exhibit 3.3 *The Seagram Co. Ltd. financial statement summaries*

	(US$m)	
	1987	1986
Consolidated income statement (year ended January 31)		
Sales and other income	3,344	2,971
Costs of goods	2,189	1,941
	1,155	1,030
Selling, general and administrative expenses	962	815
Operating income	193	215
Interest expense	84	82
Income before income taxes	109	133
Provision for income taxes	6	33
Income from spirits and wine operations	103	100
Dividend income from du Pont	151	143
Equity in unremitted earnings from du Pont	169	76
Net income	423	319

Exhibit 3.3 *continued*

	US$m 1987
Seagram balance sheet (year ended January 31)	
Assets	
Cash and short-term investments	594
Receivables	590
Inventories	1,250
Prepaid expenses	48
Wine company assets held for sale	220
Current assets	2,702
Common stock of du Pont	3,330
Note receivable from Sun Co., Inc.	51
Property, plant and equipment at cost	843
Accumulated depreciation	(344)
Net property, plant and equipment	499
Spirits/wine company investments and advances	77
Sundry assets	228
Total assets	6,887
Liabilities and shareholders' equity	
Short-term borrowings	460
United States excise taxes	61
Payables and accrued liabilities	451
Income and other taxes	58
Indebtedness payable within one year	72
Total current liabilities	1,102
Long term indebtedness	912
Deferred income taxes and other credits	882
Minority interest	35
Total liabilities	2,931
Shares without par value	
1988 – 94.8 million	
1987 – 95.5 million	257
Share purchase warrants	28
Cumulative translation adjustments	(228)
Retained earnings	3,899
Total shareholders' equity	3,956
Total	6,887

Source: Seagram Annual Report 1988.

Grand Met

Started in 1934, Grand Met went public on the London Stock Exchange in
1962 with one hotel as its principal asset. From that base, it capitalized on
good management to acquire additional quality hotels in the UK and Europe
and expanded into the related businesses of catering and building
management.

The early 1970s saw Grand Met diversifying into brewing, pub
management, distribution of wines and spirits, and gambling. Building on
its expertise in the promotion of beverages, it launched what became, in one
decade, the most popular liqueur in the world, Bailey's Original Irish Cream.
The early 1980s saw the significant addition of Intercontinental Hotels, giving
it a network of first class hotels throughout the world. Grand Met expanded
in the USA, acquiring Alpo, a large manufacturer of pet foods, and soft drink
bottling facilities in South Carolina and California – major bottlers of Pepsi-
Cola. In the USA, it also expanded into hospital management, day-care
center management and, through its 1985 acquisition of Pearle Health
Services and Diversified Products Corp., had became the foremost consumer
optical service company and manufacturer of physical fitness and exercise
equipment in the nation. It pursued further diversification into dairy
products, electronics, biotechnology as well as oil and gas.

Exhibit 3.4   *Grand Metropolitan plc financial statement summaries*

	US$m	£m	
	1987[1]	1987	1986
Statement of income (year ended September 30)			
Turnover	9298.3	5705.5	5291.3
Trading profit	931.5	571.6	487.4
Reorganization costs	15.2	9.3	27.1
Interest expense	195.9	120.2	101.3
Loss (profit) on property sales	(22.8)	(14.0)	(8.7)
	743.3	456.10	367.70
Tax	195.7	120.1	91.8
Minority interests	3.7	2.3	2.3
Loss (gain) on extraordinary items	(208.3)	(127.8)	11.7
Net profit	752.1	461.50	261.90
Ordinary dividends	168.0	103.1	87.5
Preferred dividends	0.8	0.5	0.5

Exhibit 3.4 *continued*

	US$m	£m	
	1987[1]	1987	1986
Retained profit	583.3	357.90	173.90
Profits brought forward	2618.1	1606.5	1566.6
Plus Gain (loss) on forex translation	(36.5)	(22.4)	34.5
Net premium on share issues	9.8	6.0	7.8
Less Goodwill acquired	(1062.2)	(651.8)	(137.7)
Less Bond issue capitalized reserves	0.00	0.00	(38.6)
Profits carried forward	2112.4	1296.2	1606.5
Balance sheet (year end September 30)			
Tangible assets	4441.3	2725.2	2625.7
Investments	288.8	177.2	129.8
Total fixed assets	4730.0	2902.4	2755.5
Stocks	1195.7	733.7	646.3
Debtors	1348.6	827.5	731.4
Cash at banks	184.8	113.4	88.0
Total current assets	2729.1	1674.6	1465.7
Less Creditors – amounts due in 1 year:			
Borrowings	537.3	329.7	270.0
Other creditors	1900.7	1166.3	979.7
Total current liabilities	2438.0	1496.0	1249.7
Net current assets	291.1	178.6	216.0
Total assets *less* current liabilities	5021.1	3081.0	2971.5
Borrowings	1861.0	1141.9	750.8
Other creditors	168.3	103.3	104.7
Total creditors: non-current	2029.3	1245.2	855.5
Provisions for liabilities and charges	114.7	70.4	43.9
Net assets	2877.1	1765.4	2072.1
Share capital	718.5	440.9	439.0
Profits carried forward	2112.4	1296.2	1606.5
Minority shareholders' interest	46.1	28.3	26.6
Total equity	2877.1	1765.4	2072.1

[1] Translated at the September 30, 1987 rate of US$1.6297 per pound.
Sources: Grand Metropolitan plc Annual Report 1986; *Moody's International Manual 1988.*

In 1987, Grand Met celebrated its 25th anniversary of stock exchange listing by reflecting on the route by which it had become the largest hotel, food, and beverage company in the UK (see Exhibit 3.4). For the first time, it developed its own logo to complement the many logos, trademarks and brands of its subsidiaries, products and agency relationships. Patterned on a traditional English goldsmith's hallmark, the logo consisted of three block figures in a row – a lion, a sun and an eagle – symbolizing, respectively, the UK the international market and the USA. Grand Met formulated a mission statement identifying consumer products in the food, drink and personal services as the chosen fields of activity in which its policy for maximizing shareholder wealth would be 'building brands in order to achieve good margins and sustained profitability'. It reconfirmed its use of the portfolio approach to managing its companies, allowing them a considerable degree of autonomy in return for acceptable performance.

The Events of December 1987

The closing months of 1987 found Seagram increasingly profitable, liquid and poised to begin another round of expansion by its favored method – acquisition. Consequently, few were surprised at the company's announcement on December 17 that it had reached an agreement to purchase from the Martell family all of their 40.1% of the shares of Martell. Through the acquisition, Seagram would bring its stake in Martell to 52%, and management indicated that it intended to buy out the remaining minority shareholders as well. In New York, Seagram's stock traded up by 12½ cents on the day to close at $57.375.

Seagram announced its intention to acquire Martell through its 93%-owned French champagne-producing subsidiary, G.H. Mumm & Co. The price for the shares from the Martell family was FFr 2,500 ($450) per share and the same was to be offered to other shareholders. The acquisition cost would therefore be FFr 1.49 billion ($250 million) to the Martell family and an additional $359 million to the minority shareholders for a total of $609 million, an amount within the capabilities of Seagram to raise on short notice. Trading in Martell shares on the Paris Bourse was suspended on December 17 at FFr 2,390 pending the completion of the acquisition.

The financial press speculated that Seagram's move had been precipitated by the fact that Grand Met had increased its shareholding without the Martell family's consent to 19.9% by buying shares on the open market. By law, all foreign acquisitions of the stock of French companies in excess of 20% had to be approved by the French Ministry of Finance (see Exhibit 3.5), and it was rumored that Grand Met had already filed for approval.

Exhibit 3.5 *Mergers and acquisitions in France*

France has come a long distance in relaxing controls over M&A [mergers and acquisition] deals, even by foreigners, away from the hopeless difficulties of the 1970s in overcoming often opaque government objections. France has had relatively few explicit barriers to cross-border M&A transactions, with French companies and investment banks among the most active in Europe in M&A deals. In 1987 there were 915 domestic M&A transactions in France worth over about $27 billion, with 156 French acquisitions ($5 billion) by foreign buyers and 196 foreign acquisitions ($8.3 billion) by French buyers.

Ministry of Finance approval is required for non-EC bids exceeding 20% of the target company – which is also the limit for non-EC ownership of French newspapers – and such bids can be squelched assuming the Ministry can find a matching French bid. The Ministry approval requirement has evidently discouraged many bids. Moreover

and cross

shares of

were acti\

Gov

mandato

company

a manda

Sympton

subsidiai

1988, an

supplier,

Peugeot

some of

transacti

Co

perhaps

privatize

Chirac,

ment. F

been a

George:

by the (

had a

quarter

suppor

F

$100 n

institut

severa

panies

30.9%.

proceC

somet

multiple voting rights

idly interests; the

ris Bourse in 1988

ated voting rights,

 stake in a French

% levels, as well as

least 50% owned,

:lusion of French

ition of the firm in

a French auto-parts

h group including

ance will throw up

cross-border M&A

e.

 transactions can

jor bank that was

e Minister Jacques

ters of the govern-

nat appears to have

d by a group led by

ipanies, and backed

titution that already

nterpreted in some

ported to be overtly

d at a profit of some

hat state-controlled

mbined 22.2% stake,

iese insurance com-

 general public held

ment policy on M&A

active observer, and

Source   *in Europe After 1992*
(Oxfor

The reaction from Grand Met was not long in coming. At its annual press conference held in London on December 17 to discuss year-end results (fiscal year ended October 31), management indicated surprise at the events of the previous day. M. Vernier-Palliez of Grand Met, attending Martell's annual meeting in Paris the same day, questioned the validity of Seagram's buy-out agreement and indicated that Grand Met would make a higher offer in compliance with market procedures which required that competing bids be no less than 5% higher than previously bid. Rumors emerged that Grand Met had started lobbying with officials at the Paris stock exchange and the French Ministry of Finance to nullify the Seagram–Martell agreement. But in Montreal, only a few hours later, Seagram's statement exuded confidence:

> We are delighted that the Martell family chose to deal with Seagram. We are very confident with our agreement and are optimistic that the French Government will approve the transaction. Seagram declined to comment on rumors that Remy Martin was also involved in discussions with both Seagram and Grand Met.

The next day Reuters reported that although Seagram's action was well within the French takeover rules, the fact that most small shareholders were not consulted could prompt political pressure for the government to step in. Speculation continued through the next two weeks. On December 30, 1987 Grand Met announced that it would bid FFr 2,675 ($482) per share, or $665 million in total, conditional on acceptances from at least 51% of shareholders, with comparable terms to holders of convertible bonds. Grand Met indicated that it had lodged the proposal with the stock exchange authorities on December 24, and had met on December 29 with the French takeover supervisory committee. Seagram's response reiterated its confidence in its share purchase agreement, and added:

> We continue to be hopeful that the French Government will view this agreement as positively as our two family firms [Martell and Seagram] intend it to be for the further development of the Martell business, for our employees, and for our community.

On New Year's Eve 1987, however, Reuters reported that the Paris Stock Brokers' Association gave its opinion that the Seagram bid was improper, and did not respect the requirements of Article 201 of the Securities Brokers' General Regulations requiring that the Brokers' Association must be advised of bids for purchase of the quoted firm's capital sufficient to give it control of the company. The Association stated that, despite need for official authorization for an investment from abroad, this did not mean that the transfer of a block of shares to Seagram was any different from a pure and simple direct sale, and should thus fall under rules for sale of controlling share blocks in quoted companies. Reuters noted that the Paris Stock Exchange Association had no power to block the bid: a power that rested with the Ministry of Finance.

In a public statement that day, Seagram clarified its position. It said that the transaction qualified as an exception to the 'transparency' rule requiring consultation of all shareholders because of the complexity and nature of the sale. It was a foreign acquisition contingent on French government approval. Moreover, the transaction was complicated by the various classes of shares, with the shares held by the family having greater voting rights than others. Following the execution of the transaction with Martell, however, Seagram would offer to purchase the shares of all shareholders at the same price regardless of voting class. And the transaction was being carried out according to the wishes of the Martell family, which wanted a private sale to preserve unanimity of the family.

CASE 4

Repsol, SA

Repsol, SA is an integrated oil company operating in all the hydrocarbon sectors, including exploration and production of crude oil and natural gas, transportation, refinement, and sale of oil and petrochemical products. It is a state-owned company that heads the most important industrial group in Spain, with sales of Pta 942,288 million in 1988 and 18,716 employees. In 1988, the management of Repsol, together with the government, considered the privatisation of part of the company. It was the first case of a large industrial company owned by the state being privatised.

The case describes the position of Repsol in each of the sectors in which it operates, and it shows the questions that the management of the company faced when privatising the company – size of the operation, valuation of the company, election of financial intermediaries – as well as the advantages and disadvantages of the privatisation with regard to the corporate strategy.

The Company

Repsol is an integrated oil company operating in all the hydrocarbon sectors including the exploration and production of crude oil and natural gas, transportation of oil products and liquid petroleum gas (LPG), oil refinement, production of petrochemical products (full range) and the sale of oil and oil products, petrochemical and LPG derivatives including petrol, kerosene, diesel oil, and paraffin. Repsol, SA heads a group of more than 120 companies organised into five large divisions: Repsol Exploración, Repsol Petróleo, Campsa, Repsol Química and Repsol Butano. Repsol also enjoys both direct and indirect participation in other companies in the sector. By 31 December 1988, Repsol was the largest industrial company in the country in terms of sales (Pta 942,288m) and it had 18,716 employees.

Case study by the Research Department at IESE. Prepared by Professors Eduardo Martínez-Abascal and Ahmad Rahnema, with the collaboration of Jon Sarabia, research assistant, October 1993. Reprinted here with kind permission of Professor Eduardo Martínez-Abascal, IESE. © IESE, 1993.

Repsol began operating in 1987 as a result of the reorganisation of the companies in the hydrocarbon sector which until then had all been under the umbrella of the National Institute of Hydrocarbons (NIH). Repsol was created to provide centralised management and to co-ordinate the various activities of the companies which make up the organisation today. At present, NIH holds 98% of Repsol's shares.

Operations

Production of Hydrocarbons

Repsol Exploración, SA is focused on the exploration for, and development and production of, hydrocarbons not only in Spain but also abroad. Repsol Exploración operates today in all the national oil fields and is also involved in exploration projects in another 12 countries in conjunction with foreign companies; here, Repsol principally plays the role of partner as opposed to operator.

As of 31 December 1988, Repsol had net reserves equivalent to 430.4 million barrels of oil, of which 88% was crude oil and 12% natural gas (see Exhibit 4.1). The crude oil reserves were to be found, principally, in the Middle East and also in Colombia, the UK, Spain and Indonesia. Almost all the gas reserves were located in Spain.

Repsol Exploración is trying to increase its reserves through acquisitions and exploration and has adopted a strategy of purchasing shareholdings in oil fields outside of Spain, concentrating in the areas of low geological risk. At present, these exploration activities are focused on Angola, Colombia, Egypt, other Middle East countries, the UK, Spain and Indonesia. In the past 3 years, Repsol Exploración has acquired the equivalent of 66.6 million barrels of crude oil, having increased its investments in exploration and development to Pta 36,700 million. Since 1978 exploration activity has been partly subsidised by the state to the tune of about 60%. In 1986, the company

Exhibit 4.1 *Repsol Exploración estimate of proven reserves*

Proved reserves	Thousands of barrels of crude oil	Millions of cubic feet of natural gas
As of December 1986	407,843	341,034
As of December 1987	377,877	318,334
As of December 1988	381,027	296,349

did not purchase any reserves. Between 1987 and 1988 it increased its reserves of crude oil through the acquisition of shareholdings representing 48 million barrels of crude oil at a price of Pta 34,400 million.[1]

During the past 3 years, crude oil production had increased from 114,850 barrels per day in 1986 to 132,110 in 1988 (see Exhibit 4.2). Gas production increased from 33.4 million cubic feet per day in 1986 to 69.4 million cubic feet in 1988. Oil accounted for 92% of the total production of hydrocarbons, gas represented the other 8%. In the past 3 years, Repsol Exploración produced crude oil equivalent to approximately 30% of Repsol's requirements, it being one of the strategic objectives of the company to increase this figure significantly. It is hoped that the the present reserves of crude oil and gas will keep production going for another 20 and 10 years, respectively. In 1988, Repsol Exploración sold approximately 74% of its crude production to the state under the commercial quota arrangements (see Exhibit 4.3), 24% to foreign customers and the remainder to Campsa and other Spanish companies. All the national gas production was sold to Enagas.

Exhibit 4.2 *Repsol Exploración crude oil production (thousands of barrels/day)*

	1986	1987	1988
Spain	14.4	13.0	12.0
Middle East	95.6	99.1	104.9
Other countries	4.9	4.7	15.2
Total	114.9	116.8	132.1

Exhibit 4.3 *Regulation of the oil industry*

The Spanish oil industry has been strongly regulated by the state since 1927 when a state monopoly was created over exploration, production, importation, transportation and sale of crude oil, oil products and gas. Reorganisation of the industry began in 1984 with the transfer to Campsa of the only existing distribution network for oil products. Later, in 1985, the NIH transferred part of its ownership in Campsa to the established Spanish oil refineries. Through legal enactments and subsequent agreements, a programme of transition from a state-controlled sector to one designed to fulfil the requirements of the EEC was established. The Treaty of Adhesion of Spain to the EEC and the Royal Decree (Law 5/1985) basically brought about three principal regulatory changes. In the

Exhibit 4.3 *continued*

first place, any entity within the EEC, including any other Spanish company, would be able to establish competitive retail outlets. In the second place, import restrictions on oil products would end in 1992. In the third place, and in accordance with the premise of the Treaty of Adhesion, Spain would eliminate the present system of government price-fixing before 1992.

Exploration for, and production and importation of, crude oil

The state owned all subterranean natural resources and issued exploration and production licences to companies (including foreign companies) who complied with certain legal requirements. The licensees had to sell the extracted crude oil to Spanish industry in quantities and at prices determined by the state.

Under the 'commercial quota' system, the state set a level for the quantity of crude oil (the 'commercial quota') processed annually for later distribution to Spanish refineries. The commercial quota system was devised to control the sources of supply of crude oil. The demand for crude oil over and above the commercial quota was satisfied almost exclusively by imports, an area where the state did not intervene.

Refining

All Spanish refineries operated under licences granted to them by the state which wished the refineries to purchase a proportional share of the commercial quota, according to their capacity. The Spanish oil refineries had to sell a certain amount of their production to the Monopoly which in turn sold on to Campsa. The Monopoly established the level of sales, basing them on its own estimation of the national demand, and prices. The Spanish refineries had freedom to export refined products which were not subject to, or rather exceeded, the requirements of the obligatory sales.

Historically, the Monopoly reserved to itself the exclusive right to import refined oil products. The agreement with the EEC established a procedure by which the importation of oil products from countries outside the EEC would be liberalised gradually, product by product.

Transport and sales

Before 1984, the transportation system for oil products and the network of retailers was under both the control and ownership of the state. The sales and transport networks were managed by Campsa as agent for the Monopoly, and Campsa bought and sold the oil products on its behalf. Campsa was structured to meet the requirements of the 1984 statute. This statute permitted the then operating oil refineries to purchase shares in Campsa in proportion to their refining capacities, always providing that more than 50% of the shares remained in the hands of bodies under state control. The 1984 statute envisaged that all the state assets used in the transportation and sale of oil products as well as all the stock of oil products would be transferred to Campsa. Campsa would not then be an agent of the state and would be able to buy and sell on its own account with the advantage of having the exclusive right to sell all the oil products produced by the existing Spanish refineries in Spain. These refineries would continue to be obliged to sell the petrol and diesel destined for national consumption through Campsa.

Under the 1985 statute, transportation of certain products within Spain was

Exhibit 4.3 *continued*

liberalised so that it was then possible to compete with Campsa in the retail networks. EEC organisations including Spanish companies were able to provide oil transport services and establish their own bases for these services. Under the existing law, all the service stations operated under third-party licences from the state but when these licences expired the ownership of all the service stations and their fixed assets would pass to Campsa. The remaining life of these licences was 43 years. The service stations operating under this licence system could only purchase their petrol and diesel through Campsa from the Monopoly. Today, the state continues to fix the retail price of petrol, diesel and other oil products. Under the agreement with the EEC and in terms of the 1985 statute, the sale of oil products will be liberalised, government price-fixing will be eliminated and retail sales prices will be determined by market forces. Also, under the agreement with the EEC and the 1985 statute, competition in the retail network for oil products in the road transport field will be permitted. All the present service stations in Spain form part of the network of concessions and can only sell petrol and diesel supplied by Campsa. In terms of the statute, this requirement will be maintained until after 1992. Present law and regulations in force, however, allow the existence of unlicensed service stations if they are newly built and meet certain requirements, including a requirement that they sell only imported petrol and diesel. Retail and wholesale sales of oil products of Spanish refineries and destined for sectors other than that of road transportation are also currently managed by Campsa.

Petrochemical products
The Spanish petrochemical sector has been liberalised since the 1970s. Foreign companies, whether or not they belong to the EEC, can freely import petrochemical products to Spain and establish petrochemical operations there. The only significant state intervention in this sector is in taxes and import duties. The first of January 1986 saw the elimination of import duties to coincide with Spain's entry into the EEC. The EEC import duties on petrochemical products are subject to a staged reduction. The tariffs of the other EEC countries imposed on imports of petrochemical products from Spain will be reduced equally.

Liquid petroleum gas
Repsol Butano has an exclusive licence for the retail sale of liquid petroleum gas (LPG) produced in Spain. The LPG sector is going through a process of liberalisation of import restrictions. The EEC agreement set out amounts which must be imported annually from other EEC countries which will increase annually until 1992 when LPG will be able to be imported freely from the EEC. Although, today, the prices of LPG are fixed by the state, Repsol Butano expects the position to change in 1992. There have been no import duties in recent years. Repsol Butano is subject to a special tax applicable to all participants in the LPG market.

Repsol Exploración increased its revenues 7.5% in 1987 before a fall of 14.4% in 1988 due to a decrease in sale prices, both in dollars and pesetas. Sales volume increased by around 6% p.a. The restructuring of Spanish investments and the decline in activity caused a drop in operating profits of

93.3% in 1987 only for them to recover the previous level, more or less, of around Pta 10,000 million in 1988 (the key indicators of Repsol Exploración appear in Exhibit 4.4).

Refining

Lumping together the crude oil acquisition and refining activities with the production of oil products, Repsol Petróleo, SA is the country's largest refiner with approximately 42% of the national refining capacity.

Repsol Petróleo obtains crude oil from various sources including Repsol Exploración. During 1988, Repsol Petróleo bought approximately 30 million tons of crude oil and petroleum products, 18% being purchased through the commercial quota. The rest of the purchases were made in the spot market or through short-term supply contracts; Petróleos Mexicanos (Pemex) having been the major supplier between 1986 and 1988 with an average of 20%.

Repsol Petróleo has four refineries (Cartagena, Tarragona, La Coruña and Puertollano) with combined annual refining capacity of 25 million tons. Other important assets of the company include storage facilities, an oil pipeline and tankers. Repsol Petróleo refined approximately 21.8 million tonnes of crude oil in 1988 which represented 46% of the total amount of crude oil refined in Spain. Their refineries operate at 90% capacity compared with 80% for the rest of the Spanish refineries. The ratio of conversion to distillation is 22.4% and this will increase to 28% in 1990 compared with 24% for the EEC. The method of refining used by Repsol Petróleo produces oil products (including LPG, petrol, kerosene, diesel and paraffin), oil derivatives (such as lubricants and asphalt), and basic petrochemical products (see Exhibit 4.5).

Oil products represent 92% of the production. Repsol also carries out other refining operations through Petróleos del Norte, SA (Petronor) in which it has a shareholding of 32.4%. Petronor is the third largest company

Exhibit 4.4 *Repsol Exploración: key indicators (Pta millions)*

	1986	1987	1988
Revenues	97,808	105,182	88,992
Operating profits	10,505	703	9,610
Assets	–	109,256	87,465

Exhibit 4.5 *Repsol Petróleo: production levels of principal products (thousands of tons)*

	1986	1987	1988
Oil products	19,090	18,590	19,980
Lubricants and asphalts	550	560	630
Basic petrochemical	910	940	1,050

in Spain in terms of refining capacity with a production of 11 million tons p.a., equivalent to 18% of the national refining capacity.[2]

Of the 21.7 million tons of crude oil refined in 1988, 11.6 million were sold to Campsa, 0.7 million to Repsol Butano, 3.7 million on the open market in Spain and 5.7 million to export; 1.5 million tons of products were destined to be consumed by the company itself.

The percentage of exports over sales has increased in recent years reaching 26% of the production in 1988 which represents 5.7 million tons. Around 11% of total exports were sales of petrol and 41% paraffin which is a staple product in Repsol Petróleo's range of exports. In 1988 Repsol Petróleo exported products to other countries including the USA (the principal market for unleaded petrol), Portugal, France and the UK. Repsol Petróleo's share of the Spanish market for oil-derived products was 49% in 1988. Repsol Petróleo is beginning to be involved directly in the sale of refined oil products.

Repsol Petróleo has two research and development facilities for basic petrochemical products where 170 qualified staff work, representing an expense of Pta 800 million p.a. during each of the past three years.

The revenues of Repsol Petróleo increased by 14% from 1986 to 1988 due principally to an increase in the average price while the variations in sales volume were of the order of 2% and 3% in the last two financial periods. The operating profit increased 136% in 1987 due to greater margins in the sale of lightly distilled and special combustible products. In 1988, the operating profit increased 3.7% due to a greater utilisation of capacity and better margins (the key indicators of Repsol Petróleo appear in Exhibit 4.6).

Exhibit 4.6 *Repsol Petróleo: key indicators (Pta millions)*

	1986	1987	1988
Revenues	516,677	574,531	589,684
Operating profits	16,376	38,755	40,191
Assets	–	196,509	173,511

Repsol's ability to achieve profits in this market depends on the changes in the market price of crude oil. Repsol Petróleo reduces this risk by hedging through options and futures contracts for crude and refined products.

Transport and Distribution

Campsa carries out the transport arrangements for Repsol's oil products and also its retail sales operations, being the principal oil product transport company and retailer in Spain except as regards LPG. At 31 December 1988 Repsol, directly or indirectly, owned 61% of Campsa; other refineries had about 37% and the rest was in public hands.[3]

Campsa has the only integrated network for the transportation of refined oil products excluding LPG (see Exhibit 4.3). Its network includes a system of pipelines connected to the majority of refineries and also includes significant storage facilities, fleets of lorries and tanker ships.

By 31 December 1988, the Spanish retail network for oil products in the road transport sector consisted of approximately 3,619 service stations and 1,209 petrol stations which operated under state licences. These licences required existing service and petrol stations to purchase petrol and diesel through Campsa and Spanish law provides for the continuation of this condition after 1992. At the end of 1988 Campsa had 1,106 service stations and 719 individual petrol stations servicing the road transport market. In recent years, Campsa has been actively buying service stations and was predicted to have, at the end of 1989, approximately 41% of the total number of service stations.

From June 1988, the law has permitted the building of retail service stations outside the network of concessionaires, but they can only sell products imported from other countries in the EEC and, to date, none have been built. Apart from the products for the road transport sector, Campsa also handles, directly through concessionaires as well, products for central heating, industrial use and marine and aviation lubrication.

Campsa increased its revenues by 15% in the period 1986–88 due to the increase in the tariffs and commissions of Campsa and the increase in volume of distributed products. As a result of depreciation, the running costs increased in the last two financial periods. The operating profit increased 2.2% and 9.8% in 1987 and 1988, respectively (the key indicators of Campsa appear in Exhibit 4.7).

Exhibit 4.7   *Campsa: key indicators (Pta millions)*

	1986	1987	1988
Revenues	107,918	115,148	124,591
Operating profits	12,381	15,128	16,614
Assets	–	120,912	131,609

Chemicals

Repsol's activities in petrochemical-derived products are dealt with by Repsol Química, SA. In 1988 it produced approximately 1.2 million tons of petrochemical products with a sales figure of approximately 40% of the national product (see Exhibit 4.8). As a result of strong demand, the degree of capacity utilisation of Repsol Química nearly reached 100% in 1988.

Repsol Química make polymers (which represented approximately 57% of total production and 78% of exports in 1988), intermediate products and, since 1987, specialised chemical products. Repsol Química has three principal production facilities in Puertallano, Tarragona and Santander and additional plants with a total capacity of 1.3 million tons p.a., approximately. The company invested Pta 5,500 million between 1987 and 1988 in the renovation of its plants.

Repsol Química sells its products through nine national sales offices and similar offices in other countries. In 1988, Repsol Química exports grew to 35% of total sales, two-thirds destined for EEC countries. During 1988, Repsol Chemicals purchased 73% of basic petrochemicals produced by Repsol Petroleum at market prices which represented 90% of their needs in that year. The rest of the raw materials were obtained from other Spanish and foreign sources.

Repsol Química strategy is to continue expanding its basic polymer and

Exhibit 4.8   *Repsol Química: production capacity of principal petrochemical products as of 31 December 1988 (thousands of tons per annum)*

	Total Repsol Química	Total Spain	Percentage of Repsol Química in respect of Spain
Plastics	615	1,135	54
Intermediates	382	382	100
Rubber	145	184	79

intermediate chemical activities (for example, by introducing more specialised chemicals) through constant investments in their plant and technology
and through acquisitions, principally in Europe. Repsol Química tries to
ensure the maintenance of its products' competitiveness through research
and development in applications and technology. The costs of this in the
past three years increased by approximately Pta 1,300 million p.a., which
represents more than 1% of those years' revenues.

Since the 1970s, the Spanish petrochemical industry has been liberalised
(see Exhibit 4.3).

Greater production volume and higher prices as a result of bigger
demand have resulted in an increase in the revenues of Repsol Química of
37% during the past two years. At the same time, margins have increased
by more than 30% in each financial period. The operating profits doubled
in both 1987 and 1988 (the key indicators of Repsol Química appear in
Exhibit 4.9).

Gas

Sales of LPG by Repsol are carried out through Repsol Butano, SA which
has been selling LPG for domestic and industrial use for more than thirty
years. Repsol Butano is the only wholesaler and almost the only retailer of
LPG in Spain (see Exhibit 4.3) and is the most important distribution
company of bottled LPG in Europe in terms of turnover and volume of gas
sold. The greater part of its sales consists of canisters for domestic use;
however, it also sells LPG in bulk for industrial use as fuel or raw material
in the petrochemical industry.

The consumer retail sales price of LPG is fixed by the government at
the same level as Repsol Butano pays for its purchases from Spanish
refineries and from Enagas. Repsol Butano claims its sales price per canister
to the public has been 30–40% below the sales price in other European
countries and that the prices paid to the majority of national suppliers of

Exhibit 4.9 *Repsol Química: key indicators (Pta millions)*

	1986	1987	1988
Revenues	88,047	97,079	120,860
Operating profits	1,958	15,202	31,110
Assets	–	54,509	64,743

LPG have been practically the same as those paid to foreign suppliers. Imports and sales in the LPG market have been liberalised as a result of Spain's entry into the EEC. Repsol Butano thinks that it will maintain a strong position in the LPG market due to its advantageous position in terms of storage capacity and distribution. In the last two financial periods, Repsol Butano sold approximately 2.4 million tons of LPG each year. Almost 60% of Repsol Butano's supplies were obtained from Spanish refineries and from Enagas, and the rest, which mainly came from the North Sea and the Persian Gulf, were purchased in the spot market. Repsol Butano's imports have diminished in recent years due to the increase in national production.

Bottled LPG comprised 72% of Repsol Butano's total sales in 1988. Repsol Butano supplied bottled LPG to nearly 14 million customers throughout Spain. In the period 1985–88 the LPG client base for canisters grew an average of 1.7% p.a. in volume. The process of bottling LPG was carried out at 36 locations owned by Repsol Butano throughout Spain. Once bottled, the LPG is supplied to distributors (approximately 1,000) who sell on to the final consumer for cash. Approximately 19% of Repsol Butano's revenues in 1988 were from bulk sales of LPG.

As an immediate consequence of the introduction of natural gas in certain urban markets, it is expected that part of the growth in the LPG market will switch to natural gas, albeit the total volume of LPG sales is expected to continue growing. Repsol Butano has responded to this increased competition by considerably strengthening its position in the distribution of natural gas by obtaining shareholdings in various natural gas distribution companies which has involved a total investment of pta 5,500 million. Repsol Butano has budgeted to invest between 12,000 million and 14,000 million pesetas during the next five years in a programme of investment in natural gas distribution and expects that the natural gas distribution companies in which it participates will control 50% of the national market in 1992.

As a result of the decrease in the sales price, the revenue of Repsol Butano declined by 9.3% in 1987 with almost no further variation in 1988. The sales volume of LPG has increased by more than 2% each year. Repsol Butano is subject to a tax applicable to the LPG market which the state fixes each year. The operating profit increased by 44.7% in 1987 due to the decline in raw material costs, while in 1988 it decreased by 75.7% as a result of the worsening of the relationships among the sales price, the price of raw materials and the increase in selling costs. The key indicators of Repsol Butano appear in Exhibit 4.10.

Exhibit 4.10   *Repsol Butano: key indicators (Pta millions)*

	1986	1987	1988
Revenues	123,717	112,186	112,251
Operating profits	4,907	7,100	1,722
Assets	–	120,912	131,609

Results of Repsol, SA

The operating results of Repsol have been affected primarily by the legal requirements but also by the oil price changes and the fluctuations in the dollar/peseta exchange rate.

In 1988, Repsol's revenues totalled Pta 942,288 million (see Exhibit 4.17), with an increase of 4.5% over the previous year due primarily to the increased revenues from petrochemical activity. Exhibit 4.11 shows the revenues of Repsol by sector.

Exhibit 4.11   *Repsol, SA: revenues by sector (Pta millions)*

	1986	1987	1988	Percentage 1988	Percentage growth p.a. 1986–88
Exploration and production	97,808	105,182	88,992	8	−5
Refining	516,677	574,531	589,684	57	7
Distribution of oil products	107,918	115,148	124,591	12	7
Petrochemical products	88,047	97,079	120,860	12	17
Distribution of LPG	123,717	112,186	112,251	11	−5
Less Adjustments in process of consolidation and others	−101,898	−102,079	−95,090		
Total revenues	832,269	901,482	942,288	100	6

The operating profit of Repsol in 1988 was Pta 99,214 million, with an average annual increase between 1986 and 1988 of 36.8%. Forty per cent of the operating profits come from the refining business, an activity where Repsol is well positioned. Exhibit 4.12 shows the operating results of Repsol by sector.

The greatest growth in performance has been in the petrochemical area. The largest margins are also to be found in petrochemical products. It is thought that the petrochemical product business has great potential while that of distribution will be more competitive in the future.

Exhibit 4.12   *Repsol, SA: operating results by sector (Pta millions)*

	1986	1987	1988	Percentage 1988	Percentage growth p.a. 1986–88	Percentage operating results/ revenues 1988
Exploration and production	10,505	703	9,610	10	−4	11
Refining	16,376	38,755	40,191	40	57	7
Distribution of oil products	12,381	15,128	16,614	27	16	13
Petrochemical products	7,958	15,202	31,110	31	98	26
Distribution of LPG	4,907	7,100	1,722	2	−41	1
Less Adjustments in process of consolidation and others	862	−2,264	−33			
Total operating results	52,989	74,624	99,214	100	37	11

The operating results reflect a greater national and international demand for both oil and petrochemical products and an improvement in margins due to (a) lower world crude oil prices, (b) Repsol's efforts to reduce operating expenses and personnel, (c) increased production capacity utilisation by Repsol, and (d) the production of lighter refined oil products with better margins. Exhibit 4.13 shows 1988 revenue results compared with 1986.

Repsol's net profit after tax grew to Pta 55,944 million with an average increase of 66.3% during the last two years. The net profit over sales ratio was 5.9% and return on assets was 7.7% (see Exhibit 4.17). Repsol's net profit in the past three years has been affected by additional labour costs and, especially in 1988, by the company tax provision. The nominal tax rate applicable to Repsol is 35%, however, in recent years it has been lower due to the availability of certain tax deductions.

Exhibit 4.13   *Repsol, SA: resumé of 1988 results (Pta millions)*

	Revenues	Percentage increase p.a. 1988/86	Operating results	Percentage increase p.a. 1988/86	Operating results/ revenues	Operating results/ assets
Exploration and production	88,992	−5	9,610	−4	11	11
Refining	589,684	7	40,191	57	7	23
Distribution of oil products	124,591	7	16,614	16	13	13
Petrochemical products	120,860	17	31,110	98	26	48
Distribution of LPG	112,251	−5	1,722	−41	1	4
Total	942,288	6	99,214	37	11	14

Balance Sheet

At the end of 1988 the total assets of Repsol group reached Pta 725,146 million (see Exhibits 4.14 to 4.16). The fixed assets of the group totalled Pta 487,840 million. Its capital was formed by 100 million shares of Pta 500 nominal value owned by NIH.[4] Repsol had significant reserves of Pta 293,500 million.

Exhibit 4.14 *Repsol, SA: assets by sector (Pta millions)*

	1987	1988	Percentage total assets 1988
Exploration and production	109,256	87,465	12
Refining	196,509	173,511	24
Distribution of oil products	120,912	131,601	18
Petrochemical products	54,509	64,743	9
Distribution of LPG	42,903	46,161	6
Corporate assets	200,848	221,657	31
Total	724,937	725,146	100

Exhibit 4.15 *Repsol, SA: consolidated balance sheet details*

	1986	1987	1988
Total current assets	241,342	331,531	302,752
Tangible fixed assets	337,660	313,732	316,129
Total assets	648,751	724,937	725,146
Loans and short-term debt	38,960	104,135	39,467
Long-term debt	97,217	45,199	36,486
Capital and reserves	243,532	290,807	329,615

The improvement in the treasury position of Repsol in recent years allowed a reduction in the total debt of Pta 118,600 million between 1986 and 1988. At the end of 1988, the financial accounts were greater than the short- and long-term debt together and Repsol had unused credit lines totalling approximately Pta 105,000 million.

The company hoped to pay dividends every year, one to account in the last quarter of the year and the other complementary dividend during the first half of the following year. Their payment depended on the profits achieved, on the general financial position and other factors. As a general

Exhibit 4.16   *Repsol, SA: consolidated balance sheet (Pta millions)*

	1987	1988	Percentage assets 1988
Assets			
Current assets:			
Financial accounts			
Cash, banks and credit institutions	9,437	9,839	1.4
Temporary financial investments	92,323	49,663	6.8
Loan to National Hydrocarbon Institute	21,500	50,000	6.9
	123,260	109,502	15.1
Accounts receivable			
Customers	91,856	93,593	12.9
Current account with state	–	10,006	1.4
Others	35,450	25,982	3.6
	127,306	129,581	17.9
Less Bad debt provision	−3,614	−3,774	−0.5
	124,142	125,807	17.3
Stocks			
Crude oil and natural gas	21,075	14,549	2.0
Finished and semi-finished products	41,073	32,751	4.5
Materials and other stocks	16,061	14,550	2.0
	78,209	61,850	8.5
Period adjustment	5,920	5,593	0.8
Total current assets	331,531	302,752	41.8
Fixed assets:			
Financial			
Investments in companies and other			
permanent financial investments	44,659	106,265	14.7
Loans to National Hydrocarbon Institute	33,015	–	–
	79,674	106,265	14.7
Material	737,104	773,986	106.7
Less Accumulated depreciation	−423,372	−457,857	−63.1
	313,732	316,129	43.6
Total fixed assets	393,406	422,394	58.2
Total assets	724,937	725,146	100.0
Liabilities			
Short-term debt:			
Creditors	67,488	62,763	8.7
Other suppliers	33,583	37,316	5.1
Current account with state	835	–	–

Exhibit 4.16 *continued*

	1987	1988	Percentage assets 1988
Public corporation creditors	66,594	84,020	11.7
Loan to National Hydrocarbon Institute	16,222	–	–
	87,913	39,467	5.4
Period adjustment	7,590	12,740	1.8
Total short-term debt	280,225	237,306	32.7
Medium- and long-term debt:			
Loans to National Hydrocarbon Institute	3,700	–	–
Loans	19,819	13,238	1.8
Bonds and deposits received	21,680	23,248	3.2
	45,199	36,486	5.0
Minority shareholders' interest	41,145	44,534	6.1
Capital subsidies	1,218	1,810	0.2
Provisions	28,839	44,916	6.2
State aid for exploration	37,504	30,479	4.2
Capital and reserves:			
Social capital	50,000	50,000	0.0
Reserves and net profit for period	240,807	293,500	40.5
Less Dividend to account	–	−13,885	−1.9
	290,807	329,615	45.5
Total capital, reserves and long-term liabilities	444,712	487,840	67.3
Total liabilities	724,937	725,146	100.0

Exhibit 4.17 *Repsol, SA: consolidated profit and loss account (Pta millions)*

	1986	1987	1988	Percentage revenues 1988	Percentage growth 1988–86
Revenues:					
Sales	717,034	785,008	813,102	86.3	6.5
Distribution of oil products	100,434	104,828	113,181	12.0	6.2
Others	14,801	11,646	16,005	1.7	4.0
	832,269	901,482	942,288	100.0	6.4
Expenses:					
Purchases and stock variation	471,569	489,917	500,133	53.1	3.0
Personnel	77,694	78,974	85,849	9.1	4.9
Taxes	43,315	58,484	44,462	4.7	1.3
Sub-contracted labour, supplies and services	71,739	77,748	86,508	9.2	9.8

Exhibit 4.17 *continued*

	1986	1987	1988	Percentage revenues 1988	Percentage growth 1988–86
Transport and freight	47,566	44,609	49,118	5.2	1.6
Depreciation	49,155	54,676	44,841	4.8	−4.5
Others	17,972	22,450	32,163	3.4	33.8
	779,280	826,858	843,074	89.5	4.0
Operating profit	52,289	74,264	99,214	10.5	37.7
Additional staffing costs:					
Pension plans	−	16,338	23,040	2.4	−
Workforce restructuring	9,331	1,184	−	−	−
	9,331	17,522	23,040	2.4	57.1
Financial revenues and expenses					
Financial revenues	10,181	21,169	29,114	3.1	69.1
Financial expenses	−21,506	−19,745	−18,084	−1.9	−8.3
	−11,325	1,424	11,030	1.2	−
Profit from subsidies	2,529	3,372	3,477	0.4	17.3
Minority shareholders' interest in profit for period	−6,867	−7,683	−7,588	−0.8	5.1
Pre corporation tax profit	27,995	54,215	83,093	8.8	72.3
Provision for corporation tax	7,772	9,814	27,149	2.9	86.9
Net profit	20,223	44,401	55,944	5.9	66.3

rule, the payout was never above 50% of profits. As regards the 1989 financial year, the company hoped to pay a dividend of at least Pta 90 per share.

During the past 3 years, the investments in fixed assets made by Repsol grew to Pta 141,300 million and comprised mainly the investments made by Campsa in the construction of pipelines and the purchase of service stations and by Repsol Química to increase their capacity (see Exhibit 4.18). Apart from investments in fixed assets, Repsol invested in acquisitions amounting to Pta 43,000 million between 1986 and 1988. Since 1987, exploration operations had been financed partly by the state, reaching Pta 13,000 million in the past 3 years. The company hoped to make investments in fixed assets and acquisitions to the tune of Pta 145,000 million in 1989, and between Pta 485,000 million and Pta 635,000 million in the period 1990–93 (see Exhibit 4.19).

Exhibit 4.18   *Repsol, SA: investment in fixed assets (Pta millions)*

	1986	1987	1988	Total 1986–88	Percentage total 1988
Repsol Exploración	17,196	12,773	6,715	36,684	26
Repsol Petróleo	3,807	2,556	8,648	15,011	11
Campsa	9,400	18,759	31,226	59,385	42
Repsol Química	2,359	2,180	6,438	10,977	8
Repsol Butano	3,766	6,676	8,403	18,845	13
Corporate HQ	–	–	443	443	8
Total	36,528	42,944	61,873	141,345	100

Exhibit 4.19   *Repsol, SA: breakdown of investments and acquisitions (percentage of estimated investment)*

	1989	1990–93
Exploration, development, production, and acquisition of reserves of hydrocarbon	28	33
Increases in capacity of converting and producing lightly refined products	12	7
Purchase of stocks of oil products from the Monopoly and purchases of service stations	48	45
Petrochemical research and development and acquisitions of petrochemical companies	12	15

Personnel and Management

As of 31 December 1988, Repsol had 18,726 employees of which approximately 260 held management positions. The president and vice-president of Repsol, SA managed the company aided and advised by the corporate boards and the committee of presidents of the subsidiary companies. The non-management workers were represented by three unions which negotiated the collective bargaining agreements with the Repsol subsidiaries. Since 1984, the companies that now form Repsol have reduced their respective labour forces by 10%.

The Company versus its Competitors

Apart from being the largest Spanish company in terms of both sales and profits (Pta 942,288 million and Pta 55,944 million, respectively), Repsol has an excellent commercial position in Spain with approximately 60% of the market in oil products, 40% in petrochemical products, 100% in LPG (Repsol was not only the sole wholesaler and almost the sole retailer of LPG in Spain but also the most important distribution company in bottled LPG in Europe), and hoped to control 50% of the natural gas market. It also had the largest network of service stations in Spain with 3,500 outlets.

Repsol is the largest refining company in Spain with approximately 40% of the national refining capacity. In 1988, it refined 21.8 million tons of crude oil which represented 46% of all the crude oil refined in Spain that year.

Leaving aside the 32.4% of Petronor that it controls,[5] Repsol had almost triple the sales of its nearest competitor, Cepsa, the largest private oil company in Spain which controls approximately 24% of the market in oil products and accounts for 23% of the national refining capacity. A long way behind is Petronor, owned by Repsol, with approximately 11% of the market and 17.8% of the refining capacity. Petromed accounts for a market share and refining capacity of 4% and 9.7%, respectively (see Exhibits 4.20 and 4.21).

Exhibit 4.20   *The Spanish oil sector principal competitors in 1988*

	Sales	Net profit	Assets	Own resources	Employees
Repsol	942,288	55,944	725,146	331,425	18,716
Cepsa	363,242	12,429	200,967	88,730	5,697
Petronor	172,628	38,276	85,713	49,006	801
Petromed	61,490	4,242	–	32,911	454
Asesa	13,694	–	–	–	225

Source: Mercado.

Exhibit 4.21   *Capacity of Spanish refineries as of December 1988*

	Crude oil treatment capacity (millions of tons p.a.)	Crude oil distilled in 1988 (millions of tons)	Storage capacity (thousands of cubic metres) Crude oil	Products
Repsol	25.0	21.7	3,199	3,973
Cepsa	14.5	10.8	1,410	2,410
Petromed	6.0	3.4	636	737
ERT	4.0	2.7	618	742
Petronor	11.0	9.3	1,099	1,110
Asesa	1.2	0.7	318	204
Total	61.7	48.6	7,200	9,176

Source: Campsa.

Considering these results, Repsol has a clear advantage in riding the waves of the oil market; it has its oil-fields in case of price rises and its petrochemical products in case of price falls.

As regards weak points in 1988, analysts highlighted the reduced influence of exploration activity and thought that Repsol would have to dedicate fresh resources to search for and acquire more reserves. Repsol only had cover for 30% of its raw material needs while other large European companies had 50% cover. As regards its petrochemical activity, the company has concentrated on the production of basic products whose value-added was inferior to that of products manufactured by its principal competitors.

Internationally, Repsol occupied 25th position in the world rankings of oil companies in terms of sales and 17th position in terms of profits. Repsol is a medium-sized oil company whose key indicators are comparable to the Belgian Petrofina, or the American Unocal, Sun and Coastal. Repsol's results were a far cry from those of the multinational oil groups such as Exxon or Shell, albeit its level of profitability was similar to those of the large groups in the sector (see Exhibits 4.22 and 4.23).

The Spanish oil product consumption was still only 70% of the EEC average. Given that the Spanish economy is the largest growing economy in the Community (11.8% in 1987 and 11.1% in 1988 with similar rates expected for 1989), it is expected that this consumption will increase. However, the foreign competition will increase when the EEC begins to integrate its markets. From 1991 the market in oil products will be liberalised and Repsol will have to compete with the petrol and service stations of Shell, Elf and the like: companies which can draw on international experience whereas Repsol has clung only to the Spanish market. Repsol will also have to invest in distribution.

For some foreign analysts, 'the Spanish Government has been swindling the consumer for years and protecting the oil industry from market forces'. There are concerns about how government interests will influence the policy of the company in the future. Repsol must face up to free competition after 1992 with clear deficiencies in extraction and exploration abilities and a lack of international experience in marketing and distribution. According to the analysts, 'Repsol believes that its market share is not going to change when the foreign companies come in. This is nonsense. And Repsol's expansion abroad, at least into France, is doomed to failure.'

Exhibit 4.22 *The oil sector worldwide: principal competitors in 1988 – key indicators*

	Company	Country	Sales (US$m)	Profits (US$m)	Assets (US$m)	Own resources (US$m)	Profits as percentage of			Employees
							Sales	Assets	Own resources	
1	Exxon	USA	79,557	5,260	74,293	31,767	6.6	7.1	16.6	101,000
2	Royal Dutch/Shell	UK/Neth.	78,381	5,238	85,681	45,485	6.7	6.1	11.5	134,000
3	Mobil	USA	48,198	2,087	38,820	15,685	4.3	5.4	13.3	69,600
4	British Petroleum	UK	46,174	2,155	53,030	20,830	4.7	4.1	10.3	125,950
5	Texaco	USA	33,544	1,304	26,337	8,105	3.9	5.0	16.1	40,000
6	Eni	Italy	25,226	917	36,297	8,928	3.6	2.5	10.3	116,364
7	Chevron	USA	25,196	1,768	33,968	14,788	7.0	5.2	12.0	53,675
8	Elf Aquitaine	France	21,175	1,209	28,032	9,645	5.7	4.3	12.5	73,000
9	Amoco	USA	21,150	2,063	29,919	13,342	9.8	6.9	15.5	53,423
10	Atlantic Richfield	USA	17,626	1,583	21,514	6,247	9.0	7.4	25.3	27,200
11	Usx	USA	15,792	756	19,474	5,688	4.8	3.9	13.3	58,778
12	Petrobrás	Brazil	14,806	765	13,535	6,973	5.2	5.7	11.0	67,080
13	Total	France	13,986	248	14,512	3,599	1.8	1.7	6.9	41,862
14	Pemex	Mexico	13,060	570	45,669	28,216	4.4	1.2	2.0	170,766
15	Nippon Oil	Japan	12,773	167	12,896	3,310	1.3	1.3	5.0	10,178
16	Kuwait Petroleum	Kuwait	12,078	435	21,495	14,845	3.6	2.0	2.9	15,450
17	Phillips Petroleum	USA	11,304	650	11,968	2,113	5.8	5.4	30.8	21,000
18	Petrofina	Belgium	9,898	549	9,469	3,177	5.5	5.8	17.3	23,000
19	Indian Oil	India	9,853	316	3,978	1,340	3.2	7.9	23.6	33,602
20	Petróleos de Venezuela	Venezuela	9,507	1,018	12,935	11,114	10.7	7.9	9.2	45,069
21	Unocal	USA	8,853	480	9,508	2,161	5.4	5.0	22.2	18,235
22	Idemitsu Kosan	Japan	8,814	9	10,123	337	0.1	0.1	2.7	5,497
23	Sun	USA	8,612	7	8,616	3,325	0.1	0.1	0.2	21,300
24	Coastal	USA	8,187	157	7,865	1,271	1.9	2.0	12.4	19,000
25	Repsol	Spain	7,951	480	6,400	2,909	6.0	7.5	16.5	18,716

Source: Fortune.

Exhibit 4.23 *The oil sector worldwide: principal competitors in 1988 – stock market information*

	Company	Country	Market value (US$)	EPS (US$)	Dividend per share (US$)	PER (times)	Market value book value (times)	Dividend yield (%)	Payout (%)
1	Exxon	USA	57,130	4.0	2.2	11.1	1.8	4.9	54.4
2	Royal Dutch/Shell	UK/Neth.	30,556	6.3	3.6	9.3		6.2	57.5
3	Mobil	USA	19,971	4.9	2.4	9.2	1.2	5.2	47.7
4	British Petroleum	UK	27,572	0.4	0.3	12.5	1.3	5.4	67.7
5	Texaco	USA	12,771	5.4	2.3	9.6	1.6	4.4	42.1
6	Eni	Italy	Not listed						
7	Chevron	USA	17,704	5.2	2.6	8.9	1.1	5.6	49.3
8	Elf Aquitaine	France	Not listed						
9	Amoco	USA	20,811	4.0	1.8	9.4	1.5	4.7	43.7
10	Atlantic Richfield	USA	15,412	8.8	4.0	9.2	2.3	5.0	45.6
11	Usx	USA	8,126	2.6	1.3	11.2	1.6	4.3	47.7
12	Petrobrás	Brazil	Not listed						
13	Total	France	2,158	1.7	0.8	8.8	0.6	5.6	48.8
14	Pemex	Mexico	Not listed						
15	Nippon Oil	Japan	14,629	0.2	0.0	65.9	4.0	0.4	24.6
16	Kuwait Petroleum	Kuwait	Not listed						
17	Phillips Petroleum	USA	5,503	2.7	0.7	7.2	2.4	3.4	24.3
18	Petrofina	Belgium	7,283	26.5	13.2	13.5	2.1	3.7	49.9
19	Indian Oil	India	Not listed						
20	Petróleos de Venezuela	Venezuela	Not listed						
21	Unocal	USA	4,961	0.1	0.5	180.4	2.1	2.6	476.2
22	Idemitsu Kosan	Japan	n/a	0.6	0.1				8.9
23	Sun	USA	3,844	0.1	2.7	535.4	1.0	8.4	4,500.0
24	Coastal	USA	2,076	1.8	0.3	12.7	1.6	1.2	14.8
25	Repsol	Spain	Not listed						

Source: Fortune and Disclosure.

Flotation

Repsol had been created in 1987 with the idea of preparing the company for a partial privatisation by floating part of its capital in the stock exchange. The objectives which the management of the company set out were to:

1. Secure sources of financing for the investment plan.
2. Effect a cultural change within the company.
3. Free the management of the company from political influence.

The final objective of the Repsol management was to create an integrated oil company ready to compete in both the national and international markets. This was especially important in the light of the liberalisation of the oil sector which was under way in Spain as a result of Spain's joining the EEC in 1986. The privatisation initiative came more from the managers than the owners although it was clear that it had the latter's approval.

The management of Repsol fixed the date of flotation in the stock market, one year in advance, for the spring of 1988. For six months they had been working on diverse aspects of the preparatory work. In November 1988, they would have to decide the key points of the flotation such as the size of the operation, the flotation price, the markets in which they would sell the shares, the channels of distribution, the financial intermediaries they would use, the promotion plan, etc.

The Spanish Stock Market

At the end of 1988 the Spanish stock market was enjoying a fourth consecutive year of a boom which had begun in 1985 and was only interrupted for a few months by the stock market crash in October 1987. In these years the contract volume had multiplied by five, reaching Pta 10,000 million on average daily (Pta 2.4 billion p.a.). The stock market capitalisation was Pta 10 billion, three times greater than in 1984. The number of quoted companies had gone from 334 to 368. The average profitability in these four years (1985–88 inclusive) was 43% p.a. Most importantly, though, the public, motivated by the large gains that could be made, had returned to the stock market after nearly 10 years of crisis that had almost killed the stock exchange altogether. As in other countries in Europe, the stock exchange was in fashion.

For all this, though, the Spanish stock exchange could not compete with the more developed markets of the West. The dealing system, with a call market structure, was obsolete and made for mishaps; all the deals were made through stock exchange agents who were fiduciary in character and had exclusive access to the market. The financial analysts had just appeared and were not well known. There were few institutional investors; for example, the total volume of funds managed by the Property Investment Fund was only Pta 0.5 billion, 30% of which were in equities. A report of the Bank of Spain had characterised the Spanish stock exchange as 'obscure, narrow and expensive'.

The stock market was little representative of the true economy of the country; only 20 companies represented 75% of the stock market capitalisation (banks 45%, electricity companies 25% and telephone companies 15%). The industrial companies were hardly represented at all. The amount of capital raised by quoted companies through further issues on the stock market capital had grown to Pta 385,000 million in 1987. But the fact was that quoted companies did not really use the stock market as a source of funds.

The government had just approved in June 1988 a complete reform of the stock market with a view to completely modernising it and improving the supervisory, dealing and payment systems in line with the reforms carried out in the London Stock Exchange. Under the umbrella of this process of liberalisation, brokers and dealers began to appear together with brokerage houses all structured similarly to those in the UK and America, albeit their development was still in its infancy. Studies were being made of new systems for continuous dealing using computers and for the regulation of pension funds and other bond market institutions.

The number of individual investors was estimated at 700,000 and represented 50% of the daily dealing on the stock market. It was hoped that this percentage would decrease slowly in favour of the institutional investors (investment and pension funds, etc.) as had happened in other western countries.

The Flotations Market

Stimulated by the stock market boom of the 1985–88, quite a number of companies had decided to place part of their capital on the stock market – a phenomenon almost non-existent in Spain up until that time (see Exhibit 4.24).

In general, the companies floated were small. The largest had been Acesa with a called capital of more than Pta 40,000 million in May 1987, and Endesa with more than Pta 70,000 million called in June 1988. Until mid-1988 the returns obtained by the shareholders of companies floated on the

Exhibit 4.24   *Flotations in Spain 1986–88*

	1986	1987	1988	Total
Companies floated	12	32	39	83
Capital subscribed (Pta billions)	103	310	800	1,213
Average per company (Pta millions)	8,583	9,687	20,512	14,614
Average size (sales in Pta millions)	16,130	13,330	16,747	15,924
First month average returns (%)	55.7%	6.2%	14.3%	17.2%

stock exchange had been, in general, very high (17.2% on average during the first month). The new company market was hot; many investors snapped up the whole share issue immediately whatever the quality, hoping to make an immediate profit – even on the first day – of 25% and then sell. The stock market crash of October 1987 brought about the first losses and almost stopped new flotations altogether. Normal activity was resumed in the first six months of 1988 with a strong recovery in the stock market. During those first six months almost all the new flotations were very profitable even given the inflated prices of some of them. However, by mid-1988 a number of companies had achieved a negative value on the first day of their flotation which noticeably cooled enthusiasm. Exhibit 4.25 shows the most important stock market flotations of recent years.

Exhibit 4.25   *Companies floated in Spain 1987–88*

Company	Date	Volume (Pta millions)	Percentage sold	PER (times)	Sales (Pta millions)	Employees
Acesa	15/5/87	43,700	57.6	16.0	18,856	814
Gas Madrid	15/12/87	4,495	16.0	–	10,644	960
Elosúa	28/12/87	5,294	–	13.0	69,110	1,400
Ence	12/4/88	17,725	39.3	8.9	40,662	1,209
Endesa	1/6/88	74,200	20.4	10.9	268,219	6,309
Campofrío	1/8/88	8,396	10.0	19.1	31,000	1,800
Europistas	19/9/88	7,489	29.3	11.4	3,419	210

Of the privatisations, the most important had been that of Endesa and Ence (see Exhibits 4.25 and 4.26). Endesa drew Pta 70,000 million to the stock market in June 1988, as much from outside as from within Spain, but it had notable difficulties in the flotation process and was saved by the actions of the issue manager who had foreign responsibility. The government had plans to privatise several companies.

Exhibit 4.26 *Principal privatizations in Spain 1985–88*

Year	Company	Seller	Purchaser	Capital sold (%)
1985	Textil Tarazona	INI	Entrecanales/Cima (Spain)	69.6
1985	Secoinsa	INI	Fujitsu (Japan)	69.1
1985	SKF Española	INI	SKF (Sweden)	98.8
1985	Viajes Marsans	INI	Trapsatur (Spain)	100.0
1985	Entursa	INI	CIGA (Italy/Spain)	100.0
1986	Motores Barreiros	INI	MBD (W. Germany)	38.4
1986	Pamesa	Ence (INI)	Torras (Spain)	–
1986	Seat	INI	Volkswagen (W. Germany)	100.0
1988	Ence	INI	Stock Exchange	39.3
1988	Endesa	INI	Stock Exchange	20.4

Source: The Economist Intelligence Unit.

The number of privatisations at the world level had grown considerably from an average of 15 per year in the period 1980–84 to 70 per year in the period 1985–88.

In 1986 and 1987 the accumulated value of the privatised companies grew to some US$125,000 million from practically zero. During 1988 the level decreased considerably (some US$25,000 million) due to the effect of the stock market crash in October 1987.

Japan accounted for 58% of the total value of the privatisations followed by the UK (12%), the rest of Europe (11%), Asia (8%), Latin America and others.

In the West, the leadership which the UK displayed with its programme of privatisations promoted by Prime Minister Margaret Thatcher served to put impetus into the so-called popular capitalism. The total volume of privatisations during 1984–88 had reached around US$20,000 million, the most important of which are shown in Exhibit 4.27.

Exhibit 4.27 *Principal privatizations in the UK 1984–88*

Year	Company	Size (US$ million)	Stake sold (%)
1987	British Petroleum	9,500	36.8
1986	British Gas	7,800	100.0
1984	British Telecom	4,900	50.2
1988	British Steel	4,500	100.0

Source: The Economist.

The international market for stock market flotations reached a peak in the middle of the 1980s, feeling the heat of the stock market boom in those years. It is estimated that between Europe and the USA almost $7,000 million (excluding domestic tranches) had been floated during the last year. In the USA, the total volume of initial public offerings during the past three years has reached approximately $40,000 million.

Notes

1. In 1989 their reserves increased by 25 million barrels through the acquisition of a 5% participation in a North Sea field belonging to British Petroleum for Pta 9,700 million.
2. In March 1989 Repsol purchased shares of Petronor increasing its participation in the company from 32.4% to 54.3%.
3. The acquisition by Repsol of the shares of Petronor increased the participation of Repsol in Campsa to 64%.
4. Later, on 9 February 1989, the board of directors agreed to increase the capital by Pta 100,000 million by way of a share issue of 200 million shares of Pta 500 million nominal value, with charge to retained earnings.
5. In March 1989 this percentage increased to 54.3%.

Koninklijke PTT Nederland

This case concerns the run-up to the expected initial public offering of shares in KPN in 1994. KPN was established in 1989 when the old state enterprise, the Netherlands Postal and Telecommunications Services (PTT) were incorporated, with all the shares in KPN being retained by the state of the Netherlands. The incorporation was seen as a step towards complete privatisation in the future. Data are provided on the activities, concessions, tariff control system and developments at PTT Post and PTT Telecom. The case also covers accounting principles and the long-term prospects for KPN.

From State Company to Public Company

Koninklijke PTT Nederland NV[1] (to be called KPN hereafter) was established on 1 January 1989 when the old state enterprise, the Netherlands Postal and Telecommunications Services (PTT) was incorporated. The state of the Netherlands retained all shares of KPN. The goal of this incorporation is to enhance market alertness, flexibility and commercial reality by putting the company at a greater distance from the government and creating a new legal framework within which KPN can carry out its public utility role. The incorporation can be seen as a step towards complete privatisation in the future. The present transitional phase will help the company to adapt to several market requirements and increasing competition. The initial public offering of KPN is expected in 1994. It will be the biggest flotation in the history of the Amsterdam Stock Exchange.

This privatisation plan takes place in a market expected to be the fastest-growing sector in Europe, and which has already witnessed some privatisations during the last few years. The first one was that of British Telecommunications (BT) on 3 December 1984, when the British government sold more than 3 billion ordinary shares at 130 pence per share. On

This case has been written by Professor Rezaul Kabir, Tilburg University, and Karel Scheepers, KPN, for the purpose of class discussion only. It uses fictitious future estimates. Karel Scheepers is involved in a personal capacity; the views expressed here are those of that author only and do not reflect those of KPN. © *Rezaul Kabir and Karel Scheepers, 1995.*

9 December 1991, another 1.35 billion ordinary shares were sold at 125 pence per share. The government sold its remaining holding in 1993. The highest price of BT quoted in 1992 was 437 pence, and in 1993 it was 478 pence. BT is now Britain's largest company by market capitalisation, and has a 90% share of the British telecommunications market. Analysts believe that the nature of KPN's activities can best be compared to that of the British Telecom. In 1988, Telefonica de España was privatised in Spain, and in 1991 the privatisation of Italy's state-owned telecommunications firm STET took place. Over the coming years, the privatisation of telecommunications companies in Denmark, Germany and Portugal is also expected.

Before listing on a stock exchange can take place, the price for the ordinary shares has to be set. This price should be related to the fundamental value of a KPN share. If the price is set higher than the perceived fundamental value, investors will not buy the share. If the price is lower than the perceived value, then the current shareholder (the state) will lose money because investors would have bought the share at a higher price. Although during stock exchange listing, new equity offerings are usually found to be underpriced, the fair value of a share is the starting point in determining the initial offering price.

Activities

KPN is the leading supplier of communication and information services in the Netherlands, with increasing business interests in other countries. According to its mission statement, KPN offers business and private customers a complete range of high quality products and services concentrating on the transport of information, goods and valuable items. Services are provided within the Netherlands and to and from other countries, partly under the terms of exclusive concessions assigned by the government and partly in competition with other suppliers.

KPN is the parent company of the KPN group of companies. It is managed by the board of management subject to the scrutiny of a supervisory board (see Exhibit 5.1). The company has several operating companies, the most important of which are PTT Post and PTT Telecom. PTT Post collects, sorts, conveys and distributes information, money and valuables. It also provides counter services at the post offices in a joint venture with the Postbank. PTT Telecom is responsible for electronic and optical telecommunications services, and sells and rents a wide range of terminal equipment for connection to the public infrastructure. The operating companies carry out most of their work by themselves, but some is also done by other

Exhibit 5.1 *Organisation structure of the Koninklijke PTT Nederland*

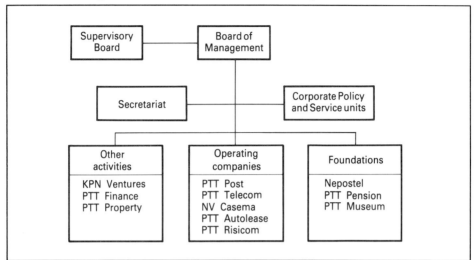

companies in which they have indirect or direct holdings. A number of support activities are undertaken in two other subsidiaries. KPN has also a majority interest of 76.5% in Casema NV (cable television) and has some other interests as well.

At the presentation of the 1992 annual report, the chairman of the board of management expressed satisfaction with the company's current financial results. As mentioned in Exhibit 5.2, the net profit after tax increased by 3.5% in 1992 to DFl 1.664 million while net turnover rose by 7.8% to DFl 15.622 million. The turnover growth achieved by PTT Telecom was in significant part realised by the business units National Networks and International Telecommunications. PTT Post handled increasing quantities of mail (individual items, printed matter, parcels and direct mail) in 1992, and the business unit PTT Post International increased its turnover by almost 17%.

Exhibit 5.2 *Group financial results of KPN in 1992 (DFl millions)*

	PTT Post	PTT Telecom	Others	Total
Net turnover	4.949	10.487	186	15.622
Total revenues	4.998	10.993	409	16.340
Earnings before interests and taxes	394	2.789	(82)	3.101
Net income	299	1.330	35	1.664

Concessions

KPN has been entrusted with two exclusive concessions by the Dutch government to perform a public utility role. KPN has delegated the postal concession to PTT Post and the telecommunications concession to PTT Telecom. According to the postal concession, KPN is obliged to transport postal items for anyone throughout the Netherlands, and to and from other countries. On the other hand, it has an exclusive concession for the distribution of letters weighing up to 500 grammes. According to the telecommunications concession, KPN is obliged to ensure the capacity and quality of the telecommunications infrastructure, operate basic services and make such services available to any person and to provide leased circuits. On the other hand, it has an exclusive concession for the installation, commercial operation and maintenance of the telecommunications infrastructure. The tendency for liberalisation is a structural environmental factor for postal, but especially for telecommunications companies. Data transport and some forms of satellite communication have already been liberalised. Legislation is expected to allow a second operator alongside KPN to provide the digital pan-European cellular system for mobile voice communication (GSM). The licence for this second mobile operator is expected to be released in 1994. According to proposals to amend the telecommunications act, as of 1995 licensed infrastructures (e.g. those of the Dutch railways, the electricity companies and the cable broadcasting organisations) may be used to provide all types of telecommunications services with the exception of telephony, and as of 1998 the telephone service using licensed installations and dedicated circuits will be liberalised. KPN finds these developments logical and reasonable, and uses the starting-point that the quality of its services and the price/effort relationship are important for customers, and therefore, for the success of KPN.

Tariff Control System

The prices which KPN can charge a consumer are controlled by a tariff control system based on a price cap. The maximum prices which an average user pays for the services provided under the terms of the postal and telecommunications concessions are linked to the indices of the governmental Central Planning Office. The maximum rates PTT Post may charge for the services it is obliged to provide are limited by the index of wage costs per employee of private sector companies; those of PTT Telecom are limited by the retail price index. KPN has the freedom to change its prices for individual services by varying percentages within the limits set by the tariff control system.

Developments at PTT Post

The achievements of PTT Post can be seen in the availability of a modern, nationwide infrastructure with an extensive network for collection, transport and distribution. International comparison indicates that PTT Post delivers high quality service and is a cost-effective company. In the Netherlands, some increase can be expected in the market for postal transport. However, the rapid advance of electronics in payment systems (cash dispensers from the Postbank) and in communications (fax and electronic mail) many put future profit under pressure. Therefore, an effort will be made to enlarge the return on the existing postal services by increased service and differentiation. PTT Post is also turning to new markets and actively developing new types of value-added service. Thus, it is not restricting itself to the national infrastructure but operating as an international integrator and is rapidly increasing its international activities by competition and cooperation with other postal companies. Since the reason for PTT Post's achievements lie in its excellent infrastructure, growth potential lies in logistic services. PTT Post wants to control the logistic services in several branches and strives for continuous improvement of quality and reduction of costs. Important cost savings can be achieved by investing in further automation of the sorting process. In 1993, PTT Post announced the operation Briefpost 2000 which aims to reduce the number of interchange centres to six large hubs where machines will sort 98% of all letters. An important reduction in the workforce is expected as a result of this operation. In February 1993, PTT Post set up a joint venture, Postkantoren BV, together with the Postbank. PTT Post and Postbank opted for closer cooperation in order to make the best use of the extensive network of post offices. The success of automatic cash dispensers necessitated a reorientation of these offices. The post offices are now being changed into modern service centres.

Developments at PTT Telecom

PTT Telecom is operating in an important growth market. The role of information in society is changing: information has become a full production factor for companies, especially for sectors like information supply, transport, distribution and services. Information has become more and more important for individuals too. The most important developments in the field of telecommunications are: the rise in fax machines, mobile communication, data communication, telematica, leased circuits, value-added services, and green numbers (so-called 06-services). These developments are mainly the result of a rapidly progressing technology and customer demands. In this context, the use of microelectronics, and in the case of transmission, digitalisation and signal transmission via glass fibre cable can be cited. PTT Telecom has already adapted its infrastructure to a large extent to modern technology. Due to deregulation and liberalisation, national and international competition is increasing. As PTT Telecom believes that the price/effort relationship is of crucial importance to meet this competition successfully, quality and efficiency improvement are key strategic issues. Competition is increasingly taking place at the European and global level: customers demand worldwide service. That is why PTT Telecom focuses on internationalisation and cooperation with other telecommunications companies. The establishment of Unisource, a joint venture with the Swedish and Swiss national telecommunications operators is, therefore, of great importance to PTT Telecom. Despite a limited home market, KPN has the benefit of a liberal legislation and a large number of internationally operating companies.

Accounting Principles

The financial data of operating companies are fully consolidated in group equity and group results (see Exhibits 5.3 and 5.4). From 1992 onwards, assets are valued at their historic cost. Before 1992, fixed assets and stocks were valued mostly at their current cost. The difference between historic cost valuation and current cost valuation, however, is not thought to be significant. Because PTT Telecom's assets dominate KPN's balance sheet, KPN strives for a market-value-based capital structure equal to the unweighted average capital structure of internationally comparable telecommunications companies with very low financial risk. Depreciation is calculated on the basis of the nominal value of tangible fixed assets as from 1992 (before 1992 depreciation was calculated on the basis of current cost). The rate of depreciation is expected to increase slightly but steadily in the future due to ever-increasing technological progress which implies a shorter economic life.

Exhibit 5.3   *Consolidated balance sheet of Koninklijke PTT Nederland NV (DFl millions)*

	1/1/89	31/12/89	31/12/90	31/12/91	31/12/92
Assets					
Tangible fixed assets	18.923	20.532	21.216	22.053	22.564
Financial fixed assets	62	68	194	142	197
Current assets					
Cash and bank balances	1.103	113	824	356	371
Other current assets	3.497	3.642	3.598	3.546	3.915
Total assets	23.585	24.355	25.832	26.310	27.047
Liabilities					
Group equity					
Shareholders' equity	7.982	9.001	9.887	10.768	11.694
Minority interests	22	25	32	34	38
Provisions	2.902	3.040	2.822	2.661	2.843
Long-term liabilities	8.166	8.297	8.764	8.126	7.832
Short-term liabilities	4.603	3.992	4.327	4.508	4.640
Total liabilities	23.585	24.355	25.832	26.310	27.047

Exhibit 5.4   *Consolidated profit and loss account of Koninklijke PTT Nederland NV (DFl millions)*

	1989	1990	1991	1992
Total revenues	13.272	14.104	15.180	16.340
Total operating costs				
Salaries	4.897	5.207	5.741	5.995
Materials and services	2.771	3.042	3.353	3.574
Depreciation	2.087	2.363	2.522	2.897
Other operating costs	735	577	660	773
Earnings before interest and taxes	**2.783**	**2.915**	**2.904**	**3.101**
Interest earned	19	91	96	58
Interest paid	549	593	608	603
Earnings before taxes	**2.246**	**2.413**	**2.392**	**2.556**
Taxes	729	850	779	887
Income from investments in affiliated and associated companies	2	4	1	(3)
Extraordinary result after taxes	(61)	–	–	–
Group result after taxes	1.463	1.567	1.614	1.666
Minority interests	(3)	(1)	0	(2)
Profit after tax	1.460	1.566	1.614	1.664

Long-term Prospects

The financial analyst of a major Dutch bank is gathering long-range estimates, after thorough investigation of the markets in which KPN operates and different macroeconomic factors – like the development of labour costs and interest rates. The US Value Line reports in its 15 January 1993 issue that the telecommunications industry continues to evolve rapidly as increasing competition, brought on by new technologies, forces regulators and incumbent wireline monopolies to react with increasing swiftness. The relative competitive environment in which some telecommunications companies are operating is shown in Exhibits 5.5 and 5.6.

Exhibit 5.5   *Relative competitive environment and valuation matrix*

	Access lines[1]	Operating margin (%)	Net debt/ net worth (%)	Competitive threat	EBITD multiple[2]
BT	44	26.8	44.0	Fair	5.0
Telefonica	34	30.2	117.9	Good	4.2
STET	40	18.6	100.2	Good	4.6
US average	49	18.8	77.8	Poor	6.6
PTT Telecom	48	27.0	66.0	Good	–

[1] Per 100 inhabitants.
[2] Defined as firm value/earnings before interest, taxes and depreciation.

Reliable sources expect a turnover growth of 6.75% for KPN in 1993. However, turnover growth will slow down afterwards due to increased competition which will affect both volume growth and prices. The forecasted growth in turnover is: 6.5% in 1994, 6.0% in 1995, 5.5% in 1996, and 5% in 1997 and the years after. The financial analyst realises the need to make correct estimates of labour costs. The increase in the workforce of KPN depends only in a limited way on turnover growth due to the fact that most of the workforce is concerned with the operation and maintenance of the postal and telecommunications network, regardless of the volume of services supplied. The labour costs per employee are thought to develop in line with the Dutch average. As a result of the current economic slowdown in the Netherlands, labour costs per employee are expected to rise only modestly in the next few years. From 1996 onwards, labour costs per employee are expected to rise at a higher rate. In order to carry out the quality improvement programme, new personnel have to be recruited. On the other

Exhibit 5.6 *Relative business risk comparison*

Company	Regulation	Competition	Non-basic activities	Political	Overall
Koninklijke PTT Nederland	L/M	L/M	L	L/M	L/M
Regional Bell Operating Co.					
Ameritech	L/M	L	L	L	L
Bell Atlantic	L/M	L	M	L	L/M
BellSouth	L/M	L	L	L	L
NYNEX	L/M	L/M	L	L	L/M
Pacific Telesis	L/M	L/M	M	L	L/M
Southwestern Bell	L/M	L	M	L	L/M
US West	L/M	L	L	L	L
International					
AT&T	L	M	H	L	M
BT	L/M	L/M	L	L	L
Cable & Wireless	L/M	H	L	M	M
Hong Kong Telecom	L/M	M	L	H	M
Italcable	M	L	L	M	M
SIP	M	L	L	M	M
STET	M	L	M	M	M
Telefonica	M	L	L	M	M

H = high, M = medium, L = low.

hand, efficiency operations will lead to a decreasing need for manpower. On balance, a slight decrease in the number of employees is anticipated. The combination of these two factors results in an expected increase in wage costs of 4.5% in 1993, 4.0% in 1994, 4.5% in 1995, and 5% in 1996 and the years after. The analyst expects other costs to remain at the 1992 level as a percentage of turnover. The dividend pay-out ratio has amounted to an average of 40% of net profit in recent years. The analyst assumes that pay-out will remain stable in coming years.

The costs of materials and services are directly related to turnover. In 1992, these were 21.9% of turnover, and in 1991, 22.1% of turnover. Due to the quality improvement programme and increased pressure on tariffs, these expenses are expected to increase by 0.5% as a percentage of turnover until 1997, and remain constant as a percentage of turnover afterwards. The analyst also wants to make an estimate of the size of net working capital which depends on the size of turnover. It can be argued that increased turnover will lead to increases in supplies, debtors and creditors. Cash and bank balances amounted to DFl 371 million at the end of 1991. KPN will strive to maintain this level in future years.

The other current assets and short-term liabilities will remain at the 1992 level as a percentage of turnover. The completion of the digitalisation of the telecommunications network will demand large investments in the next few years. In 1993 and 1994, an investment of DFl 4 billion in tangible fixed assets is expected. The digitalisation programme will be almost completed in 1995 and from then on an investment of DFl 3.5 billion per year will be sufficient (the capital expenditure is expected to rise 3% per year from 1995 onwards in line with the expected inflation).

For simplicity of calculation, the analyst decided to assume that all revenues and expenses should take place at the end of year. Because of the fact that looking far ahead is impossible, she assumes that KPN will reach a steady state after 1997, after which new investments are not expected to create or destroy any value. Microeconomic equilibrium tendencies support this opinion. The analyst has also estimated that about 50% of the provisions have debt characteristics, and the minority interests have a market-to-book ratio of 1.5. The financial analyst has also gathered some additional information thought to be useful for the analysis. These are reproduced in Exhibits 5.7 and 5.8.

Exhibit 5.7 *Comparative financial data*

Panel A: Price/earnings ratio[1]

Company	Ratio	Company	Ratio
GTE	15.1	Racal Telecom	23.6
United Telecom	15.0	McCaw Cellular	–
Ameritech	13.0	AT&T	14.1
Bell Atlantic	13.0	MCI Comm.	12.0
Bell South	14.6	British Telecom	11.0
NYNEX	11.7	Cable & Wireless	17.6
Pacific Telesis	14.7	NTT	53.7
Southwestern Bell	13.8	Telefonica	10.7
US West	12.0	STET	10.4
Telefonica de Esp.	4.8	Hong Kong Telecom	14.2

Panel B: Beta list

Betas of a few companies/industries

Company	Beta	Industry	Beta
Frans Maas[1]	0.97	Railroads[3]	0.71
Nedlloyd[2]	1.62	Electric and gas Util.[3]	0.73
Royal Dutch[2]	0.60	Petroleum refining[3]	0.86
Unilever[2]	0.78	Telephone Networks[4]	0.90
Philips[2]	1.02	Water[3]	0.60
DSM[2]	0.93	Transport[3]	0.99

Exhibit 5.7 *continued*

Betas of a few telecommunications companies/industries[5]

Telecom companies	Beta	Telecom. services ind.	Beta
British Telecom[1]	0.60	Bell Atlantic[3]	0.90
Cable & Wireless	1.15	Bell South	0.95
Ericsson	1.00	AT&T	1.35
Hong Kong Tel.	0.75	NYNEX	0.90
Racal Telecom	1.40	Pacific Telesis	0.90
Reuters	1.35	BCE INC	0.60
Telefonica Espana	0.90	Centel Corp.	1.00
Telefonica Chile	0.45	McCaw Cellular	1.75

1. *Source:* Goldman Sachs, *Presentation to PTT Nederland*, 22 May 1991.
2. *Source: Amro Share Guide,* August 1991.
3. *Source:* Wilshire Associates, Inc., *Capital Market Equilibrium Statistics*, California, 1981.
4. *Source:* Risk Management Service, July 1991.
5. *Source: Value Line Investment Survey*, 18 Jan. 1991.

Exhibit 5.8 *Financial data of some telecommunications companies*

Company	Total value ($ million)	Market value of equity	P/E ratio (1991 E)	Beta	Rating (S&P)
British Telecom	50.515	41.693	10.5	0.60	AAA
Cable & Wireless			16.4	1.15	
Hong Kong Telecom			13.6	0.75	
Telecom New Zealand	4.209	3.319	14.3		AA−
Telefonica de España	23.685	8.845	11.9	0.90	
TELMEX	22.301	20.782	8.7		
Average	25.178	18.660	13.0	0.85	
Ameritech	21.658	16.460	13.6		AAA
Bell Atlantic Corp.	26.188	19.212	13.2	0.90	AA−
BellSouth Corp.	32.046	24.054	15.5	0.95	AAA
NYNEX Corp.	22.301	20.278	13.0	0.90	A
Pacific Telesis	22.741	17.010	15.0	0.90	A+
Southwestern Bell Corp.	22.629	17.100	15.2	0.90	A
US West, Inc.	22.454	14.598	12.5	0.95	A+
Average	24.288	18.387	13.2	0.92	
ALLTEL Corp.	4.292	3.279	16.3		A+
Centel	3.925	2.450	48.1	1.00	BBB
Century Telephone Enter.	1.041	781	23.1		
Cincinnati Bell, Inc.			18.1		AA−
GTE Corp.			15.1	0.95	A−

Exhibit 5.8 *continued*

Company	Total value ($ million)	Market value of equity	P/E ratio (1991 E)	Beta	Rating (S&P)
Rochester Telephone Corp.	1.358	924	16.3	0.80	A
Southern New England Tel.	2.994	1.990	13.0	0.85	AA+
Average	2.722	1.885	21.4	0.90	

Sources: columns 1–3: Goldman Sachs, *Telephone Industry Monthly*, Aug./Sept. 1991; column 4: *Value Line Investment Survey*, 18 Jan. 1991; column 5: *Standard & Poor's Ratings Handbook*, May 1991.

Note

1. A Dutch NV is similar to a limited liability company.

CASE 6

BAT Industries plc

This case examines the abortive takeover bid for BAT Industries, the giant UK conglomerate, in 1989 by Hoylake, a consortium specially formed by three wealthy entrepreneurs for the purpose. The bid was to be financed by the issue of 'junk bonds', in essence secured on the future cash flows of BAT, and to be redeemed out of the proceeds of selling off the 'unbundled' components of BAT. BAT's own financial performance had been sluggish in the 1980s and its patchy record with acquisitions extended back to the 1960s. Its diversification policy was driven by concern with the anticipated decline in profitability of its most important single product, tobacco. After forays into paper and packaging, cosmetics, department stores and scientific instruments, it appeared to have determined on financial services as the major vehicle to restore its growth impetus.

Yet BAT appeared to be significantly undervalued by the stock market – the bid was pitched well above the market value and independent analysts assessed its break-up value even more highly. Did the market undervalue BAT or was its poor market rating a reflection of the inappropriate strategic and financial policies followed by BAT prior to the bid?

The case examines the BAT defences and documents the reasons for the failure of the bid. A surprising outcome was that BAT ended up dismantling itself: in effect doing what the bidders themselves were proposing, and also reversing an important element of its financial strategy, its dividend policy. This episode left BAT in a significantly slimmer state with two core activities: tobacco, the faithful cash cow, and financial services – but still with no apparent commercial logic. To some degree, the case illustrates the contemporary trend towards more focused activities, yet we find BAT still operating two highly diverse, mainstream activities. Are there gains which this combination of activities can offer to shareholders, otherwise unable to achieve the effects of portfolio combination? Or does scope remain for cleaving BAT into two parts?

This case has been adopted by Bill Neale as a basis for class discussion rather than to illustrate either effective or ineffective handling of an administrative situation. From: Corporate Finance and Investment: Decisions and Strategies, *R.H. Pike and C.W. Neale,* © *Prentice Hall International (UK) Ltd, 1993.*

Introduction

In July 1989, a consortium assuming the name Hoylake announced a bid of £13.4 billion for the conglomerate BAT (British American Tobacco) Industries plc. As BAT was then the third largest corporation in the UK, this event shattered the illusion held by many directors that size alone was a guarantee of immunity from assault by takeover raiders. The motive for the proposed takeover was to unbundle BAT's assets, which, according to Hoylake, were undervalued by the market. Unbundling is a latter-day euphemism for asset-stripping or breaking up the target company in order to resell the component segments at an overall profit.

A Remarkable Bid

The bid was significant for a number of reasons, apart from its sheer size. Firstly, it was launched by a company formed specifically for the purpose of mounting the bid. The founders of Hoylake were three wealthy financiers: the Australian media tycoon Kerry Packer, retailing entrepreneur Sir James Goldsmith, and merchant banker Jacob Rothschild.

Secondly, it was to be financed, not by a cash offer, but by an issue of junk bonds, the first time this financing vehicle had been used in the UK, at least on anywhere like this scale. Junk bonds are essentially IOUs, which issuers intend to redeem using the proceeds from selling the assets of the dismembered firm. They involve high risks partly because suitable buyers for the unbundled assets may be difficult to find at the right price (although skilled junk-financed takeover exponents are careful to line up buyers prior to bidding). They are also exposed to interest rate increases, which undermine their value. Due to these risks, high yields have to be offered in order to encourage the equity holders of the target to accept 'junk' in exchange for their shares. Previously, most successful asset-stripping, such as the takeover by Hanson of Imperial Tobacco, had been financed by share exchange or a combination of shares and cash/borrowing, exerting less pressure on the bidder-stripper to dispose of assets in a hurry.

Thirdly, the unbundling motivation behind the bid indicated a belief that BAT had a break-up value considerably above its market capitalisation. This aspect was especially significant as it threw into question both the wisdom of BAT's past diversification strategy and also raised doubts about the efficiency of the market's valuation of BAT. Clearly, the identity of potential bidders cannot often be predicted, but perhaps the market might have identified BAT as a potential takeover target, especially as bigger (i.e. more expensive) bids had already been successfully mounted in the USA, e.g. the junk-financed bid by Kohlberg–Kravis–Roberts for RJR Nabisco.

Fourthly, the BAT defence strategy, as revealed in its defence document, 'Building Shareholder Value', was a novel variety of tactical devices. In many respects, it amounted to a complete *volte face* of both prior financial and business strategies.

Fifthly, because of BAT's overseas ramifications, the bid raised important issues relating to regulation of takeover activity, and the ownership of major financial services concerns.

BAT's Financial Record: Implications for Diversification

More generally, the bid raised issues about the rationality of conglomerate diversification. Historically, BAT had derived the bulk of its profits and cash flow from overseas tobacco operations, in which it possessed virtual monopolies in many markets. However, acknowledging the accumulation of medical evidence on the harmful effects of smoking, BAT increasingly perceived tobacco as a declining market, at least in Western and more health-conscious societies. Consequently, it decided to use the strong and continuing cash flows from this source to buy into other activities, most notably retailing, paper and packaging, cosmetics and, eventually, financial services. Many of these diversifications, such as Macfisheries (later known as International Stores), the Yardley cosmetics business and the Mardon packaging operation were disappointing and were subsequently sold off.

By the late 1980s, BAT's profits were earned from six areas, including its share of associated company earnings. Exhibit 6.1 shows key financial data for the 'old' BAT group over the period 1984–89 from both the income statements and the balance sheets. Exhibit 6.2 shows the performance of the individual divisions in terms of turnover and operating profits, and also gives the asset base for each segment. Exhibit 6.3 shows the segmental contributions for the years 1986–90, restated to reflect the post-bid restructuring.

Exhibit 6.1 suggests that the old conglomeration of activities was not especially profitable. Over the period 1984–88, nominal operating profit grew erratically at an average annual rate of about 2.5%, EPS growth was equally sluggish at about 4% on average, while sales actually fell. Poor

Exhibit 6.1   *BAT Industries five-year summary 1984–89*

	1984	1985	1986	1987	1988	1989
Income statement for year ended 31 December						
Turnover (£m)	18,203	17,051	19,167	17,208	17,653	21,636
Operating profit (£m)	1,465	1,287	1,483	1,396	1,604	2,197
Profit after tax (£m)	873	736	869	868	1,038	1,271
Attributable to BAT shareholders	784	673	793	787	949	1,172
Extraordinary items	64	(34)	75	(36)	15	123
Profit for the year	848	639	868	751	965	1,295
Dividends (net)	151	179	209	248	299	443
Dividend per share (p)	10.30	12.10	14.30	16.90	20.10	30.00
EPS (p)	53.60	45.72	53.51	52.78	62.81	76.75
Balance sheet for year ended 31 December						
Tangible fixed assets	2,820	2,482	2,524	2,178	2,257	2,659
Investments in financial services subsidiaries	941	1,142	1,482	1,503	3,583	4,229
Other fixed assets	1,034	719	588	488	560	570
Stocks	2,640	2,238	2,146	1,810	1,939	2,235
Other current assets	2,629	2,244	2,635	2,542	1,575	1,862
Total assets	10,064	8,825	9,375	8,521	9,914	11,555
BAT Industries' shareholders' funds	4,276	3,660	4,174	3,946	3,601	4,683
Interest of minority shareholders	422	347	413	347	340	406
Shareholders' funds	4,698	4,007	4,587	4,293	3,941	5,089
Provisions for liabilities and charges	518	656	683	629	684	748
Borrowings – due beyond one year	1,986	1,453	1,338	1,171	2,089	2,374
Borrowings – due within one year	555	577	551	300	572	340
Other creditors	2,307	2,132	2,216	2,128	2,628	3,004
Total funds employed	10,064	8,825	9,375	8,521	9,914	11,555

Source: BAT Annual Report 1989

Exhibit 6.2 *Segmental performance 1984–89 (old group)*

		1984	1985	1986	1987	1988	1989
A	TURNOVER						
	Tobacco	38	37	38	35	34	33
	Retailing	25	23	21	19	19	18
	Paper	8	8	9	9	9	8
	Other trading activities	8	7	4	3	3	3
	Commercial activities	79	75	72	66	65	62
	Financial services	6	12	15	20	18	22
	Share of associated companies	15	13	13	14	17	16
	Total sales	100	100	100	100	100	100
B	OPERATING PROFITS						
	Tobacco	48	50	46	46	41	38
	Retailing	15	11	12	13	10	8
	Paper	10	12	14	13	12	9
	Other trading activities	5	4	1	1	1	1
	Commercial activities	78	77	73	73	64	56
	Financial services	9	10	18	16	24	33
	Share of associated companies	13	13	9	11	12	11
	Operating profits	100	100	100	100	100	100
C	OPERATING ASSETS						
	Tobacco	32	30	32	30	23	25
	Retailing	30	31	24	22	17	17
	Paper	10	11	12	14	11	10
	Other trading activities	10	7	9	8	6	5
	Commercial activities	82	79	77	74	57	57
	Financial services	10	14	18	22	39	39
	Share of associated companies	8	7	5	4	4	4
	Operating assets	100	100	100	100	100	100

All figures are percentages of the relevant totals.
Source: BAT Annual Reports (1984–9).

bottom-line performance was also reflected in below-par share price performance in the rising markets of the 1980s.

Exhibit 6.4(a) shows the movement of the BAT ordinary share price in relation to the FTSE 100 index over the period 1985–1991, underperforming the market prior to the bid and outperforming it following the bid. Beta values for BAT for the same period are also given in Exhibit 6.4(b).

Exhibit 6.3   *Segmental contributions 1986–90 (continuing group)*

	1986	1987	1988	1989	1990
Turnover (including associated companies)					
Financial services:					
General business	13	14	18	21	20
Life business	13	16	14	17	16
Commercial activities:					
Tobacco	64	60	58	54	57
Other trading activities	10	10	10	8	7
Continuing group	100	100	100	100	100
Operating profit					
Financial services:					
General business	20	17	27	34	(3)
Life business	8	10	10	13	21
Commercial activities:					
Tobacco	70	72	62	53	85
Other trading activities	5	5	5	3	1
Share of associates' net interest	(3)	(4)	(4)	(3)	(4)
Operating profit: Continuing group	100	100	100	100	100

All figures are percentages of the relevant totals.
Source: BAT Annual Report (1990).

The Valuation of BAT: Dividend Policy and Investment Strategy

While it is commonplace for bidders to offer above the market price for their targets, the magnitude of the bid, £13.4 billion surprised many observers when the market value was only around £8.5 billion. This prompted numerous attempts to assess the 'true' value of BAT. For example, stockbrokers Hoare-Govett reckoned that BAT's components could be sold for some £16.7 billion.

A distinction ought to be made between sum-of-the-parts valuations, which place a value on each segment of the company assuming that the individual units are quoted as separate entities, and break-up valuations, which assume that the individual parts are each sold off to the highest bidder. However, most 'after-the-event' observers were agreed that BAT had in

Exhibit 6.4 *(a) BAT share price movements relative to the FTSE 100 Share Index. (b) BAT beta values*

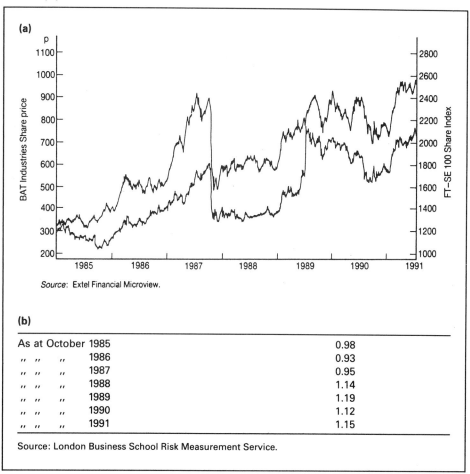

(a)

Source: Extel Financial Microview.

(b)

As at October		1985		0.98
" "	"	1986		0.93
" "	"	1987		0.95
" "	"	1988		1.14
" "	"	1989		1.19
" "	"	1990		1.12
" "	"	1991		1.15

Source: London Business School Risk Measurement Service.

some sense been undervalued by the market, but there was less agreement as to why.

Intimately connected with the issue of whether the market had correctly valued BAT, was the relationship between dividend policy and the financing of corporate diversification strategy. In a letter to the *Financial Times* (penned well before the publication of BAT's defence document), a unit trust manager attempted to explain why BAT was apparently undervalued and why a shift in dividend policy was required. The writer forcefully argued that past failure to pay higher dividends was responsible for the apparent undervaluation:

profits are not being distributed on sufficient a scale to the shareholders; they may be merely piling up in cash or equivalent form, or being ploughed back into acquisitions at prices which absorb much of the cash flow.

He went on to state:

Distributing more of your profits to shareholders raises your share price. There may be limits of prudence here, but these limits are nowhere near tested by most companies. The standard defence against high distribution – the need for re-investment for future growth – is also greatly overplayed. If assets are profitable they can be financed by many other means than retentions. Companies fool themselves if they think that retentions are 'cheap finance'. They are not. They ultimately cost the standard rate, the cost of capital, which is partly a function of the company's actual share price. High retentions depress share prices.

In its defence document 'Building Shareholder Value', highlights of which are shown in Exhibit 6.5, the BAT board recognised that BAT was a conglomerate which had grown beyond its optimum size and was insufficiently focused on its core activities of tobacco and financial services.

Exhibit 6.5 *Highlights of the BAT defence*

BAT INDUSTRIES

Building Shareholder Value

An outstanding 1989

- Forecast pre-tax profits of approximately £2 billion
  – up 22 per cent
- Forecast earnings per share of approximately 76.5 p
  – up 22 per cent
- Proposed further dividends of 20.7 p
  Total for the year of 30 pence – up 49 per cent

An outstanding future

- A group focused on financial services and tobacco with forecast 1989 pre-tax profits of approximately £1.64 billion
  – equal to the entire group in 1988
- A direct stake in:
  – Argos, one of the UK retailing success stories of the decade, with forecast 1989 trading profits of approximately £63 million
  – Wiggins Teape and Appleton, a combined international force in specialist paper and pulp, with forecast 1989 trading profits of approximately £212 million
- A higher dividend payout ratio starting in 1989
- Proposals to authorise the buy-back of up to 10 per cent of the company's shares
- The orderly divestment of US retailing and certain other businesses

It undertook to divest various assets including VG Instruments, retail stores in the USA, France and West Germany, to give away shares in Argos and Wiggins Teape–Appleton and also to pay higher dividends in the future. The defence document declared:

> The 1989 dividend payout will be significantly increased through the proposed second interim dividend of 10.3p and the proposed final dividend of 10.4p. As a result, dividend cover will be reduced from 3.1 times in 1988 to around 2.6 times in 1989. The strong cash flow and the quality of earnings of the continuing group should enable us to increase the level of payout further, reducing cover to 2.0–2.5 times in future years.

Clearly, this was a major shift in dividend policy reflecting a great belief (or hope) in the power of dividend payouts to increase share price and secure shareholder loyalty.

Attitudes of the Regulatory Authorities

A further complication in the BAT episode was the interaction between UK takeover regulations and the complexity introduced by BAT's ownership of the Farmers insurance company, acquired only in 1988, as part of its strategy of diversification into financial services. Under UK regulations, a bid must be completed within 60 days (unless another bidder emerges). American insurance industry regulations require investigation by, and the approval of, state insurance commissioners before an insurance company can change hands. The required procedures are extremely tortuous, as BAT had itself found when it acquired Farmers, having to fight off objections in state after state in which Farmers operated. Because of the expected length of the forthcoming proceedings, the UK Takeover Panel granted BAT an extension of the bid until the US authorities had pronounced. In effect, the UK takeover rules were being bent to accommodate the requirements of an extra-territorial authority.

Meanwhile, the Secretary of State for Trade and Industry, Sir Nicholas Ridley, had decided not to refer the bid to the Monopolies and Mergers Commission for investigation, as it appeared to raise no issues relating to competition, the major criterion by which the merits of takeovers and mergers were appraised at this time. Many observers felt that there were, however, broader public interest issues involved in the bid relating to the proposed method of financing.

During the US hearings, it transpired that Hoylake had lined up a buyer for Farmers, should the bid succeed, namely, French insurance company,

Axa–Midi (which had also undertaken to pay the bulk of the US legal fees, amounting to over £60 million). As a result, the US regulators were now deliberating the merits of not one but two changes of ownership.

In the event, despite the accommodating stance of the UK authorities, the bid foundered before the insurance commissioner for California, Roxani Gillespie, who apparently was concerned by Axa–Midi's proposed method of financing. The French firm intended to borrow some $4.5 billion to finance the Farmers purchase. This was regarded as likely to leave Axa–Midi with an excessively high gearing level, especially at a time when the whole US financial system was already reeling from the failure of the savings and loans associations (the US equivalent of building societies).

The bid was also killed by the collapse in junk bond financing in the USA due to rising interest rates and a series of scandals involving market manipulation by certain junk bond dealers. Interest rate increases sqeezed junk bond issuers in two ways. Firstly, the return they had to pay increased substantially as many such bonds were linked to underlying interest rates. Secondly, the higher interest rates made it harder to sell assets quickly for the handsome prices required to redeem the debt obligations.

The Impact of the Bid

Meanwhile, by 1990, BAT's profitability had improved rapidly (as predicted in the defence document) and it was clear that any new bid would have to be considerably higher, and made in cash form. The major impact of the whole saga was the realisation of significant benefits for BAT shareholders. While the US authorities were deliberating, BAT proceeded to sell off many of its now apparently superfluous activities in an effort to focus itself into a two-core business: tobacco and financial services. Not too surprisingly, BAT chairman Patrick Sheehy declared that it was BAT's strategy to do this anyway, decided far in advance of the Hoylake bid.

Whether due to panic response or the product of mature consideration, BAT was widely thought to have realised very fair values for most of its disposals (shown in Exhibit 6.6), while the proceeds for the US retail operations, Saks Fifth Avenue and Marshall Field were considerably higher than many expected. Indeed, Sir James was moved to admit that the disposal proceeds were around the top end of Hoylake's own valuations. As well as the disposals, shareholders were given free shares in the discount retail chain Argos, which realised a flotation value of around £600 million, and in the paper concern, Wiggins Teape–Appleton, which floated at £1.05 billion. Analysts reckoned that the BAT financial services interests were worth over

£7 billion, while the tobacco business was valued at about £5 billion. The overall value of disposals and the market values of flotations plus the estimated value of the remaining core significantly exceeded both the offer of £13.4 billion and the pre-bid market value of £8.5 billion.

Exhibit 6.7 summarises the progress of the bid.

Exhibit 6.6 *BAT's main divestments*

Disposals:	VG Instruments	£186m
	Breuners Retail	$92.5m
	Breuners Rental	$15m
	Marshall Fields	$1.1bn
	Saks Fifth Avenue	$1.5bn
	Ivey's	$110m
	Eurotec	£155m
	Horten AG	£140m
Flotations:	Argos	£600m
	Wiggins Teape	£1.05bn

Exhibit 6.7 *Bid timetable*

1989

11 July	Launch of £13.4 billion bid by Hoylake.
31 July	Californian regulators insist on scrutinising the effect of the bid on the Farmers insurance subsidiary.
8 August	The Hoylake offer document accuses BAT of failing in its past business strategy.
23 August	Hoylake agrees sale of Farmers for £3 billion to Axa–Midi if US authorities agree change of ownership.
15 September	Hoylake wins extension of bid timetable.
21 September	Hoylake bid cleared by Monopolies and Mergers Commission.
23 September	BAT announces break-up plans.

1990

13 February	California hearings begin.
15 March	Details of Argos demerger announced: one free Argos share for every five BAT shares held.
21 March	BAT reports 24% profits increase and dividend increase of 49%.
6 April	Argos chain of discount stores floated.
10 April	California rules against Hoylake bid.
19 April	Marshall Fields sold for $1.1 bn.
23 April	Hoylake abandons bid.
25 April	Sale of Saks Fifth Avenue to Investcorp announced.
10 May	Details of Wiggins Teape demerger announced: one free Wiggins Teape share for every three BAT shares held.
31 May	Disposal of Eurotec announced to Klockner Werke AG.
3 December	Sale of Horten AG announced for £140m to Westdeutsche Landesbank.

Crédit Lyonnais

A case on the strategy of a European universal bank. Although it had grown to be a large and successful international bank, Crédit Lyonnais's strategy took a new turn with the appointment of Jean-Yves Haberer in 1988 as chief executive. He set about transforming the 'staid, state-controlled French bank into a high-performance pan-European, universal banking institution'. Although by 1992 Haberer had already developed the beginnings of a pan-European bank, he conceived of the notion that Crédit Lyonnais would be a 'Euro-champion', nurtured by the French government to prevail in commercial warfare on the global battlefield in financial services. To reach this objective, Haberer planned for Crédit Lyonnais to grow very large, be very European, tightly control its corporate banking customers and to enjoy a 'special relationship' with the French government.

On the last working day of 1992 Jean-Yves Haberer, chairman of Crédit Lyonnais (CL), reaffirmed his aim to transform CL from a staid, state-controlled French bank into a high-performance, pan-European, universal banking institution – a consummate player in both commercial and investment banking and a veritable cornerstone of European finance – by the turn of the century. This time he could point to an important milestone on the road to his goal, a DM 1.9 billion controlling interest in the Bank für Gemeinwirtschaft, giving CL a major stake in Europe's largest and toughest financial services market: Germany. And this on the eve of implementation of the EC's '1992' Single Market initiative on January 1, 1993.

According to Haberer, the banks likely to be future leaders in Europe were Deutsche Bank of Germany, Barclays Bank of Great Britain, Istituto Bancaria San Paolo di Torino of Italy, and Crédit Lyonnais of France, i.e. the leading banks located in the leading European countries. Few others, he

Teaching case written by Professors Roy C. Smith and Ingo Walter, with the assistance of Serge Platonow. For classroom purposes only. Acknowledgement is gratefully made to Salomon Center Case Series, Svern School of Business, New York University, and INSEAD, Fontainebleau, France. Case reprinted with kind permission of Professor Walter. © Roy C. Smith and Ingo Walter, 1993.

Exhibit 7.1 *Europe's biggest banks at the end of 1991*

	Country	Total assets ($ bn)	Equity capital ($ bn)	Capital-to-assets ratio
Crédit Agricole	France	307.2	14.7	4.77
Crédit Lyonnais	France	306.3	10.5	3.41
Deutsche Bank	Germany	296.2	11.3	3.80
BNP	France	275.9	10.2	3.71
Barclays Bank	UK	258.3	11.6	4.50
ABN–AMRO Bank	Netherlands	242.7	9.3	3.85
National Westminster Bank	UK	229.3	10.5	4.56
Société Générale	France	223.8	7.1	3.16
Paribas	France	200.0	10.5	5.23
Dresdner Bank	Germany	194.5	6.5	3.33

Source: International Management, October 1992.

believed, had much of a chance. Only the leaders would have the capital strength, the domestic market share, and the intra-European networks to intimidate rivals and repel competitive threats from all sources, European or otherwise.

Haberer had chosen the grandest strategy of all. It was a strategy that would have enormous appeal to CL's sole stockholder, the French government, in its proclaimed vision that a few Euro-champions needed to be nurtured in each important industry through an aggressive 'industrial policy' of protection, subsidization, ministerial guidance, and selective capital infusions. Each Euro-champion – as many as possible French – must be capable of prevailing in commercial warfare on the global battlefield against all-comers. In financial services, according to Haberer, Crédit Lyonnais would be France's chosen instrument.

Four daring ideas outlined Haberer's plan for achieving his objective:

1. Crédit Lyonnais had to grow to be large, *very* large. The objective was to capture between 1% and 2% of all bank deposits in the 12 European Community countries. This meant capturing significant market share in multiple areas of banking and securities activities at once. Given the competitive dynamics of the financial services sector, speed was of the essence. Acquisitions of existing businesses would be made in various countries on several fronts simultaneously.
2. Crédit Lyonnais had to become very European. That meant going up against entrenched domestic competition in most of the national

EC markets simultaneously, either via aggressive expansion, strategic alliances and networks or local acquisitions. The strategy was clear, but no one tactic would suffice. Opportunism and flexibility were key.

3. Crédit Lyonnais had to exert significant control over its corporate banking customers, using deep lending and investment banking relationships with major non-financial firms and important ownership stakes in many of these same firms. Only in this way, he felt, could CL exert sufficient influence over their financial and business affairs to direct large and profitable business his way. Haberer called this *banque industrie*, a French version of the classic German *Hausbank* relationship.

4. Crédit Lyonnais had to retain the confidence of the French government. It owned the bank. It would have to inject a great deal of capital. It would have to clear the way for CL's acquisitions and ownership stakes. In would have to look beyond the inevitable 'accidents' that would occur on the road to greater glory. Crédit Lyonnais would have to become an indispensable instrument of French and European industrial policy. And this 'special relationship' would have to survive political changes in France, even changes leading to CL's own privatization.

Exhibit 7.2 *Europe's most international banks*

	Country	Assets located abroad (%)	Total assets ($ bn)
Standard Chartered Bank	UK	63.7	43
Union Bank	Switzerland	57.5	181
Swiss Bank Corporation	Switzerland	53.1	149
Crédit Suisse	Switzerland	52.4	116
Paribas	France	45.9	184
Banque Indosuez	France	45.0	68
National Westminster Bank	UK	44.3	233
BNP	France	43.8	290
Banca Commerciale	Italy	38.7	93
Crédit Lyonnais	France	36.5	285

Source: International Management, October 1992.

Exhibit 7.3 *Crédit Lyonnais's European network*

		Date of acquisition	Number of offices	Net profit FY 1991
Belgium	CL Begium	1989	34	209
Germany	CL Germany	–		
	BfG	1992	193	4[1]
Italy	Credito Bergamasco	1989	144	414
Netherlands	CL Bank Nederland	1980	100	84
Spain	CL Spain	1990		
	Banco Jover	1991	251	502
UK	CL United Kingdom	–	62	-591

1. Not including BfG.
Source: Euromoney, March 1993.

Crédit Lyonnais and *le dirigisme français*

Crédit Lyonnais first opened for business in Lyon in 1863 as a *banque de dépôts*.[1] The bank began its international operations in London during the Franco-Prussian war, and expanded throughout France and in many of the major foreign business centers in the 1870s. By 1900, it was the largest French bank in terms of assets.

With the First World War, many large-bank personnel were conscripted, and competition in French banking increased. Smaller banks took advantage of the larger banks' staffing difficulties and expanded rapidly. Beginning in 1917, *crédits populaires*, a new form of banking establishment, were allowed to be established and added to the domestic competition in France. With the 1918 Russian Revolution, sizeable deposits were withdrawn as their owners demanded that Crédit Lyonnais restitute assets confiscated by the Bolsheviks. Although profitable, CL was not making nearly the profits during the 1920s that it had enjoyed before the First World War.

During the Great Depression CL adopted a cautious approach, closing about 100 offices in France and abroad. With the onset of the Second World War, Crédit Lyonnais remained in essence apolitical, continuing the majority of its banking activities – although some foreign offices were not under the control of the main office during the German occupation. With the restoration of peace in 1945, a number of events were of central importance in determining CL's future course:

1. 1945: The French government nationalized the *banques de dépôts* – Crédit Lyonnais, Société Générale, Comptoir National d'Escomptes de Paris (CNEP) and Banque Nationale de Commerce et d'Industrie (BNCI).

2. 1966: The Ministry of Finance merged the two smaller banks, CNEP and BNCI, into BNP (Banque Nationale de Paris).

3. 1970: The president of CL, François Bloch-Lainé, adopted a strategy of partnerships with other banks in the form of Union des Banques Arabes et Françaises (UBAF), and Europartners.

4. 1973: A law was passed that allowed the distribution of shares to the employees of nationalized banks and insurance companies such as Crédit Lyonnais.

5. 1974: Election of the Gaullists led by Valéry Giscard d'Estaing, and appointment of Jacques Chaine to replace François Bloch-Lainé as chief executive of CL.

6. 1981: Election victory of the Socialists and under President François Mitterand. Appointment of Jean Deflassieux, financial advisor to the Socialist Party, to replace Jacques Chaine at CL.

7. 1982: Nationalization by the Socialists of all major French banks not already owned by the government. The government's declared objective was to influence the functioning of the banks in a direction more favorable to small and medium-sized businesses, as well as to help define and implement a new and more interventionist industrial and monetary policy. For Crédit Lyonnais, the only immediate implication was the renationalization of the shares the bank had sold to employees in 1973.

8. 1986: The Gaullists regained power in the French Legislative Assembly, with the appointment of Jacques Chirac as Prime Minister. This ushered in a period of 'cohabitation' with a Socialist president, François Mitterand. Jean Deflassieux was replaced as CL chief executive by an ardent privatization advocate, Jean-Maxime Lévêque. A privatization law authorized the public sale of 65 large industrial companies, although Crédit Lyonnais was not targeted for the first round of privatization. Groupe Financière de Paribas and the Société Générale were both successfully privatized.

9. 1988: The Socialists regained power. Privatizations were immediately suspended, and Jean-Yves Haberer replaced Jean-Maxime Lévêque as president of Crédit Lyonnais.

10. 1992: The Socialists were locked in an election battle with a Conservative and neo-Gaullist coalition led by Edouard Balladur and Valéry Giscard d'Estaing. This could lead to another period of

cohabitation, since election prospects looked bleak for the Socialists and the French presidential elections were not due until 1995. A plank in the Conservative party platform promised a resumption of privatizations to include a broad array of state-owned enterprises. Names such as Thomson, Bull, Péchiney, Rhône-Poulenc, Elf-Aquitaine, Aerospatiale, Air France, Cie. Générale Maritime, SNECMA, Usinor–Sacilor, GAN, UAP, Banque Nationale de Paris and Crédit Lyonnais were all thought to be on the list.

The successive changes of chief executives at Crédit Lyonnais with incoming governments illustrated the persistent intervention of the state in the running of companies, commonly known in France as *dirigisme*. From relative independence after nationalization in 1945, when most of the original CL board remained intact, the government had been playing an increasingly important role in defining the bank's strategic direction and the structure of its leadership. In effect, the government used the nationalized banks as an important industrial policy tool.

Regardless of the political ebb and flow, the French financial system – traditionally highly concentrated and compartmentalized – underwent substantial structural change and consistent deregulation in the 1970s and 1980s, and this opened up and developed the domestic capital market. In part, it reflected government efforts to promote Paris as a viable financial-center competitor to London, and in part it was the product of changing

Exhibit 7.4 *Crédit Lyonnais's key financial year-end figures (FFr billions)*

	1987	1988	1989	1990	1991	1992
Equity capital + equivalent	24.6	33.8	39.0	61.6	67.9	85
Total assets	899	1084	1221	1463	1587	1938
Asset growth (%)	–	20.6	12.6	19.8	8.5	22
Total banking income	27.30	30.17	35.24	40.83	46.33	49
Operating income before provisions	8.73	8.23	10.15	11.66	13.31	13.2
Provisions	5.33	6.36	6.29	6.49	9.60	14.7
Consolidated net profit	2.36	2.16	3.49	4.56	4.08	
Group share in net profit	2.23	2.063	3.13	3.707	3.162	-1.8
ROE[1] (%)	9.07	6.10	8.03	6.02	4.66	-2.1

1. ROE is group share of net profit/year-end equity and equivalent.
Source: Euromoney, March 1993; *Les Echos*, March 30, 1993.

Exhibit 7.5 *Crédit Lyonnais's principal bad debts*

Borrower	CL exposure
MGM	$1.2 billion
Maxwell	FFr 2.2 billion
Olympia and York	$350 million
Former USSR	$747 million
La Cinq	FFr 500 million
VEV	FFr 500 million–FFr 1 billion
SASEA	>SFr 570 million

Source: Euromoney, March 1993; *The Economist*, March 27, 1993.

political fashion. The financial market reforms undertaken with special vigor by the Chirac administration helped shift French corporate finance toward open capital markets and away from bank lending.

The major French banks and industrial enterprises remained tied together by strong informal relationships, a cohesion that had its roots in the *grandes écoles*, attended both by the vast majority of the leading government officials and by the senior managers of state-owned and private companies and banks. Some of the best became *Inspecteurs des Finances*, a special appointment for the brightest graduates of the élite Ecole Nationale d'Administration (ENA). This virtually ensured an individual instant prestige, lifelong admiration and responsible employment in the French government or in government-controlled entities.

Jean-Yves Haberer was a paragon of this system. He graduated first in his class at the ENA and joined the French treasury as an Inspecteur Général des Finances. He rose quickly, becoming head of the treasury while still in his forties. In 1982 he was pulled from the treasury by François Mitterand to run the newly nationalized Paribas (Compagnie Financière de Paris et des Pay-Bas). Haberer was widely resented within Paribas, and was seen as the instrument of its nationalization. During his leadership, Paribas suffered its worst fiasco, with the acquisition of the stockbroker A.G. Becker in New York, which it sold a few years later at a $70 million loss. When Paribas was reprivatized in 1986, Haberer was removed from office but subsequently appointed chief executive of Crédit Lyonnais.

Widely described as authoritarian, brilliant, intimidating and virtually friendless, Haberer was a superb politician and a good friend of the Socialists, having long-standing ties with Pierre Bérégovoy (minister of finance and later prime minister) and Jacques Delors (long president of the EC Commission). He consistently maneuvered himself into very useful positions as the Socialists' favorite banker.

Although Haberer's personal political views were said to be close to those of former right-of-center prime minister Raymond Barre, it was thought highly likely that he would be replaced in the event of a Conservative victory in the French elections of March 1993. He was still roundly disliked by the Right for serving as a 'tool' of the Left at Paribas in 1982.

Nor did Haberer's eagerness to get CL moving make many friends in the French banking world. He was perceived as a gambler, with a penchant to adopt 'go for broke' tactics. He was repeatedly criticized for grand schemes that might never have survived board scrutiny or shareholder reactions in privately-owned financial institutions.

Exhibit 7.6 *Contribution to group profits of international CL commercial banking activities (FFr millions)*

	Operating income before provision[2]		Net income[3]	
	1991	1992	1991	1992
Italy	1068	1226	414	356
Portugal	121	89	58	3
Spain	816	640	475	211
Netherlands	748	688	84	93
Sweden	6	2	1	-32
Belgium	371	278	209	159
Luxemburg	188	180	36	76
Switzerland	183	157	74	40
Great Britain	194	194	-593	-446
Woodchester	486	460	300	131
USA	779	939	1162	719
Canada	97	73	50	-129
Japan	108	45	29	55
Taiwan	86	69	45	57

1. 1992 contribution of the international activities of the commercial bank to group profits.
2. Gross operating profits.
3. Net profit.
Source: Les Echos, March 30, 1993.

The Launching Pad

By the early 1990s, Crédit Lyonnais had become a highly diversified bank that offered a complete spectrum of financial services to most client segments across much of Europe. Elsewhere, CL had holdings in Asia and in North America under its own name. In South America and Africa it generally operated under the name of either partially or wholly-owned subsidiaries.

In its drive to be a functionally 'universal' bank Credit Lyonnais offered a very broad spectrum of financial services. At the end of 1992, CL had 2,639 retail banking outlets in France, as well as an array of specialized affiliates such as the Paris stockbroker Cholet–Dupont Michaux, money-management affiliates, and niche-type businesses such as leasing. It also offered a range of insurance services (notably life insurance) and maintained a large portfolio of holdings in different French and European companies.

Operationally, Crédit Lyonnais was structured into six units:

1. The *banque des entreprises* (business bank) catered to the financial requirements of a broad spectrum of business and industry. The core function was commercial lending. For small and medium-sized businesses, Crédit Lyonnais also offered risk management products, including financial and foreign exchange options and other derivatives, asset management services covering a broad range of investments, and international development assistance such as helping to initiate cross-border partnerships and alliances. For large companies, Crédit Lyonnais services extended from fund-raising through syndicated lending, Euro-note and Euro-commercial paper distribution to large and complex financing arrangements such as project and acquisitions financing, merger and acquisitions advisory activities, and real estate financing. It also maintained leasing subsidiaries – Slibail, Slificom, Slifergie in France, Woodchester in Ireland and the UK, and Leasimpresa in Italy.

2. The banque des particuliers et des professionels (retail bank) serviced private individuals and professional clients, and carried out basic banking services such as deposits, payments services and personal loans. There had been a significant decline in demand deposit account balances in favor of interest-bearing accounts in the domestic market. Traditionally, French retail clients maintained non-interest-bearing checking accounts, but with intensified competition and changes in legislation, clients were increasingly opting for *SICAVs* – open-ended unit trusts – and especially *SICAVs monétaires*, or money market mutual funds. To attract and maintain

retail clients, CL was forced to innovate and enhance retail banking services. Debit cards, ATMs and home banking through Minitel (the French interactive telephone information system) were introduced. In addition to life insurance, Crédit Lyonnais provided personal lines (e.g. automobile) coverage through its Lion Assurances subsidiary. And for large individual and professional clients it also provided private banking services and tailored insurance plans as well as special financing arrangements – such as Inter-Fimo and Crédit Médical de France, which financed the purchase and installation of medical equipment.

3. The *banque des marchés capitaux* (investment bank) was responsible for underwriting and distributing bonds and equity new issues. In global markets, Crédit Lyonnais Capital Markets International's units – such as Crédit Lyonnais Securities in London – assured the bank's presence in foreign financial centers, while the French markets were covered by affiliates such as Cholet–Dupont. In 1991, CL was ranked first in placing domestic and Eurofranc bonds. In the derivatives sector, it accounted for about 10% of the volume on the MATIF, France's futures and options exchange. It had comparatively low standing, however, in the overall Eurobond and international securities markets.

4. A finance company, *Altus Finance*, was the former finance subsidiary of Thomson, in which CL acquired a 66% interest in 1991. During that year Altus bought a large portfolio of high yield (junk) bonds from the failed American insurance company Executive Life – a position amounting to one-third of CL's tier one capital.

5. The *gestionnaire pour compte de tiers* (fund management group) was responsible for the management of private portfolios as well as SICAVs in which private individuals held shares. CL had enhanced its offerings to include those guaranteeing capital (CAC-40 Sécurité), yield (Performance Olympique), and global diversification (Crédit Lyonnais Growth Fund).

6. As *actionnaire des entreprises*, Crédit Lyonnais had been increasing its shareholdings in other companies to further the concept of a universal bank. The notion was that, by holding substantial shares, especially in non-financial companies, CL would be able to develop a much better understanding of those companies' financial needs and influence their financing decisions. Its holding structures included:

- Clinvest, CL's *banque d'affaires*, with a diversified holding of French companies, which had been a highly profitable part of the bank;[2]
- Euro-Clinvest, a Clinvest subsidiary, with a portfolio of shares of companies in eight European countries;
- Clindus, established in 1991, had strategic and statutory holdings, principally in Rhône-Poulenc and Usinor–Sacilor, that were added to CL's balance sheet with the 'assistance' of the government;
- Innolion, a high-tech, start-up venture capital fund operating in France;
- Compagnie Financière d'Investissement Rhône-Alpes, which invested in the Rhône-Alpes region of France;
- Lion Expansion, a development capital fund for small and medium businesses and industries.

Haberer considered CL's existing structure to be an ideal basis upon which to build his *banque industrie* concept of a pan-European universal financial institution, with enough capacity to launch a simultaneous multipronged attack on an array of national markets, financial services and client segments – and to do so rapidly.

The Pan-European Building Blocks

By late 1992 Haberer had already developed the beginnings of a pan-European bank in the retail sector via an extensive cross-border branch network. This was needed to meet his target of capturing between 1% and 2% of total retail deposits in Europe, which in turn was intended to provide the 'bulk' that CL required and the basis for all of the other growth initiatives. He had in fact moved systematically in this direction since 1988.

Several acquisitions and purchases of strategic stakes in other banks had been undertaken in quick succession as CL bought local medium-sized financial institutions in Belgium, Spain, Italy and Germany. Consequently, between 1987 and 1992 the number of branches in Europe had increased threefold, and in 1991, 47% of the bank's profits came from outside France (compared with 30% in 1987).

- In Belgium, CL had rapidly expanded its local presence via aggressive branching. It tripled the number of retail and private banking clients in 18 months with a new higher-yield account called *Rendement Plus*. It offered 9% on savings deposits, compared with 3–4% offered by local banks. These rates were possible mainly because Crédit Lyonnais did not have the cumbersome and expensive infrastructure of the Belgian banks. It had only 96 employees for 32 branches in that country, three per branch; the three big Belgian banks each had at least 10 employees per branch in over 1,000 branches.

- In the Netherlands, Crédit Lyonnais had raised from 78% to 100% its stake in the Slavenburgs Bank (renamed Crédit Lyonnais Bank Nederland NV) and in 1987 had acquired Nederlandse Crediet-bank, a former subsidiary of the Chase Manhattan Bank of the USA.
- In Ireland, CL held a 48% stake in Woodchester (renamed Woodchester Crédit Lyonnais Bank), a leasing and financing company which intended to acquire a total of 40–50 retail banking outlets.
- CL had reinforced its position in the London market by buying the firm of Alexanders Laing & Cruickshank after Big Bang in 1986, subsequently renamed Crédit Lyonnais Capital Markets in 1989.
- In Spain, CL's branches had been merged with Banco Commercial Español (renamed Crédit Lyonnais España, SA), complemented by the acquisition of medium-sized Banco Jover in 1991.
- In Germany, CL in 1992 completed a deal to purchase 50.1% of the Bank für Gemeinwirtschaft (BfG) thereby ending a five-year search for a viable presence in the most important European market outside of France.

The acquisition of Bank für Gemeinwirtschaft was a key achievement, in Haberer's view. Not only was Germany the largest European banking

Exhibit 7.7   *Profits of Clinvest and Altus (FFr millions)*

	1990	1991	1992
Altus Finance	802	1,101	1,882
Clinvest	460	477	746

Source: Les Echos, March 18 and March 26, 1993; CL Annual Reports.

Exhibit 7.8 *French banks' forecasts and market statistics (local currency and local GAAP)*

16/7/93	BNP (CI)	Compagnie Bancaire	CCF	Crédit Local	Crédit Lyon (CI)	Société Générale	French Index[2]	Bank Sector[3]
Share price	533	520	224	416	687	584	160	
Issued shares	70.7	24.9	59.6	35.8	42.0	74.9		
Market value	37,683	12,952	13,322	14,872	28,862	43,725		151,415
In US$ @ 5.89	6,393	2,197	2,260	2,523	4,897	7,419		25,690
Net income								
1990	1,616	984	813	949	3,707	2,678		10,746
1991	2,936	600	917	1,075	3,162	3,369		12,059
1992	2,168	61	978	1,198	-1,848	3,268		5,820
1993E	1,073	-175	1,023	1,276	-2,931	3,374		3,639
1994E	3,684	490	1,222	1,342	-479	4,006		10,266
1995E	5,774	1,165	1,394	1,408	2,374	5,011		17,126
1996E	7,298	1,539	1,573	1,477	3,487	5,884		21,257
EPS								
1990	24.9	42.6	16.5	27.2	110.6	43.2	11.3	
1991	41.5	25.5	17.1	30.3	90.1	50.6	11.1	
1992	30.7	2.5	17.2	33.4	-49.1	45.9	10.0	
1993E	15.0	-7.1	17.3	35.7	-70.1	45.9	9.5	
1994E	48.0	19.3	20.4	37.6	-11.4	52.6	11.1	
1995E	75.2	44.8	23.1	39.4	56.5	63.6	12.1	
1996E	95.1	57.7	25.8	41.3	83.0	72.3	13.6	
DPS net								
1990	5.2	9.1	3.5	5.9	34.5	15.0	3.6	
1991	10.5	10.0	3.8	8.0	34.5	15.0	3.8	
1992	7.5	10.0	4.0	9.4	15.0	15.0	4.1	
1993E	7.5	10.0	4.2	10.7	0.0	15.0	4.2	
1994E	14.4	10.0	4.8	11.3	0.0	17.0	4.3	
1995E	22.6	11.0	5.6	11.8	19.1	19.0	4.7	
1996E	28.5	11.0	6.4	12.4	28.0	21.0	5.1	
PER								
1990	21.4	12.2	13.6	15.3	6.2	13.5	14.2	13.6
1991	12.8	20.4	13.0	13.7	7.6	11.5	14.5	13.2
1992	17.4	205.8	13.0	12.5	-14.0	12.7	16.1	12.7
1993E	35.6	-73.4	13.0	11.7	-9.8	12.7	16.9	12.6
1994E	11.1	26.9	11.0	11.1	-60.3	11.1	14.5	11.1
1995E	7.1	11.6	9.7	10.6	12.2	9.2	13.3	9.8
1996E	5.6	9.0	8.7	10.1	8.3	8.1	11.8	8.6

Exhibit 7.8 *continued*

16/7/93	BNP (CI)	Compagnie Bancaire	CCF	Crédit Local	Crédit Lyon (CI)	Société Générale	French Index[2]	Bank Sector[3]
Rel PER								
1990	150	86	95	107	44	95		96
1991	89	141	90	95	53	80		91
1992	108	1276	81	77	-87	79		79
1993E	211	-435	77	69	-58	75		75
1994E	77	186	76	77	-417	77		77
1995E	53	88	73	80	92	69		74
1996E	47	76	73	85	70	68		73
Gross yield								
1990	1.5	2.6	2.3	2.1	7.5	3.9	3.3	3.2
1991	3.0	2.9	2.5	2.9	7.5	3.9	3.5	3.4
1992	2.1	2.9	2.7	3.4	3.3	3.9	3.8	3.5
1993E	2.1	2.9	2.8	3.9	0.0	3.9	3.9	3.6
1994E	4.1	2.9	3.2	4.1	0.0	4.4	4.0	4.0
1995E	6.4	3.2	3.7	4.3	4.2	4.9	4.4	4.4
1996E	8.0	3.2	4.3	4.5	6.1	5.4	4.8	4.8
Relative yield								
1990	44	79	70	64	226	116		96
1991	83	81	72	81	212	109		95
1992	56	76	71	90	86	102		92
1993E	54	74	72	99	0	99		91
1994E	101	72	80	101	0	108		98
1995E	144	72	85	97	95	111		100
1996E	167	66	89	93	127	112		101
Book value per share								
1992	618	482	157	335	1,108	510		

1. All financial years end 31/12. Cie Bancaire net income and EPS on operating basis. Crédit Local EPS full diluted.
2. Industrial index.
3. Sector multiple is for followed companies and excludes BNP and Crédit Lyonnais, and also Cie Bancaire in 1992, 1993 and 1994. CIs - Non voting *Certificat d'investissements*.
Source: Goldman Sachs.

market, but it was also the most difficult to penetrate. Others had tried and many had failed. Those who succeeded had done so by building or buying niche-type businesses, often with indifferent results. None were taken especially seriously as major contenders alongside the three *Grossbanken*, the large regional and state-affiliated banks, and the cooperative and savings bank networks. With the acquisition of Bank für Gemeinwirtschaft, Crédit Lyonnais promised to break the mold.

In 1990, the second-largest German insurance group AMB (Aachener und Münchener Beteiligungs GmbH), had negotiated with the state-owned French insurer AGF (Assurances Générales de France) about a partnership arrangement. Besides the attractiveness of the German market, AGF was watching strategic moves by its arch-rival, the state-owned insurer UAP, whose expansion into Germany had come by way of the acquisition from Banque Indosuez of a 34% stake in Groupe Victoire, a major French insurer which had earlier purchased a German insurer, Colonia Versicherungs AG.

AGF had bought 25% of AMB stock, yet was limited to only 9% of the voting rights by the AMB board, using a special class of 'vinculated' shares. It was clearly concerned that the French company, twice its size, was out to control and eventually swallow it. Alongside the AGF acquisition of AMB stock, Crédit Lyonnais had bought a 1.8% stake in AMB as well. As part of its defensive tactics, AMB arranged for an Italian insurer, La Fondaria, to acquire a 'friendly' stake amounting to 20% of AMB shares. AGF then fought an historic shareholder rights battle in the German courts against the AMB board and a German industrial 'establishment' instinctively distrustful of hostile changes in corporate control. The defense was further bolstered by the fact that 11% of AMB stock was held by Dresdner Bank, and 6% by Munich Re. Allianz, the largest German insurer, was a major shareholder in both Dresdner Bank and Munich Re. It was a sign of the times, Haberer thought, that AGF had prevailed in the German courts and, with the help of CL's AMB shares was able to obtain AGF recognition of its voting rights – no doubt the basis for future AGF share acquisitions, possibly the La Fondaria stake.

The AGF–AMB battle provided Haberer with the opening he was looking for – appearing on his radar screen when AGF proposed that Crédit Lyonnais buy AMB's bank, the Bank für Gemeinwirtshaft, which AMB was keen to dispose of and which had been for sale for some time. BfG had been the bank of the German labor movement, plagued by poor management, periodic large losses and scandals, and a down-market client base. Nevertheless, BfG had some 200 well-situated branches throughout the country and seemed to present a one-off chance to buy a major German bank. AMB had already made great strides in turning BfG around, but a loss of DM 400 million in 1990 and a meager profit of only DM 120 million in 1991 indicated that a major capital infusion would be required in 1993. AMB was hardly interested in supplying it, and a takeover by Crédit Lyonnais was seen as a welcome opportunity to divest itself of an albatross. CL valued BfG at DM 1.8 billion; AMB valued it at DM 2.7 billion. AMB suggested that the deal could be paid for in part with the 1.8% of AGF stock held by the Crédit Lyonnais. In November 1992, Crédit Lyonnais agreed to buy 50.1% of BfG for DM 1.9 billion, effective at year-end.

Of course, acquisition battles like BfG were only the first, and perhaps the easiest, part of the building process. Certainly not all of CL's acquisitions had been easy to digest. Its purchase of the Slavenburgs Bank in the Netherlands, for example, had been the source of many headaches. Beyond a troublesome corporate culture issue, there had been a serious problem in maintaining supervision. It was Slavenburgs Bank (CL Nederland) that was responsible for large loans to Giancarlo Parretti for the purchase of MGM shares in the US (see below) – loans which CL's head office in Paris indicated it was not aware of until it was too late.

Besides outright acquisitions and aggressive expansion in the important European markets, CL employed another strategy as well – strategic alliances and networks. One of the oldest of these, Europartners, was set up as a loose association between Crédit Lyonnais, Commerzbank, Banco di Roma and Banco Hispano Americano (BHA), based on the idea of extending banking networks into neighboring countries and setting up new joint operations. Its goals were to provide a cheap mechanism to allow each of the partners' customers convenient access to basic banking services in the other countries.

But it was not long before strains began to appear in the Europartners. Over the years, Commerzbank had tightened its relations with its Spanish partner, and in 1989 BHA agreed to swap an 11% interest in its shares for a 5% stake in Commerzbank – the 1991 merger of BHA and Banco Central into Banco Central-Hispaño diluted Commerzbank's share in the merged bank to 4.5%. At the same time, there was a dispute over CL's expansion into Spain with the purchase of Banca Jover in the summer of 1991. A year earlier, Crédit Lyonnais had tried to purchase a 20% stake in Banco Hispaño Americano and was flatly rejected. BHA perceived the new action as a threat of direct competition in its home market, and suspended the relationship with Crédit Lyonnais.

Rebuffed in Spain, CL had also been thwarted in its attempt to deepen the Franco-German part of the Europartners agreement. In 1991, Crédit Lyonnais discussed swapping shares with Commerzbank, the smallest of the three German *Grossbanken* – thought to have involved 10% of

Exhibit 7.9 *International bank scoreboard*

		Assets		Capital		Performance				Market value		
		($ m)	Change from 1991 (%)	Equity ($ m)	Total capital ratio	Net income ($ m)	Change from 1991 (%)	Return on equity (%)	Real profit-ability	5/31/93 ($ m)	Market-to-book ratio	P/E ratio
1 Dai-ichi Kangyo Bank	Japan	456,484	-10.5	17,744	9.37	465	-40.9	2.63	1.010	57,672	3.1	132.9
2 Fuji Bank	Japan	454,745	-5.2	17,187	9.27	523	-36.0	3.08	1.014	60,813	3.3	111.8
3 Sumitomo Bank	Japan	448,933	-8.2	19,525	9.37	199	-80.9	1.01	0.994	65,970	3.1	335.3
4 Sanwa Bank	Japan	445,918	-5.4	17,149	9.43	818	-11.0	4.86	1.030	61,189	3.4	68.9
5 Sakura Bank	Japan	437,952	-9.0	15,608	8.96	557	-20.0	3.60	1.018	49,493	3.1	91.8
6 Mitsubishi Bank	Japan	424,348	-7.4	15,391	9.12	540	1.1	3.54	1.018	73,564	4.5	101.4
7 Norinchukin Bank	Japan	368,544	4.9	2,578	NA	370	6.2	15.55	1.029	NT		NM
8 Crédit Lyonnais	France	352,013	22.1	11,259	8.20	-139	NM	-1.37	0.979	4,445	0.6	NM
9 Industrial Bank of Japan	Japan	336,233	-2.9	12,052	8.88	356	-30.5	2.97	1.013	63,215	4.9	167.3
10 Deutsche Bank	Germany	302,030	11.3	11,806	9.50	1,134	29.8	10.03	1.060	19,729	1.7	NA
11 Crédit Agricole	France	299,231	3.5	15,579	9.10	1,058	10.3	7.12	1.059	NT		
12 Banque Nationale de Paris	France	284,795	9.7	9,314	8.70	434	-30.2	4.78	1.027	NT		
13 Long-term Credit Bank of Japan	Japan	271,688	-1.3	9,434	9.10	202	-62.8	2.15	1.006	22,336	2.3	103.0
14 Tokai Bank	Japan	270,592	-6.3	9,365	8.97	217	-50.5	2.33	1.007	24,238	2.4	50.9
15 HSBC Holdings	Britain	258,011	98.7	14,191	12.30	2,160	NM	19.10	1.226	23,782	1.9	10.0
16 Société Générale	France	257,862	16.8	7,772	9.12	645	-3.6	9.07	1.058	8,865	1.2	14.6
17 ABN–AMRO Holding	Netherlands	253,529	10.9	9,397	NA	946	10.1	10.40	1.072	8,102	1.0	9.5
18 Asahi Bank	Japan	233,263	-4.1	9,100	9.23	310	-4.7	3.44	1.018	26,856	2.7	79.7
19 Barclays	Britain	222,784	6.6	9,025	9.10	-431	NM	-4.65	0.923	11,540	1.4	NM
20 Bank of Tokyo	Japan	220,956	-11.7	8,986	9.61	361	-4.8	4.05	1.023	26,483	2.9	75.0
21 National Westminster Bank	Britain	216,787	16.8	8,599	9.80	359	NM	4.17	1.015	11,944	1.5	38.7
22 Citicorp	USA	213,701	-1.5	11,181	9.60	722	NM	6.99	1.046	9,868	1.0	16.9
23 Mitsubishi Trust & Banking	Japan	209,032	-5.8	7,460	9.77	238	-21.1	3.22	1.015	15,559	1.9	60.2
24 Paribas	France	203,900	8.5	9,987	9.00	402	NM	3.94	1.019	6,538	0.9	39.7
25 Dresdner Bank	Germany	199,516	12.1	6,318	NA	598	48.1	9.63	1.047	9,401	1.4	NA
26 Bank of China	China	197,301	28.1	10,995	NA	1,779	22.8	17.54	1.117	NT		
27 Sumitomo Trust & Banking	Japan	195,911	-3.8	7,312	10.02	213	-23.2	2.94	1.013	15,088	1.9	65.0
28 Mitsu Trust & Banking	Japan	187,127	-3.0	5,922	10.22	85	-60.1	1.44	1.001	11,520	1.8	137.7
29 Union Bank of Switzerland	Switzerland	180,768	6.9	12,888	10.00	934	10.2	7.41	1.075	16,629	1.3	17.4
30 BankAmerica	USA	180,646	56.4	15,488	11.49	1,492	32.8	12.67	1.182	15,195	1.4	10.6

Exhibit 7.9 *continued*

		Assets		Capital		Performance				Market value		
		($ m)	Change from 1991 (%)	Equity ($ m)	Total capital ratio	Net income ($ m)	Change from 1991 (%)	Return on equity (%)	Real profit-ability	5/31/93 ($ m)	Market-to-book ratio	P/E ratio
31 Westdeutsche Landesbank	Germany	164,385	19.3	6,940	8.90	145	4.0	2.87	0.993	NT	NA	NA
32 Gruppo Bancario San Paolo	Italy	161,359	15.8	6,763	NA	205	-66.1	3.37	0.986	4,596	NA	13.5
33 Bayerische Vereinsbank	Germany	153,192	10.7	4,022	9.30	278	22.0	7.27	1.022	5,186	1.5	NA
34 Daiwa Bank	Japan	152,315	-6.2	5,308	9.37	159	-41.5	3.02	1.013	15,711	2.8	92.9
35 Nippon Credit Bank	Japan	147,495	-3.7	4,869	9.00	163	-54.3	3.40	1.016	9,881	1.9	57.6
36 Commerzbank	Germany	141,803	2.9	4,390	8.34	519	53.1	12.06	1.062	5,130	1.1	NA
37 Chemical Banking	USA	139,655	0.5	9,851	11.29	1,086	NM	12.68	1.142	9,471	1.2	9.3
38 Shoko Chukin Bank	Japan	137,793	4.0	3,740	NA	165	-30.7	4.59	1.022	NT		13.0
39 Swiss Bank Corp.	Switzerland	137,764	-2.9	9,167	11.50	695	-6.1	7.66	1.071	9,193	1.1	13.0
40 Yasuda Trust & Banking	Japan	135,976	-8.7	4,749	10.26	74	-62.9	1.56	1.001	9,401	1.8	116.8
41 Hypo-Bank	Germany	134,116	13.7	3,618	8.10	231	3.4	7.01	1.020	NT		
42 Rabobank	Netherlands	128,166	7.2	7,754	NA	565	0.9	7.56	1.067	NT		
43 DG Bank	Germany	128,120	3.3	3,672	8.90	53	-69.7	1.58	0.986	NT		
44 Toyo Trust & Banking	Japan	126,933	0.8	4,091	9.79	102	-34.3	2.52	1.009	9,171	2.1	82.8
45 Zenshinren Bank	Japan	119,880	7.5	2,134	NA	127	6.5	6.13	1.024	NA		
46 Bayerische Landesbank	Germany	119,656	15.6	2,593	NA	271	49.9	11.26	1.039	NT		
47 Nationsbank	USA	118,059	7.0	7,814	11.52	1,145	NM	15.98	1.195	11,923	1.5	10.7
48 Crédit Suisse[1]	Switzerland	117,946	11.2	6,641	9.60	655	2.1	10.19	1.097	10,276	1.5	14.4
49 Intl. Nederlanden Bank	Netherlands	109,541	8.6	3,835	NA	388	4.0	10.62	1.069	9,607	1.1	10.2
50 Banca Nazionale del Lavoro	Italy	108,980	13.3	4,550	NA	50	-14.1	1.11	0.961	NT		

Japanese data are for fiscal year ended March 31, 1993. Data for all other banks are for fiscal year ended December 31, 1992, unless otherwise designated.
1. Holding company data.
NA = not available.
NM = not meaningful.
NT = not traded.
Data: IBCA Ltd.
Source: Business Weekly, July 5, 1993.

Exhibit 7.10   *(a) Gross loans to customers. (b) Total customer deposits*

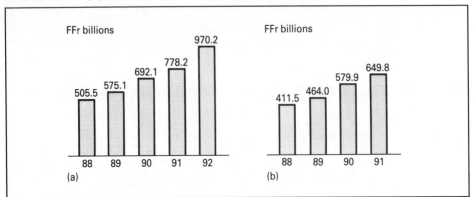

(a)

(b)

Commerzbank's equity for 7% of CL's equity. Discussions broke down over German fears that the French bank had more in mind than cementing the Europartners alliance. Commerzbank clearly did not want to be the German arm of a French bank. And there was the matter of price. Based on comparative profit figures, Commerzbank wanted a 10% for 10% share swap – even though the French bank was twice its size – because it considered itself to have a much better future in terms of earnings and market potential.

By the end of 1991 Europartners was in effect dead, although this hardly precluded strategic alliances as a further option for Crédit Lyonnais. Other partnerships have been more stable. An example was the Banco de Santander–Royal Bank of Scotland agreement, cemented by a share-swap, to create a link-up through which clients could conduct cross-border transactions at terminals located at either bank's branches. Crédit Commerciale de France had signed-up to join this alliance. And there was the proposed BNP–Dresdner deal, a cooperative agreement that involved 10% cross-shareholdings and each bank continuing to run its existing operations, with reciprocal access to branch networks but with a program of opening joint offices elsewhere, such as Switzerland, Turkey, Japan and Hungary.

The Government Link

The French economic and financial policy environment over the years had been rather unstable. When François Mitterand acceded to power in 1981, his approach to reflating the economy by increasing the size of the public sector, cutting the work week and nationalizing 49 key industrial and financial firms had led to increased imports and a deterioration of both the trade balance and international capital flows. Under those conditions, the possible solutions were either to devalue the franc and take it out of European Monetary System's Exchange Rate Mechanism or seriously to reduce monetary expansion, reduce the fiscal deficit (including cuts in spending), and stimulate the private sector.

The latter route was chosen. Taxes were cut, the capital markets were deregulated, and the French economy boomed through most of the 1980s. Finance Minister Pierre Bérégovoy, the driving force of fiscal prudence, maintained a *franc fort*, low-inflation policy throughout the period and committed the country to partial privatization, starting with the sale of minority stakes in Elf-Aquitaine, Total, and Crédit Locale de France in 1991.

Exhibit 7.11   *Senior management*

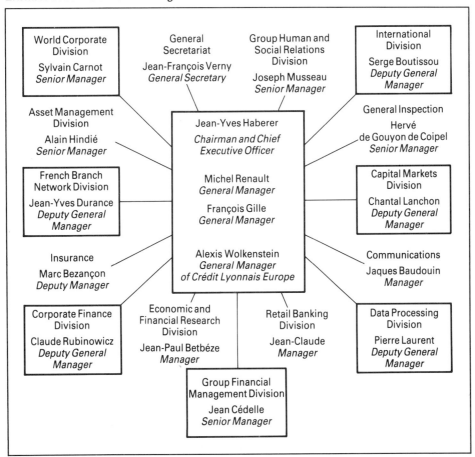

Exhibit 7.12   *Equity investments by sector (percentage net value at year-end)*

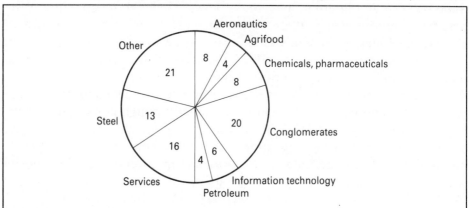

On the other hand, the Socialists had not only nationalized the big banks in 1981 when they came to power, but had continually influenced their activities since then. For example, in 1992 BNP had been asked to acquire an equity stake in Air France, and Crédit Lyonnais had been 'encouraged' to buy into the large integrated steelmaker Usinor–Sacilor – both of them inefficient state-owned firms making large losses. By linking together the state-owned equity portfolio and the equity holdings of state-owned banks, such deals could in the future allow the government to maintain control despite partial privatization of non-financial companies. There was considerable debate whether any new government that might take office in 1993 would couple a program of aggressive privatization with non-intervention in the strategic direction or the operations of banks and industry – that is, whether the micro-intervention of the past was a 'Socialist' or a 'French' attribute.

In addition to its direct and indirect equity holdings, the French government had a strong control lever through 'moral suasion' – a tradition of political meddling by bureaucrats who considered themselves able to come up with better economic solutions to national needs than the interplay of market forces. On a European level, beyond the tampering with free competition of the past and a highly protectionist stance within the EC decision process in matters of industrial and trade policy, there was concern that the French government would continue its *dirigiste* role and even try to extend it to the cross-border relationships of French firms and banks.

Harberer considered the role of the state in France as a two-edged sword. It could at times make life difficult in doing what needed to be done in carrying out his vision, but the backing of the state could provide the deep pockets and political support to overcome obstacles and setbacks that would stop ordinary banks in their tracks. Maximizing the advantages and minimizing the drawbacks meant that strong backing by the government mandarins who mattered was crucial.

The value of the government link became obvious in several 'accidents' that befell CL in its drive for growth. Specifically in wholesale lending, where balance sheet expansion could be most rapidly achieved, growth meant narrower lending margins. As the European recession began to set in during 1990 and 1991, most banks retrenched to weather the storm. Crédit Lyonnais, on the other hand, announced that it would maintain its set course and 'buy' its way out of the recession. The bank had thus taken on much riskier projects than many of its competitors, and the list of CL's lending problems in the early 1990s included (a) the Robert Maxwell affair, involving significant credit losses; (b) Hachette, the French publisher, whose television channel *La Cinq* went bankrupt; (c) Olympia and York, the failed Canadian real estate developer, where CL was the second-largest European creditor of the firm's Canary Wharf project in London; and (d) loans of over $1 billion to Giancarlo Parretti, an Italian financier (later accused of fraud), for his purchase of the Hollywood film studio MGM/UA Communications.

Rapid expansion during 1991 and 1992 did indeed provide a significant increase in CL's net banking income, In 1990 it achieved a net profit of FFr 3.7 billion, a 20% increase over 1989, although a major portion of this increase was attributable to Altus Finance. But a long list of bad debts and investments produced an equally large increase in provisions. By the end of 1991, Crédit Lyonnais was suffering serious growth pains as profits fell to FFr 3.16 billion and provisions were increased from FFr 4.2 billion to FFr 9.6

Exhibit 7.13 *Commitments outstanding at 31 December 1992 (FFr billions)*

	Gross	Cumulative provisions	Net
Film industry (including MGM)	18.727	4.540	14.187
Comfinance–Parretti group	1.217	1.096	0.121
Sasea (holding company)	0.920	0.780	0.140
Sasea (affiliates)	3.839	3.389	0.450
Scotti (including bonds issued by Pierre 1er)	3.655	2.175	1.480

Exhibit 7.14 *Contribution in 1992 of the main subsidiaries of Crédit Lyonnaise Europe to consolidated results (after consolidation restatement; FFr millions)*

	1991			1992		
	Total banking income	Operating Income banking provisions	Net profit	Total banking income	Operating Income before provisions	Net profit
CL Portugal SA	302	121	58	298	89	3
CL Espana[1]	726	432	315	908	335	145
Banca Jover	603	320	146	723	296	111
CL Bank Nederland	2,198	748	84	2,037	688	93
CL Belgium SA	816	357	177	767	284	159
CL Luxembourg SA	173	98	4	180	98	41
CL SA & CO (Deutschland) OHG	152	38	2	193	58	35
CL (Suisse) SA	428	183	74	418	157	40
Credito Bergamasco[2]	2,216	1,034	396	2,461	1,200	347
Banque Franco-Hellenique	87	52	12	96	58	22

1. Figures for 1991 concern Banco Comercial Espanol.
2. Including Banco San Marco.

billion. At 1.6% of total loans, CL's level of provisions were precarious when compared with those of other French banks. They were three times those of its main French competitors – but still better than most UK banks, for example. Nevertheless, the MGM/UA Communications controversy and CL's increasing exposure to risky loans resulted in Moody's Investor Services downgrading CL's bond rating from Aa1 to Aa2, despite the French government's continuing ownership of the bank and its own Aaa rating.

Also worrisome was the fact that CL's interest margins continued to decline as competition for deposits increased. At the same time, costs were rising as investment in technologies became increasingly necessary to keep pace with the competition, and difficulties were encountered in curbing escalating personnel costs. Assuming that margins were unlikely to improve

Exhibit 7.15 *Consolidated balance sheet*

Assets at 31 December	1991 (FFr millions)	1992 (FFr millions)
Cash, central banks, French treasury, postal accounts	29,368	22,411
Banks and financial institutions	245,977	297,974
Securities purchased under resale agreement	47,354	57,991
Loans to customers	710,907	878,454
Leasing receivables	45,927	49,507
Checks and bills receivables	75,442	66,585
Other receivables	92,558	110,195
Securities received under resale agreement	27,729	86,121
Trading securities	67,306	54,692
Securities held for sale	70,670	89,577
Investment securities	98,851	124,349
Investments in unconsolidated affiliates	27,988	39,801
Investments in companies accounted for under the equity method	17,512	23,692
– Financial affiliates	7,030	4,775
– Nonfinancial affiliates	10,482	18,917
Goodwill	3,923	4,373
Participating loans (note 16)	1,477	2,871
Fixed assets (note 18)	22,579	29,592
Total assets	1,585,568	1,938,185
Commitments and contingencies received		
Guaranties and endorsements received from financial institutions	91,124	79,253

Note: Figures for 1991 have been restated to reflect recognition of the net amount of capital notes.

Exhibit 7.15 *continued*

Liabilities and shareholders' equity at 31 December	1991 before appropriations (FFr millions)	1992 before appropriations (FFr millions)	1992 after appropriations (FFr millions)
Central banks, French treasury, postal accounts	39,258	33,960	33,960
Banks and fiancial institutions	420,219	506,736	506,736
– Demand deposits	37,238	43,333	43,333
– Term borrowings and time deposits	382,981	463,403	463,403
Securities sold under repurchase agreement	58,509	54,684	54,684
Customer deposits	317,078	419,127	419,127
Regulated savings deposits	124,109	149,854	149,854
Consumer certificates of deposit	30,040	35,830	35,830
Funds pending collection	73,703	62,752	62,752
Provisions and other accrued liabilities	105,926	134,542	135,124
Securities delivered under repurchase agreement	31,200	70,785	70,785
Trading securities	21,269	22,571	22,571
Securitized debt	295,281	361,735	361,735
– Negotiable certificates of deposit and other negotiable debt securities	192,513	242,173	242,173
– Debenture loans	78,674	89,992	89,992
– Subordinated debentures	24,094	29,570	29,570
Equity capital and equity/capital equivalent	64,898	86,374	85,027
– Equity/capital equivalent	17,862	23,037	23,037
– Reserve for general banking risks	–	3,086	3,086
– Consolidated reserves	29,701	35,241	32,718
– Capital	6,793	7,075	7,075
– Unappropriated retained earnings	433	403	675
– Minority interests	10,109	17,532	18,436
Net profit (loss) for current year	4,078	(765)	–
– Minority interest	916	1,083	–
– Group's share in net profit (loss)	3,162	(1,848)	–
– Of consolidated companies	2,760	(1,727)	–
– Of companies accounted for under the equity method	402	(121)	–
Total liabilities and shareholders' equity	1,585,568	1,938,185	1,938,185
Commitments and contingencies given			
Guaranties and endorsements given to financial institutions		47,343	26,074
Letters of credit		167,422	203,537
Guaranties, endorsements on behalf of customers, and other lines of credit		164,038	172,482
Acceptances and other		10,340	15,439
Equipment leasing commitments		12	13
Real estate leasing commitments		21	17

Source: Crédit Lyonnais Annual Report 1992.

and cost pressures would be difficult to reverse, CL would have to rely far more heavily on commission income in the future than it had in the past.

In September 1992, Crédit Lyonnais announced its group profits had plunged 92%, to FFr 119 million for the first half, compared to FFr 1.6 billion for the same period the year before. The precipitous drop was again due to an increase in provisions against bad debts, from FFr 3.4 billion for the first half of 1991 to FFr 6.3 billion for first half of 1992 – even as net banking income grew by 16% and gross operating profit before provisions increased by 33% in the same period. Forty percent of the bad debt provisions was attributed to CL Bank Nederland, the Dutch subsidiary, in connection with the MGM/UA Communications loans. In December 1992, Moody's once again downgraded Crédit Lyonnais debt to Aa3, citing 'higher risk in both the loan portfolio and the bank's strategy'.[3]

All of these problems notwithstanding, CL's performance was considered acceptable by its owner, the French Republic, with growth evidently deemed more important than profits. Still, the issue of capital adequacy could not be avoided – under either the BIS capital standards or the EC Capital Adequacy and Own Funds Directives – both to absorb the various credit losses and to support Haberer's grand design. As a state-owned bank, Crédit Lyonnais had not been allowed to raise equity capital independently. Only 5% of CL's capital was owned by shareholders, in the form of non-voting *Certificats d'Investissement*. The rest belonged either to the government or to government-controlled companies. As such, new capital infusions would have to come from the state.

Complicated arrangements had been made under French government sponsorship with five state-controlled companies during 1989–91 in order to bolster CL's capital base and at the same time solve certain industrial problems. In November 1989, CL raised FFr 1.5 billion by selling shares to the Caisse de Dépots et Consignations. In February and December 1990, share swaps with Thomson brought in FFr 6.4 billion. A deal with Rhône-Poulenc raised another FFr 1.7 billion in 1990. In 1991, at the request of Prime Minister Edith Cresson, CL invested FFr 2.5 billion in Usinor–Sacilor, and gained a 10% stake. The bank also swapped 10% of Usinor's shares for 10% of new CL shares, thereby boosting CL's shareholder equity by about FFr 3 billion. This allowed CL to consolidate its share of Usinor–Sacilor's profits and losses. It had the effect of diluting CL's earnings, but provided a neat (if temporary) solution for the steelmaker's problems.

Altogether then, by late 1992 about 28% of CL's total capital base consisted of shares in state-owned firms. In all of the share-swaps, both parties paid much higher than book values. These agreements had the effect of linking the fate of the bank to the success of the companies concerned, and also represented a powerful incentive to support these same companies in the future in the face of uncertain profitability. In any case, the resulting capital infusions were insufficient to meet the bank's needs, and the question remained what implications these cross-holding arrangements would have if and when especially Thompson and Rhône-Poulenc were privatized. The rest of the badly needed equity would have to be injected by the government.

The Grand Design

Haberer's mosaic seemed to be coming together much faster than anyone could have predicted when he took control in 1988:

- The bank's balance sheet had grown enormously under his leadership.
- CL had penetrated all of the important European markets in significant ways, including the most difficult of all, Germany.
- CL had maintained its close relationship with its shareholder, the French state, which had shown its willingness to inject capital and to tolerate even serious setbacks on the road to greater financial prominence. The bank's rapid growth and European cross-border market penetration were well suited the French government's industrial policy objective of having one large French firm as a leader in every major sector of the European economy.
- Its shareholdings in industrial companies had grown from FFr 10 billion in September 1988 to FFr 45 billion in early 1992, and it had accumulated significant equity stakes in key French industrial companies, whose strategies and financing activities it was in a position to influence. At the same time, it had provided the government with a durable industrial influence even if the affected firms were to be privatized.

According to Jean-Yves Haberer:

Our strategy considers that Western Europe will be increasingly the domestic market of major European banks for the coming decade. What we are preparing for is no longer the EC market of 1993, but the market of the years 1995 to 2000. For our corporate clients, which are large multinational groups, the location of our teams, mainly in big financial centers, is relatively unimportant. On the other hand, to offer our services to small and medium-sized corporations and individuals requires vicinity and local intimacy. We intend to build a large and profitable European banking group.[4]

Exhibit 7.16 *Consolidated income statement*

Year ended 31 December	1991 (FFr millions)	1992 (FFr millions)
Interest revenue	116,802	116,673
– *Income from money market and interbank transactions*	*34,776*	*32,836*
– *Income from customer accounts*	*76,376*	*77,733*
– *Income from leasing transactions*	*5,650*	*6,104*
Interest expense	(106,199)	(110,087)
– *Cost of money market and interbank transactions*	*(57,411)*	*(50,345)*
– *Interest paid on customer accounts*	*(29,366)*	*(28,314)*
– *Interest paid on securitized debt*	*(19,422)*	*(31,428)*
Other banking income and expenses	32,738	38,798
– *Income from the securities portfolio*	*19,298*	*23,138*
– *Other operations*	*13,440*	*15,660*
Other income	2,992	3,587
Total banking income	46,333	48,971
Operating expenses and depreciation	(33,019)	(35,761)
– *Personnel costs*	*(19,039)*	*(20,625)*
– *Taxes*	*(1,223)*	*(1,292)*
– *General operating expenses*	*(10,292)*	*(11,268)*
– *Depreciation*	*(2,465)*	*(2,576)*
Operating income before provisions	13,314	13,210
Operating provisions net of recoveries	(9,601)	(14,691)
Non-recurring items	1,498	1,270
Non-operating provisions net of recoveries	(15)	6
Employee profit-sharing provision	(170)	(99)
Income taxes	(1,350)	(340)
Earnings of companies accounted for under the equity method	402	(121)
Net profit (loss)	4,078	(765)
– *Minority interest in net profit*	*916*	*1,083*
– *Group's share*	*3,162*	*(1,848)*

Source: Crédit Lyonnais Annual Report 1992.

Various commentators, on the other hand, pointed to a number of weaknesses in the strategy, which was considered highly controversial:

1. Haberer had not considered that France's EC partners could object to French government tampering with market competition in their countries via the acquisition of local banks.

2. Haberer had not adequately addressed the problem of how to expand rapidly without buying excessive quantities of low-grade paper. He could therefore eventually create such an awful mess in CL's loan portfolio that the government would blow the whistle.
3. Haberer and his strategy were on everyone's casualty list for the political in-fighting that surely would follow the next French presidential election in 1995. Time was running very short indeed to accomplish all he was hoping for.
4. Haberer had neglected the investment banking and capital markets side of the business. Indeed, even companies in which CL had holdings – assuming sufficiently high credit standing – would prefer to use the capital markets rather than bank borrowing for their financing requirements.

Indeed, some critics combined all of these points to form a gloomy picture of Crédit Lyonnais in the late 1990s as a bank with plenty of impotent industrial shareholdings in companies that were concentrating their financing on the capital markets, plenty of acquisitions and alliances with foreign banks whose major clients were likewise defecting to the capital markets, and plenty of bad loans acquired along the way to amassing gigantic size that was of no real use.

Notes

1. A *banque de dépôts* had two functions: (a) a banking function – to collect deposits and make loans; and (b) a financial function – to underwrite new issues of debt and equity securities for its corporate clients.
2. French *banques d'affaires* were established in the 1870s for the purpose of investing in industries. By the end of the nineteenth century they were making not only business loans, but buying stakes in companies as well. In 1967 legislation abolished barriers between *banques de dépôts* and *banques d'affaires*, allowing universal banking.
3. *Euromoney*, March 1993.
4. *Euromoney* (supplement), March 1991.

Appendix: The Competitive Arena

Crédit Lyonnais in the 1990s faced increasingly stiff competition in all lines of activity at home as well as abroad – competition that could potentially thwart Jean-Yves Haberer's grand design of a pan-European universal *banque industrie*. This was the product of the size and shape of the competitive playing-field and the strategic moves of CL's rivals, both in France and in Europe as a whole.

The Domestic Competition

The French domestic market for financial services in the early 1990s had been a highly competitive one, characterized by both compartmentalized universal as well as specialized institutions – each targeting different financial activities despite the fact that deregulation had removed many of the legal barriers.

- The *caisses d'épargne* dominated the liquid savings deposit market, accounting for over 30% of such deposits.
- The *banques cooperatives*, especially Crédit Agricole, dominated the agricultural sector.
- The *banques de dépôts* (notably BNP and Société Générale) were most active in short-term industrial finance, Crédit National in longer-term loans, and Crédit Foncier in mortgage credit. All were pushing into the insurance business. In March 1989 BNP and UAP had sealed a *bancassurance* alliance, including a 10% share swap, which gave BNP a FFr 5.3 billion capital infusion and UAP 2,000 French banking outlets from which to sell insurance.
- The *banques d'affaires*, such as Paribas, were both aggressive and competent in corporate finance, although they had more in common with large financial conglomerates than did the traditional British merchant banks or US investment banks.
- The *banques étrangers*, which included Barclays Bank in the private banking sector and J. P. Morgan in the wholesale sector, were mounting fairly effective challenges in specific niches, and numerous foreign banks – including such highly-rated firms as Deutsche Bank and Union Bank of Switzerland – were attracted to France's dynamic financial markets.
- New or revitalized non-bank competitors such as the French postal savings system, finance companies such as Compagnie Bancaire (an affiliate of Paribas), and the large insurance companies were stepping-up their challenges to the large universal banks.

Certainly the most intense battle CL faced at home was to attract retail deposits. Remunerated checking accounts had been prohibited since 1967, so *SICAVs monétaires* were used as instruments to attract savings, and French banks had been pushing this form of investment aggressively. The result, however, was that the cost of funds had approached the money market rate, severely penalizing those banks which had previously lived off the cheap, unremunerated accounts – especially difficult given the rising cost of technology as banks competed to develop computerized networks offering more electronic services such as ATMs and direct telephone transactions through the domestic Minitel network.

The Pan-European Playing-field

Beyond France, the competitive playing-field was basically defined by a series of EC financial services initiatives dating back to the mid-1970s and anchored in the Single European Act 1987, which committed the EC to a single market by the beginning of 1993. By late 1992, a series of EC directives had already begun to seriously alter the European environment in banking, securities activities and insurance. These included:

1. The *First Banking Directive*. Liberalization of intra-EC banking activities can be
    traced to the 1977 First Banking Directive, which allowed banks based anywhere
    in the EC to establish branches or subsidiaries in any other member country
    (freedom of establishment) on the condition that banking regulations in the host
    country were fully observed. It also required member states to establish a licensing
    system for credit institutions, including minimum 'fit and proper' criteria for
    authorization to do business.
2. The *Second Banking Directive*. Under the Second Banking Directive 1988, a single
    EC banking license allowed credit institutions (authorized to do business in any
    one member state) to have full access to all other EC national markets for all credit
    services without separate authorization. This includes deposit-taking, wholesale
    and retail lending, leasing, portfolio advice and management, as well as trading in
    securities. In line with the broader dictates of the Basel Concordat of 1986,
    prudential control over all banks authorized to do business in the EC is exercised
    by home countries, including subsidiaries (which come under a separate 1983 EC
    directive on consolidated supervision).
3. The *Investment Services Directive*. Non-bank securities firms were slated to be
    covered by the Commission's 1988 draft Investment Services Directive, scheduled
    to go into effect in 1996. Again, home-country agencies – public authorities or
    professional self-regulatory organizations (SROs) appointed by public authorities
    – would retain the power of licensing, supervising and regulating investment firms.
    Institutions duly registered and supervised by EC home countries would in essence
    be free to establish a commercial presence and to supply securities services in any
    member country without separate authorization. Investment firms holding
    membership in stock exchanges in their home countries would likewise be free to
    apply for full trading privileges on all EC stock, options and futures exchanges.
    Close collaboration was envisaged between the EC Commission, the authorities
    responsible for securities markets and institutions, and the various banking and
    securities authorities. Again, foreign-based financial institutions would be treated
    in accordance with the principle of 'reciprocal national treatment' and, once
    certified by a member country, notionally came under the same 'single passport'
    rules as EC financial institutions as long as their home countries are not found to
    discriminate against EC-based institutions.
4. The *Capital Adequacy and Own Funds Directives*. The capital-to-assets ratio
    required of banks and securities firms impact directly their funding costs, as well
    as their ability to execute transactions, and hence their ability to offer competitive
    financing to clients. As agreed in the 1988 Basel Accord, banks were subject to a
    minimum ratio of 8% capital (composed of not less than 4% 'core' capital) to risk-
    weighted assets (defined to include off-balance sheet exposures) by the beginning
    of 1993. Besides contributing to banking stability, the Basel Accord was intended
    to promote a level playing field for credit institutions regardless of their home-base.
    In the EC context, the Basel Accord made further harmonization of capital
    standards for credit institutions largely superfluous. Comparable initiatives were
    under active discussion within the EC with respect to the securities industry in the
    form of the Capital Adequacy Directive (CAD), with respect both to securities
    firms and the securities activities of banks. The alternatives ranged from matching
    capital against position (market) risks, to minimum levels of firm capital covering
    all eventualities, along with EC-wide enforcement of maximum exposure limits.

Whatever capitalization requirements emerged in the EC would also have to be aligned between banks and non-banks doing securities business, in order to achieve regulatory parity, not least because the banking and securities activities were heavily integrated in most EC countries under universal banking structures.

5. *Conduct of Business Rules.* Whereas the EC 'single passport' for banks and securities firms was to be under the control of home country authorities, conduct of business rules regarding EC financial markets themselves would be the exclusive responsibility of host-country authorities, so that firms would have to deal with 13 different sets of rules (the 12 EC countries plus the Eurobond market), in addition to those of non-member countries. This could create serious regulatory confusion, and leave open the possibility of rule-based protectionism against non-domestic firms. It seemed likely, however, that EC rules would gradually converge toward a consensus on minimum acceptable conduct of business standards, which would seek to optimize the balance between market efficiency and regulatory soundness. Areas of particular interest with respect to conduct-of-business rules include insider trading and information disclosure.

6. Rules governing *mutual funds and unit trusts*. A 1989 EC directive governing the operation and sale of mutual funds – Undertakings for the Collective Investment of Transferable Securities (UCITS) – specified general rules for the kinds of investment that are appropriate for mutual funds and how they should be sold. The regulatory requirements for fund management and certification were left to the home country of the firm, while specific rules for adequacy of disclosure and selling practices were left to the respective host countries. Consequently, funds duly established and monitored in any EC member country and that were in compliance with UCITS could be sold without restriction to investors in local markets EC-wide, and promoted and advertised through local selling networks and direct mail, as long as selling requirements applicable in each country were satisfied. Permissible investment vehicles included high-performance 'synthetic' funds, based on futures and options, not previously permitted in some financial centers such as London. Under UCITS, (a) 90% of assets had to be invested in publicly traded companies; (b) no more than 5% of the outstanding stock of any company could be owned by a fund; and (c) there were limits on investment funds' borrowing rights. Real estate funds, commodity funds and money market funds were excluded from UCITS.

Many observers of the European financial scene commented that the symmetry of regulation and creation of a level playing field, especially as between banks and non-bank financial institutions and investment vehicles, would become an important determinant of the composition of winners and losers among financial institutions, as well as the structure of financial transactions within Europe. What seemed certain was that Europe was well on its way toward creating a highly competitive playing-field, and one that could be fully capable of rivalling financial markets elsewhere in the world.

The European regulatory setting was widely expected to continue to evolve along the lines of the universal banking model, without significant geographic or activity-based constraints, where all kinds of financial institution could compete for business across the entire financial intermediation spectrum. The various players would compete in each other's markets geographically, cross-client, and cross-product, including insurance, real estate and various areas of commerce. This environment could, in turn, provide a platform for some European financial institutions to mount serious challenges in North American and Asian financial markets.

Indeed, some observers considered financial services one of the few sectors of the European economy where the regulatory bodies were sometimes well ahead of business in promoting competitive change. Although often resisted by market participants themselves, financial services deregulation in Europe by the early 1990s had produced intense competition and pricing rivalry in many markets, an erosion of sectoral boundaries between types of financial establishments, a proliferation of new technologies, and an improved access to capital markets that shifted the balance of power away from banks and in favor of their customers.

Rivals for Pan-European Stature

Crédit Lyonnais's strategy, particularly its goal of achieving critical mass by capturing between 1% and 2% of total European bank deposits, was bound to face stiff competition in the evolving EC environment. Several classes of competitor posed very different kinds of challenge:

- There were plenty of entrenched competitors in all of the national markets in Europe that CL had to target in order to achieve its goal. Despite the EC regulations, many of the national markets were strongly controlled and relatively 'closed' to outsiders. Sometimes they were dominated by cartels, interest rate agreements and other price-fixing arrangements that bred overcapacity. Local savings bank networks, urban and rural cooperative networks, state-run savings institutions and massive local banks like ABM–AMRO and ING Groep in the Netherlands would be hard to encroach upon.

- The most direct competitors with ostensibly pan-European aspirations were Barclays Bank of the UK and Deutsche Bank of Germany. The other British banks had been focusing on the domestic market, although there was always the possibility that National Westminster or Midland Bank (owned by Hong Kong and Shanghai Banking Corporation) might try a foray on the Continent sometime in the future. Italy was in such a state of chaos that pan-European contenders were unlikely to emerge – even San Paolo di Torino – at least in the near-term. The Spanish banks clearly lacked the critical mass. The Dutch giants, ABN–AMRO and ING Groep might eventually develop European ambitions. The big Swiss banks, which clearly had the potential, were semi-detached from the EC and seemed to have strategies that targeted mainly global capital markets and private banking activities. And there was always Citibank of the USA, which had rebranded subsidiaries under its own logo in Germany, Belgium, France, Spain and Greece, and had emerged from recent domestic troubles as a powerful retail player in Europe.

- The other French banks apparently were not vying for the same pan-European position as was Crédit Lyonnais. BNP seemed to believe that to develop a 1% deposit market share by acquisition was too expensive, although its strategic alliance with Dresdner Bank AG – including a possible 10% share-swap – had been given a great deal of publicity and probably needed to be monitored. Société Générale has no apparent interest in developing retail banks beyond the French border after an abortive effort to forge a strategic alliance with Commerzbank AG of Germany.

In most European countries, CL in the retail sector would find it difficult under these conditions to benefit from the flexibility it could achieve in servicing larger (wholesale) clients. Retail banking seemed to depend on maintaining viable local-branch network. The alternatives included: (a) building-up such networks, which could be both expensive and risky; (b) buying into local retail networks, which could also be expensive and risky; or (c) strategic alliances which could be formed with local banks or other financial services firms on a mutually beneficial basis. Whatever the delivery, it was critical to have some sort of advantage 'on the ground' over local banks.

CASE 8

Dividend Dilemma at Lucas

In the year to July 1991, Lucas Industries reported after-tax profit of £50 million (1990: £140 million), and paid net dividends for the year totalling £49 million (1990: £48 million). In 1992 operating profit halved, and the £9 million after-tax loss for the year would have been a loss of £99 million without an exceptional after-tax refund of £90 million from the company's pension fund surplus. Lucas had already paid the same interim dividend as in 1991; and the question facing the new finance director was what final dividend to recommend for 1992.

Among the issues in this case are: paying dividends out of reserves; the future availability of cumulative retained profits; the tax implications of dividends; their consequences for cash and gearing; the stock market impact (for a potential takeover target); and the effect of inflation on historical cost accounts.

John Grant joined the board of Lucas Industries plc on 1 September 1992 as the group's new finance director. One of his first problems was to decide what final dividend to recommend on the ordinary shares in respect of the year ended 31 July 1992. After approval by the board of directors, the dividend decision, together with the results for the year, would be announced in mid-October; and any final dividend would actually be paid in mid-January 1993.

The year to 31 July 1992 had not been a good one for Lucas. The world recession, and the changed outlook for defence, had affected the risky and highly competitive business sectors that Lucas was in – aerospace, automotive and applied technology. Operating profits had fallen to £58 million from £113 million in 1991 (and from £207 million in 1990).

The provisional 1992 group profit and loss account and group balance sheet included the same proposed final net dividend of 4.9p per share as in the previous year (see Exhibits 8.1–8.4). With just over 700 million ordinary

This case was prepared by David Myddelton, as a basis for class discussion. © Copyright Cranfield School of Management December, 1993. All rights reserved. Case reprinted with kind permission of Professor Myddelton.

Exhibit 8.1 *Lucas Industries plc: consolidated balance sheet at 31 July (£m)*

	Draft 1992	1991	1990
Fixed assets			
Tangible: Land and buildings	312	320	288
Plant and equipment	459	450	418
	771	770	706
Investments	30	31	30
	801	801	736
Current assets			
Stocks	438	468	458
Debtors	540	573	522
Cash	278	229	229
	1,256	1,270	1,209
Creditors due within 1 year[a]	(737)[a]	(882)[a]	(773)[a]
Net current assets	519	388	436
Total assets less current liabilities	1,320	1,189	1,172
Creditors			
Falling due beyond 1 year	(429)	(284)	(248)
Provisions for liabilities and charges	(148)	(85)	(95)
	743	820	829
Capital and reserves			
Shareholders' funds[b]	725[b]	802[b]	811[b]
Minority interests	18	18	18
	743	820	829
[a]Including short-term borrowings and	189	292	174
proposed final net dividend	34 (draft)	34	34
[b]Including profit and loss account	107	167	188

shares outstanding, this would cost £34 million in net cash payments to shareholders. In addition, £11 million advance corporation tax (ACT) would be payable about three months later to the Inland Revenue.

Normally a company could offset ACT on its dividends against its UK corporation tax bill, but Lucas had not earned enough UK taxable profits. As a result, the group would only be able to recover the ACT on any final dividend if it earned sufficient UK taxable profits at some time in the future. The provisional 1992 accounts had written off, as an additional tax expense,

Exhibit 8.2   *Lucas Industries plc: consolidated profit and loss account for the year ended 31 July (£m)*

	Draft 1992		1991	1990
Turnover	2,253		2,365	2,229
Trading profit	61		107	203
Share of profits/(losses) of related companies	(3)		6	4
Group operating profit	58		113	207
Exceptional items[a]	(2)[a]			
Interest payable less receivable[b]	37[b]		30[b]	16[b]
Profit on ordinary activities before tax	23		83	191
Taxation[c]	28[c]		31[c]	44[c]
Profit (loss) on ordinary activities after tax	(5)		52	147
Minority interests	4		2	2
	(9)		50	145
Extraordinary items	–		–	5
Profit (loss) for the financial year	(9)		50	140
Dividends[d]	49[d]	(draft)	49[d]	48[d]
Amount transferred to (from) reserves	(58)		1	92
Exceptional items:				
[a]Distribution from pension fund surplus	(90)			
Provision for restructuring costs	88			
[b]Interest payable	64		48	42
Less: Interest receivable	27		18	26
Net	37		30	16
[c]See separate note 5 in Exhibit 8.4				
[d]Including proposed final net dividend	34	(draft)	34	34
After charging depreciation (net of profits on sale of fixed assets)	82		80	61

£15 million of irrecoverable ACT (1991: £14 million), of which about £4 million related to the interim dividend.

The provisional 1992 accounts showed a £5 million loss on ordinary activities after tax. After allowing for minority interests of £4 million, there would be a loss for the financial year of £9 million (1991: £49 million profit). Lucas Industries plc did, however, have a cumulative balance on the group

Exhibit 8.3 *Lucas Industries plc: cash flow statement for the year ended 31 July (£m)*

	1992	1991
Net cash flow from operating activities		
(See note 29 in Exhibit 8.4)	182	107
Net interest paid	(24)	(29)
Dividends paid	(50)	(49)
Taxation paid	(29)	(39)
	79	(10)
Investing activities		
Purchase of tangible fixed assets	(90)	(107)
Disposal of tangible fixed assets	12	9
Purchase of subsidiaries, etc.	–	(34)
	(78)	(132)
Net cash flow before financing	1	(142)
Financing		
Issue of ordinary share capital	4	15
Increase in loans	179	32
(Decrease) increase in commercial paper	(71)	43
(Increase) decrease in short-term deposits	(23)	2
Capital element of finance lease rental payments	(10)	(10)
Minority interest	–	2
	79	84
Increase (decrease) in cash and cash equivalents	80	(58)

ᵃ1990 not available.

profit and loss account at 1 August 1991 of £167 million (including profits retained in certain overseas subsidiaries).

Two items were shown as 'exceptional' on the face of the 1992 profit and loss account:

	£m
Exceptional items:	
Distribution from pension fund surplus	90
Provision for restructuring	(88)
	2

A valuation of the Lucas pension fund at 31 March 1991 revealed a surplus in excess of the 5% limit specified in the Finance Act 1986. In the absence of corrective action this would have caused forfeiture of tax relief on a

Exhibit 8.4 *Lucas Industries plc: selected notes*

	1992	1991	1990
Note 5: Taxation			
United Kingdom:			
Corporation tax	11	7	30
Deferred tax	(2)	3	(1)
Double taxation relief	(9)	(5)	(4)
Adjusted in respect of prior years	(2)	–	—
Advance corporation tax written off	15[a]	14	
	13	19	25
Overseas tax: Current	14	13	16
Deferred	–	(2)	2
Related companies' tax	1	2	1
	28[a]	32	44
Note 6: Dividends on ordinary shares			
Interim dividend paid (2.1p)	15	15	14
Proposed final dividend (4.9p)	34[a]	34	34
	49[a]	49	48
Note 29: Net cash flow from operating activities			
Group operating profit after exceptional items	60	113	
Share of losses (less profits) of related companies	3	(6)	
	63	107	
Depreciation	82	80	
Provision for restructuring	72	–	
Decrease (increase) in stocks	30	(4)	
Decrease (increase) in debtors	27	(34)	
Decrease in creditors	(75)	(33)	
Exchange adjustments on opening working capital	(17)	(9)	
Net cash flow from operating activities	182	107	

[a]Draft.

growing proportion of the fund. Eventually agreement was reached on a package involving benefit improvements of £225 million coupled with a return to Lucas of £150 million less tax of £60 million. The Occupational Pensions Board approved implementation in November 1991. It was believed that even after this corrective action a significant surplus still remained in the pension fund.

The restructuring of certain businesses was necessary to integrate operations into more modern facilities, to reduce costs and to match the future needs of customers. Of the £88 million provision in the accounts, £16 million was used before the end of July 1992, leaving £72 million outstanding in provisions for liabilities and charges.

Like most UK companies, Lucas used historical cost accounting, modified by the occasional revaluation of fixed assets. (All UK land and buildings had been revalued in 1989.) In 1992, depreciation of £8 million was charged on land and buildings, and £74 million on plant and equipment. Explicit adjustments to allow for the effect of inflation would considerably reduce reported profits for Lucas, perhaps by £30 million a year or more. Such adjustments would not be allowable for tax purposes.

Annual dividends had grown on average by over 20% a year between 1986 and 1990, as shown below. The 1991 dividend, on lower profits, had been maintained at the 1990 level; and the 1992 accounts provisionally assumed the same dividend again.

Annual net dividend per share

Year	Interim		Final		Total	Earnings per share
1986	0.64	+	2.56	=	3.20p	13.8p
1987	0.64	+	3.29	=	3.93p	16.3p
1988	1.50	+	3.75	=	5.25p	19.8p
1989	1.75	+	4.50	=	6.25p	21.3p
1990	2.1	+	4.9	=	7.0p	21.3p
1991	2.1	+	4.9	=	7.0p	7.1p
1992	2.1	+	4.9*	=	7.0p*	(1.2p)*

* 4.9p final net dividend still to be recommended and approved.

Nearly 10% of the ordinary Lucas shares were held by Lucas Pension Trust Ltd, and another 2½% by Lucas Employees Trust Ltd. Otherwise, the overall pattern of shareholdings at 31 July 1992 was fairly typical of many large companies. There were about 22,000 shareholders in all.

Size of holdings	% of total number of shareholders	% of total number of shares
1–4,000	75	3½
4,001–20,000	20½	5
20,001–200,000	3	6
200,001 and over	1½	85½

The Lucas share price gave some cause for concern. In common with many others, it had fallen sharply in the October 1987 market decline. The shares had not since regained their peak 1987 level of 190p. On 1 September 1992 the ordinary 25p Lucas shares stood at about 85p each. It was not easy to tell to what extent the expectation of a maintained final dividend was supporting the share price. John Grant was also aware of rumours in the stock market that Lucas could well become a takeover target.

The Sale of Jenapharm

This case involves the sale of a former East German pharmaceutical manufacturer, Jenapharm, by the German privatization company, Treuhandanstalt (Treuhand for short). It describes the background of the former East German economy and the role and mission of the Treuhand. The Treuhand's task is complex – the need to sell off industrial properties as rapidly as possible is complicated by unemployment and legal problems. Despite this, the Treuhand is considered a model institution to manage privatization. The case sets the stage for questions to be answered concerning the process of sale and alternative courses of action, in the face of an inquiry to purchase from a possible buyer.

In early January 1992, Fran Birgit Breuel, president of the Berlin-based Treuhandanstalt, the German privatization agency, lifted her cup of tea as she glanced out of the window of her office across the skyline of East Berlin. She had many matters on her mind that day – the Treuhand was mainly a political institution, and its purposes and methods were the subject of debate in both parts of the newly unified German republic – but her attention was drawn to an inquiry that had been received from a possible buyer regarding one of the larger and more viable companies in the Treuhand's portfolio, the pharmaceutical manufacturer Jenapharm.

For nearly nine months since she succeeded Detlef Rohwedder, the industrialist who had been murdered by terrorists in April 1991, she had been attempting to undo the results of 40 years of socialist-economic planning in Eastern Germany. The Treuhandanstalt (Treuhand for short), was the German fiduciary state trust agency in charge of privatizing the former East German enterprises. It was founded in August 1990, after the fall of the Berlin Wall, by the former socialist regime.

This case was prepared by Ralf W. H. Martens under the direction of Professor Roy C. Smith of the Stern School of Business, New York University in October 1992 for classroom discussion only. Acknowledgement is gratefully made to the Salomon Center Case Series, Stern School of Business, New York University and INSEAD, Fontainebleau, France. Case reprinted with kind permission of Professor Smith. © 1995.

The East German Economy

Germany caught the brunt of the first wave of restructuring of the former Soviet Bloc economies. First, to accelerate unification, it had to bribe the Russians, offering $30 billion in aid and troop subsidies over a two-year period (1989–1991) to get their consent to the fast track toward reunification. Germany also had to pay for the domestic integration of East Germany; it had already spent nearly $100 billion on economic unification by early 1991, and future transfer payments were expected to be even higher. It was generally understood that it would be years before subsidies and unemployment benefits would no longer be needed in East Germany on a large scale.

No-one seemed very happy with the situation in Germany after the euphoria of unification had passed. The initial impact of converting their savings into Deutsche Marks at a favorable exchange rate (1 East Mark for 1 Deutsche Mark – even though the black market rate before conversion was about 4 East Marks per Deutsche Mark) meant that many East Germans went on a spending spree, soaking up televisions, appliances, automobiles and other consumer durables. However, this happy first encounter with capitalism was replaced by the grim reality of unemployment and hard times. Citizens of the former Eastern *Länder* (states) immediately experienced a severe economic depression which they did not anticipate when they brought the wall down. Eastern labor productivity was about one-third that of West Germany, but wage rates were rising towards parity. Industrial production fell to less than 50% of the 1989 level. Unemployment, including those on short time, exceeded 30% of the workforce. Although West-German-funded public works projects, welfare and wage support payments, and small retail businesses growing up in the void left by the Communists had begun to offset the plunging industrial economy, the outlook still remained bleak in mid-1991.

The situation, however, was not entirely without hope. Economists predicted that the economic free-fall in East Germany would bottom out and recovery begin by the end of 1991. Optimists began to circulate forecasts of a 10% real growth rate for 1992 for the East – but even if this should be achieved, East Germany's GNP at the beginning of 1993 would still be 25% below where it was in 1989. And even if a 7–10% growth rate could be sustained, according to Kurt Biedenkpof, the prime minister of Saxony (one of the eastern *Länder*), per capita GDP in the East would reach only 65–70% of the West's by the end of the decade. But he added, 'As long as people see things steadily improving they will not worry so much about being equal with the West'.[1]

Meanwhile, in former West Germany, the taxpayers had to cover the bill for restructuring through higher interest charges on a great surge of government borrowings that derived from a budget deficit which by the end of 1991 was predicted to reached 4.5% of GNP. The problems of unification were threatening to contaminate Germany with the American disease – runaway budgets, huge deficits and massive borrowing requirements. New public borrowing was expected to jump in 1992 to around $110 billion (6% of GNP). Total German public sector debt outstanding was forecast to exceed 50% of GNP by 1994. It was around 40% before unity.[2]

This level of borrowing increased inflation in Germany to more than 4% in 1991, and accordingly the independent-minded Bundesbank put the squeeze on the money supply, driving real interest rates to post-war high levels of more than 5%. Not everyone in western Germany was happy with the unification situation, and loud political grumbling was beginning to be heard. Nevertheless, Chancellor Kohl sternly lectured his countrymen on their responsibilities and their obligation to help their kinsmen to the east. Although they grumbled some more, in their hearts they knew he was right.

The Role of the Treuhand

Under the former socialist regime in the GDR, all industrial property was state-owned through one or another of the large 'people's factories', or conglomerate units called *Kombinat*. The Kombinat were all converted on 1 July 1990 – the day of the treaty of economic union between the two Germanies – into either private or public companies under existing (West) German law (GmbHs or AGs). The shares of such companies – originally over 10,000 in number – were then transferred to the Treuhand for sale, rehabilitation or liquidation.

The mission of the Treuhand was:

1. To restore the business activities of the East German state to the private sector as quickly and as far as possible.
2. To establish the competitiveness of as many undertakings as possible and thereby to assure jobs and create new ones.
3. To make land available for commercial purposes.
4. To ensure that a guaranteed right of property in state-owned assets would be accorded to former East German investors after currency union.

Although a creature of public law, the legal structure of the Treuhand was similar to that of a German public corporation (AG), with a board of managing directors (*Vorstand*) of whom the majority were from West

Germany, and a supervisory board (*Verwaltungsrat*), whose function was to supervise, support and check the actions of management. Despite the western experience of the senior management, the majority of the employees of the Treuhand were formerly employed in the GDR civil service. Many of such employees, being former officials in the Communist regime, were not only lacking in the necessary commercial experience needed in a privatization agency, but carried a vested interest in prolonging things as they were.

On one hand, the Treuhand was driven by the need to sell off properties as quickly as possible (so as to end the considerable subsidies and loan guarantees it continued to provide to keep hundreds of non-viable East German companies alive); and on the other hand it was reluctant to liquidate companies, cut jobs and throw more East German workers on the welfare rolls. Further, the task of disposing of the companies quickly was complicated at first by uncertainties as to the legal ownership of land in the Eastern states (much of it once seized by the Nazis, then again by the Communists), and as to the financial responsibility to be assumed for environmental and product liabilities inherited from the past. In most situations, the Treuhand had to decide whether or not to invest in the restructuring of companies before selling them, and on the amounts of subsidies to be paid to those being kept alive.

By November 1991, the Treuhand had sold about 4,100 companies (though only 223 were sold to non-Germans) and closed only 636.[3] Its operating budget for 1991 was $22 billion, of which $12.5 billion was to be borrowed from the German government.

Although the Treuhand was supposed to work itself out of a job by the end of 1994, it still had a long way to go in privatizing some of the more complex industrial situations. Nevertheless, it has accomplished far more in the way of transferring industrial assets from the former Communist economy to the private sector than all of the rest of the Eastern European countries combined. Already it had come to be regarded as a model institution, one closely studied by privatization officials from such diverse locations as Russia, China, and Cuba.

Buying a Company from the Treuhand

To buy a Treuhand company, an investor had to search one out from a catalogue that offered almost no business or financial information. The investor then had to arrange and pay for whatever investigation he wanted – there were no audited financial statements.

The difficulties facing the accountants included evaluation of the physical assets and land of the business, and of future contracts with former Soviet Bloc countries. Former values were almost meaningless in the new DM-economy. A rule of thumb developed that valued East German capital equipment at about one-tenth of equivalent West German machinery. Future contracts with Eastern European countries were extremely difficult to evaluate, especially where the contract partner might not have been able to pay in Deutsch Marks. The status of the debts of the company, including debts to the former East German government-owned banks, was also difficult to assess without knowing whether assistance would be available from the Treuhand.

Evaluation of the market potential of companies was no less difficult. The internal market in eastern Germany was much less well-off than the western part. Though the East German standard of living could eventually improve to something like that enjoyed by the West, the great unknown was how long this would take. In the meantime, for companies to achieve viability they had to sell products outside of the East German market, which meant that they had to be well made and well priced. In most cases, to manufacture such goods would require management and financial assistance from the investor, generally investors from the West.

If an investor wanted to bid for a company, he had to state a price and submit a business plan which included an 'estimated opening balance sheet'. If there were no other bidders, and the business plan was acceptable to the staff of the Treuhand, the sale might be made. Management buy-outs were also possible if the management group could attract financing. If there were several bidders, all submissions were made to the staff, and a winner announced in due course. The winner, however, might not have been the highest bidder. If the business plan or other features of one bid seemed better than the others, the Treuhand could accept it without explanation.

Jenapharm

Jenapharm was the monopoly producer of birth control pills in the former East Germany. Its 2,000 workers (at the end of 1990) also produced steroids, antibiotics and vitamin pills, many for export to the Soviet Union. Jenapharm had been a part of the huge Kombinat centered around the Carl Zeiss optical instruments group in Jena.

In March 1991, the Kombinat, employing 27,000 workers, was taken over by the Treuhand which assumed its debts of $812 million. It sold 51% of the highly prestigious camera unit, Carl Zeiss Jena GmbH, to its pre-1945 sister company, Zeiss Oberkochen (in West Germany), for a price of

DM 0, a grant of $375 million in start-up funds, and loss compensation until 1995. The Treuhand also sold another large optical products unit, Jenoptik, to the state of Thuringia for $687 million in start-up funds and loss compensation until 1993. Forecasts showed the first profitable year for the restructured firms to be 1997.

Jenapharm was another unit of the huge Kombinat. It was the most respected pharmaceutical manufacturer in East Germany with a research department of 240 scientists. It was also considered one of the more viable companies in the group. Herr Dieter Taubert, the 39-year-old head of the company, was thought to be one of the brighter young East German managers. Soon after the fall of the wall he began taking advantage of his new freedom to add several generic drugs to the company's portfolio.

Jenapharm was one of the few larger East German companies that had a positive cash flow in the first few months of economic union, and was expecting to make pre-tax profits of DM 30 million on sales of more than DM 200 million for 1991. It had DM 16.5 million of corporate debt and DM 35 million in pension liabilities.

Meanwhile, by mid-1990, Gehe GmbH, West Germany's biggest pharmaceutical wholesaler, had already taken a large stake in the East German pharmaceutical wholesaler network. Toward the end of 1990, Gehe talked to the Jenapharm management. The discussions went well, and in January 1991 it made a formal enquiry at the Treuhandanstalt. Jenapharm's opening balance sheet, as prepared by Gehe, showed total assets of DM 230 million ($140 million). The company had made a small loss account for the second half of 1990 on sales of DM 90 million ($54.5 million), of which half came from the contraceptive pill. See Exhibits 9.1 and 9.2.

Notified by her staff of the inquiry – one of considerable importance to the Treuhand because of the visibility of the companies involved – Frau

Exhibit 9.1 *Jenapharm: opening balance sheet as at July 1, 1990 (estimated DM 000s)*

	Assets		Liabilities
Current	85,000	Current	120,000
Plant and equipment	120,000	Debts	16,500
Goodwill	5,000	Pension liabilities	35,000
Other	20,000	Shareholder's equity	58,000
	230,000		230,000

Exhibit 9.2   *Jenapharm: summary profit and loss statement (DM 000s)*

	Six months ended July 1990	Full year 1991 (est.)
Revenues	90,000	200,000
Net operating income	(2,500)	30,000

Breuel turned her consideration to how to handle the sale process from this point forward.

Notes

1. David Goodhart and Andrew Fisher, 'Stirrings of life in the East', *The Financial Times*, 13 September 1991.
2. 'Kohl's Debterdämmerung', *The Economist*, 4 April 1992.
3. The Treuhandanstalt, November 1991, as quoted in 'Hand of Kindness', *The Economist*, 21 March 1992.

The Business Strategy of Die Erste Österreichische Spar-Casse-Bank

The Sad Story of Girozentrale

Deregulation means playing a new game:

>   While most actors continue to play chess others already play bowling.

Deregulation in Austrian banking permitted the two largest Vienna based savings banks to expand by M&A activities beyond city limits, and Bank Austria also to merge with the second largest state owned bank. These moves were eroding the business of the bank of the savings banks, Österreichische Girozentrale, later called GiroCredit Bank. Since 1988 several attempts to resolve the visible problems failed because of political and personal opposition. During 1993 the much smaller 'Die Erste' was trying to get control over GiroCredit and the smaller savings banks by a holding company system which is meeting increasing resistance, with profitability of the involved banks improving. The largest savings bank, Bank Austria, does not wish to sell its shares in GiroCredit Bank without adequate compensation of some kind, and also fears the rise of a powerful group of savings banks as an important competitor.

Background

With an asset volume of Aus. Sch. 1406 billion, the savings banks constitute the largest sector in Austrian banking. Compared with that, the commercial banks account for Aus. Sch. 1,325 billion and the cooperative banks for Aus. Sch. 1,056 billion.[1] Mortgage institutions, building societies and specialised public banks have a total asset volume of Aus. Sch. 553 billion (all figures

*This case is written by Gerhard Fink and Reinherd Petschnigg as a basis for class discussion rather than to illustrate either effective or in effective handling of an administrative situation.
© Gerhard Fink and Reinhard Petschnigg, 1995. Case published with kind permission of Professors Fink and Petschnigg.*

for 1992). As the number of savings banks (91) exceeds considerably the number of commercial banks (55; end 1992), it is evident that the savings banks are on average much smaller than the commercial banks. The biggest Austrian credit institution, Bank Austria, however, is a savings bank (Aus. Sch. 562 billion). Bank Austria was established in 1991 when the biggest savings bank Zentralsparkasse und Kommerzialbank (in short Zentral-sparkasse) acquired the former Österreichische Länderbank which used to be the second largest state owned bank in Austria. The second biggest savings bank is die Erste Österreichische Spar-Casse-Bank (in short Die Erste) with an asset volume of Aus. Sch. 185 billion. Like Bank Austria, it is based in Vienna and has a large network of branches in the Austrian provinces (Austria has 9 *Bundesländer* including the capital Vienna).

From the late 1970s, deregulation in Austrian banking permitted the two large Vienna savings banks to start activities outside the city limits by establishing their own branch offices, and also by acquiring small savings banks of local importance all over the country. This made the larger savings banks stronger and even larger than before and at the same time reduced the total number of savings banks in Austria.

The bank of the savings banks, Girozentrale und Bank der Österreich-ischen Sparkassen AG (in short Girozentrale), served as the link between the various savings banks by handling payments among those banks and acted on behalf of the various local savings banks as an international merchant and investment bank. With the number of savings banks declining, Girozentrale could see its business eroding. On the one hand, more and more of the transactions between local savings banks were handled within the network set up by the larger savings banks but, on the other hand, the larger savings banks grew strong enough to become active on international markets on their own. This is particularly true for Zentralsparkasse and for Die Erste. Girozentrale also acted as a bank where the small savings banks could deposit parts of their liquidity reserve instead of depositing it with the Austrian National Bank.

Seeing its business eroding, the management of Girozentrale undertook several attempts to improve its position. The first idea was that Girozentrale could swallow Die Erste and by means of that merger would get access to a large number of clients, providing cheap money and a lot of business opportunities. This attempt failed because of conflicting views on the possible outcomes of such a merger between Girozentrale and Die Erste. A second attempt was made by Girozentrale to acquire Zentralsparkasse. This merger did not take place because of political opposition. However, the third attempt of getting access to private customers was successful when Zentralsparkasse took over Österreichische Länderbank and merged to become Bank Austria, now the largest Austrian bank in terms of employment and balance sheet total. As part of this move, Bank Austria sold one of its banks, Österreichisches Creditinstitut (in short ÖCI), to Girozentrale. Number eleven among all Austrian banks, ÖCI was feasibly large, but with 46 outlets all over Austria not large enough to provide a satisfactorily broad client base for the now merged bank with the new name GiroCredit Bank Aktiengesellschaft der Sparkassen (in short GiroCredit, total asset volume Aus. Sch. 329 billion). The minimum size for profitable business is considered to be around 150 outlets across Austria.

By swallowing a number of small savings banks in the countryside and in smaller cities in the provinces of Austria, Bank Austria acquired all together 31% of the shares in GiroCredit. Taking the same line of action, Die Erste has increased its share in GiroCredit to about 21% through the acquisition of 15 regional savings banks. The remaining independent small savings banks have watched this development with deep concern. If Bank Austria and Die Erste joined forces, they could practically dominate the business policy of GiroCredit and her relations to the other savings banks. If, however, they did not agree on a common strategy, but rather pursued non-cooperative strategies, they could block any reasonable development of GiroCredit. This was the situation as of October 1993. Everyone is convinced that this ownership distribution of GiroCredit is no longer viable and has to be changed. The management of Die Erste has become very active because, instead of being swallowed by GiroCredit, there now seems to be a chance that the much smaller Die Erste may get in to a position to gain control of the much larger GiroCredit AG (about double the balance sheet total of Die Erste).

Die Erste has proposed a plan for the restructuring of the savings banks sector aiming at (a) gaining dominance over GiroCredit by establishing a clear-cut shareholder structure in GiroCredit, and (b) transforming the heterogeneous sector into a powerful group of closely cooperating savings banks.

Before entering into the details of the proposed plan, a brief outline of the activities of Die Erste is given. Subsequently, the role of the local/regional savings banks, the position of GiroCredit, and the role of Bank Austria are discussed.

The Moving Actor in 1993: Die Erste Österreichische Spar-Casse-Bank

For the moment let us note that GiroCredit Die Erste is the second largest savings bank in Austria (Bank Austria is by far the largest). Among all

Austrian credit institutions it ranks sixth (taking the asset volume in 1992 as a yardstick[2]). In the first half of 1993, Die Erste reported the highest profitability among Austrian large banks, with an above-average fee income of more than 20% of total income (1992).[3] The ratio of operating profits to asset volume is 0.61% for Die Erste, 0.41% for Bank Austria, and only 0.28% for GiroCredit.[4]

By Austrian standards, Die Erste is a large retail bank with a strong focus on the needs of the private customer and of the large number of small and medium-sized enterprises, which are typical of the Austrian economic landscape. The bank offers a broad range of products and services to its private customers and has created eleven specialised *Kommerzzentren* with more than 200 professional business advisers who support the work of the branches when dealing with business clients. Die Erste pays particular attention to the needs of liberal professions, property developers and real estate firms.

Moreover, to enhance its attraction to customers, Die Erste created an insurance brokerage subsidiary (VMG–Die Erste Österreichische Spar-Casse-Bank Versicherungsmakler GmbH) in 1980 and thus quite soon adopted an *Allfinanz* strategy. During recent years VMG business grew at an average of more than 20% per year.

To ensure an effective distribution of its products, Die Erste has set up a network of 200 branch offices, 86 of which are in Vienna (end 1992). Two years earlier the total number of branch offices was only 139, of which 85 were in Vienna.[5] These figures reflect the expansion of the bank into Austrian provinces. Before the banking law of 1979, expansion of Die Erste across the borders of Vienna was hindered by the legally established 'region principle' which restricted business activities of savings banks to a specified geographical area. Whilst, on the one hand, opening new branches offices, Die Erste was also acquiring several savings banks in the Bundesländer, most of which disposed of several outlets in closely defined regions. The following list gives the savings banks Die Erste has absorbed since the beginning of the 1980s and which added to its network more than 60 banking outlets. There has been a considerable acceleration of this process during the last 3 years:

- Sparkasse Tulln (1993).
- Sparkassen Mariazell, Neumarkt, Neusiedl, Tamsweg (1992).
- Sparkassen Mauthausen-Grein, Grieskirchen, Gmunden, Laa an der Thaya, Radstadt (1991).
- Sparkassen Zistersdorf, Murau, St. Florian (1990).
- Sparkassen Eisenstadt, Jennersdorf (1980–89).

Contrary to its strategy in the Austrian home market, Die Erste takes a rather cautious stance as far as international business is concerned. Priority is given to the needs of Austrian firms doing business abroad. Loans to foreign clients are much less important and restricted primarily to banks and public institutions from other OECD countries. Contrary to other Austrian banks, Die Erste has avoided risky business with big private foreign enterprises.

Rather than trying to increase market share abroad, Die Erste regards international business as a necessary means to keep a sound relationship with the Austrian business client. This philosophy is reflected by a rather low intensity of market presence abroad and by the bank's geographical restriction to western Europe: Die Erste is currently running five representative offices, two of which are in Italy (Milan, Vicenza), one in London, one in Brussels and one in Madrid. Furthermore, there is a subsidiary in London dealing in securities and derivative products. Die Erste holds the view that a widespread net of branches abroad would not be appropriate and instead is creating a worldwide network of correspondent banks.[6]

Die Erste considers the efficiency and client orientation of its branches as keys to its profitability. In fact, while the branch network covers only 3.5% of all outlets in Austria, the bank has gained a larger market share in retail banking: E.g. Die Erste administers 5.7% of all Austrian savings accounts and 10% of the Austrian investment funds. Furthermore, it increased its credit volume above the overall average rate in 1992. The fact that the credit expansion did not compromise profitability is seen by Die Erste as a consequence of thorough risk analysis, risk diversification, the accompanying scrutiny during the term of the loan and the avoidance of lumpy risks. Credit business with large client enterprises is considered as particularly rather high risk and therefore subject to a strict selection process. The main thrust of credit expansion concerns small and medium-sized Austrian client enterprises which are economically weaker than larger enterprises, more dependent on the bank and, therefore, weaker in negotiating terms, too.

The enhanced efficiency of the branches and thus higher profitability is crucially dependent on the use of technology and the curbing of staff costs. Contrary to visible developments in other European countries Die Erste is rather sceptical about wholly automated, self-service branches. Hence, electronic data processing is mainly used to support bank employees in giving professional advice to the customer. At any time the *Erste-Arbeitsplatz-System* EAS (First Workstation System) enables each employee to get all necessary information and help via the terminal at his/her workstation. This also applies to ECOL, a training package at the disposal of the bank employees, for which Die Erste won an international award in 1992. Aware that staff cost is decisive for bank profitability, Die Erste had initiated a cost-cutting exercise in 1992. Despite the merger with four savings banks, total staff was reduced from 3,364 to 3,308 during this year. Furthermore, the pension scheme of the bank was adapted to the requirements of enhanced profitability.[7]

Its clear-cut strategy and its relatively good profitability (by Austrian standards) makes Die Erste an attractive partner for cooperation. In September 1993 a cooperation agreement was signed with Volksbanken AG (VBAG) which is the central credit institution of the Volksbanken sector (the whole sector has a balance sheet total of Aus. Sch. 190 billion). The Volksbanken sector is made up of credit institutions organised as cooperative banks with a traditional focus on small and medium-sized clients and is following a similar business philosophy. According to the agreement, cooperation will take place in back office areas, such as the payments system, equity and bond clearing, and electronic data processing. To emphasise her willingness to cooperate, VBAG is prepared to permit Die Erste to become its shareholder for a stake of up to 25%. The exact range of participation is still under discussion.[8]

The Establishment of a New Structure in the Austrian Savings Banks Sector

Die Erste and the local/regional savings banks are currently negotiating with Bank Austria the price of the latter's stake (about 31%) in GiroCredit with a view to restructuring the savings banks sector. In game-theoretical terms, and somewhat simplifying, the process could be described as follows: Die Erste acts as a leader, the local/regional savings banks are the followers and GiroCredit remains passive.[9]

The long-term aim of Die Erste as stated in its Annual Report 1990, is Austria-wide presence through the establishment of a tight, institutionalised cooperation with local/regional savings banks, in particular by proposed participation in these banks, where the different partners would keep their legal independence. The apparent aim of this strategy is to gain control over the whole sector (with exception of Bank Austria) with as little capital invested as possible.

To achieve this goal, Die Erste presented at the end of February 1993 a plan for enhanced cooperation and division of labour in the savings banks sector aiming at an increase in profitability (cost reduction, improvement of competitive position), 'not only for Die Erste but also for GiroCredit and the local/regional savings banks'. Under this plan, Die Erste would assume the leading role in the framework of an *Erste Österreichische Sparkassen-holding*, which would control the overall business policy of the savings banks sector.[10] It is obvious that in such a context, legal independence of local/regional savings banks would not guarantee their independence. However, if this plan succeeded, the resulting group of savings banks would be by far the largest credit institution in the country (the unconsolidated asset volume would reach roughly Aur. Sch. 840 billion).

In the proposed structure (see Exhibit 10.1, p. 162) a holding company would play the dominant role in defining the group strategy and fulfil some important functions for the group, such as:

● Developing a common marketing approach (including guaranteeing a uniform appearance of the different decentralised units *vis-à-vis* the client).
● Creating a common corporate identity, comparable to those of the cooperative banks (Raiffeisen, Volksbanken).[11]
● Taking care of Austria-wide product development, capital-raising, electronic data processing, risk-diversification in the case of large credits, etc.[12]

Moreover, excess capacities will be reduced by merging the numerous specialised subsidiaries. There are currently more than 50 leasing companies and 5 capital investment firms in the sector; with property financing companies the situation is similar.[13]

Whereas in the old structure GiroCredit did not have the power to implement a coordinated strategy of the savings banks sector (with the bottom-up approach typical for the savings banks sector such a strategy was not forthcoming), the new holding company would be able to impose certain lines of action (a top-down approach would be established). The publicly declared aim of Die Erste, however, remains to create a decentralised group of savings banks.[14]

Without the interposition of the holding company, it would be impossible for Die Erste to gain majority control of GiroCredit because Die Erste holds only 21% of GiroCredit. It would thus have to acquire the whole of Bank Austria's share (31%) to get majority control. This would be far beyond Die Erste's financial capabilities. Consequently, Die Erste will acquire only between an additional 8% and 12% of GiroCredit from Bank Austria. Another 4–8% will be acquired by local/regional savings banks, 3–6% by strategic partners (insurance companies, foreign banks), and the rest would remain with Bank Austria.

The following organisational set-up assures the leading role of Die

Erste.[15] As a first step, Die Erste, which is a savings bank with mutual status and thus has no owners from a strictly legal point of view, will convert into a stockholding company, the shares of which will be held by a foundation *Anteilsverwaltung Erste Österreichische Spar-Casse* (called Erste Foundation).

Twenty-four per cent of the shares of Die Erste[16] will be swapped for 60% of the savings banks holding company. The local/regional savings banks together with the strategic partners would get the remaining 40%. For the individual local/regional savings banks the stake will be calculated by taking into account the balance sheet total, the sum of deposits and outstanding amount of own bond issues (*Primärmittel*), the operating profit, and own funds (*Haftkapital*).[17]

If all local/regional savings banks accepted the proposed plan and if Bank Austria sold all of its GiroCredit shares, then GiroCredit would become a 100% subsidiary of the holding company. This is, however, not necessary for the plan to succeed. A 'broad consensus' among at least three-quarters of all savings banks to acquire GiroCredit shares and subsequently to exchange them for shares in the holding company should suffice, according to the chairman of the managing board of Die Erste, E. Fuchs.[18]

It is furthermore envisaged that the holding company can participate with up to 25% in the equity of the local/regional savings banks, i.e. it would achieve a blocking minority. This would represent a powerful tool for the holding company to affirm the group strategy. To what extent the 25% participation in all savings banks can be achieved will depend not only on the financial strength of the holding company but also on the willingness of the local/regional savings banks, in particular of the bigger regional banks in the provincial capitals, to transfer their own shares to the holding company.[19]

The local/regional savings banks are thus asked not only to buy GiroCredit shares, which – given the poor profitability of GiroCredit – are not necessarily the best investment opportunity anyway,[20] but also to give up some of their independence.

The Role of the Local and Regional Savings Banks

Different representatives of local and regional savings banks (G. Schmid, H. Klingan, K. Bartel) as well as the secretary general of the Savings Banks Association, G. Raab, have reacted favourably in principle to the proposed holding model. Their position, however, is characterised by the fear that they might lose too much of their independence. This fear resulted in requests for:

- Decentralised management along regional lines with powerful savings banks covering a whole Bundesland with branch offices.
- Regional mergers having priority (local savings banks such as Sparkasse Radstadt and Sparkasse Tamsweg, which have been taken over by Die Erste should be managed by (/sold to) Salzburger Sparkasse to ensure the whole coverage of the Salzburg region).[21]
- Harmonisation where necessary, but not creation of a uniform Austrian savings bank.
- Reliance on grown local structures.[22]
- Decentralised decision-making despite instructions from the holding company to local savings banks.[23]

Another request was that the new holding company should have no blocking minority (i.e. 25% or more) in the capital of the local savings banks[24] or that the participation of the holding company should be limited to 10% of the stockholder's equity.[25] In view of the state of negotiations, where a 25% participation seems to be probable,[26] some of the above-mentioned positions appear as wishful thinking.

Whatever the outcome, the willingness of a sufficient number of local/ regional savings banks to cooperate is necessary for the realisation of the project. Stick and carrot is applied to make the local and regional savings banks purchase part of the Bank Austria stake in GiroCredit and to sign up to the drafted cooperation agreement.

For non-cooperating savings banks access to central services may be restricted, e.g. to Spardat (a GiroCredit subsidiary) which is offering electronic data processing (EDP) services. The idea was aired that non-cooperating savings banks may receive less remunaration for the minimum reserves they have to keep at GiroCredit.[27] Nor should it be forgotten that Bank Austria's chairman of the managing board, R.A. Haiden, publicly considered establishing a shareholder's syndicate with Die Erste (Bank Austria and Die Erste jointly hold 52% of the equity of GiroCredit).[28] An exclusion of the other savings banks from vital GiroCredit services might be the consequence.

Having the power, Die Erste would offer representative posts to the minority holders, e.g. the chairman of the supervisory board of the holding company could be delegated by the local/regional savings banks.[29] Having gained control over the whole sector (except Bank Austria), Die Erste would be willing to change again the rules of the game and give up playing on some of the chessboards: the 'regional principle' might be revived in the holding companies model so that 'arbitrary mergers' across regional borders would not take place.[30] Another safeguard for the local/regional savings banks would be a provision stating that certain sectoral agreements can only be passed with qualified majority ensuring hereby the participation of the local/regional savings banks in the determination of the business policy of the holding subsidiaries (specialised banks). Moreover, local/regional savings banks would be offered to acquire direct stakes, for example in Spardat (EDP services), which would allow them a better defence of their interests.[31]

The consent of the local/regional savings banks to the new structure will very much depend on their own financial position. During 1992, it became obvious that rising costs and an increase in bad debts weakened the 'defence capability' of many savings banks.[32] With some better results during the first half of 1993 willingness to give up independence might be somewhat reduced. On the other hand, Die Erste, with its expansion into the Austrian provinces largely completed, can now pledge to respect the principle of 'regionality' and thus make it easier for the local/regional savings banks to cooperate.[33]

The Position of GiroCredit Bank Aktiengesellschaft der Sparkassen

GiroCredit is Austria's third largest credit institution. The former Giro-zentrale (bank of the savings banks) was renamed after the acquisition of ÖCI (Österreichisches Creditinstitut) in 1992, and has thus expanded its role from the bank of the savings banks with international wholesale merchant and investment activities to the universal bank aiming at a broader client base and offering new products.

On the one hand, the automatic business of acting as an intermediary between the savings banks is shrinking as the number of savings banks is shrinking. On the other hand the large savings banks have become strong and large enough to enter the traditional fields of GiroCredit in international banking and in doing business with the largest Austrian corporations.

The acquisition of ÖCI was the third (and this time successful) attempt to break out of the spiral of eroding business with no alternative business strategy open, because of two trends. Firstly, there is the trend to deregula-tion in Austrian banking which is permitting greater openness of local/regional savings banks *vis-à-vis* commercial banks. Thus, the latter may enter the formerly protected savings banks sector after transformation of the legal status of savings banks into stockholding companies, which simultaneously is encouraging mergers of savings banks into larger units[34] and permitting majority acquisitions in the equity of savings banks. Therefore, growing savings banks become more and more independent of the services of the bank of the savings banks (the former Girozentrale, now GiroCredit). It has to be added that the managment of GiroCredit is sometimes also attacked because of reportedly having neglected its service task to the local/regional savings banks and having given priority to regrettably unprofitable international business.[35]

On top of that, the position of GiroCredit is further weakened by the abolition of section 21 of the Savings Banks Law (*Sparkassengesetz*) on 31 December 1993. This will result in the loss of billions of relatively cheap deposits from local savings banks for GiroCredit[36] as the local savings banks are no longer obliged to place their liquidity with GiroCredit. It is typical of developments in the Austrian savings bank sector that savings banks with a balance sheet total of more than Aus. Sch. 30 billion, i.e. Bank Austria and Die Erste enjoyed an exception to the rule already before that date.

Secondly, with large enterprises becoming more sophisticated and achieving more bargaining power, they become less dependent on bank financing and are leaving only tight margins for banks.[37] Taking into account the small number of big enterprises in Austria and the high risk of large-scale international bank-lending, the prospects for a bank like GiroCredit focusing almost exclusively on these market segments are full of problems.

After the takeover of ÖCI and the adoption of a new name, Girozentrale took account of the before-mentioned developments. With the 46 Austrian branch offices of the former ÖCI (half of which are in Vienna) and a recently-opened branch in the province of Salzburg, GiroCredit now has a distribution network through which it can service new customers with new products. The traditional emphasis on merchant and investment banking for savings banks and large business clients is now complemented by the fields of small and medium-sized enterprises and high-income private clients. With the acquisition of ÖCI, GiroCredit has earned the right to enter the attractive mortgage business and business with local communities (*Pfand-und Kommunalbriefdarlehen* +16.8% in 1992) for which special licences are necessary in Austria.

GiroCredit has no alternative but to rebalance and redimension its activities. However, not all its recent activities were a success. Bad luck with several larger industry engagements further weakened its position. Now GiroCredit is actively searching for partners for the problem-ridden industrial enterprises where GiroCredit is involved with equity of credit (e.g. IGM, AKG, Hirtenberger).[38]

Therefore, GiroCredit has little room to manoeuvre at present, due to its relatively poor profitability and to the uncertainty in the composition of her future shareholders. The 'uncertain future prospects of the central savings bank' and 'high provisions for bad debts during the last years' have led the London-based bank rating agency IBCA to reduce its long-term rating for GiroCredit from A+ to A.[39]

Not least because of substantial losses in its international business (in particular in the USA and UK), GiroCredit has come under criticism from the savings bank sector in particular.[40] The takeover of ÖCI was intended to improve the competitive position in the home market and to raise long-term profitability. Moves by GiroCredit to establish outlets in all Austrian provinces are regarded with suspicion by the savings banks.[41] Views are also voiced that GiroCredit's transformation from a central savings bank into a universal bank has to be stronger and faster in order to be successful, implying that GiroCredit, if permitted, should acquire several of the small savings banks too.

As with almost all the other larger Austrian banks, GiroCredit has been suffering substantial losses in western European financial centres;[42] and as with all the others, GiroCredit is now concentrating on the development of banking operations in central and eastern Europe which are considered core markets in its strategy.

In February 1992, GiroCredit obtained authorisation from the CSFR-State Bank to open a universal bank in Prague. It will offer financial services, like payment transfers, documentary letters of credit, foreign exchange, trade finance, mergers and acquisition consulting and corporate finance (particularly for privatised companies). In 1992, GiroCredit acquired a stake in, and concluded a cooperation agreement with, the Export Development Bank (Warsaw) specialising in export promotion and export finance. GiroCredit has opened a liaison office at the headquarters of the Export Development Bank, which has nine branch offices in Poland through which clients of GiroCredit can be served. In turn, GiroCredit will train staff from the Export Development Bank in Vienna and give advice in management and distribution-related matters as well as in the establishment of new fields of business. Since 1990, GiroCredit has had representative offices in Slovenija (Ljubljana) and Croatia (Zagreb), focusing on short-term trade finance and fee-generating business.[43]

In the field of project finance, GiroCredit claims – as do Bank Austria and Creditanstalt – to be the market leader in eastern Europe. GiroCredit strives to develop further its 'dominant position' in these markets.

Besides her activities in central and eastern Europe, GiroCredit maintains branch offices in London, New York, Los Angeles, subsidiaries in Zürich, Hong Kong ('GiroCredit Vienna Asia/Pacific Ltd'), and representative offices in Berlin, Madrid, Milan, Sydney.[44] GiroCredit serves Austrian export business in these markets and is also offering its central and eastern European expertise to local clients.

Before the takeover of ÖCI, Girozentrale served as the 'international arm' for the savings banks sector. This role has now diminished as the two big Vienna savings banks (Die Erste, Bank Austria) have organised their own network of outlets and correspondent banks abroad. With the merger in 1991 of Austria's largest savings bank, Zentralsparkasse, and the second-largest Austrian commercial bank, Österreichische Länderbank, the newly merged Bank Austria can now claim a relatively important international presence[45] by Austrian standards, which makes Bank Austria fully independent from the services of the central savings bank. Bank Austria and GiroCredit are competing at the same foreign locations, e.g. in London, Prague, New York and Hong Kong.

If the plan sketched out earlier materialises, GiroCredit will come under the determining influence of Die Erste and will be integrated in a concept of division of labour in the savings banks sector.[46] This is a quite sensible solution from Die Erste's point of view, given the complementary (and the possible economies of scope) of the traditional business focuses of GiroCredit, Die Erste, and the local/regional savings banks. While Die Erste and the local/regional savings banks have a strong position in terms of raising relatively cheap savings deposits, GiroCredit can serve as seller/developer of financial services abroad, in particular in the central and eastern European countries. Taking over the central and eastern European operations of GiroCredit, Die Erste could reap considerable economies of scope and improve on its weak international presence in Europe generally. Furthermore, there might be room for rationalisation in Milan and Madrid where both GiroCredit and Die Erste have representative offices. The same is true for London, where GiroCredit has a branch office and Die Erste has a subsidiary. The GiroCredit branches (former ÖCI) might also be integrated in an overall efficiency-raising strategy of the holding company.

The Role of Bank Austria

The future role of GiroCredit will depend crucially on the outcome of negotiations between Bank Austria and Die Erste concerning the price of the former's stake in GiroCredit. For a while the divergence was considerable. While Die Erste was offering to pay Aus. Sch. 300 per share, Bank Austria wanted Aus. Sch. 400. Why exactly 400? Going back to 1992, Bank Austria was eager to find a buyer for its GiroCredit shares as it had to redress its financial position and present acceptable annual accounts to the public. Failing to find another buyer, Bank Austria sold its GiroCredit stake to its main shareholder, Anteilsverwaltung Zentralsparkasse (in short

AVZ), for a price of Aus. Sch. 400 per share. The deal was financed by a Bank Austria loan to AVZ. The loan is serviced by the dividends AVZ receives from Bank Austria.[47] Now, Bank Austria, acting on behalf of AVZ,[48] wants to sell for Aus. Sch. 400 so that it can get its loan fully reimbursed. Quite understandably, Bank Austria needs some money to consolidate its position, not least to cover part of the costs provoked by its own recent merger. Beyond that, Bank Austria must have an interest in finding a solution for GiroCredit quickly, otherwise the value of its stake would stand the risk of decreasing rapidly.

Giving away its 31% stake in GiroCredit just for cash would open an opportunity for Die Erste to create the largest Austrian bank in the medium term. If the holding company plan worked out, GiroCredit would come under the determining influence of Die Erste and the numerous subsidiaries of GiroCredit would serve as 'building blocks' for the restructuring of the sector.[49] Avoiding an obvious merger of GiroCredit with Die Erste, the holding company system would open an opportunity to transfer, division by division, to the holding company. The holding company might also take over all the subsidiaries or majority interests of GiroCredit in the various specialised daughter companies. In the end there could remain two main empty shells, GiroCredit and Die Erste. The holding company would become a new major player in the Austrian banking system. This bank would also be strong enough to continue buying the smaller savings banks and could thus gain an even larger market share than Bank Austria has today. This certainly is an option Bank Austria cannot approve of. (Ironically, purchase of the Bank Austria/AVZ share in GiroCredit could be financed only by Bank Austria itself: neither Die Erste Österreichische Spar-Casse-Bank nor the small savings banks are financially strong enough.)

The management of Bank Austria has thus to try its best to avoid both the decline of its GiroCredit shares and the rise of a powerful group of savings banks as an important competitor. The recent further deteriorating financial situation of GiroCredit, however, has made the management of Bank Austria push for a rapid solution of the 'GiroCredit problem' and thus make concessions on price and take the risk of consolidating a split group of uncoordinated savings banks into a strengthened and coherent savings banks group. Bank Austria threatened to acquire substantial units of the GiroCredit business, including its specialised subsidiaries and its branch network if the other shareholders of GiroCredit, in particular the local/regional savings banks, were not prepared to redress the financial situation of GiroCredit via capital injections and the temporary sacrifice of dividend claims.[50] The local/regional savings banks would be ill-advised to let substantial business (specialised subsidiaries and branches) drift towards the

Exhibit 10.1   *The new structure*

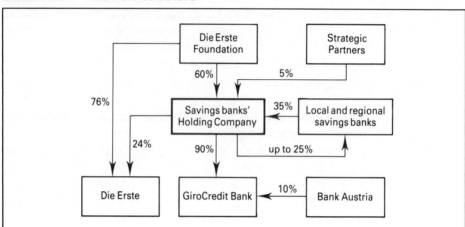

already largest bank in Austria, instead of keeping it in a structure where they participate.

In the middle of November 1993, the deadline for the 'ultimate decision' to be made by the sector was postponed once more. Reportedly, Bank Austria and Die Erste are close to reaching an agreement about the price of the shares (Aus. Sch. 350 versus 340). However, Bank Austria is seemingly determined to accept the offered price only if compensated with some of GiroCredit's equity interests in industry or specialised banking. Bank Austria will possibly tie GiroCredit, Die Erste and the local and regional savings banks into a syndicate agreement, which would prevent the new bank from entering the major business fields of Bank Austria on a larger scale.

Notes

1.   'Raiffeisenbanken' plus 'Volksbanken'.
2.   Bank Austria, CA-BV, GiroCredit, BAWAG, RZB, Die Erste.
3.   It is in particular the cooperative banks and other savings banks that have a much lower fee income (as a percentage of total income). (J. Stockinger, 'Die Struktur der Österreichischen Banken im Jahr 1992', in ÖBA, April 1993, p. 296.)
4.   Kurier, 17 August 1993.
5.   Annual Report 1992.
6.   Annual Report 1992, p. 32.
7.   Annual Report 1992.
8.   Press Release, 19 September 1993.
9.   The negotiating partner, Bank Austria, is prepared to talk about the price as soon as

professional valuations are available. The chairman of the Bank Austria's management board, R.A. Haiden, confirmed, however, that Bank Austria will keep a stake in GiroCredit and possibly invest also in other specialised subsidiaries of GiroCredit (s-Bausparkasse, s-Versicherung, Spardat) or in other savings banks. This, 'upon wish by the sector' (Press Release/APA, 29 July 1993). As the sector is composed of 91 (end 1992) savings banks, this 'wish' might reflect a certain desire by the many local/regional savings banks to have someone in the sector who would counterbalance the possibly emerging dominant role of Die Erste in GiroCredit. In any case, the publicly expressed satisfaction by Bank Austria (Haiden) with the continuing existence of the savings banks sector after a new banking law being assumed by the parliament (1993, Bankwesengesetz) (*Standard*, 13 July 1993), might well be part of a negotiating strategy aimed at raising the price for a far-reaching withdrawal from GiroCredit.

10. Annual Report 1992, p. 5.
11. W. Ulrich (vice-chairman of Die Erste), author interview, 8 March 1993.
12. *SN*, 16 August 1993; *Tiroler Tageszeitung*, 14 July 1993.
13. *Wirtschaftswoche*, 4 March 1993; *Tiroler Tageszeitung*, 14 July 1993.
14. E. Fuchs (chairman of Die Erste managing board), *Wirtschaftswoche*, 8 July 1993.
15. *Wirtschaftswoche*, 4 March 1993.
16. The exact percentage will depend upon a valuation of Die Erste; the more it is worth, the less the percentage need be to assure a majority in the holding company.
17. *Standard*, 23 April 1993.
18. *Wirtschaftswoche*, 8 July 1993.
19. ibid.
20. ibid.
21. *SN*, 16 August 1993.
22. ibid.
23. *SN*, 1 June 1993.
24. *Tiroler Tageszeitung*, 14 July 1993.
25. *Standard*, 23 March 1993.
26. Presse, 14 September 1993.
27. *Tiroler Tageszeitung*, 14 July 1993.
28. *Trend*, May 1993, p. 76.
29. According to the Erste-plan, half of the management board and half of the supervisory board will consist of Die Erste representatives (Presse, 14 September 1993).
30. *Tiroler Tageszeitung*, 14 July 1993.
31. *Standard*, 23 April 1993.
32. *Trend*, May 1993, p. 76.
33. *Wirtschaftswoche*, 4 March 1993, p. 43.
34. The concentration process in the savings banks sector looks as follows: from 174 savings banks in 1952 to 102 savings banks in 1991. By the end of 1993 there will be less than 80 savings banks in Austria. (Raab, *SN* 1 June 1993).
35. For example, W. Ulrich (vice-chairman of Die Erste), author interview, 8 March 1993.
36. *SN*, 15 July 1993.
37. See W. Gerke, 'Sinkende Zinsmarkge – steigende Provisionen?', *Bank und Markt*, June 1988, p. 5.
38. *Standard*, 10 August 1993.
39. Presse, 11 July 1993.
40. Author interview, 8 March 1993.

41. Annual Report 1992.
42. *Volkswirt*, July/October 1992, p. 11.
43. Annual Report 1992.
44. There is another representative office in Hong Kong (Annual Report 1992).
45. Eleven subsidiaries (Prague, Budapest, Laibach . . .) or majority stakes, 8 representative offices, 4 branches (New York, London, Hong Kong . . .) (*Standard*, 30 July 1993; Pressespiegel/APA, 29 July 1993).
46. Bank Austria will then remain formally part of the sector, maybe with a symbolic participation in the capital of GiroCredit. In this case it will continue to take part in the sectoral deposit insurance scheme and remain a member of the professional auditing associations of the savings banks sector.
47. *Trend*, May 1993, p. 74
48. From a strictly legal point of view, it is thus not Bank Austria that currently owns the GiroCredit shares but AVZ which is a 49% shareholder of Bank Austria.
49. *SN*, June 1993.
50. *SN*, October 1993.

Reuters' Share Repurchase

The case concerns distributions by corporations to their shareholders in the form of repurchases or share buy-backs. They are much more common and familiar in the USA than in the UK. It is an aspect of corporate finance policy: share repurchase can be used as an alternative to cash distribution by dividend.

The present case relates to the 1993 £350 million share repurchase by Reuters, the international news and financial information group, in the UK. The cash distribution was deemed successful: shareholders over-tendered nearly seven times, the share price immediately went higher and the financial press was approving.

The case examines theoretical and practical aspects of this innovative financial manoeuvre in the UK.

The Announcement

In July 1993, Reuters, the international news and financial information group, made an announcement that was generally received enthusiastically by the financial community and was followed by newspaper headline banners like 'cash splash at Reuters' (*Daily Mail*), 'Cash is no longer King' (*Times*) and 'Reuters steps gingerly off its pile of money (*Financial Times*). The announcement: Reuters would spend £350 million buying back its own shares in the largest repurchase operation in the UK since GEC's giant share buy-back in the mid-1980s. The share price immediately climbed higher, and shareholders over-tendered six-and-a-half times for the maximum amount of shares on offer (5.84% of the company's capital) by offering 38.65% of the company's share capital for cash. Later, the financial press agreed that the repurchase was timed well, skilfully executed and enhanced the company's future strategy.

This case was written by Paul Stonham as a basis for class discussion rather than to illustrate either effective or ineffective handling of an administrative situation. The case has been compiled from published sources. © Dr P. Stonham, EAP – European School of Management, Oxford, 1994.

At the time, Reuters' chairman, Sir Christopher Hogg, said:

> Reuters has been highly cash generative during the 1990s. The Board of
> Reuters has concluded that £350 million of its cash resources is surplus to
> immediate requirements and should be returned to shareholders by means of
> a share repurchase. Whilst the main purpose of the repurchase is to provide
> shareholders with the opportunity either to receive a cash distribution or to
> have an equivalent enhancement of their investment in Reuters, the Board
> believes that all shareholders will benefit from the repurchase since it should
> lead to an increase in Reuters' earnings per share.

Peter Job, Reuters' chief executive, commented:

> The Board's decision to reduce net cash balances through the proposed share
> repurchase follows a review of long-term requirements for capital for existing
> businesses, for internal investments in new programmes, and for acquisitions.
> A realistic assessment of the timing of these requirements indicated that a
> sizeable amount of Reuters' cash would continue to benefit profits only by
> virtue of being invested in money markets, and that current initiatives and
> plans could comfortably be funded from Reuters' substantial financial reserves
> and future cash flows.

What were the real motives for this disposal of apparently excess cash?
Why did Reuters, supported by its financial advisers, choose the innovative
repurchase route rather than an alternative method of returning the cash?
Were there losers as well as gainers among its shareholders? What were
analysts' and the stock market's subsequent perception of the restructured
company? These, and other questions, are addressed in this case study.

The Company's Economic Position

Reuters is a giant in its sector – international financial information and news
media. Its financial information products cover currencies, stocks, bonds,
futures, options and other financial instruments. This category accounts for
75% of total revenue (end-1992 results). It also, includes software and
systems for financial information. Reuters' two main other product
categories are: money transactions – the means by which customers use
electronic terminals to trade foreign exchange, futures and options, and
securities – and media – news, news graphics and pictures, and television
news. Transactions make up 18% of total revenue, and media 7%. Exhibits
11.1 and 11.2 show Reuters' profit and loss account and balance sheet,
respectively, for the years 1990–92.

Exhibit 11.1 *Reuters Plc consolidated profit and loss account for the years 1990–92*

For the year ended 31 December	1992 £m	1991 £m	1990 £m
Revenue	**1,567.6**	1,466.6	1,369.0
Operating costs	**(1,251.1)**	(1,176.1)	(1,081.1)
Operating profit before interest	**316.5**	290.5	287.9
Net interest receivable	**66.3**	49.6	30.4
Profit before associated undertakings	**382.8**	340.1	318.3
Profit from associated undertakings	**0.4**	0.2	1.8
Profit on ordinary activities before taxation	**383.2**	340.3	320.1
Taxation on profit on ordinary activities	**(122.6)**	(110.6)	(111.7)
Profit on ordinary activities after taxation	**260.6**	229.7	208.4
Minority interest	**0.2**	(0.1)	(1.3)
Profit before extraordinary item	**260.8**	229.6	207.1
Extraordinary item	**(24.6)**	–	–
Profit attributable to ordinary shareholders	**236.2**	229.6	207.1
Dividends	**(89.8)**	(71.5)	(62.9)
Retained profit	**146.4**	158.1	144.2
Earnings per ordinary share:			
Before extraordinary item	**61.8**	54.7	49.5
After extraordinary item	**56.0**	54.7	49.5

Source: Annual Report 1992.

The company is worldwide market leader in real-time and historic information and other services in foreign exchange, money and capital markets, with a market share of 47%. It also leads in money transaction services, with over 90% of the market, and dominates products for the equities markets (28% market share) having acquired the large US equities database Quotron from Citicorp in January 1994. The other companies in equity services are ADP, which holds 21% market share, Quick (11.5%) and Telekurs (10.5%). In commodities, Reuters comes second with 20% after Knight Ridler (22.5%), but ahead of Bonneville (13%). In energy and shipping it is the market leader with 63%.

Exhibit 11.2 *Reuters Plc consolidated balance sheet for the years 1990–92*

At 31 December	1992 £m	1991 £m	1990 £m
Fixed assets			
Tangible assets	494.4	485.1	527.1
Investments	1.8	1.6	1.7
	496.2	486.7	528.8
Current assets			
Stocks	16.8	20.0	21.4
Debtors	260.4	146.0	176.4
Short-term investments	699.8	481.5	207.8
Cash at bank and in hand	57.5	51.9	46.6
	1,034.5	699.4	452.2
Creditors: Amounts falling due within one year	(615.1)	(410.4)	(371.7)
Net current assets	419.4	289.0	80.5
Total assets less current liabilities	915.6	775.7	609.3
Creditors: Amounts falling due after more than one year	(25.9)	(30.0)	(27.0)
Provisions for liabilities and charges			
Pensions and similar obligations	(16.4)	(14.9)	(13.6)
Deferred taxation	(6.9)	(13.9)	(19.5)
Net assets	866.4	716.9	549.2
Capital and reserves			
Called-up share capital	43.8	43.6	43.4
Share premium account	36.0	24.2	17.1
Profit and loss account reserve	914.0	668.7	436.6
Goodwill elimination reserve	(153.7)	(138.4)	(138.4)
Other reserves	110.8	200.6	272.1
Shareholders' equity	950.9	798.7	630.8
Interest in shares of Reuters Holding Plc	(82.1)	(82.1)	(82.1)
Loan to Employee Share Ownership Trust	(2.5)	(1.5)	(1.5)
	866.3	715.1	547.2
Minority interest	0.1	1.8	2.0
Capital employed	866.4	716.9	549.2

Source: Annual Report 1992.

By the end of 1992, Reuters appeared to have some of the features of a mature company. In that year's annual report, the chairman referred to a process of consolidation. Up to then, the company had experienced very rapid growth, for example in the five years between 1988 and end-1992, turnover grew at less than one-quarter of the rate achieved in the previous five years, and within that period revenue growth slowed between 1990 and 1992 compared with the previous three years. This deceleration in sales growth had several causes: increasingly difficult trading conditions, greater competition, the deliberate shedding of peripheral business and the difficulty of maintaining percentage growth rates.

In 1992, Reuters held prices stable for the first time, to support customers' cost control (in 1991, one-third of revenue growth was due to price increases). Also, in 1992, favourable exchange rate movements accounted for around one-third of total revenue growth (sterling weakened against major currencies by 15% following its exit from the Exchange Rate Mechanism in September 1992). This emphasises the weaker contribution of trading revenue unadjusted for currency translation.

Reuters is looking closely at cost control in the situation of a relatively mature market. By modernising its operations, overall costs grew marginally slower than revenue in 1992, after rising 2% faster than revenue in the previous year. A high proportion of Reuters' costs are fixed, particularly staff, computer systems and supporting infrastructure costs.

The company's operating margins have declined from a high of 22.4% in 1989. Since that date, growth in both revenues and costs slowed and margins were depressed by rationalisation provisions. The 1991 and 1992 margins were further reduced by higher depreciation – in the past previous five years Reuters invested heavily in capital spending (£975 million). Despite this, the 1992 operating margin rose to 20.2% compared with 19.8% in 1991.

Dividends have tended to follow the pattern suggested by Ward (1993) for a mature business, and the company's practice in recent years has been to increase dividends ahead of earnings per share growth. In 1992, this trend accelerated, and dividend cover was reduced to below three for the first time (Exhibit 11.3). Book value per ordinary share rose by 20% in 1992 as retained profits expanded the assets base. In the five years to end-1992, Reuters' equity base trebled to £950 million. Profits also grew substantially during this period but not at the same rate. Consequently, return on equity has declined.

Reuters has considerable strengths and resources that are not recognised in its consolidated balance sheet, e.g. goodwill attached to the company's name, invulnerability to take-over by structural defence, intellectual property, and global telecommunications, business operations and a database of financial information.

Exhibit 11.3 *Reuters' financial ratios 1988–92*

Ratios	1992	1991	1990	1989	1988
Earnings per ordinary share	61.8p	54.7p	49.5p	43.6p	30.3p
Dividends per ordinary share	21.2p	17.0p	15.0p	13.0p	9.0p
Cash flow per ordinary share[1]	134.5p	126.7p	109.8p	94.4p	73.3p
Book value per ordinary share[2]	204.8p	170.9p	131.6p	98.1p	65.8p
Cash flow/book value[3]	65.7%	74.2%	83.5%	96.2%	111.4%
Profit before tax as a percentage of revenue	24.4%	23.2%	23.4%	23.8%	20.7%
Return on tangible fixed assets[4]	53.2%	45.4%	41.3%	40.9%	37.2%
Return on equity[5]	29.9%	36.2%	43.2%	53.6%	51.8%
UK corporation tax rate	33.0%	33.25%	35.0%	35.0%	35.0%

Source: Annual Report 1992.
1. Cash flow per ordinary share represents profit before taxation and depreciation divided by the number of shares in issue after deducting shares of Reuters Holdings Plc held by group companies and by the Employee Share Ownership Trust.
2. Book value per ordinary share represents adjusted shareholders' equity divided by the number of shares in issue after deducting shares of Reuters Holdings Plc held by group companies and by Employee Share Ownership Trust. Adjusted shareholders' equity is calculated after deducting interest in shares of Reuters Holdings Plc and loan to Employee Share Ownership Trust.
3. Cash flow/book value represents profit before taxation and depreciation as a percentage of adjusted shareholders' equity.
4. Return on tangible fixed assets represents profit after taxation as a percentage of average tangible fixed assets. The average is calculated by adding tangible fixed assets at the start and the end of each year and dividing by two.
5. Return on equity represents profit attributable to ordinary shareholders (after deducting extraordinary item) divided by the average adjusted shareholders' equity. The average is calculated by adding adjusted shareholders' equity at the start and end of each year and dividing by two.

Ward also talks of medium to high price/earnings (P/E) multiples for mature businesses and high earnings per share (EPS). In theory, he maintains that a mature business should sustain its strong market share, have reduced business risk (compared with an earlier growth phase), have positive net cash flow, a high dividend pay-out ratio, a high EPS, and reducing P/E multiples (the latter because growth prospects should now be modest). The share price should be stable in real terms and the company able to fund itself out of retained earnings.

Reuters fits this model partially. At end-1992 its EPS was high (61.8p) and increasing (54.7p in 1991 and 49.5p in 1990). Pre-tax profits were rising well and dividends high and rising. Nevertheless, Reuters' share price rose steadily between 1990 and 1992 in absolute terms, in relation to its sector and relative to the FT All-Share Index. This reflected the better growth prospects which might have been expected from a mature business. The company pushed into new areas in 1992 as a result of buoyant financial markets, making the year the busiest ever for new products and product enhancement. For example, phase 2 of Dealing 2000, a system for matching buy and sell orders in foreign exchange, was introduced in the UK, USA, Continental Europe, Tokyo, Hong Kong and Singapore. GLOBEX, a system that matches buy and sell orders for financial futures and options was launched by the Chicago Mercantile Exchange and the Chicago Board of Trade. There are many other examples. The company has growth prospects based on geographic expansion, new technology and penetration of new financial and business markets. In line with Ward's model, Reuters' P/E multiple fell from 30.6 in 1990, through 27.7 in 1991, to 24.5 in 1992, indicating that strong earlings growth outpaced even rising share price.

The final feature that fits Ward's model well is Reuters' cash position. Reuters has been a strongly cash-generative company for some time (Exhibit 11.4). From a £217 million cash balance in 1990, the total rose to £503 million in 1991, and £710 million in 1992. Cash flow per ordinary share rose from 73.8p in 1988 to 109.8p in 1990, and 134.5p in 1992.[1] The company funds its business largely from internally-generated cash. It has a £200 million multiple-option facility with a group of banks to provide flexibility in the management of the group's liquidity.

According to Ward's model, the reduction of business risk faced by a mature company, together with high net cash flow, should allow it to compensate through increased financial risk by using debt funding for reinvestment. This has not been the case with Reuters, which has no debt on its balance sheet.

Reuters' image as a 'mature' company is also qualified by its recent acquisition policy. Handing back £350 million to shareholders in 1993 may seem to reduce the capability for acquisitions, but this has not been the case. Not only was nearly half the 1993 cash balance retained in the company after the share repurchase, but the chairman stated specifically in his 1992 report that Reuters should not be 'cash constrained in exploiting opportunities for long-term growth'. Excessive cash, on the other hand, could lead to the temptation of an excessively ambitious acquisitions policy.

In fact, the *Financial Times* of 18 January 1994 headlined Reuters' 'aggressive return to the acquisition trail' with the news of its purchase of the screen-based financial information business Quotron from Citicorp. Reuters' acquisitions have never really stopped: in August 1993, it bought 90% of

Exhibit 11.4 *Analysis of Reuters' net cash balances 1990–92*

	1992 £m	1991 £m	1990 £m	Change 1992 £m	Change 1991 £m
Short-term investments	699.8	481.5	207.8	218.3	273.7
Cash at bank and in hand	57.5	51.9	46.6	5.6	5.3
Banking borrowings:					
Falling due within one year	(21.2)	(7.7)	(16.0)	(13.5)	(8.3)
Falling due after more than one year	(19.4)	(16.2)	(16.6)	(3.2)	0.4
Other borrowings	(4.0)	(1.3)	–	(2.7)	(1.3)
Finance leases:					
Falling due within one year	(0.6)	(1.9)	(1.9)	1.3	–
Falling due after more than one year	(2.3)	(3.4)	(2.8)	1.1	(0.6)
	709.8	502.9	217.1	206.9	285.8

(Cash balances rose 41.1% in 1992)

Source: Annual Report 1992.

Future Pager, the UK provider of pocket information; in November it acquired VAMP Health a private company supplying computer facilities to about two thousand UK doctors; in December it took a 20% stake in Safetynet, a UK computer back-up service. Again in December it bought a minority stake in AdValue Technologies, a New York company providing interactive services to advertising companies, and at the end of the same month it purchased Telekron Software Systems of California. These are not the normal strategic moves of a mature company, even if most of the acquisitions could be said to be an extension of Reuters' core business.

The Tender Offer

Reuters announced on 26 July 1993 that it proposed repurchasing up to 5.84% of its issued shares (totalling 25 million) at a price of £14 per share or the US dollar equivalent of £42 per American Depository Share (ADS), which turned out to be $63 per ADS. If the tender offer were to be fully taken up, the repurchase consideration would total approximately

£350 million. The tender offer opened on 28 July and closed on 25 August. Settlement date was to be 13 September in the UK and 15 September in the USA.

All holders of shares and ADSs were invited to sell their shares to Reuters, to a maximum of 5.84% of his/her beneficial holding. Shareholders could tender in excess of this amount which would be accepted to the extent that other shareholders did not tender the whole of their 'entitled amounts'. Such tenders would be accepted *pro rata* to the excess. Reuters indicated it would accept tenders only if a special resolution were passed in favour of the proposed repurchase by an extraordinary general meeting of shareholders (this in fact took place on 10 September). The tender offer was also conditional on a minimum of 4.25 million shares (approximately 1% of Reuters' issued ordinary shares) being received. Accepting shareholders were entitled to the July interim dividend of 6.2p net in respect of the shares tendered. Of course, they could elect not to offer all or part of their shares for sale, in which case their relative holding in the company would increase since Reuters was obliged by law to cancel the repurchased shares.

Tax Implications

The tax consequences of the share repurchase for shareholders were critical, and fairly complex overall. In addition to the purchase price there was, in general, a tax credit of approximately £3.21 (£9.63 per ADS) attaching to each share purchased. Certain UK shareholders were able to obtain a refund of this tax credit. Some US shareholders were entitled to a refund (less a 15% withholding tax) in respect of the credit, which was converted into US dollars and paid at the same time as the purchase price.

In the UK, companies pay advance corporation tax (ACT) on dividends distributed on shares (25% at the time of the share repurchase). This gives rise to a tax credit to those receiving dividends so they do not pay the tax twice. In the case of the Reuters' share repurchase, the Inland Revenue agreed that £1.16 per share bought back at £14 would be treated as a capital repayment, and therefore subject to capital gains tax. The balance of £12.84 per share was treated as a 'distribution', (i.e. equivalent to a dividend), thereby creating a tax credit of £3.21 (25% of £12.84).

The impact of the tax credit was different for different classes of shareholder. For gross income shareholders, such as individual non-taxpayers, and tax-exempt institutional funds, such as charities and pension funds, the whole of the tax credit was repayable, making the share offer worth £17.21. Around 35% of Reuters' equity was held by such funds.

In the case of individual UK shareholders, the tax credit would fully cover liability to income tax if the individual was a basic-rate taxpayer only (25%); there was no further tax to pay. If the shareholder was a higher-rate payer (40%), s/he would have to pay £3.21, or 20% of the income element and tax credit (£16.05) to bring him/her up to 40% of the gross amount.

UK-resident corporate shareholders were treated as receiving investment income equal to the total of the income element and tax credit. It was not subject to UK corporation tax, and the shareholder was able to reclaim the associated tax credit in certain circumstances. The value of the tax credit could even be increased (to 9/31) of the income element if the UK-resident corporate shareholders had in turn to pay ACT on dividends in the accounting period in which the investment income was received. There could, however, be a capital gains charge.

American shareholders (both individual and corporate) received a tax refund of the tax credit of £3.21 minus UK withholding tax of 15% of £16.05 (i.e. £12.84 + 3.21) which meant a net payment of £14.80. The US tax position was complex to say the least. American tax exempt institutional funds received more, but did not benefit to the same extent as UK tax exempt funds. It is estimated that 35% of Reuters' shareholders are American.

Benefits to Shareholders

The actual benefits to shareholders of the repurchase were complicated to work out for all but gross income funds. Although the main initial benefit came from the ACT credit, there were other factors to take into account. For example, unlike the normal UK repurchase situation, investors were allowed to buy into Reuters' shares during the offer period to qualify for the repurchase. This is similar to the American position where the record date by which shareholders had to be on the record to qualify is at the end of the offer period. There was, of course, doubt about how many existing investors would tender and how many new investors would enter the market. The strength of the interest of existing investors and new investors could affect the share price.

However, a new investor could only *guarantee* getting 5.84% of his or her shares repurchased as a result of the tender. The tax credit benefit was not worth going in for and buying up the market – even if those tendering did get more than 5.84% repurchased as a result of other shareholders not tendering, the excess was not likely to be much. The extent of the leverage involved meant that for every £100 worth of Reuters' shares bought, there was a *guarantee* of only 5.84% being repurchased and therefore being eligible for the tax credit.

Another unknown element before the repurchase operation began was the extent to which shareholders would tender all or part of their shareholding and then buy back their shares, perhaps to maintain their portfolio weighting in Reuters' stock. To the extent that this occurred, the share price would increase since Reuters' shares would be in shorter supply by 25 million shares.

The kind of calculation a new, tax exempt, investing institution (like a pension fund) would go through is as follows. For shares bought on the first day after the share repurchase, it would not be worth paying up to £17.20 because the investor could not guarantee that every share purchased would be repurchased. Supposing the investor took the view that 40% of all shareholders (mostly tax exempt funds) would tender all their shares. This meant that the investor would probably have one in eight (rather than one in twenty) shares repurchased. So two-and-a-half times 5% is in effect the maximum number of shares that the new investor could get repurchased. Therefore, the institutions could afford to pay up to 40p extra for each of eight shares at the offer price because one of them was going to be repurchased at a benefit of £3.20. In fact, the £350 million share buy-back was heavily oversubscribed, the company receiving tenders totalling 164.34 million shares (38%) for the offer of 25 million shares.

Similarly, a tax exempt institution could well decide that if the market price for the share was, say, £16, and it received £17.21 back for the share, it would happily reinvest in the share in order to return its weighting to the correct number – with the £1.21 benefit in effect coming from the government.

The financial press noted that, if the UK shareholders received a small or zero benefit via the tax credit, many would find the offer unattractive since they could sell their shares at prices higher than the £14 offer under the repurchase agreement, assuming, as everyone did, that the price would appreciate quickly following the repurchase announcement.

For US shareholders, benefits were smaller. Since their tax credit was limited to around 80p, the buy-back was unprofitable once Reuters' share price passed £14.80, which it did quite quickly.

In the case of UK and US shareholders who did not tender any of their shares, there was the benefit of now owning a relatively larger portion of the company's total shares, and of expecting to receive higher EPS assuming earnings did not drop in the foreseeable future, merely because there would be fewer shares to divide into the earnings pay-out.

Finally, shareholders could not be sure about the future behaviour of the share price, in particular whether the repurchase represented a 'signal' on the part of Reuters that the share was undervalued, and investors could expect capital gain in the future. Then there were various other factors like the recent sterling devaluation, bullish reports on the company's prospects, and so on.

Reuters' Motivations

The financial press had a field day trying to interpret the reasons that Reuters should hand back cash to shareholders. Whilst most commentators were favourably inclined, even seeing the act as a courageous one, others had more negative comments, although it must be said these were rather naive.

The *Financial Times* implied that if managers could not spend cash sensibly, they should be replaced by more imaginative types. In this newspaper's case, the criticism was reinforced by its doubts about the company's long-term growth prospects. *The Express* inquired where the money came from and commented that Reuters must have failed if it could amass so much cash – it could be accused of charging too much for its products and services.

In fact, Reuters' financial policy has been one of caution, and this had partly caused the build-up of cash. Dividend cover has been low and falling in recent years, from 3.5 in 1989 to 2.9 in 1992. At the same time, its annual cash flow has been high, leading to steeply rising net cash balances (from £20 million in 1989 to £710 million in 1992).

The chairman's 1993 statement set out the first major reason for the share buy-back: using cash excess to immediate requirements to benefit shareholders. However, this needs further questioning: why was it done at all, at this time, and in this manner?

There is no doubt that the repurchase was something of a signal, that Reuters intended to apply financial discipline and financial management to its large cash holdings. It would not be distracted by acquisitions outside its core business simply because it had the cash available. As we have seen, the company continued a policy of acquisition, buying companies and products closely allied to its existing core business. It is in the nature of Reuters' business that it requires much more in the way of capital investment than acquisitions. It is a seed corn and organic investment business. Most acquisitions the company has undertaken have contained a high element of goodwill.

Its acquisition policy is related to the nature of its business, which is people- and software-intensive rather than hardware- and asset-intensive. Reuters therefore believes it wiser to buy-in talent or make small bolt-on acquisitions rather than to make large acquisitions. Therefore a major signal was that Reuters was not a company that was going to diversify from its core business. In fact, the company had some £360 million remaining in net cash for acquisitions (and other activities) and had clear prospects of continuing high levels of cash flow in 1993 and beyond, which would satisfy any investment and acquisition requirements.

The second reason for the cash disposal was really a question of return. The company argued that shareholders were incurring an opportunity cost in allowing cash to remain on Reuters' balance sheet. At the time of the repurchase, base rate was little more than 5%. Interest rates might even fall further in the future, although the company had hedged extensively against that possibility. It certainly did not make sense for the company either to act as a bank or to be satisfied with low money market rates of return. In addition, building cash on the balance sheet would have an adverse effect on the performance of the company measured in terms of EPS.

An important factor in motivating Reuters to return cash was the fact that it had no debt on its balance sheet. In fact, Reuters had reverse gearing, and by reducing the amount of cash on its balance sheet, it reduced the negative gearing. There was therefore no question of altering the relative capital mix to the disadvantage of a class of shareholder. It gave Reuters a certain degree of comfort in returning the cash since it had a significant debt *capacity*, i.e. the ability to borrow should it need to do so.

In theory, there are advantages to a company having debt on its balance sheet – depending on which business it is in – since it would normally enjoy a better return on capital than a company not in this position. However, Reuters has never been penalised by having a 'better' capital mix, mainly because it has grown very fast and been able to use a lot of capital as a tax shield through its capital investment programme. Also, its key ratios suffered less in recession than those of companies with leverage. It was never the intention of Reuters to use debt as an alternative to cash as a form of financing. In general terms, there is less flexibility for moving leverage around by playing with the equity line in the UK than there is in the USA because of the tax dimension in the former. UK companies like Reuters are constrained by their tax capacity in capital restructuring.

Companies with large net cash balances could, in theory, be attractive take-over targets. However, this is not the case with Reuters. The company's share capital includes a founder's share of £1 which is held by Reuters' Founder's Share Company Limited. It empowers the Founder's Share Company to oppose and defeat any resolution seeking to obtain control of Reuters (control defined for this purpose as 30% of the votes at an AGM). The protection was built into the articles of agreement of the company to protect the neutrality of Reuters' provision of news and financial information. Although this offers some protection in the current market, it is still not certain that the company could survive a strongly hostile bid. However, another defence is offered by the company's P/E multiple and the high cost of acquisition. Protection against take-over was not a likely motivation for Reuters' repurchase.

A common motive for US companies to buy back shares is because they believe their shares to be undervalued. American companies are also allowed to offer a premium on share repurchases. Thus they wish to signal a price correction and *also* wish to acquire their shares at higher prices, because these become assets of the company in the form of treasury stock, i.e. they are not cancelled (as in the UK).

Alternative Means of Cash Disposal

Reuters and its advisers considered other forms of financial engineering to manage the reduction of its large net cash balance, in particular a special dividend. The disadvantage was the likely effect on EPS and analysts' perceptions of EPS declining in the future. Also, a special dividend meant that all shareholders would receive cash whether they wanted it or not, and many would be victims of the tax system depending on their individual tax positions. The share repurchase provided a choice for everyone – cash or enhanced EPS as a result of shareholders' percentage share in the company increasing. The fact that a large percentage of Reuters' shareholders were American (around 35%) also favoured a share repurchase. American institutions are much more familiar with share buy-backs and, although, the tax regime was less favourable than in Europe, it was still preferable to a special dividend.

An open-market repurchase was also considered, as an alternative to a tender offer, but rejected. Reuters was anxious to ensure that the repurchase was as tax-efficient as possible for shareholders, and open-market repurchases are not directed to existing shareholders, i.e. they are unfocused. The exercise was motivated strongly by enhancing shareholder value. As far as individual shareholders were concerned, the tender offer ensured they had easy access to the offer, and did not have to go through brokers, pay commissions and set up accounts as they would have had to do in the case of an open market offer.

Performance and Assessment

Reuters had intended to make its announcement about the share repurchase on the same day as it made public its interim results (Tuesday, 27 July 1993). However, increasing press speculation which had reached a highpoint on the previous Friday, persuaded the company to lance the speculation and make its announcement on Monday, 26 July. Dividing the announcement and presentation of the interim results proved a wise move. The repurchase announcement became more digestible.

The stock market reacted to the announcement with an immediate jump in price. On Friday, 23 July the stock price was £14.04; on Monday, 26 July at the close it was £14.40: an increase of 2.5%. The stock continued rising strongly too; a week later it stood at £15.48, an increase of 9% (see Exhibit 11.5).

The question arises: did Reuters' shares benefit from any 'abnormal return' as a result of the repurchase? (Abnormal return being defined in relation to some benchmark like the FTSE All-Share Index.) It would be possible to test statistically for the price effect of the repurchase by comparing daily total returns for Reuters' shares with the FT All-Share

Exhibit 11.5   *Reuters Holdings Plc share price from 23 July 1993 to 1 November 1993*

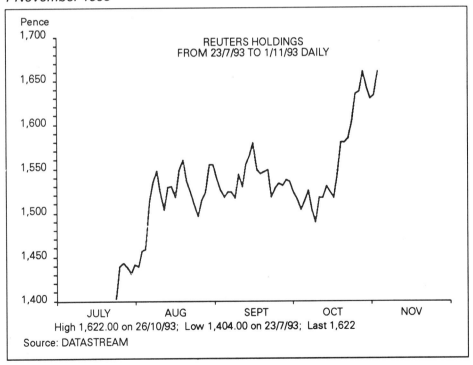

Source: DATASTREAM

Index, but it is not attempted here since in this case it is almost impossible to isolate the buy-back from other market features current at the time. Any statistical result which could not eliminate extraneous factors would be misleading. In addition, only 5.84% of the stock was being repurchased – this was hardly enough to have had a dramatic effect on stock prices. Other features of the situation which are not known are: What proportion of existing shareholders did not participate? What proportion of the stock sales were from new investors? What proportion of existing shareholders sold and then bought back again? Reuters' case is complicated by the benefit or worth of the sizeable tax credit, and its impact on different classes of investors. The 1993 interim results were released the day following the share repurchase announcement; this was an unusual combination of events. Although econometric testing may give some indication of abnormality around the announcement date and at the close of offer date, it is not likely to be instructive in the case of Reuters.

The company does not take a short-term view of shareholder value (this is stated in the chairman's 1993 interviews with the press). Reuters would not have considered a share repurchase in order to push up its share price by X amount – the kind of consideration believed to be important in US share buy-backs. The tax credit aspect was important in Reuters' external considerations; here was an opportunity to return excess cash in a tax-efficient manner. To judge whether the repurchase was successful or not on the basis of a two-to-three months' after-market in the shares would be dangerous. The company wanted to enhance shareholder value in the medium term, i.e. more than one year. With this consideration in mind, it becomes clear that the longer the period of study taken (from the buy-back event), the more important become the other factors in influencing Reuters' share price.

When Reuters' 1993 results were released in February 1994 it was clear that 1993 was a strong year. Revenue rose by 20% to £1,874 million (8% with sterling depreciation stripped out), pre-tax profits increased by 15% to £440 million and the total dividend was up 23% to 26p. Earnings per share rose by 29% from 56p to 72p, but are more accurately calculated as increasing 16p from 61.8p since earnings in 1993 were restated and adjusted for a one-off tax settlement. New cash at £450 million showed a decline from the £710 million reported at the end of 1992, but, since £350 million was spent on the share repurchase, and other sums on accelerated capital spending and acquisitions, it is clear that 1992 saw a strong cash flow to end the year at £450 million.

Reuters' share price took several jumps following the share repurchase as the market reacted to events. One was the purchase in January 1994 of

Quotron, the US financial information data service owned by Citicorp. As analysts became convinced that Reuters was serious in its bid, the shares advanced 64p on 23 December to £18.80. Then, with the announcement of 1993 year-end results and a share split of four-for-one on 8 February 1994, the share price leaped from £19.11 to close the day at £19.71 on heavy turnover. It is clear that the price effects of the share repurchase quickly became obscured by other developments which caused market reaction.

The Lessons Drawn

The strong message that comes across from Reuters' 1993 share repurchase is that the financial manoeuvre was typical of this cautious company, with a tradition of tight financial management, taking a medium- to long-term view of its business and financial strategy, and having high regard to shareholder value. The company was, and continues to be, earnings-driven rather than dividend-driven, and its choice of buy-back over special dividend was dictated by the wish to maximise the tax credit benefits of the buy-back to shareholders. The timing of the move was decided by the size of the company's net cash balance, the amount of unexhausted tax credits and the external strategy of the company combined with expectations of strong continuing cash flow.

Short-term considerations of share price were not paramount. More important were investor and analyst perceptions of the company's growth prospects even in a mature business. This is why the P/E multiple was still standing at a racy 27 in February 1994, and why the share price did not fall back after the offer period expired. Reuters absorbed the cost of the buy-back, enhanced the market's perception of the company, and increased EPS without deflecting it from its internal investment and external growth strategies.

However, the exercise could be difficult for other companies to imitate. For Reuters, the manoeuvre was a highly pragmatic one. It benefited from its financial advisers, especially the American experience of J.P. Morgan, the successful but delicate negotiations with the Inland Revenue, and good judgement in timing. For other companies, the balance of business risk and financial risk is unlikely to be the same as Reuters'. There are many contemporary examples of UK companies possessing large net cash balances, like Boots, Glaxo and Wellcome, which have followed, or are following, quite different routes to dispose of them and are making different judgements on strategy.

Finally, the environment which favours share repurchases of this type may grow more hostile in the future. The nature of ACT could change or the UK rules on share repurchases become less favourable. At the time of Reuters' share repurchase, a pragmatic judgement was made which appears to have maximised benefit to the company and its shareholders and which has a great deal to do with skilful financial management.

Note

1.   Cash flow per ordinary share represents profit before taxation and depreciation divided by the number of shares in issue after deducting shares of Reuters Holdings Plc held by group companies and by the Employee Share Ownership Trust.

Reference

Keith Ward (1993) *Corporate Financial Strategy*. Butterworth/Heinemann.

Evode Group plc

What is the value of a business? This is a fundamental question faced all too frequently in practice and for which there is no easy answer – it all depends upon the perspective taken. This case study reviews the question of value with reference to the acquisition of Evode plc by Laporte plc. Evode's share price prior to any acquisitive interest had been between 50 and 60p. Eventually Laporte paid 120p per share for the company. This case study serves to demonstrate how the price paid for Evode may well be seen to be justifiable from the acquirer's perspective. It is achieved using a discounted cash flow model evaluation known as shareholder value analysis.

Objectives

The Evode case is based on events in December 1992 and January 1993 which led to the acquisition of the Evode Group by Laporte. The case provides students with the opportunity to understand some important issues surrounding the acquisition, and to view the acquisition from the seller's and buyer's perspective.

The objectives of the case are:

1. To develop competence in applying financial analysis techniques for purposes of strategic assessment, like acquisition analysis.
2. To demonstrate how to use published information in determining future cash flows.
3. To demonstrate how to apply the general principles of shareholder value analysis (SVA) to determine the value of a company.
4. To understand the benefits of economic- versus accounting-based methods of valuation.
5. To learn to use financial management tools for strategic assessment and to support the decision-making process.

The case study assumes that a number of areas which are critical to the understanding of the acquisition process will have been covered prior to this session. These areas are:

1. Extracting data from annual reports.
2. Key business ratios for:
   ● valuation analysis;
   ● trend analysis.
3. Basic principles of forecasting.
4. Free cash flow analysis.
5. Discounted cash flow analysis.

Background

In the new year of 1993, the chairman of the Evode Group, Andrew Simon, faced the prospect of having to mount a credible defence of his company against a hostile bid from the mini-conglomerate Wassall, with more than a little apprehension.

The Evode Group was a small multinational organisation which had experienced considerable growth since the second half of the 1980s through acquisition, while its turnover grew from £95.8 million (1987) to £279 million (1991). Evode's businesses were broadly grouped in the speciality and industrial chemicals sector, and organised in five divisions:

1. Adhesives and sealants
2. Industrial coatings.
3. North American – primarily polymer compounds.
4. Plastics.
5. Chamberlain Phipps – footwear materials and components.

Mr Simon had been in some difficulty since he had announced the 1991 results at the beginning of the previous year. He had to report a nearly flat turnover performance, actually down 6% from 1990, and profit before tax down 52% to £7.3 million (£15.2 million, 1990) which after tax, extraordinary items and dividend payments resulted in a loss of £1.8 million.

Evode's poor position had resulted from a number of factors:

1. Over-exposure to the recession-hit white goods and construction sectors in the UK.
2. Its international markets, primarily the USA and EC, were affected by the worldwide economic downturn.

3. Overpaying for the acquisition of US company Chamberlain Phipps in 1989.
4. The burden created by a high level of fixed payment capital to finance the acquisition.
5. Poor management, which saw reasonably high gross margins reduce to an average operating margin of around 2% on 1991 figures.

All of this left Evode's management with little credibility.

Evode's share price had slumped to a low of 43p in August 1992 but was beginning to climb again following successful rationalisation, cost-cutting and marketing initiatives, to around the mid-fifties.

This view of the company's share price can be reconciled with a valuation undertaken using a discounted cash flow (SVA) model based upon published data shown in Exhibit 12.1. The following information was taken into consideration in determining this valuation:

- *Sales growth forecast*: 1992 figures suggests some signs of the recession lifting, and in particular strong growth in the North American polymer compound sector. In general sales growth will tend to be slow to flat until the recession ends and even then the effect may be lagged until core markets themselves grow. In 1992 Evode divested its footwear components business (Chamberlain Phipps division) thus reducing its UK-originated turnover by £31.6 million.

- *Operating profit margin forecast*: average margins had improved to 5.7% in 1992 results. Divisional analysis suggests that the polymer business already has margins in double figures and adhesives and sealants have high gross margins which are being eroded. So Evode's turnaround strategy must seek to achieve a target industry average of 10–12% medium term. In the industrial coatings division Evode will be forced to keep margins low by the intense competition and depressed state of the market.

- *Fixed capital investment forecast*: Evode needs to balance its requirement to continue to invest in its successful businesses and restructure those that are not successful to produce higher margins, with the burden of servicing its debt. Therefore, it is expected that Evode's total fixed capital investment will not exceed the depreciation estimate for the five-year period in line with its current policy. In fact, total fixed capital expenditure for replacement in the next 5 years has been estimated at £5 million, £5.5 million, £6.1 million, £7.3 million and £8.7 million, respectively. Replacement capital

Exhibit 12.1 *SVA valuation of Evode (£m)*

	Historical	Forecast					Residual
	1992	1993	1994	1995	1996	1997	
Sales	239.9	241.30	243.20	249.30	258.20	267.70	267.70
Operating profit		20.03	23.59	23.68	24.53	25.43	25.43
− Cash taxes (33%)		6.61	7.78	7.82	8.09	8.39	8.39
+ Depreciation		7.10	7.50	7.90	8.40	8.90	9.50
Operating cash flow		20.52	23.31	23.77	24.83	25.94	
− Incremental working capital investment[1]		0.31	0.42	1.34	1.96	2.09	0.00
− Incremental fixed capital investment[2]		0	0	0	0	0	0
− Replacement fixed capital investment		5.00	5.50	6.10	7.30	8.70	9.50
= Free cash flow		15.21	7.39	16.33	15.58	15.15	17.04
Cost of capital (discount factor)		1.1176	1.249	1.3959	1.5601	1.7435	
= Present value of free cash flows		13.61	13.92	11.70	9.98	8.69	

Cumulative present value of free cash flows	57.90
+ Present value of residual value[3]	83.11
= Corporate value	141.01
− Market value of debt and pref. shares	107.51
= Shareholder value	33.50
Shareholder value per share (divided by 72.71m)	0.46

1. To calculate the incremental working capital investment, multiply the forecast percentage by incremental sales.
2. To calculate the incremental fixed capital investment, multiply the forecast percentage by incremental sales. Replacement fixed capital is required to cover the cost of maintaining the existing plant and equipment.
3. To calculate the residual value, take the residual period free cash flow, i.e. where there is no sales growth, and divide by the cost of capital. Then use the discount factor for 1997 to calculate the present value of the residual value.

expenditure in the continuing period has been estimated as being £9.5 million.

● *Incremental working capital forecast*: this is another area which may benefit from tighter financial controls. However, the effect of new marketing initiatives and a severe competitive environment may force Evode into looser credit policies and higher-than-desired stock levels to maintain a good service which would force working capital expenditure up.

This information was used to generate the cash flow forecast in Exhibit 12.1, specifically via the following projections:

	1993	1994	1995	1996	1997
Sales growth (%)	0.6	0.8	2.5	3.5	3.7
Operating margin (%)	8.3	9.7	9.5	9.5	9.5
Incremental fixed capital investment (%)	0	0	0	0	0
Replacement fixed capital investment (%)	0	10	10	20	20
Incremental working capital investment (%)	22	22	22	22	22

The Lead-up to the Acquisition

On 20 November Wassall launched a hostile bid for Evode with a offer of 80p per share (£58.2 million). Wassall was run by three ex-Hanson men under the chairman Chris Miller, and had recently successfully acquired two other companies in the sealants and adhesives sector. Wassall saw Evode as a basically sound organisation, with strong market shares in UK adhesives and coatings and US plastics, which would benefit from both being unhampered by gearing and the introduction of a strong management team.

Analysts had forecast profits of £8.9 million and earnings of 3.2p for Evode in 1992, and this confirmed Wassall's view that the company would be in a poor position to fund new capital expenditure, redemption obligations, repay bank debt and pay preference and ordinary dividends. In contrast, its offer valued Evode at more than 25 times earnings and left Andrew Simon with little room to mount his defence. (On the announcement of the offer, Evode's shares jumped to 91p.)

In his defence document, presented to shareholders on 4 January 1993, Mr Simon claimed that Evode was back on the mend and announced a 40% rise in pre-tax profits to £10.2 million for 1992. However, many feared the worst as the document omitted to include a profit forecast for the current year. Evode's shares rose to 103p and Wassall announced that it was not willing to overpay for any acquisition.

The SVA assessment in Exhibit 12.1 suggesting a share price of 46p, confirmed that Evode had no options available to increase the group's value, otherwise the market would have recognised them and taken them into account. The two options that could have been considered were to:

1. increase operating cash flows, or
2. decrease the cost of capital.

Increase operating cash flows: this option was not readily open to Mr Simon in the midst of the world recession which was causing Evode's principal markets to contract, and a high level of cash outflows to meet debt repayments could not be avoided.

Decrease the cost of capital: this option also offered little or no scope as the company was already highly geared with no chance of attracting new equity investment at its current level of performance and no way of generating extra cash to repay its debt (1992 annual report revealed that divestments had only managed to raise £10 million).

Thus, the only strategic options seemed to be to sell the group or be acquired. But what was the right price to sell for? Evode's share price had already risen to 103p following the bid and Wassall had stated its unwillingness to overpay. The view expressed by one analyst was: 'A range of 100p (realistic) to 120p (maximum) would appear to be the right ball park.'

This price was determined by analysing comparable peer group companies using gross cash flow multiples (share price divided by operating profit plus depreciation, and interest received):

Peer group gross cash flow multiples

Allied Colloids	9.4
Brent Chemicals	5.4
British Vita	5.5
BTP	7.5
Croda International	6.0
Ellis & Everard	6.5
Hickson International	5.1
Wardle Storeys	9.0
Yorkshire Chemicals	9.0
Yule Catto	6.9
Average/mean	7.0

Cash flow multiples for Evode's peers in the sector were estimated as ranging from 5.4 to 9.4 with a mean of 7.0. Given recent difficulties it would be difficult to value Evode at the higher end of that range, particularly when its high gearing is taken into consideration (debt and preference shares estimated at over 20% and 35% of market value of capital employed, respectively in 1992). As a consequence this mean multiple has been used to produce the following estimated valuation of Evode's share price in which non-convertible preference share capital has been treated as debt. Convertible preference share capital has not been treated in the same manner. Although conversion looks a long-shot at present it cannot be ruled out and an allowance has been made for its conversion by way of a sinking fund to cover the potential liability of £40.7 million 9 years hence. This serves to reduce operating cash flow by £4.5 million p.a.

Evode gross cash flow multiple valuation

	£m
Operating profit	15.6
Depreciation	6.7
Interest received	0.2
Sinking fund	(4.5)
= Gross cash flow	18.0
= Gross cash flow per share	24.7p
× 7 multiple (*a*)	173.0p

	£m
Bank debt	28.5
Preference stock (US)	23.9
Less allowance for 25% gearing	(8.3)
= Total debt	44.1
= Debt per share (*b*)	60.6p
Valuation (*a*−*b*)	112.0p

Laporte – Rival Bid

On 6 January, Wassall revised its bid to 95p per share and on the same day Laporte, the UK's second largest chemical group, bought 6.1% of Evode's shares at 100p and announced its intention to make a bid above 100p. Laporte's announcement effectively outmanoeuvred what many thought would be Wassall's winning bid and allowed Evode to reject the 95p offer as inadequate.

Laporte's impending bid provided Evode with the opportunity of offering shareholders a good exit. But first Laporte had to come up with a new bid price, one which Evode would be able to recommend and be acceptable to Laporte's investors.

Laporte's appearance as white knight was no sudden move as CEO Ken Minton had been tracking Evode for seven years, first approaching Andrew Simon in 1986 and again in January 1992 following Evode's bad results.

Exhibit 12.2 *Assessment of Evode's business*

Adhesives and polymer compounds provide 'classic fit'
Ken Minton, Laporte's CEO, was reported to have claimed that Evode's two largest business sectors provided great potential for synergies from incorporation into Laporte's businesses.

Adhesives and sealants
Evode's operations have sales of £85 million from the construction and automotive sectors. Laporte already sells different adhesives to the construction sector and uses an alternative distribution network.

Polymer compounds
Although Laporte had no direct experience in this area, with sales of £85 million, the products all involved formulating chemicals (one of Laporte's strengths) and therefore also provided a good fit. The US operations were supplying high quality plastics to the food, medical and electronics sectors at good margins. The UK and Italian operations were in lower-margin markets and required repositioning.

Question marks remain over other businesses

Powder coatings
With sales of £20 million, this area was outside Laporte's expertise and its potential for margin improvement limited, therefore would be under immediate divestment consideration. Mr Minton said of the business, 'When I have to compete with big boys like these [ICI and Courtaulds], I start getting nervous.'

Plastic fabrication
Five operations with sales of £20 million were also less attractive to Laporte. Three operations – in the USA, UK and Italy – provided reasonable margins but the other two businesses required completely turning around.

Miscellaneous
Evode's remaining businesses, of which the vinyl coatings for wallpaper accounted for the majority of £40 million sales, provide no fit at all for Laporte.

Acquisition must enhance Laporte's earning in the first year
Ken Minton was committed to immediate returns from Evode and promised to tackle its margins as his first priority. In the 1980s Mr Minton improved Laporte's margins from 10% to nearly 15%.
   The improvement at Evode would come from:
   ● Better pricing policies.
   ● Extending product ranges.
   ● Reducing raw material costs.
   ● Improved manufacturing.
   ● Cutting overheads.
   ● Better marketing.
   ● Significant job losses.
Mr Minton denied the cost of rationalisation would affect earnings. Laporte had plenty of experience of cost-cutting and there would be few environmental costs.

Laporte had a strong management team and had experience in transforming a low margin bulk operation into a speciality chemicals company. Mr Minton and his team had a reputation for ruthless cost-cutting especially in non-core businesses, and had overseen the rise in Laporte's margins from 10% to 15% since 1986.

Laporte had five core businesses: organic chemicals, absorbents, metals and electronic chemicals, construction chemicals, and hygiene and process chemicals. Clear potential synergies were seen between some of these businesses and Evode. In fact, Ken Minton described the adhesive and polymer businesses as a 'classic fit'. (Exhibit 12.2 provides an anecdotal record of Laporte's assessment of Evode's business.)

As a result of detailed sector knowledge it was reckoned that the management of Laporte should be able to ensure that benefits from synergies could be achieved. Furthermore, it was believed that purchasing Evode need involve no dilution of earnings in the first year following acquisition.

Laporte offered, and subsequently paid, 120p for Evode, but was not prepared to assume any additional debt and, therefore, its offer consisted mainly of paper. The terms of its offer were:

- Twenty-three new Laporte shares for every 112 Evode shares, valuing them at 120p, or cash alternative of 115p.

- Five new Laporte shares for every 28 Evode convertible preference shares, valuing them at 104p, or cash alternative of 100p

Laporte raised £84.4 million (15.4 million new shares) via a placing and 1-for-10 open offer at 560p per share, 37.6 million new shares were issued in total. Thirty-four million shares replaced Evode's ordinary share capital, UK and US preference share capital and debt with immediate interest savings.

Laporte's shares fell 27p to 583p on announcement of the terms of the offer, having fallen 10% since the announcement of its intention to bid.

Exhibits 12.3 and 12.4 show estimates of Evode's cost of capital pre-acquisition and Laporte's cost of capital post-acquisition.

Exhibit 12.3 *Estimate of Evode's cost of capital pre-acquisition*

Beta (β)	1.53
Equity risk premium (ERP)	4%
Risk-free rate (Rf)	9.26%
Cost of equity: K$_e$ = Rf + (β x ERP)	15.38%
Cost of debt	11.055%
Cost of preference shares (K$_p$)	
US preference shares: estimated yield	7%
UK preference shares: estimated yield	10.1%

Weighted average cost of preference shares
Total value of preference shares £65.61m

$$\text{US preference shares} = \frac{40.754}{65.61} = 62\%$$

$$\text{UK preference shares} = \frac{24.855}{65.61} = 38\%$$

$$\mathbf{K_p} = \begin{array}{l} 62\% \times 7\% = 4.3\% \\ 38\% \times 10.1\% = \underline{3.84\%} \\ 8.14\% \end{array}$$

Capital structure

Equity =	Market capitalisation	=	74	= 40.77%
	Equity + Debt + Pref.		181.51	
Debt =	Total debt	=	41.9	= 23.08%
	Equity + Debt + Pref.		181.51	
Preference =	Preference shares	=	65.61	= 36.15%
	Equity + Debt + Pref.		181.51	

Cost of capital = Equity (15.38% x 40.77%) + **Debt** (11.055% x 23.08%) +
Preference shares (8.14% x 36.15%)
= 11.76%

Exhibit 12.4 *Estimate of Laporte's cost of capital post-acquisition*

Beta (β)	1.11
Equity risk premium (ERP)	4%
Risk-free rate (Rf)	9.26%
Cost of equity: Kê = Rf + (β x ERP)	13.7%
Cost of debt	6.9%

Cost of capital = Equity (13.7% x 75%) + **Debt** (6.90% x 25%) = 12.00%

PART 2

Corporate Finance and Restructuring

Introduction

Stock exchanges in Europe have experienced a bumpy ride in the late 1980s and early 1990s. After the great crash in October 1987 the markets boomed with the apparent ending of the recession in the early 1990s. Yet, underlying these short-term trends is a longer-term one which indicates that equity financing is falling as a percentage of all financing forms. This is certainly the case in the past two decades where it has been discouraged by the growth in debt finance, heavier government borrowing, innovation in bond markets and an increasingly short-term attitude by investors.

Nonetheless, the first few years of the 1990s have been characterized by a rising tide of new issues and rights. Privatization alone has been estimated to add 10% to the capitalization of European bourses by the end of this decade. Other factors encouraging equity markets have been the liquidity stimulus offered by derivatives, and the recession which stimulated demand by investors faced with low interest rates which seemed intractable.

The first two cases in this section, by Roy Smith, Ingo Walter and Hugh Thomas, concern the financing of the giant Eurotunnel project in the 1980s. In the first case, Barclays Bank undertakes a detailed study of the invitation to underwrite a debt issue by Eurotunnel. In the second, W.H. Clarkson Pension Investments considers a sub-underwriting of a Eurotunnel equity issue, involving warrants.

Turning from underwriting aspects of new capital issues, Anthony Neuberger presents a case (case 17) on the rapidly growing business services company, Saatchi and Saatchi. In 1988, the company sought an injection of new money by a flotation, to finance expansion into the burgeoning consultancy market. The equity market was disenchanted with the company, so Saatchi and Saatchi opted for an issue of convertible puttable preference shares.

In case 22, Anthony Neuberger and Thomas Ryan examine the abortive

195

flotation in 1992 by the $3 billion GPA aircraft leasing group. The share issue was aborted because all the signs were registering an expensive failure. Several reasons were discussed, including overpricing the issue, and a personality cult in the company's management.

In the case of EuroDisney (case 23), by Amir Zafar and Matthew Davis, the share issue was probably too successful in the light of subsequent developments. The authors examine the pricing of EuroDisney's 1989 public share issue within the framework of traditional share valuation theories. Following oversubscription and a large premium on the opening share prices, investors' hopes soon turned sour.

As well as cases on large public share issues, this section includes examples of the financing of smaller companies. In the Devro case (case 18), Ken Robbie and Mike Wright examine a major management buy-out which took place in 1991 at a time when the value of the buy-out market in the UK was contracting. The Devro buy-out had to be conservatively structured in terms of debt/equity, and the financing was complex, involving equity, subordinated debt, a vendor loan, and senior debt. The equity itself was split into three classes.

Robbie and Wright also provide an example (case 19) of small company financing – Brunton Curtis Outdoor Advertising – in which venture capital was raised by second-time entrepreneurs. Second-time entrepreneurs have become a feature of the venture capital scene over the past decade, and it is now quite common for founders of businesses who sell their companies to start new businesses. The case features questions of the attractiveness of second-time entrepreneurs to venture capitalists and the advantages of venture capital as a form of finance.

Another smaller company, BCS Computer Systems Ltd, is the subject of case 20 by Barry Howcroft and Grahame Boocock. Seeking to raise new finance, the company's directors considered various financing possibilities, including an injection of equity by the directors, venture capital and government grants.

A further group of three cases concerns restructuring exercises by the management or shareholders. In one company, IBM, the share ownership structure was reorganized (case 21); in the second, Wellcome Trust, a large secondary offer of shares was made (case 15 and 16), and in the third, Amazonia Plantations, a loan conversion was set up (case 26).

For IBM, Theo Vermaelen and Kees Cools examine the company's share repurchase of 1989. The offer resulted in a substantial increase in the share price, even after the tender had been priced at a sizeable premium to market price. The case evaluates the method chosen to finance the repurchase.

In the cases of the Wellcome Trust, Paul Stonham investigates the 1992 secondary share offering of Wellcome plc shares by their dominant holder, Wellcome Trust. The outcome was the largest fully-paid non-privatization offering of shares ever to take place. The use of what was at the time an innovative offer technique in the UK – book-building and over-allocation – caused widespread comment in the financial community.

In the instance of the third company in this group, Amazonia Plantations, Christian Wolff looks at the implementation of a package of measures taken to restructure the finances of a South American plantations company, including conversion of loans into equity, and the buying-off of short-term loans at a discount.

The remaining two cases in this section concern foreign direct investment (FDI in the UK, case 24) and a takeover (GMA–MA case 25).

Clive Collis presents data on foreign direct investment in the UK, looking especially at the three regions (Scotland, Wales and the West Midlands) which received the largest share of FDI flows during the second half of the 1980s.

Oriol Amat and Xavier Puig investigate the financial aspects of an acquisition by a French insurance company, GMA, of a Spanish insurance company, MA, seeking to gain entry into the Spanish insurance market by acquiring a minority controlling stake in MA.

Eurotunnel (A)

Debt

A project financing case based on the early stage of financing the Eurotunnel. The Eurotunnel project was the largest privately financed infrastructural project of the century. Barclays Bank was approached by the Arranging Banks with an offer to join a group of some 40 second-tier banks underwriting a £5 billion loan to the Eurotunnel System. In fact, it was asked to give a pre-underwriting agreement. The case study considers the events prior to signing the underwriting agreement, the terms and conditions of the credit facilities and the project economics. Barclays Bank's head of Project Finance was required to make a concise, well reasoned recommendation on whether or not to participate. This case should be read in conjunction with the background information provided in the appendix to case 14 'Eurotunnel: Equity' on pages 208–43.

'Salt in the wound!' Ian Morrison, assistant to the Project Finance Division manager of Barclays Bank of London, glumly thought to himself on February 14, 1986, as he looked over the financing plan for the Eurotunnel System, a project to construct a rail tunnel between the UK and France under the Channel. A scant three weeks before, President François Mitterrand of France and Prime Minister Margaret Thatcher of the UK had jointly announced that their governments would award the concession to construct the Eurotunnel System to the Channel Tunnel Group – France Manche (CTG–FM) consortium. The announcement meant that the effort which Barclays had expended as co-promoter of the rival, more ambitious EuroRoute bridge and tunnel project had been in vain. And, equally annoying, National Westminster Bank, Barclay's chief competitor in the UK and a shareholder in CTG–FM, was leading the group of Arranging Banks organizing a £5 billion loan for the Eurotunnel System. Natwest, Midland

This case was prepared with the assistance of Dorothea Bensen and Hugh Thomas by Professors Roy C. Smith and Ingo Walter of INSEAD and the Stern School of Business, New York University, as a basis for class discussion rather than to illustrate either effective or ineffective handling of an administrative situation. © *Roy C. Smith and Ingo Walter, 1995.*

Bank, Banque Indosuez, Banque Nationale de Paris and Crédit Lyonnais (the Arranging Banks) were offering Barclays the chance to join the victors as one of a group of some 40 second-tier underwriting banks.

The instructions which the head of Project Finance Division had given Ian had been clear: in analyzing what was to be the largest privately financed infrastructural project of the century, Ian was to ignore Barclay's previous work with EuroRoute. He was to make a concise, well reasoned recommendation of whether or not to participate in the Eurotunnel System financing on the merits of the System itself. 'Wimps!' muttered Ian as he settled down to his task. 'For a few billion more, Britain and France could have had the best bridge and tunnel road and rail link in the world. Now, we get two holes in the ground.'

The Invitation

The invitation which Barclays had received was to give pre-underwriting commitment to underwrite. The commitment would be conditional on the occurrence of several key events and the amount of the commitment was to be £40, £50, £80, £120 or £160 million, subject to reduction at the option of the Arranging Banks. Owing to the size, complexity and unusual nature of the transaction and the length of time anticipated between commitment and syndication, the Arranging Banks on behalf of Eurotunnel were first requesting a letter of commitment. They anticipated that in six months or so this would be replaced by a full underwriting agreement which would set the stage for syndication. In March 1986, however, the intended borrower had as yet had no corporate existence, the intended construction contract had not yet been drafted, and the purpose for which the loan was to be made had not yet been legalized by the governments of the UK and France. Therefore, it was considered premature to sign an underwriting.

As Ian understood the situation, however, the Arranging Banks had good reason to approach the market in this slightly unorthodox way. It was essential for them to boost the amount of underwriting commitments – rumored to be in the neighborhood of £4.3 billion – to the full £5.0 billion budgeted for total credit facilities in order to preserve political momentum and demonstrate to the equity market that the whole System's debt financing was 'locked up'. Only then could they hope to tap the equity market successfully. And clearly, they could gain from the additional British political clout which would accompany the entry of Barclays into the ranks of the underwriters. Eurotunnel's political storms weren't over yet.

Events Prior to Signing of the Underwriting Agreement

The following events would have to occur before the underwriting agreement could be signed:

1. The concession would have to be signed by the British and French governments.
2. New corporate entities, Eurotunnel, SA, Eurotunnel plc and their general partnership would have to be established.
3. The corporate entity for the contractor would have to be established and the construction contract negotiated and signed.
4. The Channel Tunnel Bill, to ratify the treaty and the concession would have to be passed by the UK parliament.
5. Parallel legislation would have to pass the French National Assembly. In addition, an order for the acquisition of the land for the French terminal would have to be obtained.
6. A suitable site for the dumping of spoil would have to be provided.
7. A second offering of equity (called Equity II) of £150 million would have to be made.

In addition, the Arranging Banks anticipated that approval for the construction of the high-speed Paris–Calais TGV rail line, on which the trains would travel at average speeds of 185 mph would be forthcoming from the French government. A natural extension of the existing TGV rail network, the construction of this line would be critical to the achievement of a Paris–London rail travel time competitive with air travel time. A similar TGV line was not anticipated to be constructed in the UK in the near future.

While this process was being implemented, the French National Assembly elections scheduled for March 1986 would occur. And as the Thatcher government was already late in its third year, there was a good chance of there being a parliamentary election in the UK before syndication.

Terms and Conditions of the Credit Facilities

The invitation contained a summary of the terms and conditions of the anticipated Credit Agreement.

Amount
The total amount was to be denominated in three currencies as follows (reference rate £1.00 = FFr 10.00 = US$1.50):

	£ equivalent
Amount	*at reference rate*
£2,600 million	£2,600 million
FFr 21,000 million	£2,100 million
US$450 million	£300 million

Of the total amount, it was anticipated that 80% would be available for general use and 20% would form a cost overrun, standby facility.

Conditions Precedent
Following the signing of the Credit Agreement, a further three conditions would have to be fulfilled in addition to the normal conditions precedent in Euromarket syndicated loans:

1. A third tranche of equity, Equity III, would have to be floated to raise total paid in capital to £1.0 billion and, from that, capital expenditures in excess of £700 million would have been made.
2. Specified costruction progress would have been made.
3. The banks would be reasonably satisfied with the construction program and cost control structure.

Availability, Repayment and Refinancing
The facility was to be available for drawings for a period of 7 years from signing. Drawings were to be in the form of cash or letters of credit to secure third-party loans.

Repayments were to be made out of the cash flow of Eurotunnel with final repayment being no later than 18 years from the day of signing. The cash flow in Exhibit 13.1 shows anticipated repayments for the first 11 years of normal operations. It was anticipated that unamortized loans would be refinanced at the maturity of the loan.

Eurotunnel would be allowed, upon payment of a fee, to prepay in full the outstanding amounts at any time after the opening of Eurotunnel to regular traffic. Early repayment could be made without fee payment after two complete summers of operation at the rate of 20% per year of the total amount subject to maintaining certain ratios. Assuming that Eurotunnel proved profitable, early refinancing was highly likely.

Fees Eurotunnel would pay the syndicate banks fees as follows:

- To the Arranging Banks: ⅛% flat on the total amount raised.
- To underwriting banks: ⅞% flat on the underwritten amount to each bank *pro rata* to its underwriting.

Exhibit 13.1 *Base case cash flow projections (£m)*

	1993	1994	1995	1996	1997	1998	1999	2000	2001	2002	2003
Source of funds											
Profit before tax	70	108	199	373	350	422	508	614	716	823	927
Depreciation	103	158	159	160	162	167	169	171	173	176	184
Issue of long-term debt	321	0	776	352	361	452	0	0	0	0	0
Issue of capital	0	52	25	0	0	0	0	0	0	0	0
Total	494	318	1159	885	873	1041	677	785	889	999	1111
Use of funds											
Asset purchases	262	37	0	0	0	39	0	0	0	9	108
Debt repayment	0	0	799	493	478	561	111	102	111	122	133
Dividends paid	0	0	181	173	229	290	318	308	377	442	513
Tax paid	0	15	84	103	128	158	175	192	251	290	331
Subtotal	262	52	1064	769	835	1048	604	602	739	863	1085
Change in non-liquid working capital	-3	-7	-11	-11	-10	-12	-7	-14	-10	-12	-20
Change in liquid funds	229	259	84	105	28	-19	66	169	140	124	6

- Pre-loan commitment fee: ¼% p.a. on committed amounts from March 14, 1986 until the signing of the Credit Agreement.
- Regular commitment fee: ⅛% p.a. on the undrawn amount (but not including amounts covered by the additional commitment fee) from the date of signing the Credit Agreement until the end of the availability period.
- Additional commitment fee: ¼% p.a. on the undrawn amount budgeted to be used in the current half year and ⁵⁄₁₆% p.a. on any amounts drawn over the budgeted amount.

Interest   For drawings of up to 80% of the total facility, the interest rate would be bank cost of funds in the relevant currency plus a margin of 1¼% p.a. before completion and 1% after completion. If, three years after the opening of Eurotunnel to regular traffic, conditions permitting refinancing had not been satisfied, the margin would revert to 1¼% p.a.

For drawings in excess of 80% of the total facility (i.e. use of the standby facility) interest would be bank cost of funds in the relevant currency plus a margin of 1¾% p.a. prior to completion and 1¼% after completion. If, three years after completion conditions permitting refinancing had not been satisfied, the margin would revert to 1½%.

For drawings in excess of 90% of the total facility, the standby margins would be increased a further ⅛%.

Exhibit 14.7 illustrates background market yields at October 31, 1987.

Security   All assets of Eurotunnel, including the System, the concession and the bonds of the contractor, would be pledged to the lending banks so that, in the event of a default, full control and benefit would revert to them.

Negative Pledges   Eurotunnel would not be able to carry any other business, except concerning the System, without bank permission. Eurotunnel would be able to undertake no borrowing except under the credit agreement.

Events of Default   A number of events would allow the banks discretion to take various unilateral actions including the enforcement of the security. These events included: (i) the default cover ratio tests not being met; (ii) the opening of the System being delayed for more than one year; (iii) an unremedied breach of Eurotunnel's obligations, and (iv) once repayments started, the amounts outstanding under the credit agreement exceeding a certain amount.

Default Cover Ratios   Eurotunnel would not be entitled to make drawings if the ratio of the present value of the forecast net cash flow (as estimated by information from Eurotunnel, the maitre d'oeuvre and certain consultants) to bank outstandings was below 1.2; to partially refinance if it was below 1.3, or to pay dividends if it was below 1.25. The dropping of the ratio below 1.0 for 90 days or more would constitute an event of default.

Third-party Loans   It was anticipated that the European Investment Bank, (EIB) an international lending agency of the EEC, would be keen to make funds of up to £1 billion available on a fixed rate, long-term basis at concessional rates of interest. EIB was not prepared to take project risk during the period of construction but would be prepared to take the risk of Eurotunnel once the System was operational. It therefore was anticipated that EIB's advances would be guaranteed by letters of credit drawn under the credit agreement and that, following project completion, these would be allowed to lapse. Detailed terms had not been discussed.

Multicurrency Options   Although the obligations under the commitments were to be denominated in pounds sterling, French francs and US dollars as given above, it was anticipated that the credit facility could include multicurrency facilities at the option of Eurotunnel.

Project Economics

Having worked on the EuroRoute feasibility analysis, Ian Morrison was acutely aware that the key to project viability lay in the cost and revenue assumptions which underlay the projected cash flows, the degree to which those assumptions were likely to vary from their projected values, and the sensitivity of the cash flows to that variation. There were, after all, only three sources of cash inflows: traffic (road and rail) tolls, additional equity and refinancing debt. If Eurotunnel was unprofitable, the warrants expiring in 1992 (£110 million), 1994 (£52 million) and 1995 (£25 million) would not be exercised, and debt refinancing could be problematic. And the degree of reliability of traffic forecasts stretching into the twenty-first century had yet to be established.

Eurotunnel had provided, in addition to its 'best guess' cash flow projections (called the base case), the results of a number of sensitivities. These tested the effects of changes in key variables on project performance. The sensitivities included:

A. Increasing construction costs and owning group costs by 10%.

B. Delaying tunnel opening by six months and encountering construction and operating cost overruns of £270 million.
C. Reducing revenues by 15% throughout the concession period.
D. High speed Paris–Eurotunnel railway services not being introduced.
E. Real interest rates increasing by 2% throughout (i.e. from a bank cost of funds of 8.5% p.a. to 10.5% p.a.).
F. Inflation being assumed to rise in 1% stages from 5% in 1987 to reach 9% in 1991, reverting to 6% in 1994 and thereafter.
G. Severe downside case: a combination of cases B, C and E.

Exhibit 13.2 summarizes the results of these sensitivities compared with the base case.

As Ian settled into his task, he jotted down, in no particular order, the kinds of issue which his analysis would have to discuss: project structure, viability, financial returns to bank, political issues, current loans market, credit support, bank recourse, completion risk, economic risk, political risk, financial risk, and so on.

Exhibit 13.2 *Sensitivities compared with base case*

	Banks's maximum exposure (£bn)	Date of minimum final repayment	First debt cover ratio	First permitted refinancing	Permitted dividends
Base case	4.068	2005	1.29	1996	1995
A	4.654	2005	1.15	2002	1998
B	4.646	2005	1.14	2002	1999
C	4.116	2005	1.10	2004	2001
D	4.058	2005	1.25	1996	1995
E	4.347	2005	1.15	2000	1999
F	4.709	2005	1.26	1996	1996
G	5.193	2008	0.85	none permitted	2008

Exhibit 13.3 *Pricing on Euromarket transactions January–February 1986*

Borrower	City of Sheffield, UK
Amount	£20 million
Tenor	10 years
Type	Deferred purchase facility
Spread	LIBOR + ¼% years 1–3; LIBOR + ⅜% thereafter
Front-end fees	1/16% for £3 million; ⅛% for over £3 million
Commitment fees	1/16% on the undrawn portion
Lead manager	Banque Paribas

Exhibit 13.3 *continued*

Borrower	Shipping Corp. of India
Amount	£42 million
Tenor	7½ years
Type	Pre-delivery ship financing
Spread	LIBOR + ⅜% for first 4 years; LIBOR + ½% thereafter
Front-end fees	3⁄16%
Commitment fees	¼% on the undrawn portion
Lead manager and guarantor	State Bank of India
Borrower	Halifax Building Society, UK
Amount	£200 million
Tenor	10 years
Type	Sterling floating rate notes
Spread	LIBOR + ⅛%
Issue price	100
Lead manager	Morgan Grenfell
Borrower	Republic of Turkey
Amount	US$233 million
Tenor	8 years
Type	Project loan for power plant; co-financing with World Bank
Spread	LIBOR + 1¼% for first 3 years; LIBOR + 1⅜% thereafter
Borrower	Government of the Philippines
Amount	$2.9 billion
Tenor	10 years
Type	Sovereign refinancing
Spread	LIBOR + 1⅝%
Borrower	Mass Transit Railway Corp. of Hong Kong
Amount	HK$1 billion (approximately US$128 million)
Tenor	7 years with put and call options at 5 years
Type	Bearer participation notes
Spread	LIBOR + ¼%
Lead managers	Manufactures Hanover and others
Borrower	Alpargatas SAIC (Argentina), a private sector corporation
Amount	$28 million
Tenor	5 years
Spread	Either LIBOR + 2⅛% or US Prime + 1¾%
Lead manager	Citicorp and Morgan Guaranty
Borrower	Société National des Chemins de Fer (SNCF)
Guarantor	Republic of France
Amount	$600 million
Tenor	10 years
Type	Securitized notes and Floating Rate Notes
Spread	LIBOR + ¼%
Call option	3 years
Lead manager	Crédit Lyonnais

Eurotunnel (B)
Equity

A project financing case on raising the equity component of the Eurotunnel project. In 1987, W.H. Clarkson Pension Investments Ltd was invited to sub-underwrite a £770 million offer-for-sale equity financing of the Eurotunnel project – the third consecutive equity offering for this venture. Clarkson also had the opportunity to bid for shares in Eurotunnel as an investor, with any bids being offset against the firm's sub-underwriting exposure. The divisional manager and treasurer of Clarkson have to decide whether to be a sub-underwriter in Equity III and whether to invest on Clarkson's own account in Eurotunnel. The case includes information on the structure of the financing deal and the underwriting, the distribution system, returns to investors, and market sentiment before the share issue. Data on the background to the Eurotunnel project are provided as an appendix to this case.

London, November 20, 1987. W.H. Clarkson Pension Investments Ltd. 'It might be the best annuity since the Suez Canal. Then again, it might be the most expensive engineers' toy since the Humber Bridge. And quite frankly, my dear Jill, I haven't the faintest idea of which it is. Why do you ask? Are we trying to decide if we're going to get stuffed by Robert Fleming?' smirked Geoff Racher, Division Manager, to his colleague Jillian Ponsonby, Treasurer.

Jillian stiffened visibly. 'It may come as a surprise to you, Mr. Racher, to know that my job with respect to the Eurotunnel IPO is to decide whether or not Clarkson will act as a sub-underwriter for the issue. It may also come

This case was prepared by research assistants Dorothea Bensen of INSEAD, Fontainebleau, France and Hugh Thomas of the Stern School of Business, New York University, under the direction of Professors Roy C. Smith and Ingo Walter of the Stern School of Business, New York University and INSEAD as a basis for class discussion rather than to illustrate either effective or ineffective handling of an administrative situation. © Dorothea Bensen and Hugh Thomas, 1995.

as a surprise to you to know that sub-underwriting, when engaged in judiciously and with due regard to risk and return, can be a very profitable activity indeed. Your job is *precisely* to tell me whether or not Clarkson will bid to invest in Eurotunnel. And you are also *supposed* to know what your kindred number-crunchers in the other investment houses in the City think. Time is running out. And furthermore, I am not your *dear* Jill!'

'Of course, she's right,' Geoff mused as he watched Jillian stalk away. 'And she knows that I'll decide by the end of the day whether Clarkson will be investing in the deal. Pity she doesn't have a sense of humour, though,' he reflected as he turned back to the prospectus.

The Deal

The prospectus, dated November 16, 1987, outlined the terms under which the British contingent of an international syndicate of underwriters was offering 45.9% of the equity of Eurotunnel plc (EPLC) and Eurotunnel, SA (ESA) (together referred to as Eurotunnel) to the British investing public through the issuance of 220 million combined shares (units) with warrants attached. Eurotunnel had been established to construct and operate the proposed £6 billion railway tunnel under the Channel between the UK and France. The offer for sale – which would raise £770 million in equity financing and bring the total equity raised since Eurotunnel's founding to £1.023 billion – was the third consecutive equity offering, and hence was known as Equity III.

Equity II, a private placement of £200 million worth of units launched just over a year earlier, in October 1986, had been undersubscribed in the UK and demand in the US had been low. Its failure in those markets was widely attributed to political and organizational uncertainties, leading to doubts as to whether the project would ever be built. The British sub-underwriters had avoided major losses, however, thanks partly to over-subscription in France, Japan and Germany – and partly to the efforts of the Bank of England in pressuring investment houses in the City to subscribe for the units.

Clarkson had been invited to sub-underwrite in Equity III, and had to respond by the end of the day. Clarkson would also have an opportunity to bid for shares in Eurotunnel, a decision which had to be made by November 27. If Clarkson also were to bid to purchase shares as an investor, those bids could be set off against the firm's sub-underwriting exposure.

Eurotunnel in November 1987

In November 1987 the project was on a firmer footing than it had been a year earlier. All political and legal hurdles on the route to construction had been cleared, and the market perceived the management to have been strengthened (see Exhibit 14.1). The syndication of the £5 billion project credit agreement, completed in October 1987 with over 130 banks joining the 50 underwriters in the financing, had been a success. Of course, not a penny of the £5 billion facility could be drawn prior to the successful completion of Equity III. And the stock market crash of October 1987 had added a new element of uncertainty.

By November 1987, the Eurotunnel board of directors comprised many of the leading financial and corporate figures of France and the UK. Directors of Eurotunnel included directors of British Petroleum, British Steel, Caisse des Dépôts et Consignations, Crédit Agricole, Crédit Foncier, Crédit Lyonnais, Glaxo, Hambro, Indosuez, Midland Bank, Moët Hennessy–Louis Vuitton, National Westminster Bank, Plessy, Peugeot, RTZ, Shell, Société Générale de Belgique, Morgan Grenfell, Standard Chartered and UBAF, to name but a few. The largest British shareholders after the Equity II offering were Standard Life, Legal and General, Prudential and the BP International Oil Group. The principal French shareholders were Compagnie Financière de Suez, Caisse des Dépôts et Consignations, Caisse Centrale des Mutuelles Agricoles and UAP, France's largest insurance company.

Equity III

Equity III was structured as an initial public offering of units, each of which was made up of a single share in the UK company, EPLC, and a single share in the French company, ESA. Units would be listed on both the International Stock Exchange in London and the Bourse in Paris. Under the articles of association of both EPLC and ESA, shares of EPLC and ESA were not permitted to be sold separately; hence, the shareholding of the EPLC, ESA and the joint entity, Eurotunnel, would be identical.

Attached to each unit was one detachable warrant to purchase additional units in Eurotunnel. By exchanging 10 warrants together with the exercise price of 230p per share of EPLC plus FFr 23.00 per share of ESA, a warrant-holder could purchase at any time between November 15, 1990 and November 15, 1992 one unit of additional equity in Eurotunnel.

Exhibit 14.1   *Chronology: March 1986–October 1987*

1986

March
: Socialist president Francois Mitterrand names Jacques Chirac, leader of the Gaullist Rassemblement pour la Republique, as the new prime minister following rightist victory in general elections, ushering in a period of cohabitation. Chirac confirms continued support for Eurotunnel.

April
: Channel Tunnel Bill encounters unexpectedly strong opposition from environmentalists and Flexilink in the British House of Commons.

May
: Channel Tunnel Bill further delayed due to violation of required parliamentary procedures.

June
: Eurotunnel delays Equity II placing.

August
: Channel Tunnel construction contract signed between Eurotunnel and Transmanche.

October
: Equity II averts undersubscription only after considerable pressure from UK government.

December
: Banque Indosuez and Robert Fleming named to jointly lead-manage Equity III, scheduled for spring 1988.

1987

February
: Alastair Morton, chairman of Guinness Peat named to succeed Lord Pennoch as UK co-chairman of the board of Eurotunnel.

April
: Equity III postponed until October 1987.

May
: European Investment Bank commits in principle to lend £1.0 billion to Eurotunnel based on bank counter-guarantees during construction period and project risk thereafter.

: Eurotunnel signs agreements with British Rail and La Société Nationale des Chemins de Fer Français, with railways guaranteeing, for first 12 years of tunnel operation, payment of 60% of tunnel tolls, with shortfalls to be met from other operations.

June
: French laws numbers 87-383 and 87-384 passed by National Assembly authorizing president to ratify treaty with the UK and concession with Eurotunnel.

: Alastair Morton announces that Barclays, Lloyds and Standard Chartered have joined the loan underwriters.

: Eurotunnel signs £73.5 million equivalent French franc–pound sterling bridge loan with Banque Indosuez, BNP, Crédit Lyonnais, Crédit Agricole, Caisse des Dépôts et Consignations, Midland, Robert Fleming, Morgan Grenfell, Warburgs and Belgamanche, with repayment to be made from Equity III proceeds.

July
: In the UK general election, Margaret Thatcher's Conservatives win a majority of seats in the House of Commons. Election is considered to be a vote of approval for Conservative Party's 8-year long government.

: Channel Tunnel Bill receives royal assent.

: Treaty between France and UK is ratified and concession comes into force.

: Underwriting of £5 billion project loan is finalized. European Investment Bank signs £1 billion loan.

September
: In general syndication of £5 billion project facilities, 130 banks worldwide commit to provide funds.

: Campaign for Equity III begins.

October
: Stock markets crash worldwide.

: Equity III launched.

The Underwriting

Equity III was a fully underwritten offering divided into three tranches, a French tranche, a UK tranche and an international tranche. In December 1986, Eurotunnel had awarded jointly to Banque Indosuez and Robert Fleming & Co. the mandate to lead-manage and underwrite Equity III. The lead managers had subsequently expanded the underwriting team to include other issuing houses from France (Banque Nationale de Paris, Crédit Lyonnais, Caisse des Dépôts et Consignations and Caisse National de Crédit Agricole) and the UK (Morgan Grenfell & Co. Ltd, S.G. Warburg & Co. Ltd, County Natwest Ltd. and Samuel Montagu & Co. Ltd). After discussions among Eurotunnel, the underwriting banks and interested international investment banks in late October and early November 1987, it was decided that the French tranche should be made up of 101 million units, underwritten at a price of FFr 35 per unit, the UK tranche be made up of 101 million units, underwritten at a price of 350p per unit, and the international tranche would comprise 18 million units at a price of 175p plus FFr 17.50 per unit. Hence, the structure of the underwriting was as shown in Exhibit 14.2.

A Canadian tranche had been withdrawn at the last moment, after the stock market crash of October 17th was found to have severely weakened the capital of the Canadian underwriter, Wood Gundy. The offering was to follow the schedule set out in Exhibit 14.3.

Exhibit 14.2   *Eurotunnel lead underwriters*

Country/region	Lead underwriter	Number of units in the tranche
France	Banque Indosuez	101,000,000
UK	Robert Fleming	101,000,000
International comprising:		18,000,000
USA	Salomon Brothers	1,800,000
Belgium/Luxembourg	Générale Bank	2,160,000
Middle East	Al Bank Al Saudi Al Fransi	4,500,000
Rest of Europe	Indosuez	2,520,000
Japan	Nomura	4,320,000
Rest of the world	Robert Fleming and Morgan Grenfell	2,700,000

Exhibit 14.3 *Schedule of offering events*

November 13	Underwriting agreement entered into
November 16	Selling period starts
November 27	UK and French offers to close
November 29	Final number of units offered to be settled
December 3	Payment
December 9	Renounceable letters of acceptance to be sent
December 10	Listings to be filed in London and Paris
January 22	Last date for renunciation
March 7	Definitive certificates to be sent

The UK Tranche

Both the UK and the French tranches were to be placed according to standard IPO practices in those countries. In the UK, the underwriters had preplaced 42 million units of the total 101 million with certain institutional investors, leaving only 59 million to be sub-underwritten and allocated to bidders. Bidders would complete their application forms (see Exhibit 14.4) and turn them in to one of 27 receiving centers throughout the UK before 10.00 a.m. on Friday, November 27. The bids would be tabulated over the next two days, and by the following Monday morning, the City would know whether or not the issue had been a success.

Total fees on the UK tranche were to be 4½% of the principal, from which the lead manager would pay out all other fees. One per cent was reserved for management fees, 1% for underwriting fees and 2% for selling commissions. Geoff was not sure what the sub-underwriting fee would be, but guessed that the underwriters would give up 1% to 1¼%, retaining for themselves ¼% to ½%. He also assumed that those institutional investors who committed to preplacement would be compensated by receiving the full selling and underwriting commissions. In the event of oversubscription in one tranche and undersubscription in another, reallocation of shares would occur with the fee structure of the reallocated shares being adjusted to the level of the receiving tranche.

In France, units were to be distributed largely through the banking system on a first come, first served basis.

Return to Investors

Investors in Eurotunnel looked to the stream of dividends which would be available from passenger and freight revenues, net of operating expenses and debt service during the 49 years from the projected completion of the Eurotunnel System to the end of the concession (see the appendix to this case). The life of Eurotunnel, from the investors' perspective, would be divided into three distinct periods:

1. The construction period, from 1987 to the end of 1992, when equity funds and loans would be drawn to finance construction.

Exhibit 14.4   *Application form for UK investors*

Before completing this form, you should read carefully the notes opposite.

To: Robert Fleming & Co. Limited, Morgan Grenfell & Co. Limited, S. G. Warburg & Co. Ltd, Eurotunnel plc and Eurotunnel, SA.

I/We offer to purchase _____ units with New Warrants   [1]

on and subject to the terms and conditions set out in the full prospectus dated 16 November 1987 relating to the UK Offer, comprising listing particulars regarding EPLC and ESA (the 'Prospectus'), at a price of 350p per Unit (with one New Warrant attached)

and I/We attach a cheque or banker's draft for the amount payable of £ _____   [2]

signature	date

[3]

If you wish to receive travel privileges and are an individual eligible for travel privileges or are applying on behalf of a child, write YES in the box. If you do not write YES in the box, you will not be entitled to any travel privileges. Details are set out in the section of the prospectus entitled 'Travel Privileges'.   [4]

Please use block capitals   [5]

Mr/Mrs/Miss/Ms or title	forename in full
surname	
address	
	postcode

◀------- Pin here a cheque or banker's draft for the amount in Box 2 payable to 'Eurotunnel UK Offer' and crossed 'Not negotiable'   [6]

Exhibit 14.4 *continued*

[1] Put in Box 1 of the application form (in figures) the number of Units with New Warrants for which you are applying. You may only apply for one of the numbers of Units with New Warrants indicated below:

Number of Units with New Warrants for which you are applying	Amount payable
100	£350
200	£700
300	£1,050
400	£1,400
500	£1,750
750	£2,625
1,000	£3,500
1,250	£4,375
1,500	£5,250
2,000	£7,000

Above 2,000 units with New Warrants applications must be in the following denominations:

Applications	Multiples of
2,000 to 10,000 Units with New Warrants	1,000
over 10,000 Units with New Warrants	10,000

[2] Using the right-hand column of the table above, put in Box 2 of the application form (in figures) the amount payable.

[3] Sign the application form in Box 3 and date it.

The application form may be signed by someone else on your behalf if he or she is authorized to do so. An agent should enclose the power of attorney appointing him (unless he is a Selling Agent, Financial Intermediary or UK Clearing Bank as defined in the Prospectus) and should state clearly the capacity in which he signs.

A corporation must sign under the hand of a duly authorized official whose name and capacity must be stated.

[4] If you are an individual and wish to claim travel privileges, write YES in Box 4 of the application form.

If you do not write YES in Box 4, you will not be entitled to any travel privileges. Please read the section of the Prospectus entitled 'Travel Privileges' before completing the box.

[5] Put in Box 5 your full name and address in capitals. Only one application should be made for the benefit of any person.

Applications may only be made by persons over 18. However, a parent, grandparent or guardian of a child under 18 may apply for the benefit of a particular child. To apply for the benefit of a child, you should put your own name in Box 5 and, after your surname write 'a/c' followed by the full name of the child and the child's date of birth. Applying for one or more children will not prevent you from making a single application for your own benefit.

The right is reserved to reject multiple or suspected multiple applications.

Exhibit 14.4 *continued*

---

[6] Pin to Box 6 where indicated a cheque or banker's draft for the amount you have entered in Box 2. The cheque must be made payable to 'Eurotunnel UK Offer' and crossed 'Not negotiable'. A separate cheque or banker's draft must accompany each application.

The payment must relate solely to this application. No receipt will be issued.

The cheque or banker's draft must be drawn in pounds sterling on an account of a branch of a bank in the UK, the Channel Islands or the Isle of Man and must bear a UK bank sort code number on the top right-hand corner. If you do not have a cheque account, you can obtain a cheque or banker's draft from your building society, your bank or a third party, in which case you should print your name on the back of the cheque or banker's draft.

An application form may be drawn on a person other than the applicant or by banker's draft, but any moneys returned will be sent by cheque crossed 'Not negotiable–a/c payee only' in favour of the applicant.

You must return your completed application form together with a cheque or banker's draft for payment so as to arrive by 10:00 a.m on Friday, 27 November 1987 (or by 3:30 p.m. on Thursday, 26 November 1987 if the form is taken by hand to one of the additional receiving centres listed at the end of this document).

Photocopies of this application form will not be accepted in any circumstances.

---

2. The start-up period, from 1993 to mid-1995, when the System would be tested, actual traffic and operating costs could be compared with projections, new debt would be issued to replace the construction period loans, various construction guarantees would expire (or be called in the event of nonperformance) and warrants would be exercised or allowed to expire.

3. The main operation period, from mid-1995 until the expiry date of the concession in 2042, when dividends would accrue to unit-holders.

In all three periods, unit-holders would be subject to potential capital gains and losses on the market values of their units and (in the construction and start-up periods) on their warrants. Starting from the main operation period, dividends would be expected to grow as the project debt was amortized and the toll rates increased with inflation. The prospectus outlined projections of dividends payable to unit-holders (see Exhibit 14.5).

In addition to dividends, Eurotunnel offered to individual subscribers in Equity III travel privileges as shown in Exhibit 14.6. The perks were intended to attract retail investors, especially British residents.

Exhibit 14.5 *Projected dividends (£m)*

1993–1998: year ending 31 December	1993	1994	1995	1996	1997	1998
Turnover	488	762	835	908	986	1,072
Profit before taxation	70	108	199	273	350	422
Profit for the year available for distribution	62	88	158	217	277	328
Dividends: total	–	149	169	217	277	328
per unit	–	£0.39	£0.44	£0.56	£0.71	£0.85

Later years: year ending 31 December	2003	2013	2023	2033	2041
Turnover	1,586	3,236	6,184	11,356	17,824
Profit before taxation	927	2,410	4,897	9,152	14,453
Profit for the year available for distribution	566	1,476	2,986	5,605	8,880
Dividends: total	566	1,476	2,986	5,605	8,880
per unit	£1.46	£3.80	£7.70	£14.44	£22.88

The above projections incorporate inflation assumed to be 4% in 1987 rising to 6% by 1991 and remaining at 6% thereafter.
Source: November 1987 prospectus.

Exhibit 14.6   *Travel privileges offered to subscribers in Equity III*

Number of units purchased and held	Travel privilege
100	One return shuttle trip to be taken within 12 months of the system opening
500	One return shuttle trip per year for the first 10 years of operation
1,000	Two return shuttle trips per year until the end of the concession period
1,500	An unlimited number of shuttle trips until the end of the concession period

Market Sentiment Before the Share Issue

In Paris, confidence in Equity III was strong, as it had been since Eurotunnel's inception. The mood in the City, however, was cautious. Managers of performance-related funds such as unit trusts and investment trusts were not keen on it because of the seven-year gap between the investment and the initial dividends. Pension funds had reservations about whether the degree of risk was appropriate, or even legal, for them to take on. Insurance companies were the most enthusiastic among the institutional investors. But the opinions of the private investor would not be known until after the issue closed.

The *Financial Times* summed up much of the City's sentiment about Equity III in an article on November 7, 1987:

> If it works, it will be quite a remarkable coup. Amid the worst stock market conditions in recent memory and just days after the BP issue entered record books as the world's biggest flop, investors are about to be asked to put £770 m worth of shares in a hole in the ground which will certainly not produce a penny of revenues until, at least, 1993. . . . [T]he banks have insisted that there should be a tranche of equity funding in place – as the occasionally earthy Mr Alastair Morton, Eurotunnel's UK co-Chairman, put it 'to provide some insulation between their bums and a hard floor . . .'
>
> If investors are to buy their shares, however, they will require more in return than some vague feeling that they are fostering international goodwill, and to this end the Eurotunnel consortium has attempted to forecast what [their] profit will be.
>
> It is an odd picture. For the first seven years, there is nothing but construction costs and debt. But once the tunnel comes into operation in 1993, the tolls begin to flow in like water and with operation costs low in proportion

to income, a large proportion of these revenues goes straight through to dividends. Eurotunnel forecasts that the yield on the issue price will be 18% in 1994, 34% in 1996 and 60% in 2003.

Dividends of that order suggest that the capital value of the shares will rise to bring yields into line with other investment returns. Eurotunnel calculates that someone looking at the estimated dividend stream over the life of the concession until 2042 will be prepared to pay £34 a share when the dividends start to flow in 1995. That compares with a likely offer price of 350p; so investors might hope to see their shares multiply in value seven times in seven years.

That is a very attractive rate of return. Yet it rests on some heroic assumptions about the chances of completing the tunnel on time and to budget, and about whether the projected traffic flows will live up to expectations.

According to a London manager of one Japanese bank which is supporting the project: 'The only thing you can be sure of is that none of the traffic forecasts is likely to be right. But if you drive down to Dover and see the queues of cars waiting to cross the Channel, you are either impressed or you are not. We were impressed.'

Exhibit 14.7 illustrates background market yields at October 31, 1987.

Geoff Racher's Problem

In theory, Clarkson's decision was twofold: (i) whether or not to be a sub-underwriter in Equity III and (ii) whether or not to invest for its own account in Eurotunnel.

Geoff, a self-proclaimed realist, considered the sub-underwriting decision to be strategic and unrelated to Eurotunnel. Either Clarkson was to remain a sub-underwriter or it wasn't. If it decided to remain a sub-underwriter, Clarkson would maintain the reputation that it would accept virtually every offer that came along, regardless of the merits of the deal or whether or not Clarkson was bidding as an end-investor. On the successful deals, Clarkson would collect the sub-underwriting fees for no work. On the unsuccessful deals, it would take the fees and its pro-rata share of the unsold shares. In theory, a sub-underwriter could decide which offers to accept, but Geoff felt that if a sub-underwriter declined more than a tiny fraction of invitations, it would receive no more invitations – and it would certainly receive no invitations to sub-underwrite the good deals.

In the final analysis, however, Geoff knew that his ideas on sub-underwriting were irrelevant. Jillian, he knew, would make that decision. And the critical input to her decision – at least in theory – was his bidding strategy. Whether or not Clarkson was to sub-underwrite, Geoff would have to determine the proper method for assessing the risk/return tradeoff of the project. He would have to assess systematically the attractiveness of Eurotunnel to Clarkson. Add he would have to make a comment on the City's perception of the project. Geoff's work for the day was well defined.

Exhibit 14.7 *Market yields as of October 31, 1987*

	Long-term bond yields (%)	
	Government issues	Corporate issues
France	10.95	11.28
UK	9.22	11.00
USA	9.04	10.25

	Three month Eurocurrency rates (%)
Euro Dollars	7.62
Euro French Francs	9.00
Euro Sterling	9.44

Exhibit 14.8 *Dividend yields and P/E ratios in world markets 1981–86*

Dividend yields (%)

	1981	1982	1983	1984	1985	1986
Australia	6.19	7.67	5.65	4.30	3.60	2.70
Belgium	7.50	6.50	5.20	4.60	4.80	3.30
Canada	4.49	4.03	4.22	3.70	3.13	2.99
France	8.25	8.11	5.30	4.80	3.70	2.60
Germany	5.83	4.89	3.34	3.61	2.47	2.74
Hong Kong	n/a	7.90	6.32	5.99	3.50	2.92
Italy	2.52	2.89	4.30	6.28	2.56	2.36
Japan	1.58	1.61	1.19	1.09	0.99	0.78
Netherlands	7.90	7.20	4.80	4.80	4.50	4.20
Switzerland	3.39	3.05	2.44	2.64	1.85	1.87
UK	5.65	5.05	4.62	4.62	4.45	4.45
USA	5.00	4.10	3.50	4.30	3.60	3.40

Exhibit 14.8 *continued*

P/E ratios	1981	1982	1983	1984	1985	1986
Australia	n/a	n/a	n/a	7.8	12.9	17.8
Belgium	11.9	12.9	10.7	9.7	10.5	12.7
Canada	8.6	19.1	22.4	15.2	14.4	17.4
France	7.4	9.3	15.6	14.4	14.2	19.2
Germany	10.7	11.9	17.0	12.9	13.9	14.4
Hong Kong	14.7	5.8	7.2	8.1	14.1	16.3
Italy	41.2	22.4	17.5	15.1	27.4	27.5
Japan	21.1	22.8	27.7	31.3	33.7	50.3
Netherlands	5.7	5.5	7.2	7.7	9.3	11.8
Switzerland	11.1	11.6	11.9	10.0	13.0	13.3
UK	11.1	12.4	13.7	12.7	12.4	13.7
USA	8.0	10.2	11.7	9.6	12.7	14.2

Source: Goldman Sachs.

Appendix   Eurotunnel – Background

Note   This background material is for use in analyzing case 13, 'Eurotunnel – Debt' and case 14, 'Eurotunnel – Equity'. It was prepared with the assistance of Dorothea Bensen and Hugh Thomas by Professors Roy C. Smith and Ingo Walter of INSEAD and the Stern School of Business, New York University. It is intended to be used as a basis for class discussion rather than to illustrate either effective or ineffective handling of an administrative situation. © Roy C. Smith and Ingo Walter, 1995.

Scheduled for completion in 1993, the Eurotunnel System would join the rail network of the UK with that of France and mainland Europe providing a fast, frequent, reliable and comfortable cross-Channel transport link. The System, a twin-bore rail tunnel, rail equipment, rolling stock, terminals and associated infrastructure, was a technically straightforward engineering project, although its immensity would require that construction be implemented with great logistical coordination. Initiated at the same time as the EEC members' ratification of the Single European Act to create, by 1992, a single internal European market, the Eurotunnel System was a powerful economic and symbolic initiative. And its method of financing, with private capital bearing the risks of a large, international, long-term infrastructure development, was a method untested in world capital markets since the breakdown of the European imperial order three-quarters of a century before.

Historical Background

Since the time Napoleon first seriously considered the construction of a tunnel between the UK and France in 1802, plans for linking Britain with the mainland periodically had been redrafted only to be shelved. In 1882 tunneling actually started on the UK side. Abandoned soon after, the unfinished tunnel still yawns, its structural integrity preserved in the chalk bedrock near Dover.

In 1973, president Georges Pompidou and prime minister Edward Heath signed a treaty to construct a twin-bore rail tunnel under the Channel. Tunneling began in 1974 but, in the wake of the defeat of Mr Heath's Conservative government by the Labour Party led by Harold Wilson, the treaty lapsed without ratification by Parliament and, again, tunneling was abandoned.

In the early 1980s, investigations began into the possibility of the construction of a fixed link financed purely by private capital (see Exhibit 14.9 for chronology). Studies, commissioned by the UK and French governments, culminated in the publication of a report by the Anglo-French Study Group in 1982. The report was favorable to the construction of a rail link, but it was widely believed at the time that the report would join its predecessors in the archives, unimplemented.

In March 1984, Banque Indosuez, Banque Nationale de Paris, Crédit Lyonnais, Midland Bank and National Westminster Bank (together, the Arranging Banks) presented to the governments of the UK and France a report detailing how a fixed link across the Channel might be financed with private capital. Subsequently, the Arranging Banks teamed up with some of the largest construction companies in the UK (Balfour Beatty, Costain, Tarmac, Taylor Woodrow and George Wimpey) and France (Société Générale d'Entreprises, Spie Batignolles and Société Auxiliare d'Entreprises) to form the Channel Tunnel Group Limited of the UK and France Manche, SA (CTG and FM respectively). CTG-FM was a general partnership to develop and lobby for what would become the Eurotunnel System. With such experience behind it, CTG-FM was the consortium the most advanced in its plans when, following an initiative by Prime Minister Thatcher in the UK and President Mitterrand in France, their governments issued, in April 1985, a joint invitation to promoters to submit bids for the financing, construction and operation of a fixed link across the Channel without recourse to government funds or guarantees.

From the ten bids submitted in October 1985, four major contenders were identified, one of which was the CTG-FM Eurotunnel System. In January 1986, not surprisingly, the Eurotunnel System was selected as the winning bid. Thereafter, Mr Mitterrand and Mrs Thatcher signed the treaty by which they agreed (subject to government ratification) to the construction of the System and specified that each of their governments would sign a concession with the appropriate corporate national entity of the winning bidder: CTG in the UK and FM in France.

The concessions would give to CTG–FM the right to build and operate the System over a period of 55 years from the date of ratification. It would be free to determine its own commercial policy, including the setting of tariffs. No competing fixed link would be allowed to be built without CTG-FM's approval before the end of 2020, in effect giving CTG–FM the right of first refusal over the construction of a road link. At the end of the concession, in 2042, the System would become the property of the British and French governments.

Government action in support of Eurotunnel was not without opposition. A month after the announcement of the invitation to promoters, a group of ferry owners, port interests and environmentalists established Flexilink, an pressure group dedicated to the prevention of the construction of a fixed link between England and France. Flexilink began a publicity campaign in which it forecast a severe price war between the fixed link and ferry operators if the fixed link went ahead. Following the announcement of the winning bid, Flexilink accused Eurotunnel of manipulating statistics in its estimates of the capital cost of the tunnel, likely tariffs and traffic, arguing that the cross-Channel traffic market would suffer a slowdown in

Exhibit 14.9 *Chronology to February 1986*

June 1982	UK parliamentary study recommends a privately financed twin-bore tunnel.
May 1984	Joint study by five French and UK banks published in support of project financing of a twin-bore rail tunnel. UK government seen to be unenthusiastic.
October 1984	French and UK government discussions to clarify stand on cross-Channel fixed link.
November 1984	Margaret Thatcher on French television says it would be 'wonderful' if Channel Tunnel would be built.
January 1985	Anglo-French government working party group on the fixed link set up.
February 1985	Sir Nicholas Henderson, ex-British ambassadour to Bonn, Paris and Washington, appointed chairman of the Channel Tunnel Group.
April 1985	UK and French governments invite investing public to submit, before the end of October 1985, bids to build and operate a fixed link across the Channel financed wholly by private capital.
May 1985	Group of ferry companies establishes Flexilink, an organization to campaign to prevent the construction of a fixed link.
November 1985	Four bids from a field of ten are announced to be under consideration (figures are construction costs only estimated by bidding groups):
	● EuroRoute: £4.8 billion part-bridge, part-tunnel road and rail link.
	● CTG–FM: £2.6 billion twin-bore rail tunnel.
	● Eurobridge: £5 billion 23-mile composite fiber suspension bridge.
	● Channel Expressway: £2.5 billion twin-bore road tunnel with separate rail tunnel.
	House of Commons holds debates on the fixed link. Further details are sought from competitors regarding railway usage terms.
December 1985	France and the UK provisionally agree that duty-free sales will be allowed in the fixed link.
	British Rail and Société Nationale des Chemins de Fer reach preliminary agreement with main three bidding contenders.
January 1986	In continuing debate over the bids, rival consortia attempt to form alliances but banks supporting CTG–FM state that commitments of financing are not transferable to different projects.
	French and UK governments, after consultations with advisors Schroders, Chase Manhattan, Crédit Commercial and Morgan Guaranty, announce that CTG–FM's bid is the winning bid, saying that it was the best researched and detailed plan, responding to environmental concerns and having the advantage of a short construction schedule.
	CTG–FM raise £50 million in seed capital in Equity I issue.
February 1986	French and UK governments sign a treaty authorizing the construction of the fixed link.
	Sir Nicholas Henderson resigns as chairman of Channel Tunnel Group and is succeeded by Lord Raymond Pennock, director of Morgan Grenfell Group, deputy chairman of the Plessy Corporation and director of Standard Chartered Bank.

growth and that the tunnel would prove to be unprofitable, ending up as a drain on the UK taxpayers. Flexilink's campaign was in accord with the thinking of the British National Union of Seamen, which was also vigorously opposed to Eurotunnel because of the potential loss of jobs on the cross-Channel ferries. They feared that about 6,000 jobs would be lost in the Dover and Folkestone area once the tunnel was in operation.

French public opinion was generally in favor of the fixed link, especially since, during the construction period, Eurotunnel would bring needed jobs to the depressed Normandy area. The situation was less clear-cut where the prosperous southeast of England was in no need of construction employment opportunities and where concerns to preserve the environment might turn some sectors of the public against Eurotunnel.

The System

The Eurotunnel System was to comprise:

- Twin rail tunnels and a service tunnel under the Channel (see Exhibit 14.10).
- Two terminals, one at Folkestone near Dover in the UK and the other at Coquelles near Calais in France (see Exhibit 14.11).
- purpose-built shuttles to carry passenger and freight vehicles between the terminals (see Exhibit 14.12).
- Inland clearance depots for freight at the French terminal and at Ashford near Folkestone in the UK.
- Connections to nearby road and rail infrastructure.

The two main tunnels, of 7.6 m internal diameter, would each have a total length of just under 50 km, comprising 3 km under the French mainland, 38 km under the seabed and 8 km under the British mainland. In addition to the two main tunnels, a service tunnel of 4.8 m internal diameter was to be built, linked to the main tunnels by cross-passages. The service tunnel would provide ventilation to the main tunnels, permit the carrying out of routine safety and maintenance work, and provide a safe refuge in case of need. Two crossovers were planned between the rail tunnels to allow trains to continue to operate at reduced frequencies on a single track during periods of tunnel maintenance.

Corporate Structure

The corporate structure of Eurotunnel could be accurately described as a dual-bodied, single-headed transnational hybrid. Shown in Exhibit 14.13, it involved parallel groups of companies with common shareholders but separately registered and located in the UK and France, and joined together in a general partnership.

CTG and FM had already entered into an association constituting a partnership under English law and a *société en participation* under French law for the purpose of the operation and maintenance of Eurotunnel. Profits and losses (after financing and other costs but before depreciation and tax) were to be divided equally between CTG and FM. As of March 1986, the rest of the corporate structure was still on the drawing board, but it was planned to be implemented shortly, creating Eurotunnel plc and Eurotunnel, SA as legal entities.

Exhibit 14.10 *Rail and service tunnels*

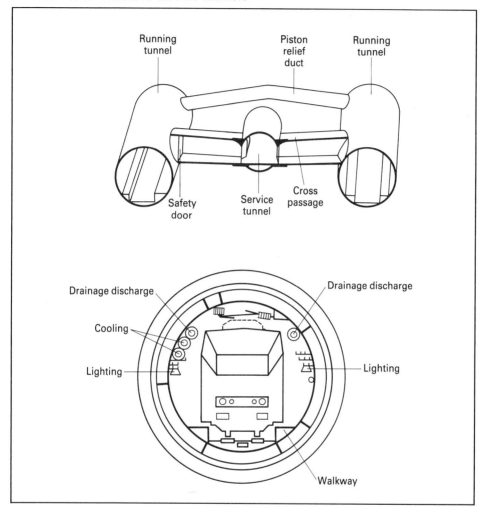

Eurotunnel Finance Limited and Eurotunnel Finance, SA would manage the finances of the partnership. Eurotunnel Developments Limited would enter into joint arrangements with third parties to hold and develop property in the UK not required for the building of the Eurotunnel System, to exploit opportunities brought about as a result of the construction and operation of the System and to promote traffic.

Organization and Management

Eurotunnel was to operate from a single head office in London where the majority of its staff were to be located. An office in Paris was to serve particular requirements in France such as

Exhibit 14.11 *The terminals. (a) Folkestone, UK. (b) Coquelles, France*

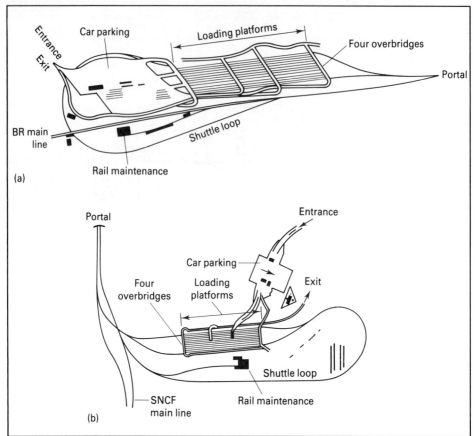

local land acquisition, statutory and accounting activities. Eurotunnel was to have three divisions: (i) finance, (ii) operations and project, and (iii) commercial.

The finance division was to include the treasurer's department, responsible for managing Eurotunnel's financial resources, the controller's department, responsible for all accounting and budgeting functions, and the taxation department, responsible for taxation advice and coordination.

The operations and project division was to be made up of the operations department, responsible for defining the operational requirements, optimization parameters and maintenance policy of the System; the project administration and control department, responsible for the establishment of project procedures, flow and dispatch of information, project forecasts and reporting, cost and time control, and review of quality assurance and safety procedures proposed by the contractor; and the project design and construction department, responsible for control and approval of the design and the works, incorporation of Eurotunnel's requirements into the design, certification of payment, approval of programmes, issuance of instructions and decisions to the contractor and the maitre d'oeuvre,

Exhibit 14.12   *The shuttles*

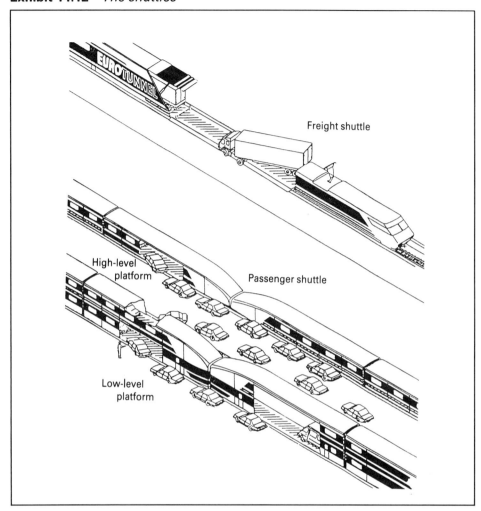

the administration of the construction contract and the maitre d'oeuvre contract, and the administration of variations and claims.

The commercial division was to comprise the commercial/technical coordination department, responsible for ensuring that the commercial needs of the company were taken into account during the optimization process of the System design; and the commercial department which was to determine the needs of the marketplace through contact with future user groups, establish internal traffic forecasting methods, liaise with external traffic and revenue consultants, establish the internal procedures for ensuring that user needs were met, negotiate contracts and tariffs, and identify and manage sources of ancillary revenue in the terminal areas and shuttles. From approximately thirty months prior to the opening of the

Exhibit 14.13 *Corporate structure of Eurotunnel*

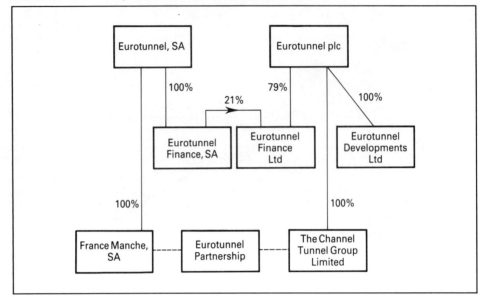

System, full client account, sales and marketing departments were planned to be progressively introduced.

The chief executive was to be responsible for the management of Eurotunnel in close consultation with the co-chairmen of the board. His responsibilities were to be carried out through meetings with executives in Eurotunnel's divisions and through formal meetings of the chief executive's committee, the finance task force and the executive group. The chief executive's committee was to be responsible for implementing the joint board's overall strategic policies.

Construction

Construction was to be carried out by the contractor, Transmanche Link, under a single general obligation to design, construct, test and commission a fully operational system within seven years of signing the construction contract. Transmanche Link was a joint venture of Translink of the UK and Transmanche Construction of France, the first being a joint venture between Balfoure Beatty, Costain, Tarmac, Taylor Woodrow and Wimpey, all of the UK, and the second being a *groupement d'intérêt économique* between Bouygues, Dumez, Société Auxiliare d'Entreprises, Société Générale d'Entreprises and Spie Batignolles, all of France. In effect, then, those promoters and initial Equity I shareholders of CTG–FM who were construction companies were to become the contractors under a separate contractual obligation.

It was planned that the construction contract be divided into three main parts, the target works, the lump sum works, and the procurement items.

- Target works, comprising the tunnels, and underground structures accounting for about 50% of the contract price, would be paid for on a cost plus 12% profit basis. If the actual cost were less than the targeted cost, the contractor would receive 50% of the savings but, if it were more, he would pay 30% of the cost overrun up to a ceiling of 6% of the target cost.

- *The lump sum works*, comprising the buildings and infrastructure of the terminals, the fixed equipment and the mechanical and electrical elements of the system, were to be paid for on a lump sum basis, with the contractor either enjoying totally savings for delivering the lump sum works under budget or paying totally for any cost overrun.

- *The procurement items* were principally the locomotives and the shuttles. These would be subcontracted by the contractor. Payment of the subcontracted bid price would be made directly and fully by Eurotunnel to the subcontractors. Since the contractor was to supervise bidding for and implementing of the subcontracts, it would be paid its direct costs for carrying out this work plus about 12% of the value of the procurement items.

  In addition, the contractor was liable to pay damages of about £350,000 per day up to 6 months and £500,000 per day thereafter for every day which the project was delayed beyond the final completion deadline.

The obligations of the contractor were to be secured by a performance bond equal to 10% of the total value of the contract which would be released upon System completion. In addition, 5% of the amount due to the contractor on progress payments would be withheld or covered by a bond during the construction period and would be released in two installments, 12 and 24 months respectively from System completion. The five French and five British parent companies of the contractor would also give general guarantees covering 100% of the contractual obligations of the contractor with the joint liability of each of the French parents and the several liability of each of the UK parents to be limited to 50% and 10%, respectively.

The contractor would be entitled to no release from obligations due to strikes of its own labor; however, general strikes interrupting the required flow of goods or materials would be cause for completion date extension. Similarly, the contractor would be liable for delays and cost overruns caused by accidents or flooding but could be released from obligations to the extent that delays or cost overruns were caused by changes in specifications by Eurotunnel or the actions of the British and French governments, or if the bedrock conditions were different from those determined by Eurotunnel.

To supervise the work of the contractors, determine progress for release of progress payments, assess budget performance and provide an objective assessment of the work to the lending banks, Eurotunnel intended to appoint the reputable and otherwise uninvolved firms of W.S. Atkins & Partners and Société d'Etudes Techniques et Economiques to serve jointly as maitre d'oeuvre. The maitre d'oeuvre, expected to employ up to 100 persons on-site, would also be responsible for supervising standards of safety and quality of construction.

Eurotunnel was to be built by boring the three parallel tunnels (i.e. two train tunnels and one service tunnel) through the bedrock beneath the Channel. Studies determined that there were three principal strata along the route chosen for the tunnel, as shown in Exhibit 14.14

Since chalk marl, the second stratum from the surface at a depth of about 100 m, provided an ideal tunneling medium, impermeable to water but relatively soft, it was planned to locate the maximum possible length of the undersea tunnel, 90%, through it, and to restrict as much

Exhibit 14.14 *Planned course of Eurotunnel through the bedrock*

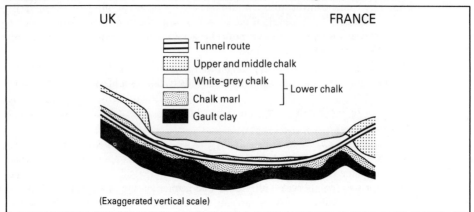

(Exaggerated vertical scale)

as possible tunneling through the fractured chalk of the surface stratum, where there was the risk that water would be encountered in fissures. The most difficult tunneling conditions were expected to be encountered in the section near the French coast, where tunneling through the first stratum was unavoidable. There, the 'closed face' method of boring would be used as opposed to the faster 'open face' method usable on the chalk marl. By constantly probing the ground 100 m ahead of the face, it was considered that water-bearing fissures could be detected and grouted, preventing serious water inflow.

This technique would also minimize the risk of ground collapse in the fissured upper stratum. The chalk marl was considered stable enough to be safely left unsupported over a small length for a short period of time, enabling the lining for the most part to be erected immediately behind the shields of the tunnel-boring machines. If the ground conditions so required, the UK machines would have the facility for sealing the face in an emergency, allowing building the tunnel lining inside the tail-skin of the tunnel-boring machines. On the French side, because the ground was generally less stable, this method was to be used at all times. Once completed, it was considered that only a major earthquake could cause a collapse and flooding of the tunnel.

To prevent fire in the tunnels during construction, combustible material in the tunnels was to be kept to a minimum; fire extinguishing equipment was to be kept at all locations, key personnel were to be trained to deal correctly with fires, heat sensors to trigger equipment shut-off were to be installed on any potentially combustible pieces of equipment, and strict rules were to be observed regarding use of welding and oxyacetylene equipment in the tunnels. Care would be taken to ensure that ventilation systems were correctly controlled and could be reversed or shut-off, whilst minimizing the danger of suffocation, and that emergency breathing apparatus or air supplies would be available at the working face.

It was widely appreciated that, as planned by Eurotunnel, the construction of the System would not be a difficult technical exercise. Compared to the much delayed Saikan Tunnel between Hokkaido and Honshu in Japan, where the rock was hard and highly fissured and the zone was earthquake prone, conditions for construction of Eurotunnel were excellent. Moreover, the simplicity of the design – which had been a key factor in its selection by the British and French governments – increased the chances of the System being completed on time and within budget.

Financing

To build the System and run Eurotunnel, its subsidiaries and associated companies from ground-breaking to opening it was estimated that approximately £4.8 billion was needed to be used as follows:

	£bn
Construction costs	2.8
Corporate and other costs	0.5
Provision for inflation	0.5
Net financing costs	1.0
Total	£4.8 bn

A detailed breakdown of these costs is given in Exhibit 14.15. To meet these costs plus unanticipated cost overruns, it was planned to raise funds as follows:

	£bn
Equity	1.0
Loans	5.0
Total	£6.0 bn

To help cope with the tricky problem of raising £6 billion for a greenfield project without third-party guarantees, Eurotunnel planned to raise financing in several stages:

1. Prior to selection by the French and UK governments, the Arranging Banks had obtained strongly worded letters of intent from 33 banks to underwrite loans of approximately £4.4 billion.
2. Upon selection, in January 1986, the founding shareholders contributed equity of £50 million into CTG–FR in what was known as Equity I.
3. The Arranging Banks then worked to increase the numbers of underwriting banks for the loan financing to 40 in the spring of 1986 and to formalize their several obligations in a binding commitment to underwrite a £5 billion syndicated loans. Syndication was planned to follow signing the construction contract and completion of Equity II.
4. It was planned that in June 1986 the second issue of shares, Equity II would occur. This issue would raise a further £150–£250 million.
5. Signing of the underwriting agreement and general syndication of the £5 billion debt would then follow. Drawdown would not be allowed to occur, however, until the full £1 billion of equity had been raised and a large portion of it had been spent.
6. Equity III, by which the balance of the £1 billion equity would be raised, was planned for the first half of 1987.

Following completion of the System, in its first full year of operation, it was anticipated that 79% of Eurotunnel's total costs would be accounted for by capital charges, i.e. interest and depreciation. Capital charges as a proportion of total costs were estimated to decline steadily thereafter, particularly from 2012 onwards. Moreover, it was anticipated that project debt could be prepaid and cheaper financing could be easily arranged, further lightening the debt burden.

Exhibit 14.15 *Expected cost summary (£m)*

	1986	1987	1988	1989	1990	1991	1992	1993	Total
Construction[1]	14	168	504	575	671	507	300	22	2,761
Owning group[1]	37	103	81	74	70	66	73	61	565
Inflation	–	3	30	68	118	130	110	30	489
Net financing[2]	8	49	29	95	160	245	327	111	1,024
Total	59	323	644	812	1,019	948	810	224	4,839

[1] Up to opening of the tunnel and at April 1987 prices.
[2] Up to 30 June 1993, at current prices.

Estimate of owning group costs prior to System completion

	£m
Management	146.8
Operations	38.1
Office	20.6
Finance	51.6
Insurance	65.0
Land and property	29.1
Parliamentary	15.1
Maitre d'oeuvre	72.7
Provisional sums	126.3
Total	£565.3m

Net financing costs

	1987	1988	1989	1990	1991 on
Inflation rate	4.5%	4.5%	5.0%	5.5%	6.0%
Real interest rate	5.0%	4.5%	4.0%	3.5%	3.0%
Interest rate (before margin)	9.0%	9.0%	9.0%	9.0%	9.0%
Interest received on credit balances	8.5%	8.5%	8.5%	8.5%	8.5%

Revenues – Sensitivities

The two largest direct customers of the System were to be the national government-owned railway companies British Rail (BR) and Société Nationale des Chemins de Fer Français (SNCF), whose relationship with Eurotunnel was to be defined under contract. Half of Eurotunnel's revenues were anticipated to come from the railways. Thus, in the preselection months of November 1985 to January 1986, the competing contractors had spent much effort ardently courting BR and SNCF to secure their commitments to contract to use the fixed link.

The other half of Eurotunnel's revenues were to come from road vehicles. The vehicles, together with their drivers and passengers were to be transported in specially designed shuttles running at speeds of up to 160 kph between the terminals. Different types of shuttle would transport passengers and freight. During the journey, drivers and their passengers would normally remain in their vehicles.

Eurotunnel expected to have competitive advantage over existing cross-Channel services, i.e. ferry and hovercraft services between various ports and airline services between major cities. Eurotunnel's services would not be as vulnerable to the adverse weather conditions in the Channel which disrupt ferry, and particularly hovercraft, services. Eurotunnel planned to operate all year round, and with a higher frequency of service compared with that offered at equivalent times by existing operators.

A schematic chart showing a comparison of the shuttle's journey time with those of the ferry and hovercraft services between Dover and Calais is given in Exhibit 14.16. The total times in the chart are for journeys between a common point on the M20 motorway in the UK and a common point on the A26 autoroute in France, through which points the bulk of road traffic on the Dover–Calais route is expected to pass. It should be noted that the chart compares ferry, hovercraft and shuttle services outside periods of exceptional demand and in good weather conditions.

In France, SNCF was proposing a new, high-speed railway line between Paris and Brussels and a branch constructed to the French terminal of Eurotunnel. The construction of these lines would enable the new passenger trains to travel at speeds of up to 300 kph in France and Belgium, and, with planned improvements to traditional tracks on the UK side, would permit direct rail services between London and Paris and London and Brussels taking approximately 3 hours and 2½ hours, respectively. Exhibit 14.17 compares travel times on

Exhibit 14.16 *Comparison of journey times between Dover and Calais*

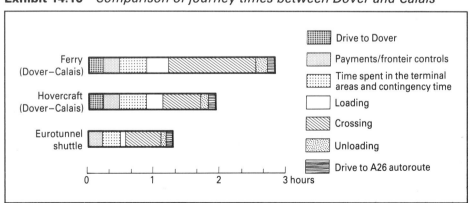

Exhibit 14.17   *Comparison of journey times between London and Paris*

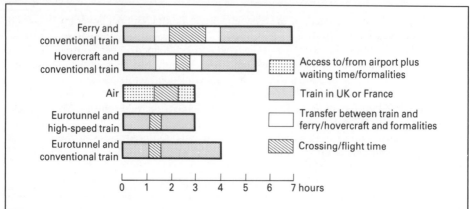

major scheduled services between the city centers of London and Paris taking into account the introduction of a high-speed train service.

To assess the likely future demand for the tunnel and the resultant revenue prospects over the concession period, Eurotunnel selected SETEC Economic from France, Wilbur Smith Associates from the USA (WSA), and Alastair Dick and Associates from the UK (ADA) as marketing consultants. The SETEC/WSA/ADA's market assessment approach comprised:

1. A review of past trends in passenger and freight traffic by sea and passenger traffic by air between the UK and mainland Europe by consumer categories.
2. An assessment of likely total traffic flows in 1993 and thereafter.
3. An estimate of Eurotunnel's share of this future market ('diverted traffic'), by allocating traffic flows by routes and mode of transport.
4. A forecast of the additional traffic that is likely to be created as a consequence of the existence of the tunnel ('created traffic').
5. An estimate of the revenues to be generated from the above traffic and from ancillary activities.

Their assessments, summarized in Exhibit 14.18, were based on the following key assumptions:

(a) High-speed railway services between London and both Paris and Brussels would be available at the start of operations.
(b) Duty-free facilities would be permitted throughout the concession period.

The SETEC/WSA/ADA study concluded that Eurotunnel was economically feasible. It projected that the total cross-Channel market would grow from 48.1 million passenger trips and 60.4 million tonnes of freight in 1985 to 88.1 million passenger trips and 122.1 million tonnes of freight by 2003 and concluded that Eurotunnel would be able to attract a large proportion of this growing market. On the passenger side, as Eurotunnel would require no pre-booking, the service would be substantially faster and more convenient and reliable than existing ferry services (for through-rail passengers between London and Paris, for example, the service

Exhibit 14.18 *Market data and projections*

Historical growth and forecasts for cross-Channel traffic

	1975–1985 Annual growth rate (%)	Actual 1985	1985–1993 Annual growth rate (%)	Forecast 1993	1993–2003 Annual growth rate (%)	Forecast 2003	2003–2013 Annual growth rate (%)	Forecast 2013
Passengers (million p.a.):								
Foot	6.6	35.6	3.4	46.4	3.0	62.6	2.5	80.3
Car	3.6	7.3	3.5	9.6	2.8	12.6	1.6	14.7
Coach	11.4	5.2	6.0	8.3	4.5	12.9	2.7	16.9
Total	6.5	48.1	3.7	64.3	3.2	88.1	2.4	111.9
Freight (million gross tonnes p.a.):								
Unitized	6.9	27.0	4.9	39.8	4.1	59.7	3.6	85.4
Non unitized	3.5	33.4	3.7	44.6	3.4	62.4	3.1	84.4
Total	5.0	60.4	4.3	84.4	3.8	122.1	3.4	169.8

Estimate of Eurotunnel's share of the market

	1993[1] Tunnel traffic	Share of global market to tunnel (%)	2003 Tunnel traffic	Share of global market to tunnel (%)	2013 Tunnel traffic	Share of global market to tunnel (%)
Passengers (million trips p.a.)						
Shuttles						
Car	6.0	6.3	7.5	59	8.3	57
Excursions	2.2	76	2.7	75	3.0	75
Coach	4.2	51	5.9	46	6.9	41
Total shuttles	12.4		16.1		18.2	

Exhibit 14.18 *continued*

Estimate of Eurotunnel's share of the market

	1993[1]		2003		2013	
	Tunnel traffic	Share of global market to tunnel (%)	Tunnel traffic	Share of global market to tunnel (%)	Tunnel traffic	Share of global market to tunnel (%)
Railways						
Diverted from coach	2.5	30	4.6	36	6.9	41
Diverted from sea	6.2	97	5.3	97	4.3	96
Diverted from air	5.8	16	8.0	15	10.4	15
Total railways	14.5	—	17.9	—	21.6	—
Total	26.9	42	34.0	39	39.8	36
Freight (million gross tonnes p.a.)						
Shuttles						
Unitized: Roll-on, Roll-off	7.5	24	10.3	22	13.0	20
Railways						
Unitized: RoRo diverted to rail	1.0	3	1.5	3	2.1	3
Containers and wagons	3.4	37	4.9	37	7.0	37
Nonunitized: Bulk	2.4	5	2.9	5	3.4	4
New vehicles	0.5	37	1.0	35	1.7	34
Total railways	7.3	—	10.3	—	14.2	—
Total	14.8	17	20.6	17	27.2	16

Exhibit 14.18 *continued*

Estimate of created traffic

	1993[1]		2003		2013	
	Price-induced	Other	Price-induced	Other	Price-induced	Other
Passengers (millions trips p.a.)						
Car shuttle	0.3	—	0.4	0.4	0.4	0.5
Coach shuttle	0.5	—	0.7	0.5	0.8	0.6
Rail	2.0	—	2.5	1.0	3.1	1.4
Total	2.8	—	3.6	1.9	4.3	2.5
Freight (million gross tonnes p.a.)						
Roll-on, Roll-off shuttle	—	—	0.2		0.2	
Rail: unitized	—	—	0.3		0.4	
Total	—	—	0.5		0.6	

Forecast of total revenues at 1987 prices

	1993[1]			2003			2013		
	Diverted	Created	Total	Diverted	Created	Total	Diverted	Created	Total
	£ million			£ million			£ million		
Shuttle									
Car	130.9	7.2	138.1	163.7	15.9	179.6	182.0	20.9	202.9
Coach	34.7	2.5	37.2	47.3	6.1	53.4	54.7	8.0	62.7
Roll-on, Roll-off	75.6	—	75.6	103.7	2.0	105.7	131.0	2.3	133.3
Subtotal	241.2	9.7	250.9	314.7	24.0	338.7	367.7	31.2	398.9

Exhibit 14.18 *continued*

Railways								
Tolls	173.8	13.8	187.6	195.5	22.8	218.3	211.9	20.9	232.8
Contribution to operating costs	18.2	1.6	19.8	25.7	3.4	29.1	31.7	4.1	35.8
Subtotal	192.0	15.4	207.4	221.2	26.2	247.4	243.6	25.0	268.6
Ancillary	40.3	2.1	42.4	50.9	5.0	55.9	57.2	6.5	63.7
Total	473.5	27.2	500.7	586.8	55.2	642.0	668.5	62.7	731.2

1. Stated as for a full year of operation.

would be twice as fast as and far more convenient than existing rail–sea–rail services) and would be competitive with air services in terms of cost and, operating from city center to city center, time. SETEC/WSA/ADA projected that Eurotunnel would gain in 1993 some 42% of the passenger market. For rail freight, as Eurotunnel would provide for the first time a through service which would avoid transshipment, allowing rail freight to and from the UK to become competitive with road freight, with a consequent potential for an environmentally attractive shift of goods traffic off roads and onto rail, SETEC/WSA/ADA projected that in 1993 some 17% of freight traffic would go through Eurotunnel. These proportions were projected to decline to 36% of passenger traffic and 16% of freight traffic by 2013.

The study also concluded that Eurotunnel's existence, and the general lowering of the cost of travel it should bring, would lead to the creation of a certain amount of new traffic. On the basis of SETEC/WSA/ADA's forecasts, Eurotunnel would, in its first full year of operations, carry a total of some 30 million passengers and 15 million tonnes of freight.

Revenues would come from three sources: (i) shuttle fares, assumed at opening to match the then prevailing fares for Dover–Calais ferries, in turn estimated to be 20% lower in real terms than 1986 prices for freight, and 5% lower in real terms than 1986 prices for passengers, (ii) railway charges and tolls, (iii) ancillary revenues, for example catering and duty-free sales to passengers passing through the terminals, and payments in respect of the use of the tunnel as a conduit for cables.

The total income expected by SETEC/WSA/ADA in 1993, stated for a full year of operations, was some £500 million in April 1987 prices, rising to some £642 million in 2003. The split between the sources of this income in 1993 is expected to be shuttle 50%, rail 41% and ancillary 9%.

As the base case was predicated on UK GDP growth rates of 2.15% p.a. from 1985 to 2003 and 2.0% thereafter, French GDP growth rates of 2.25% p.a. and Belgian GDP growth rates of 1.9% p.a., sensitivities to determine the effects on revenues of variation in growth rates of 0.5% p.a. were calculated as shown in Exhibit 14.19. Other sensitivities relative to the SETEC/WSA/ADA base case were calculated as shown in Exhibit 14.20.

SETEC/WSA/ADA also studied the impact of changes on revenues in case of nonavailability of high-speed railway services, assuming 4 hour transit time London–Paris and 3 hours 40 minutes London–Brussels. They concluded that, assuming a base case of 100, projected revenues would decrease by 1%.

Prognos, AG of Switzerland reviewed the forecasts produced by SETEC/WSA/ADA and judged that the models developed were adequate tools to forecast both global cross-Channel traffic and tunnel traffic for passengers and freight. While a sensitivity test, using

Exhibit 14.19 *Effect on revenues of varying GDP growth rates by 0.5% p.a.*

	1993		2003	
	Increase	Decrease	Increase	Decrease
Passengers	104.9	95.1	107.0	93.0
Freight	106.2	93.8	112.4	87.6
Total	105.1	94.9	108.5	91.5

Exhibit 14.20 *Effect on revenues of varying critical assumptions*

Changes relative to base case	Cases (index 100 – basic assumptions)					
Ferry tariffs	90.0	90.0	100.0	110.0	110.0	110.0
Tunnel tolls	90.0	100.0	90.0	110.0	100.0	110.0
Revenue change						
Car passengers	89.5	80.4	113.3	110.7	122.0	90.8
Coach passengers	89.5	91.3	98.0	110.7	108.7	101.9
Lorries (RoRo)	90.3	89.5	100.9	109.7	110.5	99.2
Container/wagons	88.8	92.0	96.6	111.3	107.9	103.1
Total traffic						
revenue	**93.6**	**91.0**	**103.3**	**106.5**	**109.8**	**97.4**

socioeconomic parameters developed independently by Prognos revealed significant differences in traffic volume by type of traffic, the test confirmed the overall level of the SETEC/WSA/ADA revenue forecasts. Prognos concurred with SETEC/WSA/ADA's view that the ability of ferry operators to reduce their tariffs in response to the tunnel is very limited. Prognos believed that a price war would be to the disadvantage of ferry operators in the long term and therefore not in their interest. SETEC/WSA/ADA and Prognos differed in their view on the assessment of competition from air services. Prognos believed that the liberalization of European air transport would lead to price cuts which will reduce air fares, and consequently through-rail passenger traffic, further than was assumed by SETEC/WSA/ADA. They also believed that traffic build-up would be slower than assumed. The impact of such changes on SETEC/WSA/ADA's forecast would be to reduce total projected tunnel revenues by 9.5% in 1993 and 3.9% in 2003.

Exhibit 14.20 illustrates the effect on revenues of varying pricing and traffic assumptions.

Operating Risks

It was widely considered that fire would pose the most serious operating risk. A conflagration could spread quickly as petrol-filled vehicles caught alight. Hundreds of people caught in the close confines of the tunnel could be killed by flames and highly noxious gases. A possible remedy, the segregation of passengers and vehicles during the journey, had been rejected as it would increase loading times and adversely affect Eurotunnel's time competitiveness.

The shuttle trains and the tunnel were designed to incorporate the most up-to-date fire prevention and fire-fighting technology. A continuous walkway alongside the track linked by connecting passages to the central service tunnel was to facilitate evacuation of passengers in case of emergency. In the event of a serious blaze, each wagon would be capable of being automatically uncoupled from the train so that the fire can be isolated. Locomotives would be situated at either end of the shuttle to allow exit either in Britain or France. Fire doors would be designed to prevent fire and noxious fumes spreading to other wagons and allow passengers time to escape. Fire curtains would be able to contain a fire and stop any fumes spreading to any other wagon for at least 30 minutes.

The prospect of trains colliding head-on would be ruled out by the construction of two separate rail tunnels side by side. Under normal conditions, trains would be permitted to

Exhibit 14.21 *Cash flow projections*

	1993 £m	1994 £m	1995 £m	1996 £m	1997 £m	1998 £m	1999 £m	2000 £m	2001 £m	2002 £m	2003 £m	2013 £m	2023 £m	2033 £m	2043 £m
Turnover [1]	488	762	835	908	985	1,072	1,158	1,254	1,356	1,466	1,586	3,236	6,184	11,356	17,824
Operating costs [2]	(86)	(145)	(155)	(168)	(183)	(206)	(216)	(235)	(255)	(277)	(304)	(631)	(1,207)	(2,246)	(3,604)
Depreciation	(103)	(158)	(159)	(160)	(162)	(167)	(169)	(171)	(173)	(176)	(184)	(234)	(271)	(328)	(383)
Interest, net	(229)	(351)	(322)	(307)	(291)	(277)	(265)	(234)	(212)	(190)	(171)	39	173	370	616
Profit before taxation	70	108	199	273	350	422	508	614	716	823	927	2,419	4,879	9,152	14,453
Taxation	(7)	(18)	(38)	(53)	(69)	(88)	(198)	(240)	(279)	(321)	(361)	(934)	(1,893)	(3,547)	(5,573)
Profit after taxation	63	90	161	220	281	334	310	374	437	502	566	1,476	2,986	5,605	8,880
Transfer to reserves	(1)	(2)	(3)	(3)	(4)	(6)	(7)	(9)	(5)	–	–	–	–	–	–
Profit for the year available for distribution	62	88	158	217	277	328	303	365	432	502	566	1,476	2,986	5,605	8,880
Dividends payable	–	149	169	217	277	328	303	365	432	502	566	1,476	2,986	5,605	8,880
Per unit	–	£0.39	£0.44	£0.56	£0.71	£0.85	£0.78	£0.94	£1.11	£1.29	£1.46	£3.80	£7.70	£14.44	£22.88
1. Turnover is derived as follows:															
Shuttle	251	384	423	463	505	551	599	652	709	770	836	1,763	3,527	6,682	10,650
Rail	194	314	341	368	396	430	459	493	530	569	612	1,191	2,105	3,641	5,526
Ancillary	43	64	71	77	85	91	100	109	117	127	138	282	552	1,033	1,648
Total	488	762	835	908	986	1,072	1,158	1,254	1,356	1,466	1,586	3,236	6,184	11,356	17,824
2. Operating costs are analysed as follows:															
Fixed expenses	53	88	92	99	107	117	126	137	148	161	174	314	562	1,006	1,604
Variable expenses	33	57	63	69	76	89	90	98	107	116	130	317	645	1,240	2,000
Total	86	145	155	168	183	206	216	235	255	277	304	631	1,207	2,246	3,604

3. The figures for 1993 represents trading only from the opening date in May to December. Dividends in 1994 and 1995 include distribution of reserves carried forward from earlier year.

4. On the basis of the assumption relating to inflation, £1 in July 1987 is approximately equivalent to £1.45 in 1994; £1.83 in 1998; £2.45 in 2003; £4.38 in 2013; £7.84 in 2023; £14.05 in 2033 and £22.39 in 2041. Although dividing the projected figures by these values does not give the same result as if no inflation had been assumed in the projections, it does provide an approximate equivalent in July 1987 prices of the figures shown.

Exhibit 14.21 *continued*

Bases and assumptions

Traffic and revenue

For the purpose of their forecasts of traffic and revenue, Eurotunnel's traffic and revenue consultants have made certain macroeconomic assumptions, the most important of which relates to the growth in UK gross domestic product. It has been assumed that UK gross domestic product will grow at 2.15% per annum between 1985 and 2003 and at 2.00% per annum between 2003 and 2013. After 2013 a decreasing growth rate in traffic volumes has been assumed, declining to zero by 2042. They have made other basic assumptions as follows:

(i)   Currently envisaged international agreements and conventions regarding trade and passenger movement will remain in effect throughout the forecasting period. In particular, the current proposals for the internal market within the European Community have been taken into account.

(ii) No national or international emergencies will arise which will abnormally affect cross-Channel traffic.

(iii) No alternative fixed link across the Channel will become operational during the concession period.

(iv) Ferry companies will continue to operate cross-Channel services both before and after the System becomes operational.

(v)   The System will be adequately marketed, signposted, advertised and maintained to encourage maximum usage.

(vi) Tariffs for Eurotunnel shuttle services will on average be the same as those for ferry services on the Dover–Calais routes and will remain constant in real terms.

(vii) Revenues derived by Eurotunnel from through-rail services will be based upon the usage charges and contribution to operating costs set out in the railway usage contract. The provisions of that contract will be implemented and the proposed high-speed railway linking Paris, Brussels and the French terminal will be constructed and operational by the time the System opens.

(viii) Eurotunnel will be able to make duty- and tax-free sales to passengers using shuttle services.

Financial and other

For the purpose of the projections of profit, the following assumptions have been made by the directors:

(i)   The System will be built according to the specifications of and costs set out in the construction contract and will open to traffic during May 1993, at which time it will become fully operational for all forms of shuttle and train traffic.

(ii) All necessary approvals will be obtained from the intergovernmental commission and the safety authority without conditions which require material changes to the System or its operation as currently proposed.

(iii) Traffic and revenues will be as forecast by the traffic and revenue consultants, modified to reflect the partial year of operation in 1993, updated to July 1987 values and adjusted for inflation on the basis set out below.

(iv) Corporate and other costs between 21 January 1986 and the start of operations will be £642 million at July 1987 prices.

(v)   The equivalent of £770 million of equity funding will be raised through this issue at the prices per unit set out in this document.

(vi) The equivalent of £101 million will be raised in November 1992, £52 million in December 1994 and £25 million in June 1995 by the exercise of warrants.

Exhibit 14.21 *continued*

Bases and assumptions (continued)
Financial and other

(vii) The tax regimes in the UK and France will not change and the published protocol to the UK/France double tax convention will be ratified.

(viii) Subject to compliance with the terms of the credit agreement, following the start of operations all profits available for distribution under UK and French law will be distributed each year as dividends to shareholders. Where necessary, surplus cash in any group company will be available to finance dividends.

(ix) The FFr exchange rate will be £1:FFr 10.0 throughout the period to the end of the concession and no losses or gains will arise on transactions in other currencies.

(x) Inflation will increase revenues, overheads, operating costs and capital expenditure at the following rates per annum:

1987	4.0%
1988	4.5%
1989	5.0%
1990	5.5%
1991 and thereafter	6.0%

(xi) Interest will be received on cash balances at a rate of 8.5% per annum throughout the concession period.

(xii) Revenues and costs (excluding depreciation and tax) will be shared equally between the concessionaire companies. The Channel Tunnel Group Limited (CTG) and France Manche, SA (FM).

(xiii) The travel privileges for subscribers to this issue will not significantly affect Eurotunnel's revenues, operating costs or taxation.

---

travel in one direction only. Computer-controlled signalling, monitoring and override devices would be installed alongside the track and inside the shuttles as well as in 'control towers' at either end of the tunnel to prevent trains from running into the back of each other.

Sensors and highly sensitive surveillance equipment would be installed in passenger terminals at either end of the tunnel to combat the possibility of a terrorist attack. The tunnel, buried between 17 and 40 m below the seabed, was thought to be impossible to bring down by conventional explosives. A bomb inside a shuttle wagon could inflict damage in the immediate vicinity, but it was believed that the design of the fire curtains would limit the number of casualties and prevent any subsequent fire from getting out of control.

The Wellcome Share Offering (A)
Strategy

In 1992, Britain's number one medical research charity, The Wellcome Trust, made the largest fully-paid non-privatisation secondary offering of shares ever to take place on the UK Stock Exchange and internationally. Since the Trust was the dominant shareholder in the drug company Wellcome plc, such an offering was clearly of major strategic importance to both organisations. This case explores the strategic thinking behind this giant share sale and concludes that it provided attractive benefits to the Trust and the 'Company'.

The Wellcome Share Offering: Strategic Aspects

The Offering

Number One, Park Square West is a handsome Regency building just a few steps from one of the entrances to London's Regent's Park. It was from his first floor office that the chairman of The Wellcome Trust, Roger Gibbs, contemplated the events that were just about to take place in July 1992 – the largest fully-paid non-privatisation secondary offering of equity shares ever to take place on the UK Stock Exchange, and internationally as well. Eventually, 288 million shares were sold for £2.3 billion.

How is it that The Wellcome Trust, Britain's distinguished and largest medical research charity (with assets nearly 10 times the size of those of its nearest UK rival – see Exhibit 15.1) came to be the instigator of such a dramatic share-selling blockbuster?

This case was written by Paul Stonham as a basis for class discussion rather than to illustrate either effective or ineffective handling of an administrative situation. The author is grateful to executives of the organisations concerned for discussions on the events of this case study. Responsibility for the final version of this case study rests with the author only. © European Management Journal, 1993.

Exhibit 15.1 *Top UK trusts 1991 (£m)*

	Grants	Assets
Wellcome Trust	58.40	3,250.00
Tudor Trust	15.78	117.16
Gatsby Charitable Foundation	11.84	198.66
Leverhulme Trust	11.20	330.00
Royal Society	10.67	28.86
Wolfson Foundation	8.64	54.74
Henry Smith (Estates Charities)	7.49	100.00
Baring Foundation	7.25	38.64
Rank Foundation	7.19	107.49
Monument Trust	7.07	74.63

Source: Charities Aid Foundation.

History of The Wellcome Trust's Funding

The answer goes back a long way. On 27 September 1880, two American pharmacists, Silas Burroughs and Henry Wellcome, both of whom later became British subjects, established a partnership in London, Burroughs, Wellcome and Co. Later, this and subsequently-established businesses were taken over by the Wellcome Foundation Limited (WFL), which was incorporated. Sir Henry Wellcome died in 1936 leaving the share capital of WFL to be held on charitable trust (now known as The Wellcome Trust), the objectives of which are the advancement of research in human and animal medicine and the support of the history of medicine.

To date, the Trust has funded some headline-catching research successes, such as:

- The first study in the UK into what turned out to be AIDS. Current work is on the leading edge of AIDS research.

- Greater understanding of spongiform encephalopathy ('mad cow disease').

- Techniques to assist the survival of premature babies.

The Trust also has a reputation for funding 'Cinderella' areas of research – those fields finding it hard to gain financial support from other sources. These include mental health, skin diseases, vision and tropical medicine. These do not readily attract the interest of commercial pharmaceutical companies.

In 1986, the Trust transferred its shares in WFL to Wellcome plc ('the Company') in exchange for ordinary shares in the Company.

Although the Trust and the Company may be synonymous in the mind of the general public, linked through the name Wellcome, they are in fact completely separate. In common with other UK charities, the Trust is subject to supervision by the Charity Commissioners and the UK courts. Consent was required by the Charity Commissioners in 1986 to allow the Trust to exchange its shares in WFL for shares in the Company, now newly-formed as a holding company for the Group.

The research programmes funded by the Trust are administered totally separately from the Company's research, and are directed towards different aims. The Trust exercises its rights as a shareholder (and, of course, a dominant shareholder), but plays no role in the management of the Company. It has no representation on the board of the Company.

In 1986, the Company was floated publicly and given a Stock Exchange quotation. At that time, the Trust owned 100% of the stock of the Company but, as Roger Gibbs put it

> The Trust decided it had too much of its assets in one basket, and considered it important to diversify its portfolio. The Trust portfolio was being used, as it is now, to finance medical research.

The best way to diversify was to achieve a stock market listing. So the Trust disposed of approximately 21% of its holding in the Company. A new holding company, Wellcome plc, was formed for the Wellcome Group as a whole. The Wellcome Foundation Limited continued in being as a private company and the principal operating subsidiary of Wellcome plc. As well as the new listing, the Company issued 5% new shares for cash and also issued employee share options. So, up to 1992 and the share offering of that year, the Trust held approximately 73.5% of the Company's ordinary shares.

The Trust said in the 1986 prospectus for going public that it would sell no more shares until at least two years had elapsed. The Trust explained that it wished the whole investment world to appreciate the qualities of Wellcome more fully and also to give the Company time to grow. Both these things came true. In those two years alone, turnover increased by 25%, pre-tax profits by 76% and earnings per share nearly doubled. Over the same period, the shares of Wellcome became scarce (pharmaceuticals are a defensive stock, and Wellcome was held more tightly as it showed good growth).

In 30 June 1990, the chairman and chief executive, Sir Alfred Shepherd, retired. There were two successors for his joint role, Sir Alistair Frame as chairman and John Robb as chief executive. From the Trust's point of view, it seemed an inappropriate time to consider again selling more shares. It would have given the market the wrong signal. The Trust decided to wait until the new management had made its impact, and a further two year period was thought suitable. Again, its confidence was fully justified; turnover increased by 31%, pre-tax profits by 60% and EPS by 58%. In addition, the Company underwent considerable strategic and structural reorientation for the long run in that period.

By the spring of 1992, The Wellcome Trust, with the help of its financial adviser, was of the opinion that the time could now be right to divest itself of more Wellcome plc shares. In the background to this decision were several factors affecting the Trust's operations.

First, although it was experiencing a rapidly rising income (7.8% annual average RPI – indexed over recent years), the director of the Trust, Dr. Bridget Olgivie, reported in 1991 that demands on its resources had never been greater, resulting in a progressive decline in the percentage of applications that could be funded in whole or in part.

Second, higher education institutions in the UK had faced continual reductions in their resources for more than a decade. With even less government help forthcoming, the demands on the Trust's fund would accelerate.

The Reasons for Diversifying

With the demand for its funds ever increasing, the Trust took a closer look at the structure of its income. Again, it believed it was over-concentrated on holdings of Wellcome plc shares. Wellcome shares are growth stock, yielding (in early 1992) about 1.5%, in contrast with a market average of around 4.5–5%. Clearly, by switching its investments out of Wellcome into higher-yielding stock, the Trust could improve its annual income. Also, since capital appreciation of Wellcome shares had been strong in recent years, the value of the 73.5% holding made up over 95% of the value of the Trust's income-earning assets in early 1992. This was an imprudent weighting of the Trust's investment portfolio.

To the suggestion that in the long run, growth stocks earn the same as high dividend stocks through capital growth, the Trust replied that portfolio diversification was as important as the achievement of income growth. In fact, Wellcome share dividends were increasing faster than the market average, but the stock price was going up faster still, resulting in reducing yield.

In addition to this, the Trust's charitable status precludes it from dispersing its capital, only its income. The Company's high capital growth (characteristic of pharmaceutical stocks) is not of great value to a charity for this reason. The yields on pharmaceutical stocks are low because so much of the profit is ploughed back into R&D.

Pharmaceutical stocks are volatile. Exhibit 15.2 shows a steady average rise in price of Wellcome's shares from 1986 to 1992, but much volatility around the trend. Market reaction to scientific reports on drugs like AZT (Retrovir) shows swift price response. Exhibit 15.2 shows the market effect of a scientific report published by a research worker, Dr. Griffiths, which claimed that scientific trials combining AZT (an anti-AIDS drug) and Zovirax (an anti-viral drug for herpes) prolonged the life of AIDS patients by three times. It caused Wellcome shares to increase from £9.70 to £10.66 in a short space of time ('combination statement'). A 'calm-down statement' from Wellcome plc, which markets both drugs, reduced the price to nearer £10.00, temporarily. From an investment point of view, The Wellcome Trust believed it prudent to diversify into less volatile stocks, even though over the years the Company has been an excellent investment.

Although the time may have been right for the Trust to think of reducing its holdings of the Company's shares, it was clearly of great concern to the Company. The relationship between the two organisations has always been close, and there was never any question of the Trust making totally self-interested decisions itself about its stockholdings in Wellcome plc. Apart

Exhibit 15.2   *Wellcome absolute share price 1986–92*

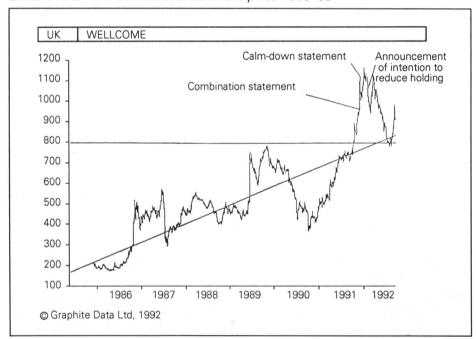

from anything else, a 74% shareholder can clearly have an impact on a company if it decides to make a big strategic move.

Wellcome plc

From Wellcome plc's (the Company's) point of view, an outsider might have said that the Trust's proposed divestment of a large part of its shareholding in the Company might have looked like a *fait accompli* – take it or leave it. But this was never the relationship in the past, and was certainly not the manner in which the decision was reached in early 1992. Consultation between the Trust and the Company was close. Apart from the fact that the Trust was *the* major shareholder in the Company, the latter has always benefited from the academic prestige of the Trust and, by association through the name Wellcome, with the power and reputation of the Trust in the field of medical research. Consultation also took place with the Trust's and the Company's financial advisers.

The proposed share offering therefore had to be seen against the background of the Company's fortunes in early 1992. Clearly, the success of the offering to the Trust and the benefit to the Company depended on the current state of development of the Company and its competitive potential.

Analysis of Wellcome plc

The Company is a major international pharmaceutical group, ranking among the global top 20 drug companies, measured by sales. Its business is the research, development, manufacture and marketing of human healthcare products for sale in both the prescription medicine and over-the-counter (OTC) markets. At the close of business on 22 June 1992, Wellcome had a market capitalisation of approximately £7.9 billion, making it the 15th largest UK registered company quoted on the UK Stock Exchange.

The Company has over 17,000 employees in total, of whom 31% work in the UK and 27% in the USA. Approximately 20% of employees are engaged in R&D, largely in the UK and USA. It has over 40 operating subsidiaries worldwide, with major manufacturing units in the USA, UK, Italy, France and Spain.

The USA, the world's largest prescription market and OTC pharmaceutical market, is also Wellcome's largest national market, accounting for 43% of all sales from continuing operations in 1992 (£793 million). The UK is the Company's second largest national market (8% of sales) and, in the rest of Europe, the Group's three largest markets are France, Italy and Germany. European sales total £590 million (25% of sales). Japan is the world's second largest national pharmaceutical market and Wellcome's third largest national market in terms of sales (£128 million). The Company's other international sales account for 17% of its total pharmaceutical market and sales of £188 million in 1992.

Wellcome's products span the prescription medicines, anti-virals, neuromuscular blocking agents, antiinflammatory, arthritic and respiratory drugs, cardiovascular drugs, central nervous system drugs, anti-cancer drugs, immunosuppressants and antibacterials. Non-prescription (OTC) medicines comprise cough and cold, tropical anti-infectives and analgesic products. The Company's flagship product is Zovirax, a leading world product in the treatment of genital herpes, shingles and cold sores; in 1992, this product earned £586 million or 34% of Wellcome's total sales of continuing operations. Its next best-selling product is Retrovir (AZT), the leading therapy in the treatment of HIV and AIDS; 1992 sales of Retrovir were £213 million or 12% of total sales of continuing operations. Other Wellcome key products for the 1990s are: Exosurf, a lung treatment for premature babies; Wellferon, used in treating chronic hepatitis-B infection; Lamictal, used for add-on therapy in epilepsy; and 256U and 882C which are expected to be launched in 1995/96 to replace Zovirax.

Wellcome has a very good record in R&D and for turning R&D into new products – it has launched 11 original products in the past nine years. These include Lamictal (1991), Wellbutrim (1989), Wellferon and Exosurf. Current research includes fundamental studies into aspects of breast cancer, and the Company is licensing products from other organisations to complement its own research (like Campath 1H, a genetically-engineered humanised monoclonal antibody licensed from Cambridge University – for use in cancer therapy; and RheothRx, licensed from the CytRx Corporation – to combat lung and breast cancer).

The Company's strength in R&D has not been equally matched until recently by its marketing successes. Zovirax, which was launched in 1981, only recently reached its full sales potential of nearly £600 million annually, and soon the patents are due to expire in certain parts of the world. Retrovir is now well known because AIDS has become a household word, and its sales have grown steadily with higher incidence of AIDS. Before 1990, Wellcome plc had a strongly 'academic' feel about it, where research could carry on for its own sake rather than for reasons of commercial viability. That emphasis was corrected with the advent of new management in 1990, although there had been some refocusing on strictly commercial criteria from the time of the Stock Market flotation in 1986. The new chief executive, John Robb, commented:

> Marketing is terribly important. We have a great reputation in research and development, but not a comparable reputation in marketing. We used to think, if we got the research and development right, the products would sell themselves.

John Robb's new marketing emphasis has included an expanded salesforce in the USA and Japan, and co-marketing agreements with companies elsewhere in the world, like Sigma Tau in Italy, Boehringer Mannheim in Mexico, Hoechst in Germany and Sumitomo in Japan. There are also joint ventures in Japan (Nippon Wellcome – jointly owned with Sumitomo) and in Brazil and Indonesia. The threat to the sales of Zovirax caused by the end of patent life is being met by the development of two new drugs, 256U and 882C, and the pursuit of approvals from regulatory authorities to sell some form of Zovirax without prescription. The threat of competition from alternative drugs to Retrovir is being met by development of treatments with Retrovir in combination with other therapies, although it is known that Glaxo is developing a new AIDS drug, 3TC, as an alternative to Retrovir, and putting millions of pounds into its development.

John Robb has also refocused on the group's R&D. The Company still remains committed to excellence in research, but a project management approach has been adopted, which was perfected by Glaxo in the 1980s. The system involved dropping compounds which fail to reach development targets on time. Since September 1989, the number of compounds in development has fallen from 78 to 34. Product development is expensive – it costs between £100 and £150 million to bring a drug to market. Those drugs that are fully developed will be launched in all possible markets to justify the money invested in them.

With the advent of the new management in 1990, a process of divestment of businesses within the group began. The objective was to dispose of operations which no longer fitted the Company's mission as a research-based organisation. The process of disposing of non-core business was largely completed in 1992. In 1991, the Company sold Calmic International, its hygiene services business, to Rentokil, and its vaccines operations to Medeva, the British pharmaceutical group. At the beginning of 1992, it sold its environmental health division to Roussel Uclaf of France, for £48 million. And in the same year, International Murex Technologies bought Wellcome's diagnostics business for £15 million.

Restructuring through disposals has taken place widely in the pharmaceutical industry. Fisons sold its UK consumer healthcare business to Hoffmann–La Roche of Switzerland for £90 million in 1992. Fisons used the proceeds to cut its borrowings. The Company also sold its US and Canadian healthcare business in 1992 for $140 million to Ciba–Geigy, the

US subsidiary of the Swiss chemicals group. Hoffmann–La Roche, on the other hand, expanded its OTC business in 1992, partly by the UK acquisition, which doubled its UK OTC turnover, and partly by acquiring Nicholas, the European OTC business of the US group Sara Lee for $790 million. This was all part of Hoffmann–La Roche's strategy to expand its presence in OTC medicines.

The pharmaceutical industry as a whole, and of course Wellcome plc, are currently facing demanding legislation and price controls in many countries. The debate is most active in the USA where 47% of the Company's sales occur. Some drug groups have introduced voluntary price freezes to reduce pressure from Congress. In June 1992, the German government announced proposals to freeze drugs prices for two years in the world's third largest pharmaceutical market. In Japan, the world's second largest market, price cuts have become the norm. In general, the whole industry is facing greater pricing pressure both on existing drugs and new products. It stems from the providers of healthcare, both government and privately funded. The background is increasing demand for drug products as the population ages (the 'greying effect') and elderly patients require more treatment and medication. Also, people expect and demand better healthcare, and research yields new therapies. The pharmaceuticals sector is an easy target to aggressively attack costs; it is also politically sensitive.

Wellcome is better placed than many drug companies to meet this challenge. Its sales growth is driven by volume growth and product mix improvements, rather than by price increases alone. Its R&D portfolio is targeted towards such products. Wellcome will benefit in one respect from this healthcare provider pressure – the encouragement towards greater self-medication. It will profit from the expected switch of Zovirax to OTC for the treatment of cold sores in Europe and genital herpes in the USA. It is estimated that 30 million people in the USA are affected by herpes, and that between 15% and 40% of Europeans regularly suffer from cold sores.

Price control mechanisms operate differently from country to country and can result in large price differentials between markets that can be aggravated by currency fluctuations. These price differentials are exploited by traders (parallel importers) who purchase branded products in lower-priced markets for resale in higher-priced markets. In the European Community, parallel importing is made easier by the fact that price levels for particular products vary widely from country to country, while Articles 30 to 36 of the Treaty of Rome provide for freedom of movement of goods. This enables importers to take advantage of price differentials by moving products from lower-priced to higher-priced member states.

The new management has already been mentioned. Since July 1990, with the appointment of Sir Alistair Frame and John Robb, three new executive directors have been appointed, reducing the average age of the executive directors to 51. But the most important change was in management philosophy – primarily instilling a greater sense of commercialism and purpose throughout the whole organisation. A new geographic reporting structure was put in place. The group was decentralised with more individuality and responsibility, but financial controls were tightened under central supervision. The new emphasis on marketing has already been described – with its focus on boosting the salesforce and setting up co-promotion deals.

The management also introduced several other new strategic initiatives. One was a concentration on Wellcome's core business of prescription medicines and OTC products. Second, a more commercial approach to R&D, and a closer relationship between R&D and marketing, designed to ensure timely and successful product launches. Third, an increased emphasis on the financial returns generated from Wellcome's business, particularly in relation to sales, trading margins, earnings per share and cash generation.

A financial analysis of Wellcome reveals a healthy position in 1992 and strong growth in previous years; the influence of the new management from 1990 is seen clearly.

The Company has experienced continually rising turnover. From £1,469 million in 1990, it has risen to £1,603 million in 1991 and £1,699 million in 1992. The increase in 1992 was 16.7% for continuing operations. Excluding currency effects, underlying growth was up 18%. Price increases accounted for only 3% of growth. This indicator is well in line with Wellcome's emphasis on volume growth, given the current pressure on world pharmaceutical prices.

Pre-tax profits have showed similar strong growth. From £315 million in 1990, they have risen to £403 million in 1991 and £505 million in 1992, an average rate of 26%. The pre-tax profit margin increased from 21.7% in 1990 to 24.9% in 1991 and 27.7% in 1992. John Robb believes he has realistic expectations of achieving a 30% margin during his period as chief executive. But there is still scope for further improvement, as is apparent from industry averages; e.g. Glaxo 32%, SmithKline Beecham's (SKB) pharmaceutical division 28% and Fison's pharmaceutical division 27%. The changing sales mix, with emphasis on the newer higher-margin products, coupled with continued cost containment, should lead to margins at the higher range being likely.

Wellcome is particularly healthy in cash terms. The disposal of non-core and low-margin businesses has added to cash inflows (£104 million up to March 1992). In addition, trading cash inflows have been continually positive. At year-end in August 1992, Wellcome was sitting on a cash pile of £410 million, a doubling of its net cash position from £198 million in 1991, compared with £17.4 million in 1990. Whilst this is a formidable position to be in, it still does not compare with Glaxo's massive current cash surplus of £1,200 million. The natural reaction to this strategy is to infer that Wellcome is in a good position to make acquisitions. If this were so, logical targets would be to strengthen the infrastructure in Continental Europe and the Far East in the field of consumer health, or perhaps acquisitions in the strongly-growing US market.

Against the background of shareholders' funds of £868 million in 1990, £1,101 million in 1991 and £1,177 million in 1992, net cash in percentage terms was 2% in 1990, 18% in 1991 and 29% in 1992. This is a very creditable achievement. The management has also added to cash by considerable gains at the operational level, with special emphasis on control over working capital.

Wellcome's tax charge is very high by industry standards: 37.5% against Glaxo's 28%, SKB's 33% and Fison's 25%. The main reasons for this are the high tax rates charged on Wellcome's overseas business, which is a large proportion of the total. Moreover, the Company does not have manufacturing facilities in a tax haven. Some progress has been made in reducing the overall rate from 42% in 1987 to the present figure.

Historically, Wellcome has a cost-of-goods-sold line largely around its peer group average, but in 1992 this improved following the divestment of its non-core business, resulting in percentage points about 1.5 to 2 better than its international competition. But at 22.6% cost of goods sold as a percentage of group sales in the first half of 1992, this figure was still well above the 18% achieved by Eli Lilly and Syntex.

Wellcome has consistently spent above the peer group average on selling, general and administration, and although the Company is making determined efforts to reduce this spend as a proportion of sales, it is likely to remain above average for the foreseeable future. Also, the increase in the size of the salesforce in overseas markets, and more advertising on new and existing products, will further raise costs in this field.

Exhibit 15.3 shows share performance since 1986. Since 1990, earnings per share (EPS) have increased on average by 23%, dividends per share by 42% and dividend cover has decreased by 9%. Actual and forecast earnings growth is well above market and sector average.

Robert Fleming Securities, merchant banking advisers to The Wellcome Trust, forecast a high EPS growth rate in 1992, amounting to 23% compound for the following five years. This rate is superior to those expected from other leading pharmaceutical companies, e.g. Glaxo and SKB (both

Exhibit 15.3 *Wellcome plc: share statistics*

	1992	1991	1990	1989	1988	1987	1986
Earnings per share	36.0p	29.3p	22.7p	19.7p	15.1p	11.2p	7.8p
Dividends per share	13.0p	10.0p	6.5p	5.05p	3.6p	2.81p	2.11p
Dividend cover (times)	2.8	2.9	3.5	3.9	4.2	4.0	3.7
Share price at end of the financial year	817p	746p	475p	708p	496p	471p	178p
Share price during the financial year:							
High	1,173p	746p	785p	756p	570p	514p	234p
Low	704p	367p	423p	400p	292p	178p	156p

1. The ordinary shares were offered for sale to the public at 120p each.
Source: Wellcome plc Annual Report 1992.

UK) with 16% and 15%; Merck, Pfizer and Eli Lilly (all US) with 18%, 20% and 14%, respectively; and Sandoz and Roche (both Swiss) with 15% apiece. Wellcome stood at an end-financial year 1992 P/E of 28× and 22.5× for year-end August 1993, which compares with Glaxo at 23× for year-end June 1992 and 19× for year-end June 1993, and Smith Kline Beecham at 17× for year-end December 1992. A comparison with Glaxo is the most suitable. Both are pure pharmaceutical companies and use the same accounting standards. They have similarly high standards of research and comparable quality of management. Wellcome's more demanding P/E is justified by superior growth prospects, smaller size and, more importantly, lower risk profile (i.e. it is not dependent upon one large, maturing product with the simultaneous introduction of many new products).

If Wellcome's key financial ratios are examined, they are all very favourable (see Exhibit 15.4). With the possible exception of the tax ratio (for reasons explained earlier), there is near continual improvement over the past four years in all ratios. Returns on equity and capital, and all profit margins are impressive, and employee-related ratio improvements are spectacular. The ratios indicate both external (market) achievements and internal (cost and operating) efficiencies over the past four years.

Exhibit 15.4   *Wellcome plc: key ratios*

Description	26/8/89	1/9/90	31/8/91	29/8/92
Return on shareholders' equity (%)	20.13	22.59	22.32	26.47
Return on capital employed (%)	27.27	28.97	29.69	34.39
Operating profit margin (%)	20.24	21.21	24.50	27.69
Pre-tax profit margin (%)	20.05	21.66	24.84	28.77
Net profit margin (%)	12.23	13.72	15.75	18.09
Income gearing (%)	8.84	8.49	5.50	4.23
Borrowing ratio	0.29	0.26	0.18	0.16
Stock ratio (days)	53.26	55.61	51.83	40.73
Debtors' ratio (days)	91.56	88.34	83.60	75.92
Creditors' ratio (days)	69.16	69.47	75.91	81.59
Working capital ratio	2.36	2.00	2.15	2.21
Sales per employee (£)	69.243	77.913	85.848	99.514
Operating profit per employee (£)	14.017	16.523	21.030	27.560
Capital employed per employee (£)	55.934	63.852	76.207	87.089
Tax ratio (%)	39.07	36.89	36.77	37.25
Cash earnings per share (%)	26.02	29.94	36.93	44.49

Source: Datastream.

Attitude of Wellcome plc

What of the position and attitude of Wellcome plc in early 1992 to a proposed large transfer of ownership of its shares? Clearly, the Company had always known of the possibility and, since 1986 when it went public, had a sizeable proportion of its equity (around 26%) held in non-Trust hands. The Company had to take into account the fact that it had an external 26% shareholding and ensure that whatever was proposed was not going to be of disbenefit in any way to them by giving preference to the 74% shareholding. Since the time the Company went public, it has taken all its shareholders seriously. Even though it had a majority shareholder, it tried to cultivate the other key shareholders.

Existing shareholders would be sensitive to the stock market impact of offloading such a large quantity of shares all at once. One would expect a general stock market reaction to mark down the share price – large secondary share offerings carry with them a certain amount of risk. What are the chances that such an offering takes place in a stock market where there is excess demand, i.e. when the price is likely to rise? There are both general market conditions to consider, sector conditions and the market sentiment for the particular stock in question.

In 1991, stock markets did not perform particularly well, although pharmaceutical stocks gave a glittering performance. But by the beginning of 1992, the pharmaceutical sector had begun underperforming, particularly by about April when investors switched out of defensive stocks, such as pharmaceuticals, into cyclical companies. But Wellcome shares were running high; since the Company's flotation in 1986, investors had seen a five-to sixfold increase in price. The original flotation price was £1.20; in 1992, a price high of £11.31 was achieved. This, in itself, may have contained the seeds of a problem – would investors resist the temptation to take their profits on such a satisfying capital appreciation in the stock – with the obvious implication for the share price.

Volatility of Wellcome's stock has been mentioned before – reflecting the general market volatility of pharmaceutical stocks which are particularly sensitive to scientific discovery. This volatility was also increased by the very tight market in the stock – there was only about 25% of the stock in the market at any one time, and about 70% of that free float was accounted for by some 30 institutions who saw it as a core holding and did not often trade. This feature would almost certainly provide an immediately depressing effect on a post-share price offering. Wellcome's problem would be the psychologically damaging effect of such a price movement. Clearly, this difficulty would arise when a large proportion of Wellcome's shares were sold, but it increased the importance of getting the timing of an offering right so as to minimise the possibility of a fall in share price immediately. A greater than doubling of Wellcome's share price between the beginning of 1991 and the end of that year was a very good background to the possibility of a second offering as long as it was not believed that the Company had exhausted its growth potential at that date.

Wellcome's capital structure is low-geared. Only about £179 million was held in bonds and foreign currency loans in 1992 by the group, against shareholders' funds of £1,174 million. This position means the Company has to pay close attention to dividends and dividend policy as the main direction for its stream of income arising from trading operations and investments. As with most companies, the 'signal' aspect of dividends is important, but with Wellcome the stock market response is even more sensitive with its present capital structure. This reinforces the effect of the stock being tightly held, as mentioned above.

Wellcome's shares were considered 'scarce' in early 1992 – because of the tight holding, low turnover and concentration in the hands of the Trust. But the shares are ranked high in the FTSE 100 and regarded as blue chip

Exhibit 15.5 *Geographical breakdown of sales by customer location, 1991*

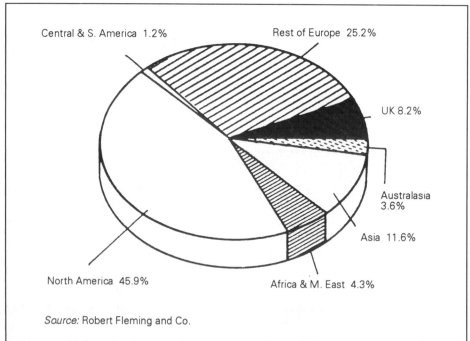

Central & S. America 1.2%

Rest of Europe 25.2%

UK 8.2%

Australasia 3.6%

Asia 11.6%

North America 45.9%

Africa & M. East 4.3%

Source: Robert Fleming and Co.

by institutions. Most UK institutions felt underweight in this stock at this time and, everything else being equal, welcomed the opportunity to increase their holdings. This feature of the stock would help to offset what would normally be a depressing effect on the price of offloading a large quantity of the stock on the market.

With the advent of the new management in 1990, greater emphasis was placed on visibility amongst the general public. It was felt by the management that the name Wellcome was not well known by the public at large, less so than perhaps Glaxo or Smith Kline Beecham, and it would be to the advantage of Wellcome to achieve a broader shareholder base than it had achieved so far. The association with The Wellcome Trust was of course highly beneficial so far as scientific reputation was concerned, but again neither were well known by the public at large. Greater visibility had, of course, advantages in terms of consumer interest if Wellcome's products were to be sold OTC as well as on prescription. From this point of view, Wellcome could only benefit from a wider spread of retail shareholding following a disposal of part of the Trust's holdings.

The same would apply to new institutional holdings of the Company's shares. A greater spread, possibly among institutions with a more active portfolio view of the Company's shares, would increase investor interest in the stock – with more of the stock more easily available in the market and a better turnover in the market. There would more likely be greater press comment.

One of the major factors encouraging the Company to accept a 1992 redistribution of its shares was the current mismatch between the geographical patterns of its sales and that of its shareholdings. As Exhibits 15.5 and 15.6 show, the largest part of Wellcome's sales are made in North America – 45.9% in 1991, and 35.4% of net assets were located there; 54% of profit came from North America. Yet only 2% of the Company's shares were held in North America. Glaxo and SKB are listed in the US and had 27% and 35% shareholdings there, respectively. The same was true of Europe excluding the UK and Japan: nearly 37% of sales were made to these areas in 1991, but negligible shareholdings found there. By contrast, the UK accounted for 8.2% of sales and 19.5% of net assets and the overwhelming majority of shareholding, even outside the Trust's own holdings.

In the case of the USA, visibility of Wellcome would also be improved by a share listing. Burroughs Wellcome is strongly represented in the USA, it has 2.1% of the US market by value and ranks 18th in terms of pharmaceutical sales. Also, sales in the USA are growing faster than the market overall – most of this growth came through volume growth and product mix rather than price increases. Therefore, Wellcome considered it

Exhibit 15.6   *Geographical breakdown of trading profits*

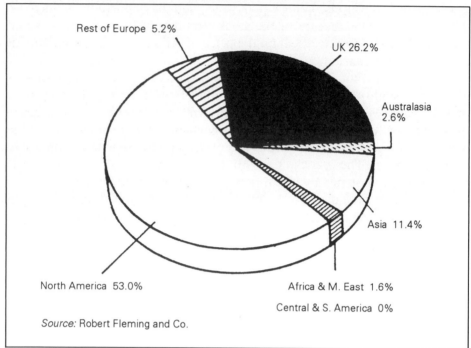

Source: Robert Fleming and Co.

appropriate and important to get its name and business better known in the USA by a stronger holding of its shares there and a listing in the stock market. This would perhaps be made more important by the fact that Burroughs Wellcome's salesforce was relatively small in the USA (a total of 658), compared with some of the major league players who number several thousand. Even with current moves to strengthen the US salesforce, it would still only be the size of one of Merck's divisional salesforces. Although the offering would be a secondary one in the USA, the Company knew there was unmet demand for its shares there, so it would, in effect, be like an initial public offering.

     In the rest of Europe (excluding the UK) Wellcome is similarly under-represented in comparison with the size of these markets. This is revealed by the dominance of Zovirax in product sales compared with the limited sales of the other products within the Group's portfolio. Even with current growth of 16% (in local currency terms) against a general market trend of under 10%, Wellcome has not made good penetration of these markets, and it was important to gain greater visibility through wider spread of ownership of

Wellcome shares, made more urgent by preparing for the string of new products awaiting European approval.

Finally, the Japanese market is vital in Wellcome's strategy. It is the world's second largest market and yet represents only 7% of Wellcome's sales. It is also a highly individual market characterised by a high degree of fragmentation (even the largest player holds a less than 5% share), domination by domestic pharmaceutical companies, a medical system in which doctors both prescribe and supply the drugs, and a huge number of wholesalers and salesmen. Given these features and the strong Japanese business culture, Wellcome believed it helpful to get as many shares in Japanese hands as possible, to alter the perception of Wellcome as a desirable investment stock as well as purveyor of products.

In all its non-UK markets, Wellcome realised that building up an investor base in not easy. Glaxo has 25% of its shares held in the USA, but it has taken some 5–6 years to build up to that level. At the same time, Wellcome is now putting in place a fairly extensive investor relations programme in overseas markets, especially in the USA, in order to raise the profile of the Company as an investment vehicle.

From the Company's point of view, another disadvantage of a share structure that is concentrated in the hands of one dominant shareholder (the Trust) is that it would be difficult to raise additional capital through a rights issue, particularly a shareholder who has no extra cash to take over the rights. With the Company's shares held in a greater number of hands and with a more international spread of shareholders, the chances of successful rights issues would be increased. This factor could not be held as of overwhelming importance, because by late 1991 the company had built up a large cash surplus, and was forecast to increase it even further. But that situation could change in the future, and could be advantageous.

The Offering Decision

In early 1992, discussions began to take place between the Trust and their advisers on the former's wish to diversify its investment portfolio by selling off a proportion of its equity stake in the Company.

The Trust had for a long time signalled its intent to follow this course, as far back as 1986 when it disposed of its first tranche of 26.3% of Company shares. But further disposals were held back until an 'appropriate time'. By late 1991 and early 1992, over four years had elapsed since the 1986 flotation and the 21% divestment of the Trust's shares in Wellcome plc. The Trust now had several reasons for wishing to dispose of a larger proportion of its

Wellcome plc shareholdings. There were legal reasons why the Trust could not readily dispose of its Company shareholding – in its will, the Trust required the approval of the Charity Commissioners to reduce its holding to below 50.1%. In fact, as discussions progressed between the Trust and the Company and with the help of financial advisers, the Trust applied for approval in March 1992 and got it. It gained approval to reduce its holding from 73.6% to 25%, but not lower. If it reduced to this level, it would need to sell around 417 million shares.

The Decision Case

By about November 1991, when the Company's results were known for that year, discussions began between the Trust and the Company. The Trust *could* reduce its holding of the Company's shares to 25%, but decided that a reduction of 30–40% would be more appropriate, if a diminution of the size could be effectively managed through the stock markets and yield acceptable financial results.

On 2 March 1992, an announcement was made to the Press that the Trust would dispose of a large quantity of its shares, the exact amount was

Exhibit 15.7   *The arguments favouring the share divestment*

Wellcome Trust	Wellcome plc
Increased demand for the Trust's research funds	Good performance by Wellcome plc stock prior to offering, although general stock market performance weak
Reduced government funding of pharmaceutical research	'Scarcity' of Wellcome stock would be rectified; Trust's stock tightly held
Over-concentration of Wellcome plc stock in the Trust's investment portfolio	Greater visibility amongst investors and the public at large
Need for higher income from investment portfolio	Better match between geographical pattern of sales and assets and that of shareholding
Pharmaceutical stocks unusually volatile	Easier to raise cash through rights issues in the future
Inappropriate exercise of the Trust's fiduciary duties	Better stock market turnover of Wellcome's shares and greater liquidity of stock
Timing decided by appointment of new Wellcome plc management	Excellent growth prospects for Wellcome plc, measured by several indicators

The Share Offering

not specified but, at that time, it was believed to be of the order of 330 million shares. This marked the culmination of all the Trust's and the Company's negotiations and represented an optimum timing for them, taking into account guidance from their financial advisers. Exhibit 15.7 summarises those factors which encouraged the Trust and the Company, leading to their joint decision to make the share offering. The skilful manner in which that offering was made is the subject of Part B of this case study.

Exhibit 15.8 *Wellcome plc: profit and loss account for the year ended 29 August 1992*

	1992 (£m)	1991 (£m)
Turnover:		
Continuing operations	1,699.4	1,455.8
Discontinued operations	62.6	150.5
Total	1,762.0	1,606.3
Cost of sales	(392.5)	(393.9)
Gross profit	1,369.5	1,212.4
Other operating costs	(881.8)	(817.8)
Trading profit	487.7	394.6
Net interest receivable	17.0	8.3
Profit on ordinary activities		
before taxation	504.7	402.9
Tax on profit on ordinary activities	(189.2)	(147.1)
Profit on ordinary activities		
after taxation	315.5	255.8
Minority interests	(6.4)	(6.7)
Profit on ordinary activities		
attributable to shareholders	309.1	249.1
Extraordinary items	(50.9)	(1.4)
Profit for the year attributable		
to shareholders	258.2	250.5
	(111.9)	(85.7)
Profit retained for the		
financial year	146.3	164.8

Source: Wellcome plc Annual Report 1992

Exhibit 15.9   *Wellcome plc: balance sheet as at 29 August 1992*

	Group	
	1992 (£m)	1991 (£m)
Fixed assets:		
Tangible assets	818.0	811.0
Investments	2.2	3.1
	820.2	814.1
Current assets:		
Stocks	196.6	228.1
Debtors	366.5	367.9
Investments	569/7	362.1
Cash	23.3	33.4
	1,156.1	991.5
Creditors – amounts falling due within one year		
Loans and overdrafts	(89.7)	(80.5)
Other	(430.0)	(375.8)
Net current assets	636.4	535.2
Total assets *less* current liabilities	1,456.6	1,349.3
Creditors – amounts falling due after more than one year		
Loans	(93.2)	(117.2)
Other	(4.3)	(3.9)
Provisions for liabilities and charges	(155.1)	(100.6)
Minority interests	(26.6)	(26.9)
Total net assets	1,177.4	1,100.7
Capital and reserves		
Called-up share capital	215.2	214.3
Share premium account	64.5	54.5
Profit and loss account	897.7	831.9
Shareholders' funds	1,177.4	1,100.7

Source: Wellcome plc Annual Report 1992

The Wellcome Share Offering (B)
Technical Execution

When London merchant bank Robert Fleming and Co. managed The Wellcome Trust's offering of shares on the London stock market in 1992, it did so in a very skilful manner. At least one notable feature of this offering was its size – the largest fully paid non-privatisation secondary offering of shares ever to take place on the London Stock Exchange and internationally.

The study discusses Fleming's choice of share-offering technique – book-building with over-allocation and a greenshoe option, an innovative technique on the UK domestic equity market. It then charts the month-by-month progress of the deal. From a number of points of view, the offering is considered successful. An attractive price was obtained, a much broader institutional and geographical spread of shareholding was achieved, and the market was efficiently stabilised against the background of a freely-falling stock market.

Introduction

On 2 March 1992 it was announced to the press that the Wellcome Trust (the UK's largest medical charity) had decided to sell some portion of its 73.6% shareholding in Wellcome plc, the multinational pharmaceutical corporation (the 'Company'). For Roger Gibbs, chairman of the Trust, this represented months of negotiation with the Company and talks with both sides' financial advisers. For the UK stock market it meant that the Trust could reduce its holding to 25% and dispose of up to 417 million shares, although a sale of

This case was written by Paul Stonham as a basis for class discussion rather than to illustrate either effective or ineffective handling of an administrative situation. The author is grateful to executives of the organisations concerned for discussions on the events of this case study. Helpful comments were received on both parts of this case study by faculty and students at a seminar of the Centre for Studies in Money, Banking and Finance in Sydney in early 1993. Responsibility for the final version of this case study rests with the author only. © European Management Journal, 1993.

around 300 million shares was more likely. In any event, the prospect was for a share offering which would be the largest non-privatisation sale of equities ever known on the London Stock Exchange as well as a major international offering.

The implications for the strategy of the Trust and the Company were very important and have been explored in Part A of this case study ('Strategic Aspects'). The manner in which the offering was made was highly skilful and the subject of much careful planning. The second part of the case study focuses on the technical execution of the sale.

Choosing the Lead Bank

In 1986 the Wellcome Foundation obtained a Stock Market listing, became Wellcome plc, and the Trust divested itself of 20% of the Company's equity. At the same time, the Company raised £50 million by issuing 5% new shares. With the sale of 20% equity and 5% new shares, the Trust ended up with 75% of the Company's stock. At this time, the Company was capitalised at about £1 billion.

The institution chosen to take the Company to the stock market was Robert Fleming and Co. Ltd, a London merchant bank. The flotation was considered very successful. Fleming and Co. was equity-orientated, although relatively small in the game of equity offerings. The flotation was, at that time, one of the largest seen on the London Stock Exchange. From 1986 onwards Flemings had been retained by the Trustees, advising them on the potential for further divestment and other matters.

In 1992, Flemings was again chosen to manage the Trust's second divestment, this time of blockbuster size. It was chosen from a list of 15 contenders and may not have seemed an obvious choice at the time. However, it had managed the 1986 flotation well, and its expertise in equity management had grown in the intervening years. It is also worth mentioning that, in 1992, Flemings was the second largest manager of equities in the UK ($50 billion) and the second most profitable bank in the UK – its return on equity and return on capital were the highest among UK merchant banks in 1992. Roger Gibbs commented,

> We knew the institution well, we had great respect for it, and we thought they would do a good job for us – as in fact it turned out.

The Trust appointed Flemings as financial adviser, global co-ordinator and book runner for the offering. The two principal executives involved at Flemings were Philip Bradley, director of corporate finance, and Ian

Hannam, director of capital markets. Ian Hannam had recently been recruited from Salomon Brothers, and had an excellent track record in equity operations. Financial adviser to Wellcome plc was Baring Brothers and Company.

Structure of the Offering

In the UK, new shares are traditionally sold by offer for sale, or bought deal/ underwriting. Using this method, the company selling new shares allots them to an issuing house (lead bank), and the shares are then offered in turn to the general public. They are priced at the start of marketing. During the period in which the listing particulars and offering documents are being prepared, the lead bank uses its contacts in the financial world to determine a likely total demand for the shares. With this information and in agreement with the vendor company, a fixed price is determined at which the shares will be offered. This is the price announced on 'impact day', the start of the official offer period. It also marks the issue of the listing particulars.

Normally, an offer for sale is underwritten (or guaranteed) and further underwritten by sub-underwriters in the case of a large flotation. The principal underwriter may or may not be the lead bank. For a commission, underwriters commit themselves to buy any shares remaining unsold at the end of the offer period. At the end of the offer period acceptances and payments are received, shares allotted to investors and dealing in the shares begins. There are also other ways of issuing new shares like sales by tender and placings.

Flemings considered the underwriting route, and rejected it. There were several reasons why they eliminated this route. The main theoretical advantage of an underwriting is that it reduces uncertainty. The uncertainty is passed on to the underwriter and the company issuing the shares is assured of their price. But it is an expensive procedure, and the greater the risk the greater the underwriting cost. In the UK the commission charged is around 2%, but more seriously there is a discount as well which could amount to 10% under the current market price.

In the case of the Wellcome stock, the share price was volatile and so there would have been difficulty in deciding a long-term stable price in the case of an underwriting. Underwriting the Wellcome stock would have been possible only at a very large discount. In February 1992 Wellcome's stock stood at around £11 per share, and figures of about £6.50 were being mentioned as underwriting possibilities, which was out of the question. Underwriters were made extra cautious by memories of the huge British

Petroleum share flop of 1987, when they had signed underwriting commitments just before the UK stock market went into free-fall on Black Monday.

The underwriting method would also have proved difficult in the light of the size of the Wellcome offering. It was considered doubtful if the banks had sufficient capacity or liquidity to underwrite £2 billion worth of stock.

Finally, Flemings pointed out that the Wellcome share offering was a secondary one – all the shares sold were existing issued and listed shares – there were no new shares being issued. Consequently, the Stock Exchange's rules applying to the issue of new shares did not apply. There was no requirement to produce listing particulars or a Companies Act prospectus. Most importantly of all, the pre-emptive rights of existing shareholders, by which a new issue must offer shares pro-rata to existing shareholders, did not hold. Why, therefore, argued Flemings, should the Trust not consider a more effective means of disposing of a large part of its shareholding?

The Book-building Technique

Flemings looked at the book-building technique of offering shares as a preferable alternative and recommended it to the Trust (see Exhibit 16.1). The principle behind book-building is that the lead bank markets the stock without naming the exact share price and before the prospectus is complete. During a pre-designated offer period, investors can tender for shares, indicating the likely size and price they are prepared to accept. The term 'book-building' comes from the way the bank builds up demand during the period from these indications. At the end of the stated book-building period, the size of the offer and the single share price are fixed ('strike price'), the offering document is finalised, and the shares allotted. Immediately after this, underwriting occurs for a few hours just prior to the announcement of trading, and there is a very limited underwriting risk.

Essentially, the book-building technique is an exercise in coping with volatility. Whereas with the underwriting process the risk is passed on to the underwriter, with this technique the risk over share price and over the balance of supply and demand is reduced or eliminated by the bank having much more flexibility in dealing in the market. This flexibility also gives the bank the opportunity to acquire a lot more information. Flemings obviously wanted to achieve the highest share price possible, but also to provide the Trust with a compromise between maximum revenue and maximum turnover, as well as encouraging a share price rise in the aftermarket.

The first advantage of the process is that it therefore matches price with

Exhibit 16.1   *The advantages of book-building*

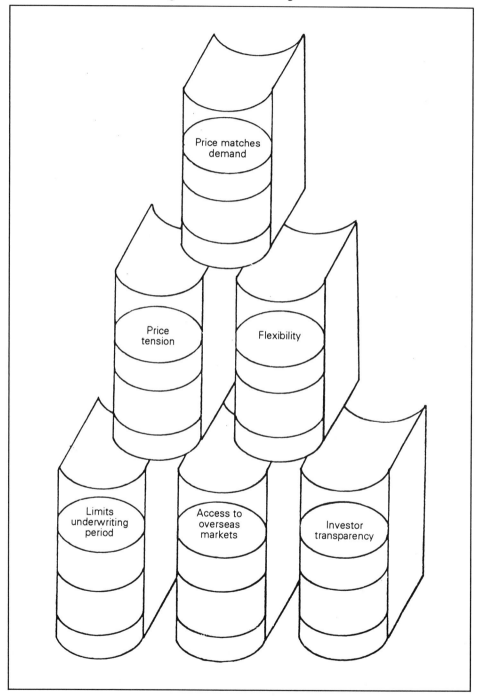

demand more accurately than front-end underwriting with price and size fixed at the outset. The avoidance of a large underwriting discount could also help to deter stags (short-term buyers aiming to sell off quickly at a higher price). Allied to this is the advantage of being able to size the offering according to demand. This is because price and size are fixed at the end of the book-building process.

Secondly, book building has the added advantage of investor transparency, giving Flemings valuable information on the state of demand for Wellcome's stock and enabling it to balance demand and price. Every investor indicating demand greater than £100,000 of shares had to disclose who the beneficial owner was. Quality of investor mattered too; Flemings wished to know if investors were serious and long-term, or were merely looking to make a quick buck or even to short. The bank wanted to ensure a healthy aftermarket in the stock. This was perfectly legal and covered by section 212 of the Companies Act 1985, which gives UK companies investigative powers of this nature.

Thirdly, book-building enabled the creation of price tension between investors, with all investors competing against each other in a single offer, as in an auction. Pricing tension was also created between UK institutions and demand overseas.

Fourthly, this mechanism is well understood overseas, particularly in the USA where Wellcome was seeking to build up shareholder representation to match its operational strength. Book-building suits the distribution capacity of overseas financial houses.

Finally, book-building avoids the creation of an underwriting overhang of stock. If a significant amount of stock is actually taken up by underwriters in the event of shortfall of share sales, subsequent sales can depress the aftermarket share prices.

Fleming's Approach as Global Co-ordinator and Adviser

Fleming's approach to this challenging task was first of all to emphasise teamwork and 'the best person for the job'. Not only was this an enormous transaction, but an enormous number of people around the world were involved. Nine syndicates of banks were appointed across the globe including a UK syndicate, and lead managers appointed for each syndicate. The syndicates were chosen with great care and lead managers interviewed competitively in London. Their task was to market the shares effectively in each region they represented. Flemings believed that one of the advantages of the Trust choosing them as global co-ordinator was that being smaller in the league of global international operators (like Goldman Sachs or Salomons), they were not subject to the same jealousies and hidden agendas, and were therefore better able to create effective teams, and act as a leader.

Next Flemings put in place the basic structure of the offering. As well as the syndicate structure (somewhat similar to Eurobond offerings), the bank insisted on a 'level playing-field' throughout the world. Every investor – Japanese, American, Chinese, or whatever – was to be treated in exactly the same way when it came to putting in their bids during the book-building exercise. There was no discrimination, and no special discounts such as were offered in the earlier BT offering in the UK. At the end of the book-building process investors knew there would be a single issue price around the world based on the bids. There was also one offering document when book-building closed which, although possessing differing local information, e.g. for Japan or Canada, contained the same core information within different wrap-around information. As well as the institutional offer, Flemings also set up a retail offer in the UK, again with no special discounts as in the BT offering, and this proved eventually to be very successful.

The sale was of fully paid shares. Again this was unlike BT's earlier offering, and was intended to prevent arbitrage where investors in partly paid shares have time value in the delay in paying for them. Flemings did not want investors taking punts on the value of the time element of the partly paid. Another advantage of fully paid shares is that US investors are familiar with them, and Flemings was hoping specifically to appeal to US investors. The structure also included an over-allotment option, explained more fully later in this case study.

Flemings also insisted on complete control throughout the process. Although teamwork was also essential, the bank led and commanded this transaction from the outset. It avoided the kinds of problem that the GPA offering ran into through loose controls. The press was also kept well informed, and was basically supportive.

The Timetable

Exhibit 16.2 shows the timetable of the offering from announcement on 2 March to the end of the stabilisation on 20 August. This timetable does not show the lengthy negotiations between the Trust, the Company and the advisers that took place before 2 March. There were essentially five major phases in the offering timetable: consultation, education, pre-marketing, book-building, and allocation and stabilisation.

Exhibit 16.2 *The Wellcome share offering timetable*

1992	
2 March	Announcement by Trust of intention to sell
mid-March	Due diligence begins
31 March	Lead Managers appointed
20 April	Ministry of Finance (MoF) approval (Japan)
30 April	Court order granted
7 May	Confidential pre-filing of F-3 with SEC
early May	Due diligence ends
mid-May	Verification begins
4 June	Announcement of structure and intention to proceed; publication of preliminary offering circular, US 'pink herring' and Canadian; preliminary offering memorandum; F-3 filed in USA; execution of the orderly marketing agreement and retail selling agents' letter; retail marketing begins, share information office opens; briefings to brokers to begin
8 June	Filing of draft summary prospectus with Japanese MoF
mid-June	Meetings with institutions and managers
18 June	Pre-filing of securities registration statement (SRS) with MoF
22 June	Verification ends
24 June	Execution of international tender offer agreement. Global co-ordinator's agreement, receiving banker's agreement and other agreements
25 June	Announcement of provisional size of the offer; publication of impact day international offering circular, US 'red herring' and Canadian offering memorandum; filing of SRS and first amendment to F-3
6 July	Book-building begins
21 July	UK public offer closes 3:30 p.m.; share information office closes
23 July	Second amendment to F-3; F-3 declared effective
24 July	Last time for receipt of bids by managers – 5:00 p.m.; book-building ends
25–26 July	Analysis of book and determination of tender price and allocations
26 July	Purchase memorandum executed in escrow
27 July	Purchase memorandum released from escrow; announcement of tender price and allocations – 8:30 a.m. suspension of trading on LSE ends; New York Stock Exchange listing effective – 2:30 p.m. (London time); filing of post-effective SRS
3 August	Settlement
5 August	Share certificates posted to the public

Source: Practical Law for Companies, November 1992.

Phase 1: Consultation (2 March–10 May)

After the announcement of the share offering, Flemings, the Company and the Trust went through a series of 'beauty parades' by which they selected lead managers for the regional syndicates across the world. The process was selective, but consultative as well, in that the managers and their institutions contributed to the structure of the offering from their experience and local knowledge. Co-managers and other distributors within the syndicate were selected in this phase (see Exhibit 16.3). At this early stage too, syndicates were made aware of the transparency conditions attached to investors bidding in amounts larger than £100,000.

Once the syndicate structure was in place, Flemings established a 'pot system' for allocating selling commissions. Traditionally, in the UK, the person who takes the order actually earns all the commission on the deal. Flemings split the commission so that the order-taker received half of the selling commission, and the other half of the commission was available to the syndicate to decide which of its finance houses it should be awarded to in the light of information provided and perspective on the stock.

Phase 2: Education (11 May–3 June)

By 11 May the offering had still not gone out to investors. This phase covered the period when Flemings was educating the syndicate members and the various finance houses in the syndicates who would help in distributing the stock. Research analysts and salespeople from the syndicates were briefed by the Company's management in London at a two-day symposium, and similarly in the USA. These meetings enabled the analysts to obtain information to write their research report to distribute to investor institutions.

Flemings identified 700 'flagship' investing institutions worldwide (high-quality, long-term investors), which the bank believed to be key and who would have a significant amount of interest in investing in the stock. During this phase the regional syndicates were constructed fully, i.e. all the additional finance houses and people needed to distribute the stock were put in place.

Phase 3: Pre-marketing (4 June–5 July)

On 4 June Flemings went 'live' and actually launched this offering. Up to this stage the market had been told of the Trust's intentions, subject to market conditions and external events like the UK general election, etc. Flemings confirmed the offering timetable and the basic structure of the offering, e.g. a tender offering with a book-building phase, and international syndicates.

This phase consisted essentially of talking to investor institutions. The syndicates had previously been educated in the Company and the share

Exhibit 16.3 *Syndicate structure*

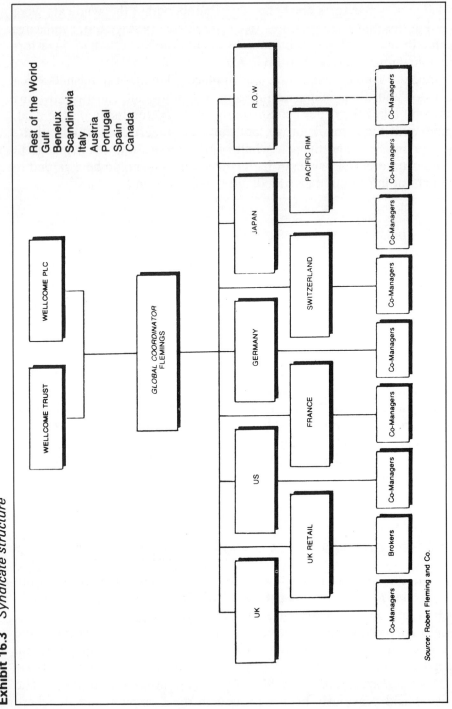

Rest of the World
Gulf
Benelux
Scandinavia
Italy
Austria
Portugal
Spain
Canada

Source: Robert Fleming and Co.

offering and were briefed to visit institutions all around the world and 'spread the gospel'. During the programme, 700 flagship investors were visited by lead manager analysts, and Fleming's own analysts made over 100 institutional visits.

In the case of the USA, a 'pink herring' document was published on 4 June, which was basically a preliminary draft of the offering document. It contained most of the information that was eventually contained in the final prospectus but was briefer in terms of the offering size and pricing. The purpose of the 'pink herring' document was to enable the marketing of the offering in the USA to commence. Wellcome stock was traded in the form of American depository receipts in the USA, but it did not have a listing, and was quoted in Pink Sheets. Marketing the stock was forbidden by the Securities and Exchange Commission in the absence of a file registration with the SEC. Hence the 'pink herring'. In the UK, the preliminary offering circular was published simultaneously; this was also a draft of the UK and international offering document giving preliminary information to investors.

On 25 June, Flemings called all the syndicate institutions back to London to assess what they thought the likely demand would be internationally. The results of these discussions were that Flemings was able to size the offer, i.e. give an indication of what the bank thought the size of the offer should be. They came to the conclusion that it should be around 330 million shares, subject to subsequent increase or decrease. Thus, on 25 June ('impact day'), a 'red herring' document was issued in the USA (part of the first filing with the US Securities and Exchange Commission), and its equivalent issued in the UK, the offering circular, was published. The syndicate pre-marketing period was therefore used to assess preliminary demand for Wellcome's shares.

Phase 4: Book-building (6 July–24 July)

Phase 4 represented a critical period in managing and building up the demand for Wellcome's shares. On 6 July, the book was opened and investors were able to put their bids in. Investors were given a three-week period in which to indicate the size and price of their bids.

The process was managed by a sophisticated computer system originally developed by Price Waterhouse for the 1991 BT sale and further refined for its own purpose by Flemings. Two vital features incorporated in the program have been mentioned already. One was investor transparency. When managers reported in larger investors, they were required to file full details of these institutions.

The other feature was a set of criteria which categorised investor institutions by quality. There were five categories, in descending order of quality:

1. Existing shareholders – these were given first preference.
2. 'Flagship' – high quality institutions with serious intentions to hold the stock long-term.
3. Good investors.
4. Moderate investors.
5. Others.

Investors could enter any of three types of pricing bids, in descending order of points earned in terms of allocation of shares:

1. Strike price – those institutions who accepted in advance the single price decided by Flemings at the end of the book-building process.
2. Fixed price – institutions which put in bids at a single fixed price at different levels of size.
4. Market price plus or minus a percentage – institutions converted these bids into fixed prices when tenders were closed.

As well as rewarding investors for the type of bid, Flemings awarded extra points for 'aggressiveness' of bid, i.e. investors who applied early and/or bid high fixed prices were given more points in the allocation priority.

All these scale factors – type of institution, type of bid and aggressiveness of bid, were programmed into the computer to give quality profiles of investor institutions in order to rank them in priorities for allocation.

Investors could change their bids at any time during the book-building process since they were only putting in indicative offers. They could cancel their reservation of shares at any point, even after the allocation had been made.

As was mentioned earlier, syndicates competed against each other in seeking business in their regions. Each day the London 'war room' would judge whether individual syndicates were performing well or badly. Those which were considered under-performing would be encouraged to improve.

With the daily information reported into London by syndicate managers, Flemings was able to draw up a price/demand diagram plotting the level of demand at a range of prices. The bank also had the institutional profiles of large investors in its monitored share register. By 25 July, Flemings was able to record that it had in fact a total demand for 370 million shares at 8.00 per share. Using the points system and institutional profiles, it decided it was appropriate to cut back demand to 310 million shares.

Although the Trust could probably have sold this number it eventually agreed with Flemings, it was wary of destroying the aftermarket. Clearly, a proportion of this number would unload their shares on the aftermarket shortly following allocation, with a consequently depressing effect on the price. A mechanism called the 'greenshoe' over-allotment option was put into place to cater for this.

As Exhibit 16.4 shows, the computer program incorporated layers of reporting. Each day, managers at level 1 reported indicative bids in full detail from what were eventually 1,100 institutions and over 40,000 private investors. At level 2, regional bookrunners from the 9 syndicates worldwide reported in to the book-building global co-ordinator where the demand was sized, and eventually price and allocation fixed.

The Over-allocation Option

During the negotiations, the Trust had really decided it wished to sell 270 million shares, which would reduce its holding in the Company from 75%. But Flemings had agreed with the Trust prior to book-building that it would have the ability to over-allocate 40 million shares. This would give the bank a degree of flexibility in balancing the aftermarket. It could eliminate or reduce excess demand in the market – demand excess to long-term requirements of investors – by 'selling short'. It hoped to have the option to acquire shares that were for speculative purposes.

The bank could buy back over-allotted share contracts by market purchases, but there are obvious snags. If share prices were subsequently to go up, and Flemings had only the option of buying back in the market to deliver the over-allocation – in other words, if it had an uncovered short – it would incur a loss. The short position could only be eliminated by this method by the bank buying back at a price higher than the offering price. Thus, it was during the next phase of the offering that Flemings used another option, innovative to the UK, to overcome this potential problem.

Phase 5: Allocation and Stabilisation (25 July–20 August)

During this period, Flemings, in conjunction with its syndicate managers and the Trust, was able to allocate the shares according to the criteria it had set up – earliness, quality and aggressiveness. The computer was instructed to allocate 310 million shares on the basis of these criteria, but included in this analysis was a host of qualitative factors introduced by the Trust, Flemings and the syndicate managers which resulted in re-allocation between syndicates and between particular institutions. They could be positive or

Exhibit 16.4 *Computer systems*

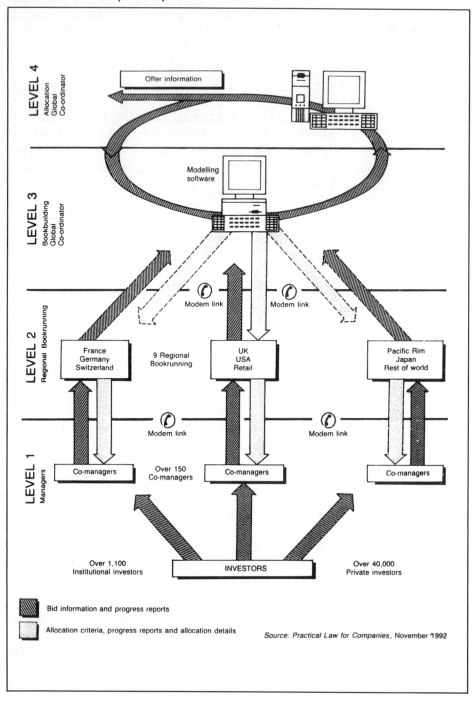

Source: Practical Law for Companies, November 1992

negative factors so that despite the computer saying an investor was allocated 0.25 million shares, the fact that the investor was known to be low quality resulted in a nil allocation.

The 'Greenshoe Option'

On 27 July, Flemings told the market that the Trust had sold 270 million shares with a right to allocate a further 40 million shares, but the market did not know if Flemings would over-allocate the entire 40 million shares. There was no legal requirement for the bank to do this.

In order to avoid the risk of a loss on this uncovered short selling position, Flemings in fact covered it by agreeing an option with the Trust to acquire additional Wellcome shares to cover this short position – in fact up to 15% of the shares actually sold. This was the 'Greenshoe option' named after an American company who first used the technique during a new issue of shares. The advantage of such an option is that it can be used to satisfy excess demand when the share price is rising, or, in this case, to reduce or eliminate speculative demand in the market by buying back shares. The greenshoe option gave Flemings valuable flexibility.

It was a matter of choice that the size of the greenshoe option and the over-allocation were the same. Flemings chose that position because it did not want an uncovered short. But it was not necessary and the over-allocation could have been greater.

The Stabilisation

On 27 July, the stabilisation period began. It was the Monday following the close of book-building on 24 July. During the book-building period in which theoretical demand was being built up, although demand for Wellcome's stock was rising, stock market prices and the price of Wellcome's shares went down and down. This was no surprise since some people were known to be shorting Wellcome's shares – selling Wellcome's stock in anticipation of a later fall in the price of the stock in the offering. This would, of course, realise them a profit. There was now an incentive for institutions to 'talk the shares down', for their own benefit.

However, on the morning of Thursday, 23 July, the day before the book closed, Flemings put out an announcement to say that they would not be accepting any bid below £8, so this stopped the shorting.

When the market opened on 27 July, market-makers' price for Wellcome's shares immediately went to £8 and stayed there (see Exhibit 16.11). Institutions selling beyond that level could have depressed the price below £8 which Flemings did not want. It therefore bought shares with the knowledge that it could buy up to 40 million shares under the Greenshoe option from the Trust.

After stabilising the price at around £8, the whole market, and Wellcome's share price turned worse. The effect was compounded for Wellcome's stock because, as the market was falling overall, and Flemings were undertaking to buy at £8, institutions began to sell Wellcome's stock at what was obviously a relatively attractive price. After a few days' trading, Flemings allowed Wellcome's price to drop to £7.80 since the market was falling heavily and there was no point in supporting the stock against a fall in the market.

As a result of the over-allotment or short selling of 40 million shares, Flemings had received £8 a share for them and was sitting on £320 million plus deposit interest – which was quite a tidy sum. So the bank used this power to buy back 22 million shares, making the total allotment of shares 288 million. The balance of the money was used to pay the Trust, to exercise the greenshoe option, and to buy the 18 million shares of over-allotment to cover that amount of over-allocation. Fleming had 30 days to tighten up demand, to fine-tune the immediate aftermarket, and it resulted in a net deal of 270 million plus 18 million shares.

During the stabilisation process, TOPIC screens showed the fact that Flemings was stabilising the price at £8. This is a requirement of the Financial Services Act. In effect, the market for Wellcome's stock was being stabilised. Any profits or losses incurred on the deal as a result of stabilisation accrued to the deal.

Flemings did not buy shares at above £8 because that would have resulted in an immediate loss since it had allocated shares at £8, but on the other hand, it was judged that if there was any expense incurred in buying the shares, Flemings would fund it. If the share price went above £8, Flemings could sell, i.e. go more short, because it could buy from the Trust at £8. In retrospect, had Flemings known the size of the actual demand in the market, it could have done the deal at 288 million shares, or over-allocated the additional 22 million shares. But it was Flemings' way of dealing with the uncertainty. Had there been certainty, there would have been no need for such a complex procedure.

The other way of coping with the uncertainty would have been to take up an unduly conservative position on the shares with the probable result that could be seen with all the early UK privatisations – the shares quickly going to an enormous premium, with the vendor, and all serious shareholders, the losers. Stabilisation, using the over-allocation and greenshoe options, allowed Flemings to match supply and demand as closely as possible to reality in a very uncertain market. In effect, it was making the market more perfect by intervention, although like the UK government trying to prop up sterling in 1992, it could have some effect, but could not really defy the markets. Flemings saw reality in allowing the stabilisation price to drop to £7.80 when institutions were selling heavily to realise cash at a time when Flemings was buying Wellcome's stock at £8.

In the case of the Wellcome share offering, it was an advantage that no new cash was being raised. As we have seen in Part A of this case study, the Trust was wealthy, but it required a higher yield from its investment portfolio. The Trust was an enormous investor selling one investment to replace it with another – diversifying. The Wellcome share price went down in a falling market, so that the Trust was only interested in how Wellcome's share price fell relative to other share prices, or the FTSE 100. It was the net effect that mattered. The problem would have been quite different if Wellcome had been cashing in its shares and placing the money on deposit in a bank.

Stabilisation could have given rise to legal problems. It could have been accused of creating a false market or of insider dealing – dealing with inside information. Both of these traps, however, are recognised in the SIB Conduct of Business Rules (Part 10) which allow stabilisation of share price offerings as legitimate if it is carried out with the object of helping the market to function properly. In this case, the false market and insider dealing provisions of the Financial Services Act and Company Securities (Insider Dealing) Act are not involved.

During the stabilisation period, the merchant bank, Barclays de Zoete Wedd (BZW), understood this mechanism perfectly and made money by announcing that they would establish a managed investment for the Wellcome Trust. They offered to buy shares (from an approved list) from investors who wanted to realise cash to buy Wellcome shares. For this they charged a minimum commission and no spread. To the Wellcome Trust, BZW said they would sell these shares to Wellcome, in exchange for the proceeds Wellcome was receiving from the sale of its shares at the mid-price, no spread. In effect, BZW acted as a middleman in a swap of Wellcome shares. Clearly, it was difficult for the Trust to reinvest £2.3 billion in shares as a result of its offering – it would have moved the market. BZW assisted this process, smoothed the reinvestment and matched two complementary desires. It was brilliant; Flemings regretted that it did not think of it first.

Smith New Court, another UK merchant Bank, also set up a warrant which enabled investors to insure against relative under-performance by Wellcome. If Wellcome's shares under-performed the index by more than 9% from the issue price, the warrants had value. They could be exercised at any time during the three-month period up to 27 October.

The UK Retail Offering

Retail investors in the UK were offered the possibility of taking part in a public offer, through retail agents. They could only apply for shares at the single tender price – there were no incentives or discounts such as applied in the earlier BT issue. Maximum application was £100,000 and minimum £1,000, and the shares were fully paid in one instalment. Transparency was also applied to retail investors, and retail agents were required to report details of investors applying for shares in excess of £50,000. Existing Wellcome shareholders were given priority allocations of up to £5,000 at the tender price.

Wellcome's retail shares were very successful, resulting in over 46,000 investors at the close of stabilisation. The Trust had the advantage that it had no mission to increase wider share ownership such as the UK government had when it privatised BT. It would have had legal problems with the Charity Commissioners if it had been seen to increase wider share ownership as well as fund medical research. At the time Wellcome made its public retail offer, several other retail offers had failed, including Anglia Windows, MFI, Taunton Cider, *Daily Telegraph*, Dr Pepper, Seven Up, Revlon, and, of course, the cancelled GPA flotation.

Wellcome's retail offer was conducted principally by direct mail, targeting high net worth individuals from bought-in mailing lists. This was a luxury that the BT issue did not have. And, of course, Flemings had the advantage of the flexibility and greater information provided by its computer system over some of these other offers.

Evaluation of the Wellcome Share Offering

On 18 October 1992, *The Observer* (Melvyn Marckus and George Parker-Jervis) commented,

> The 'greenshoe' mechanism for buying and selling shares in the £2.3 billion
> sale of drugs-combine Wellcome's shares three months ago has earned
> merchant bank Robert Fleming applause from the City.

This was valid comment. At the end of the stabilisation period, the Wellcome Trust had reduced its shareholding in Wellcome plc from 73.5% to 39.9% and received £2.3 billion. From Wellcome plc's point of view, it now had a much broader institutional and geographical shareholding spread – 1,100 institutional investors in 24 countries. The offering resulted in 46,000 retail investors, and US shareholdings in Wellcome's shares increased from

1% to 10% (over 20% of the free float). Flemings had efficiently stabilised the market for Wellcome shares using the greenshoe and over-allocation options, and made an attractive market at a good price against the background of a freely falling London Stock Market, 13% in the UK and 18% in Japan in the previous three months. These are the highlights of the offering.

The geographical distribution of the shares was a mixed success. As one would have expected, the major pharmaceutical markets, the UK, USA and Japan, absorbed most of the shares (90%). This raised the question of whether such a large syndicate of banks (120) was really necessary. But this is hindsight, and under what were clearly difficult market conditions in 1992, it was difficult to fix in advance exactly what the pattern of demand would be. It was a time when investment advisers were emphasising cyclical stocks and not defensive ones like pharmaceuticals.

About 48% of the shares were allocated to existing shareholders and 11.7% to retail investors worldwide. Sixty per cent of the shares went to the UK, including 14.4 million retail shares sold by a network of 68 retail brokers. The USA took 25% of the shares amounting to 70 million, including 50% of all retail shares. Japan took 5% of shares, Switzerland took 4.5% and France and Germany together 2.1% of the remaining 10%. It is quite clear that lead manager Morgan Stanley did a very good selling job in the USA, and Nikko in Japan, the latter covering 80% of Japanese sales single-handedly. Continental Europe and Canada were disappointing, with Germany taking 4 million shares and selling them back in the first two days. Canada took less than 1 million shares.

From the banking syndicates' point of view, the exercise was very profitable. Total commissions paid out to participants amounted to £75 million, of which £34 million went to UK institutions, consisting of underwriting, management and selling fees.

Flemings were successful in ensuring a stable aftermarket. In the three days following the offering, fewer than 4 million shares traded before New York opened on the first day, and then, following arbitrage, 13 million shares were traded. The following day only 1.6 million shares were traded in the UK and 758,000 in the USA. The bank had succeeded in preventing a large dumping of shares by its quality control of investors at the book-building stage.

Flemings can take credit for their efficient handling of the book-building exercise, the over-allocation option and the stabilisation of share price, all against the background of what had become a very weak market.

As Exhibit 16.5 shows, Wellcome's share price on 28 February was 1,126p. Between that date and the date when the offer closed, 24 July, the share price had fallen to 826p, a drop of 26.6%. The FTSE 100 index dropped in absolute value only 7.2%, so Wellcome's price fell a heavy 21.0% over the period relative to the FTSE 100. The falling market in general, and bear raids on Wellcome's stock had caused damage.

But this picture is not as bad as it seems. Wellcome's price, at 826p, was still between six and seven times the level at which the stock floated in 1986. It had only exceeded 800p in the eight months preceding the offering. Exhibit 16.10 shows that in the twelve months prior to close of offer on 24 July, Wellcome's absolute price increased 14.1%, the FTSE 100 index decreased 7.9%, and therefore Wellcome's shares increased relative to the FTSE 100 index by 23.0%. The stock is very volatile; if a trend line is fitted to Exhibit 16.14 (1986–92), it would have recorded around £9 in 1992.

From the beginning of the pre-marketing phase to 24 July, the performance of Wellcome's stock was little different overall to the FTSE 100 index and the FT All Share Index – slightly inferior – all measurements were down.

During the stabilisation phase, however (27 July–20 August), Flemings succeeded in keeping Wellcome's share price reasonably stable, starting the period at 800.5p, and ending on 20 August at 802.0p. But the weight of the offer was enormous – 288 million shares sold – so it was clearly a success to achieve that volume of sales at a steady price.

In fact, the longer-term aftermarket proved Wellcome's stock had a very healthy reception by the stock market. Between 27 July and 12 October, Wellcome's price increased from 800.5p to 963.0p, a percentage increase of 20.3. During this period, the FTSE 100 increased only 8.9%, making Wellcome's relative increase 10.6%.

It has been questioned whether the over-allocation and greenshoe options would have worked as well in a rising market as in a falling one, in other words, was the mechanism asymmetrically efficient? In a rising market (had it been possible to be clairvoyant), Flemings could have done an underwritten deal. But book-building would have been more profitable because as the price moved up, demand would have moved up with it. If the market had been rising, Flemings would not have bought any shares in the market, they would probably have exercised the greenshoe option for 40 million. It would not have been possible to underwrite in a falling market, except at a huge discount, and it may therefore not have been possible to do a deal at all. In a falling market, the book-building exercise and over-allocation option allowed Flemings to do a deal. The only reason for over-allocating was to stabilise. Had Flemings not thought the price was going down it would not have tried stabilisation.

The book-building mechanism has been followed in the Eurobond

Exhibit 16.5 *Wellcome absolute share price and relative to FTSE 100: announcement to close of offering (28 February 1992 to 24 July 1992)*

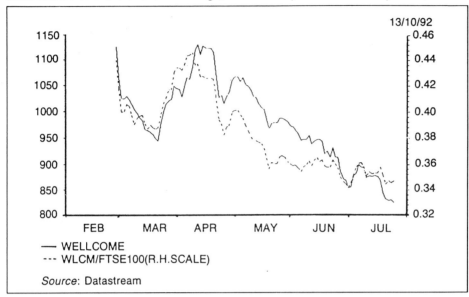

Exhibit 16.6 *Announcement – 28 February 1992 to 24 July 1992: Wellcome relative to UK health and household sector*

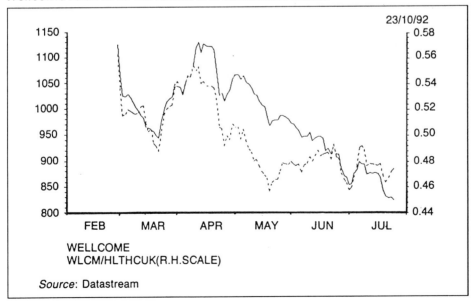

Exhibit 16.7   *Announcement – 28 February 1992 to 24 July 1992: Wellcome relative to US health and household sector*

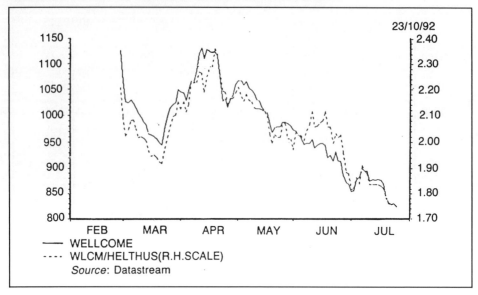

Exhibit 16.8   *Wellcome absolute share price and relative to FTSE 100: launch to close of offering (4 June 1992 to 24 July 1992)*

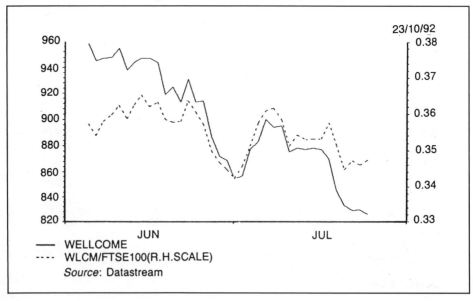

Exhibit 16.9   *Launch – 4 June 1992 to 24 July 1992:*
Wellcome relative to FT All Share

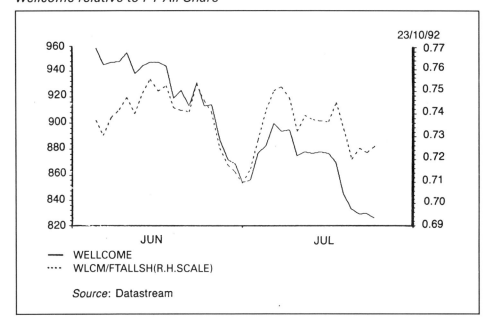

Exhibit 16.10   *Wellcome absolute share price and relative to FTSE 100:*
12 months prior to close of offering (24 July 1991 to 24 July 1992)

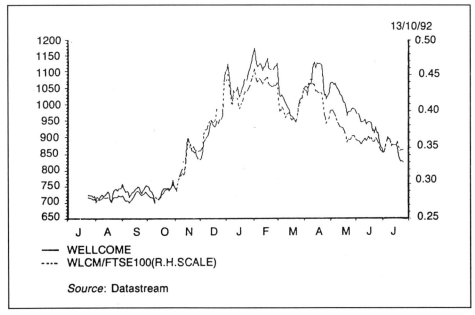

market and US equity markets for many years, but it is innovatory in the UK domestic equity markets. Regulators are taking a close interest in it. It will be interesting to see if it becomes more common in future years, although a major current obstacle to its rapid development in the UK is the pre-emptive rule.

Exhibit 16.11   *Wellcome absolute share price and relative to FTSE 100: stabilisation period (27 July 1992 to 20 August 1992)*

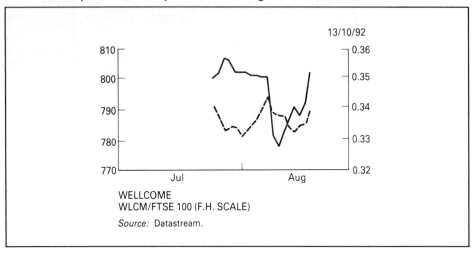

Exhibit 16.12   *Wellcome absolute share price and relative to FTSE 100: post-offering period (27 July 1992 to 12 October 1992)*

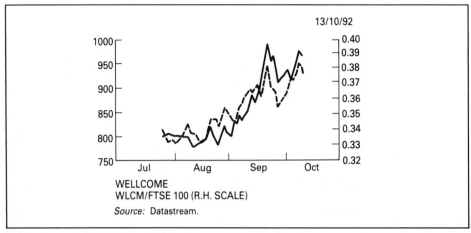

Appendix   Share Price Performance Graphs

Exhibit no.

Announcement – 28 February 1992 to 24 July 1992

16.5	(a)	Wellcome absolute price:	28 February	1126p
			24 July	826p
			% change	−26.6%
	(b)	FTSE 100 absolute value:	% change	−7.2%
	(c)	Relative to FTSE 100:	% change	−21.0%
16.6	(a)	Relative to UK Health and Household (Datastream):		−15.8%
16.7	(a)	Relative to US Health and Household (Datastream):		−20.8%

Launch – 4 June 1992 to 24 July 1992

16.8		*Relative to FTSE 100*		
	(a)	Absolute price:	4 June	958p
			24 July	826p
			% change	−13.8%
	(b)	FTSE 100 absolute value:	% change	−11.4%
	(c)	Relative to FTSE 100:	% change	−2.8%
16.9		*Relative to FT All Share*		
	(a)	FT All Share:	% change	−12.5%
	(b)	Wellcome relative to FT All Share:	% change	−1.5%

Over the 12 months prior to close – 24 July 1991 to 24 July 1992

16.10	(a)	Absolute price:	24 July 1991	724p
			24 July 1992	826p
			% change	−14.1%
	(b)	FTSE 100 absolute value:	% change	−7.9%
	(c)	Relative to FTSE 100:	% change	+23.9%

Stabilisation – 27 July 1992 to 20 August 1992

16.11	(a)	Absolute price:	27 July	800.5p
			20 August	802.0p
			% change	+0.2%
	(b)	FTSE 100 absolute value:	% change	+0.5%
	(c)	Relative to FTSE 100:	% change	−0.3%

Post-offering – 27 July 1992 to 12 October 1992

16.12	(a)	Absolute price:	27 July	800.5p
			12 October	963.0p
			% change	+20.3%
	(b)	FTSE 100 absolute value:	% change	+8.9%
	(c)	Relative to FTSE 100:	% change	+10.6%

FTSE 100 – 28 February 1992 to 24 July 1992

16.13	(a)	Absolute value:	28 February	2562.1p
			24 July	2377.2p
			% change	−7.2%

Wellcome Share Price – flotation to October 1992

16.14	(a)	Absolute value:	28 February	211p
			24 July	982p
			% change	+364.0%

Exhibit 16.13 *Absolute value of FTSE 100 Index:*
announcement to close of offering (28 February 1992 to 24 July 1992)

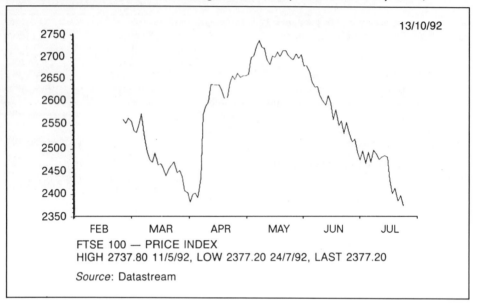

13/10/92

FTSE 100 — PRICE INDEX
HIGH 2737.80 11/5/92, LOW 2377.20 24/7/92, LAST 2377.20

Source: Datastream

Exhibit 16.14 *Wellcome absolute share price:*
announcement to close of offering (28 February 1992 to 24 July 1992)

CASE 17

Saatchi and Saatchi

In 1988, Saatchi and Saatchi, the owner of two of the world's big three advertising networks, raised £175 million through the issue of convertible preference shares. The case describes the reasons that Saatchi's wanted to raise the capital, and its plans to build itself up into the world's largest business service company. The company's reasons for issuing convertibles rather than either straight debt or straight equity are also explained.

The convertible itself contained a number of innovatory features, most notably a 'rolling put' which allowed investors to put the shares back to the issuer between five and ten years after issue. The terms of the issue are set out in summary form in the case.

The case provides a good basis for examining why companies issue securities, and raises a number of issues concerned with security design. It can also be used to demonstrate how hybrid securities can be valued.

Saatchi's had never been shy about its ambition to become the world's largest business service company. By 1988, their two global advertising networks (Saatchi and Saatchi Advertising Worldwide and Backer Spielvogel Bates Worldwide) were ranked numbers two and three in the world. Their consulting arm, though much smaller, was growing rapidly. Saatchi's growth, part organic, part by acquisition, had been phenomenal, with revenues having increased one-hundredfold and earnings per share having grown at an annual compounded rate of 36% over the previous decade. But growth requires capital, and with shareholders' funds of only £40 million supporting a turnover 100 times as large, new capital was urgently needed.

This case was written by Anthony Neuberger as a basis for class discussion rather than to illustrate either effective or ineffective handling of an administration situation. © Anthony Neuberger, 1995.

In the Beginning

The two brothers, Charles and Maurice Saatchi, sons of an Iraqi-Jewish immigrant, set up the advertising agency in London in 1970 with £100,000 capital. Charles, the elder brother, was a talented copywriter who had gone into advertising straight from school. Maurice graduated from the London School of Economics, and had worked for a time in magazine publishing.

The agency was launched with some panache. The brothers took a full page advertisement in the *Sunday Times* to announce the launch of the new agency. Its early output included an advertisement for contraception which is remembered to this day; it showed a 'pregnant' man with the caption, 'Would you be more careful if it was you that got pregnant?'

By 1973, the new agency had won a number of prestigious accounts. In the annual league table for that year, it was placed 26th with billings[1] of £5.1 million, some way behind the leader, J. Walter Thompson with £41.1 million. Saatchi's made their first significant takeover that year when they bought the agency E.G. Dawes for £220,000. That agency had billings of £1.6 million in 1973.

The step which turned Saatchi's into a public quoted company was largely unplanned. In 1975, the board of the advertising agency group Compton UK Partners was looking for a merger with a young dynamic agency in order to rejuvenate the company. Compton UK, which ranked number 11 in the league table in 1974 with billings of £17.4 million, had a strong client list but a lacklustre reputation. It was listed on the London Stock Exchange; only a small proportion of the equity was owned by the directors; 30% was held by Compton Communications of New York. Saatchi and Saatchi only came into the picture as possible partners when they tried to persuade Compton advertising managing director Ted Rimmer to come and work for them. He was much impressed by the young agency and advocated a merger. Following the merger, the Saatchi directors ended up with 35% of the merged equity. While not having a majority shareholding, the brothers had effective control since they jointly had the largest single stake in the merged company.

The next few years were highly successful ones for Saatchi's. They succeeded in generating some very substantial new business (Allied Breweries, BP, IBM, Procter and Gamble). They gained public notoriety through their hard-hitting campaign for the Conservative Party in the 1979 General Election when the Conservatives took power from the Labour Party. Perhaps their most famous advertisement was a poster showing a long queue of people waiting to receive unemployment pay under the caption 'Labour isn't working'.

In that same year, the London agency of Saatchi's moved to the top of the league table with billings of £67.5 million, ousting J. Walter Thompson. Saatchi's was growing by acquisition as well as organically. A list of major acquisitions is at Exhibit 17.1. The first big acquisition after the merger with Compton UK was the purchase of Garrott Dorland Crawford Holdings, a privately owned network of advertising agencies and financial service firms. Saatchi's acquired it in 1981 for a total price of £5.6 million, of which £1.5 million (funded by a rights issue) was paid up-front, with the rest payable in the following two years, depending on achievement of certain financial targets.

The pattern for Saatchi acquisitions had been set. They would be uncontested. Existing management would remain in place, at least initially. They would be financed by issuing new equity. The purchase price would be spread over several years, and would depend on performance.

In 1982 Saatchi's went international by taking over Compton Communications, the New York based advertising group which already had a 20% stake in Saatchi's London agency through the merger with Compton UK some seven years earlier. Compton Communications was larger than Saatchi's with total billings of $650 million; it comprised not only the New York advertising agency, but also a network of agencies worldwide, and a collection of specialist advertising agencies. The price was $55 million, with the down-payment of $31 million again being financed by the issue of 8 million shares.

Saatchi's first major acquisitions outside advertising took place in 1984 when it acquired one of the leading US market research companies, Yankelovich, Skelly and White for $13.5 million. In the same year, they took a much bigger step by acquiring the Hay Group, an international US-based consultancy specializing in human resource management. This was significant both because of its size – a price of up to $125 million, including $80 million up-front – and because it showed that Saatchi's were trying to turn themselves from an advertising company to a more broadly based business service company.

The Underlying Strategy

Where was Saatchi's heading? The conventional wisdom at the time was that there was a natural limit to the size of an advertising agency. The relationship between an agency and its client had to be based on trust so that they could discuss frankly the product's strengths and weaknesses, strategies for brand promotion and areas of vulnerability. If two agencies merged, they would

Exhibit 17.1 *Saatchi and Saatchi: major acquisitions 1978–87*

Figures after the acquisition are the initial down-payment + the maximum additional subsequent earn-out payment. Except where indicated, the companies acquired are advertising agencies. Figures in brackets relate to the company's performance in the year preceding the acquisitions; profit figures are pre-tax.

1978	Hall Advertising (Edinburgh)	£0.25m + £0.75m
1979	O'Kennedy-Brindley (Dublin)	£0.315m
1981	Garrott Dorland Crawford Holdings (UK)	£1.5m + £4.1m (billings £50m)
1982	Compton Communications (New York)	$30.8m + $24.5m (billings $650m, profits $8m)
1983	McCaffrey & McCall (New York)	$10m + $7.5m (billings $140m, profit $3.6)
1984	Cochrane Chase Livingston (California)	$1.4m + $1m
1984	Harrison Cowley (UK regional advertising, PR and recruitment agency)	£7.5m in convertible unsecured loanstock
1984	Hedger Mitchell Stark (London)	£1.2m + £1.8m
1984	Yankelovich Skelly and White (NY-based market research and Boston-based human resource management)	$13.5m ($20m T/O, $1.3m profits)
1984	Hay Group (International Human Resource Management)	$80m + $45m (T/O $105m, profits $12.9m)
1985	Hayhurst (Canada)	£3.75 +
1985	Campaign Advertising (New Zealand)	£0.43m +
1985	Sharps Advertising (UK)	£1.1m + (billings £28m)
1985	Grandfield Rork Collins (London)	£4m + £6m (billings £45m)
1985	Marlboro Marketing (New York Sales Promotion)	$14m + to make 9 × future average earnings
1985	Kleid (US Direct Marketing)	$4m + $11m
1985	Siegel & Gale (US Corporate Communications)	$2m + to make 10 × future average earnings
1985	Clancy Shulman & Associates (Connecticut Market Research)	$2m + (T/O $1.46m profits $0.27m)
1985	Rowland (New York Public Relations)	$10m + to make 10 × future average earnings (T/O $7.3m, profits $2.17m)
1986	Dancer Fitzgerald Sample (New York)	$75m + $25m (billings $876m)
1986	Backer & Spielvogel (US)	$56m + $45m ($385m billings)
1986	Ted Bates Worldwide	$400m + $50m (billings $3,107m, profits $64.5m)
1987	Cleveland Consulting (Logistics Consultant)	$2m + to make 9.5 × future average earnings
1987	Peterson (Litigation Services)	$42m + $142m (T/O $48m, profits $12.2m)

expect to lose accounts of clients who were competing with each other. Size is also difficult to combine with creativity and originality.

Saatchi's, however, saw the advantages which come with size. First came their perception of market consolidation. They pointed to the increasing emergence of global companies, competing globally. Following Theodore Levitt, the marketing guru, they distinguished between multinational and global companies. Multinationals adjust their products and practices to the countries where they operate, at high relative costs. The global corporation operates with resolute constancy as if the world were a single entity. The global corporation with its low relative costs would dominate the markets. A global corporation would want to use service companies which could themselves readily operate globally.

This was not to deny that national and regional market segments exist. They do, but Saatchi's argued they were becoming less important, not only within Europe, but also worldwide. The companies which had succeeded in establishing global brands would increasingly dominate their competitors because of economies of scale. Saatchi's, with its worldwide network of agencies, could service global brands globally, while at the same time use its local market knowledge to tailor the impact specifically to local circumstances.

In support of their view that their clients were consolidating, they pointed to the fact that in the five years up to 1986, the share of world advertising expenditure of the top 100 US companies had risen from 12% to 17%. The advertising industry itself was consolidating rapidly. Over the same period the number of major multinational advertising agencies had shrunk from 12 to 8, but their share had increased from 12% to 20%. The problem of conflict of interest had been solved by Interpublic, which until 1986 was the world's largest advertising group. It owned a number of advertising networks which were run totally separately. In April 1986, the sixth, twelfth and sixteenth largest US advertising agencies, with combined billings of over $5 billion in 1985, combined to form the world's largest agency, Omnicom. If Saatchi's were to dominate the advertising industry, it would have to move quickly.

The other strand in their thinking was the growing importance of know-how relative to tangible assets. They saw service industries, and particularly business service industries such as advertising and consultancy, as being the growth industries of the future. This represented both an opportunity and a challenge. Economies of scope and scale apply in know-how industries just as much as in other industries. Size means the ability to serve global customers, to cross-sell services, to retain better talent, to get superior media-buying clout (consolidation was occurring in the media, with the emergence of global multi-media empires like News International, Time, Inc., and Bertelsmann), and to benefit from improved information systems and wider experience. The challenge was to manage a global know-how-based industry effectively. Know-how assets are different from physical assets: they go home at night. If dissatisfied, they leave, taking clients with them. They demand and need autonomy to work effectively. Scale economies are hard to realize. A company which knew how to manage know-how globally would reap the rewards of dominating a fragmented and rapidly growing market.

Saatchi's believed that they had the skills. They gave individual agencies autonomy. They paid well by industry standards. They were ready when necessary to rationalize operations, merging agencies and replacing existing management. They were also able to reap global economies of scale by cross-referrals both between advertising agencies in different countries and between advertising and consultancy. Through their stock market quote, they had ready access to capital markets.

It was logical to diversify out of advertising, an industry which was growing at well under 10%, and expand into consulting which, on their rather broad definition, was more than six times as large as advertising and growing at 20% annually. The consulting industry was far more fragmented than advertising, with no firm having more than 1% of the market. Saatchi's argued that it was ripe for consolidation, and that they, with their ability to manage a global know-how business and ability to raise capital from the equity markets, would be well placed to compete against the incumbent firms, most of which were partnerships.

The Acquisition of Ted Bates

Ted Bates was the third largest advertising agency with worldwide billings of $3,100 million in 1985, as compared with Saatchi's $4,500 million. It was known for having developed a theory of advertising based on the notion of the unique selling proposition (USP). Bates had the reputation of being a competent, if somewhat dull, agency. It was unusually profitable; its pre-tax profits in 1985/6 were $64.5 million, which gave it a ratio of profit-to-income (not billings) of 16.8% compared with under 10% for other major quoted US agencies. The price paid by Saatchi's was $450 million (of which $400m was paid up-front in cash).

Saatchi's put Ted Bates together with Dorland (UK) and another US agency acquired in 1986, Backer & Spielvogel, to form a completely separate international advertising network from Saatchi and Saatchi. Some $400 million of business was lost as a result of the merger, but the advantages of having two separate networks were well illustrated by the handling of the account of Dixon, the electrical goods retailer. As a result of the merger, Dixon found that their account was being handled by the same network which handled their rivals, Woolworth. Saatchi's responded by moving the entire team working on Dixons' account from Backer Spielvogel Bates to Saatchi & Saatchi, and thus kept the account.

The Run-up to the Convertible Issue

Following the major acquisitions of 1986, 1987 was largely devoted to rationalizing the two advertising networks. Some small acquisitions were made, largely on the consulting side. An unsuccessful approach was made to take over the Midland Bank, the smallest of the UK's 'Big Four' high street banks, which was a potential target following large third world loan write downs and a disastrous acquisition of a Californian bank. The approach was regarded as somewhat cheeky since Midland's market capitalization was still more than twice that of Saatchi's. Rebuffed by Midland, Saatchi's also made an abortive approach to the middle-sized investment bank Hill Samuel. The rationale for going into financial services was an extension of that used for consulting – a know-how based industry with much scope for cross-selling of products.

By 1988, the company was ready to make some more large acquisitions. The basic strategy of expanding into consulting remained intact. However, the stock market was no longer as attractive a source of funds as it had been. Having been a darling of the stock market, Saatchi's was now looked on with some suspicion. The word 'megalomania' became increasingly prominent in press commentary. Many people felt that Saatchi's had overpaid, particularly for Ted Bates, and had yet to demonstrate that it could deliver the advantages of scale.

The goal of creating the dominant business service company in the world filled some with foreboding. When Saatchi's predicted in 1987 that the world market for consulting services would be worth well over $200 billion by 1991, and that ten firms would account for a third of it, investors had reasonable grounds for suspecting massive new share issues to pay for the acquisition of several billion dollars of consulting turnover. By June 1988, Saatchi's shares were trading on a P/E multiple of 8.7. Critics pointed to Saatchi's propensity to issue equity capital (the capital history is at Exhibit 17.2), and foresaw rapid dilution as Saatchi's used equity to buy companies paying ten times pre-tax profits.

The City's worries about Saatchi's were perhaps a natural reaction to the excessive euphoria about the company's prospects in the first half of the 1980's. Earnings per share growth of over 40% cannot be sustained for ever. But there were other reasons for concern. First, the departure of Martin

Exhibit 17.2   *Saatchi and Saatchi: five year performance*

	1983	1984	1985	1986	1987	1988
Earnings per share (p)	13.2	19.9	31.6	38.2	45.9	
Dividends per share (p)	4.4	6.3	9.8	11.8	14.5	
Share price (p): High	273	380	510	697	698	577
Low	163	245	365	427	435	325

All figures adjusted for capital changes

Capital history

		(millions)
Shares in issue June 1983		16.1
Aug. 1983	1 : 2 scrip issue	+ 8.1
Dec. 1983	ADRs issued in USA	+ 4.2
Dec. 1984	Issued in part-payment of purchase of Hay	+ 10.4
		38.8
Apr. 1985	1 : 3 scrip issue	+ 12.9
Jan. 1986	Rights issue (£393m)	+ 57.6
		109.4
Mar. 1987	1 : 3 scrip issue	+ 36.6
Mar. 1987	Placing (£63m)	+ 9.7
Payment for miscellaneous acquisitions		0.6
Shares in issue June 1988		156.3

Sorrell, Saatchi's much respected finance director, in 1986 to set up his own international advertising agency WPP (which took over J. Walter Thompson) weakened confidence. Second, the attempt to take over the Midland Bank in 1987 suggested to some observers that the Saatchi board dangerously overestimated its own skills. Third, advertising agencies were felt to be overpriced in the more sober mood after the crash of 1987. As a result, Saatchi's share price had been particularly hard hit, and had substantially underperformed the market (see Exhibit 17.3).

And yet Saatchi's felt that their strategy was paying off handsomely. Their financial figures showed that they could not only grow rapidly, but they could also grow profitably. They had evidence that cross-referrals worked; 213 of their clients were using 3 or more of Saatchi's 16 service lines, up from 50 clients a year earlier.

If the equity market no longer looked a promising source of capital, debt markets looked still less attractive. Saatchi's balance sheet as at September 1987 is at Exhibit 17.4. As can be seen, it had very little debt; bank loans, overdrafts and loan stock totalling £32.5 million were heavily outweighed by cash of £200 million. But Saatchi's suffered from the problem

Exhibit 17.3   *Saatchi's share price (adjusted for capital changes)*

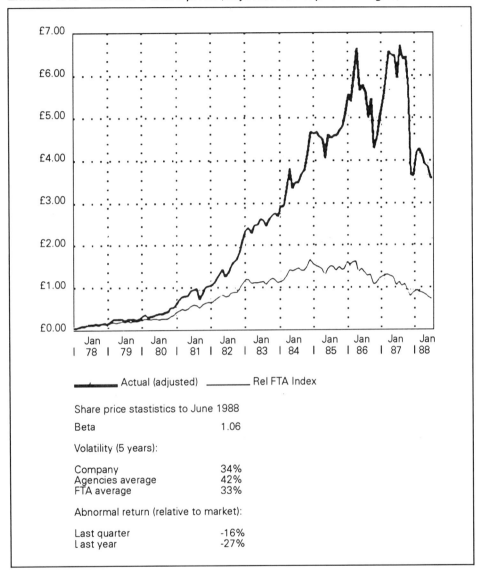

Share price stastistics to June 1988

Beta   1.06

Volatility (5 years):

Company	34%
Agencies average	42%
FTA average	33%

Abnormal return (relative to market):

Last quarter	-16%
Last year	-27%

faced by all acquisitive companies which buy know-how companies. The purchase price being far in excess of the net book value, acquisitions lead to massive goodwill which under UK accounting rules [2] has to be written off immediately. For that reason, the accounts show capital and reserves at a mere £40 million, and this was more than fully accounted for by convertible

Exhibit 17.4   *Saatchi and Saatchi: financial statements*

Consolidated Profit and Loss Account
for the years ended 30 September 1987 and 1986

	1987 (£m)	1986 (£m)
Turnover	3,954.2	2,087.0
Revenue (gross profit) (Note 1)	773.8	443.9
Profit ordinary activities before taxation	124.1	70.1
Taxation on profit on ordinary activities	(45.3)	(25.7)
Profit ordinary activities after taxation	78.8	44.4
Minority interests	(2.9)	(0.7)
Preference dividends	(6.3)	(6.3)
Profit for the financial year attributable to ordinary shareholders of the company	69.6	37.4
Ordinary dividends	(22.6)	(13.5)
Retained profit for the financial year	47.0	23.9
Earnings per ordinary share (Note 2)	45.9p	38.2p

Consolidated Balance Sheet as at 30 September 1987 and 1986

	1987 (£m)	1986 (£m)
Fixed assets	133.5	119.4
Current assets (Note 3)	781.8	764.2
Creditors: (Note 4)		
Amounts falling due within one year	(744.6)	(692.3)
Net current assets	37.2	71.9
Total assets less current liabilities	170.7	191.3
Creditors: (Note 4)		
Amounts falling due after more than one year	(84.4)	(47.6)
Provision for liabilities and charges (Note 13)	(39.4)	(44.4)
Minority interests	(6.7)	(8.3)
	40.2	91.0
Capital and reserves		
Called up share capital (Note 5)	115.1	110.4
Reserves (Note 6)	(74.9)	(19.4)
	40.2	91.0

Exhibit 17.4 *continued*

Consolidated Statement of Source and Application of Funds
for the years ended 30 September 1987, 1986 and 1985

	1987 (£m)	1986 (£m)	1985 (£m)
Source of funds			
Profit before taxation	124.1	70.1	40.4
Adjustment for items not involving movement of funds:			
Depreciation	18.7	10.7	6.1
Exchange transaction adjustments	(7.8)	2.6	(1.4)
Total generated from operations	135.0	83.4	45.1
Issue of ordinary shares	61.5	392.9	78.1
Issue of convertible preference shares	–	–	95.9
Issue of debentures	1.3	43.0	2.0
	197.8	519.3	221.4
Application of funds			
Dividends, including those paid to minorities	(26.8)	(14.1)	(5.1)
Taxes paid	(24.2)	(18.6)	(12.7)
Purchases less sales of tangible fixed assets	(37.1)	(20.8)	(4.5)
Acquisition of subsidiaries	(16.5)	(397.2)	(143.7)
Deferred consideration and reorganization costs paid	(62.1)	(46.0)	(8.6)
Acquisition of fixed asset investment	(3.2)	(9.4)	(0.6)

Net increase in long-term loans,
   creditors and provisions and
   decrease in long-term debtors
	27.1	20.8	2.6

	(142.8)	(485.3)	(172.6)
Changes in working capital			
Work in progress	(1.4)	(1.3)	3.9
Debtors	18.9	(65.6)	(9.7)
Creditors	(42.8)	83.8	29.5
	(25.3)	16.9	23.7
Increase in net cash balances and **current asset investments**	29.7	50.9	72.5

Exhibit 17.4 *continued*

Notes to the accounts

1. Revenue is after net interest receivable of £23.8m (1986 = £17.1m).
2. Based on 151.6m shares (1986 = 98.0m).
3. Including £200.3m cash (£170.3m).
4. Including £53.9m deferred purchase consideration on acquisitions. Further sums not provided for would become payable over the next five years depending on future level of profits. These would not exceed £107.7m.
5. Fully paid

	1987	*1986*
156.0m ordinary shares of 10p	15.6	10.9
99.5m 6.3% conv. cum. red. £1 prefs	99.5	99.5
	115.1	110.4

The preference shares are convertible into ordinary shares 1989–2015 at the rate of 18.713 ordinary shares per £100 of preference shares.

6. **Movements in reserves:**

	£m
At beginning of year	(19.4)
Premium or ordinary shares issued, less expenses	60.5
Goodwill from deferred consideration payments	(66.7)
Additional goodwill from reorganisation of 1986 acquisitions	(70.8)
Goodwill from acquisitions in 1987	(14.0)
Transfer from P&L account	47.0
Exchange translation and capitalization of reserves	(11.5)
At end of year	(74.9)

---

cumulative redeemable preference shares with a face value of £100 million. Further acquisitions more than fully funded by debt would lead to the company showing negative capital on its balance sheet.

Although this did not totally exclude the possibility of raising straight debt, this and the lack of tangible assets suggested that any debt the company issued could not be of investment grade – they would have to issue junk bonds. They would have to pay a substantial premium – perhaps 200 to 250 basis points spread over long-dated treasury bonds. With short-term rates at 9.3% and 5 year treasuries yielding 10%, this made long-term debt look very dear. As the cash flow statements (at Exhibit 17.4) show, Saatchi's had a strong interest in minimizing the costs of servicing any new capital raised. Also the issuing of junk bonds would not help Saatchi's image as the leading business service company.

Saatchi's thoughts inevitably turned to hybrid financing. To avoid having negative capital, the new security should be classed as equity on the balance sheet. But an issue of ordinary shares was ruled out by the likely adverse response by the market. This indicated some kind of preference share which had a regular payment (like a bond). A straight preference share is very similar to an unsecured, subordinated bond. Saatchi's would have to offer a very high coupon level to sell such a security. To make the issue more attractive to investors, it could be made convertible into ordinary shares. This would provide a sensible sharing of risk between the investor and the company. The company was confident that its strategy would succeed, and its share price rise. If it were right, the investor would benefit because he could convert into ordinary shares. If it were wrong, the investor would be protected because he would have a guaranteed yield on the preferred share.

In practice it was virtually inevitable that the preference shares would be converted. Assuming typical terms, the preference shares would be redeemable at par in fifteen years if not converted, but the share price would only have to rise by around 10% for conversion to be more attractive than redemption. The share price had more than doubled over the past five years; for it not to increase by 10% over the next fifteen years, something would have to go badly wrong. So dilution would be deferred, not avoided. But the delay in conversion to ordinary shares would be useful; it would allow time for the strategy to pay off in terms of higher earnings. Furthermore, even on a fully diluted basis, the earnings per share impact of an issue of convertible shares would be less than for an issue of ordinary equity because the new shares would be issued at a premium to the share price at the time of issue rather than at a discount.

Convertible preferred stock could be seen as a kind of deferred equity issue. But it had further advantage over an issue of ordinary shares. Under the UK Companies Acts, it was difficult to offer significant quantities of new shares directly to new investors; existing shareholders had pre-emptive rights on any new issue. The convertible preferred stock provided a way of selling equity to new investors on the Euromarket. This was obviously attractive for a company which wanted to be seen as a global player. It would enable them to tap a wider capital market for funds, and this could reduce their cost of capital.

The terms of a convertible are reasonably standard. The Saatchi share price stood at about £4.00. This suggested that the preference shares should be convertible into ordinary shares at the rate of some £4.40 nominal of preference shares for every ordinary share (a 10% premium). UK long-dated treasury bonds were yielding just under 10%. Investors would expect a substantial premium if they were buying unsecured, subordinated preference shares. On the other hand, the conversion rights had substantial value. This suggested a coupon of around 10.5% on the preference shares.

The idea of paying a premium over treasuries and also offering conversion rights did not seem very appealing. The cost of servicing the shares would still be high. Another suggestion was put forward. Saatchi's should guarantee to buy any unconverted preference shares back from investors after 5 years at a 20% premium to the issue price. Investors would then accept a much lower yield. If they were offered a coupon of 6.75%, then they would know that at worst they could put the preference shares back to Saatchi at a profit after five years, getting an all-in return of 10%, the same as on treasury bonds. From Saatchi's viewpoint, the lower coupon would be extremely welcome. At the same time the probability that they would have to make good on the guarantee was small. Investors would only exercise the right to put the shares if Saatchi's share price failed to appreciate by 20% or so over five years. Given Saatchi's share price performance in the past, and the fact that the shares were starting from an undemanding P/E multiple of 8.7, that looked improbable. Even in the unlikely event that the shares were put back to them, Saatchi's would have succeeded in raising unsecured, subordinated five year debt finance at the same rate as the UK government.

The company did decide to raise £171 million net through the issue of convertible puttable preference shares through a specially created subsidiary domiciled in the Netherland Antilles; the terms of the issue are summarized in Exhibit 17.5

Exhibit 17.5 *Terms of the convertible puttable preference shares*

Saatchi & Saatchi Finance NV, a fully owned subsidiary of Saatchi & Saatchi plc. issued 176,478,516 of 6.75% redeemable convertible preference shares 2003 of £1 each at par on 20 June 1988.

Conversion

Each preference share is convertible into ordinary shares at the rate of £4.41 nominal of preference share for each ordinary share. Conversion can take place at the investor's option at any time between 1 October 1989 and 8 July 2003. The mid-market closing price of the ordinary shares on 16 June 1988 was £4.01.

Dividends

Each preference share has the right to receive from the issuer a fixed cumulative dividend of 6.75% payable annually on 15 July each year from 1989 to 2003, and will accrue until the share is redeemed or converted. The payment of preference dividends shall take priority over payments to any other class of shareholder.

Any outstanding preference shares will be redeemed at their face value, together with accrued dividends, on 15 July 2003.

Exhibit 17.5 *continued*

Investor Put

The investor can require the issuer to redeem the preference share on 15 July of any of the following years at the percentage of face value shown in Table 1 (together with accrued dividends).

Table 1

Redeem on 15 July	at
1993	119.71%
1994	124.91%
1995	130.62%
1996	136.91%
1997	143.82%
1998	151.43%

(These figures are designed to give the investor who puts his shares on any of these dates a redemption yield of 9.98%).

Issuer call

The issuer can redeem the preference shares in the twelve months following 16 July in each of the years in column 1 of Table 2 for the percentage of face value in column 2, provided that the average closing price of the shares in the month preceding the issue of the redemption notice exceeds the percentage of the conversion price in column 3.

Table 2

Year from 16 July	Redeem at	if share exceeds
1989	104%	135%
1990	103%	135%
1991	102%	135%
1992	101%	135%
1993	100%	135%
1994	100%	137%
1995	100%	142%
1996	100%	149%
1997	100%	156%
1998–2002	100%	100%

So for example, the issuer could give notice in December 1990 that he would redeem the preference shares at 103% of their face value provided that the average share price in the preceding month had exceeded 135% of the conversion value of £4.41, that is £5.95.

In addition, the issuer has the right to redeem the preference shares on 15 July in the years 1993–98 inclusive at the prices indicated in Table 1.

If the issuer gives notice to redeem the shares, he has to pay accrued interest to the date of redemption, and has to give thirty days' notice, during which time preference shareholders are free to convert their preference shares into ordinary shares.

Exhibit 17.5 *continued*

Guarantee

All payments due to investors are guaranteed by Saatchi & Saatchi plc even if the issuer, its Netherland Antilles subsidiary, does not have the distributable reserves itself to pay out dividends. In the event of the guarantor or one of its principal subsidiaries defaulting on any other substantial legal liability, or in the event of substantial tax changes, the preference shares become redeemable at a price which gives investors a redemption yield of 9.98% on the money invested.

In addition, there are provisions protecting preference shareholders from the effects of new share issues and share splits, and covenants to prevent the issue of new equity capital of greater seniority than the preference shares.

Author's note: This exhibit reflects my understanding of the terms of the security. It is intended to be used for teaching purposes, and is not in any way authoritative. The interested reader is advised to consult the original document.

Notes

1. Billings refer to the total media spend by the client which passes through the agency; the agency typically keeps about 15% of the billings. The figures are supplied by the individual agencies and are normally based on the card rate for advertising rather than the actual rate the agency is able to negotiate.
2. Under US rules, goodwill is amortized against the P&L account over forty years.

Devro

A Large Management Buy-out
Subsequently Floated

*The management buy-out process involves considerable attention to
initial financial structuring and to planning for the realisation of
investment made by equity and other financial backers. Devro provides
an example of a large buy-out which had been attempted several times
before finally being completed in early 1991, a difficult point in the history
of the buy-out industry. The case describes the background to the
transaction, the areas which require to be examined before a buy-out can
take place and financial structuring issues. Developments after
completion of the transaction are followed in the case in order to
examine the initial restructuring which was carried out, and the
background to the company's flotation on the stock market in June 1993.
Questions are asked concerning the method of exit and the longevity of
buy-outs.*

Introduction

During 1990 and 1991 the UK management buy-out market showed a serious
contraction in value as equity and debt providers reacted to the overpricing
and over-leveraging of the late 1980s. Declining economic and financial
prospects and increasing evidence of poor performance of some earlier buy-
outs, including well publicised bankruptcies, reinforced these concerns.
Devro, a buy-out which had been attempted unsuccessfully several times in
the 1980s, however, provided a timely reminder when it was completed in
April 1991 that major buy-outs could still be financed on the right terms.
At £107.7 million Devro was the fourth largest buy-out to be completed in
the UK in 1991 and the second largest ever in Scotland. This case describes

*This case was written by Ken Robbie and Mike Wright as a basis for class discussion rather
than to illustrate either effective or ineffective handling of an administrative situation.* © *Ken
Robbie and Mike Wright, 1995.*

the background to a buy-out transaction, the areas which need to be examined before a buy-out can take place, financial structuring and planning for an exit.

The Company

Devro, previously owned by Johnson & Johnson the US healthcare group, had developed in the late 1950s from their Ethicon subsidiary's Development and Research Organization (hence the name Devro). While searching for new absorbent materials with which to make surgical sutures, they had been testing collagen, a protein found in the connective tissue of cattle hide. Although in the end not used for surgical sutures the researchers saw an application, as collagen was edible, as a suitable material for sausage casing, replacing the traditional use of animal gut.

By 1990 Devro had grown into an international producer of sausage skins, marketing the product in over 45 countries with variations to reflect local tastes. The company was estimated to supply over 70% of the UK and almost 50% of the world sausage markets. The company employed 1,000 staff in total, with the largest operation in Scotland where it employed 600. In 1990 Devro had a turnover of £70 million and operating profits of £17.6 million. Devro was, in essence, organised through three separate geographical divisions – the UK, USA and Australia – with each reporting directly to the parent rather than through an internal Devro structure.

The Divestment and Purchase Process

Sausage casings, however, did not represent a core activity for the healthcare parent and a change in ownership of Devro had been discussed for many years. With Johnson & Johnson's reputation as a fair employer, the possibility of a management buy-out had seemed appropriate to some managers. Significant personal dangers can exist in proposing such a transaction. As early as 1984, a buy-out bid by the Scottish managers resulted in the dismissal of all but one of the senior executives, while the survivor lost his post as managing director in January 1990 after seeking Scottish managers' involvement in a US-based management buy-out attempt which failed.

However, by 1990 the seriousness of Johnson & Johnson's intention to sell the company was apparent, with the appointment in July 1990 of Goldman Sachs as advisers to them in the potential sale. In July, Charterhouse Development Capital which had been involved in the 1984 buy-out proposal and which had been unsuccessful on the grounds of price, received information on the company but subject to the proviso that no contact be made directly with Devro. While this restricted Charterhouse significantly, they were able in August to give an indicative offer subject to general due diligence, only to find that Goldman Sachs intended to seek a wider range of potential purchasers. Following the distribution of information memoranda in November and a presentation in early December 1990, Charterhouse were able to make an offer for Devro subject to specific due diligence just before Christmas, and, following the acceptance of this, full access was allowed to the management.

Three of the important areas which had to be thoroughly investigated before financial structuring could be finalised and the transaction completed were: Devro's sales performance and market position; review of historical and planned financial position; and the composition of the management team. These investigations had to be carried out at a time in the middle of the Gulf War when logistics such as air flights to some of the company's important markets were particularly difficult.

A specialist consultancy firm was engaged to study the markets in which Devro operated and its competitive position. A major problem was the lack of published accounting information on competitors, given that the few major competitors were privately owned or divisions of large organisations. A major element of this analysis was extensive interviews with Devro's customers in its principal markets.

One of the leading international accountancy practices was used as reporting accountants to carry out the financial investigation and review historical and planned performance. This process was complicated by the organisational structure and international nature of Devro. As described earlier, the three operating divisions were not consolidated. Each sent financial reports directly to Johnson & Johnson. Furthermore, the taxation and currency aspects of such an international transaction required very careful examination to ensure the structuring of the buy-out was fiscally, legally and financially sound.

Given the divisional structure which meant that Devro did not have a head office and the possibility of competing national management teams (as indicated by the earlier failed buy-out attempts) very careful consideration was given to the composition and roles of the management team. The chairman and chief executive was a former senior board member of Johnson & Johnson who had been involved in providing strategic advice to the Devro management during 1990. The other senior management consisted of the joint managing directors of the European operations, the Australian managing director and the president of the US operations. While the new holding company was to be registered in Scotland with all administrative, accounting and company secretarial operations run from there, the chairman and chief executive was to be based in London.

Financial Structuring

The buy-out was financed at a time when the UK buy-out industry was under significant pressure. The UK economy was in recession, interest rates remained high and there was increasing concern as to the effects on buy-out returns of overpricing and over-leveraging in the late 1980s. Consequently, many banks which had been willing providers of senior debt in the late 1980s were no longer providing finance for new transactions. To counter these problems the Devro buy-out had to be seen to be conservatively structured in terms of its debt/equity ratio, especially since the company had major financial requirements for new product development and process upgrades. Additionally, the company would want to take advantage of other forms of finance which could be available (e.g. vendor loan notes and mezzanine) as well as the international nature of its business.

The financing structure is shown in Exhibit 18.1 and involved the use of equity, subordinated debt, a vendor loan and senior debt. Charterhouse, through Charterhouse Development Capital and the Second Charterhouse Buy-out Fund, was the arranger and underwriter of the equity which was then syndicated to other equity 'players' including Baring Capital Investors, Botts & Co., Citicorp Venture Capital, Clydesdale Bank Equity, NatWest Ventures, Dunedin Ventures and Standard Life Assurance. As in almost all UK buy-outs, the equity was split into ordinary shares, another class of ordinary shares for institutions, and preference shares. The last type of shares gave institutions a running return on their equity investment as well as redemption rights. Management had an initial share in the equity of 15%, although this could be increased through the use of a ratchet mechanism dependent on achievement of a predetermined institutional return. Other employees were to be invited to participate in a share option scheme at a later date.

Despite problems in the UK mezzanine market at the time, it was possible to provide £12.2 million of mezzanine financing arranged by Mezzanine Management and with First Britannia Mezzanine Management as the lead provider. This facility had an 8 year term with a margin over LIBOR of 350 basis points. As with most mezzanine deals, the return for the mezzanine providers' increased risk relative to senior debt came not only from the higher interest rate spread but also from some aspect of

Exhibit 18.1 *Devro buy-out financial structuring*

	£m
Equity	
●Ordinary shares (management)	0.3
●Ordinary shares (Charterhouse DC and others)	1.7
●Preference shares (Charterhouse DC and others)	28.3
Total equity	30.3
Vendor loan	
●Vendor loan (Johnson & Johnson)	2.2
Subordinated debt	
●Mezzanine (Mezzanine Management)	12.2
Senior debt	
●7 year form loans (Industrial Bank of Japan, First National	
Bank of Chicago, Royal Bank of Scotland and others)	58.0
●Australian loan guarantee	5.0
●Working capital facility	5.0
Total debt	68.0
Total financing	112.7

Source: CMBOR/BDCL/Touche Ross.

participation in the equity. In this case, the mezzanine holders were issued with warrants for 5.5% of the equity on exit.

The transaction also contained a small vendor loan. While the amount in this case was relatively low, such finance has been a significant element of large UK buy-out transactions in 1991, providing an additional financing source especially where mezzanine finance might have been seen to be too costly.

The senior debt took the form of three facilities: £5 million for working capital, a further $5 million Australian loan guarantee (for tax purposes) and a £58 million seven year term loan at 200 basis points over LIBOR and amortised over the life of the deal. While the share of debt in the total financing was higher than in the majority of 1991 buy-outs, it was judged by the lead bankers to allow adequate asset cover and strong cash and interest cover ratios. The debt arrangers were the Industrial Bank of Japan, First National Bank of Chicago and the Royal Bank of Scotland. The use of the last two reflected the geographical coverage of Devro's activities, with the Royal Bank (then) also being the parent of Charterhouse. The Industrial Bank of Japan became an active participant in both mezzanine and senior debt provision in UK buy-outs in 1990–91, helping to fill a gap caused by the retreat of some other banks following disappointing experiences.

An unusual feature of the senior debt arrangement was the decision to syndicate the deal to other banks before completion of the transaction: in most buy-outs debt and equity will first be underwritten in time for the completion of the buy-out, but syndication will not take place until after that point. In Devro's case, the difficult state of financial markets at the time necessitated this less usual approach. By completion, full syndication had taken place to six other financial institutions.

Post Buy-out Performance

Following the buy-out a series of initiatives was implemented to focus the activities of Devro in order to improve profitability. Despite the initial costs of these measures and the recessionary conditions, turnover and profits improved in 1991. This improvement was even more marked in 1992 (Exhibit 18.2) when the operating margin was a record high of 26.7%. However, as a result of the high levels of debt incurred at the time of buy-out, net profit levels were lower in both 1991 and 1992 than in 1990, the last full year before buy-out.

Exhibit 18.2   *Devro: consolidated profit and loss account*

	Year ended 31 December		
	1990 (£000)	1991 (£000)	1992 (£000)
Turnover	72,939	76,538	82,735
Cost of sales	42,280	44,741	47,340
Gross profit	30,659	31,797	35,395
Net operating expenses	14,415	14,227	13,285
Operating profit	16,244	17,570	22,110
Net interest (receivable)/payable	(6)	7,123	8,977
Profit before taxation	16,250	10,447	13,133
Tax on profit on ordinary activities	5,847	2,290	3,628
Profit for the financial year	10,403	8,157	9,505
Dividends payable	10,775	208	1,415
Retained (loss)/profit for the year	(372)	7,949	8,090

Source: Devro listing particulars.

With a high proportion of the costs of manufacture being of a fixed nature, sales improvements were able to be translated into margin improvements. Nevertheless, there was considerable emphasis on improving manufacturing efficiencies. Additionally, group structures were reorganised leading to the integration of the largely autonomous divisions comprising Devro Europe, Devro Americas and Devro Pacific. This development into a centrally coordinated business with a worldwide infrastructure gave the group a truly international focus thereby enabling it to take full advantage of worldwide trade and development opportunities. Given the maturity of many of the company's markets, particular focus was placed on new product and process development as well as the emerging markets of the Pacific Basin, Eastern Europe and South America. In particular, interest was being shown in China and the former Soviet Union where collagen-based products had achieved little penetration.

Importance had also been placed on collagen film which had been commercially launched in 1990 and is used predominantly for the wrapping of cooked meats such as ham. Sales of this product more than doubled in 1992. Plans were under way for expanding this part of the product range and further improving quality, thereby expanding both the total market and the company's market share.

Turnover and operating efficiency improvements were also accompanied by financial changes (Exhibit 18.3). Considerable emphasis was placed on generating cash flow by measures such as rigorous control of capital expenditure, debtors and stock levels. Consequently, net cash flow from operating activities reached over £25 million in 1992, the company generating cash significantly in excess of the original buy-out debt repayment schedule.

The Exit

In June 1993, Devro was floated on the stock market through an offer for sale and placing which raised £76.6 million net of expenses and gave the company a market capitalisation at the initial float price (170p per share) of £224 million.

The flotation allowed both management and institutional shareholders to sell shares thereby realising gains on their original investment, and provided a market for existing shareholders while allowing further opportunities for employees to invest in the company (two executive share option schemes and a sharesave scheme were established in May 1993). Additionally, the directors felt that, as a result of the reduced level of debt and through having access to opportunities that arise from being a quoted company, the group

Exhibit 18.3 *Devro: consolidated balance sheets*

	As at 31 December		
	1990 (£000)	1991 (£000)	1992 (£000)
Fixed assets	21,833	43,230	43,848
Current assets			
Stocks and work in progress	8,097	9,419	9,862
Debtors	15,951	10,528	12,150
Cash at bank and in hand	1,717	3,118	8,089
	25,765	23,065	30,101
Creditors: amounts falling due within one year	25,558	15,334	16,633
Net current assets	207	7,731	13,468
Total assets less current liabilities	22,040	50,961	57,316
Creditors: amounts falling due after more than one year	—	68,150	61,295
Provisions for liabilities and charges	4,908	2,592	4,791
	4,908	70,742	66,086
Net assets (liabilities)	17,132	(19,781)	(8,770)
Capital and reserves			
Called up share capital	12,781	303	304
Share premium account	—	30,060	30,072
Profit and loss account	4,351	4,891	15,658
Other reserves	—	(55,035)	(54,804)
Shareholders' funds	17,132	(19,781)	(8,770)
Net cash flow from operating activities	19,467	19,750	25,430

Source: Devro listing particulars.

would be able to commit further resources to pursuing its strategy and increasing research and development expenditure.

To encourage a float, bonuses aggregating £1.2 million were paid to most employees.

As well as allowing existing shareholders to realise gains, flotation also enables a complete capital restructuring of the company. Under this the preference share capital of £28.3 million was redeemed at par and the mezzanine and senior debt facilities repaid. Thus £51.6 million of loan repayments were made whilst a new working capital facility of approximately £20 million was advanced by the First National Bank of Chicago.

References

Chiplin, B., Wright, M. and Robbie, K. (1993) *Management Buy-outs in 1993: The Annual Review from CMBOR*. Nottingham: CMBOR.

Dixon, R. (1991) 'Venture capitalists and the appraisal of investments, *Omega*, vol. 19, no. 5, pp. 333–344.

Green, S. and Berry, D. (1991) *Cultural, Structural and Strategic Change in Management Buy-outs*. London: Macmillan.

Jensen, M.C. (1989) 'Eclipse of the public corporation', *Harvard Business Review*, Sep./Oct.

Jones, C.S. (1992) 'Accounting and organisational change: an empirical study of management buy-outs', *Accounting, Organisation and Society*.

Kaplan, S. (1991) 'The staying power of the LBO', *Journal of Financial Economics*, vol. 26, pp. 217–254.

Mueller, D.C. (1988) 'The corporate life-cycle', in S. Thompson and M. Wright (eds), *Internal Organisation, Efficiency and Profit*. Oxford: Philip Allan.

Palepu, K. (1990) 'Consequences of leveraged buy-outs', *Journal of Financial Economics*, vol. 27, no. 1.

Ruhnka, J., Feldman and Dean (1992) 'The "living dead" phenomenon in venture capital investments', *Journal of Business Venturing*, vol. 7, pp. 137–155.

Singh, H. (1990) 'Management buy-outs: distinguishing characteristics and operating changes prior to public offering', *Strategic Management Journal*, July/Aug.

Wright, M. and Coyne, J. (1985) *Management Buy-outs*. Beckenham: Croom-Helm.

Wright, M., Robbie, K. and Coyne, J. (1987) *Flotations of Management Buy-outs*. London: CMBOR/Spicer and Pegler Associates.

Wright, M., Dobson, P., Thompson, S. and Robbie, K. (1992) 'How well does privatisation achieve government objectives', *International Journal of Transport Economies*, October.

Wright, M., Thompson, S., Robbie, K. and Wong, P. (1993) 'Management buy-outs in the short and long term', paper presented at the Babson College Entrepreneurship Research Conference, March, University of Houston.

Wright, M., Robbie, K., Romanet, Y., Thompson, S., Joachimsson, R., Bruining, J. and Herst, A. (1993) 'Realizations, longevity and the life cycle of management buy-outs and buy-ins: a four country study', *Entrepreneurship Theory and Practice*, vol. 18, Winter 1993, pp. 89–109.

Wright, M., Robbie, K., Thompson, S., and Starkey, K. (1994) 'Longevity and the life cycle of management buy-outs: a contingency approach to corporate governance', *Strategic Management Journal*, vol. 15, pp. 215–27.

CASE 19

Brunton Curtis
Outdoor Advertising

A growing feature of venture capital over the past decade, which has reflected the resurgence of an entrepreneurial culture in the UK, has been the emergence of the second-time entrepreneur. It is now becoming quite common for founders of business who sell their companies to start new businesses and sometimes to buy back at a later stage the businesses they have sold. Successful entrepreneurs who sell their business may have significant personal financial resources as a result, but they may still require support from a venture capital firm. This case follows the history of two experienced managers in the outdoor poster advertising industry who form a company which is successfully sold a few years later. After remaining in a managerial capacity for a year after the sale, they then leave to form another company. While able to finance their new start-up for a short time, venture capital is required to help fund a major acquisition. Questions are raised concerning the attractiveness of second-time entrepreneurs to venture capitalists and the advantages of venture capital as a form of finance.

Introduction

An important feature of the UK economy over the past decade has been the growth of venture capital, and with it the resurgence of an entrepreneurial culture. As entrepreneurs sell the ventures they have grown, issues arise as to whether they wish to repeat the venture in a different form, whether they are particularly attractive candidates for venture capital finance should they wish to develop another venture, and if they can apply the experience learnt in the first venture in an effective way in subsequent ventures. This case study examines two entrepreneurs who set up a company, merged it with a larger, privately owned company before selling out some time later. They then

This note was written by Ken Robbie and Mike Wright as a basis for class discussion rather than to illustrate either effective or ineffective handling of an administrative situation. © Ken Robbie and Mike Wright, 1995.

formed another company which sought venture capital at a relatively early stage and then trebled the company's size through an acquisition requiring a further round of venture capital financing.

The First Venture

In 1985, Steve Curtis and Ron Brunton founded Brunton Curtis Outdoor Advertising (BCOA). Both had extensive experience in the outdoor advertising industry. Curtis had been service, operations and regional manager for Mills and Allen and latterly for Maiden Outdoor Advertising. Brunton had been in sales management with Mills and Allen since 1965. The team had complementary skills: Curtis specialising in on-site acquisitions, operations and finance and Brunton on sales. The company was initially financed by a small amount of personal equity and bank overdraft.

In 1987, BCOA merged with the privately owned Alban Communications, doubling the group's size and providing working capital facilities for further growth. Brunton and Curtis retained share holdings in the enlarged company. By 1988 the company had a turnover of £1.6 million and had an operating profit of £58,000 (Exhibit 19.1). In August 1989, Manx and Overseas Investments (a Section 535 listed company) purchased BCOA for over £2 million, adding the company to their existing interests in the sector (Dolphin Media Group) which had been formed from earlier takeover activity. The two founders of BCOA cashed out half of their shares, rolling the other half into Manx and Overseas Investments shares; both Brunton and Curtis stayed on to manage the new company which had a total of over 2,305 forty-eight-panel sheets. Sensing the effects of the recession on the over-ambitious expansion of the parent company together with their own desire to work for themselves, the two founders left in April 1990 to found Poster Power. In April 1991, Manx and Overseas, following serious cash flow problems, sold Dolphin to Mills and Allen.

Exhibit 19.1 *Trading performance of Brunton Curtis Outdoor Advertising 1986–88 (£000)*

	1986 (£000)	1987 (£000)	1988 (£000)
Turnover	118	1,008	1,600
Operating profit	(31)	38	58

The Second Venture

Brunton and Curtis formed Poster Power three months after leaving Dolphin with the aim to develop another outdoor poster advertising group, specialising in transactions which were not of interest to the large national companies. The two founders were able to take advantage of the knowledge learnt from the previous venture by being highly selective in the sites acquired while having the immediate advantage of access to sites. The initial financial structure included equity of £10,000, director loans of £30,000 apiece and an unsecured overdraft from the Royal Bank of Scotland of £160,000.

In November 1991 the Monopolies and Mergers Commission (MMC) ordered Mills and Allen to divest Dolphin as the group had a market share of 33.8% of the 48-sheet and larger sized roadside panel market. As early as July 1991, Poster Power had obtained a management contract to run Dolphin's outside advertising activities and to advise in their disposal on a six-month rolling contract basis. Brunton and Curtis started investigating the idea of bidding for the Dolphin Group but found that the £13 million sought by the vendor was an impractical amount for a relatively new company, despite their track record. Indeed the vendor, which itself was owned by the French group Avenir Havas, SA, was faced with a problem in finding a buyer as large companies in the sector could themselves run into problems with the MMC while smaller companies did not have sufficient funds to mount a bid. Lengthy negotiations were held with one particular potential purchaser for the whole group, but these discussions eventually fell through. It was believed that the potential purchaser had been prepared to offer only half of the price paid by Mills and Allen for Dolphin.

In June 1992 the Office of Fair Trading (OFT) gave Mills and Allen a deadline of fifteen months to dispose of Dolphin. Brunton and Curtis saw an opportunity emerging but thought that additional finance would be required. In the first venture they had not thought of venture capital and had found the early participation of a trade investor helpful at the time. To develop this second venture they felt that venture capital would be more appropriate and would probably involve them in ceding less equity. Problems existed in finding an appropriate venture capitalist as at this stage the amounts required appeared too small to be of interest to many venture capital firms approached. Alternatively, if Poster Power were to make an offer for the entire Dolphin group, a potential venture capitalist might be discouraged by the small size of Poster Power and the relative youth of the management team who were essentially working for themselves. After a considerable search, finance was obtained from Greater London Enterprise (GLE), which specialises in relatively small investments in the London area. Two senior members of the GLE staff also had extensive advertising industry experience. Managers were impressed by GLE in that they did appear to know relatively more about small businesses than many other venture capitalists and had some start-up/early stage experience. In November 1992, GLE subscribed for £100,000 of ordinary shares, giving them 29% of the issued share capital, and provided a £100,000 loan. At the same time the Royal Bank of Scotland overdraft facility was reduced to £50,000.

This refinancing strengthened Poster Power's balance sheet significantly and would assist with some further expansion of the company. Mills and Allen (M&A) were now coming under considerable pressure to divest Dolphin. The takeover talks with a third party having collapsed, Brunton and Curtis now made an offer (at a very low price) for the whole Dolphin operation. This bid was not unexpectedly rejected but they were given the go-ahead to buy part of the group. Even this smaller move would involve a quantum leap forward for Poster Power. The company was then making a modest profit with a turnover of slightly over £500,000 (Exhibit 19.2). The business plan which was formulated to justify the acquisition envisaged that turnover would more than treble immediately and would reach £3 million by 1996, by which time the group would have a profit before tax of over £500,000. The acquisition combined with organic growth forecast in the 1994–96 period would result in Poster Power controlling almost 1,000 panels by 1996.

Negotiations with M&A started in December 1992 for the selective purchase of some of the outdoor advertising sites, as well as with prospective financiers. The acquisition was completed on 27 May 1993 for over £900,000 with finance in place, of which £500,000 was provided by a new venture capitalist, Barclays Development Capital; GLE had only a limited capacity for providing further funds on this scale. As a result, Poster Power Advertising was able to acquire a portfolio of 450 forty-eight-sheet Dolphin Outdoor Advertising sites in the Meridian and Anglia television regions as

Exhibit 19.2   *Trading performance of Poster Power and Brunton Curtis 1991–94 (£000)*

	1991 (£000)	1992 (£000)	1993 (£000)	1994[1] (£000)
Turnover	281	567	832	2,373
Operating profit	(8)	33	51	281

1. Projected.

well as a number of high profile billboards in London. The company obtained
a market share of 18% in the Anglia region, 26% in the Meridian region and
5% in the Carlton television regions which are seen as the 'golden triangle'
by the advertising industry. The enlarged Poster Power reverted to the
Brunton Curtis Outdoor Advertising name.

References

MacMillan, I.C., Zemann, L and Subbanarasimha, P.N.S. (1985) 'Criteria distinguishing
    successful from unsuccessful ventures in the venture screening process', *Journal of
    Business Venturing*, vol. 2, pp. 123–137.
Ronstadt, (1986) 'Exit stage left', *Journal of Business Venturing*
Silver, A.D. (1985) *Venture Capital: The Complete Guide for Investors*. New York: John
    Wiley.
Starr, J and Bygrave, W. (1991) 'The assets and liabilities of prior start-up experience: an
    exploratory study of multiple venture entrepreneurs', in Churchill *et al.* (eds), *Frontiers
    of Entrepreneurship Research 1991*. Babson, Ma.
Starr, J, Bygrave, W. and Tercanli, D. (1993) 'Does experience pay? Methodological issues
    in the study of entrepreneurial experience', in S. Birley and I. MacMillan (eds),
    Entrepreneurship Research: Global Perspectives. Elsevier Science Publishers.
Wright, M. and Robbie, K. (1993) *Venture Capitalists and Second Time Entrepreneurs*.
    Nottingham: CMBOR.

BCS Computer Systems Ltd

The directors of BCS Computer Systems Ltd have identified potential for major growth through a new product, COMPS; the name is derived from the fact that it offers a complete maintenance and planning system. The further development and marketing of COMPS will require significant additional funding over the next twelve months. In the light of the information given, and the possible risks involved, the reader is asked to formulate an appropriate financing package which would enable BCS to exploit fully this profitable growth opportunity.

This case study is based upon a real company, but it is not called BCS Computer Systems Ltd and it is not located in East Anglia. Likewise, the new product which forms the main body of this case does exist, but its actual name does not resemble that given.

Background

BCS was formed in 1980 by the two joint managing directors, who still own the shares on a 50/50 basis. Each director has vast experience in this field, having been involved in the business PC market since it began in the late 1970s. They developed their selling skills at the same large office reprographic equipment company until they left to set up BCS.

Based in Ipswich, the company has since expanded considerably over the past decade:

1st year sales £340,000	Employees	7
1992/93 sales £1,960,000	Employees	21

When the company was formed, Commodore was the leading microcomputer manufacturer in the marketplace. BCS rapidly became one of the top 20 Commodore dealers (of some 350 nationwide) and the company had the honour to be appointed one of the small number of Commodore

This case was written by Grahame Boocock and Barry Howcroft and Ian Shepherdson as a basis for class discussion rather than to illustrate either effective or ineffective handling of an administrative situation © Grahame Boocock, Barry Howcroft and Ian Shepherdson 1995.

business centres. This was an early recognition of the quality of service offered by BCS and of its expertise in the business applications of microcomputers.

In 1984/5 IBM entered the personal computer market. After selling a variety of IBM 'clone' systems for approximately two years, BCS gained coveted IBM dealership status. However, fierce competition in the market for stand-alone PCs prompted the directors of BCS to develop the system sales side of the business.

This change of policy, implemented over recent years, has led to rapid growth for BCS. In essence, BCS has established a strong base in a number of business areas; it caters for the needs of a range of business customers, with the emphasis shifting to the sale, and subsequent maintenance, of larger systems to correspondingly larger customers. The capital base of the company has been steadily built up and gross margins have improved.

Apart from the COMPS project, which is described separately below, BCS currently operates the following departments:

1. Accountancy practice support – this department operates the exclusive East Anglia dealership for the most popular range of software used in accountancy practices. This division accounted for approximately £300,000 turnover in the year to March 1993, with a contribution to gross profit of around £130,000. The sales from this division can also lead to standard business systems (refer to (2) below) – the accountants often recommend BCS to their clients.

2. Core business sales – covers all non-specialist system sales. BCS markets a range of standard packages used by businesses for, *inter alia*, stock and production control, and all their word-processing needs. Sales from this division were £750,000 in 1992/3, with a contribution to gross profit of approximately £250,000. Although this margin is lower than the directors would like, some 80% of these customers take out maintenance contracts with BCS after the initial warranty period expires.

3. Maintenance and service – is the most profitable department in the company, with sales currently expanding by nearly 50% per annum. For the last financial year, turnover from this source was £230,000, resulting in a contribution to gross profit of around £195,000.

   Income accrues from the annual renewal of system sales maintenance contracts and also from contracts arising from the sale of new systems, i.e. after the expiry of the given warranty period (see core business sales above). Furthermore, this division has been successful in generating new business, even where the initial system was not sold by BCS.

4. Other – BCS maintains small sections dealing with software support, networks and programming; these make only modest contributions to the output and profitability of the company (indeed, some of them make small losses at present). BCS also employs staff for its own administrative and accountancy requirements.

The COMPS Product

The COMPS project is the brainchild of one of the directors of BCS. The directors are now convinced that this maintenance planning system presents BCS with a superb opportunity to market a high-margin product on a national basis.

All machinery requires regular checks and maintenance to ensure its correct functioning and the prevention of unplanned breakdown. In addition, statutory regulations demand that safety checks are carried out on equipment which may present a hazard to the user.

In many organizations a minimum of plant maintenance is carried out. Money expended is classed as an addition to manufacturing costs and engineers are constantly under pressure to contain these costs to a minimum. As a result, situations develop over several years whereby constant breakdowns and production downtime place the engineer in conflict with management to obtain resources to deal with a problem which is not of his making. By this stage, maintenance labour costs are spiralling.

Planned preventative maintenance is the answer to this problem. There are approximately 10 competitor products on the market, but the directors of BCS believe that: 'COMPS is a totally comprehensive, flexible software package designed specifically for the management and control of maintenance regardless of the type of business. It has been designed, written and is supported by engineers with direct field experience in maintenance, manufacturing and computer systems.'

The main target market is corporate businesses with a manufacturing bias or heavy maintenance requirements. Clients will primarily be in the manufacturing sector, although airports, transport undertakings and computer companies would qualify. By computerizing its planned maintenance and fault prevention, any company with plant to maintain on a regular basis can cut costs on production downtime. As the average cost of installation is £20,000, however, the COMPS system is unlikely to be cost-effective for smaller companies.

The first sites were supplied with the prototype product in 1990. With the cooperation of past clients, it was possible to test COMPS under working conditions (refer to Exhibit 20.1).

In the summer of 1991, it was decided that the product was ready for general release, supported by a marketing campaign which commenced in September 1991. A total of 600 enquiries were received over the next nine months. Although the majority of COMPS enquiries did originate in the

Exhibit 20.1 *Suffolk Agrochemicals*

Extract from *Plant Manager Monthly,* January 1991

Suffolk Agrochemicals installed a computer system to improve maintenance planning. That objective was achieved, together with other benefits arising from improved communications between departments which led to better understanding of maintenance needs.

The story begins 12 years ago when Peter Taylor became maintenance manager at Suffolk Agrochemicals. His particular headache was in planning maintenance work around the demands of batch production which varies to suit seasonal work.

At Suffolk's site, for example, active ingredients are processed to form liquid, powder or granular end-products. Production has to be timed to suit the demands of farmers in the UK and abroad – about 75 per cent of the production is exported. The processing includes blending, milling, grinding and pumping as well as filling, weighing and packing operations. With close to 5,750 identifiable fixed assets (as well as mobile and portable equipment), the maintenance requests increased to 150 per week.

It was inevitable that computers would be needed to plan and schedule the maintenance workload. Suppliers of computerised maintenance systems, however, seemed to think that all manufacturing was carried out on fixed equipment working in continuous cycles. Hence, Taylor relied essentially upon manual systems; by the end of 1988, the manual system had become bogged down by paperwork.

Fortunately he found a company (BCS Computer Systems) with a new product – a COMPS prototype – which could be tailored to any manufacturing situation. This was installed in June 1989. The system includes details of assets, routine specifications, preventative maintenance jobs, and fault/project work.

Taylor admits that the time taken to capture and enter data into the system should not be underestimated. After the first nine months, for example, he and his staff had entered about 35 per cent of the necessary information, i.e. 2,000 fixed assets; 145 routine specifications; 420 preventative maintenance jobs; and, 100 company addresses. Even at that stage, the system was handling between 800 and 1,000 fault/project requests and 350 preventative maintenance job requests.

The efficiency of the plant is increased by the fact that maintenance work can now be planned in advance to take place in breaks in the production schedule. Management can also quickly and easily call up reports on equipment, workload, faults and so on. Not only is the productivity of the maintenance planning operation improved – Taylor estimates two extra people would have been required on the old manual system to handle a similar workload. At the same time communications between departments have been greatly improved. For instance he believes that the production planners and plant managers have a much better understanding of the maintenance needs.

southern half of the country, it soon became evident that BCS, from being a primarily local sales outlet with clients almost exclusively in East Anglia, could quickly become a supplier on a national basis.

BCS has invested almost £175,000 in the COMPS project to date, principally research and development, and marketing costs. Sales of the COMPS system were over £500,000 in the year to March 1993, contributing over £200,000 to the gross profit for that period. There was some heavy discounting to encourage early sales, but the gross margin on COMPS is expected to improve significantly from now on.

The Future Strategy for BCS

The consensus of opinion within the computer industry is that firms such as BCS can prosper only be moving away from their dealership roots. Richard Price, an industry expert with a major firm of management consultants, recently stated that:

> There are good reasons why dealers should go into vertical markets. Research has shown that the average annual growth in computer system sales to corporate clients is about 20%, compared to an 8% growth in sales of packages to small and medium-sized businesses. One of the reasons for this may be that vertical markets are not being tackled by suppliers in the aggressive way that the corporate market has been, leaving the door open to dedicated centres.

The directors of BCS firmly believe that this policy should be adopted. The development of the COMPS product allows BCS to move forward on three fronts (i.e. product development, dealership and maintenance), hence the desired vertical integration is achieved. In future, priority will be given to the high margin elements of the business, the COMPS and the maintenance departments.

With many hundreds of computerized planned maintenance systems installed in the market as a whole, current COMPS penetration is small, but a significant number of sales have been to blue-chip companies.

The sales effort so far has been based on direct sales by a team of three BCS employees. A dealer network is shortly to be established, although the benefits of this network may not immediately become apparent. The intention is that salespeople and dealers should follow up enquiries resulting from a national marketing campaign, as well as contacting potential clients from their own customer base. In addition, a series of roadshows are planned in conjunction with a market leader in project management software. Magazine advertising will be used only in support of these roadshows – BCS has been very successful in achieving free publicity by being mentioned in prominent articles by top industrial journalists.

Once the product has been successfully sold and installed there is an opportunity for 'add-on' sales of software in related products. These are not included in the sales projections.

In the light of progress to date, it is now possible to forecast sales with a greater degree of accuracy. Sales for the coming year should approach £850,000, and the contribution to gross profit should be around £470,000 in the 1994 audited figures. As the national network of dealers starts to supplement the direct sales team, it is projected that the COMPS annual turnover will reach a minimum of £1.6 million by 1997, at a gross margin of around 60%.

For the maintenance department, projected turnover for the year ending March 1994 is £350,000, at a very healthy gross margin of 80–85%. This rate of growth is in line with past increases; turnover is forecast to rise to £850,000 by 1997. Some additional staff will obviously be required to support the increased activity in this department.

The core business sales and accountancy practice support departments are expected to grow at a more modest 10% per annum. There will be some rationalization of the remaining activities and some services will be discontinued.

The Financial Implications of the Strategy

Financial information is given in Exhibits 20.2 and 20.3.

BCS bank with the National Bank (a major UK clearing bank group) and their present bank overdraft limit is £300,000. This facility is secured by a standard bank debenture, giving a fixed charge over fixed assets and debtors and a floating charge over stock. However, the directors estimate that BCS will require additional funding of £300,000 for at least the next twelve months. This request mainly arises in respect of the investment in working capital required to meet the forecast increase in sales for COMPS.

In the past, 40% of system sales were leased, hence BCS received funds immediately from the leasing company. This percentage has fallen to around 10%, because the larger customers purchasing COMPS have insisted on generous credit terms. Apart from having money tied up in debtors, BCS will also have to invest in stock in advance of the sales drive. Furthermore, BCS's main suppliers have recently imposed tighter credit terms. As the customers' experience with the product is taken into account, there will also be further expenditure associated with refining COMPS.

Exhibit 20.2 *BCS Computer Systems Ltd audited accounts*

Balance sheet as at 31 March

	1993		1992	
	£	£	£	£
Fixed assets				
Office equipment, vehicles, fixtures and fittings		217,000		141,000
Current assets				
Stock and WIP	447,000		314,000	
Debtors	430,000		216,000	
Cash	1,000		1,000	
Current liabilities				
Trade creditors	280,000		189,000	
Bank overdraft	260,000		123,000	
Preferential creditors	45,000		27,000	
Sundry creditors	8,000		31,000	
Hire purchase (current)	74,000		33,000	
NET CURRENT ASSETS		211,000		128,000
Longer-term liabilities				
Hire purchase	38,000		18,000	
European Community loan	59,000			
Provisions				
Outstanding maintenance contracts	136,000		75,000	
NET ASSETS		195,000		176,000
Financed by:				
Share capital		2,000		2,000
Reserves		193,000		174,000
		195,000		176,000

Profit and Loss Account for the year ended 31 March 1993

	£	£
Sales	1,960,000	1,365,000
Cost of sales	1,147,000	817,000
Gross profit	813,000	548,000
Distribution/admin. costs	720,000	477,000
Depreciation	48,000	27,000
Interest payable	26,000	25,000
Pre-tax profit	19,000	19,000
Taxation	–	4,000
Retained profit	19,000	15,000

Exhibit 20.2 *continued*

Notes to the Accounts

1. 'Outstanding maintenance contracts' in the balance sheet refers to the value of unexpired sales maintenance contracts; this item has not been taken into account in calculating the gearing figure.

2. BCS has produced a cash flow forecast indicating that the additional funding of £300,000 is an accurate reflection of the company's needs. This forecast has been compiled on the basis that the required funding is in the form of debt.

3. The 1992 and 1993 audited figures incorporate contributions of £52,000 and £105,000, respectively, towards the costs of developing COMPS to date.

4. A summary of projected financial information is as follows:

	£000 (year ending March)			
	1994	1995	1996	1997
Turnover	2,300	2,900	3,500	4,350
Gross profit	1,209	1,557	1,974	2,527
Net profit	64	283	481	858
Capital and reserves	259	541	1,022	1,897

Exhibit 20.3 *BCS ratio analysis*

Audited accounts			1993	1992
Net worth (£000)			195.0	176.0
Borrowing (£000)			357.0	141.0
Gearing (%)			183.0	80.0
Gross margin (%)			41.5	40.1
Net margin (%)			1.0	1.4
Interest cover (times)			1.7	1.8
Current			1.3	1.3
Acid test			0.6	0.5
Debtors/sales (days)			80.0	58.0
Stock/cost of sales (days)			142.0	140.0
Creditors/cost of sales (days)			89.0	84.0

Forecasts (year ending)	1994	1995	1996	1997
Gross margin (%)	52.6	53.7	56.4	58.1
Net margin	2.8[1]	9.8	13.7	19.7

1. (Assuming additional £300,000 included as short-term borrowing?).

Additional investment in working capital will also be necessary to finance the 10% increase in turnover on the non-COMPS activities. The forecast increase in maintenance activity should not, of course, require significant increases in stock levels.

No major capital expenditure is projected for the foreseeable future. The company's rented premises are in an ideal location and in a good state of repair. The fixed assets will be upgraded over the next twelve months, but the outlay will only be modest. In particular, BCS's own computer systems should be adequate, although some minor extensions may be necessary.

International Business Communications

This case focuses on the 1987 repurchase tender offer by IBC for 40% of its shares. After considering other alternatives to improving the UK stock market's opinion of IBC's shares, the IBC management accepted its financial advisers' opinion to go for a share buy-back. To that date, the repurchase would be the largest in UK history and the first repurchase tender offer. The case deals with the financing of the deal, and a decision by the investment manager for Prudence Investments to sell or hold on to the 200,000 remaining shares in IBC after he had sold the maximum allowable (300,000) under the tender arrangements. The investment manager turned to analysts' reports for guidance.

On February 20, 1989, Michael Bell, CEO of International Business Communications (IBC), had many reasons to be pleased. He had just succeeded in increasing IBC's share price from 99p to 140p by a technique common in the USA, but novel in the UK: a share repurchase tender offer for 40% of IBC's shares. The move was lauded by the financial press as a 'novel way to increase the earnings',[1] 'the end of an illogical aversion towards share repurchase in Europe',[2] and as 'an alternative to the MBO'.[3]

Company Background

IBC was formed in November 1985 as a shell company, wholly owned by Michael Bell and Victor Burley, each owning 50% of the shares. On January 3, 1986, the company arranged a reverse takeover of RTD, a publicly quoted Irish engineering company. As a result, IBC started trading on the London

This case was written by Theo Vermaelen, Professor of Finance at INSEAD, with the help of Kees Cools and David Douglas as a basis for class discussion rather than to illustrate either effective or ineffective handling of an administrative situation. © INSEAD, Fontainebleau, France, 1993.

Stock Exchange on January 6, 1986 when the shares opened at 78p per share, capitalizing the group at £11.8 million. In the first annual report, Michael Bell, founder and CEO, outlined the basic strategy of the group. IBC's goal was to capitalize on the 'information society'. Given the pace of change and the speed and increasing ease of communication, he believed there was tremendous scope for providing information 'at the right time, in the most convenient way and at a competitive price'. The group would be mainly engaged in supplying business information through publications, conferences and training seminars on legal, financial and scientific issues. In order to achieve its strategic objectives the company started growing through acquisitions in the publishing business and divested unrelated businesses, acquired through RTD. From January 1986 through September 1987, IBC made 5 acquisitions of financial and business publishing companies and sold RTD's engineering interests, mostly to management for little consideration. In all, the acquisition part of the purchase price was paid by issuing shares of IBC, although in each case, shareholders also received a cash alternative.

The largest acquisition was announced on September 5, 1987 when IBC made a £98 million offer for Barham Co. Barham was best known for the investor tipsheets *Fleet Street Letter* and *Penny Share Guide*. However, unlike IBC, Barham was involved in a wide range of fields, with publishing providing only 40% of 1986 operating revenues of £4.5 million. A third came from advertising and market research and the remainder was split between property services and typesetting. At the time of the acquisition of Barham, IBC was worth approximately £50 million (200p share price and approximately 25 million shares outstanding). As a result of the acquisition, the number of IBC shares increased from 25 million to 60 million.

The Crash

The timing of the Barham acquisition was a little unfortunate. One-and-a-half months later, the stock market crashed. From October 17 to November 5, IBC's share price fell from 205p to 92p, a more pronounced decline than the FTSE index, which fell by 30% in the same time period. Analysts were particularly concerned about two facts. First, at the worst possible time, IBC had acquired a company heavily involved in investor tipsheets. It was felt that the traumatic experience of the crash would create a lot of doubt in investors' minds about the value of investment advice provided by newsletters such as *Fleet Street Letter* and *Penny Share Guide*. Second, on November 5 it was disclosed that four officers of the company had sold 1.2 million shares held by insiders (see Exhibit 21.1). On that day the stock price fell by 22p.

Exhibit 21.1 *IBC: insider ownership until 20 February 1989*

Director	31-Dec-86	31-Dec-87	31-Dec-88	20-Feb-89
M.G. Bell	2,436,452	2,346,402	2,146,402	1,502,482
N.G. Coles	1,563,113	1,013,113	863,113	489,428
J.J. Haines	1,602,356	1,602,356	1,602,356	1,121,756
S.R. Stein	2,312,609	1,002,609	602,609	0
J.W. Geevers	2,127,731	1,800,000	1,950,000	1,000,000
K.H. Komhoff	1,007,391	657,391	507,391	0
F.J.P. Madden	4,666	1,666	1,666	1,666
D.M. de Groot	24,999	34,999	34,999	34,999
P.S. Rigby	31,879	31,879	31,879	31,879
S. McAlpine	0	61,222	0	0
I.J. Forsyth	0	149,367	261,205	165,693
Total directors	11,111,196	8,701,004	8,001,620	4,347,903
Total shares outstanding	24,030,736	60,277,243	62,568,117	37,541,281
Directors as % of total	46.2%	14.4%	12.8%	11.6%

During the next 14 months, IBC failed to recover from the crash: although by December 31, 1988 IBC's stock price had increased to 99p the increase was in line with general market movements. During this period, IBC had made two major acquisitions. In April, IBC acquired *Direct Response* magazine and on November 4 it bought Pirola Editoria, Italy's oldest publishing house, for £5.9 million. In contrast to IBC's previous acquisitions, both companies were paid for by cash. IBC tried to raise cash by selling noncore businesses acquired through the Barham acquisition. IBC's unrelated activities included advertising, marketing research and design, typesetting, light engineering and property consultancy. Exhibit 21.2 lists all IBC's subsidiaries by the end of 1987. During 1988, IBC sold Smedley McAlpine, an advertising agency for £975,000 cash to its management on November 4. However, on November 18, the company announced that it could not, as planned, sell Teacher Marks, its property consultancy division 'because of adverse market conditions'.

The Share Repurchase

By mid-December 1988, Michael Bell felt increasingly unhappy about the stock market's opinion of IBC's prospects. He believed that the market had overreacted to the October 1987 crash by assuming that investors would shy

Exhibit 21.2   *IBC: company subsidiaries, December 1987*

Name	Nature of Business
Agra Europe (London) Ltd (72% owned)	Publication and distribution of agricultural intelligence bulletins
ASM (Accessories) Ltd	Manufacture of specialist medical equipment
Euroforum BV (incorporated in The Netherlands)	Business to business information
Fleet Street Publications Ltd[1]	Publication and sale of newsletters
International Business Communications Ltd	Business to business information
International Business Communications Pty Ltd (incorporated in Australia) (85% owned)	Business to business information
International Business Communications (Holdings) US, Inc. (incorporated in Massachussetts, USA)	Business to business information
International Insider Publishing Company Ltd	Publishing and electronic information
Marcus Bohn Associates Ltd[1]	Sales and management training
Pirola Editore SpA (incorporated in Italy)	Publication and sale of newsletters (acquired 2 December 1988)
Research and Auditing Services Ltd[1]	Market research
Springett Associates Ltd[1]	Design consultancy
Summerfield Lerner Ltd[1]	Advertising agency
Swinton Electro-plating (Lancs) Ltd	Electroplating
Teacher Marks Deal Ltd[1]	Commercial property consultancy
Topic Typesetting Ltd[1]	Typesetting, page make-up and artwork services
Towers Noble Ltd[1]	Graphic design

1. These subsidiaries were acquired in 1987 as a result of the offers for Barham Group plc.

away from investors' newsletters. In the June 1988 semi-annual report he tried, unsuccessfully, to change the market's opinion by pointing out that:

> although promotion has been suspended altogether for some of its financial newsletters, such as *Penny Share Guide* and *Fleet Street Letter*, subscription renewals were still running at 90 percent.

In spite of all efforts to convince the market, the stock continued to languish and was now trading at 99p. Moreover, in the two weeks after the announcement of the cancelled Teacher Marks sale, IBC stock price had fallen (relative to the market index) by 15%.

IBC management had considered a buyout of the company, but Oliver Pawle, director of UBS Phillips and Drew (P&D), IBC's advisers, had recommended against it. He estimated that a buy-out would saddle the company with as much as £110 million of debt. Moreover, a MBO would create a conflict of interest between their management and the company's shareholders. Instead P&D advised IBC to go 'for a halfway house: buy back 40% of its shares at 150p, a premium of 50.5% to the company's stock price of 99p on January 4. The offer would expire at noon on February 10.

This repurchase would be the largest stock repurchase in UK history and the first repurchase tender offer. Prior to the Companies Act 1981, share repurchases were illegal in the UK. Since then, several hundred companies had made share repurchases in the open market, but usually for very small amounts (less than 1% of the number of shares outstanding). Although share repurchases were legal, the Companies Act specified that they had to be paid out of distributable profits. Moreover, the tax treatment of share repurchases (see Appendix) was discouraging buy-backs, relative to paying out dividends.

Phillips and Drew got around the Companies Act by creating 'distributable profits' in the holding company. Although the exact procedure was not disclosed, the method essentially involved setting up two wholly owned subsidiaries and then selling existing business 'at fair market value' to these subsidiaries to create £43.8 million of distributable profits in the holding company. As IBC filed a consolidated tax statement, this construction had no tax consequences. P&D also assured IBC that because of the Barham acquisition, it would not be liable to ACT tax. For arranging the deal P&D was paid £750,000.

Financing

The £37.5 million purchase cost of 40% of the 62.6 million outstanding shares (i.e. approximately 25 million shares) was financed by a £67.5 million credit facility, provided by Morgan Guaranty. This credit line was also to be used to refinance some outstanding debt (at that time IBC owed £24 million short-term bank debt and £3.4 million of long-term debt; see Exhibit 21.3).

A sum of £29 million was borrowed in Dutch florins at the local interbank rate (6% at the time) plus 1.5%, and the remainder was borrowed in sterling at LIBOR plus 1.5%, but capped at 13.5%. As, at the time of the repurchase, Euroforum, IBC's Dutch subsidiary was expected to generate

Exhibit 21.3 *IBC: consolidated balance sheets (£000)*

Year ending 31 December	1985	1986	1987	1988
Cash	1,264	4,643	1,714	1,145
Investments	0	79	522	0
Debtors	576	2,299	11,457	17,142
Stocks	188	340	702	2,514
Prepayments	181	593	867	817
Total current assets	2,209	7,954	15,262	21,618
Tangible Fixed Assets	420	9,058	42,346	10,426
Intangible Fixed Assets	6	1,669	6,575	75,753
Total assets	£2,635	£18,681	£64,183	£107,797
Bank Debt	0	248	5,556	24,181
Total Creditors	1,022	2,355	5,626	8,158
Income received in advance	433	939	2,126	2,624
Corporation Tax payable	177	1,103	3,900	7,282
Dividend Payable	0	541	1,527	1,053
Other Creditors	583	1,605	12,403	16,319
Total current liabilities	2,215	6,814	31,138	59,617
Long Term Debt	0	142	5,133	1,863
Long Term Hire Purchase	0	49	727	1,197
Corporation Tax payable	0	142	473	106
Purchase of Subsidiaries	0	0	4,437	200
Other Creditors				105
Total long-term liabilities	0	333	10,770	3,471
Deferred Tax and other Provisions	49	178	2,007	2,453
Minority Interest	30	95	770	1,080
Called up share capital	945	2,403	6,028	6,257
Loan held for Conversion	0	0	0	0
Share Premium Account	6	5,467	6,443	6,588
Revaluation Reserve	0	1,668	4,040	23,431
Other Reserves	(673)	477	484	(3,745)
Profit and Loss account	63	1,246	2,503	8,645
Total equity (book)	341	11,261	19,498	41,176
Total equity (market)	11,800	23,350	60,012	62,060
Total liabilities and equity (book)	2,635	18,681	64,183	107,797

cash flows of £2.7 million, the Dutch-florin-denominated debt was expected to be serviced without any major currency exposure.

The loan agreement specified that IBC was supposed to pay back

£10 million in 1989 and in 1990, followed by payments of £7 million, £11 million, £12 million and finally £8.5 million in 1995. Robert Mason, vice-president at J.P. Morgan estimated that, as IBC was planning to make disposals, they would realize £15–20 million over the next few years. In addition, Morgan specified minimum interest coverage ratios of 1.3 during the first year, 1.5 during the next year and 2 thereafter.

The Announcement

The repurchase announcement was made in two stages. On January 6, 1989, IBC announced that it was 'examining a number of options to buy in shares'. The actual announcement of the specifics of the tender offer was made on January 26. Exhibit 21.4 shows IBC's stock price and the FTSE Index around the announcement.

In the prospectus, Michael Bell pointed out the reasons for the repurchase:

> 'They offer shareholders the immediate opportunity to realize a significant amount of their holding at a substantial premium to the market price. The tender price of 150p per share represents a premium of 47% over the closing middle market quotation of 102p of 5 January, 1989, the quotation two business days prior to the announcement that the Company was examining a number of options to buy-in its shares and a premium of 21% over the closing middle market quotation on 25 January, 1989, the day immediately prior to the announcement of these proposals.
>
> They allow shareholders to maintain their percentage interest in the Company and to participate fully in the future growth of the Company which the management confidently expects to achieve. The Directors believe that the Company is well positioned to take advantage of a growing market for business information in the UK and Europe. It is a market leader in both conferences and business newsletters which are both strongly cash generative businesses. Although the substitution of debt for equity will increase the gearing of the Company, it also enhances the potential for rapid earnings per share growth.
>
> The Tender Offer will help to remove any overhang of stock arising from the Barham Group plc acquisition and should lead to a greater shareholder concentration amongst firm, long-term investors.
>
> The Executive Directors will be increasing their proportionate equity participation in the Company assuming that the Tender Offer is fully subscribed. The Directors believe that management incentives and equity participation are essential ingredients in developing a successful business. The Board therefore intends to draw up proposals for a new performance related Senior Executive Share Option Scheme. When these proposals have been formulated they will be presented to shareholders for approval.

Exhibit 21.4 *IBC's stock price performance around the time of the stock repurchase announcement*

	IBC price	FTSE Index	Abnormal return[1]	Cumulative abnormal return
2 Jan. 1989	99	926.6	0.00	0.00
3 Jan. 1989	99	921.2	0.58	0.58
4 Jan. 1989	99	926.5	−0.57	0.01
5 Jan. 1989	102	930.0	2.61	2.62
6 Jan. 1989	113	935.8	9.62	12.24
9 Jan. 1989	114	945.5	−0.16	12.09
10 Jan. 1989	114	947.7	−0.23	11.86
11 Jan. 1989	114	947.4	0.03	11.89
12 Jan. 1989	114	955.6	−0.86	11.03
13 Jan. 1989	114	961.8	−0.65	10.38
16 Jan. 1989	114	966.8	−0.52	9.86
17 Jan. 1989	115	965.0	1.06	10.92
18 Jan. 1989	115	976.0	−1.13	9.79
19 Jan. 1989	119	985.5	2.46	12.24
20 Jan. 1989	121	989.0	1.31	13.55
23 Jan. 1989	122	993.1	0.40	13.95
24 Jan. 1989	122	1001.1	−0.80	13.16
25 Jan. 1989	123	1000.6	0.86	14.02
26 Jan. 1989	138	1010.7	10.51	24.52
27 Jan. 1989	140	1034.1	−0.85	23.67
30 Jan. 1989	139	1051.1	−2.35	21.33
31 Jan. 1989	140	1055.0	0.35	21.68
1 Feb. 1989	139	1050.2	−0.26	21.41
2 Feb. 1989	139	1053.0	−0.27	21.14
3 Feb. 1989	139	1067.9	−1.40	19.74
6 Feb. 1989	138	1056.9	0.31	20.05
7 Feb. 1989	137	1070.8	−2.03	18.02
8 Feb. 1989	139	1082.8	0.33	18.35
9 Feb. 1989	143	1075.9	3.48	21.83
10 Feb. 1989	143	1065.1	1.00	22.84
13 Feb. 1989	140	1053.4	−1.01	21.83
14 Feb. 1989	141	1060.9	0.00	21.83
15 Feb. 1989	141	1060.3	0.06	21.89
16 Feb. 1989	140	1055.2	−0.23	21.65
17 Feb. 1989	140	1058.9	−0.35	21.31
20 Feb. 1989	139	1069.4	−1.70	19.60

1. The abnormal return is computed as the difference between the return on IBC and the *FT* All Share Index.

In addition, the prospectus disclosed that pre-tax profit of 1988 had increased from £5.317 million to £13.333 million (Exhibit 21.5). Although this was a dramatic increase, it was not entirely unexpected as in September

Exhibit 21.5   *IBC: consolidated income statements (£000)*

Year ending 31 December	1985	1986	1987	1988
Total sales	5,937	15,226	29,031	66,551
Cost of sales	3,528	8,678	13,671	33,044
Depreciation	0	296	953	1,710
Gross profit	2,409	6,252	14,407	31,797
Admin. expenses	1,732	4,603	9,632	17,329
Operating profit	677	1,649	4,775	14,468
Exceptional items	0	0	0	0
Other income	8	85	390	298
Interest income	88	198	614	339
Interest expense	13	76	462	1,772
Pre-tax profit	760	1,856	5,317	13,333
Corporation tax	136	431	1,446	4,161
Overseas tax	9	200	458	676
Total tax	145	631	1,904	4,837
After-tax profit	615	1,225	3,413	8,496
Minority interests	121	2	74	162
Net profit on ordinary items	494	1,223	3,339	8,334
Extraordinary items	0	606	296	659
Net income	494	1,829	3,043	7,675
Dividends	0	683	1,776	1,891
Retained earnings	494	2,512	1,267	5,784
EPS (pence)[1]	5.2	7.0	11.0	13.4
Beta				1.02

1. Excluding extraordinary items and based on the average number of shares outstanding over the year.

1988, the company announced semi-annual pre-tax profits of £6.364 million, slightly less than 50% of the annual figure.

Ted Miller's Problem

On February 20, Ted Miller was wondering what to do next. As an investment manager for Prudence Investments he had tendered all his 500,000 IBC shares. As in total 59.5% of the outstanding shares were tendered, IBC had set up a rationing scheme that purchased relatively fewer shares from shareholders who tendered larger fractions of their holdings. Exhibit 21.6 shows more specifically how it worked. Hence, as Miller had tendered all his shares, he would be able to sell approximately 300,000 shares to the company at 150p per share.

He was wondering what to do with the remaining shares: to sell in the open market or to hold out for the long run. Ted Miller had considerable success with investing in US companies after they made repurchase tender offers. However, one thing here was different: in contrast to the typical managerial behaviour in the US, a large number of IBC's officers and directors were tendering or selling out. The tendering behaviour was mentioned in the offering document:

> Messrs Haines, Coles, Stein and myself intend to sell in aggregate 1,857,486 shares representing approximately 35.6% of our shareholdings. In addition Messrs Noble and Teacher, directors of subsidiaries may tender all or part of their holdings. Mr Geevers and Mr Komhoff will not tender their shares but may sell in the market up to 50% and 100% of their holdings, representing 1,482,391 shares.

Miller turned to some analysts' reports. In general, analysts were optimistic about the first segment of IBC's business: conferences, courses and seminars (see Exhibits 21.7 and 21.8 for some historical data). During the last year, the number of conferences held in Europe had increased by 14%. With the opening of European markets only three years away, the need for business people to acquire greater knowledge of opportunities and challenges facing them was increasing and it was expected that conferences would become an increasing source of information. Moreover, the training

Exhibit 21.6

Per 1,000 shares owned	
Number tendered	Number purchased
0–400	All
500	433
600	466
700	499
800	532
900	565
1,000	598

Exhibit 21.7 *Historical business segment data (£000)*

Business segment	1986 Sales	1986 Operating profits	1987 Sales	1987 Operating profits	1988 Sales	1988 Operating profits
Conferences, courses/seminars	7,638	826	13,859	2,065	14,378	7,664
Publishing	4,977	620	8,213	2,134	18,376	4,098
Advertising and marketing	–	–	3,541	266	16,639	1,329
Other	2,611	203	3,418	310	16,758	1,377
	15,226	1,649	29,031	4,775	66,151	14,468

Exhibit 21.8 *Geographical breakdown of operating profits*

Country	1986 Sales	1986 Operating profits	1987 Sales	1987 Operating profits	1988 Sales	1988 Operating profits
UK	88	71	83	78	83	80
Europe	16	29	16	21	12	15
USA and Australia	1	0	1	1	5	5
	105	100	100	100	100	100

requirements of certain professions favored IBC's continued growth. For example, the Law Society requirement of continued professional education for solicitors and the annual growth in solicitors of more than 10%, guaranteed a continuing demand for seminars and conferences. Overall, strong growth, ignoring acquisitions, of around 15% per year was expected.

The publishing side of the business created more worries. Seventy-five per cent of 1988 profits came from *Fleet Street Letter* and *Penny Share Stock Guide*, investor tipsheets that were bought mainly by small investors who were attracted to the bull market of the 1980s. This business segment was highly sensitive to share price movements. Although in 1988 IBC managed to increase tipsheet profits by cutting all advertising after the 1987 crash, it was unlikely that this experiment could be repeated. Growth (assuming no acquisitions) would not exceed 5% per year.

The third segment, advertising and marketing, were noncore businesses that were also risky: a downturn in the economy would make companies cut their advertising and marketing budgets. The spectacular growth in 1988 was merely a result of incorporating fully the turnover of Barham subsidiaries (Springerfield Lerner, Research and Auditing Services, Topic Typesetting and Towers Noble). Without further acquisitions, growth would be modest (between 5% and 10%). Moreover, these activities had a stable but relatively small pre-tax profit margin of 8%.

Finally, analysts accepted J.P. Morgan's estimate that the 'other' businesses would be sold for £20 million during the next two years to repay the debt.

Notes

1. *Financial Times*, February 2, 1989.
2. *Euromoney*, June 1989.
3. *Corporate Money*, February 13, 1989.

Appendix   The Tax Treatment of Share Repurchases and Dividends

From the *firm's* perspective, the amount used to repurchase shares, over and above the weighted average price of the shares, counts as a distribution of capital. This is the same treatment as a dividend. For example, if a company buys back 100,000 shares at £4 and the firm issued 500,000 shares at £3 (say, 5 years ago) and 500,000 shares at £1 (say, 10 years ago), the repurchase will be considered as a distribution of £200,000.

When a company pays a dividend, D, the firm must make an advance corporation tax payment (ACT) of:

$$\text{ACT} = \frac{D \times t_m}{1 - t_m}$$

where t_m is the rate of imputation, which in the UK is that basic rate of personal tax. Since 1988, t_m is equal to 25%, so that per pound of dividend, the company pays an ACT tax of $0.25/0.75 = £0.33$. Thus in the numerical example above, the repurchasing company would have to pay £66,000 ACT. The ACT paid can be reclaimed against mainstream corporation tax if the firm has enough taxable income to offset. ACT can be carried forward if there is not enough taxable income. However, the repurchase could be a problem for IBC, which had foreign-sourced profits (ACT credits are useless against foreign-sourced profits).

While at the corporate level, the tax treatment of dividends and distributions of capital (through share repurchases) is similar, the tax treatment at the *investor* level differs fundamentally. A UK investor who receives a *dividend*, D, pays personal income taxes on the grossed up dividend $D/(1-t_m)$ and gets a tax credit of $D \times t_m/(1-t_m)$, so that, after personal taxes, a dividend of D is worth:

$$\frac{D \times (1 - t_p)}{(1 - t_m)}$$

where t_p is the investor's marginal income tax rate. Hence, for an investor with a marginal tax rate equal to the basic rate, no further taxes on dividends are due. For such an investor, the double taxation of corporate profits has been entirely eliminated. As, since 1988, t_m is 25% and the highest marginal tax rate is 40% the maximum tax on dividends is currently 20%. Investors with marginal tax rates below t_m are eligible for tax refunds. Specifically, a tax-exempt investor (such as a pension fund) can reclaim the entire ACT $(= Dt_m/(1-t_m))$. Hence, in contrast to the USA, tax-exempt investors have a high preference for dividends.

In contrast to the investor who receives a dividend, the investor whose shares are *repurchased* does not receive a tax credit, but is liable for capital gains taxes. Capital gains is assessed on the price at which they are purchased minus the original cost of the shares.

In short, unlike the USA, in the UK it will generally be tax inefficient to buy back stock as an alternative to paying a dividend. An investor cannot use ACT tax credits to offset capital gains tax liabilities, and capital gains are taxed at the same rate as dividends. In addition, share repurchases for large fractions of the firm's outstanding equity may create significant costs for UK companies that do not have profits against which ACT credits can be offset.

GPA Group plc

GPA grew from virtually nothing in 1975 to become one of the world's largest aircraft leasing companies. It buys and sells planes, leases them from investors and on to airlines. By 1992, GPA was turning over $2 billion a year and had 320 employees. It had $20 billion of aircraft on order, accounting for nearly 10% of the world's aircraft production. The company was based in Ireland and was privately owned. It decided to go public and was valued at around $3 billion. At the last minute the flotation was aborted.

The case describes how the company grew and the strategies it followed from start-up to the flotation. Among the issues raised by the case are the functions of specialised financial intermediaries and the role of leasing. The rapid growth and huge increase in the value of the company also raises questions about the ways in which financial intermediaries can create and capture value, and in particular the degree to which GPA's success was due to providing a much needed service or to taking very large positions in the aircraft market.

A tired and dishevelled Tony Ryan trudged out of Nomura's palatial City offices at 5.30 on Thursday morning. For the previous 48 hours, with hardly a pause, he and his team of executives and advisers had fought to save the flotation of GPA, the $3 billion Irish aircraft leasing company he had founded with £5,000 17 years ago . . . what was to have been the crowning moment of his career had turned to ashes.

(*Sunday Times*, 21 June 1992)

Later that morning, the company issued the following statement:

In the light of the indications of worldwide demand for the company's ordinary share capital, the Board of GPA Group plc, having consulted its advisers, has decided that it would not be in the interests of the company and its shareholders to proceed with the initial public offering at the present time.

This case was written by Thomas Ryan under the supervision of Anthony Neuberger as a basis for class discussion rather than to illustrate either effective or ineffective handling of an administrative situation. © *Thomas Ryan, 1995.*

Background

GPA's business is aircraft finance. It buys planes, leases them to airlines, sells planes to investors and leases them back. Tony Ryan founded GPA in 1975 to provide aircraft leasing services. It is based at Shannon, on the west coast of Ireland, Ryan remains the key player in GPA. Said one Dublin banker, 'If Tony was killed in an aircrash, the quality of leadership would not be there.'

Born in 1936, Ryan claims a family history in the transport business – his father was a train driver, while his grandfather was a railway station master. In 1958, he joined Aer Lingus (the national Irish airline) as a dispatcher. As Ryan explained:

> One evening in 1974 when I lived in Asia, I stopped to watch a food vendor whom I passed each day. He was a banana chip maker. His business was to slice, cook and sell bananas to passers-by. He was extraordinarily skilful, not only in slicing hundreds of bananas into thousands of perfect pieces, but also at selling his product. He impressed me and made me think. I felt it a pity that such marketing, technical talent and energy was devoted to a process which sold for a mere penny. There and then I determined that when I went into business on my own account I would apply my energies to developing and marketing a big-ticket product which could sell for vastly more.

The next year he raised £45,000 from Aer Lingus and Guinness Peat to add to his own £5,000 and entered the aircraft leasing market. In the early years, GPA acted as a broker. Ryan and his executives criss-crossed the globe seeking customers for other people's surplus aircraft.

In 1979, the company started purchasing aircraft for its own account. It believed there was a ready market for leasing used aircraft. In 1980, it got the necessary boost to its equity base when Air Canada took a stake that valued the group at US$25 million. In 1986, Air Canada and Japanese investors subscribed for a further equity issue which valued the firm at US$150 million. This enabled GPA to serve the deregulated and rapidly expanding North American market. This was also the year in which GPA placed its first order for a new aircraft direct from the manufacturer.

Guinness Peat, the founder shareholder which gave its name to the group, sold out its shares for $240 million in 1988, in a deal which valued the whole of GPA at $1.56 billion.

By 1992, GPA was turning over $2 billion a year and making $250 million a year in profits, mainly from leasing and trading planes. It had $20 billion of new aircraft on order, accounting for 8–10% of worldwide commercial aircraft production. GPA was still a private company. Its balance sheet was becoming stretched. Some of its major shareholders (particularly

Aer Lingus and Air Canada) were, for their own financial reasons, keen to reduce their stake in the business. This was the background to the attempt to float the group which was aborted in June 1992.

Group consolidated statements of cash flow, balance sheets and profit and loss information for recent years are shown in Exhibits 22.1 to 22.3.

Management

Ryan has a reputation for being hard on his 317 employees, regarding the exceptional as normal and the normal as substandard. The average marketing executive spends 170 nights a year away from Shannon, and clocks up some 140,000 air miles.

While the number of employees may seem remarkably small in relation to the group's earnings, it is actually well staffed compared with its competitors. Substantial resources are devoted to forecasting supply and demand for different types of aircraft. The main operations room bears a remarkable similarity to a war room. Within seconds, full information on every commercial aircraft in the world can be called up for display on one of the three movie screens. Maps can show the location of individual or types of aircraft and the position of GPA marketing agents.

To create the necessary credibility and obtain top-class management and political advice, GPA assembled a board whose members' previous positions included Irish prime minister, British chancellor of the exchequer, chairman of ICI, vice-chairman of Chrysler Corporation, president of Mitsubishi Corporation and commissioner of the European Community.

The Civil Aircraft Industry

Since 1970 air travel, measured in revenue passenger miles (RPMs – the number of fare-paying passengers carried multiplied by the distance flown in miles) has grown at 7–8% per annum, substantially faster than the rate of worldwide GDP growth. From mid-1990 the industry experienced a decline which it attributed to the worldwide economic slowdown and the Gulf War. This resulted in the sight of some 10% of the world aircraft fleet parked in the Mojave deserts of California, as airlines took delivery of previously ordered aircraft and retired older planes.

There are three significant commercial aircraft manufactures: Boeing and McDonnell Douglas of the USA and the European Airbus consortium, which together account for over 90% of all new civil aircraft orders.

Exhibit 22.1   *GPA Group plc: consolidated cash flow statements ($m)*

| | Year ended March 31 | | |
	1990	1991	1992
Cash flows from operating activities:			
Profit before preference dividends	242	262	268
Adjustments to reconcile net profit to net cash provided by operating activities:			
Provision for aircraft maintenance	71	80	134
Depreciation and amortisation	115	126	179
Gain on sale of aircraft, property, plant and equip.	(129)	(189)	(174)
Share of retained earnings of associated companies (net of of dividends received)	21	(32)	(19)
Changes in operating assets and liabilities (net of acquisitions):			
Accounts receivable and other assets	(206)	(176)	(8)
Accounts payable and other liabilities	156	131	69
Other	(17)	(20)	(47)
Accrued aircraft maintenance liability	(32)	(57)	(62)
Net proceeds of aircraft sales	1,305	1,217	1,185
Net cash provided by operating activities	1,526	1,342	1,525
Cash flows from investing activities:			
Purchase of aircraft	(1,466)	(1,250)	(2,135)
Investments in and advances to associated companies	(133)	(139)	(124)
Deposits and predelivery payments	(502)	(675)	(322)
Other	(10)	(47)	23
Net cash used by investing activities	(2,111)	(2,111)	(2,558)
Cash flows from financing activities:			
Redemption of preference shares			(77)
Proceeds from sale of share capital	206		101
Dividends paid	(114)	(71)	(97)
Increase in indebtedness	3,378	4,907	4,342
Indebtedness repaid	(2,862)	(3,831)	(3,124)
Net cash provided by financing activities	608	1,005	1,145
Net increase in cash	23	236	112
Cash at beginning of year	16	39	275
Cash at end of year	39	275	387

Exhibit 22.2   *GPA Group plc: consolidated balance sheets ($m)*

Consolidated Balance Sheets (US$m)		At March 31	
	1990	1991	1992
Assets:			
Cash	39	275	387
Accounts receivable	237	406	389
Net investment in finance leases	14	75	76
Investments (principally in associates)	260	440	430
Aicraft	1,870	2,656	4,241
Deposits and aircraft predelivery			
payments	553	623	816
Other assets	89	114	160
Total	3,062	4,589	6,499
Liabilities, share capital and reserves:			
Accounts payable	76	102	104
Accrued expenses and other liabilities	355	600	804
Indebtedness	1,637	2,713	4,162
Provision for liabilities and charges	101	127	199
Total liabilities	2,169	3,542	5,269
Share capital outstanding:			
Ordinary shares	4	94	95
A Ordinary shares		9	9
Preference shares	10	1	101
Total nominal value	14	104	205
Share premium	546	455	382
Retained earnings	333	487	642
Other reserves		1	1
Share capital and reserves	893	1,047	1,230
Total liabilities, share capital and			
reserves	3,062	4,589	6,499

Manufacturing is a labour-intensive process. The key to economic manufacturing is to operate plant at close to capacity. Over the medium term (18 months to 2 years) capacity can be increased or cut back, but over the short term it is inflexible. While there has traditionally been some element of aircraft customisation, largely in respect of seating capacity, the product is very standardised.

New aircraft demand is highly variable. This cyclicality is aggravated by the 1–3 year lag between order and delivery. As a consequence, airlines deliberately over-order when demand is high in the knowledge that they can

Exhibit 22.3 *GPA Group plc: profit and loss information ($m)*

Profit and Loss Information	Amounts in accordance with Irish GAAP Year ended March 31				
	1988	1989	1990	1991	1992
Revenues:					
Aircraft leasing	197	368	470	582	837
Sales of aircraft and related assets	422	661	1,480	1,285	1,127
Fees, commissions and other income	31	13	12	22	46
	650	1,042	1,962	1,889	2,010
Gross profit:					
Aircraft leasing	41	52	80	93	89
Sales of aircraft and related assets	43	90	125	184	175
Fees and commissions	30	13	12	22	31
Other	9	6	5	9	11
	123	161	222	308	306
Selling, general and administrative expenses	19	18	17	63	44
Operating income	104	143	205	245	262
Share in results of associated companies	3	15	42	36	17
Profit on ordinary activities before taxation	107	158	247	281	279
Profit after taxation and minority interests	101	152	242	262	268
Preference dividends	21	26	36	20	19
Profit available to holders of Ordinary shares	80	126	206	242	249
Earnings per Ordinary share:					
Basic	0.64	0.81	1.19	1.23	1.19
Fully diluted	0.54	0.70	1.05	1.10	1.15
Dividends per Ordinary share	0.17	0.22	0.30	0.30	0.30

resell any planes they do not need at a profit. Conversely, when signs of over-capacity appear, orders can drop away rapidly.

In 1989, for example, manufacturers' order books were full for 4–5 years ahead. Aircraft deliveries in 1991 were at record levels – some 800 aircraft for a total of $44 billion (see Exhibit 22.4). But orders were already falling sharply, coming down from a peak of $71 billion in 1990 to $32 billion in 1991.

Looking ahead, deliveries are expected to fall to some 530 aircraft in 1997, but demand is then expected to rise again as demand builds up, and as aging aircraft are replaced by modern, quieter planes. Longer-term, analysts (including those at GPA) are predicting a growth rate of over 5% for the worldwide commercial aircraft fleet.

The entry of Airbus to challenge the US duopoly increased the extent of price competition and discounts of 5–10% from list price are not unusual for larger orders. Indeed, GPA's purchasing power has reputedly enabled it

Exhibit 22.4 *Commercial aircraft deliveries (excluding former Soviet Union)*

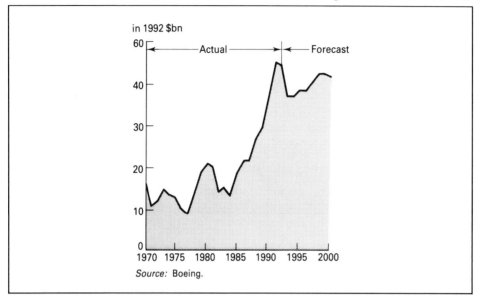

in 1992 $bn

Source: Boeing.

to get discounts as large as 15–20%. Selling terms are normally one-third in advance with the remainder on delivery. The nature of the buying decision has changed from one dependent on the close relationship between the manufacturer and the airline's engineering department to one emphasising aircraft lifetime costs.

The used aircraft market has grown to rival the new market in terms of the number of planes traded each year. It is characterised by the presence of intermediaries such as aircraft brokers. The manufacturers have not traditionally played a significant role in this market, but have recently started to accept 'trade-ins' to win sales. The market operates efficiently.

Aircraft Technology

There have been two radical technological innovations in the last thirty years: the introduction of jet engines in the late 1950s and of wide-bodied planes in the early 1970s.

In the aftermath of the second oil crisis of 1973, many observers expected that higher fuel prices, noise restrictions and newer engine technology would make such aircraft as the B727, B737 and DC9 obsolete. Prior to 1973, fuel costs amounted to 12% of total aircraft operating costs, but by 1979 fuel costs represented 25% of total operating costs. However, the subsequent decline in real oil prices changed the trade-off between purchase cost and life-time operating costs, and saved the older aircraft.

The expected life of a typical aircraft, aided by additional maintenance, has extended from 15 years in 1970 to 30 years in 1986. As a result, by the end of 1986, only 857 out of the 9,202 jets manufactured had been retired.

The Airlines

Following widespread losses in the airline industry in the years of the Great Depression, the US airlines were regulated by the Civil Aeronautics Board (CAB) from 1938. Its policies included severe restriction on industry/route entry and exit and setting fares to allow even the most inefficient airlines to continue in operation.

Price-based competition was in effect prevented by the CAB, so airlines were forced to compete on the basis of service. Airlines tried to distinguish themselves with faster and more comfortable planes. Equally, cost savings due to new technology were not passed to consumers.

As a result of deregulation, route networks became more variable in both length and traffic density. It also inspired the introduction of hub-and-spoke systems which increased demand for smaller, shorter-range aircraft. The increased congestion and related landing slot constraints ultimately produced a demand for larger aircraft.

The major carriers buy new aircraft to meet both expansion and replacement needs. They sell old aircraft (say, aged 15 years) to international airlines outside the USA and Europe and to charter airlines. During the 1970s they did not consider buying used aircraft because of the absence of a secondary market for relatively new planes and because of the incentives inherent in the US regulatory environment. But by the mid-1980s, even such carriers as American and United had made substantial used aircraft purchases.

Most airlines owned their own planes outright, though up until 1985 some 20% were leased on financial leases. Financial leases are long-term leases which extend for virtually the entire economic life of the plane. The lessee is responsible for operating and maintaining the plane. At the end the lessee normally has the right to purchase the plane for a nominal sum. From an economic point of view there is little difference between taking a financial lease, and buying a plane outright while financing the purchase with a long-term loan secured on the plane itself. However, it is the lessor who can claim the capital allowances on the plane, and the entire lease payment (and not just the interest component) is tax deductible by the lessee and taxable for the lessor. From 1978, the accounting treatment has reflected the economic reality, and under US accounting rules, firms have been obliged to account for financial leases as if they owned the underlying assets.

Since 1985, there has been rapid growth in the proportion of planes which were on operating leases. These are short-term, typically 5–7 year leases where the plane reverts to the lessor at the end of the lease. Operating leases are attractive to airlines for a number of reasons. The major aircraft manufacturers work to long lead times. The operating lease allows a carrier to expand its fleet although it may have failed to order adequate aircraft in advance. Many airlines are in a financially weak position because they are relatively new or because the have suffered in a deregulated market. Deregulation has made earnings very volatile, with US airlines collectively showing operating profits of $3 billion in 1988 followed by losses averaging $3 billion a year over the next three years.

In Europe, liberalisation has proceeded at a somewhat slower pace. But as competition has intensified, profitability has declined and so too has the readiness of governments to provide financial support for national flag carriers. In the fastest growing area of the world for aviation – the Asia/Pacific region – there has been little move towards deregulation.

By the end of the 1980s some 16% of the world's fleet was subject to operating leases, and GPA expected this proportion to grow to 23% by the mid-1990s.

Aircraft Prices

Aircraft prices have held up remarkably well over the years. The price of a Boeing 737-200A, a typical third-generation jet which was introduced in the early 1970s and still forms the backbone of the world's fleet, appreciated in value by some 10% per annum over the period 1975–86, against an inflation rate of 6.7%. More recent indicative second-hand prices for a variety of planes are given in Exhibit 22.5. Since 1990, prices have dropped back sharply, falling by some 20% or more.

GPA's Philosophy

Maurice Foley, GPA's president, explains the company's thinking about the business by saying that, 'an aircraft is not just a commodity but an opportunity to add value, especially through flexibility'. He sees aircraft as

Exhibit 22.5 *Second-hand airplane prices*

Generation	Introduced	Type	Size	Estimated prices ($m)	
				Jan. 1987	Oct. 1990
Second	1964–	B-737-100	Small	5.0	2.4
Third	1972–	B-737-200A	Mid	7.5	5.8
Fourth	1979–	B-737-300	Mid	22.0	22.0
(quiet jets)		MD-82	Mid	17.5	18.5
		B-747-200B	Jumbo	25.0	44.0
		A-310-200	Large	30.0	39.0
Fifth	1986–	F-100	Small	19.0	24.0
(state-of-art)		B-767-200	Large	30.0	39.0

an investment product and notes that practically all investment products are distributed by intermediaries because investors do not have the expertise or the knowledge.

Foley argues that GPA attracts new funds to the aircraft industry. 'The reason that GPA is becoming more important and profitable is that it is serving real needs and doing things that are needed in the market. No successful business can be built on a myth; it has got to be built on a market.'

GPA is much concerned with the returns that it offers its shareholders. The returns on an operating lease are not particularly exciting. But by having gearing of 66%, a 10% return on assets can be turned into a more acceptable 30% return on equity. By setting up substantial loan facilities with a consortium of banks, secured on its assets generally rather than on specific planes, GPA can raise money at good rates without restricting its freedom of action.

As one analyst explained: 'The airlines can use GPA with its strong position in the capital markets to attract funds at much better rates than they could get themselves on their own overstretched balance sheets. The banks like lending to GPA rather than to the airlines directly because they can diversify their risks. Much better to lend to GPA than to lend to some third world airline and face all the country and credit risk that that implies.'

The Leases

Most of the fleet is leased to carriers under operating leases whereby GPA retains title to the aircraft and bears substantially all of the risks and rewards associated with ownership, including the residual value of the aircraft.

Lease terms are largely standardised within the firm. Most leases are dry leases where the lessee is responsible for all operating expenses. The lease terms require certain levels of maintenance and specify the required condition of the aircraft at the expiry of the lease.

The leases have either a fixed rate or a rate dependent on market interest rates. The margin on leases depends on a number of factors including the age of the aircraft, the perceived credit risk of the lessee, demand for a particular aircraft type, competitive conditions and the terms of the lease. In recent years, the group's lease margins have declined for a number of reasons. Firstly, the company has an increasing proportion of newer aircraft which command lower lease margins than older aircraft, because lease rates have not kept pace with the growth in new aircraft cost. Secondly, the proportion of leased-in aircraft (which command lower margins since the group does not bear the residual risk) has increased as the group has expanded its aircraft selling programme. Finally, the slowdown in the civil aviation market has depressed margins throughout the industry. At 31 March 1992 the majority of leases had terms in excess of five years, and the average remaining lease period was 5.6 years.

The Lessees

GPA actively manages the credit risk by a number of mechanisms. Exposure to specific countries and customers is controlled by formal concentration limits. GPA normally requires security for the lessee's obligations. Rentals are typically payable monthly in advance, and include a three month deposit. The lease terms provide for various remedies, including repossession, in the case of default. The regular monitoring includes reviews of the operations and performance of the lessor, and daily checks on all receivables. While the firm has experienced no problems to date in reclaiming physical control of repossessed aircraft, GPA carries political risk insurance against losses arising from inability to effect repossession.

GPA also carries out a substantial part (around one-fifth) of its leasing through a network of joint venture companies which it has formed with different manufacturers. Each of the companies deals exclusively with one manufacturer, and in the group's view, they give it a unique marketing advantage over other leasing companies.

The geographical composition of group leasing profits is as shown in Exhibit 22.6.

Exhibit 22.6   *GPA Group plc: geographical composition of group leasing profits*

| | Year ended 31 March | | | |
| | 1988 | | 1992 | |
	$m	%	$m	%
Group[1]				
North America	9.8	21	11.1	10
Central and South America[2]	12.1	26	33.0	30
Europe	15.4	33	28.6	26
Asia/Pacific[3]	4.5	9	28.2	26
Rest of the world	5.3	11	8.5	8
Total	47.1	100	109.4	100
Joint venture companies	5.8		20.4	
GPA	41.3		89.0	

1. This table shows 100% of leasing gross profit for GPA and the joint venture companies. The leasing gross profit of the joint venture companies is shown to enable this to be reconciled to GPA's aircraft leasing gross profit.
2. Principal countries in which the group is active in the Central and South America region include Brazil, Chile and Mexico.
3. Principal countries in which the group is active in the Asia/Pacific region include Indonesia, Malaysia, the People's Republic of China, the Philippines, the Republic of Korea and Singapore.

The Fleet

The company concentrates on aircraft with wide customer acceptance and flexible operating characteristics. In recent years this has meant a focus on fourth generation aircraft which meet the latest noise regulation requirements and also offer fuel efficiency benefits. The composition of the fleet on 31 March 1992 is shown in Exhibit 22.7.

The group's owned fleet of 315 aircraft was valued by BK Associates, Inc. of New York, for prospectus purposes, at 6.5 billion at 31 March 1992. Of these, the joint venture companies owned in total 82 aircraft with a value of $1.9 billion. This current fair market value was defined as 'the price most likely to be agreed upon in an arm's length transaction between an informed and willing buyer and an informed and willing seller without undue pressure on either buyer or seller to buy or sell'. The valuation employed two valuation bases:

1. On prices obtained in recent sales of aircraft types comparable to the aircraft being valued.

Exhibit 22.7 *Composition of GPA's fleet*

Manufacturer	Aircraft type	Generation	Owned	Leased-in	Total
Boeing	B-737-3/4/500	Fifth	56	52	108
	B-737-200	Third	35	2	37
	B-757-200	Fourth	2		2
	B-767-200ER	Fifth	1		1
	B-767-300ER	Fifth	5	2	7
	Other Boeing		3	2	5
McDonnell Douglas	MD-82/3/7	Fourth	37	13	50
	MD-11	Fifth	1	2	3
	DC10	Third	2	3	5
	DC8	First	30		30
	DC9	Second	21	5	26
Airbus	A300	Third	5		5
	A320	Fifth	16	12	28
Fokker	F100	Fifth	26		26
Other jets			10		10
Turboprop/other			65	1	66
Total			315	94	409

2. Where insufficient data were available under (1), by comparing the direct operating costs of the aircraft being valued with those of a new replacement aircraft of known cost.

Competition in the Operating Lease Business

The prospectus noted that the over-supply of available aircraft facing the civil aviation industry emphasised the already highly competitive nature of the market for aircraft leasing and sales. These difficulties resulted in 'an increased proportion of non-revenue earning aircraft in the Group fleet, a significant erosion in the Group's lease margins and certain of the Group's lessees experiencing financial difficulties'.

The competitors include:

1. Aircraft lessors such as Ansett Worldwide Aviation Services and International Lease Finance Corporation (acquired by American Insurance Group in 1990) which have broad-based fleets.
2. Specialists who operate in specific markets or specific aircraft types.
3. Airlines, aircraft manufacturers, banks, airline brokers and other financial institutions who may have access to larger financial resources than the group.

GPA's share of the operating lease market is about 20%, but it is heavily concentrated in the new plane sector where it has over 40% of the market. Among global lessors, GPA has a 48% share of new plane deliveries and options.

Aircraft Sales

As part of its strategy, the firm sells aircraft from its portfolio. It will often sell the planes to a consortium of investors, and then lease back the planes from them, leasing them on to an airline. This allows the group to realise the value of any manufacturer's discount on the purchase of the aircraft, to release the invested equity, to repay any associated debt and to realise the value inherent in the lease receivables.

The group thus takes the credit risk of the ultimate lessee. The investor consortium normally retains the asset risk inherent in the residual value of the aircraft, but in certain circumstances the group may be obliged to repurchase aircraft previously sold. At 31 March 1992 such commitments amounted to $303 million over the period 1993–2002. At that date, the directors estimated that the market value of aircraft covered by such undertakings exceeded the underwritten value.

Purchase Commitments and Options

The group had entered into significant future purchase commitments with aircraft manufacturers for new aircraft over the period to the year 2000. It also acquired a number of options to purchase new aircraft in the future. The prospectus noted:

> Because of the long lead time required in the manufacture of aircraft, GPA believes it has benefited from placing significant purchase orders and, as a major customer of aircraft manufacturers, believes it has obtained favourable pricing terms and flexibility in the timing of deliveries.

The agreements typically require the group to make a deposit for contracted aircraft delivery; this is refundable only in the event of certain actual or anticipated delivery delays. Option considerations are non-refundable. The group's cost in respect of those commitments and options is shown at Exhibit 22.8.

Ryan claims to be relaxed about the commitments, explaining, 'I sleep like a baby. I wake up every 10 minutes screaming.' More seriously, GPA

Exhibit 22.8 *GPA Group plc: orders and options*

Group Orders and Options
At 31 March, 1992

	Nine months ending 31 Dec. 1992	Year ending 31 Dec. 1993	1994	1995	1996	1997	1998	1999	2000	Total 1992–2000
Number of aircraft										
Firm orders										
GPA	51	61	43	23	19	16	11	13	4	241
Joint venture companies			4	7	5	4	3	3	2	28
Group	66	80	62	30	26	16	11	13	4	308
Options										
GPA			31	62	43	27	13	13	3	192
Joint venture companies			4	7	5	4	3	3	2	28
Group	0	0	35	69	48	31	16	16	5	220
Cost ($m)[1]										
Firm orders	2,152	2,619	2,325	1,171	1,079	831	567	807	349	11,900
Options			1,001	2,467	2,012	1,391	942	905	336	9,054
Total	2,152	2,619	3,326	3,638	3,091	2,222	1,509	1,712	685	20,954

1. The costs (in $ USm) are stated at prices applicable in January 1992 (these prices have escalated by approximately 1% since that date) and do not take into account adjustments arising from contractual price escalations after this date. Such adjustments are based, among other things, on changes in labour, materials and fuel indices in the USA and elsewhere. The costs assume that all options will be exercised.

reckons that it could readily ride a recession since it could afford to cut rentals considerably yet remain ahead on a cash basis while showing an accounting loss. And, they note, the portfolio of planes is still there to be traded if necessary.

Given the state of the industry, during financial 1992, the group exercised 14 options, rescheduled 28 options and did not exercise 16 others. By agreement with manufacturers, it had orders for 11 aircraft and rescheduled delivery of 5 aircraft.

Financial Exposures

The group conducts its business almost entirely in US dollars. It manages its interest rate exposure on a portfolio basis using duration-weighted hedging techniques, recognising the interest rate sensitivity of the group's assets and liabilities and the period to repricing.

GPA borrows substantial amounts at predetermined margins over US LIBOR. It uses hedging techniques to limit the impact of changes in market interest rates.

Accounting Policies

The financial statements are prepared under Irish generally accepted accounting principle (GAAP), which are substantially similar to those operating in the UK.

Gross profit is reported net of all direct costs allocated to each activity. Interest expense (or lease in costs in respect of leased aircraft), depreciation and certain taxes are allocated in their entirety to aircraft leasing.

Depreciation is calculated on a straight-line basis, using an estimated useful life of 25 years from the date of manufacture and a residual value of 15% for aircraft and engines. In contrast, Singapore Airlines provides 80% of cost over 10 years, Cathay Pacific depreciates its aircraft over 5–15 years, and British Airways over 12–20 years.

GPA takes all the profit on sale and leaseback transactions at the time the transaction is completed.

Financing

The Group's aircraft purchase commitments exceed the sources of committed funding available to it. If it were unable to obtain access to the necessary funds, GPA would be obliged to default on purchase commitments and incur the related penalties. GPA's committed facilities at March 1992 were as shown in Exhibit 22.9.

The revolving secured committed credit facility was provided by a syndicate of 73 banks. The maximum amount committed of $2.4 billion reduces on a quarterly basis from December 1990 until September 1996, at which point the commitment will expire. Upon each reduction, GPA is obliged to repay any excess over the reduced committed amount. The facility, like most of GPA's debt, is floating rate.

The majority of financing for the joint venture companies is transaction-specific and is secured on their assets. The status as at March 1992 is shown in Exhibit 22.10

Exhibit 22.9 *GPA's committed facilities at March 1992 ($m)*

	Committed	Drawn down
Short-term borrowings (including the current portion of long-term borrowings)	742	451
Long-term borrowings		
Secured revolving committed credit facility	2,075	1,155
Other secured indebtedness and finance lease obligations	1,052	561
Other loans	1,995	1,995
Total long-term borrowings	5,122	3,711
Total indebtedness	5,864	4,162

Exhibit 22.10 *Financing for the joint venture companies as at March 1992 ($m)*

Company	Committed	Drawn down
GPA Airbus Limited	408	126
GPA Fokker Limited[1,2]	325	207
Irish Aerospace–MD Limited	321	318
GPA Jetprop Limited[1,2]	92	34
GPA Rolls Limited[1]	68	65
Total	1,214	750

1. The accounts of these companies have been consolidated in GPA's financial statements.
2. The borrowings of these companies are guaranteed by GPA.

ALPS

At the time of the offering, GPA was in advanced negotiations for the creation of the first aircraft-backed publicly traded security, under the name 'Aircraft Lease Portfolio Securitisation 92-1 Limited (ALPS). It was proposed that ALPS would buy 14 aircraft with a market value of $500 million from GPA from the proceeds of public senior debt issues and private placements of subordinated debt. The debt securities would neither be obligations of, nor guaranteed by, GPA, although it would contribute between $50 million and $70 million, primarily by way of subordinated debt. GPA would continue to manage the aircraft and would also assist with the remarketing of the aircraft when they were required to be sold.

Shortly before the closing date for the offering, GPA successfully made the first issue of securitised aircraft leases, as outlined above.

Shareholders

The main shareholders in GPA at the time of flotation are listed at Exhibit 22.11. The plan was to raise $850 million by selling 85 million new shares at $10 each. This would have valued the equity of the group after the flotation at $2.86 billion.

Exhibit 22.11 *Shareholders*

Shareholders	Ordinary shares owned beneficially prior to the offer (millions)	
Mitsubishi Trust and Banking Corp.	25.6	11.3%
Air Canada	21.7	9.6%
Aer Lingus	19.9	8.8%
Prudential Insurance Company of America	15.4	6.8%
Long-Term Credit Bank of Japan	13.8	6.1%
Irish Life Assurance	5.4	2.4%
Kawasaki Enterprises	4.2	1.9%
Bank of Nova Scotia	3.5	1.5%
Mitsubishi Corporation	2.9	1.3%
Nippon Total Finance	2.8	1.2%
Deutsche Bank	2.4	1.1%
Dr Tony Ryan	18.3	8.1%
Other employees	14.5	6.9%
Others	79.2	34.9%
Total	226.8	100.0%

One of the objectives of the flotation was to provide an exit mechanism to existing shareholders. Some of these, such as the Irish airline Aer Lingus, were experiencing cash shortages as a result of the decline in airline profitability. The asset represented by their GPA holding was a non-core asset which could be usefully liquidated to support their core business.

The advisers pointed out that the threat of a large sale by existing shareholders either at the flotation or afterwards would depress the share price, and thus prejudice the flotation. The company agreed with its existing shareholders that they would not sell more than 20% of their holdings. This would mean that $600 million of the new money raised would go to the company and $250 million to existing shareholders.

When it became clear that the flotation would not succeed, the issue was pulled. Opinions on the reasons for the failure were varied. Some people argued that the sale itself was mishandled; the issue was overpriced. The substantial blocks of shares left in the hands of unwilling shareholders meant that any upside movement was likely to be limited. With little prospect of the shares moving to a large premium in the short-term, investors were quite happy to hold back to see how the shares performed knowing that they would be likely to be able to pick up shares in the market. Others pointed to the fact that, by this time, the market had become disenchanted with the aviation sector which had substantial excess capacity, with the financial sector and with companies dominated by a single personality.

EuroDisney

The EuroDisney case attempts to examine the ill-fated attempt by the US-based Walt Disney Corporation to transfer their successful theme park concept to mainland Europe. The case begins by analysing the Disney investment decision in terms of the theories relating to the growth of multinational corporations, using as a framework the geobusiness model developed by Robock and Simmonds.

The case then goes on to examine the pricing of the public share issue that financed the project. This examination – conducted within the framework of traditional share valuation theories – involves a critical look at the offer for sale prospectus that accompanied the share issue along with the assumptions and forecasts implicit within. The case ends by looking at some of the reason that the Paris-based park has failed to live up to the high expectations that accompanied the share float.

The purpose of this case study is threefold. Firstly, we attempt to analyse the decision of Disney to expand its theme park and resort concept into Europe – and in particular France – in terms of the traditional theories relating to the growth of multinational corporations. Secondly, we critically examine the process by which Disney arrived at the price at which to offer the shares in the company operating the park; during this examination we discuss the applicability of traditional share valuation theories used in Disney's approach. Thirdly, we attempt to examine some of the reasons behind the apparent failure of the EuroDisney park to live up to expectations.

Introduction

Once upon a time a man named Walt Disney drew a simple black and white picture of a mouse named Mickey. Even given his vivid imagination, Walt,

This case was written by Amir Zafar and Matthew Davies as a basis for class discussion rather than to illustrate either effective or ineffective handling of an administrative situation.
© *Matthew Davis and Amir Zafar, 1995.*

at the time, must have found it difficult to conceive what this simple drawing would one day lead to. Sixty-five years on from his debut, Mickey Mouse has spawned a multibillion dollar worldwide business and the name Disney has become one of the most recognisable and marketable brands in history.

The early success of Disney was attributable to its ability to produce innumerable cartoon characters that not only had an instant and durable appeal to children of all ages, but whose appeal stretched beyond social, national and cultural boundaries. Apart from Mickey Mouse, characters ranging from the bumbling Goofy to the mischievous Donald Duck are instantly recognisable to millions of people throughout the world, despite the fact that they have long since passed into middle age.

The original characters were initially restricted to appearing in 5–10 minute reels. However, by the late 1930s, Disney had begun to expand into the more ambitious and lucrative feature film market – so began the golden era of Disney films with classics such as *Snow White*, *Dumbo*, *Peter Pan*, *Pinnochio* and *Jungle Book* gaining worldwide acclaim for their excellence. These films proved not only to be worldwide box office hits but also provided, along with the original Disney characters, a platform for the expansion of character-related merchandising – including the sale of music, clothes, toys and comics.

The move into the theme park market did not come until the mid-1950s. Walt Disney dreamt of creating a park that not only provided a showcase for his characters but which also provided visitors with a complete entertainment experience – a park where visitors could spend the whole day divorced (as far as possible) from the real world.

The first park, Disneyland, was opened in 1955 at Annaheim near Los Angeles. The park proved an immediate success and by 1971 a second park – The Magic Kingdom (based on similar design concepts to Disneyland) – was opened in Orlando to exploit the market on the east coast of the USA. Disney further developed the theme park concept in the USA through the opening in Orlando of the EPCOT Center in 1982 and the Disney–MGM Studios theme park in 1989 – the Orlando park then constituting Walt Disney World.

Painstakingly designed, the parks feature numerous attractions spread across a number of 'themed' areas, ranging from Fantasy World – an area where childhood fantasies are brought to life – to Frontier Land – where attractions are designed to give visitors a feel for the Wild West faced by America's early settlers. And, of course, around every corner there is a familiar Disney character ever eager to please the visitor.

Up until 1989, the year of the EuroDisney share offer, Disneyland and Walt Disney World had between them attracted approximately 600 million visits. Such a volume of visits boosted ancillary service industries – primarily the hotel and motel industries. Disney attempted to exploit this through their 'resort concept' which attempted to make the parks themselves the focal points of a holiday destination. The areas around the parks were developed to provide accommodation – ranging from 5-star hotel complexes to campsites – and other facilities such as golf courses, shopping malls, water sports amenities, and night-time entertainment complexes were established. The development of the resort concept was vital to the growth of Disney since the combination of the resorts and the parks had a synergistic effect, with each feeding off the another.

Through a constant process of changing and updating attractions, and the continual marketing of the Disney brand itself, the theme parks and resorts prospered. Despite the influences of the 'Star Wars' culture on children, Disney theme parks have retained their place in the hearts and imaginations of millions of children and adults alike as a dream holiday destination.

Reasons for Expansion Abroad

Having firmly established the success of the theme park and resort concept in the USA, Walt Disney's next step was to take the concept abroad. This step was marked by the opening of Tokyo Disneyland in 1983.

What are the factors that influence a firm's decision to expand activities abroad? There have been numerous classical theories advanced to explain the growth of multinationals. We examine the case of Walt Disney through the use of the 'geobusiness model' developed by Robock and Simmonds (1989). The model is useful since it provides a framework within which the sometimes diverse classical theories can be applied.

The geobusiness model identifies three variables as being vital in determining whether a company stretches its business activities beyond its own national boundaries, these being:

1. Conditioning variables.
2. Motivating variables.
3. Control variables.

Conditioning Variables

In essence, conditioning variables determine whether an opportunity exists for a company to expand its global horizons. Most classical theories would identify market imperfections as being one of the primary factors resulting in opportunity arising. Stephen Hymes (1976) identified these market imperfections as existing globally in both the product and factors of production markets resulting in certain firms acquiring a competitive advantage over others. He argued that firms would invest abroad if there was opportunity to exploit this advantage. Hymes identified product differentiation as being one of the key sources of this competitive advantage. This argument had originally been developed in more detail by Richard Caves (1971).

Product differentiation arises when goods and services provided by competing enterprises are 'distinguishable . . . by minor physical variations, brand name and subjective distinctions created by advertising' (Caves 1971). Such product differentiation in essence creates barriers to entry by other firms and hence enables companies that possess these benefits to exploit them and thereby make supernormal oligopolistic profits. Indeed, Hymes described a successful differentiated product as a 'unique asset'.

The theme park and resort concept developed by Disney is in many ways a unique asset to Disney. Indeed the Disney theme park can be described as the ultimate in differentiated products since no other theme park can be a Disney theme park. The uniqueness of Disney parks has been the cumulative result of over 50 years of 'brand marketing' – brand marketing that was in place the first moment a Disney character appeared on the movie screens.

Disney theme parks maintain a unique position in the consciousness of millions of people, young and old alike. Every new Disney film release, every minute of Disney TV on our screens and every product endorsed with a Disney image is carefully tailored to reinforce the favourable images people have of Disney. This image is inextricably linked to the theme parks.

Certainly, therefore, it can be argued that Disney does have a unique, differentiated product in the theme park market. Given the existence of this unique asset, Caves identifies two conditions that need to be fulfilled in order for a firm to exploit this asset abroad. Firstly, the marginal costs incurred in establishing this asset (the asset in question being product differentiation) must be low relative to the returns earnable. Secondly, the exploitation of the asset must necessitate foreign production or foreign supply.

Caves' second condition is satisfied by virtue of the fact that the product in question – the theme park – can only fully service overseas target markets provided they are located in the target market.

But what about the first condition? The marketing of Disney has not been confined to the USA. Film releases are international, Disney TV now broadcasts worldwide and product endorsements take place on a worldwide basis. The internationalisation of the brand was established long before

Disney made the decision to take its parks abroad. Thus the transfer of the Disney park concept out of the USA to other countries did not in theory require heavy advertising and marketing costs to maintain the uniqueness of the asset – this had already been established.

Motivation Variables

The second set of variables identified in the Robuck and Simmonds model are classified as motivation variables. Given that the opportunity exists for foreign expansion, what are the motivational factors that actually result in the foreign investment decision being made?

Classical theory would identify Walt Disney's primary motivation as being that of market seekers. These theories suggest that where a firm is endowed with very firm-specific strengths, then over time – as these strengths develop – the domestic economy may become too constraining. Growth potential is not realised and the firm-specific strengths may begin to erode through a combination of 'competitor catch-up' and lack of use. Classical theory, therefore suggests that firms in this situation would try to capitalise on these strengths by expanding into untapped markets abroad.

Walt Disney have over the years developed very firm-specific strengths – in particular, strengths relating to the theme park industry. These strengths are particularly evident in two areas. Firstly, there are the strengths that have been built up in the area of marketing and brand establishment, and secondly there are those skills that Disney has developed in the conceptual design of the parks themselves. While the name Disney was clearly influential in attracting visitors to the US parks in the first instance, quite clearly if these parks were not well designed and failed to meet expectations, visitors would not continue to be attracted. The design of the parks themselves is a continual process. Disney recognises that in order to maintain market leadership the parks need continually to be redesigned and updated with new attractions.

Having achieved market dominance in the USA, and having gauged the level of interest abroad by taking account of the number of foreign visitors visiting the US parks, the expansion of the theme park concept abroad may have been influenced to some extent by the above motivational factors.

Having established the need to seek out another market, the actual target needs to be selected. Two primary factors in the selection decision are:

1. The potential economic strength of the target market – in order to determine the potential long-term viability of the project. This process would involve the predator company undertaking a process

of economic scanning, concentrating on key economic indicators such as per capita income, interest rates, inflation rates and consumer spending patterns.

2. The possibility of obtaining favourable financing arrangements from investing in one country as opposed to another. This was a factor of particular importance in Walt Disney's decision to expand the park concept into Japan, as we discuss later.

Control Variables

The third set of variables identified by Robuck and Simmonds in the foreign investment decision process are known as control variables. In essence, these variables cover government-induced policies that may act as an incentive or disincentive to investment abroad as opposed to investing in the domestic economy. Incentives could range from the provision of loans at favourable rates to favourable tax breaks. Disincentives could include restrictions on the expropriation of profits. Indeed, we shall come to see that the decision to invest in France was influenced to a certain extent by inducements offered by the French government.

The above analysis has enabled us – via the Robuck and Simmonds geobusiness model – to examine Walt Disney's decision to expand the theme park concept abroad in terms of relevant classical theories on the growth of multinationals.

Method of Expansion

The decision to expand abroad is only part of the investment decision. The second broad area that a firm needs to address is the method of expansion. There are basically three ways a firm can expand its activities abroad:

1. The firm can export the unique asset it has under its control – servicing the overseas demand from the home base.
2. The firm can license the exploitation of the asset to a foreign firm in return for licensing fees and royalties.
3. The firm can invest directly in the foreign target market.

Given the nature of the theme park, option 1 was not available to Disney on the basis that the park must be situated in the target market. However, both options 2 and 3 have been used by Disney – the former in Japan and the latter in France.

Tokyo Disneyland

The first expansion of the Disney theme park concept took place in Japan. Given the existence of the Disney brand asset the decision to expand into Japan can be attributed to three main reasons:

1. The very rapid rise in the material wealth of the Japanese since the end of the Second World War has been accompanied by an equally rapid move away from traditional Japanese culture towards Western – and most particularly US – influences. This process of westernisation, accelerated by the existence in Japan of a very heavily US-influenced media, is particularly evident among the younger generations who appear to have used their new-found wealth to rebel against traditional Japanese values. The impact of the strong US influences is evident, for example, in the massive success enjoyed by US rock bands and by the popularity of North American sports such as baseball. This heavy cultural presence made the Japanese particularly susceptible to the images portrayed by Disney – if Americans enjoyed a day at Disney then the Japanese wanted it too.

2. Along with the positive cultural aspects, Disney identified that Japan offered large, concentrated target population centres. The population of Japan at the beginning of the 1980s was approximately 110 milliom, almost five times that of California, despite being smaller geographically. The 50 km radius around the Tokyo Disneyland was identified as having a population of about 30 million, this being approximately three times that of Los Angeles. Given the wealth of the Japanese there was certainly a market there to be tapped.

3. The third, not insignificant factor behind the reason for the expansion into Japan can be classified as financial. The early 1980s had been a period of heavy capital spending by the Disney Corporation, with 1983 marking the opening of the EPCOT Center in Orlando and the launch of Disney TV. This expansion had necessitated heavy borrowing in the USA. The Tokyo Disneyland project offered a way of expanding the resort concept abroad without the need for Disney to increase its debt burden significantly. Disney's partners, Oriental Land, could provide the site – having a value of approximately $650 million – as well as the financing for the project itself. Disney in turn were responsible for providing the Disney name along with the conceptual design work for the park in

return for royalties of approximately 10% of ticket sales and 5% of merchandising and food sales.

Factors 1 and 2 in terms of the Robock and Simmonds model were the market-seeking motivational variables Disney needed to expand into Japan. Factor 3 can also be classified as a motivational variable, but this time a resource-seeking variable, the resource in question being the availability of cheap borrowing.

Although not connected directly to the theme park project, itself Disney managed to secure a Japanese syndicated bank loan of approximately 15 billion at, according to Disney, considerably lower rates of interest than were available in the Western financial markets. The loan was used to ease the debt burden in the USA and was also used as a hedge against the foreign exchange risk of the royalty income since the royalties from Tokyo Disney-land were to be used to repay the loan.

Walt Disney therefore had no direct interest in Tokyo Disneyland – and as such had limited their risk from the possible failure of the venture. However, Tokyo Disneyland proved to be anything but a failure. Consequently, Disney did not benefit from the success of the venture as much as they would otherwise have done. This 'lost' income must have weighed heavily on the minds of Disney executives when determining the nature of the interest to be held in EuroDisneyland.

Expansion into Europe

The next logical step in the expansion of the Disney theme park and resort complex appeared to lie in Europe, and Disney began seriously investigating the idea in 1983. With the Disney brand name already well entrenched in the minds of European children and adults alike, a demand for the park concept seemed to be evident in the large number of European visitors to the Disney parks in the USA. Disney executives hoped that this popularity represented the tip of a much larger market on mainland Europe itself. Having established that a market potentially existed, the question of the timing of the expansion arose.

Along with the rest of the industrial world, the early 1980s represented a period of recession and slow growth for Europe. Faced with the second oil price shock of the decade in 1978–79 governments in Europe almost unanimously attempted to tackle the potential threat of stagflation with a series of restrictive fiscal and monetary policies. This general policy – followed partly as a consequence of the effects of the expansionary policies pursued in the aftermath of the first oil price shock in 1973–74 and partly as a general change in the political climate in favour of the right – whilst being generally successful in the fight against inflation aggravated the deflationary impact of the oil price rise and resulted in recession.

By the end of 1982 the worst aspects of the recession seemed to be over. As inflation was brought under control governments found they could loosen monetary policy, and interest rates were allowed to fall. The combination of falling inflation and interest rates had the effect of increasing both consumer and business confidence.

The increase in consumer confidence which was primarily a result of the fall in the cost of borrowing was reflected in an increase in the demand for consumer durables and new housing – the latter giving a much needed boost to the construction industry. Despite the positive impact of the increase in consumer expenditure, the main driving force behind Europe's move out of recession came from the investment impetus provided by the business sector. This increase in the level of business investment was the result of four main factors:

1. An increase in the level of business optimism that had arisen as a result of low inflation and the consequent wage moderation that had followed – the latter due to a lowering of inflationary expectations as well as to the impact of unemployment.
2. Lower costs of borrowing along with the stagnation of capital spending in the first years of recession encouraged an acceleration in the replacement of old and obsolete equipment.
3. An upturn in the inventory replacement cycle consequent upon the increase in consumer expenditure.
4. An increase in the rate of returns being earned by companies as a result of productivity gains and a failure to pass on all the effects of the fall in oil prices in the form of price reductions.

Given the levels of consumer and business confidence in the period 1983 onwards, forecasts for the growth of the European economies into the 1990s and beyond were generally optimistic – this optimism was heightened by the potential impact of the following events:

1. The boost in both consumption and investment demand expected as a consequence of the removal of intra-European barriers to trade by 1992. Some analysts suggested that the effect of '1992' on European output could be as high as 5%.
2. The move away from centrally administered planning in the former Eastern Bloc countries. It was anticipated that the unharnessing of

the entrepreneurial spirits as a result of the move into the free market would boost intra-European trade and growth.

3. It was hoped that the general move towards greater harmonisation of European economic policy – as illustrated by '1992' and cooperation in the Exchange Rate Mechanism – by enabling more even growth patterns across Europe would boost growth via synergistic intra-European trade.

Given the development of the European economy in the period 1983 onwards it is of no surprise to find that Disney executives found the time ripe for expansion into Europe. The next choice involved the selection of the country into which expansion should take place. In essence, this would involve assessing the merits and demerits of each of the main potential hosts: France, Germany, the UK, Italy and Spain.

Choice of France

Following the framework established in the Robock and Simmonds model, the process of selecting the country in which to base the EuroDisney park would have involved the following:

1. The narrowing down of the broad motivational variables for direct investment in Europe established as a consequence of the economic scanning of the general European economic climate.
2. The consideration of any control variables, in essence, government-induced incentives or disincentives influencing the choice of location.

Motivational Variables in respect of France

Having established the existence of a potential market in Europe – both now and, more particularly, in the future, given the prospects for growth – there was a need for Disney executives to examine motivational variables on a specific country-by-country basis. On the assumption that the primary motive of Disney to expand into Europe was on the basis of market-seekers, we could identify the following factors as being most relevant to Disney in the process by which potential hosts were eliminated from the reckoning:

1. Geographical location.
2. Perceived tourist culture.

3. Economic background and the potential of the chosen host to support the venture.

Geographical Location

One of the key considerations of Disney executives in establishing a theme park in Europe was to make the appeal of the park as pan-European as possible and thereby establish as broad a potential market as possible. The decision to name the park EuroDisney as opposed to linking the name to an individual country or region was consistent with this pan-European approach.

Vital to the potential economic success of EuroDisney, therefore (as recognised in the share prospectus), was going to be the ability of the park to attract visitors not only from the chosen host nation but also from surrounding countries. Therefore the base for EuroDisney was required to have as wide a population catchment area as possible.

On the basis of this criterion, countries such as Spain and Italy, despite being two of the five largest economies in western Europe, appeared to be ruled out. Being geographically on the periphery of western Europe these countries did not appear to have the scope for being a catchment for the other main western European economies.

The UK, although close to the main large population centres of western Europe suffered from the disadvantage of not being on the mainland continent – although this may have proved to be only a short-term problem given the progress being made on the Channel Tunnel.

On the other hand, Germany and France appeared to have more scope for achieving the greatest catchment population for a potential EuroDisney market. In particular, France seemed to be the ideal base, with common borders with the other three major Continental economies as well as the Benelux countries in addition to being in close proximity to the UK.

Perceived Tourist Culture

Much of the success of the original US-based Disney parks has been as a result of Disney's ability to establish the theme parks as holiday destinations. For this concept to work in Europe, the region in which the park was eventually situated had to be regarded as a desirable holiday destination by Europeans – in essence, a place where people would be happy to spend their annual vacation.

Despite efforts by the German Tourist Board, Germany still does not carry the same kudos as a holiday destination as France. Part of the reason for this is the industrial background of Germany – which creates negative images in the minds of tourists – and the fact that the climate in Germany is generally less favourable than in many areas of France.

France, on the other hand, is far more attractive in the mind of the average tourist – whether these attractions lie in the romantic and historical images of Paris or in the warmer climes of the South of France. Indeed, the attractions of France are so large and varied that they appeal as much to the French as anyone else. This is illustrated by the fact that in the mid-1980s the spending of French tourists abroad – in terms of total household consumption – was only about half that of other EC counterparts.

Therefore, from the point of view of Disney executives it may have appeared to be easier to get people to visit a Disney park in France, in essence letting EuroDisney ride on the back of France's popularity as a tourist destination, than to try to encourage people to visit somewhere like Germany.

Economic Background

Given the need to appeal to the population of the Continent as a whole, the need to establish the potential for economic growth in Europe – and most particularly western Europe – was essential. Nevertheless, the need to ascertain growth prospects on a country-by-country basis was also important since it would be natural to assume that the greatest supporters of the potential park would come from the host country.

Economic scanning on a country-by-country basis could focus on a number of different economic performance criteria and indicators. Some of the primary indicators as to whether a market is able to sustain a new product include the absolute size of the economy as measured by, for example, the GDP (on a total as well as per capita basis), interest rates, inflation and unemployment rates as well as indicators of potential future growth provided in forecasts by organisations such as the OECD and the IMF.

In terms of absolute size and per capita income, western Europe is dominated by five large economies. In order of size these are Germany, France, Italy, the UK and Spain. However, given the fact that other motivational variables such as geographical location and tourist desirability had been used to narrow down the potential sites to France, it would only really have been necessary to ensure that the growth and potential for growth in the French economy was consistent with the patterns emerging in the rest of Europe.

All of the main western European countries had participated in the growth of the European economy in the period 1983 onwards. There was, however, a variation in the speed at which the different economies moved out of recession into growth. In general, those countries that tackled the problem of inflation most vigorously and successfully in the period 1978–81 emerged out of recession first – most notably this was the case for Germany and the UK. Countries such as France, Italy and Spain, however, were, generally speaking, slower to move onto the recovery path, although once on this path, growth was equally strong and sustained.

For France in particular, the period from the mid-1980s onwards saw a rapid increase in growth. The growth of the French economy in the period was boosted by levels of disinflation greater than in other EC countries. This disinflation resulted in particular from the effects the high unemployment levels (resulting from the pursuit of tight financial policies) and the commitment to shadow the Deutschmark in the ERM had in moderating the level of labour price increases. Disinflation and wage moderation boosted business confidence and French competitiveness and, through increasing rates of return achievable, resulted in an increase in the level of productive investment. Given this investment-driven growth in France, the potential for the growth in the French economy into the 1990s appeared, along with the rest of Europe's, to be strong.

Given the geographical advantages of France and its perceived desirability as a tourist destination, the economic situation and prospects for growth in the 1990s only further enhanced France's credibility as a suitable host for the park.

Control Variables in respect of France

As indicated in the Robock and Simmonds model, motivational factors in respect of a foreign investment decision can be strengthened or mitigated by the effect of control variables – in essence, the impact of potential host government investment incentives or disincentives.

Even given the importance of the motivational variables in favour of France, described above, the impact of the incentives offered by the French government to Disney cannot be underestimated in the final decision to locate the park just outside Paris.

Motivated by the potential massive boost an influx of visitors to a Disney park could provide the local economy – through job creation and the related income multiplier effects – the French government (and in particular President Mitterand) made no secret of its desire to have the park situated in France.

The French proceeded to offer Disney a number of powerful incentives – incentives that were far greater than anything that other potential host governments were prepared to offer. These incentives were formalised in the Master Agreement signed by the French government and Disney in March 1987. The main inducements offered were as follows:

1. The 5,000 acre site on the periphery of Paris was offered to Disney at 1971 prices – resulting in a saving to Disney of approximately FFr 10,000 per acre.
2. The government offered to undertake a considerable programme of infrastructure development related directly to the park itself at no cost to Disney. This infrastructure work included: (a) the building of extensive road and rail links, including the promise of a fast train connection between EuroDisney and the Channel Tunnel, and (b) the provision of extensive underground works, most particularly in respect of sewerage systems.
3. Advantageous tax rules with regard to the write-off of the considerable costs of construction.
4. The offer of almost FFr 4.8 billion of loans at interest rates almost 2% below market rates.

Given the powerful combination of the motivational factors in favour of France and the incentives provided by the positive control variables given by the French government, the choice of France as the host for EuroDisney appeared to be justified.

Development and Method of Financing

Primarily as a consequence of the desire to maximise the potential catchment area of the proposed park, the site chosen for EuroDisney was Marne-la-Vallée, an area approximately 30 kilometres east of Paris with approximately 132 million Europeans living within one day's journey of the park.

The development of the site itself was to consist of two initial phases:

1. Phase 1A – scheduled for completion in 1992 – comprising the construction of the Magic Kingdom (based on the design concepts of the original Disney parks in the USA) and the associated resort facilities.
2. Phase 1B – scheduled for completion in 1996 – comprising a theme park based on the Disney–MGM Studios at Walt Disney World in Orlando.

The initial construction costs of phase 1A which basically consisted of establishing the level of facilities needed to make the park operational were estimated in the share prospectus at approximately FFr 14.9 billion. With FFr 4.5 billion of the total cost syndicated through a number of leading continental banks, the remainder of the financing was shaped by:

1. The requirements of the Master Agreement signed with the French government in 1988.
2. The desirability of finding some way of making early use of tax losses certain to be incurred in the first years of the company's operations.

As discussed earlier, one of the factors motivating the decision of Disney to select France as the host country was the level of inducements offered by the government. One of the key inducements was the offer to Disney of FFr 4.8 billion of loans through the French public sector savings bank at rates of interest almost 2% below the market levels of interest. One of the conditions of the Master Agreement, however, was that 51% of the owner companies formed be offered to the public – given the nature of EC regulations this involved by necessity a pan–European share issue.

However, in determining the nature of the vehicle for this share issue, regard had to be paid to the optimal group structure, that is the group structure that would minimise the costs of borrowing as far as possible. In order to try and achieve this, Disney enlisted the help of Banque Indosuez – which had made a name for itself arranging the financing for Europe's other major capital project, the Channel Tunnel. With the help of Banque Indosuez, Disney was able to establish a corporate structure that not only enabled EuroDisney to obtain funds cost efficiently but which also enabled Disney to maintain control.

The company actually operating the park was set up as EuroDisneyland Société en Commandite par Actions (SCA) – this was the vehicle for the 51% public share issue in 1989. SCAs are characterised by having a tiered shareholder structure:

● Associate Commandites, or the general partners of the SCA, who take on unlimited liability in return for the right to appoint the managing director.
● *Commanditaires* who relinquish their right to appoint or dismiss the managing director in return for limited liability.

Disney managed to take on the role of general partner, and thereby assume complete control over the appointment and dismissal of management, through a wholly-owned subsidiary EuroDisneyland, SA.

In order to obtain financing benefits, however, it was necessary to set up a third company. The company – EuroDisneyland Société en Nom Collectif (SNC) – was used as the vehicle to enable Disney to take early advantage of the large operating losses and tax allowances that would arise in the first few years of the project. The SNC, with characteristics similar to that of a partnership, would carry the costs of construction and lease the assets to the operating company. As a consequence, the costs of depreciation and interest (during construction) – now resulting within the SNC as opposed to the SCA – could be set off against the income earned within the SNC.

Due to the advantage furnished on the French partners – approximately 83% of the equity of the SNC was provided by French institutional investors – they agreed to advance loans of approximately FFr 2 billion to the operating company at effective rates of interest of only approximately 7% as opposed to market rates approximating to 10%. It was envisaged that at the end of the lease period of 20 years the assets would be purchased by the operating company at the depreciated book value and the financing company dissolved. As a consequence of the arrangement EuroDisney was able indirectly to take advantage of the large tax allowances in the first years of construction much earlier than would have been the case had it only had the option of setting these allowances against its own operating profits. The result of this was to improve the dividend profile for potential investors.

Share Valuation

EuroDisney came to the market in October 1989 as a greenfield venture. EuroDisney was a new business, with no track record and no earnings history. This posed a significant practical problem for EuroDisney management and its financial advisors: how do you value a company that has no history?

EuroDisney responded to this practical problem with a theoretically well established approach: the dividend valuation model. The dividend valuation model states that: the current share price is totally determined by the anticipated future dividends, discounted at the investor's expected rate of return. The average expected rate of return on a share, in turn, represents the company's cost of equity. An investment is attractive to the investor who expects it to provide a rate of return that exceeds the rate required by that investor given the associated risk.

Valuing a share based on the present value of the expected future dividend stream is a concept which is familiar to all current and past students of financial management. However, the difficulties in applying the assumptions of this theoretical model to practical situations are equally well known. What will future dividends be? Will dividends be constant or will they grow? If they grow, what will be the growth rate? What is the impact of tax? What is the impact of inflation? What is the appropriate cost of equity to use as a discount rate?

The assumptions that EuroDisney made in order to derive the opening share offer price were summarised in a financial model ('the model'). The model consisted of a detailed forecast of earnings and dividends to the year 2017, and an assumed price/earnings ratio of 12.5 thereafter.

The analysis of how EuroDisney applied the dividend valuation model leads to two strands of discussion. Firstly, how realistic were the assumptions in the model regarding future earnings and dividends? Secondly, how valid was the implied cost of equity?

The Model

The model consisted of projected profit and loss accounts for the year commencing 1 April 2016, and cash flow projections for the same period. It was also assumed that at the end of this period EuroDisney would be capitalised at 12.5 times profit available for distribution for the year ending 31 March 2017. The major assumptions contained within the model were reviewed by an independent consultancy firm, Arthur D. Little, Inc. (ADL). A sensitivity table was also included in the prospectus to show the effect of variations in certain of the key assumptions (see Exhibit 23.1).

Exhibit 23.1 *EuroDisney: net income and sensitivity table*

	1990	1991	1992	1993
Actual net income for the year ended 30 September (FFr million)	381	249	(188)	(5,300)

	Worst	Expected	Best
Attendance	10 million	11 million	12 million
Per capita spending	−10%	*	+10%
A 6-month delay in the opening of the Magic Kingdom	*	*	*
Construction costs of phase 1A higher by 10%	*	*	*
Resort and property development income	−10%	*	+10%
Inflation	3%	5%	7%
Real interest rates	+1%	*	−1%
Residual value (P/E ratio in 2017)	10.5	12.5	14.5
* Specific sensitivities not stated in prospectus.			

It would be very easy at this point to apply the considerable benefit of hindsight and criticise the assumptions in the model to the extent that they proved inaccurate. To criticise a forecast merely because it did not match reality would demonstrate not only a lack of awareness of the uncertain and dynamic nature of the business environment but also a lack of appreciation of the purpose of forecasts. However, in this case it is interesting to review the methodology adopted by EuroDisney and consider the reasonableness of the underlying assumptions.

The Principal Assumptions

1. Attendance.
2. Per capita spending.
3. Operating Expenses.
4. Cost of construction.
5. Resort and property development income.

1. Attendance
At first sight, attendance predictions appeared conservative. EuroDisney estimated the first year attendance to be 11 million visitors. This figure was consistent with the average first year attendances achieved at the Magic Kingdom theme parks in Florida and Japan.

Several studies, both internal and external, were commissioned by EuroDisney in order to predict the expected attendance levels. The latest of these studies prior to the share issue was carried out by ADL in 1989. The purpose of this study was to 'verify and confirm the methods and assumptions used in previous studies, and to make its own estimates of attendance potential'.

ADL believed there were a number of factors that contributed to the high attendance levels at Disney-designed theme parks. These factors included the following:

1. The design and scope of a Magic Kingdom theme park are such that a complete visit requires more than one day.
2. The quality and capacity available at Disney hotels allow the demand for longer stays to be satisfied.
3. The level of recognition of the Disney name and the quality of the experience make Disney theme parks popular holiday destination resorts.

ADL was of the opinion that these factors distinguished Disney-designed theme parks from existing theme parks and amusement parks in Europe, which are smaller and basically designed for single-day visits. Therefore, in determining potential penetration rates and the number of annual visits per guest in order to derive projected attendance levels at EuroDisney, ADL relied largely on the experience at Disney-designed theme parks.

ADL concluded that because of the larger number of people living within a convenient travelling distance of EuroDisney, the assumed attendance figures in the model could be achieved with market penetration rates at or below those experienced at other Disney-designed theme parks.

The assumed first year attendance of 11 million was below the range of potential initial attendance estimated to be between 11.7 million and 17 million in the ADL study. Attendance at the Magic Kingdom was then assumed to grow over the period covered by the financial model at an average compound rate of 2% per annum. This growth rate compares with average growth of 3.8% for the other Magic Kingdom parks in California, Florida and Japan, and incorporates the effect of new attractions and the opening of a new theme park, scheduled for 1996.

Initial attendance at the second theme park was expected to be 8 million, with growth estimated to be 2% per annum for the first 10 years, then 1% per annum for the next 10 years to 2016. This prediction was based largely on the experience at Walt Disney World, where the opening of a second theme park, the EPCOT Center, added 11 million guest visits in its first year.

2. Per Capita Spending

Predictions were made of per capita spending at the two theme parks under four headings: admissions, food and beverage, merchandise, and parking and other. The assumptions were based on experience at Disney theme parks and adjusted to local conditions. In a separate report, ADL evaluated the reasonableness of the assumed admission prices. ADL reviewed the admission prices charged in Paris for major competing attractions in terms of entertainment value and also the prices charged by European theme and amusement parks. ADL's reviews indicated that the predicted admission prices for EuroDisney, whilst higher than those charged at other European theme and amusement parks, were considered low when related to Paris prices for quality adult-oriented entertainment, and seemed consistent with prices charged for other family-oriented attractions.

ADL also evaluated the assumed prices for food and beverages at EuroDisney. ADL analysed the prices paid in Paris, examined food and beverage prices at other European theme and amusement parks, and reviewed typical food and beverage expenditure patterns in France as compared with the USA. ADL concluded that the assumptions regarding food and beverage expenditure were reasonable.

With respect to estimated merchandise sales, ADL decided that there was no comparable experience in the Paris region of the type of small retail shops, exposed to a high volume of visitor traffic which are found at Disney-designed theme parks. Therefore, ADL concluded that it was reasonable to base EuroDisney merchandise sales estimates on experience at other Disney-designed parks.

3. Operating Expenses

The main elements included in the operating expenses assumptions were labour costs, cost of sales, maintenance expenses, general and administrative expenses, property and business taxes and the base management fee.

Labour costs, cost of sales, maintenance expenses and general and administrative expenses were all based on Disney-experience, adjusted for EuroDisney-specific and other local market factors. Labour costs included a premium of 10% over the market average in order to attract high quality employees.

Under the company's articles of association, the management company, a wholly-owned Disney subsidiary, was entitled to annual fees consisting of a base fee and management incentive fees. The base fee was calculated as a percentage of total revenues less 0.5% of after-tax profits, initially set at 3%, rising to 6% after a maximum of 5 years after the opening of the Magic Kingdom. The management incentive fees consisted of a sliding percentage of adjusted pre-tax cash flow, and a fixed 35% of any pre-tax gain on the sale of hotels.

4. Cost of Construction

The cost of the Magic Kingdom construction was estimated to be FFr 9.5 billion, as part of a total cost of FFr 14.9 billion for phase 1A as a whole. The construction of the second theme park was estimated to cost FFr 5.9 billion. These estimates were based on Disney's experience of theme park construction.

5. Resort and Property Development Income

Based on Disney's experience, which had indicated that the most profitable use of land around a Disney theme park was hotels, Eurodisney planned a hotel construction programme consisting of 18,200 rooms. The hotels were classified according to service and proximity to the Magic Kingdom, ranging from 4-star deluxe to 2-star hotels.

The model assumed that hotel occupancy rates would rise from 68% in the first year to 80–85% by the third year of operation. This compares with an average occupancy rate of 94% at Disney-operated hotels at Walt Disney World over the past 15 years. The projected hotel performance was based on local studies and on comparisons with the performance of hotels surrounding Disney's other parks. It was assumed that each hotel would take two years to build, and would be entirely financed by debt at an interest rate of 9–10% per annum.

The model assumed that of the total 18,200 rooms to be built, only the 500 rooms of the Magic Kingdom Hotel would be owned and managed permanently by EuroDisney. The remainder would be owned and operated for 2–4 years after construction, and then sold to third parties at a profit.

Evaluation of Assumptions

The attendance predictions have, in fact, proved relatively well-founded, although figures for the second year of operation have been reported to be down on the previous year. The 11 millionth visitor entered the EuroDisney theme park only a few weeks after the anniversary of its opening in April 1993. The seasonality of attendance levels was underestimated, however, and without winter discounts EuroDisney may have fallen well short of the first year attendance prediction.

Before the park opened in 1992, EuroDisney dismissed concerns that attendances would be adversely affected by the notorious autumn and winter weather conditions in the Marne-la-Vallée region. EuroDisney pointed to the experience at the Tokyo park, which had thrived despite an unpredictable climate. EuroDisney had believed that design-features such as covered walkways and heated restaurants and stores would ensure that EuroDisney did not become merely a fair-weather park.

However, EuroDisney has had problems attracting the required number of visitors outside the summer season. EuroDisney, which has very high fixed cost commitments, needed to achieve consistently high year-round attendances if it was to be as successful as the prospectus envisaged. With the benefit of hindsight, this was probably an over-optimistic assumption. No other European theme park or amusement park remains open throughout the year. The Walt Disney name may well be synonymous with magic and fantasy, but this alone provides little protection against the elements.

Per capita spending assumptions have also proved over-optimistic. Visitors have spent significantly less on food and merchandise in the theme park and at its hotels than EuroDisney expected. European visitors have found prices to be too expensive. The high initial set-up costs meant EuroDisney was obliged to set an admission price of around £100 for a family of four. At that price, many customers are reluctant to spend even more money on the expensive food and merchandise which is on sale at the site.

The depressed state of the property market in the Paris region has not only deprived EuroDisney of the expected revenues from the anticipated sale of hotels, but has also scuppered the ambitious plans for commercial and residential property development in and around the resort.

Hotel occupancy rates have also fallen short of expectations. Visitors to EuroDisney have preferred to make short visits. Many have stayed in hotel accommodation in Paris, which is generally no more expensive than at EuroDisney, and make a one-day excursion to the theme park. This compares with visitors to the US Disney theme parks who tend to stay for at least one week.

It is easy to look back at the assumptions contained in the prospectus and conclude that they were too optimistic. However, we must remember that the EuroDisney forecasts were extensively researched via internal and independent studies, and were made at a time when it was not unreasonable to predict relatively healthy European economic conditions for the early 1990s.

However, the prospectus contained one implicit assumption that can be questioned. Disney assumed that it would have little difficulty transferring American culture to western Europe. The whole EuroDisney outlook and ethos was American. Employees are called 'cast members', and beards, moustaches, stockings, suspenders and eyeliner are not allowed.

The principal assumptions themselves were very much based on the experiences at Disney's US theme parks, rather than those of their European counterparts. The theme park phenomenon was relatively new to France, and yet Disney believed visitors to EuroDisney would possess largely the same tastes and spending habits as Americans.

Some relatively small concessions were made to the undiluted American formula: some of the restaurants provided higher quality food, French was the predominant language spoken, and the main parade attraction was timetabled for midday in an attempt to avoid overcrowding in the cafés and restaurants. (The French prefer to sit down for lunch between 12.30 and 2.30 rather than 'graze' throughout the day). Nevertheless, the impact of the alcohol ban within the Magic Kingdom, language difficulties, the adverse reaction to Disney's stringent rules concerning employees' appearance, European eating and spending habits (including differences between visitors from one European country and another) and the fact that Europeans, unlike Americans, are reluctant to take their children out of school to visit a Disney theme park, have all caused unexpected headaches for EuroDisney.

The cultural problems are highlighted by the experiences of Euro-Disney's competitors, who have not suffered as badly as a result of adverse European economic conditions. The Asterix theme park in France, for example, has fared remarkably well since EuroDisney opened. It seems that the French favour homegrown, rather than American, cultural attractions.

These cultural aspects should have been researched more effectively, incorporating a greater awareness of the diversity and peculiarities of European tastes. At the time of the 1989 share offer, EuroDisney had supreme confidence in the venture, and until the theme park opened, this confidence seemed to be shared by investors. However, this confidence resulted in complacency. It is clear that EuroDisney almost believed that the Mickey Mouse symbol alone would be enough to break through all cultural obstacles.

Sensitivity Analysis

All forecasts are subject to varying degrees of risks and uncertainty since future cash flows cannot be predicted with absolute certainty. The degree of risk associated with an investment opportunity should be reflected in the cost of equity. However, it is also important to evaluate the impact of the variability of cash flows on that cost of equity. One method that can be used is sensitivity analysis.

The EuroDisney prospectus included a sensitivity table (shown in Exhibit 23.1) which estimated the effects of varying certain assumptions on the expected rate of return. Potential investors were provided with extra information which enabled them to identify areas which were critical to the success of the project. The information was far more sophisticated than mere single-value forecasts.

However, the sensitivity table analysed the effect of each change independently. No attempt was made to portray the overall effect of different scenarios. Perhaps it is unrealistic to expect a company to divulge the total effect of a range of possible scenarios, from the most optimistic to the nightmare scenario, given the cost of preparing such information. Anyway, such an analysis may mislead potential investors, who may believe that those scenarios presented are the only ones possible in reality.

One weakness of any sensitivity analysis is that it does not indicate how likely it is that a variable will change by the given amount. Was it equally likely that initial attendance would be 1 million above or 1 million below 11 million? Was it as likely that per capita spending would be up 10% against forecast as it was that inflation would be 1% higher than forecast? The chosen variation in the assumptions used in the table seems very arbitrary. However, EuroDisney would argue that at least the information provided demonstrated how sensitive the rate of return was to illustrative changes in certain key variables. Potential investors could then apply their own judgement as to how likely these outcomes were.

A financial forecast that covered a period extending 27 years from the date of preparation without some form of sensitivity analysis would be simplistic and inadequate. However, investors might well ask how a forecast covering such a long period could hope to be accurate? Some of the variations in key assumptions included in the sensitivity table failed to capture actual experience. The second phase (phase 1B), which was to provide vital additional revenues from 1996 onwards, has been postponed. If the forecast has proved unrealistic after just 5 years, how accurate is a forecast covering 27 years likely to be?

The Discount Rate

The two main determinants of the cost of equity are interest rates and a premium for risk. Risk consists of two elements: business risk and financial risk. Business risk is defined as the risk associated with a firm's projections of its future operating income, or in other words, it relates to the riskiness of its assets. Financial risk is defined as the shareholders' risk over and above basic business risk resulting from financial gearing.

Business Risk

Business risk relates to the riskiness of a company's assets and results from the type of business it engages in. For EuroDisney, the main sources of business risk included economic, cultural, climatic and competitive factors.

The success of EuroDisney was directly related to the health or otherwise of the European economies. If Disney had known that there would be a recession in Europe, it may not have continued with the EuroDisney venture. Obviously, the recession has affected many different types of business. However, it has had a profound affect on the tourist industry.

Given that EuroDisney hoped to attract a significant number of visitors from outside France, the value of European currencies relative to the French franc is another important economic factor. Experience has shown that the depreciation of sterling, the peseta, the lira and the Irish punt relative to the franc, has made EuroDisney a very expensive holiday. In fact, it has become almost as expensive as a trip to the real thing on the other side of the Atlantic.

EuroDisney estimated that 50% of total visitors would be French. Cultural issues were very relevant to the success or otherwise of EuroDisney. The extent to which EuroDisney could sell the very American Walt Disney theme to Europeans, and the French in particular, was a crucial factor. Of all Europeans, the French are arguably the fiercest defenders of their own nationalistic and cultural values. Prior to its opening, the theme park was condemned by one French critic as a 'cultural Chernobyl . . . a horror made of cardboard, plastic and appalling colours, a construction of hardened chewing gum and idiotic folklore taken straight out of comic books written for obese Americans'.

EuroDisney brushed this aside, asserting that most French people would ignore the issue of cultural invasion, which was 'a debate only for the intellectuals', who would probably bring their children to EuroDisney, anyway. In a further bid to counter the fears of American cultural imperialism, EuroDisney officials were also quick to point out that many of the Disney characters and stories, such as Snow White, Pinocchio and Peter Pan, did in fact originate in Europe.

The variability of EuroDisney's cash flows is also influenced by the nature of the climate of the Paris region. The American Disney parks enjoy almost guaranteed year-round sunshine. EuroDisney's attendance levels are clearly sensitive to less predictable weather conditions, particularly in the colder and wetter winter months.

The final major source of business risk facing EuroDisney is competition. Other European theme and amusement parks include the Asterix Park, north of Paris, Alton Towers in the UK, Efteling in Holland, Walibi in Belgium and the Europa-Park in Germany. As well as this, EuroDisney could also be said to be competing in the wider family-entertainment and tourist industries, and ironically it even faces competition from the American Disney parks themselves.

Financial Risk

There are basically two main categories of shareholder in EuroDisney. Walt Disney retained 49% of the shares and the bulk of the remainder were offered to the public via the 1989 prospectus. Even at this very broad level of analysis, it is clear that the risks for Walt Disney as a shareholder in this venture were quite different from those of other shareholders.

The financial arrangements were such that Walt Disney received income through royalties, incentives and a management fee, even before dividends were considered. To the other shareholders this arrangement in effect increased the level of financial risk involved. The royalties and management fee represented, in the same way that interest payments do, a fixed commitment to be met before profits could be distributed.

On top of this source of financial gearing, there was also a significant element of conventional debt in the capital structure. The prospectus indicated that the phase 1A construction (estimated to cost FFr 14.9 billion) would be financed by FFr 11.3 billion of debt. EuroDisney had planned to repay much of this debt using the proceeds from the sale of hotels within the EuroDisney complex. However, the depressed state of the French property market has prevented this, pushing gearing well above anticipated levels.

How Realistic Was the EuroDisney Cost of Equity?

Back in the autumn of 1989, a UK investor could have achieved a rate of return of around 10% by investing in 20-year maturity treasury bills. This perhaps would have been as near a risk-free investment as possible at the time. In contrast, the EuroDisney cost of equity implied an expected return of 13.3%, giving a premium of just over 3% for the risks involved. The question to ask is whether this represented an adequate rate of return given the uncertainties associated with the venture?

In 1989, EuroDisney issued a pre-prospectus document (the pathfinder prospectus) in order to gauge the likely level of interest in the share offer. This document suggested three possible initial share prices: FFr 60, FFr 65 and FFr 70. This range must have been based on an initial calculation using a predetermined estimated cost of equity. (The prospectus gives no indication of how the cost of equity was derived.)

Given the extremely positive response to the proposed share issue, EuroDisney decided to set the initial share price slightly above the top of the quoted range. The share offer was oversubscribed 5 times, and shares opened at a substantial premium on the offer price. In Paris, shares touched FFr 91 on the first day of trading, which was consistent with prices on the grey market, which had been operating since the time the offer was launched.

It is clear that, at the time, investors believed that the rate of return on EuroDisney shares was more than adequate compensation for the perceived risks involved. Indeed, the share price peaked at FFr 165 in March 1992, before the park had even opened and without any change in EuroDisney's own forecasts.

In a perfect capital market, securities will be valued at a price which offers a fair return for the specific risks involved. Securities that are undervalued (in relation to the associated risk) will be bought, and securities that are overvalued will be sold, until equilibrium prices are reached. However, perfect markets depend on a number of factors, including rational decision-making by investors. One might wonder whether in the period up to April 1992, EuroDisney investors, and many investment analysts, became so carried away by the Disney fantasy, that they had lost touch with reality themselves.

'It Can't Fail!'

Without question, EuroDisney is proving to be a financial nightmare for Disney executives. Larger than expected opening year losses accompanied by an almost daily deterioration in the future prospects for the park have put the continued viability of the park in doubt.

A considerable part of the disappointment regarding the performance of EuroDisney can be attributed to the failure of EuroDisney to live up to the very high expectations of both private and institutional investors alike.

The high expectations for EuroDisney can largely be put down to the 'Eisner factor' and the image of ruthless efficiency Walt Disney has cultivated. The powerful figure of Michael Eisner has dominated Disney for the past decade. His success in turning the fortunes of Walt Disney around in the USA – demonstrated by an increase in the market capitalisation of Walt Disney between 1984 and 1988 of $8.6 billion (reflecting a fivefold increase of individual share prices) – earned him not only a legendary reputation in the leisure and entertainment industry but also earned him $40 million in 1988.

Given the success enjoyed by Walt Disney under his guidance, there was an understandable expectation that EuroDisney would also be a success. However understandable these expectations, it is perhaps a little disappointing that seasoned investment analysts were carried away with this Eisner euphoria to the extent that, at the time of the share issue, the possibility of failure was not even contemplated. This anticipation of success resulted, as we have already seen, in the price of EuroDisney shares spiralling up to unrealistic levels (a spiralling that was reflected in the grey market even before the shares were being publicly traded).

What were the reasons behind the apparent failure of the venture? The downturn in the European economy was certainly a factor. Given the growth in the European economy in the period 1983 onwards and the optimistic forecasts for sustained growth into the 1990s, Disney executives were entitled to believe that the timing of their investment decision in Europe was justified. They, along with many so-called economic experts, did not foresee the fact that Europe at the end of the 1980s was about to enter a deep recession. There were a number of factors that were perceived to be the cause of this downturn in economic growth.

The end of the 1980s saw a marked tightening in monetary policies in western Europe. This tightening was primarily the result of two factors:

1. The late 1980s had seen the re-emergence of a certain degree of inflationary pressures. In a manner consistent with the early 1980s, governments tackled this by tight financial policies that resulted in a fall in the real money supply.
2. The emergence of these inflationary pressures was particularly evident in the newly created German Republic. One of the primary causes of this increased pressure was the impact on the money supply of the conversion of the East German Östmark into Deutschmark at rates apparantly ungoverned by economic realities. In an effort to contain inflation the Bundesbank proceeded to tighten monetary policy by raising interest rates. These increases sent a deflationary pulse through the other western European economies via the Exchange Rate Mechanism as governments attempted to maintain currency levels within agreed bands. The committment of the French government, in particular, to the ERM central rates resulted in an unrealistically high value for the franc, making French holidays relatively more expensive for other Europeans than would have been the case had the franc been allowed to drift to a more realistic level.

The deflationary impact of the tight monetary policies was exacerbated by the loss of consumer and business confidence brought on by the onset of hostilities in the Gulf as a result of the Iraqi invasion of Kuwait. Although the initial rise in oil prices was contained, the uncertainty created by the outbreak of war in an area of vital strategic importance certainly had a deflationary effect, particularly in the business world. The outbreak of war had a direct impact on the tourist industry as the threat of terrorist activities persuaded people to take their holidays locally.

In addition to the above factors, the expected boost to demand expected from the former communist regimes of Eastern Europe failed to materialise. It was evident in the example of the former Soviet Union that the structures necessary to support the successful running of a market economy did not exist. In addition, growing political and ethnic tensions in the region – vividly captured in the conflicts in the former Yugoslavia – appear to prevent the sustained growth of these regions for the foreseeable future.

The impact of these factors was not such as to prevent EuroDisney meeting targeted attendance levels in the first year but they may have conspired in reducing attendance levels below predicted levels in subsequent years. In addition, it may have adversely affected the level of per capita spending once visitors were inside the park.

Another consequence of the poor economic climate in Europe has been a slump in the property market in France. EuroDisney has been unable to sell its hotels as planned, and so has been unable to contain its rising debt burden.

However significant the effects of the recession in Europe, much of the apparent failure of EuroDisney can be attributed to the failure of both Disney executives and investment analysts to predict how well a Disney theme park in Europe would perform.

Given our analysis of the Robock and Simmonds model, Disney executives were probably justified in thinking that a potential market for their product existed in Europe. However, it appears that certain decisions that were made – most particularly in respect of location and pricing – were mistaken.

In terms of our Robock and Simmonds model, the selection of France as the host appeared justified – however, the location of the site on the outskirts of Paris (although maximising potential population catchment) failed to take account of climatic factors. One of the key factors to the success of the park is its ability to attract visitors throughout the year. Whilst this happens to be the case in the warm climates of California and Florida the expectation that visitors would be attracted to a Disney park in the middle of a North European winter appeared to be somewhat unrealistic. Attendance levels have proved to be so poor over the winter months that park workers have had to be laid off and a number of heavy discount schemes have been put in operation in an attempt to attract visitors. Although Disney deny this to be the case, the closure of the park over the winter months is now on the agenda of Disney executives.

With the benefit of hindsight, certain commentators now give the opinion that Spain would have served as a better base given the similiarity of its balmy climate to that of Florida and California.

Pricing is another major area where Disney seems to have been over-optimistic. It would appear that the cost of admission – approximately £100 for a family of four – are proving to be increasingly beyond that which visitors are prepared to pay. Whilst it is true that the admission prices are roughly equivalent to those charged at the US parks, it would appear that this basis of comparison is not valid, perhaps because visitors to the USA are prepared to pay a premium since the parks there are the originals and a favourable climate is almost guaranteed. Whilst it is true that attendance levels were met in the first year, the high prices have been one of the contributing factors to the disappointing attendance levels in subsequent years.

A by-product of admission prices being too high has been that the level of spending by visitors once inside the park has been well below that predicted. This has been another critical factor in the disappointing income levels at the park.

Hotels and other accommodation around the park also appear to have been over-priced. In particular – unlike the US market where there is an ample supply of good quality motel style accommodation – there appears to be a shortage of accommodation that would be within the range of middle income earners. The impact of this has been that at even the peak tourist times the levels of occupancy at the hotels have been below those experienced in the USA and, more particularly, those predicted in the financial model.

The dual impact of the high admission prices and accommodation charges has been the realisation that the US Disney parks were somehow robbing the European market. Competitively priced package trips to the US parks have proved popular with European tourists despite the opening of EuroDisney. For example, all-inclusive two week package trips to Orlando are available in the UK at prices starting from £200 per person. It would appear that Disney executives underestimated the continuing appeal of US Disney parks, especially in the light of the price differentials between the US and the European parks.

As at the end of the 1993 financial year, the survival of EuroDisney depends crucially on a successful renegotiation of the £2.4 billion of debts held by the banks. Without this – and possibly substantial cash injections from Walt Disney itself – the future for the park looks bleak.

Whilst EuroDisney's prospects appear very unpromising, Walt Disney, and indeed the French government, have a very great deal to lose if EuroDisney fails. With the support of such a well-established financial giant as Disney, perhaps EuroDisney will eventually succeed. EuroDisney officials have recently stressed that the shares should be seen as a long-term investment, and that very good returns could still be achieved in two to three decades' time. However, this is a far cry from the optimism contained in the share offer prospectus back in 1989. It remains to be seen whether a EuroDisney theme park situated near Paris can ever be profitable.

References

Caves, R. E. (1971) 'International corporations: the industrial economics of foreign investment', *Economica*, February.

Davis, E. W. and Pointon, C. (1994) *Finance and the Firm*, Oxford University Press.

Hymes, S. H. (1976) *The International Operation of National Firms: A Study of Direct Investment*, MIT Press.

IMF, *World Economic Outlook*, 1983 onwards.

OECD, *Economic Survey*, 1983 onwards.

Robock, S. H. and Simmonds, K. (1989) *International Business and Multinational Enterprises*, Irwin.

S. G. Warburg and Company (1989) *EuroDisneyland SCA: Offer for Sale*. London: Warburg.

Foreign Direct Investment in the UK

An Overview and Three Regional Case Studies

The study begins by providing a definition of foreign direct investment (FDI), summarising Dunning's explanation of why international production takes place and examining the changing patterns of world FDI. This is followed by an account of the UK's share of FDI from the world's major source countries and a discussion of the UK as a host country for FDI. It is shown that at the beginning of the 1980s nearly two-thirds of the stock of FDI in the UK was from the USA but that in recent years flows of FDI to the UK from Europe and Japan have grown in importance. A brief discussion is provided on the factors attracting FDI flows to the UK from the major sources and comments are made on the impact of FDI on the economy. A synoptic evaluation of probable future trends of FDI flows to the UK is provided. As an introduction to three regional case studies, there is an analysis of the regional distribution of FDI flows to the UK. Regional case studies are provided for the West Midlands, Wales and Scotland. In each case there is a discussion of recent trends in FDI, the sectoral composition and subregional distribution, the most important locational factors and the main impacts of FDI on the regional economy.

Introduction

Foreign direct investment (FDI) takes place when a firm from one country sets up a branch or subsidiary company in another country, or increases an existing investment there, or when it buys a controlling interest in a firm in another country, or when strategic alliances such as joint ventures are created. The agents of FDI are transnational corporations (TNCs) and

This case was written by Clive Collis as a basis for class discussion rather than to illustrate either effective or ineffective handling of an administrative situation © Clive Collis, 1995.

multinational corporations (MNCs). TNCs are companies operating in at least two countries, including the home country. Where a company has operations in a number of countries it is referred to as an MNC. FDI differs from portfolio investment, the latter referring to the case where shares in a (foreign) firm are bought purely for financial purposes rather than to gain control.

FDI plays an important role in the UK economy (DTI English Unit, 1991) and its regions (Collis, 1992). In 1989, as a proportion of GDP, the UK attracted more FDI than any other country. This investment amounted to £5,670 million, and in absolute terms, was more than any other country except the USA. In 1989, foreign-owned companies (FOCs) contributed 15% of all new capital investment undertaken in the UK, a proportion which rose to 20% in 1990. The cumulative total of FDI made in the UK during the 1980s exceeded £22,000 million with the number of foreign investment projects averaging 340 per annum in the second half of the 1980s. The main types of FDI made in the UK between 1984 and 1990 were start-ups (41%) and reinvestment/expansions of existing operations (44%). Acquisitions accounted for only 9% and the remaining 6% were joint ventures with UK companies.

Within the UK, the regions which received the largest shares of FDI flows during the second half of the 1980s were Scotland, Wales and the West Midlands. Between 1983 and the last quarter of 1988 Scotland's share of FDI projects remained stable (21% in 1983 and 22% in 1988), that of Wales rose (from 13% to 18%) and that of the West Midlands increased markedly (from 6% to 16%). In contrast to the rise in importance of the West Midlands as a location for FDI flows to the UK, the South-east region's share of flows of FDI projects fell from 25% to 18%.

Explaining FDI: Dunning's Eclectic Paradigm

There are numerous explanations of why international production, via FDI, takes place. Dunning's 'eclectic' explanation incorporates the elements contained in a number of other explanations (Dunning, 1991). His argument is that firms will engage in international production when they possess 'owner-specific' advantages over indigenous rivals, when these can be 'internalised' and when 'location-specific' advantages are present. An example of an owner-specific advantage is the exclusive ownership of a brand name for a product. Whereas rivals in other countries cannot produce legally such a branded product there, the owner of the brand can do so. The internalisation of owner-specific advantages occurs when the advantages are best exploited by firms themselves rather than through licensing them to indigenous firms in other countries. Internalisation often occurs when firms have invested large sums of money on research and development activity. They set up their own production facilities abroad rather than selling or leasing the technology. Examples of location-specific factors, which determine the location of production abroad, are the existence of a particular market or the availability of cheap labour or other production resoures too. The extent and pattern of international production, through FDI, is the result of the interplay of these three factors.

The Global Context: Changing Patterns of World FDI

Recent developments in world FDI exhibit a number of contrasts with previous patterns of FDI. Major changes have occured in the *source* of FDI, its *destination*, and the *sectors* in which FDI has concentrated (Dicken, 1992).

The upsurge in world FDI which occurred after 1946, particularly in manufacturing, was led by the USA. This reflected its economic strength at the time. The second most important *source* nation was the UK. By the mid-1980s, Japan and West Germany had emerged also as major sources of FDI and this reflected their achievement of economic prosperity and power. By the 1990s other Pacific Rim countries, such as Hong Kong, South Korea, Taiwan, Singapore and Malaysia, had emerged as sources of FDI. In addition to this shift in the geographical origin of world FDI, there have been changes in the geographical *destination* of FDI. In the early post-war years the majority of FDI was located in developing countries. However, by the late 1980s three-quarters of all FDI in the world was located in the developed market economies. A key feature of this concentration of FDI in developed economies has been the rise in importance of the USA as a host nation. In 1975 the stock of inward investment in western Europe (41%) was nearly four times greater than that in the USA (11%). By 1985 the stock of FDI in the USA (29%) just exceeded that in western Europe (28.9%). However, changes in this situation have occurred as a result of the Single European Market (SEM). There has been a recent upsurge in FDI in western Europe from America and Japan. Bachtler and Clement (1991) attribute this to the 'potential size and anticipated growth of the European market, though also the perceived threat of protectionism'.

In addition to these shifts in the source and destination of world FDI there has also been a change in the *sectors* in which investment by foreign-owned companies (FOCs) has taken place. Historically, FDI was concentrated in natural-resource-based sectors such as mining and foodstuffs for export. Although these sectors still retain some importance there has been a shift of investment to manufacturing and, more recently, to service sectors. This is in conformity with the sectoral shifts which have taken place within national economies. Within manufacturing there are three broad types of sector which have a particularly large FOC presence. These are: techno-logically advanced sectors such as pharmaceuticals, computers, scientific instruments, electronics and synthetic fibres; large volume, medium-technology consumer goods industries, for example motor vehicles, tyres, televisions and refrigerators; and mass production consumer goods indust-ries supplying branded products such as cigarettes, soft drinks, toilet preparations and breakfast cereals. Within services, FDI is concentrated in trading (i.e. retail and distribution), in banking, finance and insurance and in other business and commercial services such as accountancy and legal services. FDI in distribution is often the first step made by a FOC in a location as part of a progression towards investment in assembly and manufacturing. The growth of FDI in the financial sector may, to a large extent, be explained by the deregulation of financial markets and the abolition of controls on international capital movements.

The UK's Share of FDI from the World's Major Source Countries

TNCs from the USA are a major source of FDI and account for 40% of the world total. Within Europe since the 1950s, there has been shift in American FDI away from the UK and towards Continental Europe. For example, in 1956 almost 60% of USA manufacturing investment in Europe was in the UK. This was six times more than in either West Germany or France. By 1988 the UK's share, whilst still being the largest, had fallen to less than 30%; on the other hand, Germany's share had increased to 21%. This change reflected the desire of many USA companies to be located in the core of the EU market. In addition, there has been a growth of American manufacturing investment in Ireland and, to a lesser extent, in Spain. These investments in peripheral countries of the EU reflect both the pull of cheap labour sources and the effect of regional incentives. Thus, although the UK remains a favoured European location for manufacturing investment from the USA, there is strong competition from Germany and growing competition from Ireland.

The leading European sources of FDI are the UK, Germany, Switzerland and Holland and, to a smaller extent, France, Italy and Sweden. Between 1950 and 1970 West Germany created one-third of the foreign manufacturing subsidiaries established by the largest European MNCs. The biggest concentration of West German FDI in manufacturing is the USA (32% in 1987). Within EU destination countries the UK faces strong competition from France, Belgium, Spain and Italy. The UK's share of West-German FDI in manufacturing in the EU in 1987 was only 10.3%, but nevertheless this is an important component of FDI in the UK.

There was a significant take-off in FDI from Japan in the 1960s. Its world share of FDI rose from 0.7% in 1960 to 11.7% in 1985 (Dicken, 1992). Within Japanese FDI overall, manufacturing is much less important than services. The geographical location of Japanese FDI has moved away from developing countries to developed economies: the USA hosts 40% and Europe 16% of Japanese FDI. This move reflected both the introduction of protective barriers against Japanese imports and the high value of the Japanese yen which affected the competitiveness of exports. In 1987, in manufacturing, some 48% of Japanese FDI was in North America and only 10% in Europe. Within Europe, the UK is the most favoured location for Japanese manufacturing FDI.

The UK as a Host for FDI

Whilst the UK may be a minor destination for FDI from a particular source, that source may constitute a major component of FDI in the UK itself. Thus, whilst the UK's share of American FDI is smaller than previously and the UK attracts a small proportion of total West German and Japanese investment, these sources are crucially important to the UK itself.

The stock of FDI in the UK at the beginning of the 1980s was made up of 62% from the USA and 15% from other EU countries. Flows of FDI to the UK during the 1980s have diminished the importance of the USA and increased the importance of the EU. Japan emerged as a major source of UK FDI (Dicken, 1992; Young et al., 1988).

The position in the 1990s may be summarised as follows. The major sources of flows of FDI to the UK are the USA, Japan and Europe (West Germany within the EU and Sweden and Switzerland within the rest of Europe). Whilst the proportion of FDI flowing to the UK from the USA declined in the 1980s the USA remains the UK's major source country for FDI projects. The increase in the flow of FDI from Japan during the 1980s was from $4 billion in 1980 to $33 billion in 1987. Between 1984 and 1990 some 28% of inward investment flows came from other EU countries, particularly Germany (DTI, 1991).

The recent flow of Japanese investment into the UK has been influenced by the trade barriers, the SEM and the high value of the yen. German investment has, in large part, been a result of the search for cheap labour and the penetration of the UK market from within. In addition to market factors, it is also language and cultural similarities which explain the large US investment in the UK.

It is extremely difficult to assess the overall impact of FOCs on the UK economy. A major problem is to establish a counterfactual, i.e. what would have happened to the UK economy if there had been no FDI in the UK? The more limited approach normally adopted is to examine the impact of FDI on a host economy in terms of its effects on: the balance of payments, employment and productivity, technology transfer and innovation, and on market structure. A review of the evidence on these impacts has suggested that in the case of the UK there is probably a net benefit to the economy from FDI (Young *et al.*, 1988).

The UK as a whole is faced with increased competition in attracting FDI (Collis, 1992). Competition for US manufacturing investment in particular is strengthening, not only from Germany but from Ireland and Spain. With respect to FDI from other EU countries the trends are not wholly favourable since the main beneficiary of the increasing amount of investment has been the USA. However, given the success of existing investment by Japanese companies in the UK, the UK is likely to remain a favoured location for Japanese FDI. There is also potential for attracting some of the rapidly rising amount of FDI from other Pacific Rim countries. Nevertheless, there are a number of factors and perceptions which may adversely affect the UK. These include perceptions about the skills and attitudes of the labour force, concerns over infrastructure provision, and weakened financial incentives since the abolition of regional development grants in 1988. There is also a danger that the completion of the SEM is reinforcing the attractiveness of the London–Paris–Hamburg 'golden triangle' and that this will be reinforced now the Channel Tunnel is open.

Recent Trends in the Regional Distribution of FDI in the UK

Exhibit 24.1 shows the regional distribution of the flows of overseas inward investment into the UK regions (Collis and Roberts, 1992) for most of the 1980s. The figures reveal a significant fall in the flows of overseas inward investment to the South-east. Both Scotland and Wales retained their strong positions as host regions to FDI. The West Midlands rose considerably in prominence.

In the case of foreign investors, the locational choice is dictated by the

Exhibit 24.1 *Regional distribution of the flows of foreign direct investment in the UK 1983–88*

Regions	1983		1985		1988 (first 9 months)	
	Projects (%)	Jobs (%)	Projects (%)	Jobs (%)	Projects (%)	Jobs (%)
Scotland	21	28	15	18	22	20
Wales	13	13	12	8	18	19
West Midlands	6	14	17	15	16	25
South-east	25	18	23	21	15	8
North-east	8	6	8	8	7	5
Northern Ireland	5	6	4	5	6	6
Yorkshire and Humberside	4	3	4	12	5	6
East Midlands	5	3	5	2	5	4
North-west	9	6	8	8	4	5
South-west	4	3	4	3	2	2
Total	100	100	100	100	100	100
UK total numbers	236	30,800	377	44,400	224	25,887

The jobs are those associated with projects over the long term and are the total of new and safeguarded jobs. In addition to the long term or 'hypothetical' nature of jobs, there are other problems associated with IBB data, particularly for inter-regional comparisons, such as inconsistency in methods of counting projects and jobs.

Source: Extracted from Roberts, Noon and Irving (1988), Collis, Noon, Roberts and Gray (1989) and Collis (1992). Derived from IBB data.

objective of minimising costs whilst having access to markets for inputs and outputs (Hill and Munday, 1992). This implies that a number of locational factors are important: labour costs, regional financial incentives and communications infrastructure. Econometric evidence for the regions of the UK shows that financial incentives and access to markets are substantial influences on the regional distribution of new foreign inward investment. Within the UK these factors have been particularly beneficial to Wales and the West Midlands in recent years.

The characteristics which constitute 'overheating' (a tight labour market, shortage of land, traffic congestion) adversely affected the South-east during the 1980s. The West Midlands benefited from a central location with good international, national and local communications providing access to markets. Wales benefited from a stable population of existing overseas investors, good industrial relations and a welcoming approach by national and local authorities. Scotland benefited from the concentration of academic institutions which contributed a flow of professional, technical and skilled labour. Financial assistance has also been a significant factor for Wales, Scotland and, since 1984, has been a beneficial factor for the West Midlands.

Case Studies of FDI in the UK Regions

The West Midlands

Readers are referred to Roberts *et al.*, 1988; Collis *et al.*, 1989, 1990; Collis, 1992; Collis and Roberts, 1992.

It was not until the mid-1980s that the West Midlands emerged as a major recipient of flows of FDI (see Exhibit 24.1 above). Between the beginning of 1984 and the end of 1986 these FDI flows came mainly from the USA and Canada (42%), the EU (34%) and the Far East (12%). Compared with flows in the UK as a whole this represented a lower proportion of investment projects from the USA and Canada and a higher proportion from the EU and Japan. In the later 1980s the under-representation of investment from the USA increased as did the over-representation from the EU. The result was that the EU became the largest source of FDI in the West Midlands. By the end of the 1980s 39% of the stock of FDI in the West Midlands had come from the EU and 37% from the USA and Canada.

The predominant sectors in which FDI has taken place in the West Midlands are distribution (particularly for West German companies) and metal goods, engineering and vehicles (the predominant sectors for North American investors). Recently some investments in financial and business services have been arriving, particularly from the USA and Japan.

The main activities undertaken by foreign investors in the West Midlands are sales, marketing and warehousing, distribution and servicing activities, followed by assembly and manufacturing. There is a tendency for investors initially to establish sales and marketing activities and then later to progress to the assembly and manufacture of final products. However, Japanese companies are entering the cycle at a later stage, as assemblers and manufacturers, replacing exports because of trade barriers and the completion of the SEM.

For the West Midlands there is detailed survey evidence available on location-specific factors. Evidence is available both for the stock of existing investors and the flow of new investors. Exhibit 24.2 shows the results for the 1987 survey which were obtained from responses from nearly one-half of the existing stock of foreign investors (299 out of 614 companies). The results for the 1989 survey are for new locators and are based on responses from 35 companies.

Exhibit 24.2 *Factors in FOCs' choice of the West Midlands as a location*

Locational factors	1987 survey	1989 survey
National and regional communications	1	2
Local accessibility	2	1
Availability of premises	3	4
Cost of premises	4	3
Availability of labour	5	7
Skills of the workforce	5	5
Availability of land	7	11
Cost of land	10	17
Local markets for products	9	9
Local component supplies	11	16
Presence of other FOCs in West Midlands	14	8
High quality environment	12	12
Financial assistance	13	10
Other reasons	8	*

* Additional questions were asked in the 1989 survey, based on 'other reasons' given in the 1987 survey.

Source: Collis and Roberts (1992) 'FDI in the West Midlands: an analysis and evaluation', *Local Economy,* vol. 7, no. 2.

Both surveys revealed the importance of the communications infrastructure: the major attraction of the West Midlands was a central location, one with good national and regional communications and good local accessibility. A commonly cited 'other' factor in the 1987 survey was proximity to Birmingham Airport and this factor ranked sixth amongst new locators in the 1989 survey. This reflects the importance of good international communications in the location decision. It is noticeable also that labour factors were important in both surveys. As regards financial assistance, the core of the West Midlands became an assisted area in 1984 and thereafter regional selective assistance became available to companies locating there. Therefore this factor showed up as more important for new locators than for the existing stock who were not eligible for regional assistance, although some of the latter had received financial help under local authority schemes. However, a number of well established FOCs pointed out in the 1987 survey that the extent of further investment in the West Midlands was being positively influenced by the availability of regional financial assistance.

Within the region the location of FOCs in evenly divided between the West Midlands county area (Birmingham, Coventry, Dudley, Sandwell, Solihull, Walsall and Wolverhampton) and the shire counties (Hereford and Worcester, Shropshire, Staffordshire and Warwickshire). There is a fairly even spread of FOCs through the shire counties but within the West Midlands county area there is a concentration of FOCs in Birmingham and, to a lesser extent, in Coventry. For the West Midlands county area and Hereford and Worcester, FOCs from North America are particularly important. In Staffordshire, FOCs from EU countries, particularly Germany, are significant. In neither the county area nor any of the shire counties are FOCs from the Far East present in large numbers. However, of the small percentage of FOCs of Japanese origin located in the region, the main locations are the West Midlands county area and Shropshire (particularly the Telford area).

There has been no comprehensive analysis of the costs and benefits of FDI for the West Midlands but evidence exists with respect to a number of effects. It has been estimated that up to 100,000 direct jobs were being provided by FOCs located in the West Midlands in 1989. In a number of cases jobs have built up over a lengthy period. For example, in 36 of the North American companies aggregate employment grew from 984 jobs to 7,442 jobs since their original location in the West Midlands. Evidence suggests also a significant contribution made by foreign companies to the skills of the workforce through employee training. There is also evidence of training customers and suppliers.

Local sourcing of inputs does occur and a growth in local component supply has taken place recently. However, there is considerable scope for much higher proportions of the input requirements of FOCs to be supplied by local companies in the West Midlands. The capital equipment purchases of FOCs in the West Midlands tend to be more local than is the case for supplies of materials and components. In the case of local business services (financial, accountancy and legal) there is considerable use of local sources. There is also evidence that between one-third and one-half of FOCs located in the West Midlands carry out research and development activity there.

Whilst FOCs located in the West Midlands export final products out of the UK, particularly American investors, they also sell to the West Midlands and the rest of the UK. It is, in fact, the rest of the UK which is the main market for investors from North America, the EU and the rest of Europe. This is consistent with their choice of the West Midlands as a location, its central position and good communications providing good market access to the rest of the UK.

Wales

Readers are referred to Morris, 1987; Welsh Affairs Committee, 1988; Hill and Munday, 1991; Collis 1992.

The take-off period for FDI in Wales occurred in the mid to late 1960s. In 1971, FOCs employed 35,500 people in manufacturing in Wales, 11% of total Welsh manufacturing employment. The numbers employed in overseas owned manufacturing in Wales rose to over 53,000 in 1979 but dropped to 40,000 in 1983. However, by 1986 the numbers had risen again to 44,500. By 1990 the number of employees was 56,000 representing 22% of the Welsh manufacturing workforce or 6% of all employment. The growth trend in foreign-owned manufacturing employment in Wales from the early to late 1980s reflects the overall boom in FDI to Wales which took place over that period.

There is both a sectoral concentration of FDI in Wales and an over-reliance on particular source countries. Employment in FOCs in Wales is concentrated in the electrical and electronics industries (23% in 1988) and, to a lesser extent, in motor vehicles (12.6%), chemicals (10.7%) and metal manufacture (9.0%). In 1986, 66% of foreign-owned manufacturing employment in Wales was in North American-owned companies with only 12% in EU-owned companies and 10% in Japanese companies. Recent flows overall have not substantially changed the stock position but the fastest growth in the 1980s was from Japanese and EU sources. The position for all overseas investment in Wales in 1988 was that 26,600 jobs were in 98 companies of American origin (and 3,600 in 9 Canadian companies); 7,600 jobs in 66 companies from the EU; 3,000 jobs from 23 companies from Sweden and Switzerland and 6,900 jobs in 15 companies from Japan.

An interesting feature of the period 1983–90 was the relationship between new investment projects and expansions of existing projects. Whilst there were 67 new North American investment projects secured, there were also 88 expansions. However, the capital investment in new North American projects was much higher than in expansions. For Japanese-owned companies it was also the case that the number of expansions exceeded the number of new projects but in this case capital investment in expansions was nearly as high as for new projects. Companies from Europe undertook more new investments than expansions but the total investment in expansions was greater than in new projects.

There are considerable subregional differences in the location of FDI in Wales. With respect to the amount of manufacturing employment in FOCs there were marked differences in 1983 with Mid-Glamorgan and West Glamorgan (and Llanelli) having disproportionately high shares (33% and 24% respectively). Gwent's share was 19% and Clwyd's 10%. Dyfed, Gwyned and Powys had extremely small shares. In the period 1983–87 the attractiveness of Mid-Glamorgan persisted but Gwent and Clwyd improved their positions markedly. These three counties together, with only 50% of the population, attracted 75% of jobs and capital investments from abroad. It is the effect of the M4 corridor that has been crucial to south-east Wales. The contrasts within the north, between Gwyned in the north-west and Clywd in the north-east, stem from the latter having better communications and market access and a larger labour market.

The two main factors in attracting FDI to Wales as a whole are financial incentives and labour availability. Other factors include the development of communications and market access (notably the M4 motorway), good industrial relations, the availability of factories and serviced sites, and a welcoming attitude by regional and local investment promoters together with good aftercare. Moreover, the evidence suggests that foreign locators are satisfied with their locational choice. However, there are disadvantages also. Evidence from companies rejecting Wales as a location has revealed the existence of managerial and skilled worker shortages, a weak service infrastructure (office services, employment services) and lack of a clearly defined and coherent 'image' for Wales (particularly compared with Scotland). However, in 1990 Welsh Development International was created to market Wales, replacing a situation where WINvest (an arm of the Welsh Development Agency) was only one of a number of promotional agencies.

There is some evidence available about the benefits of FDI to Wales. The major benefits have been in terms of direct employment, diversification of the industrial structure, and managerial and work-practice improvements. However, whilst it is the case that the survival rate of foreign branch establishments is good, there is considerable concern over the branch-plant syndrome. The characteristics of branch-plants are deemed to be: low levels of decision-making authority and a lack of high-level functions such as research and development; low levels of integration into the regional economy in terms of purchases of raw materials, components and business services, and a predominance of 'screwdriver' assembly operations.

The evidence suggests that Wales exhibits many of the characteristics of a branch-plant economy. In general, FOCs have not established research and development centres in Wales, there is a low level of raw material and components sourcing and, particularly in the electronics industry, assembly plants employ a high proportion of females at relatively low wages. However, it is the case that some Japanese investors are developing local supply networks and therefore integrating more into the regional economy.

Scotland

Readers are referred to Hood and Young, 1982; Young, 1989; National Audit Office, 1989; Collis, 1992.

FDI in Scotland has been dominated by the USA as a source country. The period 1965–75 was the most important for new openings of American-owned companies. At its peak, in 1975, manufacturing companies of American origin accounted for 14% of Scotland's manufacturing employment. During the 1970s there was also a growth in the number of European manufacturing units, many being acquisitions of indigenous companies. In total, in 1975, there were 108,200 people employed in 280 foreign-owned manufacturing units in Scotland. In 1981 there were 288 foreign-owned manufacturing units, but employment had fallen to 80,457 jobs. By the beginning of 1988 there were 344 foreign-owned manufacturing units in Scotland, employing 70,300 people, over 18% of all manufacturing jobs in Scotland.

Within manufacturing the main sectors of foreign ownership in Scotland have been electrical and electronic engineering, mechanical engineering and instrument engineering. The main spatial concentration has been in the Strathclyde region. It was in Strathclyde, and in electrical and mechanical engineering that major job losses occurred between 1976 and 1981. In that period there were a number of closures of foreign-owned manufacturing units which, at their maximum employment levels, provided nearly 45,000 jobs in Scotland. Most of the jobs lost, in a total of 61 closures, were in a small number of large, well established companies such as Singer, Goodyear and Chrysler. Whilst the reasons for these closures were complex, in many cases a major factor was dissatisfaction with labour performance.

Whilst there is detailed information available on the reasons that the particular companies which closed made Scotland their original choice as a location, most of it relates to choices made too long ago to be relevant today (e.g. Singer in 1867). However, the choice of Linwood as a location for Rootes/Chrysler/Peugeot in the early 1960s does illustrate the effects of regional policy instruments. The push factor was the refusal of an Industrial Development Certificate for expansion at the Coventry site and the pull factor was the regional financial assistance available in Scotland. In this case, other factors of relevance were labour supply, transport and dock facilities and the adjacent location of a pressed steel plant.

The availability of regional financial assistance has, in fact, been of significance to many of the foreign investors' decisions to locate in Scotland. Until its abolition in 1988, the regional development grant meant that regional assistance was automatic and predictable, features stressed by foreign direct investors as important. In addition, 'tailor-made' regional packages of selective assistance have been a feature of Scottish incentives since the late 1970s and have helped attract new FDI. Whilst financial assistance has been an important determinant of locational choice, the motivation to invest abroad has been market access. American parent companies have generally defined the area of market operations for Scottish plants, initially to supply the UK but subsequently the wider European market. Another factor of particular importance for Scotland as a locational choice is the availability of professional, technical and skilled labour. In this respect Scotland has benefited from its relatively large number of universities. The fact that the quality of jobs created by FDI in electronics is higher in Scotland than in Wales partly reflects this.

Locational choice has also been affected by the method of entry of FDI. Historically, investments from the USA have been in greenfield sites in Scotland, often because the parent company previously had no direct manufacturing overseas. The later arrival of EU investment was more usually through acquisition and the location was therefore predetermined.

The major benefit of FDI to Scotland has been the direct jobs created, an important consideration in a region of high unemployment. Other benefits include the exporting activities of FOCs located in Scotland and the development of a trained cadre of managers within them. However, concern has been expressed about the low levels of local sourcing undertaken by FOCs, particularly in electronics, and the rather low levels of R & D undertaken by foreign-owned plants in Scotland.

References

Bachtler, J. and Clement, K. (1991) 'Inward investment in the UK and the Single European Market', *Regional Studies*, vol. 24.

Collis, C. (1992) 'Overseas inward investment in the UK regions', in P. Townroe and R. Martin (eds), *Regional Development in the 1990s: The British Isles in Transition*. London: Jessica Kingsley.

Collis, C. and Roberts, P. (1992) 'Foreign direct investment in the West Midlands: an analysis and evaluation', *Local Economy*, vol. 7, no 2.

Collis, C., Noon, D., Roberts, P. and Gray, K. (1989) *Overseas Investment to the West Midlands Region* (second report). Coleshill: West Midlands Industrial Development Association.

Collis, C., Noon, D., Berkeley, N. and Roberts, P. (1990) *Benefits of Inward Investment to the West Midlands*. Coleshill: West Midlands Development Agency.

DTI English Unit (1991) *Knock-on Effects of Inward Investment: England Overview*, London: HMSO.

Dicken, P. (1992) *Global Shift: The Internationalisation of Economic Activity*. London: Paul Chapman Publishing.

Dunning, J. (1991) 'The eclectic paradigm of international production: a personal perspective', in C. Pitelis and R. Sugden (eds), *The Nature of the Transnational Firm*. London: Routledge.

Hill, S. and Munday, M. (1991) 'Foreign direct investment in Wales', *Local Economy*, vol. 6, no. 1.

Hill, S. and Munday, M. (1992) 'The UK regional distribution of foreign direct investment: analysis and determinants', *Regional Studies*, vol 26, no 6.

Hood, N. and Young, S. (1982) *Multinationals in Retreat: The Scottish Experience*. Edinburgh: Edinburgh University Press.

Morris, J. (1987) 'Industrial restructuring, foreign direct investment and uneven development: the case of Wales', *Environment and Planning A*, vol. 19.

National Audit Office (1989) *Locate in Scotland*, Report by Comptroller and Auditor General, House of Commons. London: HMSO.

Roberts, P., Noon, D. and Irving, P. (1988) *Overseas Investment to the West Midlands Region*. Coleshill: West Midlands Industrial Development Association.

Welsh Affairs Committee (1988) *Inward Investment into Wales and its Interaction with Regional and EEC Policies*. London: HMSO.

Young, S. (1989) 'Scotland v Wales in the inward investment game', *Frazer of Allander Quarterly Economic Commentary*.

Young, S. Hood, N. and Hamill, J. (1988) *Foreign Multinationals and the British Economy*, London: Croom Helm.

CASE 25

GMA–MA

This case is based on GMA, one of the main French insurance groups, and its strategy for entering the Spanish market. Special emphasis is given to the possible acquisition of MA, an important Spanish insurance company, which is still independent.

The two main aspects in the case are:

1. *To become acquainted with the process of acquisition, from the moment of receiving a brief up to the final proposal of a concrete deal.*
2. *To know and evaluate the strategy of gaining control with a minority stake and following this, increases in capital.*

Introduction

GMA is one of the leading companies in the French insurance sector. It has a minimal participation in foreign markets. With a view to the Single European Market in 1993, the board of directors decided as a priority aim to widen the company's horizons abroad, and to attempt to get a foothold in Spain. The following are the special requirements:

1. The proposed strategy of implantation must bear in mind that GMA wants to enter the whole Spanish market and not just one particular sector.
2. GMA has a special interest in entering the life insurance branch and is least interested in the automobile insurance branch. However, its main interest is generally in entering the Spanish market as soon as possible by whichever route.

This was written by Oriol Amat and Xavier Puig as a basis for class discussion rather than to illustrate either effective or ineffective handling of an administrative situation. Names of the companies have been disguised. © Oriol Amat and Xavier Puig, 1995.

Structure of the Spanish Insurance Sector

The insurance sector is one of the most dynamic within the Spanish economy at present. This is due to the fact that in recent years Spanish society has adapted to the models of other developed countries. The wide differences which existed between Spain and other countries with respect to premiums per inhabitant are gradually disappearing, which would suggest a future increase in the volume of total premiums.

The rise in the sector is due not only to its quantitative growth but also to the qualitative changes in demand regarding the offer of products and services which vary according to the objectives they need to meet.

However, in spite of its attraction, entry to the Spanish market is a complex business. The sector is dominated by companies which belong to the Spanish banking sector and by multinational insurance companies. There are few possibilities of making an acquisition which will give the buyer an immediate position of importance on the market.

The case study aims to show the difficulties which would be faced on entering the insurance sector in Spain, given its structure. The report also outlines various possible strategies to gain a favourable position on the Spanish market. Exhibits 25.1–25.4 provide some information about this sector.

Structure of the Forty-five Leading Companies in the Sector

Companies Listed on the Stock Market
In Spain, insurance companies are not usually listed on the stock market. Of the few which are, it is not usually possible to buy significant blocks of shares in them.

Among the 45 companies in the previous list, several are insurance companies listed in the Madrid and/or Barcelona stock markets (see Exhibit 25.5).

Companies Controlled by Spanish Banking Groups
Excluding the companies listed on the stock market, Exhibit 25.6 shows insurance companies which are controlled by banking or national savings groups.

Companies Controlled by Multinational Groups
A third group is that of the companies controlled by international groups, shown in Exhibit 25.7.

Exhibit 25.1 *Insurance in the EC's twelve member states (distribution of premiums in percentage)*

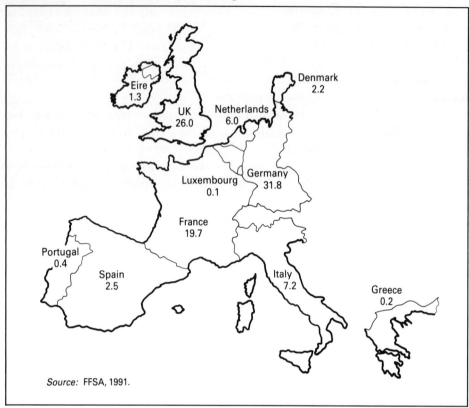

Source: FFSA, 1991.

Exhibit 25.2 *Percentage annual increase of insurance premiums in Spain*

1. Likely development with a view to 1992: 20% each year
2. 1991
    (a) Overall   20.5%
    (b) Life   31.5%
    (c) Multi-risk policy   18.3%
        (i)   Car   22%
        (ii)   Illness   15%
        (iii) Fully comprehensive   26%

Source: FFSA, 1991.

Exhibit 25.3 *Classification of the 45 leading companies in Spain in 1991*

Ranking	Companies	Parent Group	Total Premiums (Pta million)
1	Euroseguros	BBV	260.624
2	La Union Y El Fénix	Banesto	105.229
3	Grupo Vitalicio	Banco Central – Generali	101.844
4	Caser	Conf. Cajas Ahorro	64.965
5	La Estrella	Banco Hispano	55.064
6	Mapfre Mutual de Seguros	Corporacion Mapfre	43.511
7	Mutua Madrileṇa Automovil	Mutualidad	35.221
8	Catalana de Occidente	Family Group	33.098
9	Plus Ultra	Norwich Union Ins.	29.392
10	Cresa Aseguradora	Ibérica Allianz–Ras	27.563
11	Mapfre Vida	Corporacion Mapfre	27.056
12	Winterthur Seguros	Winterthur	25.454
13	Musini	INI	25.298
14	Santa Lucia	Grupo Privado	23.768
15	Uniseguros	Banco Zaragozano	23.318
16	Cenit	Banco de Santander	23.318
17	Aurora Popular	BBV	21.807
18	Nationale Nederlanden	Grupo Nederlanden Dutch Group	20.371
19	Sanitas	BUPA	19.296
20	Assicurazioni Generali	Grupo Generali	18.755
21	Ocaso	Private Group	18.502
22	Asistencia Sanitaria	Private Group	18.391
23	AGF Seguros	AGF	18.289
24	Mutua General de Seguros	Mutualidad	17.360
25	Sud America	A Sul America	16.734
26	Aegon	Aegon Group	16.332
27	Zurich	Zurich Group	15.569
28	Bilbao	NV Amev Group	15.467
29	UAP Iberica	UAP	15.111
30	Schweiz	Schweiz	14.391
31	MA	Private Group	14.060
32	Credito y Caucion	Catalana de Occidente Consorcio Compen. Seg	13.876
33	Ercos	Allianz–Ras	12.927
34	Mare Nostrum	Axa–Midi	12.916
35	Paternal Sica, LA	Axa–Midi	10.274
36	Eagle Star	Eagle Star Group	9.756
37	Dapa	Athena	9.398
38	Mapfre Industrial	Corporacion Mapfre	9.138
39	CEP Vida Seg. y Reaseg.	Caixa d'Estalvis Penedes	8.894
40	Adriatica	Allianz–Ras	8.759
41	Hércules–Hispano	Banco Exterior	8.558
42	Hispania	Zurich Group	8.430
43	Pelayo Mutua	Mutualidad	8.051
44	Union Iberoamericana	Zurich Group	8.032
45	Previasa	Private Group	7.887

Exhibit 25.4 *Structure of the 45 leading companies in the insurance sector*

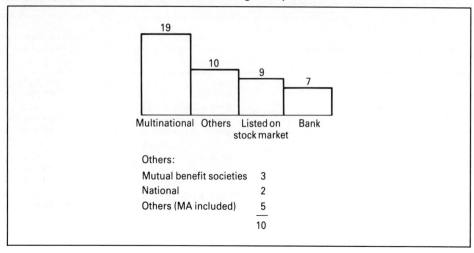

Others:

Mutual benefit societies	3
National	2
Others (MA included)	5
	10

Exhibit 25.5 *Insurance companies listed in the Madrid and/or Barcelona stock markets*

Company	Parent group	Ranking
Mapfre Mutual de Seguros[1]	Corporacion Mapfre	6
Mapfre Vida[1]	Corporacion Mapfre	11
Ercos	Allianz–Raz	33
La Estrella	Banco Hispano	5
Hércules–Hispano	Banco Exterior	41
La Unión y el Fénix	Banesto	2
Grupo Vitalicio	Banco Central–Generali	3
Catalana de Occidente	Family Group	8
Credito y Caucion[1]	Catalana de Occidente	32

1. It is the parent company which is listed on the stock market.

Exhibit 25.6 *Insurance companies controlled by banks or national savings groups*

Company	Parent group	Ranking
Euroseguros	BBV	1
Caser	Conf. Española de Cajas de Ahorro	4
Plus Ultra	BBV	9
Uniseguros	Banco Zaragozano	15
Cenit	Banco de Santander	16
Aurora Popular	BBV	17
CEP Vida Seg. y Reaseg	Caixa d'Estalvis Penedes	39

Exhibit 25.7 *Insurance companies controlled by international groups*

Company	Group	Ranking
Cresa	Allianz–Ras (Austria)	10
Winterthur	Winterthur (Switzerland)	12
Nationale Nederlanden	Dutch Group (Holland)	18
Sanitas	BUPA (UK)	19
Assicur Generali	Generali Group (Italy)	20
AGF Seguros	AGF (France)	23
Sud America	A Sul America (Brazil)	25
Aegon	Aegon Group (Holland)	26
Zurich	Zurich Group (Switzerland)	27
Bilbao	NV Amev Group (Holland)	28
UAP Iberica	UAP (France)	29
Schweiz	Schweiz (Switzerland)	30
Mare Nostrum	Axa–Midi (France)	34
Paternal Sica	Axa–Midi (France)	35
Eagle Star	Eagle Star Group (UK)	36
Dapa	Athena (France)	37
Adriatica	Allianz–Ras (Austria)	40
Hispania	Zurich Group (Switzerland)	42
Union Iberoamericana	Zurich Group (Switzerland)	44

Other Companies

Finally, the fourth group consists of companies in which mutual benefit societies, cooperatives, private and public groups have stakes. This group is shown in Exhibit 25.8

Exhibit 25.8 *Insurance companies controlled by mutual benefit societies, cooperatives, private and public groups*

Company	Created or with stakes	Ranking
Mutua Madrileña Automovil.	Mutual Benefit Society	7
Musini	INI	13
Santa Lucia	Private Group	14
Ocaso	Private Group	21
Asistencia Sanitaria	Private Group	22
Mutua General de Seguros	Mutual Benefit Society	24
MA	Private Group	31
Credito y Caucion	Catalana de Occidente Consorcio Compens. Seguros	32
Pelayo Mutua	Mutual Benefit Society	43
Previasa	Private Group	45

Strategies

The following are strategies which could be followed to enter the insurance market in Spain via the stock exchange:

1. Acquisition.
2. Collaboration agreements or joint ventures.
3. Create a new company (*ex-novo*).

Acquisition

1. Taking a controlling interest (immediate or gradual) in a medium-sized company with:
   (a) over 5 billion premiums;
   (b) an extensive geographical coverage;
   (c) a large variety of products.
2. Taking a minority interest in a large company with over 20 billion premiums.
3. Complete acquisition of the various small companies in order to create a holding company with:
   (a) fewer than 5 billion premiums;
   (b) no serious problems (accidents/technical provisions).

Bearing in mind the structure of the Spanish insurance sector, as follows:

1. companies belonging to banking groups;
2. companies belonging to multinational groups;
3. companies listed on the stock market;
4. other companies (private groups, mutual benefit societies, etc.).

Exhibit 25.9 has been drawn up to assess the best acquisition strategy.

Exhibit 25.9 *Bank acquisition strategies*

	Bank group	Multinational group	Stock market	Others
Majority %	No	No	No	Selective negotiations
Minority	Possible (direct negotiation with bank[1] improbable)	No	Yes (minority portion)	Yes
Various	n/a	n/a	n/a	n/a

Collaboration Agreements or Joint Ventures

Collaboration agreements or joint ventures might be arranged with:

1. large companies in the sector, to develop specific products (e.g. agricultural insurance);
2. one or more companies with financial or banking services with a good network of commercial branches (e.g. savings banks).

Recommended Acquisition Strategy

The controlling interest strategy is the one recommended, i.e. over 5 billion premiums. It is felt that such a strategy is possible only with regard to some of the companies listed in the group 'Others'. In particular, in this group, only one showed interest in being acquired – MA.

It would be highly unlikely that the companies which are controlled by Spanish banking groups would be prepared to yield most of their share capital. Only a minority stake would be possible following negotiations with the parent banking company.

With regard to the companies listed on the stock market (Madrid and Barcelona), the following must be observed:

1. Four of them are dominated by banking groups:
   - La Estrella   Banco Hispano
   - Hércules–Hispano   Banco Exterior
   - La Unión y el Fénix   Banesto
   - Grupo Vitalicio   Banco Central
2. Another of the companies listed on the market belongs to a foreign group:
   - Ercos   Allianz–Ras
3. The four remaining companies are controlled by non-banking Spanish groups.
   - Mapfre Mutual de Seguros
   - Corporacion Mapfre   } Mapfre Mutual Benefit Society
   - Mapfre Vida   } Private group
   - Credito y Caucion/Catalana de Occidente

If a minority stake interest is required in one of the companies listed on the stock market, it would only be technically possible in two of them:

- Corporacion Mapfre
- La Unión y el Fénix

This is because, having studied Exhibit 25.10, it can be seen that the free floating of these two companies, even though the percentages are small, make them the only companies which are in any way accessible (15.7% and 11.5% respectively).

However, according to a stockbroker firm, in three months 200,000 Mapfre shares (1.07%) and 70,000 Union y el Fénix shares (0.6%) could be bought. These acquisitions could be doubled and blocks could be bought on the stock market. This looks quite feasible, the problem being, though, that this would create buying pressure which would bring about a rise in the share price.

The most viable strategy is that of collaboration agreements or joint ventures with Spanish financial institutions with a solid commercial network. Most of these institutions do not have developed insurance products available as yet or they have only recently introduced them. They need the know-how but they already have the network. In turn, GMA has the know-how but needs a commercial network in Spain.

The big problem is that we are usually talking about an agreement with a savings bank, and this type of company usually has a local network but it is almost never on a national scale.

With regard to the possibility of creating an *ex-novo* company, this means a great deal of time is needed, with the added handicap that the present situation in the sector makes it difficult to hire good professionals.

Report on MA

Overview

Classification (1991)

- Ranking: 14th
- Market share: 1.71%
- Net turnover: Pta 21,347 million

Background

- 1936–1988: Mututal benefit society
- 1988: Limited company
- Share capital: Pta 1,761 million

Exhibit 25.10 *Data for the financial year 1991*

Stock market	Nominal value	Papers (market listed)	Adm. capital (Pta million)	Nominal value (yr. total)	Capital (Pta million)	Days quoted (%)	Nominal vol./cap. (%)	Last estimate quoted (Pta)
Mapfre Cats*	500	14,026,390	2,013	1,472,978,250	9,351	248	15.7	7,490
Ercos Madrid	1,000	1,750,000	1,750	8,338,000	1,750	10	0.4	5,000
La Estrella Barcelona/ Madrid	500	2,000,000	1,000	4,928,500	1,000	44	0.4	6,150
Hércules–Hisp. Barcelona/ Madrid	500	1,920,000	960	49,401,000	960	222	5.1	8,450
La Unión y el Fénix Cats*	500	10,080,000	5,040	582,463,500	5,040	239	11.5	6,870
Grupo Vital Barcelona	500	6,534,000	3,267	5,708,500	3,267	38	0.1	11,000
Catal. Occid. Barcelona	1,000	2,250,000	2,250	5,814,000	2,250	26	0.2	15,000

* Computer Assisted Trading System

Shareholders' Distribution

- Share capital controlled by members of the board of directors: 27%
- Share capital held by 430,000 shareholders (old mutual benefit society members): 73%
- Share capital under company control: 27%

Portfolio Structures (1991)

- Motor: 92%
- Legal defence 4.5%
- Travel insurance: 2%
- Others: 1.5% (life)

Portfolio Development

Year	Premiums	%
1988	7,919	100
1989	14,003	176.8
1990	13,489	170.3
1991	21,347	269.2

Summary (1991)

- Number of branches: 99
- Number of agents: 6,105
- Number of agents controlling 80% of portfolio: 1,176

Technical Provisions

- Insufficiency: independent firm calculation: 9,508 M.

Insurance Credit

- Sectoral average: 15%
- MA: 22.9% (1990)
     25.7% (1991)

Fixed Assets

- Balance sheet: Pta 2,400 m
- Market value estimate: Pta 6,000 m

Technical/Financial Situation

Our opinion of the technical financial situation of MA Ltd is as follows.

Fixed Assets
The tangible fixed assets represent 93.8% of the total fixed assets and
basically correspond to the value of the company's computer equipment and
furniture. The accumulated depreciation for this reaches 41.8% which, given
the speed with which computer equipment becomes technically obsolete, is
an important consideration in this context.

Total Investment in Fixed Assets
The evaluation in the balance sheet of the item 'land and buildings' amounts
to Pta 2,400 million, while its market value estimated by the company
amounts to Pta 5,846 million.
      The value in the balance sheet of 'land and buildings' related to
technical provisions is Pta 2,601 million which makes up 86% of the total.
With the object of insurance cover, the value is put at Pta 3,255 million, while
the market value would be Pta 5,406 million according to the company.

Investments
The investment in fixed interest makes up 91% of the total, which illustrates
a shrewd performance on the part of the company. It would be necessary to
know what the heading 'other investments' entails to be able to judge the
value of the remaining percentage.

Credit
An item in the company balance sheet which makes up Pta 5,572 million is
'credit against policyholders' and this is 25.7% of the total of premiums and
net increases on cancellations (net trade). In 1990, this was 22.9%, well
above the average for the sector. If we consider that this is around 15%, it
can be seen that Pta 596 million provision is too low against outstanding
premiums.

Technical Provision for Lending
The balance sheet value of this provision, contrasting with the total value
of premiums and net increases on cancellations, insurance other than
life insurance and net trade, produces the ratio of 46.5, which in 1992
was 53.4.

The technical provision for lending in the automobile branch makes up 96.6% of the total of these provisions and with regard to premiums, a ratio of 47.15 was achieved for 1991. Bearing in mind that this same ratio was 75.55 in 1990 for the automobile branch of the Spanish insurance sector, the shortfall of provisions rises to Pta 5,760 million.

A significant point is that accidents in the automobile sector in 1990 made up 82.84% of the total misadventures, while the forecasts for 1991 indicate that it has risen to 98.1%. This means that the provision ratio should rise for lending/premiums and net increases on cancellations, so that the shortfall ratio should rise. If this ratio over the accidents was maintained, the shortfall would be Pta 8,600 million.

Technical Provisions for Risks Already in Progress
The balance sheet value of this provision amounts to Pta 8,008 million, of which Pta 7,371 million corresponds to the automobile branch. The relation between this provision and the total of premiums and net increases on cancellations was, for this particular branch, 38.38% in 1990. In MA the ratio is 36.3% which means that it is below Pta 422 million.

We must indicate here that we are calculating the provision over the total of premiums and net increase on cancellations in the branch, when we know definitely that this figure should be reduced in the sum corresponding to the policies which have not been cancelled and are pending payment, and which is very high. Bearing this in mind, the shortfall for risks already in progress is around Pta 312 million.

Memorandum Accounts
This item on the balance sheet needs to be checked for its contents given that the sum is very high.

External Management Expenses
The external management expenses make up 12.8% of the total of premiums and net increases on cancellations for the financial year, which leaves them 1% higher than the average in the automobile sector.

Accident Policies
The company's accident policies in 1991 made up 80% of total premiums, while in 1990 it was 74%. This increase reflects what happened in the sector, and presumably is not due to an inadequate selection of risk policies.

Conclusions

Analysis of the technical and financial figures for MA Insurance and Reinsurance allows us to draw the following conclusions:

1. The quantity of premiums acquired by the company, over those needed to made a possible deal for a takeover of shares, must be corrected by taking into account the quantity of premiums which correspond to the policies issued and which are pending cancellation because they are unpaid.

2. The allowance of technical provisions is not sufficient. A preliminary study shows insufficiency in the following:
   (a) technical provisions for lending: Pta 5,760 million.
   (b) technical provisions for risk polices already drawn: Pta 312 million
   (c) technical provisions for premiums which are pending payment: Pta 596 million.

   Together these amount to Pta 6,668 million. If we were to consider the increase in accident policies in 1991, the insufficiency would reach Pta 9,508 million.

3. An increase in capital in the immediate future is essential for the company to cover the solvency margin which it is legally bound by.

A Strategy Proposal for the Takeover of MA

Strategic framework

The shareholding situation within MA at present is the following:

1. Members of the board of directors control 27% of the company's share capital. They are willing to jointly sell their stake if given a good offer.

2. The remaining 73% is in the hands of 430,000 shareholders, who are old mutual benefit society members. This means that the company control is in fact dependent on the purchase of the 27% block.

This peculiar distribution of shares, in which 73% is widely dispersed, means that control of the company can be taken by the purchase of the 27% block. We therefore put forward a strategy which covers two stages:

1. The acquisition of 27% of the capital.

2. An increase in capital.

Given the technical and financial situation of the company, a third stage is suggested with two aims:

1. To capitalize the company, which is essential for its future viability.
2. To increase the participation of GMA, on the assumption that due to its wide dispersion, the other shareholders will not be involved in the increase in capital. This implies that GMA will take on the cost of restructuring the company, and in exchange will gain approximately 85% of its share capital.

The final result would be a takeover of a company with a solid structure and a market share of 1.71%, which ranks it 14th among Spanish companies, according to UNESPA figures for 1991.

Strategy Costs

The figures which we will use as reference to value the cost of the suggested strategy are:

1. Initial share capital (k_0) of Pta 1,761 million.
2. Stake to be bought: $27\% \times 1,761$ million = Pta 475.5 million.
3. Total premiums and net increases of cancellations in 1991 (net trade): Pta 21,347 million.

The cost analysis will be carried out using two assumptions:

1. Insufficient provisions to cover: Pta 6,668 million.
2. Insufficient provisions to cover: Pta 9,508 million.

Insufficient Provisions to Cover: Pta 6,668 million
The increase in capital needed would be 15×1, which would be:

- possible capital to subscribe in the increase: $15 \times 1,761$ = Pta 26,415 million.
- Subscription of 27%: Pta 7,132 million.
- Share capital (very probable) following increase (k_1): $1,761\text{m} \times 7,132\text{m}$ = Pta 8,893 million.
- Final stake by GMA:

$$\frac{7,132 + 475.5}{8,893} = 85.5\%$$

Purchase of 27% at the price of Pta 1 per premium peseta. The total cost for GMA would be:

- Purchase of 27%: 27% × 21,347 m = Pta 5,764 million.
- Increase in capital costs: Pta 7,132 million.
- Total cost: 5,674 m + 7,132 m = Pta 12,896 million.

With regard to the volume of premiums this would be:

$$\frac{\text{Total cost}}{85.5\% \times \text{Premiums}} = \frac{12,896\ m}{85.5\% \times 21,347\ m} = \text{Pta}\ 0.706/\text{premium peseta}$$

Maximum price to be paid for the 27% of the capital for the average total cost of the operation is to be Pta 1 per premium peseta. The total cost will be:

$$85.5\% \times 21,347 = \text{Pta}\ 18,252\ \text{million}.$$

The cost of the increase is Pta 7,132 million so the maximum cost of the purchase of 27% will be:

$$18,252\ m - 7,132\ m = \text{Pta}\ 11,120\ \text{million}$$

In terms of the volume of premiums it will be:

$$\frac{\text{Maximum cost}}{27\% \times \text{Premiums}} = \frac{11,120\ m}{27\% \times 21.347\ m} = \text{Pta}\ 1.93/\text{premium peseta}$$

Insufficient Provisions to cover: Pta 9,508 million
The increase in capital needed would be 20 × 1 which would be:

- Capital to subscribe in the increase: 20 × 1,761 = Pta 35,220 million.
- Subscription of 27%: Pta 9,509 million.
- Share capital following the increase: 1,761m + 9,509m = Pta 11,270 million.
- Final stake by GMA:

$$\frac{9,509 + 475.5}{11,270} = 88.6\%$$

Purchase of 27% at the price of Pta 1 per premium peseta. The total cost for GMA would be:

- Purchase of 27%: 27% × 21,347m = Pta 5,764 million.
- Increase in capital costs: Pta 9,509 million.

● Total cost: 5,764m + 9,509m = Pta 15,273 million.

In terms of the volume of premiums this would be expressed as follows:

$$\frac{\text{Total cost}}{88.6\% \times \text{Premiums}} = \frac{15,273\text{ m}}{88.6\% \times 21,347\text{ m}} = \text{Pta } 0.807/\text{premium peseta}$$

Maximum price to be paid for 27% of the capital for the average total cost of the operation to be Pta 1 per premium peseta. The total cost will be:

$$88.6\% \times 21,347 = \text{Pta } 18,913 \text{ million}$$

The total cost of the increase is Pta 9,509 million, so the maximum cost of the purchase of 27% would be:

$$18,913\text{ m} - 9,509\text{ m} = \text{Pta } 9,404 \text{ million}$$

In terms of the volume of premiums this is expressed as follows:

$$\frac{\text{Maximum cost}}{27\% \times \text{Premiums}} = \frac{9,404\text{ m}}{27\% \times 21,347\text{ m}} = \text{Pta } 1.63/\text{premium peseta}$$

Final Considerations

Exhibit 25.11 summarizes the proposed strategy and its cost.

Exhibit 25.11 *Provision and premium increase considerations of acquisition*

Insufficient increase		Cost 27%	Total cost	Cost of Pta/premium	Max. 27% Pta/premium
Pta 6,668 m	7,132 m	5,764	(85.5%) 12,896 m	0.706	1.93
Pta 9,508 m	9,509 m	5,764	(88.6%) 15,273 m	0.807	1.63

This data and the alternative strategies open are sufficient to enable GMA to make a decision whether or not to make an acquisition bid for MA.

Amazonia Palm Oil Plantations

*This is a case about a development project which was in part undertaken
by a Dutch development bank. The project involves investment in palm
oil plantations and processing units in Brazil. Liquidity problems, losses
and payment arrears introduced the necessity to restructure the
company financially. Two different scenarios are under consideration.
Both scenarios would be accompanied by conversion of a loan and
considerable refinancing. The economic environment is highly
inflationary, which poses questions about international capital
budgeting. In addition, the restructuring brings out an interesting conflict
of interest between shareholders and creditors.*

Introduction

The Amazonia Corporation palm oil plantations and processing units are
located near the mouth of the Amazon River in north-eastern Brazil.
Amazonia consists of two plantations, covering a total surface of 16,125
acres. The end-products, palm oil and palm kernels, are sold predominantly
in the local market through agents. Only 15% of total production was
exported in 1990.

Amazonia was started in 1967 as an experimental project. The
Nederlandse Financierings en Ontwikkelingsmaatschappij (NFO) got
involved with Amazonia in 1976 as a shareholder (25%) and creditor. NFO
is a Dutch development bank. In 1980 an expansion took place and NFO
increased its equity and debt stakes in Amazonia. At the same the
Development Finance Corporation (DFC), a branch of a well-known
supranational organization, and the Botra Trading Group became involved.
In 1987 Botra obtained a 51% stake in Amazonia's equity. The Botra

*This case was written by Christian C.P. Wolff, on the basis of materials kindly provided by Mr
K.R.J. de Waal. The case was written as a basis for class discussion rather than to illustrate
either effective or ineffective handling of an administrative situation. For reasons of
confidentiality some names have been disguised. © Christian C.P. Wolff, University of
Limburg and Amsterdam Institute of Finance, 1993.*

Trading Group is a Brazilian conglomerate. Group turnover amounted to about US$ 350 million in 1990.

Liquidity problems, losses and payment arrears induced Botra to replace Amazonia's entire management by Botra employees in late 1990. This measure resulted in successful crisis management. The new management implemented a package of measures to restructure Amazonia's finances, including conversion of Botra loans into equity and buying off expensive short-term cruzeiro loans at a discount. The latter operation was financed through additional loans from NFO and DFC.

In 1990 NFO hired a consultant to inspect Amazonia's books. No irregularities were found and the consultant was positive. Liquidation of collateral securities as a response to Amazonia's current problems did not appear lucrative under the current circumstances. Research on the spot by one of NFO's departments, in close collaboration with DFC, led to the proposal to restructure Amazonia's finances. DFC had the program screened by one of its agricultural experts.

The Current Situation and Problems

Amazonia comprises two plantations: Partuba (9,845 acres) and Abra (6,280 acres). *Partuba* is the area where Amazonia was started. It can be reached easily by road and by boat. Two factories to extract palm oil are present, with capacities of, respectively, 20 and 10 fresh fruit bunches (FFB) per hour. The investments involve good infrastructure, about 100 houses for employees, a school, a hospital, etc. Of a total of 12,500 acres of plantation, about 2,700 acres were destroyed by the so-called yellow disease in the period 1985–89. Factory no. 2 (capacity 10 FFB/hour) was opened in 1986. This factory was in operation only for about 3 months before it was closed because of lack of fruit. It is well conserved and currently awaits a better future.

The *Abra* area was purchased in 1985. It is also easily reached by road and by water. A plantation of 6,280 acres was realized in the years 1986–90. Compared with Partuba, Abra's climatological conditions for palm oil are superior. In the vicinity of Abra, 22,000 acres of plantation were developed successfully by competitors.

Amazonia's current problems can be summarized as follows:

1. Nonproductive investments:
   (a) the Abra plantation: an investment of about $ 7 million, largely realized with internally generated funds. The first trees will soon lead to production. An oil extraction factory could not be realized and there is no alternative in the vicinity;

(b) factory no. 2 at Partuba: an investment of about $ 2.5 million, also largely internally funded. The factory is closed. The shortage of fruits follows from the destruction of considerable acreage by a disease. The purchase of fruits from outgrowers was disregarded.

2. The total plantation acreage of Partuba is about 12,500 acres of which 2,700 acres were destroyed by yellow disease. These were mainly old plants that needed replacement in any case. With the assistance of experts the disease is now under control, after years of experiments. Three more years of small-scale experimentation will take place before the lost acreage will gradually be replanted on a large scale from 1995/96.

3. Extreme drought periods in 1987, leading to reduced production in 1988 and 1990.

4. Deterioration of world market prices of palm oil from 1985. In addition to the drop in world market prices, Amazonia was hurt by the economic downturn in Brazil.

5. Liquidity problems induced the previous management to obtain unfavorable short-term cruzeiro loans with real rates of interest in the range of 24–70%. From late 1989, shareholder Botra was also forced to provide liquidity. A total of about $3.5 million of short-term cruzeiro loans were obtained. Through capitalization of interest, the amount outstanding is now about $ 7 million.

6. The previous management was weak in cost control, production efficiency, marketing and finance. Top management resided in São Paolo, far from the plantations. Communication with shareholders and creditors was insufficient.

Crisis Management

Mr Antonio Scheinkman, who had proved himself within the Botra Group, was appointed chief executive officer in late 1990. The entire board was replaced at that time. A number of measures were taken:

1. Amazonia's financial and commercial management was overhauled and important changes were implemented.

2. The number of employees was reduced by about 250. In July 1991 only 520 persons were employed by Amazonia. At the Abra area only the security guards were kept and maintenance took place only when funds were available.

3. The main office in São Paolo was closed and sold. The new management chose to operate from the Partuba plantation.
4. Measures were taken to reduce costs and increase operational efficiency.
5. The supply of management information was improved. A strategic plan was formulated for presentation to shareholders and creditors.
6. Financial restructering took place. Some loans were converted into equity. Expensive short-term cruzeiro loans were restructured with the help of NFO and DFC. Confidence of these foreign creditors was regained.
7. Nonproductive investments are to be dealt with either by selling on Abra and factory no. 2, or by completion of Abra and relocation of factory no. 2, in which latter case additional funding (equity and debt) is needed, probably from new participants.
8. Marketing was improved: geographical dispersion of customers, higher sales prices through judicious timing of sales, emphasis on starting up direct sales (rather than through agents), penetration in new market segments.
9. Cash-generating complementary activities were initiated, such as purchase of fruits from small farmers, exploitation of wood in the Abra area, transportation of fruits from Abra to Partuba, cultivation of other crops on that part of the Partuba area which will not be available for palm tree growth in the next three years.

The Market

The international market for palm oil is dominated by Malaysia and Indonesia. On December 19, 1991 a tonne of palm oil cost US$ 372 (CIF, London). At the same time a futures contract February/March 1992 traded at US$ 380. For the next five years or so a considerable increase in demand and production is anticipated. The position of Brazil as a palm oil producer is relatively modest. Per capita consumption of oils and fats is low in Brazil.

Amazonia's end-products, palm oil and palm kernels, are mostly supplied to Brazilian margarine and soap producers in the south of the country. The European market is less interesting for Amazonia because of Malaysian competition and high transportation costs. Amazonia's production is easily absorbed by the local market. In line with international trends, local consumption grows steadily because of the positive price difference with soy and favorable characteristics compared with animals fats. Amazonia's new management aims to achieve greater geographical dispersion of customers, to sell more of its products directly (i.e. not through agents) and to pick favorable moments to sell the end-products. In 1991, 80% of sales was shipped to 10 customers. The largest of these customers absorbed 30%. In 1990, 50% was sold to the largest customer and 5 companies purchased 80% of Amazonia's outputs. Depending on stocks and spot prices in the international market, Amazonia will also export its output. Currently 15–25% of total output is exported.

Sales projections are based on a net sales price ex-factory of US$ 350/metric tonne palm oil and US$ 140/metric tonne of palm kernels. Sensitivity analyses were performed at sales prices of plus and minus 10%. These sensitivity analyses correspond to the historical trend in world market prices. Despite the problems with the Brazilian economy and the dip in prices, Amazonia was able to realize an average price of US$ 350/metric tonne in 1991.

Compared with Malaysia, Amazonia's comparative advantage lies in short delivery times and the ability to supply small quantities. Customers, therefore, need not keep extensive stocks, which would result in high financing costs in Brazil. The Brazilian government actively stimulates palm oil production and consumption. Stimulation by means of tax reductions is expected in the near future.

Analysis of Amazonia's financial position and profitability

The official financial accounts of Amazonia are presented in Exhibit 26.1. The figures are in cruzeiro and are somewhat difficult to interpret. The monetary corrections in the balance sheet and the profit and loss account were implemented to reflect the impact of Brazil's extremely high inflation rate. (Some basic economic data can be found in Exhibit 26.2, which summarizes NFO's country risk assessment of Brazil.) Because of the high inflation rates and despite the monetary corrections, Amazonia's financial accounts give a distorted picture of reality.

Because of the problem sketched above, Amazonia also kept balance sheets (at least with respect to fixed assets) and profit and loss accounts in historical US dollars. Amazonia's goal is to keep financial accounts in US dollars on a monthly basis. Cash flow figures in dollars are already available. The figures in Exhibit 26.3 are all in dollars. They were not audited but do give a reasonably accurate impression of reality.

Exhibit 26.4 reports pertinent price and quantity data, including interim figures as at September and November 1991. Determining factors behind recent losses are:

Exhibit 26.1 *Amazonia Corp. financial statements: key data*

	Year-end 1991[1]	Year-end 1990	Year-end 1989
Balance sheet (Crz millions)			
Balance sheet total	19,215	2,000	197
Shareholders' equity	9,248	423	118
Working capital	−4,229	−673	−51
Profit and loss account (Crz millions)			
Gross sales	2,003	508	20
Net sales	1,701	441	19
Interest expense[2]	8,644	1,420	67
Monetary correction[3]	11,522	583	66
Net income	3,223	−694	7
Exchange rates			
Crz/US$	1,068	170	11.3
Crz/DFl	625	100	5.9
Treasury bill rates (3 month)			
Brazil	15.3%	26.2%	34.0%
Netherlands	9.5%	9.3%	8.9%
USA	4.0%	6.7%	7.8%

1. Estimate.
2. Including exchange losses on foreign currency loans and inflation effects on local loans.
3. Difference between monetary corrections on fixed assets and on shareholders' equity.

Exhibit 26.2 *NFO country risk assessment: Brazil, December 1991*

Indicators	3-year average[1]	Est. 1991	Est. 1992	Qualification
Balance of payments/external debt				Weak
Current account/GDP[2]	0.3%	0.2%	0.2%	
Exports of goods/GDP	8.0%	7.6%	8.5%	
Int. reserves/imp. of goods	5.9 mo.	4.9 mo.	4.5 mo.	
Gross external debt/GDP	27.3%	24.5%	24.3%	
Gross external debt/exports	305.0%	281.5%	249.6%	
Debt service ratio[2]	32.7%	35.3%	32.5%	
Net interest/exports	18.8%	19.3%	20.2%	
Macroeconomic policy				Unacceptable
Government surplus/GDP	−3.5%	−0.5%	n.a.	
Inflation	1,484%	250%	130%	
Real economy				Weak
Real economic growth	−0.5%	−2.0%	1.5%	
Fixed investment/GDP	24.4%	25.6%	25.9%	
Political and social situation				Weak
OVERALL ASSESSMENT[3]				UNACCEPTABLE

1. Yearly average over the period 1988–90.
2. Excluding short-term debt.
3. At the same time Institutional Investor rated Brazil 26.5 out of 100, ranking the country 66th of 113 nations, behind Uruguay (31.2) and before Costa Rica (22.5). Euromoney rating: 3.57 out of 10. Ranked 81st of 126 countries, behind Jamaica (3.70) and before Ecuador (3.44).

Exhibit 26.3 *Amazonia Corp. financial statements: key data*

Year-end	1991	1990	1989
Balance sheet (US$000)			
Balance sheet total	18,606	18,660	18,635
Fixed assets (net)	17,758	17,511	16,895
Shareholders' capital	9,789	11,801	11,470
Debt financing	7,876	6,354	6,798
of which:			
NFO/DFC	1,835	1,590	1,852
Local banks	1,943	3,366	3,698
Botra	4,098	1,398	1,248
	7,876	6,354	6,798
Profit and loss account (US$000)			
	1990	1989	
Net sales	5,793	8,413	
Interest expense	2,944	2,433	
Net income	−2,012	331	
Cash flow	−1,513	1,064	

Exhibit 26.4 *Amazonia Corp.: price and quantity data*

	Est. 1991	Nov. 1991	Sept. 1991	1990	1989	1988
Palm oil production (tonnes)	11,996	10,972	8,509	13,431	15,248	12,630
Palm kernels (tonnes)	n/a	n/a	2,148	3,435	3,882	3,212
Sales palm oil (tonnes)	n/a	n/a	9,737	14,778	17,379	12,176
Sales palm kernels (tonnes)	n/a	n/a	2,011	3,437	3,865	2,959
Sales price palm oil (US$/tonne)	350	345	353	334	380	447
Sales price kernels (US$/tonne)	n/a	144	108	n/a	n/a	n/a
Costs/tonne palm oil[1]	n/a	n/a	301	n/a	n/a	n/a

1. Excluding financing costs, but including kernel revenues (by-product).

1. The downward trend in production volume in 1990 and 1991 because of insufficient fertilization, due to liquidity problems, and the effects of earlier droughts.
2. Reduced sales prices, which appear to be picking up again.
3. Extremely high interest charges on local cruzeiro loans including those obtained from Botra.

Amazonia's reconstruction measures during 1991, including extra costs due to reorganization, release of personnel, writing off bad debts and settlement with the tax office, will take effect in 1992. The total reconstruction cost incurred amount to US$300,000–400,000. This amount had an impact on the 1991 cost price per tonne of palm oil.

Amazonia's financial position transpiring from the dollar-based figures is reasonably good. An independent consultant provided an estimate of the total value of Amazonia's assets of $19.5 million. Amazonia's management estimate its value at about $25 million.

Prospects and Plans for the Future

Two scenario's for Amazonia's future are considered by the management:

Scenario 1   Sale of the Abra plantation and factory no. 2. The combined market values are estimated to amount to about $8.0 million. Because of current economic conditions in Brazil, it would probably take 1–3 years to effect the sale. The proceeds would be used in part to reduce bank loans of about $3.85 million. Amazonia would continue operations on a smaller scale. The area of the Partuba plantation that was destroyed by yellow disease would be replanted from 1996 onwards. This investment can be financed out of cash flow.

Scenario 2   Continuation of Abra and relocation of factory no. 2 from Partuba to Abra. Under this scenario the destroyed Partuba area would also be replanted. Total investments amount to about $6 million over the period 1991–94.

Both scenarios would be accompanied by:

1. Conversion of the entire Botra loan (about $4.9 million at the end of 1991) into equity. In 1991 about $0.8 million interest was paid on the loan.
2. Reconstruction of NFO/DFC loans totalling about $2.2 million (NFO: $1.3 million) at the end of December 1991. Repayment in 5 years; 1992 is grace period. Interest will be revised to conform to market conditions.
3. It is suggested that the expensive short-term cruzeiro loans of about US$1.86 million be refinanced with NFO/DFC loans at a discount of 40%. Because the reconstruction will probably be effected in March 1992, the cruzeiro loans will increase to about US$2.1 million in March through capitalization of interest. The projections

calculate with refinancing to the extent of US$1.3 million (40% discount). NFO and DFC have offered to convert the remaining $0.85 million into equity on the same terms as the Botra loan. In addition to a reduction of principal of $0.85 million, this operation would save Amazonia about $1 million in interest payments over the period 1992–94.

4. Appraisal of all fixed assets, possibly followed by revaluation.

Exhibit 26.5 provides data on Amazonia's capital structure before and after conversion, both in cruzeiro and US dollars.

Exhibit 26.5 *Amazonia Corp.: capital structure before and after conversion (December 31, 1991)*

	Amounts in cruzeiros (000)[1]			Amounts in dollars (000)[1]	
	Before conversion	Conversion[2]	After conversion	Before conversion	After conversion
Equity	9,248,303	6,072,367	15,320,670	8,659	14,345
Capital increase NFO/DFC[3]		106,800	106,800		100
Total equity	9,248,303	6,179,167	15,427,470	8,659	14,445
Botra loan[4]	5,279,443	−5,279,443	0	4,943	0
Bank loans[5]	1,982,311	−1,982,311	0	1,856	0
NFO loan	1,359,994	690,528	2,050,522	1,273	1,920
DFC loan	982,503	498,859	1,481,362	920	1,387
Total debt[6]	9,604,251	−6,072,367	3,531,884	8,993	3,307
Total debt + equity	18,852,554	106,800	18,959,354	17,652	17,752

Distribution of shares	Before conversion		After conversion	
	%	No. shares × 1,000	%	No. shares × 1,000
Botra	50.95	111,869	63.14	237,198
NFO	16.26	35,689	14.20	53,349
DFC	9.61	21,099	9.11	34,209
Others	23.18	50,889	13.55	50,889

1. Exchange rate Crz 1,068/US$.
2. The intrinsic value per share remains the same before and after the conversion.
3. NFO and DFC each put up additional equity capital of $100,000 consisting of:
   - an effective payment of $50,000;
   - a reconstruction fee of $50,000 to be paid in shares by Botra.
4. The Botra loan is converted into equity.
5. Bank loans are refinanced (60%) pro-rata by NFO and DFC.
6. Increase of short-term loans in the period January–March 1992 is not taken into account.

In Exhibits 26.6 and 26.7 cash flow projections as prepared by NFO for scenario 1 and scenario 2, respectively, are presented in dollar terms. These tables include net present value (NPV) calculations and sensitivity analyses. Under scenario 1 it is assumed that Abra will be sold in 1994. Revenues and costs pertaining to Abra have not been included in Exhibit 26.6.

NFO has calculated NPVs using an annual discount rate of 12%. This percentage corresponds to the market rate on foreign dollar-denominated loans. Only operational cash flows (cash flow + interest − investments) are discounted, excluding initial investments and residual values which are assumed to cancel because of continuous reinvestment. Sensitivity analyses were undertaken with variations of plus and minus 10% on the base sales price of palm oil.

Continuation of Partuba without Abra would lead to considerable replantation investments from 1996 onwards, after repayment of loans. Because of this and because of the reduced productivity of older, healthy palm trees, liquidity and profitability will worsen in the years 1997–2005 under scenario 1. The problem of reduced productivity can be addressed by continuing Abra. From 1993 this area will be fully productive. Considerable investment in replacing factory 2, however, renders scenario 2 relatively risky.

NFO's Position

Amazonia is one of the oldest projects in NFO's portfolio. NFO got involved with Amazonia in 1976. At the end of 1987 the first payment arrears occurred. From 1988 onwards, Amazonia has not met its obligations at all, apart from several small payments.

NFO granted loans to Amazonia in 1976 (loan 1) and 1980 (loan 2). Loan 1 involved an original principal of DFl 2.85 million at an interest rate of 5% annually. The original principal of loan 2 was DFl 2.0 million at 9.5% interest. At the end of 1991 NFO was owed about DFl 2.24 million, including remaining principal, interest and penalties. NFO and DFC loans are essentially mortgages on fixed Partuba assets (on equal terms, pro-rata).

NFO's current equity holdings in Amazonia consist of 5.59 million ordinary shares (corresponding to 6.47% of Amazonia's ordinary share capital and 2.55% of total equity). In addition, NFO holds 30.10 million preference shares (38.06% of total preferred stock and 13.71% of total equity), which do not carry voting rights. Because of the extremely inflationary environment the face value of the shares was dropped in April 1988. On March 31, 1991 an independent expert valued NFO's ordinary stock at DFl 429,000 and NFO's preferred stock at DFl 2.31 million.

Exhibit 26.6 Amazonia's cash flows: scenario 1 – Partuba with replantation/without Abra and factory no. 2 (US$ thousands)

Year	1992	1993	1994	1995	1996	1997	1998	1999	2000	2001	2002	2003	2004	2005
Net sales	5,070	5,074	4,785	4,646	4,554	4,762	3,934	3,598	3,285	3,032	2,951	2,987	3,230	3,596
− Costs, expenses	−3,444	−3,456	−3,409	−3,316	−3,314	−3,261	−3,145	−3,141	−3,118	−3,315	−3,146	−3,194	−3,050	−3,283
Operating profit	1,626	1,618	1,376	1,330	1,240	1,001	789	457	167	−283	−195	−207	180	313
− Depreciation	700	700	700	700	700	700	700	700	700	700	700	700	700	700
− Interest	315	315	236	0	0	0	0	0	0	0	0	0	0	0
Net profit before tax	611	603	440	630	540	301	89	−243	−533	−983	−895	−907	−520	−187
− Tax 35%	214	211	154	221	189	105	31	0	0	0	0	0	0	0
Net profit	397	392	286	410	351	196	58	−243	−533	−983	−895	−907	−520	−187
Cash flow	1,097	1,092	986	1,110	1,051	896	758	457	167	−283	−195	−207	180	313
Sale of Abra and factory 2			4,700											
Total cash-in	1,097	1,092	5,686	1,110	1,051	896	758	457	167	−283	−195	−207	180	313
− Investments	368	242	283	372	524	647	832	826	801	893	872	738	675	686
− Repayment loans	0	856	2,569	0	0	0	0	0	0	0	0	0	0	0
Cash balance	729	−6	2,834	738	527	249	−74	−369	−634	−1,176	−1,067	−945	−495	−373
Cumulative cash	729	723	3,557	4,295	4,822	5,071	4,996	4,627	3,993	2,817	1,750	805	310	−63
Sensitivity analysis														
Net profit base sales 100%	397	392	286	410	351	196	58							
− sales 110%	727	722	597	711	647	473	314							
90%	68	62	−39	108	55	−125	−304							
Cash balance base sales 100%	729	−6	2,834	738	527	249	−74							
− sales 110%	1,059	324	3,145	1,039	823	526	182							
90%	400	−336	2,510	436	231	−72	−436							
Cumulative cash base sales 100%	729	723	3,557	4,295	4,822	5,071	4,996							
− sales 110%	1,059	1,383	4,528	5,567	6,390	6,916	7,098							
90%	400	64	2,574	3,009	3,240	3,168	2,731							
Calculation NPV[1]														
− CF (Cash flow + Interest − Investment)	1,044	1,165	939	738	527	249	−74	−369	−634	−1,176	−1,067	−945	−495	−373
Palm oil price US$/TO NPV														
110% 385 | 4,818 | CF 110%	1,374	1,495	1,250	1,039	823	526	182	−50	−306	−873	−772	−646	−172	−74
100% 350 | 2,527 | CF 100%	1,044	1,165	939	738	527	249	−74	−369	−634	−1,176	−1,067	−945	−495	−373
90% 315 | 118 | CF 90%	715	835	615	436	231	−72	−436	−729	−963	−1,479	−1,362	−1,244	−818	−733

1. NPV calculation based on period 1992–2010.

Exhibit 26.7 Amazonia's cash flows: scenario 2 – Partuba with replantation/with Abra (US$ thousands)

Year	1992	1993	1994	1995	1996	1997	1998	1999	2000	2001	2002	2003	2004	2005
Net sales	6,406	6,784	7,374	7,857	8,289	8,228	7,954	7,618	7,214	6,891	6,763	6,524	6,498	6,637
− Costs, expenses	−4,583	−5,141	−5,331	−5,321	−5,385	−5,312	−5,195	−5,192	−5,168	−5,368	−5,181	−5,210	−4,956	−5,129
Operating profit	1,823	1,643	2,043	2,545	2,904	2,916	2,759	2,426	2046	1,526	1,582	1,314	1,542	1,508
− Depreciation	700	850	1,000	1,000	1,000	1,000	1,000	1,000	1,000	1,000	1,000	1,000	1,000	1,000
− Interest	435	555	584	481	367	252	216	180	144	108	72	36	12	0
Net profit before tax	688	238	459	1,064	1,537	1,664	1,543	1,246	902	418	510	278	530	808
− Tax 35%	241	83	161	372	538	582	540	436	316	146	179	91	186	283
Net profit	447	155	298	691	999	1,082	1,003	810	586	272	332	181	345	525
Cash flow	1,147	1,005	1,298	1,691	1,999	2,082	2,003	1,810	1,586	1,272	1,332	1,181	1,345	1,225
New local funds for Abra														
− Local long-term loans	1,000	1,000	1,000											
− Equity	2,000													
Total cash-in	4,147	2,005	2,298	1,691	1,999	2,082	2,003	1,810	1,586	1,272	1,332	1,181	1,345	1,225
− Investments	3,966	750	1,277	469	568	792	952	947	941	1,009	1,068	896	894	974
− Repayment loans	0	956	1,056	1,156	1,156	300	300	300	300	300	300	200	100	0
Cash balance	181	299	−35	66	275	990	751	563	345	−37	−37	85	351	251
Cumulative cash	181	480	445	511	786	1,776	2,527	3,090	3,435	3,393	3,361	3,446	3,796	4,047

Sensitivity analysis

Net profit	1992	1993	1994	1995	1996	1997	1998
base sales 100%	447	155	298	691	999	1,082	1,003
− sales 110%	864	596	778	1,202	1,538	1,616	1,520
90%	31	−440	−278	181	460	547	486

Cash balance	1992	1993	1994	1995	1996	1997	1998
base sales 100%	181	299	−35	66	275	990	751
− sales 110%	598	740	444	577	814	1,524	1,268
90%	−235	−296	−612	−445	−264	455	234

Cumulative cash	1992	1993	1994	1995	1996	1997	1998
base sales 100%	181	480	445	511	786	1,776	2,527
110%	598	1,337	1,782	2,359	3,172	4,697	5,965
90%	−235	−531	−1,143	−1,588	−1,852	−1,397	−1,163

Calculation NPV[1]

− CF (Cash flow + Interest − Investment)	1992	1993	1994	1995	1996	1997	1998	1999	2000	2001	2002	2003	2004	2005
	−2,384	810	605	1,704	1,798	1,542	1,267	1,043	789	371	366	321	463	251

Palm oil price US$/TO NPV[1]

			1992	1993	1994	1995	1996	1997	1998	1999	2000	2001	2002	2003	2004	2005
110%	385	7,594	CF 110%	−1,967	1,251	1,085	2,214	2,337	2,076	1,784	1,538	1,258	819	775	745	885	683
100%	350	4,106	CF 100%	−2,384	810	605	1,704	1,798	1,542	1,267	1,043	789	371	366	321	463	251
90%	315	336	CF 90%	−2,800	215	29	1,193	1,254	1,007	750	548	320	−172	−162	−234	−2	−180

1. NPV calculation based on period 1992–2010.

If NFO were to liquidate its interest in Amazonia, the nonvoting character of a large portion of its stock would be a hindrance. Under the current circumstances the preferred stock would not be an interesting portfolio investment to third parties. The very poor economic climate in Brazil does not attract many investors, foreign or local. A recession, currency transfer problems with the Central Bank and very high real rates of interest characterize the current economic environment. In this context it does not appear well-timed to liquidate stock or to execute the mortgage on Partuba. Restructuring Amazonia's operations and finances (together with DFC) is NFO's current goal. Cooperation from the Botra Trading Group is a necessary condition to realize this goal.

PART 3

Risk Management

Risk Management

Introduction

The first few years of the 1990s have seen continuing instability of foreign exchange rates as well as their short-term volatility. It has given rise to the development of financial instruments to hedge against adverse movements which can damage profit margins in international transactions and investment flows. The instability is now more acute as the result of the collapse of the European Exchange Rate Mechanism and the widening of its permitted fluctuation bands.

Most of the cases presented in this section are concerned with perception of currency risk by companies and their strategy and measures taken to avoid it, including the adoption of hedging instruments with a contractual base. There is just one case which is not company-focused. That case is by Keith Redhead and examines basis risk in futures and options contracts.

The first of the company-focused cases is written by Donald Lessard and Ahmad Rahnema and concerns the Spanish food company Ibersnacks, SA. Issues are raised about the cost and risk of financing in foreign currency and the impact of exchange rate movements on the operating profitability of the firm. The case considers the relationship between financial and operating risk and helps understand choice between risk and return.

H. Lee Remmers looks at financial risk management in the context of a hypothetical airline, Euroair. Companies that trade internationally could be in the business of currency trading as well as their product/service business. The extent to which currency trading is added to the core activities depends upon attitudes towards risk. Choosing the wrong strategy can result in losses, which may be actual or opportunity losses. The choice between hedging instruments, for example, forwards versus options, is seen to have considerable importance for company performance.

The next case, by Elroy Dimson and Paul Marsh, examines Hallgarten Wines, a UK importer buying wines priced in Deutschmarks and French francs. Hallgarten reprints its price list annually and between reprints is susceptible to changes in the price of wine, including changes arising from exchange rate movements. Hallgarten has a requirement to measure its currency exposure and then decide on risk management techniques, possibly hedging with currency options and futures.

Evi Kaplanis and Antonio Mello consider a Swedish high-technology company, Svenska Neuhaus. This company anticipates a future receipt of sterling and is considering whether and how to hedge this exposure. Techniques available include the forward market and the money markets. An alternative would be to use the Deutschmark as a proxy for the Swedish krona and to hedge with futures or options.

Jaguar Cars has always had exposure to variable exchange rates as such a large proportion of the company's UK luxury car production is sold overseas, mainly in the USA. Evi Kaplanis and Mike Staunton look at Jaguar's currency hedging strategy in the late 1980s, in particular selling currency forward. The hedging policy of arch-rival Porsche is compared and it is noted that Porsche has less aversion to options than Jaguar but continues to use the currency forward market.

In the final study, which focuses on the markets for hedging corporate risks, Keith Redhead considers the efficiency of hedging with currency (and stock index) futures in the case where changes occur in the difference between (cash market) price and the corresponding futures price (called 'basis'). Such changes in basis can occur as a result of price changes. Illustrations are provided which give a methodology for calculating the number of contracts required which provide an improved hedge.

Ibersnacks, SA

This case examines the issues associated with the cost and risk of financing in foreign currency and raises questions regarding the impact of exchange rate movements on the operating profitability of the firm. It addresses the question as to whether foreign currency financing is risk-increasing or risk-reducing. The case considers the relationship between financial and operating risk and helps to consolidate understanding of choices involving risk and return.

In early August 1992, Javier Pérez, the CFO of Ibersnacks, a Spanish firm that produces and sells sweet and salty snack foods throughout Spain, was considering how to finance a substantial increase in working capital associated with a new line of products to be distributed through supermarkets and other wholesale channels.

With the gradual opening of the Spanish money markets, and the increasing sophistication of Spanish banks, he faced a much wider range of choices than the traditional peseta loan at a rate that was neither strictly fixed nor strictly floating, but adjusted sporadically in line with market movements.

Company Background

Ibersnacks, SA, is one of Spain's largest producers and distributors of a wide array of sweet and salty snack foods. Ibersnacks products are sold through an extensive field salesforce. The company's sales organization consists of 1,300 salespeople who cover approximately 200,000 accounts throughout the Spanish territory.

Ibersnacks has many competitors within its industry (see Exhibit 27.1). Some offer a broad range of other food products, and some have

This case was written by D.R. Lessard and A. Rahnema as a basis for class discussion rather than to illustrate either effective or ineffective handling of an administrative situation. © IESE, 1993.

Exhibit 27.1 *Spanish snack foods market in 1991 (Pta millions)*

Company	Sales	Market share	Origin
Productos Pepsico	26,500	28.2%	USA
Ibersnacks	21,500	22.9%	Spain
Borges	11,000	11.7%	Spain
Unichips–Crecspan	7,800	8.3%	Italy
KP Larios	5,500	5.9%	UK
Cohesol–Importaco	5,000	5.3%	Spain
Representaciones Mirasir	5,000	5.3%	Spain
Comercial Levantina de Frutos Secos	3,000	3.2%	Spain
Almenderas Llopis	2,500	2.7%	Spain
Coop. Uteco Castellón	2,300	2.4%	Spain
Productos Churruca	2,200	2.3%	Spain
Other	1,700	1.8%	Spain

substantially large financial resources. The principal competitors are Spanish companies that produce and sell their products almost entirely in the local market. However, over the past few years, several companies from other EU member countries and a US multinational had entered to the Spanish market by taking over local firms.

Relative competitive strength is dependent upon distribution capacity, range of product, retailers' mark-up, brand image, quality and reliability. Price is the most important competitive factor when all other considerations are equal, and price reductions usually accompany improvements in production costs.

While labour is 100% local, Ibersnacks uses local and imported raw materials in the manufacture of its products. Many of the raw materials are imported or their prices are determined in currencies other than the Spanish peseta (see Exhibit 27.2).

Exhibit 27.2 *Cost structure of Ibersnacks*

Component	Percentage of total prod. cost	Percentage imported	Price currency
Raw materials:			
Potatoes	30	75	DM
Dry nuts	25	50	US$
Plastics packaging material	10	–	US$
Edible oils	5	50	US$
Labour	20	–	Pta
Manufacturing overheads	10	–	Pta

Ibersnacks' records since 1989 had been outstanding. Sales had increased by about 20% annually and reached Pta 21,500 million in 1991 as the company pursued its goal of increased market share.

Net income reached Pta 1,201 million and return on equity increased to 19% (see Exhibits 27.3 and 27.4 for financial information).

Exhibit 27.3 *Ibersnacks, SA: profit and loss account (Pta millions)*

	1989	1990	1991
Sales	15,159	17,846	21,474
Cost of sales	11,415	13,473	16,148
Gross margin	3,744	4,373	5,326
Marketing and selling expenses	1,198	1,588	2,114
General and administrative expenses	834	939	1,094
Financial expenses	247	309	414
Other expenses	156	184	221
Income before taxes	1,309	1,353	1,483
Provision income taxes	246	257	282
Net income	1,063	1,096	1,201

Exhibit 27.4 *Ibersnacks, SA: balance sheet (Pta millions)*

	1989	1990	1991
Assets			
Cash	115	126	140
Accounts receivable	2,465	2,983	3,654
Inventories	2,354	2,852	3,327
Other current assets	996	1,110	1,241
Total current assets	5,930	7,071	8,362
Fixed assets (net)	3,668	4,875	5,833
Total assets	9,598	11,946	14,195
Liabilities and equity			
Short-term borrowings	1,719	1,911	2,303
Accounts payable	1,650	1,787	2,012
Income taxes payable	240	275	321
Accrued liabilities	82	181	293
Total current liabilities	3,691	4,154	4,929
Long-term debt	1,892	2,681	2,954
Common equity	1,869	1,869	1,869
Retained earnings	1,315	2,411	3,612
Total liabilities and equity	9,598	11,946	14,195

Management's goals include annual sales growth of 20%, nearly twice the growth rate of the market served. The growth is largely self-financed, based on a target return of 20%, a willingness to use debt and a policy of paying no dividend. Sales are invoiced in the local currency, with a collection period of 60 days.

The Financing Decision

In August 1992, Pérez was considering how to finance a Pta 50 million request for additional working capital needed for the introduction of a new line of product. After discussing the issue in the board meeting, Pérez decided to explore different financing alternatives. On the following day he contacted his bank and expressed Ibersnacks' interest in raising funds for covering its working capital needs in any currency if the price was reasonable. He requested that the bank prepare a formal offer.

Two days later, Pérez received an offer from his bank. In addition to the possibility of borrowing in pesetas, his bank offered the following possibilities:

1. US dollar, Deutschmark, or any other major world currency on a three month floating basis at LIBOR + 75 basis points (bps).
2. Peseta on a three month floating basis at MIBOR + 50 bps.

Pérez recalled from his studies that it was risky for a firm to borrow in a currency other than its own, but also recognized that with a gap of about 9% between the dollar and peseta interest rates, he could gain a major competitive advantage by availing himself of the cheaper finance. Further, he knew that some of his major competitors, subsidiaries of US, UK or Italian firms, often financed local operations in currencies other than the peseta. (Current interest rates are shown in Exhibit 27.5.)

In order to make a final decision, Pérez reviewed the historical development of interest rates and exchange rates in major currencies as well as commentary on currency movements in the Spanish and international press. Pérez noted that views on where the peseta would go over the next few months against most major currencies were mixed. With an appreciation of about 10% over the last three months, the peseta had been strengthening against the US dollar while weakening against the major currencies of the European Monetary System (see Exhibit 27.6). Some experts, including Spanish senior politicians and business organizations' officials, stated publicly that the Banco de España policy to maintain a strong peseta in the European Monetary System (EMS) was damaging the competitiveness of

Exhibit 27.5 *Interest rate for major currencies 1992*

		3-month LIBOR					3-month MIBOR
	US$	DM	£	FFr	Lit	ECU	pta
January	4.07	9.48	10.62	9.86	11.72	10.32	12.88
February	4.07	9.57	10.36	9.94	11.74	10.24	12.75
March	4.34	9.68	10.61	10.01	11.83	10.13	12.57
April	4.13	9.72	10.62	9.93	11.92	10.04	12.55
May	3.92	9.75	10.08	9.81	11.97	10.11	12.50
June	3.95	9.71	9.96	9.99	12.99	10.42	12.62
July	3.45	9.75	10.16	10.13	15.15	10.74	12.95
August[1]	3.38	9.81	10.19	10.31	15.00	10.98	13.25

1. As of 14 August 1992.

the Spanish economy; and hence, they called for a devaluation of the peseta. They argued that Spain's failure to devalue to offset its higher cumulative inflation relative to its key trading partners had increased the price of domestic inputs in foreign currency terms to the point that it was virtually impossible for Spanish business to remain competitive, despite greater productivity, wage moderation, innovation, etc.

However, there was substantial disagreement over the degree, if any, of overvaluation of the peseta. Those that argued it was overvalued noted that from 1985 – just prior to the entrance to the EC – to July 1992, the consumer price index (CPI) of Spain had a cumulative inflation differential of 18.9% relative to the CPI of the other EC countries. Taking into account that the peseta appreciated 1.4% within this period against the other EC currencies, Spanish total loss of competitiveness had been 20.3%: a significant figure for exporters to bear, or for national companies to fight against foreign competition.

Others, including key government economic officials, however, noted this calculation was misleading since the CPI includes goods and services that are not traded internationally. Using an industrial price index, they pointed out, the inflation differential of Spain with respect to the other EC countries from 1985 to July 1992 had been only 0.7%. Adding to this figure the aforementioned 1.4% appreciation resulted in only a 2.1% loss in competitiveness, a figure well within the reach of Spanish firms.

The government, using the industrial price index, argued that a loss of competitiveness of 2.1% within seven years was not alarming; but those who dealt with, for example, the tourism industry, considered the accumulated differential inflation of 20.3% to be much too high.

Exhibit 27.6   *Spanish peseta appreciation against major currencies, exchange rates and volatility, May–August 1992 (Pta per unit of foreign currency)*

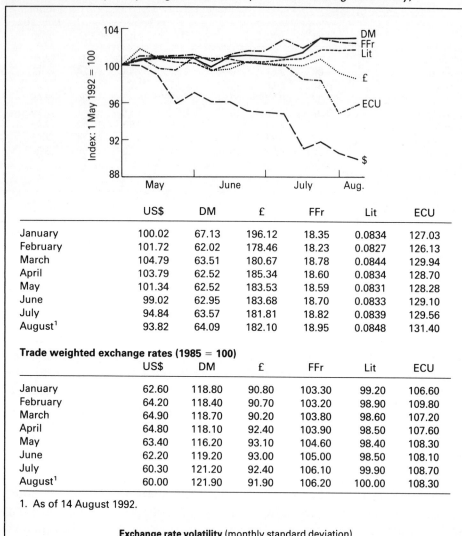

	US$	DM	£	FFr	Lit	ECU
January	100.02	67.13	196.12	18.35	0.0834	127.03
February	101.72	62.02	178.46	18.23	0.0827	126.13
March	104.79	63.51	180.67	18.78	0.0844	129.94
April	103.79	62.52	185.34	18.60	0.0834	128.70
May	101.34	62.52	183.53	18.59	0.0831	128.28
June	99.02	62.95	183.68	18.70	0.0833	129.10
July	94.84	63.57	181.81	18.82	0.0839	129.56
August[1]	93.82	64.09	182.10	18.95	0.0848	131.40

Trade weighted exchange rates (1985 = 100)

	US$	DM	£	FFr	Lit	ECU
January	62.60	118.80	90.80	103.30	99.20	106.60
February	64.20	118.40	90.70	103.20	98.90	109.80
March	64.90	118.70	90.20	103.80	98.60	107.20
April	64.80	118.10	92.40	103.90	98.50	107.60
May	63.40	116.20	93.10	104.60	98.40	108.30
June	62.20	119.20	93.00	105.00	98.50	108.10
July	60.30	121.20	92.40	106.10	99.90	108.70
August[1]	60.00	121.90	91.90	106.20	100.00	108.30

1. As of 14 August 1992.

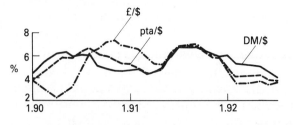

Exchange rate volatility (monthly standard deviation)

Other observers argued that the peseta would fall against other major currencies once the German Bundesbank reduced its interest rate; indeed, they argued that although the peseta was already overvalued on entering the EMS in June 1989, the authorities were in no position to bring the exchange rate to a more sustainable level until recently. In their opinion, Spanish monetary policy suffered the paradox of being 'too credible'. The deflationary policy of the Banco de España inevitably meant high interest rates; and financial markets, believing that price stability (and thus a stable currency) would be achieved eventually in Spain, found the peseta extremely attractive.

According to these observers, the prevailing tension in the Exchange Rate Mechanism as a result of Denmark's unexpected rejection of the Maastrich Treaty on monetary union in a referendum on 2 June, and uncertainty over the results of the 20 September Maastrich referendum in France, provided an excellent opportunity for the Spanish authorities to adjust the exchange rate. The hopefully more realistic perception of the exchange rate risk in the peseta would make it easier for the Banco de España to pursue its fight against inflation.

In choosing among these financing alternatives, a number of considerations seemed pertinent. Ibersnacks' present and future need for funds, the 'cost' of the principal alternatives under different future scenarios, the report of the tax treatment of foreign exchange gains and losses (see Exhibit 27.7), and the possibility of taking advantage of the low dollar rate without fully exposing the company to a potential devaluation of the peseta against the dollar were issues meriting careful thought. This, the first foreign exchange financing of Ibersnacks, could set a precedent that would influence future financing decisions.

Exhibit 27.7   *Spanish tax system*

Corporate Rates
The current corporate tax rate on ordinary income is 35%. However, the income of non-resident entities operating in Spain without a permanent establishment is taxed at a rate of 25%.

Spanish legislation treats capital gains as normal income taxable at the regular 35% corporate tax rate. Capital gains realized by non-resident entities are also taxed at this rate.

Loss Relief
Tax losses may be carried forward and offset against future taxable income for a period of five fiscal years. No provision is made for the carryback of tax losses.

Exhibit 27.7 *continued*

Foreign Exchange Gains and Losses

Foreign currency transactions are accounted for in pesetas at the rate of exchange prevailing at the transaction date. Exchange gains and losses arising on settlement of balances are taken to profit and loss account when they arise.

Balances receivable and payable in foreign currency at year-end are expressed in pesetas at the rate of exchange prevailing at year-end. Unrealized foreign exchange losses, determined for groups of currencies with similar maturity or market trends, are charged to expenses, while unrealized exchange gains, similarly determined, are deferred.

Exceptionally, unrealized foreign exchange losses incurred prior to 1990 when new accounting principles came into force, are capitalized as assets and amortized on a straight-line basis over a period of three years, or permitted by regulations designed to comply with the new accounting principles.

If Foresight were as Clear as Hindsight . . .

Managing Currency Fluctuations

This case argues that internationally-trading companies have to make up their minds what business they are in – their product/service business alone or currency trading as well. It is suggested that there is a middle ground to these stark alternatives. It involves any number of currency hedging alternatives. Through the medium of a theoretical airline case study, EuroAir, the case explores several strategies. Which of them is best depends on the taste of EuroAir's management and shareholders for risk.

Imagine this company's predicament. Costs have risen sharply. Volume has fallen dramatically. Competition is more cut-throat than ever. Profit margins are razor-thin and may well disappear. New equipment costing $100 million or more per unit has been ordered in such huge amounts that not only its management and bankers, but also the national government, wonder where the funds will be found to pay for it. Yet management knows that the firm cannot survive without investing heavily. What is this company? Easy. Any major airline today. Is this a risky business? Must be one of the most.

If they do not have enough risks already, many airlines face yet another: unpredictable currency fluctuations. The airlines are to a large degree a dollar business. Fuel is priced in dollars; on many international routes, American carriers price aggressively – and in dollars; aircraft, spares and much auxiliary equipment is priced in dollars. Currency risk is an especially serious problem for European airlines which have been committing billions of dollars to modernize their fleets. If the dollar were to appreciate significantly, the equipment on order will cost a lot more Deutschmarks, pounds, francs or pesetas.

This was written by H. Lee Remmers as a basis for class discussion rather than to illustrate either effective or ineffective handling of an administrative situation. © European Management Journal, *1991.*

Many 'experts' believe the dollar is substantially *undervalued* at the present time. The data in Exhibit 28.1 does show that the dollar is worth a lot less today than it was just a few years ago. There is an old saying that what goes up generally comes down again. The reverse is also often true. From what the graph shows, should one now assume that the dollar has bottomed out and will soon begin to rise? A lot of people have views on this. For many, the dollar can be expected to appreciate. But when this will happen and by how much, only time will tell. In the meantime, decisions must be taken and risks assumed.

Given the current state of affairs in the airline industry, it seems unlikely that many company directors are going to add to their headaches by allowing their currency position to be left willy-nilly to the whims of the market place. But who knows? This may prove to be the most profitable course of action. Take the case of Lufthansa, the principal German airline. Its experience with currency volatility has been well documented.[1] As reported in early 1985, it placed an order with Boeing for some $500 million of new aircraft – with delivery and payment in roughly a year's time. At that time, the dollar was at an all-time high against the Deutschmark. There was strong sentiment in the markets that the dollar would fall but, because of political uncertainties, when this would occur and to what extent it would fall was the subject of

Exhibit 28.1   *Spot exchange rates of the ECU against the US dollar (January 1986–January 1991)*

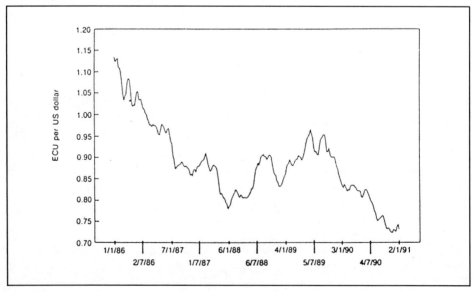

endless debate. Lufthansa decided to do what many do in such circumstances: it hedged half of the $500 million by purchasing dollars forward, while leaving the other half open. As things turned out, this course of action cost Lufthansa some DM 250 million *more* than if the entire $500 million had been unhedged. Reportedly, the airline's management came under severe criticism from those benefiting from hindsight. Apparently the critics believed Lufthansa should have left the entire position unhedged. Wouldn't this be *speculation* in most people's book?

Does the Lufthansa example offer some guidance for what European airlines should do today? In my opinion, it is helpful in that it clearly shows the difficulty in dealing with uncertainty and risk-taking. I believe that corporate management, boards of directors, shareholders and other interest groups must make up their minds as to what business they are in. If it is the airline business, fine; management should hedge the currency risks and know exactly how many francs, Deutschmarks, pounds or ECUs[2] they will pay for their equipment. If they are in the airline *and* the currency trading business, then OK; why not take a view and try to profit on currency movements? If their view turns out to be correct, the equipment will cost less, profits will be higher, and *perhaps* those responsible will get praised for clear foresight. If they get it wrong . . . well, let's hope that the accountants can camouflage the damage – otherwise the head-hunters will have some new clients. However, I believe there is some middle ground worth exploring.

In the discussion that follows, a fictitious company which we will call EuroAir is used to provide a case study. Its route structure includes Europe, the Middle East, the Far East and the North Atlantic. The latter route is an especially important source of revenue, but margins have suffered from intense competition. EuroAir's currency of account is the ECU. The equipment it has on order totals more than $1.5 billion it has options to purchase additional aircraft over the next 3 years worth about the same amount. Since its currency of account is the ECU the purchase of Boeings for dollars opens it up to a very large currency risk. EuroAir's management believes there is more than enough risk from its airline business and has decided to insulate the company cash flows from currency fluctuations. The hedging example will be based on a $100 million exposure for one year.

EuroAir has at least a half dozen currency hedging strategies it could consider. First of all, *do nothing*. It is not impossible that the dollar purchase of aircraft actually provides a hedge for an already exposed dollar position. Management should ask themselves, 'what would happen to our revenues and margins if the dollar strengthened?' A stronger dollar could mean higher ECU revenues on certain routes such as over the North Atlantic. Passenger and cargo volume might rise and if the American carriers were price leaders in that market, a stronger dollar would convert into more ECUs. On the other hand fuel costs would rise in terms of the ECU. A detailed analysis of the economics of the industry would be needed to determine the overall impact. If indeed changes in the value of the dollar did affect revenues then equipment purchases in dollars could provide a natural hedge.

If, on the other hand, revenues were insensitive to changes in dollar rates, to leave the purchase unhedged would be an implicit bet on a weaker US currency. This strategy, we have argued earlier, would be speculation, adding to the high degree of risk the company already faces. This can be seen from Exhibit 28.2.

Let us assume that the management of EuroAir has determined it will need to hedge the aircraft purchase. There are basically two approaches: (1) lock-in, or (2) set a ceiling on the ECU cost

To lock-in the ECU cost would mean hedging with a forward contract or taking a position in the money market. Although either would virtually guarantee the ECU cost of the aircraft purchase the forward contract hedge with a bank to buy $100 million at a rate fixed at the outset would be in almost all circumstances the more cost efficient. In the graphs that follow the forward exchange rate for a twelve month contract was ECU 0.7350 per dollar. This means that the $100 million aircraft purchase would cost ECU 73.5 million,

Exhibit 28.2 *EuroAir hedging strategies: pay-offs from a $100m aircraft purchase*

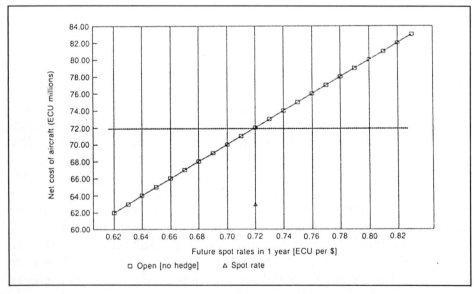

ECU 1.5 million over what it would cost at the current spot rate of ECU 0.72 per dollar.

Exhibit 28.3 shows that the forward contract will produce a gain if the dollar rises, or loss if it falls, by the end of a year's time. This outcome, added to ECU cost of the aircraft at different rates (Exhibit 28.2), will always add up to a net *hedged* result of ECU 73.5 million – hence the rate is *locked-in* whatever happens to the dollar exchange rate. But this is the obvious drawback of this strategy. If the dollar weakens, the aircraft will cost the same as if it were to strengthen. The forward hedge could be seen as a bet that the dollar will rise above the current forward rate. A better strategy would be to use a hedge that would set a ceiling on the cost if the dollar were to rise, but allow the airline to profit if it were to fall. EuroAir could hedge half of the purchase price, but this could give them the Lufthansa experience all over again. This means some kind of an option hedge.

The simplest of these would be to buy a call option. Exhibit 28.4 shows the gain or loss *at maturity* from buying a $100 million call with the strike price set at the present spot rate. The cost of this option would be ECU 3.68 million – almost 5%.

The net cost of the aircraft would be capped at ECU 75.68 million, the strike price plus the cost of the option. This is shown by Exhibit 28.5. Note the comparison with the net results from the open position and the forward

Exhibit 28.3   *EuroAir hedging strategies: pay-offs from a forward contract*

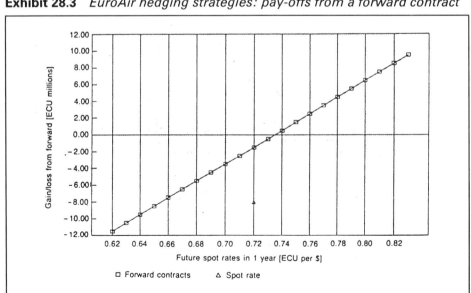

Exhibit 28.4 *EuroAir hedging strategies: pay-offs from a call option*

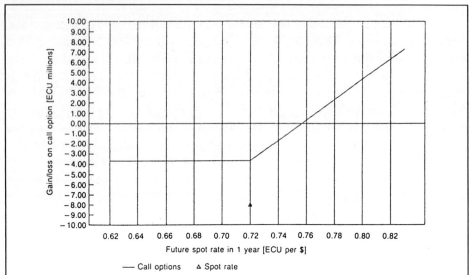

hedge. This hedge gives the company the possibility of benefiting from a further fall in the value of the dollar, yet limits the risk if the dollar strengthens. Is this speculation? The call option hedge is nothing more than an implicit bet against the dollar, but with limited risk. Is this a sensible thing to do given the recent pattern of the ECU/dollar exchange rate seen in Exhibit 28.1? If the dollar strengthens much more than 2% from its present level, the forward hedge would certainly be better. Furthermore, the EuroAir board may be loathe to pay a premium of ECU 3.68 million *up front* for what is something less than a sure thing.

Using a bit of financial engineering, the company could come up with another option hedge that might be more attractive. Options can be combined with forwards or other options in a variety of ways to gain risk-return characteristics that could not be obtained otherwise. For example, a long[3] put option and a long forward in the same amounts taken together will replicate a long call option. Similarly, a long put position can be obtained by selling forward and buying a call in the same amounts. Of course, such a synthetic instrument would rarely be of interest to a company wishing to hedge a currency exposure. It is simpler to buy the put or call in the first place. However, if a long forward contract were to be combined with a long put which was for a lesser amount, a *synthetic call* could be engineered with different characteristics than could be obtained from buying a call directly.

Exhibit 28.5 *EuroAir hedging strategies: pay-off comparison of forward hedge, call option hedge and open strategies*

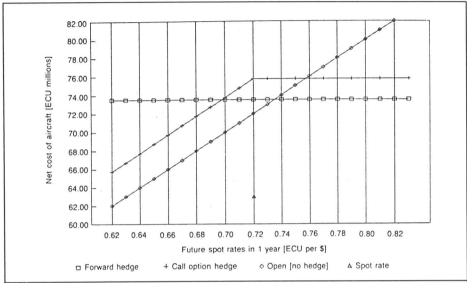

To illustrate, a $100 million long put option and long forward contract *together* would produce virtually the same pay-off line at expiration as that of the call option shown in Exhibit 28.4. A $100 million long forward contract by itself has the pay-off line shown in Exhibit 28.3. If the forward contract were combined with a $50 million long put, the result at expiration would resemble a long call (Exhibit 28.4), but at less than half of the cost and with an upward sloping profit line that was about half as steep (22½° instead of 45°). By combining the gain or loss from this synthetic call option with the cost of the aircraft at different future spot rates, we obtain the results shown in Exhibit 28.6. The maximum cost of the aircraft with this hedge becomes ECU 74.67 million with an up-front cost of ECU 1.17 million for the put option. The drawback of this hedge is that there is less potential gain if the dollar weakens further. Called a synthetic call hedge here, it is sold by banks under such names as *participating forward*. It may be packaged so that the option premium is paid at maturity rather than up front. Of course, the company could construct this hedge by itself, buying the component parts from one or more banks or on a financial futures exchange.[4]

Another example of financial engineering is a hedge constructed of two options. This comes with different names in the bank OTC[5] market: *zero cost option, range forward, cylinder*. For hedging the purchase of the aircraft, EuroAir would buy a $100 million call option and sell (short or

Exhibit 28.6 *EuroAir hedging strategies: pay-off comparison for 100% forward hedge, synthetic call and open strategies*

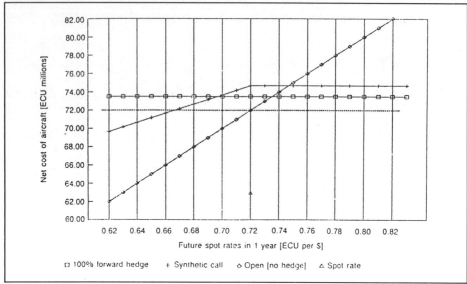

write) a $100 million put option. The strike prices are generally set *out-of-the-money*.[6] Combined with the purchase cost of the aircraft under different future spot rates, this hedge sets both a ceiling and a floor to the net result. Depending on the strike prices set for each option, the ceiling and floor can be adjusted to achieve different risk-return objectives. Strike prices can also be set so that the premium paid on the call is covered by that received from the short put – the *zero cost option*. The example shown in Exhibit 28.8 is this type of hedge. Exhibit 28.7 shows the pay-off at expiration of the two options. The long call has a strike price set at ECU 0.77, and costs ECU 1.58 million. The short put has a strike price of ECU 0.71 and provides a premium income exactly equal to the cost of the call. No cost to EuroAir and a guarantee that the net cost of the aircraft will be no higher than ECU 77 million or lower than 71 million. This can be seen from the graph in Exhibit 28.8.

We have looked briefly at four different hedging strategies.[7] Which of these is best for EuroAir? *Ex ante*, it is difficult if not impossible to say. It depends on the taste of the airline management and shareholders for risk. The three option hedges are all an implicit bet on the dollar becoming weaker over the next 12 months. The call option hedges need a dollar cheaper by some 5% to be superior to the forward contract hedge. The protection they offer against a more expensive dollar is inferior to the forward by

Exhibit 28.7   *EuroAir hedging strategies: pay-off comparison of buy $100m call and sell $100m put options*

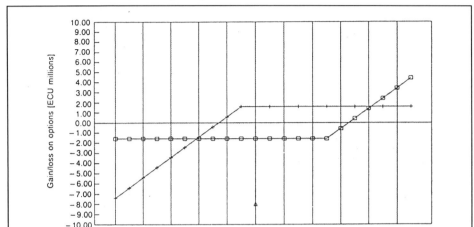

ECU 1.17 million (synthetic call) and ECU 2.23 million (call). The zero cost option in the most favourable scenario would be ECU 2.5 million better than the forward, but would leave the airline ECU 3.5 million worse off in the event that the dollar rose significantly. The risk–reward trade-off appears tilted in favour of *locking in* the exchange rate.

The situation facing Euro Air is just about the opposite to that Lufthansa faced in 1985–86. Then the dollar was greatly overvalued; in early 1991, it was for many market observers somewhat undervalued. By hedging partially, Lufthansa suffered what most people could call an opportunity loss. If not appearing in the company accounts as a loss, it was real enough and caused the management plenty of grief. EuroAir can face a real loss if it chooses the wrong hedging strategy *and* also an accounting loss that will be plain to see. The reader may have his or her own view on the future course of the dollar and the appropriate hedging strategy for EuroAir. To me, in late February 1991, the forward contract looked best. The odds seemed stacked in favour of a strengthening dollar over the next 6 to 12 months. It was not the time for options. At the present time (mid-May 1991) with the dollar at ECU 0.82, the superiority of the forward hedge appears confirmed. Look in at the end of this year to see whether this decision was still the correct one.

Exhibit 28.8 *EuroAir hedging strategies: pay-off comparison of forward hedge, zero-cost option and open strategies*

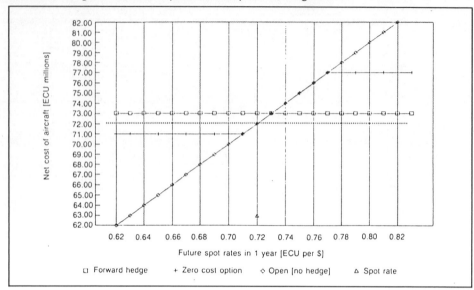

Notes

1. See for example, 'Where options would have made a difference', *Intermarket Supplement*, Philadelphia Stock Exchange, November 1986; Neil McGeown, 'Lufthansa: a case study in options', *Market Perspectives*, Chicago Mercantile Exchange, vol. 4, no. 8, 1986.
2. The ECU (European Currency Unit) at present includes the Deutschmark, French franc, Belgian franc, Netherlands guilder, Danish krone, Irish punt, lira, drachma, peseta, escudo and sterling. About two-thirds of the ECU's value consists of four currencies: Deutschmark, guilder, French and Belgian francs.
3. In market parlance, *long* means to buy or hold an asset; *short* means to sell an asset. Hence a short forward means that one sells forward (currency); a long put means that one buys a put option.
4. Futures on only a few currencies are traded: Deutschmark, sterling, Swiss franc, Australian and Canadian dollars, and yen. Although introduced on both the Chicago and London futures markets, the ECU contract has not been successful.
5. OTC: over-the-counter, i.e. not traded on an organized exchange, but between banks via telephone and electronic communication.
6. The terms *out-of*, *at-*, or *in-the-money* are commonly used in the options market. They refer to where the option's strike price lies in relation to the spot price (sometimes the forward or futures price) at the time the option transaction takes place. A call option with a strike price of ECU 0.75 per dollar would be *out-of-the-money* if the spot price

is ECU 0.72; you could not exercise this option profitably until the spot price rose above ECU 0.75.

7.   Actually five if we accept that the airline may have a natural hedge from its operations (i.e. that its profits move in tandem with changes in the value of the dollar). In this case, the four *financial* hedges would be unnecessary – they could even create an exposure where one did not exist before.

CASE 29

Hallgarten Wines Ltd

Hallgarten is a prominent UK wine importer, specializing in German and French wines. Wine is purchased for forward delivery, as well as in the spot market. Transactions are denominated in Deutschmarks or francs, and payment made when the wine clears the bonded warehouse, where it can remain for up to a year. Hallgarten promotes its wines through an extensive, illustrated price list, reprinted annually. Once the price list is fixed, Hallgarten is exposed to adverse wine price fluctuations. Exchange rate variability is a particular concern here. Hallgarten is looking at alternative methods of managing and hedging its exposure, perhaps using currency options and futures. But first it needs to decide just how exposed it is.

Peter Hallgarten's travel schedule is inflexible: it can be varied by, at most, a few days. December in particular is a busy month. As chief executive of Hallgarten Wines Ltd he must travel throughout Europe to determine the quality of the new harvest. There is always pressure to visit a large number of wine-producing areas, while making sure that sufficient time is set aside for seeing existing suppliers.

In October 1986, Peter Hallgarten therefore assigned several days for working at home to review his current business plans. A factor which caused him considerable concern was the variability of exchange rates. Volatile currencies were a problem which Peter had learned to live with, but recently a number of proposals had been put to him which required consideration.

This case was written by Elroy Dimson with the assistance of Cecilia Reyes and Mike Staunton as a basis for class discussion rather than to illustrate either effective or ineffective handling of an administrative situation. We are grateful to Peter Hallgarten for his help, and to Shantan Acharya for research assistance on our earlier draft. For reasons of confidentiality some items of internal company data have been disguised. © Elroy Dimson and Paul Marsh, 1987.

The House of Hallgarten

Peter Hallgarten's family have a longstanding involvement in the German wine industry, and in 1898 Peter's grandfather, Arthur Hallgarten, started his own wine brokerage company. In 1933, Arthur's son Fritz sought refuge from Germany and established Hallgarten Wines Limited as the London importer for German wines. He specialized in estate bottled wines with original labels, and also a generic range of German wines. Peter, the son of Fritz Hallgarten, initially studied for a career in chemistry but in 1958 joined the family wine company.

Peter and his company are well known and highly respected in the wine and spirit industry. Hallgarten Wines is operated, however, with a small and tightly knit workforce. There is a sales director reporting to Peter, as chairman; and in 1986 the company employed 30 sales, warehouse, delivery and administrative staff. The company imports around 2 million (70 cl) bottles per year. Its turnover is over £4 million, and the firm has a capital employed of around £1 million. Exhibit 29.1 provides summary financial data on the company.

The UK Wine Market

In recent years UK wine consumption per head has increased marginally (from 8 litres in 1978 to some 9 litres in 1987) but is still minimal compared with France's per capita consumption of 89 litres and the European average of 45 litres per capita (down from 50 litres in 1978).

World wine production is dominated by Europe, with approximately 80%, led by France with 22%. West Germany accounts for 8% of world production, and in 1983, its exports of 240 million litres (about 15% of its total production) went primarily to the UK (98 million litres) and the USA (57 million litres). The total UK table wine market, including still and sparkling wine, both imported and UK produced, amounted to 380 million litres, accounting for some £2 billion of consumers' expenditure. The bulk of the UK wine market is made up of imported still wines. In 1983, they accounted for 92% of the market by volume and 88% by value.

Germany ousted Spain from its position as third largest supplier to the UK market in 1978 and overtook Italy in 1980. In 1983 Germany accounted for 27% of total imported still wine clearances compared with French wines which accounted for 46% by value (but only 38% by volume). Trade estimates suggest that the shares for off-licence (supermarkets and specialist retailers) and on-licence (pubs and restaurants) sales are respectively 65%

Exhibit 29.1 *Hallgarten Wines Ltd: consolidated accounts*

Balance sheet	1985	1984	1983	1982	1981
		£000 for year ending 31 December			
Tangible assets	105	100	111	80	83
Investments	20	20	20	30	28
Fixed assets	125	120	131	110	111
Stocks	493	633	573	519	521
Trade debtors	1,139	1,227	1,077	960	1,007
Other current assets	50	50	50	175	35
Current assets	1,682	1,910	1,700	1,654	1,563
Total assets	1,807	2,030	1,831	1,764	1,674
Current liabilities	876	1,134	997	1,005	935
Net assets	931	896	834	759	739
Shareholders' funds	925	874	818	756	735
Other long-term liabilities	6	22	16	3	4
Capital employed	931	896	834	759	739
Profit and loss account					
Sales	4,448	4,433	4,213	3,863	3,790
Trading profit	120	136	105	105	137
Depreciation	32	31	25	24	24
Operating profit	88	105	80	81	113
Investment income	9	22	11	7	0
Profit before interest	97	127	91	88	113
Interest paid	7	1	2	8	8
Net profit before tax	91	126	89	80	105
Tax	39	69	26	58	n/a
Profit after tax	52	57	63	22	n/a
Dividends	1	1	1	1	n/a
Retained earnings	51	56	62	21	n/a

and 35% by volume. Within the off-licence trade, the approximate split between supermarkets and specialist retailers is 60: 40.

The structure of trade in wine importing and wholesaling has changed radically over the past decade. Many of the functions of broker, shipper, agent, importer and wholesaler have now been integrated vertically, sometimes with that of the grower, in other cases with the retailer's function. There is a variety of routes by which wine reaches the consumer. Another feature has been the growth of own-labels which predominate in the supermarket trade, and it has been estimated that own-labels now account for over 55% of all supermarket wine sales. Indeed, the Sainsbury group claims to be the largest wine retailer, with up to a 15% share of the table wine market.

In the UK, there are two components in the tax applied to wine: customs duty and value added tax (VAT). Duty is independent of the value of wine, but is applied according to the alcohol content. A typical wine with less than 15% alcohol will incur duty of £0.98 per litre. VAT (15% at the time of writing) is applied to wine after the addition of duty.

Wine Prices

Sales of German wines were reported by a prominent German wine house (Deinhard) in early 1984 to fall in the following price brackets: under £2 per bottle, 20%; £2–£3 per bottle, 66%; over £3 per bottle, 14%. Interestingly, prices appear not to have increased since then; a store check at the end of 1986 at supermarkets and specialist shops in London revealed prices such as the following: Goldener Oktober £2.69, Johannisberger Erntebringer 1981–2 £3.69, Crown of Crowns £2.45, Black Tower £2.25, Blue Nun £2.99, Bereich Nierstein 1984 £1.99, and Deinhard Green Label £3.95. Own-label and Euroblend products were available at significantly lower prices than these. These prices have in the recent past increased by less than the general rate of inflation, currently around 3% per annum.

The lower the quality of wine, the more its price will also reflect the supply of competing wines from other producing countries. For example, prices have been affected on occasions when unexpectedly large quantities of Italian or Californian wine have been dumped on the market. Exhibit 29.2 shows that domestic wine prices, in the UK, Germany and France, have been considerably more volatile than the general level of retail prices.

The prices of the best wines, since they are distinctive, fluctuate according to the quality of the vintage and the quantity produced in each category. Most producers of these best wines retain a certain proportion of each harvest for subsequent sales and, in addition, there are regular auctions of wine, such as those held by Christies in London. Over the longer term, prices also seem to vary with the business cycle, but there still remain considerable differences between the price movements of individual wines, even those produced in the same region. Finally, the prices at which importing firms can sell their inventories more or less parallel the fluctuations in the price of the current crop. These effects can be seen clearly in

Exhibit 29.2   *Domestic wine prices in the UK, Germany and France, 1980–85*

This figure displays the monthly levels of domestic wine prices and the corresponding retail price index (RPI) levels for the UK, Germany and France, rebased to 100 as at 31 December 1979. The annual percentage inflation rates for the three countries (estimated for 1986) were as follows:

	1980	1981	1982	1983	1984	1985	1986
UK	18.1	11.9	8.7	4.6	5.0	6.1	3.5e
Germany	5.5	6.0	5.3	3.0	2.5	2.2	0.1e
France	13.5	13.3	12.0	9.5	7.7	5.8	2.8e

Sources: Datastream, Bulletin Mensuel de Statistique and Preise und Preisindizes für die Ein und Ausfuhr.

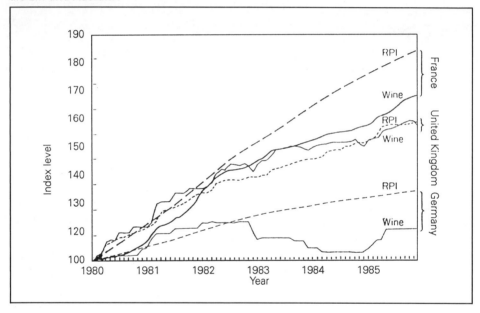

Exhibit 29.3, which records the retail prices (adjusted for inflation) of several representative types of wine.

Products and Prices

Unlike France, where the grading of quality wines is largely geographical, in Germany exactly the same vineyards that produce quality wine (QmP, the top quality, and QbA, a middle level) can also produce table wine (Tafelwein) and Landwein (a superior German Tafelwein, from one of 15 specified districts). Although Liebfraumilch (a QbA) is the most widely

Exhibit 29.3 *Retail wine prices in the UK adjusted for inflation, 1970–86*

Year	Bordeaux second growth	Burgundy second growth	Red Burgundy	Vintage Port	Cham-pagne	Alsace	Moselle	Rhine
1970	100	100	100	100	100	100	100	100
1972	103	136	134	108	118	112	225	195
1974	172	171	172	188	166	181	127	144
1976	107	167	150	141	107	80	83	80
1978	142	277	183	145	136	119	95	70
1980	178	273	257	130	157	122	130	65
1982	152	373	203	132	137	96	114	52
1984	137	271	274	163	134	126	84	53
1986	145	223	238	188	155	98	103	68

Compiled from Berry Brothers and Rudd price lists 1970–86. The figures are based on the retail price (but excluding customs duty) for the year in question for a currently mature vintage for a representative wine. The prices have been deflated by the retail price index and expressed in index form with 1970 = 100.

exported, Germany also produces many fine wines, virtually all from the late-ripening Riesling grape. The House of Hallgarten is best known for its Liebfraumilch, Niersteiner, Piesporter, sparkling Schloss and other German wines, where good quality and reliability are important to both the trade buyer and consumer. In addition, there are recently introduced lines such as Hallgarten's new top quality QmP branded range, Kabinett, Spätlese and Auslese.

The House of Hallgarten in fact offers a full list of German and French wines, as well as a range of liqueurs and fine spirits. German wine accounts for some 70% of the company's turnover, while French wine now represents nearly 30%. This proportion has increased over recent years as a result of Peter's continuing policy of diversification away from German wines, a policy which has also taken him into selling small quantities of Portuguese, Israeli and English (Isle of Wight) wines. In August 1986, Hallgarten Wines disposed of the distribution rights for the range of Royal Liqueurs invented by Peter during the 1970s and early 1980s, which had previously accounted for 3–5% of the firm's turnover. Consequently, by late 1986 about 99% of Hallgarten's sales revenue was attributable to its wine business.

The firm sells 300–400 different lines, and promotes them with a 20-page lavish, colour illustrated price list, summarized in Exhibit 29.4. A typical print run for the price list is about 5,000 copies, with a cost which depends on artwork requirements, but which might be £4,000–5,000 per revision, plus distribution expenses.

Exhibit 29.4 *House of Hallgarten price list, December 1986*

Category	Number of varieties	Price range (£)
French table wines and vin de pays	9	1.73–2.16
Bordeaux red wines	22	2.08–43.00
Bordeaux white wines	7	1.95–4.17
Loire wines	6	1.88–4.66
Chablis	5	5.50–6.83
Burgundy-Côte d'Or/Maconnais	32	2.68–10.42
Beaujolais/Midi/Provence	12	2.15–7.00
Rhône Valley wines	22	2.20–10.66
Chateauneuf-du-Pape wines	9	4.66–6.08
Vin Doux Naturel	2	5.16–5.66
Alsatian Rhine wines	5	2.32–4.33
Champagne/sparkling wines	5	2.33–7.67
Euroblend/Tafelwein/Landwein	3	1.60–2.42
Liebfraumilch/Own-label QbA	6	1.63–1.92
Moselle	16	1.82–3.64
Rheinhessen	10	1.97–2.70
Rheingau/Nahe/Palatinate	7	1.96–2.50
Palatinate/Nahe Estate Bottled	11	2.30–4.83
Rheinhessen/Franconia/Baden estate bottled	12	2.45–4.17
Rheingau estate bottled	1	2.57–4.25
Moselle estate bottled	15	2.23–4.89
Saar estate bottled	11	2.42–4.42
Ruwer estate bottled	11	2.25–7.25
Beerenauslesen	11	6.75–11.25
Trockenbeerenauslese	5	14.33–33.50
Eiswein	4	9.33–13.50
Connoisseur selection	7	3.58–5.42
Portuguese wines	5	3.33–6.42
English wines	1	2.33–2.33
Grenadine/Cooler	2	1.17–1.90
Liqueurs and fine spirits	8	3.08–8.83

This table summarizes a glossy 20 page price list. All prices are in £ per bottle (approximately 70 cl), and includes customs duty but not VAT.

Trade buyers, such as restaurant proprietors, set their own prices on the basis of the wholesale costs they expect to incur. Consequently, if Hallgarten pays more than expected for a particular wine, the costs cannot easily be passed down the trading chain, for this would impose on the trade buyer the expense of reprinting menus and wine list. It is equally difficult to withdraw a product which appears on the current Hallgarten list. If the goodwill of customers is to be fostered, Hallgarten can adjust prices only when the price list is reprinted. As with most other wine suppliers, this occurs once a year. On-licence buyers (such as restaurants and hotels) account for around 35% of Hallgarten's sales by volume.

The difficulty of recovering cost increases is a problem not only with the less expensive wines that are mostly enjoyed when young and for which up to a year's inventory may be held. It is also a problem with the fine wines, for which Hallgarten's stock would also have to be replenished at a higher price. Thus, with his price list fixed for up to a year in advance, Peter Hallgarten's margins are obviously eroded by adverse movements in wine prices.

The German grape harvest usually takes place over a period of two months from mid-September onwards. Most everyday wine is made to be drunk within two years of the harvest, though Riesling QbA and the highest quality (QmP) wines may not reach their peak for 5 or 7 years. This gives rise to varying time-scales for the production of different qualities of wine. Exhibit 29.5 indicates these time-scales and shows that Hallgarten can be exposed to adverse wine price fluctuations for a protracted period. Partly because of this, Peter has recently increased the proportion of his stock which he buys in the 'spot' market, rather than for forward delivery (see below).

Wine sales tend to peak in anticipation or the Christmas and New Year period, and final-quarter sales are higher than in the rest of the year. There are, in addition, month-to-month fluctuations in demand, most notably the surge which precedes the spring Budget, when an increase in tax on wines and spirits is often expected. Exhibit 29.6 provides a sales breakdown for Hallgarten Wines over the 12 months of the year.

Terms of Trade

When an importer such as Hallgarten Wines seeks to buy wine, there are various practices which are standardized in the industry. One is that wine transactions are denominated in the currency of the exporting country. In Hallgarten's case, the producer usually invoices Hallgarten Wines before the goods leave Germany. The German wine exporter sends a bill of exchange to Hallgarten with the shipping documents. The bill requires Hallgarten to pay for the goods on terms agreed with the producer. By adding the word 'accepted' and his signature, Peter Hallgarten 'accepts' the debt indicated on the bill of exchange, and, typically one week after they have left Germany, the goods arrive in the UK. The accepted bill of exchange is sent to the German supplier. The supplier either waits 2–3 months until Hallgarten Wines is due to pay in full, or discounts the bill at a local bank. After

Exhibit 29.5   *Illustrative production and selling timetable for European wines*

<table>
<tr><td colspan="2" align="center">Standard White Wines
(such as Liebfraumilch)</td></tr>
<tr><td>Typical list price (excluding VAT)</td><td>£1.70–£2.50</td></tr>
<tr><td>Annual quantity (bottles)</td><td>0.5 million</td></tr>
<tr><td>Harvest month</td><td>October 1986</td></tr>
<tr><td>Quantity and price agreed[1]</td><td>November 1986–February 1987</td></tr>
<tr><td>Bottling period</td><td>February–December 1987</td></tr>
<tr><td>Arrival in UK</td><td>February 1987–March 1988</td></tr>
<tr><td>Sales period</td><td>March 1987–May 1988</td></tr>
<tr><td colspan="2" align="center">Better White Wines
(such as Moselle)</td></tr>
<tr><td>Typical list price (excluding VAT)</td><td>£2.50–£3.50</td></tr>
<tr><td>Annual quantity (bottles)</td><td>0.7 million</td></tr>
<tr><td>Harvest month</td><td>October 1986</td></tr>
<tr><td>Quantity and price agreed[1]</td><td>November 1986–February 1987</td></tr>
<tr><td>Bottling period</td><td>February–December 1987</td></tr>
<tr><td>Arrival in UK</td><td>February 1987–March 1988</td></tr>
<tr><td>Sales period</td><td>March 1987–May 1988</td></tr>
<tr><td colspan="2" align="center">Standard Red Wines
(French)</td></tr>
<tr><td>Typical list price (excluding VAT)</td><td>£2.50–£3.50</td></tr>
<tr><td>Annual quantity (bottles)</td><td>0.4 million</td></tr>
<tr><td>Harvest month</td><td>September–October 1986</td></tr>
<tr><td>Quantity and price agreed[1]</td><td>June 1987</td></tr>
<tr><td>Bottling period</td><td>June 1987 onwards</td></tr>
<tr><td>Arrival in UK</td><td>August 1987–July 1988</td></tr>
<tr><td>Sales period</td><td>September 1987–December 1988</td></tr>
</table>

1. The dates shown for agreeing quantity and price apply to the major contract buyers, for example, of standard white wines. Whereas these buyers tend to purchase forward, smaller importers currently tend to buy on a 'spot' basis from producers throughout the calendar year.

60–90 days, when the bill has matured, payment is made by Hallgarten's bank to the owner of the bill.

A second practice is that frequently the wine is purchased for forward delivery, and as much as two years may elapse between the date when firms contract for the purchase and the date when delivery occurs. Large importing firms generally contract for about two-thirds of their purchases in late autumn, the remaining purchases being spread over the year. Whereas large importers find it economical to buy in bulk, smaller firms such as Hallgarten Wines have found it more profitable to decline to finance large inventories: they have, in effect, forced their storage costs onto the producer. During

Exhibit 29.6 *Seasonal breakdown of Hallgarten sales*

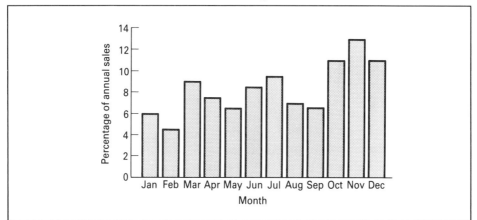

1986, Peter Hallgarten has therefore increasingly resorted to purchasing wine in the 'spot' market. Over the last year, about half of all his purchases were bought for immediate delivery to the company. The other half of his purchases were bought forward, often for delivery in 60–90 days' time, but sometimes with delivery after 120 days or more. Practices in the trade have, however, been changing frequently, and Peter considers that in a relatively short period, the proportion which he buys 'spot' could easily change.

A third practice is that payments to the wine exporter by the importer are often timed to occur at the end of the month in which the wine clears the customs houses. Since customs duty is not paid until the wine is released, the imported wine may then remain in the importing firm's bonded warehouse for up to a year.

Finally, the discount and credit arrangements extended by importers to their customers tends to be fairly standardized. A rule of thumb is that an average gross sales margin of 18–20% is required for a wine importer to break even (Hallgarten Wines achieves 20%). However, for very large customers the margin is trimmed to 10–12%, while for direct sales (or 'brokerage') business a margin of 5% is regarded as acceptable. The margins which Hallgarten negotiates, as well as the company's standard credit terms (1/30, EOM, net 60), are thus typical of their competitors.

Currency Exposure

Peter Hallgarten insists that his company is primarily a wine importer and wholesaler, and not a commodity or currency trader. However, there are occasions when he has bought and then resold wine in an overseas market, without taking physical delivery of the product. These opportunistic transactions have generally been profitable. Similarly, he periodically seeks an opinion from his bank manager on the strength of sterling, relative to the Deutschmark or French franc, before deciding whether to buy the appropriate quantity of foreign currency in the forward market.

The bank manager will usually supplement his opinion with a quotation for forward purchase of his chosen currency. If Peter accepts the quotation, the resulting contract commits Hallgarten and the bank to exchange sterling for another currency at the agreed rate of exchange, and on the date specified in the contract. Peter also uses rates published in the *Financial Times* as a guide to the cost of forward cover, though these quotations are in fact the rates for commercial contracts, i.e. in amounts of £25 000 or more, and with only a limited range of maturity dates. When Peter makes a forward purchase of foreign currency, he normally enters into a negotiated contract with his bank, where the amount and delivery date are specified to suit the company's needs. Though some banks have indicated that a commission would be payable, Hallgarten's bank does not charge a fee for arranging forward cover. However, Peter has noticed that the buy–sell spread tends to be wider for his negotiated contracts than that quoted in the press.

If forward purchase is cheaper than buying foreign exchange in the spot market and/or if he expects the foreign currency to appreciate, then Peter will consider hedging at least part of his exposure. He therefore finds that it is a normal part of his business for him to speculate on the sterling/ Deutschmark and sterling/franc exchange rates. He sees this as inevitable for an importer in the position of Hallgarten Wines. Moreover, he points out that if he can trade in currencies more shrewdly than his competitors, then the firm's trading income will be enhanced.

Recently, currencies have been very volatile (see Exhibits 29.7 and 29.8), and the performance of Peter's bank manager in predicting exchange rate movements has been, to say the least, disappointing. As an alternative, Peter has considered whether to use a specialist firm to provide forecasts of the relevant exchange rates. However, he is not certain how he would choose between the many forecasting services which are available.

Hedging Alternatives

Another avenue would be to hedge exchange rate exposure using currency futures or options contracts. Peter had previously rejected these instruments as being too sophisticated for a firm the size of Hallgarten, but recently

Exhibit 29.7 *Volatility of the DM/£ and FFr/£ exchange rates*

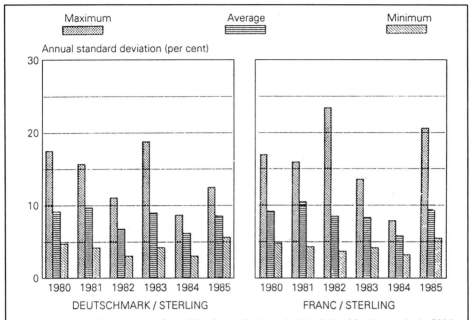

This Exhibit is based on a series of volatilities (annualized standard deviations) for changes in the DM/£ and FFr/£ exchange rates. Volatilities were estimated from daily data within each month, starting in January 1980. For each calendar year, the exhibit plots the mean of the 12 monthly volatilities and the highest and lowest of these twelve estimates. The mean of all the volatilities is: DM/£ 8.3% and FFr/£ 8.7%. The correlation between daily percentage changes in the DM/£ and FFr/£ exchange rates over this period is 0.49.

Exhibit 29.8 *Month-end £, DM and FFr interest and exchange rates, 1980–86*

Year and month	12-month percentage Eurointerest rate			DM/£ exchange rate		FFr/£ exchange rate	
	UK	Germany	France	Spot rate	12-month forward	Spot rate	12-month forward
1980: 1	16.00	8.63	13.50	3.93	3.68	9.21	9.01
2	17.13	9.44	15.00	4.04	3.77	9.49	9.32
3	17.69	10.25	15.00	4.19	3.93	9.67	9.45
4	14.75	8.69	13.25	4.08	3.87	9.53	9.41
5	15.00	8.56	12.88	4.17	3.94	9.70	9.52
6	14.25	8.19	12.63	4.14	3.92	9.62	9.48
7	13.44	7.88	11.88	4.19	3.98	9.69	9.55
8	15.25	8.19	12.63	4.28	4.02	9.96	9.73
9	14.44	8.75	13.31	4.33	4.12	10.05	9.95
10	14.94	8.62	12.69	4.65	4.40	10.71	10.50
11	14.00	9.44	13.00	4.54	4.36	10.54	10.45
12	15.88	9.06	12.69	4.68	4.47	10.85	10.71

Exhibit 29.8 *continued*

Year and month	12-month percentage Eurointerest rate			DM/£ exchange rate		FFr/£ exchange rate	
	UK	Germany	France	Spot rate	12-month forward	Spot rate	12-month forward
1981: 1	13.13	9.38	12.75	5.03	4.86	11.58	11.54
2	12.13	12.75	13.38	4.73	4.75	11.10	11.23
3	12.38	11.56	13.13	4.71	4.68	11.12	11.19
4	12.63	12.13	13.88	4.74	4.72	11.22	11.35
5	13.00	12.81	17.00	4.81	4.80	11.44	11.85
6	13.38	12.44	20.00	4.65	4.61	11.09	11.74
7	14.63	12.50	20.13	4.58	4.50	10.86	11.39
8	14.25	12.50	24.00	4.53	4.46	10.89	11.82
9	16.13	11.75	23.50	4.15	4.00	9.97	10.61
10	16.00	11.44	19.00	4.16	4.00	10.44	10.71
11	14.44	9.69	18.13	4.33	4.15	10.90	11.25
12	15.88	10.38	18.63	4.30	4.10	10.90	11.16
1982: 1	14.69	10.31	17.19	4.35	4.18	11.06	11.30
2	14.00	9.94	16.88	4.34	4.19	11.06	11.34
3	13.63	9.19	19.50	4.31	4.14	11.13	11.71
4	13.69	8.50	19.88	4.19	4.00	10.93	11.53
5	13.44	8.56	20.88	4.20	4.02	10.96	11.68
6	13.19	9.38	18.75	4.27	4.12	11.84	12.42
7	12.00	9.13	18.25	4.27	4.16	11.87	12.53
8	10.81	8.50	20.50	4.30	4.21	12.02	13.07
9	10.50	7.94	19.63	4.29	4.19	12.11	13.11
10	9.56	7.00	19.38	4.29	4.19	12.11	13.20
11	10.31	7.06	19.75	4.01	3.89	11.34	12.31
12	10.44	6.00	20.00	3.84	3.69	10.88	11.83
1983: 1	11.38	5.94	17.88	3.75	3.57	10.63	11.25
2	10.81	5.63	18.63	3.69	3.51	10.46	11.19
3	10.69	5.38	15.13	3.57	3.40	10.70	11.12
4	10.13	5.38	16.50	3.84	3.67	11.51	12.17
5	10.38	6.00	17.25	4.06	3.90	12.19	12.95
6	10.13	6.00	18.00	3.89	3.74	11.68	12.52
7	10.63	6.00	16.75	4.02	3.85	12.06	12.73
8	10.56	6.50	17.00	4.03	3.89	12.14	12.84
9	9.88	6.31	16.25	3.94	3.82	11.97	12.66
10	9.75	6.19	15.00	3.93	3.80	11.95	12.52
11	9.63	6.50	16.75	3.95	3.84	12.03	12.81
12	9.88	6.44	14.50	3.95	3.82	12.08	12.59
1984: 1	9.94	6.44	14.38	3.96	3.83	12.11	12.59
2	9.50	6.25	16.75	3.88	3.77	11.96	12.75
3	9.38	6.13	15.88	3.73	3.62	11.51	12.19
4	9.44	6.25	14.13	3.79	3.68	11.63	12.12
5	10.88	6.81	15.00	3.79	3.65	11.62	12.05

Exhibit 29.8 *continued*

Year and month		12-month percentage Eurointerest rate			DM/£ exchange rate		FFr/£ exchange rate	
		UK	Germany	France	Spot rate	12-month forward	Spot rate	12-month forward
	6	10.69	6.81	14.50	3.76	3.63	11.54	11.94
	7	12.38	6.63	13.81	3.78	3.59	11.60	11.75
	8	10.81	6.25	12.88	3.79	3.63	11.62	11.84
	9	10.81	6.06	12.13	3.77	3.61	11.58	11.72
	10	10.63	5.94	12.13	3.68	3.53	11.29	11.44
	11	10.00	5.69	11.75	3.70	3.56	11.34	11.52
	12	10.25	5.63	11.50	3.66	3.50	11.19	11.32
1985:	1	12.19	6.19	11.50	3.57	3.38	10.92	10.85
	2	12.63	6.56	11.88	3.63	3.43	11.05	10.98
	3	11.94	6.25	11.88	3.85	3.66	11.77	11.76
	4	12.13	6.13	11.25	3.83	3.63	11.69	11.59
	5	12.19	5.69	10.25	3.94	3.71	11.99	11.78
	6	12.06	5.69	11.50	3.96	3.73	12.07	12.01
	7	10.81	5.00	11.88	3.99	3.78	12.16	12.28
	8	11.06	4.75	11.88	3.89	3.67	11.90	11.99
	9	11.00	4.75	11.50	3.75	3.54	11.44	11.49
	10	11.31	5.19	11.13	3.77	3.56	11.50	11.48
	11	11.19	4.75	10.19	3.74	3.52	11.40	11.30
	12	11.75	4.88	12.50	3.54	3.32	10.84	10.91
1986:	1	12.69	4.69	13.00	3.38	3.14	10.33	10.36
	2	11.75	4.44	11.00	3.23	3.02	9.93	9.86
	3	10.31	4.50	10.13	3.45	3.25	10.62	10.60
	4	9.56	4.50	7.50	3.36	3.20	10.69	10.49
	5	9.50	4.81	7.56	3.43	3.28	10.91	10.71
	6	9.63	4.69	7.38	3.37	3.22	10.75	10.53
	7	9.97	4.69	7.38	3.12	2.97	10.15	9.91
	8	9.63	4.38	7.44	3.03	2.88	9.93	9.73

Barclays Bank had launched its BERO (bearer exchange rate option) certificates (Exhibit 29.9). A sterling put BERO (giving Peter the right throughout the next 6 months to buy Deutschmarks at the current exchange rate) would cost about £250 for £5,000-worth of cover. The BERO certificate could be purchased and sold over the counter at the local bank (see Exhibit 29.10(b) for specimen quotations).

Peter was quite interested in the BERO concept since this constituted a 100% guarantee of protection against adverse currency fluctuations while Hallgarten would still benefit from any favourable movement in the exchange rate. But he was doubtful whether the BERO was the best way to

Exhibit 29.9 *Specimen premiums for a £5,000 currency option certificate as at 28 February 1986*

Barclays BERO Certificate

SPECIMEN PREMIUMS – DM/STERLING BEROs

Premiums for BEROs (which represent the total cost for the rights under the certificates) are based like other currency options on the following:

option (strike) price in relation to the current exchange rate
period of the option (or time left to expiry date)
prevailing exchange rate volatility
prevailing forward margins (which themselves are a function of interest rate differentials).

The table below gives examples of typical sale and repurchase premiums in £ sterling of one £5,000 sterling put (DM call) and sterling call (DM put) BERO certificate, at different exchange rates. It is based on strike prices of sterling puts at 3.15 and 3.20 and sterling calls at 3.30 and 3.35 with a 6 month expiry date.

CURRENT RATE: *3.10*

	Puts			Calls	
Strike	*Sale*	*Repur*	*Strike*	*Sale*	*Repur*
3.15	354	329	*3.30*	52	33
3.20	411	389	*3.35*	40	23

CURRENT RATE: *3.15*

	Puts			Calls	
Strike	*Sale*	*Repur*	*Strike*	*Sale*	*Repur*
3.15	298	272	*3.30*	69	47
3.20	353	328	*3.35*	52	34

CURRENT RATE: *3.20*

	Puts			Calls	
Strike	*Sale*	*Repur*	*Strike*	*Sale*	*Repur*
3.15	252	224	*3.30*	89	65
3.20	298	272	*3.35*	70	48

CURRENT RATE: *3.25*

	Puts			Calls	
Strike	*Sale*	*Repur*	*Strike*	*Sale*	*Repur*
3.15	208	181	*3.30*	114	88
3.20	253	225	*3.35*	90	66

CURRENT RATE: *3.30*

	Puts			Calls	
Strike	*Sale*	*Repur*	*Strike*	*Sale*	*Repur*
3.15	173	144	*3.30*	142	116
3.20	209	182	*3.35*	115	89

CURRENT RATE: *3.35*

	Puts			Calls	
Strike	*Sale*	*Repur*	*Strike*	*Sale*	*Repur*
3.15	140	114	*3.30*	177	150
3.20	175	146	*3.35*	142	116

CURRENT RATE: *3.40*

	Puts			Calls	
Strike	*Sale*	*Repur*	*Strike*	*Sale*	*Repur*
3.15	114	87	*3.30*	214	190
3.20	142	116	*3.35*	176	149

CURRENT RATE: *3.45*

	Puts			Calls	
Strike	*Sale*	*Repur*	*Strike*	*Sale*	*Repur*
3.15	90	68	*3.30*	258	237
3.20	116	89	*3.35*	213	189

Source: Barclays Bank.

hedge his exposure. He therefore decided to examine other approaches to managing the foreign exchange risk of the company. The most obvious alternative was to use currency futures.

Currency futures are in essence forward contracts which are bought and sold in a specialized marketplace. The futures contract, like a forward

Exhibit 29.10 *Forward, futures and options quotations as at 8 September 1986*

Contract	Bid and offer quotations for various contract maturities				
(a) Forward contracts	*Spot rate*	*1 month*	*3 month*	*6 month*	*12 months*
DM/£ Forward	3.064–78	3.047–67[1]	3.020–40	2.984–04	2.912–35
FFr/£ Forward	10.041–71	10.033–71	10.029–70	10.025–66	10.015–57
(b) BERO certificates	*17 Oct.*	*17 Nov.*	*17 Dec.*	*17 March*	*17 June*
£/DM Call @ 3.10	—	—	57–72[1]	76–95	—
@ 3.15	—	—	33–45	52–70	—
@ 3.35	—	5–15	—	—	—
@ 3.40	—	5–15	—	—	—
£/DM Put @ 2.95	—	—	43–58	96–115	—
@ 3.00	—	—	72–87	133–155	—
@ 3.30	—	416–426	—	—	—
@ 3.35	—	495–505	—	—	—
(c) Futures contracts	*Spot rate*	*3 month*	*6 month*	*9 month*	*12 month*
$/DM Futures	0.4837–39	0.4840–44[1]	0.4857–62	—	—
$/£ Futures	1.4868–75	1.4860–75	1.4715–30	—	—
(d) Traded options	*October*	*November*	*December*	*March*	*June*
$/DM Call @ 0.48	0.95–07[1]	1.33–44	1.63–75	2.25–38	2.70–88
@ 0.49	0.48–57	0.85–95	1.14–25	1.75–88	2.22–38
@ 0.50	0.18–26	0.50–60	0.76–87	1.35–47	1.82–95
$/DM Put @ 0.48	0.45–55	0.80–90	1.03–15	1.50–65	1.85–00
@ 0.49	0.95–06	1.30–45	1.53–65	2.00–15	2.35–50
@ 0.50	1.67–78	1.95–10	2.15–27	2.60–75	2.92–07
$/£ Call @ 1.40	8.40–90	8.55–85	8.80–30	9.30–80	9.95–25
@ 1.45	4.00–25	4.70–05	5.20–50	6.10–50	6.80–30
@ 1.50	1.30–60	2.10–45	2.70–05	3.80–25	4.50–00
@ 1.55	0.20–45	0.75–05	1.30–60	2.25–60	2.95–35
@ 1.60	—	—	0.55–75	1.25–55	1.85–15
$/£ Put @ 1.40	0.05–30	0.60–90	1.20–50	2.80–10	4.10–60
@ 1.45	0.80–10	1.90–20	2.75–15	4.75–15	6.30–80
@ 1.50	3.00–30	4.40–75	5.35–75	7.50–95	9.10–60
@ 1.55	6.75–25	8.00–30	8.85–20	10.85–35	12.40–90
@ 1.60	—	—	13.00–45	14.70–20	16.15–75

1. Quotations are given with the lower value first, as illustrated here. A forward rate quotation of 3.047–67 means that the bank sells at the commercial rate (that is, over £25,000-worth of currency) of 3.047, buying at 3.067. A BERO price of 57–72 means that the bank buys a £5,000 face value certificate with a maturity of 1 month and strike of 3.10 for £57, selling at £72. The futures quotations, which are for units of DM 125,000 and £25,000 respectively, have a similar interpretation to the forward rates. Finally the traded options, which have units of trading of DM 62,500 and £12,500, respectively, are quoted in US cents per DM or £: thus, the quotation of 0.95–07 means that the broker buys an October $/DM call with a strike of 0.48 for 0.95 cents and sells for 1.07 cents per DM.

contract, is an agreement to exchange one currency for another; but unlike the forward contract, the maturity dates and the value of the contract are standardized. This makes it cheaper and easier to close out a position in a currency. In London, currency futures contracts were traded on the London International Financial Futures Exchange (LIFFE). Unfortunately, though contracts were available in Deutschmark and sterling, these (and other) currencies were traded on LIFFE against the dollar, while it was necessary to use the Philadelphia Stock Exchange to buy futures on the French franc (also traded against the dollar).

Peter was aware that trading in the currency futures market involved commission payments negotiated between the individual client and the broker or member of the exchange, and that margin payments were also required. An attraction for Hallgarten Wines was that, unlike forward contracts, use of the futures market would not automatically consume lines of credit. However, Peter was doubtful about whether this was a real benefit, since the company would have to ensure that it could adequately meet margin calls. Exhibit 29.10(c) provides specimen quotations for futures on the Deutschmark and sterling.

Peter's other alternative was to buy foreign exchange protection by means of a currency option, not necessarily a BERO. In exchange for paying the appropriate premium, Hallgarten would have the right, but not the obligation, to buy or sell a set amount of one currency against another at a fixed rate on or before a specified date. As the option holder, Hallgarten would benefit from a favourable movement in the exchange rate while being protected from any adverse movement. Traded options on the $/£ and $/DM exchange rates (only) were traded on LIFFE and the London Stock Exchange, while other currencies were traded in Philadelphia, Chicago and elsewhere (see Exhibit 29.10(d) for specimen quotations). Over-the-counter currency options were also available in many banks for most currencies, though their face values would have been normally much larger than that of the BERO.

Peter Hallgarten had also read about other forms of currency protection. Salomon Brothers, for example, offered a 'range forward' contract, while Citicorp Investment Bank's 'cylinder options' are similar. Those contracts specified a range of exchange rates between two currencies which would apply when the contract matured, but the exchange rate was guaranteed not to exceed or fall short of the limits which were stated in the contract. These types of contract were available in various currencies; but at the time the contracts were all against the dollar, so Peter thought it would require some ingenuity to use this approach to hedging exchange rate exposure.

Given the hedging methods that were available to him, Peter started work on developing a strategy for Hallgarten Wines Limited. He was particularly keen that his policy for dealing with the exchange risks and other international financial risks encountered by the company should be practical and easy to implement.

CASE 30

Svenska Neuhaus

*This Swedish high technology company (identity and country disguised)
has won a bid to install a control system for a UK chemical plant. A
payment of £4 million is due in 3 months' time. Svenska's senior
management is concerned about exchange risk, and is discussing with
its bankers whether to hedge their exposure. Hedging could be achieved
using the forward market, the money market, or via the Deutschmark. In
the latter case, they could hedge using currency futures or options. This
case provides data on interest rates, spot and forward exchange rates,
and currency option and futures prices. Svenska need to decide whether
to hedge, and if so, how.*

On the morning of 8 January 1985, Rolf Lindorn, the chief executive of
Svenska Neuhaus, heard that the company had just won a bid to install a
fibro-optical control system for a UK chemical plant. This new system was
developed entirely by Svenska Neuhaus and was the only one capable of
competing with similar products offered by American and Japanese firms.
Svenska Neuhaus had been awarded the 1984 prize for Storsta Svenska
Exportframgang for this invention, and everyone still remembers how
pleased Rolf Lindorn looked when he walked onto the stage to receive the
award from the prime minister.

The following day (January 9), Rolf Lindorn and Ulf Ericson, the chief
financial officer of Svenska Neuhaus, met with Ove Holbeck of Enskilda
Banken to discuss financial issues related to the contract. Neuhaus' bid
amounted to £4.4 million (Exhibit 20.1) and 9% of this had already been
paid by the UK firm that morning as a deposit. The balance was due when
installation was completed. Neuhaus' chief engineer was pretty confident
that this would be within the next 90 days (the completion date in the contract
was 10 April 1985).

---

*This case was prepared by Evi Kaplanis and Antonio Mello as a basis for class discussion rather
than to illustrate either effective or ineffective handling of an administrative situation. © Evi
Kaplanis and Antonio Mello, 1987.*

Exhibit 30.1 *Details of the Svenska Neuhaus bid made on 12 December 1984*

	SKr million	£ million
Materials	25.0	2.4
Direct labour costs	9.6	0.9
Direct overhead costs	6.9	0.6
Total costs	41.5	3.9
Profit factor	5.1	0.5
Total	46.6	4.4

Converted at the closing exchange rate for the day (SKr 10.58 / £).

The meeting focused on the exchange risk related to the outstanding amount of £4 million. Ove Holbeck was concerned about the value of the pound. He was worried that it might depreciate against the other major currencies and consequently against the Swedish krona which was pegged to a trade weighted basket of currencies (Exhibit 30.2).

Exhibit 30.2 *Weights used in the trade weighted currency index for Swedish kronor*

Currency	1984 weightings	1983 weightings
US dollar	19.1	18.1
Deutschmark	16.2	16.6
Sterling	13.2	13.0
Norwegian krone	9.4	9.3
Danish krone	8.2	8.5
Finnish markka	7.2	7.4
French franc	5.5	5.6
Dutch guilder	5.1	5.2
Belgian franc	3.8	3.7
Italian lira	3.6	3.7
Japanese yen	2.7	2.7
Swiss franc	2.2	2.3
Austrian schilling	1.5	1.6
Spanish peseta	1.2	1.2
Canadian dollar	1.1	1.1

The Swedish krona was pegged to the European currency snake between 1973 and 1977, since when it has been tied to a trade-weighted currency index. The weights of the currencies in the basket are revised each year at the end of March and are calculated as a proportion of each country's average share in Sweden's foreign trade over the previous 5 years, with double weighting attached to the US dollar. The percentage weightings from April 1984 (and the prior year weightings) are as shown in the table.

Source: Riksbanken.

Mr Holbeck explained to Rolf Lindorn and Ulf Ericson that they had several options. Firstly, they could do nothing. This would leave Svenska Neuhaus exposed to fluctuations in the Swedish krona/British pound exchange rate. Thus if sterling appreciated against the Swedish krona, there would be a currency gain, while if it depreciated, there would be a currency loss.

Alternatively, they could hedge their exchange exposure. Mr Holbeck explained that if Svenska Neuhaus wished to hedge using the forward market, it would have to sell sterling forward. He told Lindorn and Ericson that Enskilda Banken was prepared to buy sterling at the 90-day forward quotation of Skr 10.33/£.

To hedge using the money market, Svenska Neuhaus would have to borrow pounds in London now, convert them into kronor at the current spot rate (Exhibit 30.3), invest the proceeds in Sweden, and repay the pound loan in 3 months with the proceeds of the contract. Mr Holbeck suggested that a sterling loan could be arranged at 0.5% above the prime lending rate (Exhibit 30.4) and Enskilda was prepared to pay 11.00% on a 3 month Swedish krona deposit account.

Finally, Mr Holbeck suggested that hedging could be achieved through the Deutschmark – in other words, the DM could be used as a proxy for the Swedish krona, since the movements of these two currencies are largely correlated (Exhibit 30.5). Three options were available to Neuhaus if it decided to hedge through the DM. First, it could hedge using the money market. Second, it could hedge using currency options (Exhibit 30.6).

Exhibit 30.3 *Spot and forward exchange rates and Eurocurrency interest rates*

(a) The pound spot and forward exchange rates (9 January 1985)

	Close	*3 months forward*
Sweden	10.31–10.32 (SKr/£)	3.5–4.125 ore discount
Germany	3.6025–3.6125 (DM/£)	3.875–3.625 pfennig premium
USA	1.1415–1.4225 ($/£)	0.46–0.42 cents premium

(b) Eurocurrency interest rates (market closing rates (9 January 1985)

	Sterling	*US dollar*	*DM*
3 months	9.9375–10.0625	8.25–8.375	5.5625–5.6875

Source: Financial Times, 10 January 1985.

Exhibit 30.4 *Comparison of money supply and interest rate figures*

	Money supply percentage rise on year ago		Money market		Commercial banks		Bond yields		Eurocurrency	
	Narrow (M1)	Broad[1]	Overnight	3 month	Prime lending	3 month deposit	Government longs	Corporates	3 month deposit	Bonds
Australia	10.2	11.4	10.50	14.20	13.50	13.80	13.70	14.70	12.57	12.87
Belgium	4.3	10.1	8.40	10.75	14.00	10.40	11.65	11.48	10.75	n/a
Canada	−2.6	3.9	10.25	9.70	11.25	9.75	11.92	11.85	9.85	11.91
France	5.6	7.8	10.75	10.75	11.50	10.75	11.83	12.94	10.63	11.67
Germany	2.5	4.0	5.50	5.75	8.00	5.23	7.20	7.08	5.57	7.48
Holland	4.6	7.3	5.88	5.88	7.50	5.88	7.60	7.79	5.88	7.54
Italy	10.4	11.5	15.88	16.00	17.00	11.50	13.10	13.25	14.38	n/a
Japan	3.4	7.7	6.19	6.29	5.50	3.50	6.55	7.10	6.22	7.16
Sweden	n/a	3.4	13.50	11.55	14.50	11.25	12.04	12.50	11.75	n/a
Switzerland	1.9	7.7	2.94	4.88	7.50	4.25	4.77	5.07	4.75	5.52
UK	18.7	11.1	5.25	10.19	10.50	9.94	11.03	12.76	10.06	11.36
USA	5.0	9.9	8.38	7.95	10.75	7.85	11.84	12.70	8.38	11.48

Interest rate % per annum (8 January 1985, except bonds which are 4 January 1985)

Other rates in London: 3 month treasury bills 9.2%; 7 day Interbank 9.1%; clearing banks 7 day notice 6.1%. Eurodollar rates (LIBOR): 3 months 8.4%; 6 months 9.0%.

1. M2 except Australia, Canada, Switzerland, USA, West Germany. M3, Japan. M2+ certificates of deposit, UK £M3. Definitions of interest rates quoted available on request. *Sources:* Chase Manhattan, Chase Econometrics, Banque de Commerce (Belgium), Nederlandse Credietbank, Crédit Lyonnais, Svenska Handelsbanken, ANZ Bank, Crédit Suisse First Boston. These rates are indicative only and cannot be construed as offers by these banks.

Comment: On both measures of West Germany's money supply, the 12 month rate of monetary growth picked up in November – while in Holland, both measures slowed in October. French banks cut their prime lending rates by half a point to 11.50%; Italian banks cut theirs by a full point, to 17%.

Source: The Economist.

Mr Holbeck explained that although options were expensive, they not only provided the company with insurance against adverse exchange rate movements but also offered a potential gain when exchange rates moved favourably. Third, they could hedge using the futures contract (Exhibit 30.7). Mr Holbeck provided Mr Ericson with information on interest rates, forward rates and industrial exchange rates (Exhibits 30.2–30.8).

Ericson and Lindorn realized that 'no action' implied that they accepted the exchange risk. On the other hand, they recognized that hedging was costly.

Exhibit 30.5 *Historical monthly spot exchange rates*

Date (end of month)		DM/$	SKr/$	£/$
1982:	January	2.3085	5.6510	0.5309
	February	2.3860	5.7910	0.5508
	March	2.4142	5.9510	0.5613
	April	2.3327	5.8120	0.5591
	May	2.3452	5.8595	0.5583
	June	2.4598	6.0920	0.5753
	July	2.4545	6.0910	0.5747
	August	2.4972	6.1685	0.5812
	September	2.5276	6.2905	0.5908
	October	2.5668	7.4340	0.5976
	November	2.4872	7.4610	0.6203
	December	2.3765	7.2945	0.6194
1983:	January	2.4475	7.4520	0.6532
	February	2.4212	7.4395	0.6574
	March	2.4265	7.5090	0.6761
	April	2.4581	7.4930	0.6404
	May	2.4871	7.5531	0.6491
	June	2.5419	7.6425	0.6534
	July	2.6435	7.7470	0.6575
	August	2.6867	7.9080	0.6657
	September	2.6391	7.8220	0.6686
	October	2.6264	7.8170	0.6688
	November	2.6970	7.9600	0.6827
	December	2.7238	8.0010	0.6894
1984:	January	2.8139	8.1800	0.7125
	February	2.6058	7.7890	0.6716
	March	2.5900	7.7160	0.6932
	April	2.7174	7.9975	0.7161
	May	2.7333	8.0710	0.7219
	June	2.7842	8.1840	0.7393
	July	2.8964	8.3960	0.7657
	August	2.8870	8.4563	0.7630
	September	3.0253	8.5750	0.8013
	October	3.0296	8.6194	0.8214
	November	3.0963	8.8025	0.8339
	December	3.1480	8.9895	0.8647

Source: International Financial Statistics.

Exhibit 30.6 *Currency option prices (Philadelphia Exchange) on 9 January 1985*

Exercise price ———→

Contract size ———→

Spot exchange rate (cents/£) ———→

Option and under-lying	Strike price	Calls–last			Puts–last		
		Mar	Jun	Sep	Mar	Jun	Sep
12,500 British pounds–cents per unit.							
BPound	.110	r	r	r	1.10	s	r
114.37	.115	1.95	3.35	4.40	3.15	4.60	5.80
114.37	.120	0.65	1.65	r	6.70	r	8.50
114.37	.125	r	0.75	1.50	r	r	r
50,000 Canadian dollars–cents per unit.							
CDollr	...75	r	r	r	0.33	r	r
75.75	...76	0.34	r	r	0.76	r	r
75.75	...78	0.04	s	s	r	s	s
62,500 West German marks–cents per unit.							
DMark	...31	1.16	1.71	r	0.34	0.67	0.90
31.77	...32	0.59	r	r	0.78	1.17	r
31.77	...33	0.30	0.74	r	r	r	r
31.77	...34	0.15	0.45	r	r	2.39	r
31.77	...35	r	0.30	s	r	r	s
31.77	...36	r	0.19	s	r	r	s
31.77	...37	0.02	s	s	r	s	s
125,000 French francs–10ths of a cent per unit.							
FFranc	.105	r	r	3.55	r	5.05	r
6,250,000 Japanese yen–100ths of a cent per unit.							
JYen	...39	0.82	1.33	r	0.46	r	0.85
39.29	...40	0.36	r	r	r	r	r
39.29	...41	r	0.48	r	r	r	r
39.29	...42	r	r	0.50	r	r	r
62,500 Swiss francs–cents per unit.							
SFranc	...37	r	r	2.56	0.36	r	r
37.90	...38	0.87	1.55	2.09	0.79	r	r
37.90	...39	0.48	1.09	1.73	r	r	1.95
37.90	...40	0.23	r	r	r	r	r
37.90	...41	0.10	0.45	r	r	r	r

Price on January 9, 1985 for the option to buy/sell £1 ←———

Total call vol. 7,676   Call open int.   101,985
Total put vol. 3,601   Put open int.   50,412

r–Not traded.   s–No option offered.   o–Old.
Last is premium (purchase price).

Exhibit 30.7 *Currency futures prices on 9 January 1985*

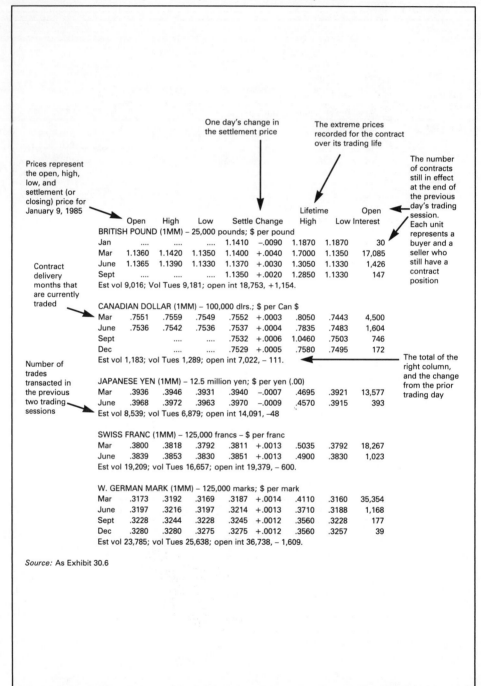

One day's change in the settlement price

The extreme prices recorded for the contract over its trading life

Prices represent the open, high, low, and settlement (or closing) price for January 9, 1985

The number of contracts still in effect at the end of the previous day's trading session. Each unit represents a buyer and a seller who still have a contract position

	Open	High	Low	Settle	Change	Lifetime High	Low	Open Interest
BRITISH POUND (1MM) – 25,000 pounds; $ per pound								
Jan	....	....	....	1.1410	–.0090	1.1870	1.1870	30
Mar	1.1360	1.1420	1.1350	1.1400	+.0040	1.7000	1.1350	17,085
June	1.1365	1.1390	1.1330	1.1370	+.0030	1.3050	1.1330	1,426
Sept	....	....	....	1.1350	+.0020	1.2850	1.1330	147
Est vol 9,016; Vol Tues 9,181; open int 18,753, +1,154.								

Contract delivery months that are currently traded

CANADIAN DOLLAR (1MM) – 100,000 dlrs.; $ per Can $								
Mar	.7551	.7559	.7549	.7552	+.0003	.8050	.7443	4,500
June	.7536	.7542	.7536	.7537	+.0004	.7835	.7483	1,604
Sept	....	....	....	.7532	+.0006	1.0460	.7503	746
Dec	....	....	....	.7529	+.0005	.7580	.7495	172
Est vol 1,183; vol Tues 1,289; open int 7,022, – 111.								

Number of trades transacted in the previous two trading sessions

The total of the right column, and the change from the prior trading day

JAPANESE YEN (1MM) – 12.5 million yen; $ per yen (.00)								
Mar	.3936	.3946	.3931	.3940	–.0007	.4695	.3921	13,577
June	.3968	.3972	.3963	.3970	–.0009	.4570	.3915	393
Est vol 8,539; vol Tues 6,879; open int 14,091, –48								

SWISS FRANC (1MM) – 125,000 francs – $ per franc								
Mar	.3800	.3818	.3792	.3811	+.0013	.5035	.3792	18,267
June	.3839	.3853	.3830	.3851	+.0013	.4900	.3830	1,023
Est vol 19,209; vol Tues 16,657; open int 19,379, – 600.								

W. GERMAN MARK (1MM) – 125,000 marks; $ per mark								
Mar	.3173	.3192	.3169	.3187	+.0014	.4110	.3160	35,354
June	.3197	.3216	.3197	.3214	+.0013	.3710	.3188	1,168
Sept	.3228	.3244	.3228	.3245	+.0012	.3560	.3228	177
Dec	.3280	.3280	.3275	.3275	+.0012	.3560	.3257	39
Est vol 23,785; vol Tues 25,638; open int 36,738, – 1,609.								

Source: As Exhibit 30.6

Exhibit 30.8 *Daily exchange rates: SKr/£*

Week commencing	Monday	Tuesday	Wednesday	Thursday	Friday
12 November 1984	10.735	10.750	10.740	10.740	10.705
19 November 1984	10.725	10.642	10.610	10.570	10.557
26 November 1984	10.495	10.545	10.570	10.557	10.563
3 December 1984	10.560	10.600	10.625	10.560	10.592
10 December 1984	10.610	10.560	10.580	10.525	10.565
17 December 1984	10.530	10.477	10.430	10.395	10.465
24 December 1984	10.452	n/a	n/a	10.430	10.430
31 December 1984	10.405	n/a	10.385	10.405	10.400
7 January 1985	10.380	10.365	10.315		

n/a indicates not available (public holiday).

Jaguar Cars

A Case on Foreign Exchange Exposure

Jaguar, a luxury UK car manufacturer, is exposed to exchange rate fluctuations since a large proportion of its sales are in dollars whilst its costs are in sterling and Deutschmarks. This case raises some interesting issues regarding the rationale for hedging foreign exchange exposure within an internationally competitive environment.

From 1979 to 1981 Jaguar Cars lost £120 million. The cars that the company produced at the time were unreliable and badly finished. In addition, the strength of sterling, at an average rate of $2.33 in 1980, was given as another explanation for the losses. The variability of exchange rates has caused great concern in Jaguar, since a large proportion of their revenues comes from overseas, mainly the USA, while most of the company's raw materials and components are bought in the UK.

The Company and its History

In 1922, William Walmsley and William Lyons formed the Swallow Sidecar company to build motorcycle sidecars. In 1935 the company was floated on the Stock Exchange and in March 1945 it changed its name to Jaguar cars.

The company produced a series of successful sports cars. In 1960 Jaguar doubled its capacity by purchasing the Daimler company. Jaguar, however, was still small compared with its European and American competitors. This put the company at a disadvantage in terms of development and distribution costs. In 1966 Jaguar cars merged with the British Motor Company to form British Motor Holdings, and in 1968 BMLC was formed from a merger of BMH and British Leyland.

This case was written by Evi Kaplanis and Mike Staunton as a basis for class discussion rather than to illustrate either effective or ineffective handling of an administrative situation. © *Evi Kaplanis and Mike Staunton, 1990.*

In 1980 John Egan was appointed chief executive of Jaguar. Bill Hayden from Ford later described the progress of Jaguar in the 1980s as follows:

> In 1980 Jaguar was on its knees. What few cars it made were of appalling quality and the government was about to turn the lights out. John Egan has more than trebled production over the past 10 years, introduced a new saloon and still managed to invest half a billion dollars on new equipment.

Jaguar became an independent company through privatization in August 1984. Exhibit 31.1 provides some financial data on the company.

Exhibit 31.1 *Jaguar Cars financial data*

Year	Total turnover (£m)	US turnover (£m)	Profit (£m)	Total sales (000 cars)	US sales (000 cars)
1980	166	–	(52)	16	3
1981	195	–	(36)	14	5
1982	305	–	6	21	10
1983	472	–	49	29	16
1984	634	–	42	33	18
1985	746	469	87	38	21
1986	830	544	83	41	25
1987	1,002	555	61	47	23
1988	1,076	468	28	50	21

The Market for Luxury Cars

The most important market for luxury cars is the USA. Exhibit 31.2 gives the distribution of sales by area for Jaguar, Mercedes-Benz and BMW.

Exhibit 31.2 *Distribution of sales (% by value)*

Company	Home market	USA	Rest of Europe	Other
Jaguar	30	42	16	12
BMW	32	19	32	17
Mercedes	48	15	23	14

The major competitors of Jaguar in the US luxury car market are predominantly based in West Germany. Mercedes-Benz and BMW are both much larger than Jaguar with 1989 sales exceeding 500,000 cars, and Porsche, with annual sales of around 30,000 cars, is a similar size (see Exhibit 31.3). Some, however, argue that Jaguars are closer substitutes for Cadillacs than Mercedes or BMW because of their smooth ride, soft seats and the easy steering.

The scale advantage of Mercedes and BMW ensures that they are less dependent than Jaguar on the luxury segment of the market (see Exhibit 31.4). The chairman of BMW, Eberhand van Kuenheim, considers that the only truly serious opposition for BMW is Mercedes, saying that Jaguar's output of 50,000 units annually is simply too low, representing a world market share of only 0.1% compared with BMW's 1.4%.

Jaguar's position, and its dependence on the US luxury car market, is indeed closer to that of Porsche. Porsche's chairman, Heinz Branitzki, states that:

> In the future, the Porsche for beginners is a used Porsche. The £20,000 segment is definitely a thing of the past; I would like to concentrate on the £40,000 plus, but the air up there is quite thin. We are not Mercedes, and don't sell cars like Mercedes. Our ambition is to provide sheer driving pleasure.

Exhibit 31.3 *US luxury car market 1987 (thousands of cars)*

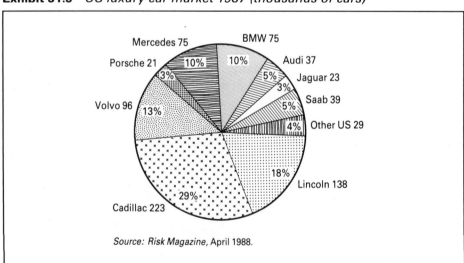

Mercedes 75 — 10%
Porsche 21 — 3%
BMW 75 — 10%
Audi 37 — 5%
Jaguar 23 — 3%
Saab 39 — 5%
Other US 29 — 4%
Volvo 96 — 13%
Lincoln 138 — 18%
Cadillac 223 — 29%

Source: Risk Magazine, April 1988.

Exhibit 31.4 *Prices and production shares of luxury cars*

Jaguar			BMW			Mercedes			Porsche		
M	P	PS	M	P	PS	M	P	PS	M	P	PS
XJ6	21	75	3	11	69	COMP	15	32	944	32	n/a
V12	33	6	5	16	18	MID	18	53	911	42	n/a
XJS	27	19	6	37	1	S	49	15	928	57	n/a
			7	41	12						

M model, P price (£000), PS production share (%).

Jaguar's Currency Hedging Strategy: April 1988

Jaguar has substantial currency exposure which derives from the fact that 70% of its output is exported, whilst its production is concentrated in the UK. Prior to privatization in August 1984, Jaguar had left its foreign exchange exposure largely uncovered, in line with British Leyland policies. By early 1985, Jaguar wanted to be more certain of its forward revenues and had started to implement forward hedging.

Jaguar's finance director, John Edwards, describes that forward sale policy:

> We basically stick to managing our major exposure, the US dollar. Our aim is to sell forward 75% of the estimated dollar receipts on a rolling twelve month basis. When there are occasions, either for reasons of taking advantage of very good exchange rates or where we feel we would like to lock in a profit number for a period, then we extend this cover to more than 75% and more than twelve months. In the spring of 1985 we were able to sell up to two years forward at rates which proved in 1986/87 to be very beneficial in terms of profit contribution.
>
> Since 1985 we have continued this policy and we are now [February 1988] in a position where we have locked in 95% of anticipated receipts of 1988 at $1.55 to the pound and 40% of 1989's anticipated exposure at around $1.70.
>
> There is a very little questioning from analysts of anything other than cash flow exposures. As the translation impact goes through reserves and not through the P&L, it is very rarely considered.
>
> We find that people only want to know about the US dollar. However, we do have exposure to currencies of other countries to which we export cars. We are long in all European countries (other than Germany) and every other market. In Germany we have started to buy considerable numbers of components and particularly the new XJ6 has substantial costs in Deutschmarks. What we have done here is to leave the exposure open as we

are looking towards a balanced position on this currency, as sales increase in Germany.

Treasurer Michael Lane amplifies Jaguar's policy:

> As a company we need to give ourselves time to react. It is no good getting up one day and saying we are losing money – let's cut costs. What dollar hedging does is give us time to make the necessary adjustments (in production, marketing and sales, and cost structures) to such a degree that we will still be profitable. Hedging is just buying time, nothing else. Banks are quoting us rates around 1.75 for the early part of 1989 and are only prepared to give us the stronger rate of 1.70 for the end of 1989. We don't think it is worthwhile increasing our 1989 hedging ratios now because we think the dollar will strengthen between now and then, which will allow us to lock in our 1989 receipts at a better rate than is currently available.
>
> The problem with options is that we have to pay for them. We have to pay to get a benefit which is unknown, as opposed to the premium cost which is the only certainty. We have looked at options many times and have rejected them, principally on the cost of the premiums. We just don't think it is worth our while to pay these premiums when we can sell forward at rates that are acceptable to us. What's more we have been very successful in the forward market.

Exhibit 31.5 gives the average rates achieved by Jaguar and the average spot rates and forward rates for the period 1984–89. Exhibit 31.6 gives quarterly spot and forward exchange rates since 1976. Exhibit 31.7 shows the relationship between Jaguar's share price and the Deutschmark and dollar exchange rates during the period 1984–89.

Exhibit 31.5 *Dollar/sterling spot and forward rates (annual averages)*

Year	Spot rate	1-year forward rate	Rate achieved by Jaguar
1984	1.34	1.24	
1985	1.29	1.27	1.26
1986	1.47	1.42	1.28
1987	1.64	1.61	1.44
1988	1.78	1.75	1.55
1989	1.63	1.58	1.70

Exhibit 31.6 *Dollar/sterling exchange rates*

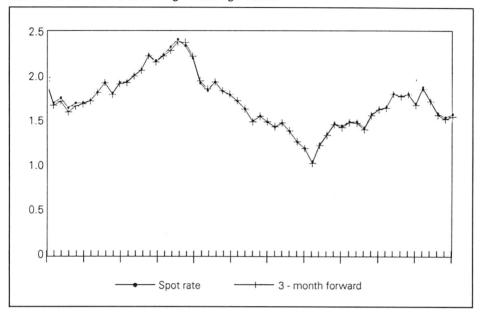

Exhibit 31.7 *Relationship between Jaguar's share price and exchange rates, 1984–89*

R(Jaguar)	= 2.64 + 0.35 R($US) + 1.31 R(DM)	$R^2 = 0.13$
R(Jaguar)	: Monthly % return from Jaguar shares	
R($US)	: Monthly % return to UK investor holding $US	
R(DM)	: Monthly % return to UK investor holding DM	

Porsche's Hedging Policy

Jaguar's views are echoed by Porsche, one of its main German rivals. Finance director Hans Vollert says:

> We have been hedging our dollar receipts for a few years and have not been convinced of the value of options. We do not use options on a large scale because we think they are too expensive. It doesn't make any sense to use them in an environment which has seen the dollar heading down consistently. We are not very optimistic about the dollar and so we will continue to use the forward market.

Porsche's policy has been to sell 6–9 months forward. Consequently, as at April 1988, Vollert had hedged all incoming dollar receipts up till October that year at a $/DM rate of 1.80–1.90. Porsche has no intention of extending its hedging horizons as far ahead as those of Jaguar.

Until March 1989 Porsche had shared Jaguar's aversion to options. 'Then', says finance director Hans Vollert, 'we changed our minds. Now we are partly using options – mainly zero-cost – to cover 20–25% of our dollar/ Mark transaction exposure.'

This conservative strategy, which involves buying put options at the same time as selling calls (forgoing some of the potential gain, but offsetting some of the premium paid) is used for about half Porsche's hedging; the company is currently covered about 50% for 1989 at a level of around DM 1.85 = $1.

The change of heart at Porsche came after a period of months considering the possibilities, given that the dollar was drawing ever closer to a level where it might rebound.

Calculating Numbers of Futures and Options Contracts required for Hedging

*When hedging instruments are used to reduce exposure some risk
remains, in particular basis risk. Futures prices may not move precisely
in line with the currency (or other) prices and as a result hedges may be
imperfect. This case study describes a technique for removing one
source of basis risk.*

Basis is the difference between a spot (cash market) price and the
corresponding futures price. Changes in basis reduce the efficiency of
hedging with futures. One source of basis change arises directly from price
movements. Futures prices tend to stand at premiums (or discounts) to cash
market prices. This relationship between futures and cash prices, which is
based on cost of carry, extends to the relationship between changes in futures
prices and changes in cash prices. In the absence of a change in cost of carry,
a futures premium would entail the extent of movement in the futures price
exceeding that of the cash price. This means that basis changes as a result of
price changes. The analysis that follows demonstrates that this source of basis
change can be eliminated by an appropriate calculation of the number of
futures contracts, a calculation that may seem to be counter-intuitive.
Initially the analysis will be based on stock index futures but will
subsequently be extended to the case of currency futures.

To determine the number of contracts when hedging with stock index
futures, consider the hypothetical situation in which the FTSE 100 Index
stands at 2,000, the FTSE 100 Futures Index stands at 2,200, and the portfolio
to be hedged has a current market value of £550,000 and a beta of one. Two
alternatives for the calculation of the requisite number of contracts are (at
£25 per index point):

$$\frac{\text{Value of hedged portfolio}}{\pounds 25 \times \text{Spot index}} = \frac{\pounds 550{,}000}{\pounds 25 \times 2{,}000} = 11 \text{ contracts}$$

and

$$\frac{\text{Value of hedged portfolio}}{\pounds 25 \times \text{Futures index}} = \frac{\pounds 550{,}000}{\pounds 25 \times 2{,}200} = 10 \text{ contracts}$$

The effectiveness of these alternatives can be judged in the context of two scenarios: (1) an immediate 10% fall in the market, and (2) the spot index being at 2,000 on the futures maturity date. In both cases the portfolio is hedged by a short futures position.

In scenario 1 the decrease in the value of the portfolio is £55,000. In the absence of any change in interest rates or expected dividend yield the futures index would also exhibit a 10% fall to 1980. So the profit on each futures contract is $220 \times \pounds 25 = \pounds 5{,}500$. At £5,500 per futures contract the £55,000 fall in the value of the portfolio is compensated for by 10 contracts. This suggests that the futures index should be used in the denominator when ascertaining the requisite number of futures contracts.

In scenario 2 the value of the portfolio remains at £550,000. If futures are held to maturity they should provide an effective increase in the value of the portfolio based on the relationship between the initial spot and futures indices $(2{,}200/2{,}000 = 1.1$, that is a 10% increase in the value of the portfolio).

The achievement of this outcome requires a futures profit of £55,000. Convergence implies that the futures index falls by 200 so that the cash flow from each futures contract is $200 \times \pounds 25 = \pounds 5{,}000$. A total cash flow of £55,000 thus requires the use of 11 contracts. This implies that the index to be used in the denominator when calculating the number of futures contracts is the spot index.

The implication of this analysis is that the number of futures contracts to be used depends upon when they are likely to be closed out. If they are likely to be closed out immediately then the futures index should be used in determining the number of contracts. If the futures contracts are to be held to their maturity date the spot index should be used. A closing out date between these extremes would suggest an index between the spot and futures indices based upon interpolation.

The Need for Leverage

When closing out takes place immediately after a futures position is established the futures profit or loss includes the futures premium and hence is more than is required to offset cash market movements. The futures coverage thus needs to be leveraged downwards. This is achieved by dividing the exposure by the futures index, which will include the futures premium. Consider the following data:

Cash exposure	£1,000,000
FTSE 100 futures price	2,500
Current FTSE 100 index	2,451
Futures premium	2%

A 100 point fall in the FTSE 100 Index would entail a 102 point fall in the futures price. As a result, the £40,800 cash market loss would be offset by a profit on

$$\frac{£40,800}{102 \times £25} = 16 \text{ futures contracts}$$

Sixteen futures contracts relate to a current cash exposure of:

$$16 \times 2451 \times £25 = £980,400$$

The exposure covered is leveraged down in order to offset the distorting effect of the futures premium.

An Illustration

The merits of using a weighted average of spot and futures prices, rather than the futures price, in ascertaining the appropriate number of futures contracts can be illustrated by the following example.

Futures contracts with four months to maturity are to be used to hedge a portfolio over a three month period. The following information is available.

Value of S&P 500 Index	200
Value of portfolio	$10,200,000
Risk free interest rate	10% p.a.
Expected dividend yield on S&P 500	4% p.a.
Beta of portfolio	1.34

The spot index, interest rate and expected dividend yield imply a fair futures price of 204 (the futures premium being based on 10% p.a. minus 4% p.a. over four months). If the actual futures price is equal to the fair futures price then each futures contract would relate to $204 \times \$500 = \$102,000$ of stock. Using the futures index in the denominator indicates a requisite number of contracts equal to:

$$1.34 \times (\$10,200,000/\$102,000) = 134$$

whereas using a weighted average of the futures and spot prices would involve a denominator based on an index of $200(0.75) + 204(0.25) = 201$. The denominator would thus be $201 \times \$500 = \$100,500$ and the implied number of contracts would be:

$$1.34 \times (\$10,200,000/\$100,500) = 136$$

Exhibit 32.1 shows three possible index values after three months, the corresponding fair futures prices (on the assumption of unchanged interest rates and expected dividend yields), and the portfolio values inclusive of dividend receipts. Exhibit 32.2 shows the futures profits (losses) from a short futures position over the hedge period, and the resultant value of portfolio plus futures, when 134 contracts are used, and Exhibit 32.3 shows the futures profits (losses) and the resultant value of the portfolio and futures combined when 136 futures contracts are used.

The risk-free rate of return on the initial portfolio value would have provided $10,455,000 after 3 months. It can be seen that using the futures price to determine the number of contracts sold neither completely eliminates risk nor approximates portfolio performance to the risk-free rate of interest. Using an average of the initial spot and futures prices, weighted by the anticipated time to closing out, completely eliminates risk and generates a performance close to that provided by the risk-free rate of interest (the remaining deviation from the risk-free rate of return arises because multiplication by beta is a procedure which provides only an approximation).

Exhibit 32.1   *Three-month index values, fair futures prices and portfolio values*

Value of index after 3 months	180.0	200.0	220.0
(Fair) Futures price	180.9	201.0	221.1
Value of portfolio after 3 months	$8,883,180	$10,249,980	$11,616,780

Exhibit 32.2   *Futures profits/losses and portfolio values*

Profit (loss) from futures	$1,547,700	$201,000	($1,145,700)
Value of portfolio plus futures	$10,430,880	$10,450,980	$10,471,080

Exhibit 32.3 *Futures profits/losses and value of portfolio plus futures*

Profit (loss) from futures	$1,570,800	$204,000	($1,162,800)
Value of portfolio plus futures	$10,453,980	$10,453,980	$10,453,980

Currency Futures

The requisite number of contracts depends on the currency of the sum to be hedged (for example, sterling or US dollars, against which the derivatives are quoted) and upon the expected point in time at which closing out will occur. This analysis uses the Chicago Mercantile Exchange sterling currency contracts and assumes an awareness that the locked-in rate depends on the closing out date – the spot rate if contracts are closed out immediately, the initial futures rate if contracts are held to maturity, or an average of the two weighted according to the period of time for which the contracts are held.

Suppose that there is a need to hedge £10,000,000 against US dollars and that the pound is trading at a 2% premium against the dollar. Spot £1 = $1.50 and 6-month futures £1 = $1.53. Further suppose that the £10,000,000 is covered by 160 sterling currency contracts (160 × £62,500 = £10,000,000). Now consider two scenarios:

1. An immediate rise in the pound to £1 = $2.00, followed immediately by closing out (with no change in relative £/$ interest rates).
2. A rise in the pound to £1 = $2.00 by the futures maturity date, with closing out on the futures maturity date.

In the first case, the futures price would rise to $2.04. The cash market loss would be $0.50/£, whereas the futures profit would be $0.51/£ (because the futures profit includes the premium). So the initial number of contracts should ideally be margined down to an extent that offsets the premium. This could be achieved by dividing the initial dollar value of the hedged sterling by the futures price.

$$\$15,000,000/\$1.53 = £9,803,922$$

In principle, futures contracts corresponding to £9,803,922 (in practice probably 157 contracts) should be entered into.

In the second scenario the futures price reaches $2, providing a futures profit of $0.47/£. The effective price of sterling is thus $1.53 – the number of contracts does not need to be margined. In other words, a number of contracts equivalent to the initial dollar value of the hedged sterling divided by the initial spot exchange rate would be appropriate.

$$\$15,000,000/\$1.50 = £10,000,000$$

One hundred and sixty futures contracts (£10,000,000/£62,500) are required. If contracts are to be closed out or exercised before maturity, the requisite number of contracts would lie between 157 and 160 and be a direct function of time to closing out (approaching 160 as the closing out date approaches the maturity date of the contract).

In order to ascertain the number of contracts needed to hedge a dollar sum, a sterling equivalent must be found. Consider two possibilities:

1. Hedging $15,000,000 with a view to closing out almost immediately (that is, hedging an imminent sum of $15,000,000).
2. Hedging $15,300,000 with a view to holding the futures contracts to maturity (that is, hedging a sum of $15,300,000 anticipated for 6 months hence).

In both cases, suppose that the initial spot rate is £1 = $1.50 and the initial (6-month) futures price is £1 = $1.53. Suppose, further, that the spot price moves immediately to £1 = $2 in the first case, and to £1 = $2 by the futures maturity date in the second.

In the first case the sterling value of the dollars falls from £10,000,000 to £7,500,000. At £1 = $2 the requisite dollar profit from futures would be $5,000,000. This would be obtained from contracts relating to £9,803,922 ($15,000,000/$1.53) since the futures profit per £1 would be $0.51, bearing in mind the 2% premium. So the appropriate number of contracts would be based on dividing the dollar sum to be hedged by the initial futures exchange rate.

In the second case the dollar profit from the futures required to ensure that the $15,300,000 is worth £10,000,000 (that is, to ensure that the $15,300,000 is converted at the original futures price) is $4,700,000. This would be obtained from futures based on £10,000,000, since the futures profit would be $0.47 per £1. Again, the appropriate number of contracts is based on dividing the dollar sum to be hedged by the initial futures exchange rate.

So whether the futures are to be closed out almost immediately or are to be held to maturity, the dollar sum should be divided by the initial futures price of sterling in ascertaining the sterling value to be covered by futures. It follows that whenever the contracts are to be closed out the dollar sum should be divided by the initial futures rate. So the number of contracts is independent of the point in time at which the exposure is due to appear (the date on which the currency flow is expected).

This conclusion conflicts with the intuitive idea that the exchange rate at which conversion takes place should be the forward rate relating to that point in time, which would be a weighted average of the initial spot and futures exchange rates.

The Role of Basis

The reason for ascertaining the appropriate number of sterling contracts to cover a dollar-denominated exposure by dividing the dollar sum by the futures exchange rate (relating to the futures maturity date) rather than by the implied forward rate (relating to the date of the exposure) can be seen in terms of avoiding part of the basis risk. If the interest rate structure between the two currencies remains unchanged, movements in the general level of exchange rates would cause changes in basis. With futures prices at a discount (or premium) against the spot, futures price movements would be smaller (or larger) than the spot price changes. As a result basis changes, and hedges would tend to be imperfect.

To compensate for such changes in basis, numbers of futures contracts need to be factored up or down. In the case of a futures discount, the number of contracts needs to be factored up by the same percentage as the discount. In the presence of a premium, factoring down by the same percentage as the premium would be appropriate. Dividing the dollar sum to be hedged by the futures price, rather than by an implied forward price for the exposure date, would provide the factoring required. A futures discount leads to an increase in the number of contracts by the required percentage; vice versa for a premium.

An Illustration

The points raised can be illustrated by means of a hypothetical example. It is 28 October and prices for sterling currency futures are:

| December futures | $1.7595 (18 December maturity) |
| March futures | $1.7475 (18 March maturity) |

A treasurer anticipates that $20 million will be received on 18 January and decides to hedge the exposure using the March futures. On 18 January the new spot (offer) rate is $1.90.

The implied forward rate for 18 January can be obtained by interpolating between the December and March futures prices; it is $1.7555.

The number of contracts suggested by the implied forward rate for 18 January is:

(20,000,000/1.7555)/62,500 = 182 (to the nearest whole number)

whereas the number of contracts suggested by using the March futures price as the divisor is:

(20,000,000/1.7475)/62,500 = 183 (to the nearest whole number)

There has been no change in the interest rate structure between the currencies, so that the futures discount remains at the same percentage. The January–March discount was $0.008/$1.7555 = 0.004557. The new money value of the futures discount will be $1.90 × 0.004557 = $0.0087, which implies a new March futures price of $1.90 − $0.0087 = $1.8913.

The profit from each March futures contract is therefore ($1.8913 − $1.7475) × 62,500 = $8,987.5. The two hedging strategies generate futures profits of:

$8,987.5 × 182 = $1,635,725 (£860,907.9)

and

$8,987.5 × 183 = $1,644,712.5 (£865,638.2)

Meanwhile, the loss on the underlying exposure was ($20,000,000/$1.7555) − ($20,000,000/$1.90) = £866,449.8.

The hedging strategy using the March futures price for determining the number of contracts produces the more efficient hedge. The factoring up of the number of contracts largely compensates for the 0.07 cent change in basis, though the compensation was less than complete since some rounding down was required in order to ascertain the nearest whole number of futures contracts.

Implications for Fixed Hedging with Options

An options contract could be regarded as a futures contract that is contingent upon the option being in-the-money at exercise. Therefore, analysis relating to futures should have implications for options. In fact, synthetic futures positions can be achieved by combining long and short option positions. Analysis relating to futures should be applicable to synthetic futures and hence the constituent components of synthetic futures. The analysis relating to the determination of the appropriate number of futures contracts thus has implications for the determination of the requisite number of option contracts. In particular, in the equation:

$$\frac{\text{Value of hedged stock}}{\text{Size of option contract} \times \text{Stock price}} = \text{Number of contracts}$$

the stock price could be the spot price, the synthetic futures price or a weighted average of these dependent upon the likely date of exercising or closing out the option. The suggestion (which is perhaps counter-intuitive) is that the sooner the likely closing-out date the more important the synthetic futures price is to the determination of the number of option contracts needed.

Implications for Hedging with Swaps and Warrants

The adjustments of futures and options hedges suggested in the foregoing analyses have been modest. A small proportionate factoring up or down can improve hedge efficiency but the absence of such adjustments might not be seen as too problematical, particularly in the light of other sources of hedge imperfections. The modest extent of the adjustments arises from the tendency for futures premiums and discounts to be relatively small. The small premiums/discounts in turn arise from the short periods of time to maturity.

When longer-term instruments, such as swaps and warrants, are used, the premiums/discounts between spot and futures (or synthetic futures) prices become much more significant. A 2% premium over 6 months may not seem too important but a 20% premium over 5 years has considerable significance for hedge ratios. Swaps can be regarded as portfolios of forward contracts and warrants as long term options. Adjusting sizes of swaps and numbers of warrants in order to eliminate part of basis risk, as suggested by the analysis of this article, would be an important exercise with considerable significance for hedge efficiency.